The Zelator

Ecce nunc patiemur philosophantem nobis asinum?
(What, shall we allow a fool to play philosopher with us?)

(Lucius Apuleius, *The Golden Ass*, bk X, xxxiii)

The Zelator

*A modern initiate explores the
ancient mysteries*

◄○►

Mark Hedsel and David Ovason

C

CENTURY · LONDON

This edition published by Century Books Limited 1998

1 3 5 7 9 10 8 6 4 2

Copyright © 1998 Mark Hedsel

All rights reserved

Century
Random House UK Ltd, 20 Vauxhall Bridge Road, London SW1V 2SA

Arrow Books Ltd
Random House UK Ltd, 20 Vauxhall Bridge Road, London SW1V 2SA

Random House Australia (Pty) Limited
20 Alfred Street, Milsons Point, Sydney,
New South Wales 2061, Australia

Random House New Zealand Limited
18 Poland Road, Glenfield,
Auckland 10, New Zealand

Random House South Africa (Pty) Limited
Endulini, 5a Jubilee Road, Parktown 2193, South Africa

Random House UK Limited Reg. No. 954009

A CIP catalogue record for this book
is available from the British Library

Papers used by Random House UK Limited are natural, recyclable products made from wood
grown in sustainable forests. The manufacturing processes conform to the environmental
regulations of the country of origin.

ISBN 0 7126 7807 7

Typeset by MATS, Southend-on-Sea, Essex
Printed and bound in the United Kingdom by
Mackays of Chatham PLC, Chatham, Kent

Contents

Acknowledgements

The most precious thing of all, said Goethe's Green Snake, is friendship. Friendship has the power to see through the shadows, into the light within, and it is in this power that we trace the worth of such a gift.

Yet, an esotericist cannot write or speak of the light without also thinking of the darkness, for he or she knows that the flame and the shadow are one and the same thing. A wise esoteric conceit holds that one may learn more from one's enemies than from one's friends. However, the very fact that an enemy can help implies that any encounter with an enemy is a potential gift of knowledge. From this we must assume that everyone we have met in life, for howsoever a brief a moment, is worthy of our thanks.

Yet, there are certain meetings – certain friendships – which seem bereft of any shadow. Mark Hedsel once told me of a strange meeting he had with an initiate in Chartres. The man appeared as from nowhere, and by explaining an esoteric symbol to Mark, revealed to him the solution to a problem which had troubled his mind for several years. The stranger left as mysteriously as he had come, even before Mark had time to express his thanks, or learn his identity. The meeting was almost archetypal, for many real encounters are of this kind – deep in spiritual space, yet so transient in time as to pass by unacknowledged. I know that Mark, given an opportunity to acknowledge his debt, would have thanked this unknown initiate now, along with a hundred other men and women who eased his questing along the valley Path.

I would like to thank Mark Booth, who encouraged Mark Hedsel to write this book, and I would like to thank the editors, Roderick Brown and Liz Rowlinson, who guided the manuscript through the press with such sensitivity and kindness.

Prologue

. . . man is not Man as yet.
Nor shall I deem his object served, his end
Attained, his genuine strength put fairly forth,
While only here and there a star dispels
The darkness, here and there a towering mind
O'erlooks its prostrate fellows . . .

. . .

Such men are even now upon the earth,
Serene amid the half-formed creatures round
Who should be saved by them and joined with them.

(Robert Browning, *Paracelsus*, from the 1867 ed. of The
Poetical Works of Robert Browning, vol. I, pp. 190 and 192)

I first saw Mark Hedsel in October 1955, at the Archer Gallery, in Westbourne Grove, London. He was talking to Dr Morris, the almost-destitute owner of the gallery, and to that most remarkable artist, Austin Osman Spare, who had a selection of paintings, pastels and drawings on exhibition at the gallery.[1]

Dr Morris had to some extent taken Spare under her wing, and had arranged this exhibition in order to help him earn enough money to keep body and soul together.[2] I later discovered that Spare knew that this would be his last exhibition: he had said to a friend that he would be dead within the year.[3]

I recognized Spare from photographs I had seen. I had been impressed by his poetry, and by the stories I had heard about his strange abilities. It was an interest in this which had brought me to the gallery, and to the dawning realization that Spare was one of the unrecognized geniuses of our century. He was no longer as famous as he had been: part of this was due to the loss of his studio and pictures in the early years of the Second World War, as a result of Nazi bombing.[4] Some of those familiar with

1

magical curse law had suggested that this loss was a direct result of Spare's own uncompromising attitude to Hitler. It seems that, in 1936, Spare had been asked to paint the dictator's portrait at Berchtesgaden, and had rejected the Führer in no uncertain way.[5] It was testament to the strength of the artist that he was prepared to stand alone in the face of almost universal appeasement.

The minute I saw Spare's face, I realized just how appropriate was his name: he was indeed *spare*.[6] Whether I sensed this wildness of spirit from his shock of greying hair, from the intensity of his eyes, or from the ragged appearance of his ill-fitting clothes is hard to say. From his poetry I had expected him to be intense, yet self-assured – serene in his spiritual insight; yet his face seemed to be restless, even tortured. Electric forces seemed to ray from the hair upon his face. His sparse moustache seemed to press down into his jaw, drawing his mouth into a thin and compact line, as though life-experiences had pushed him into a severity at variance with his spiritual knowledge. Even his intense intellectual quality, so clearly expressed in the high forehead, seemed to be pulling him asunder: his mind was lifted upwards by the shock of wild hair, yet drawn earthwards by the weight of his heavy dark eyebrows. Calm and intense, amidst this warfare of hair, were the most powerful eyes imaginable. I was pleased that he didn't glance towards me, for I imagined that the full stare of those eyes might well strip one soul-naked. It was no surprise for me to learn some years later that Spare had admitted during an interview on BBC radio that, were he so inclined, he could kill a man with a curse.[7]

Although my attention was taken at first by Spare, I could not help also looking at his companion. Even among that group of distinguished artists and poets who had come to pay Spare tribute this man stood out as someone of special calibre. I felt *compelled* to study him.

I did not know who Mark Hedsel was, but I could see from his quiet, sophisticated posture and the assuredness of his gestures that he was a person of extraordinary being. At the same time, I had that uncanny yet undeniable feeling that I had met him before. Do we always have a momentary presentiment when we glimpse a fragment of our destiny, I wonder?

It was difficult to determine his age, but I judged him to be in his late 20s. Although the weather was not particularly cold that October day, he had a dark blue scarf wrapped around his neck, and he wore a beret, in the French manner. Under his arm he carried a small leather satchel. The contrast with Spare was striking. The artist also had a scarf around his neck: it was a checked scarf, and, being tucked into his inner coat, suggested the dress of a rough Cockney.[8] In contrast, Hedsel was a dandy

– he wore his scarf flowing loosely around his neck, allowing it to fall elegantly over the top of his coat. It was, I imagined, such a touch of cultivated refinement that one would have experienced in the appearance of that urbane occultist, the mysterious Comte de Saint-Germain.[9] Indeed, when I first looked at Mark Hedsel, quite unaware of how our lives would intertwine in later years, my mind called up an imagination of that fastidious and totally misunderstood initiate who wandered with such ease through the pre-Revolutionary courts of 18th-century France.

In later years, I discovered that this final exhibition of Austin Spare's paintings had left its traces in the lives of several people. Two very remarkable women – each in their own different ways deeply interested in reincarnation – had been to the Archer Gallery, within a few days of my own visit. Both are still alive: one is in her 80s, and the other well into her 90s. Even so, I am pleased to report that they are still my friends, and that both recall this exhibition as significant for British art. Both were wise enough to purchase works from those on display.[10]

I was a poor student in 1955, and it never entered my mind that one day I would own the extraordinary pastel by Spare with which I fell in love at the exhibition (plate 1). Over 30 years later, one of these women – knowing of my interest in him – selected the picture from her own extensive collection of arcane art, and gave it to me.

Austin Spare had been very poor, which may explain why the pastel was so cheaply framed. I was delighted to find, when I lifted the wooden panel from the inappropriate framing, that, in the corner, Spare had signed the picture with his characteristic AOS monogram. As I held the pastel up to the light to peer at the signature, I had no need to hunt out the old gallery catalogue in search of the title: it had remained engraved upon my soul for all those 30-odd years.

Spare had called the pastel *Blood on the Moon*.

Of course, when I first saw the picture at the Archer Gallery, I had wondered what the title meant. I was far too young to have the courage to approach Spare himself in search of an explanation. Later, when I talked to my friends, and even to the lady who bought it, I discovered that no one knew why Spare had given the picture that strange title. I had read enough of Spare's writings to know that there would be a deep meaning hidden away somewhere, for he had been immersed in the magic of hieroglyphic lore, but by the time I began to look attentively for it, Spare had passed away, taking with him, as I imagined, any possible answer to my question.

As it happens, I eventually did find out what the title meant, but this meaning has little relevance to my account of how I met Mark Hedsel.[11] The reason why I mention the enigma of its title at all is because of the remarkable thing that happened later, when I encountered Mark Hedsel for the second time.

On a Thursday afternoon, almost a month after seeing Mark Hedsel in the Archer Gallery, I called at the Atlantis Bookshop in Museum Street. I wanted to find a second-hand copy of Wilhelm's translation of the oriental esoteric classic *The Secret of the Golden Flower*.

So far as I can recall, in those days, there were only two esoteric bookshops in London – the famous Watkins of Cecil Court, run by the learned esotericist, John Watkins,[12] and the Atlantis, which was owned by Michael Juste, a highly proficient arcanist.[13]

My first encounter with Michael Juste, two years earlier, had been very strange, even perturbing. In 1953 I was only 15 years old. Although I already had an interest in arcane thought, I really knew nothing. At that point in my life, I had decided that instead of going to university, I would attend art school to study painting, and the first time I pushed open the door of the Atlantis Bookshop, I was clutching a sketchbook in one hand and a small portfolio in the other.

When I cast my mind back to that important time in my life, I seem to recall that the Atlantis was still lit by two gas lamps. Undoubtedly, electricity was available, but Michael Juste seems to have insisted on using the old gas lights above what had formerly been the fireplace. I can still hear the hiss from the gas mantles in the otherwise silent shop, and I can remember how dark and gloomy it was – not a place where one could examine books with any ease. One had the feeling that the Atlantis was meant to serve as something quite other than a bookshop.

When I walked into the shop, and my eyes had grown accustomed to the half-light, I saw two faces looking intently at me. Both had deep-set penetrating eyes and flowing locks. In the gloom, they were so similar that it took a moment or so for me to realize that one was a life-sized bronze bust – a static version of the live individual who, after smiling at my confusion, introduced himself as Michael Juste.

'We've met before,' he said, almost casually, his eyes seeking out my own, as though anticipating confirmation of his words.

'I don't think so,' I said. I was quite new to London, and knew perhaps only half a dozen people in the entire city.

'Yes. We met in Egypt. You were a scribe in that life, too.'

He was not showing off. He was quite matter of fact, and there was a disconcerting sureness in his voice.

4

I should have been taken aback by his words, but there was something so comforting and certain about them that it was only afterwards I began to realize how strange the conversation had been.

'Well, in this life, I shall be a *painter.*' I held up my sketchbook. That morning, I had crouched on the window-seat of Christopher Wren's former house on the south bank of the Thames to sketch the marvellous view of St Paul's through the bombed warehouses. Wren had purchased the house in order to watch the new cathedral rising from the charred remains of the old: now, from the same casement window, it was possible to see his cathedral rising from other charred remains. I flicked open the pages to this pen-drawing and held it towards him.[14]

He took the book, and nodded at the picture. There was a trace of impatience in his voice: 'You were a scribe then. *You will be a scribe again.* In this life.' He handed the sketch back to me, rather brusquely.

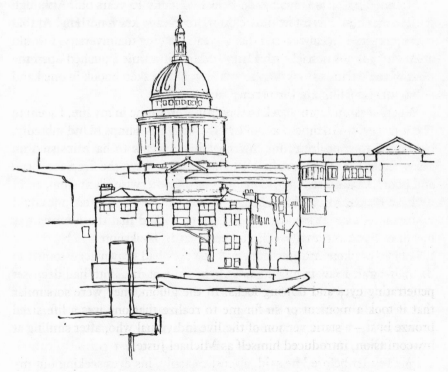

Sketch of St. Paul's Cathedral, across the Thames, from the former house of Sir Christopher Wren. Drawn c. 1953.

Two years after that encounter, I was in the shop again. The spring-bell above the door rang, and Mark Hedsel walked in. Wearing the same scarf and beret, he looked like a dapper version of a left-bank French student.

Over his shoulder he carried a satchel, which he swung down on to the desk, alongside my own portfolio. There was something strange about the gesture, for he had taken the straps between his thumb and forefinger, holding his palm outwards towards us. I presumed that he was making some form of greeting to Michael: I had read about such confraternity signals, but had never seen one before.

Michael turned to me and asked, 'What is your name?'

'David Ovason.'

'Well, David, this is Mark Hedsel. I suspect you'll find you have many things in common.' As he spoke, he glanced at us both in turn, as though to imply that there was a special meaning behind his words.

'I saw you at the Archer Gallery,' I ventured, as Mark held out his hand towards me.

'Austin's exhibition?'

I nodded, as I shook his hand. 'You were talking to Austin Spare.'

'I've met him only a few times.' Mark turned to Michael. 'He had sold eight pictures before we left.'

'Well,' put in Michael with a laugh, 'that will save him going to the pub for a while.'

'He drinks a lot?' I asked, rather surprised.

'No,' Mark said. 'He hawks his pictures around. He's a genius, acting like a tinker. Sometimes he shows his works in pubs.[15] If you ask him, he'll draw your portrait for a few shillings.' He addressed Michael once again. 'There it is in a nutshell. English genius. The lone Ego, eccentric and poor. An outcast.'

'Like Blake,' Michael laughed.

'In more ways than one,' agreed Mark. (I did not know what they meant at that time. Later I discovered that Spare claimed to have been Blake in a previous lifetime.)

There was a pause, during which Mark looked at me intently. His profile was sharp-cut, his face well-formed and youthful, but there was a mature quality in his eyes that suggested he must be much older than 30: they were kind, penetrating and wise – undoubtedly, his most remarkable feature. One felt he was watching and assessing, yet entirely without suspicion.

'Would you like to go for a coffee, David?' Mark's gaze was still very steady, even when asking such an ordinary question, as though his interest was not in the question, nor in the answer, but in the one being questioned. Already, I had formed the notion that he was involved in a secret school of hidden learning, and my heart was racing.

I nodded, and picked up my sketchbook. As I did so, the heavy top flap of the book swung open, and knocked a glass off the desk. It fell to the bare linoleum, and smashed. Embarrassed, I bent down to pick up the pieces. I dropped the broken shards into the jagged remains of the glass, and put it on the desk.

'I'm really sorry.'

'It's alright,' said Michael, brushing aside my apologies. 'You'd better hold it under the tap . . .'

At first, I could not understand, but then I saw that he was staring at my finger, which was bleeding.

I put the sketchbook down on the desk once more. Michael went to the back of the shop, and pulled open a door which led on to a flight of stone steps. Following his directions, I went down into the cellar of the bookshop for the first time.

The atmosphere was uncanny, yet not unpleasant. I felt protected. Later, when I began to learn about the secret world of magic, I remembered that cellar, and understood why the atmosphere had been so strange: it became clear to me that Michael had magically attuned the interior with a ritual to ensure that only those genuinely interested in arcane things would be able to enter. The cellar was overflowing with rare occult books, pictures and arcane bric-à-brac, such as magical objects, ritual lamens (magical pectorals) and pointing sticks, and other curiosities. What intrigued me most was that there were so many paintings, pastels and drawings by Spare in the chaos. Crammed into bookshelves, and piled quite without order on the floor, were vast numbers of books, and although I had no time to examine these, I was amazed to see among them beautifully tooled vellum bindings with titles by such occultists as Agrippa, Dee, Gichtel and van Helmont.[16]

I washed my finger, removing from it a broken splinter of glass. I tore strips from toilet paper, and made a rough bandage to stem the flow of blood. Then I climbed the stairs back to the bookshop.

As I entered the shop, the two looked up in surprise as though I were an intruder. They seemed to be sharing a joke.

'Look,' Mark said to me, pointing at my sketchbook, which still lay open on the desk. On the left-hand page was a water-colour sketch I had made a few weeks earlier. It was a picture of the horned Diana, loosely based on an illustration I admired by Boris Artzybasheff (plate 2).

'Look,' Mark repeated.

The blood from my cut finger had run in a rivulet across the picture. It was a congealing red lightning flash, splitting the soft blue of the night sky, and piercing through the naked belly of the sky-borne Diana.[17]

'You see – *blood on the Moon*,' said Michael Juste.

I was shaken. I had told no one of my interest in Spare's painting. Were they showing me that they could see right into my thoughts, even into my soul? Were these two already possessed of that higher vision of which I had read in the arcane books of those who wrote on the secrets of initiation? Suddenly, I felt hopelessly out of my depth in the presence of such men.

Of course, in those days I was young, and it was much later that I realized Michael and Mark had not been thinking of the title of Spare's picture at all. Their attention had been drawn to the image of Diana in my sketchbook, for they had both seen the alchemical significance of the blooded picture.[18]

When they saw the blood running across the image of the Moon, they immediately read into it the same hidden meaning. They saw in this image the meeting of Sun and Moon. In alchemy, the union of Sun and Moon – expressed in such diverse yet related symbols as the meeting in sexual congress of King and Queen, or in the androgyne male-female

Solar King and Lunar Queen in union: figure from the
1550 edition of the alchemical Rosarium Philosophorum

figure beloved of 16th-century engravers – is an important stage in the production of the Secret Stone, the discovery of which is the aim of the alchemists. Within the context of our meeting, they saw the blood on the Moon as a sign that I would become involved in the *conjunctio* of alchemy – which is to say that I would become interested in initiation. They were far too experienced as occultists not to recognize that every act – even a seeming accident – is filled with inner meaning.

Half an hour later, I was sitting with Mark in the nearby Italian coffee house, the Roma, which was usually thronged with readers from the British Museum library. While I burned to ask Mark about the blood, I did not have the courage to raise the matter then. Consequently, I remained convinced for some months that he and Michael had been able to read my thoughts.

Mark kept the conversation on arcane subjects. We discussed in particular several interesting trends in contemporaneous arcane schools, and the secret initiation literature which was beginning to emerge from them. I recall discussing with him the enigmatic *All and Everything* of Gurdjieff[19] (which I had not read at that point), the unfinished autobiography of Alice Bailey,[20] and the Evans-Wentz version of the Tibetan *Book of the Dead*.[21]

Suddenly, from the general topic of books, he turned to personalities, and I was immediately out of my depth. He asked if I knew who had initiated the Austrian esotericist, Rudolf Steiner. The question surprised me: I had heard that Steiner had been involved in Masonic activities, and it had been rumoured that he had been an associate of Theodor Reuss, in the esoteric group, the *Ordo Templi Orientis*, but the idea that Steiner had been initiated by any modern group had never entered my head. Mark Hedsel did not appear to be surprised that I merely shrugged at his question, to show that I could not answer it.[22]

Although the conversation had floundered in my own ignorance, Mark quickly redirected it. From Steiner, he led the talk back, with little difficulty, to Theosophy, about which I knew a little, and then further back to the Hermetic Brotherhood of Luxor,[23] about which (once again) I had to admit I knew nothing. It was clear that he was trying to find out from which direction I was coming, and where I was going, yet his questions were always kindly, and always articulately phrased. From the very beginning, I perceived something of the depth of the man. I did not dream that in the distant future our friendship would ripen in a creative way. I did not anticipate that our lives would take such different directions, and that many years would pass before we would sit once again discussing such matters. The seeds were planted in the Atlantis

Bookshop, when the solar blood poured on to the Moon, yet it took 42 years – a lunar cycle – before Mark Hedsel brought to completion his account of an extraordinary journey alongside some of the Masters of the modern world.

'Michael had been right, after all,' I remarked to Mark, when we met to discuss his book, on the last Monday of August, 1991.

'How so?'

'I did become a writer.'

'You became a *scribe*,' he corrected gently. The truth was that I *had* become a scribe, working with hieroglyphics rather than with words. Perhaps that is why I had decided to become a painter before I went on to university to study literature. A picture is more primal to the idea, as a word merely *conjures* images: the written word is, by definition, a secondary source. A face might launch a thousand ships, but a description of a face is unlikely ever to induce a single boat to raise sail.

'Well, now I will be the picture,' said Mark, 'and you must help me put myself into words.'

'I don't understand. What picture?' The years had passed, yet I still found his well-articulated phrases enigmatic. 'What picture?' I repeated.

'I am to be the picture of the Fool in the Tarot pack.'

My eyes must have narrowed, as I looked at him. Whatever one might say of Mark Hedsel, it was clear that he was no fool, and, so far as I knew, never had been. I looked at him more closely. He had changed – we all had changed in those 40-odd years. His scarf and beret had gone. They had been replaced by a smart business suit and an expensive silk tie, yet somehow he did not look much older. If he were a fool, then he was a very well-disguised fool. As I studied him, the old image of the ageless French initiate, the Comte de Saint Germain, floated once again into my mind, like a beckoning ghost.

'A Fool?' I asked. 'What do you mean?'

He laughed. 'I suspect that you'll find out as we work on the book together. You will be the limner.' He sipped his coffee. 'You know the Fool card of the Marseilles deck?'

I nodded. This old design showed a Fool, staff in hand, walking along a road.*

He tapped his forehead. 'It's all locked up in here. I'll hand you the key.'

---

* This is shown on page 17.

'A sort of autobiography?' I hoped so. I would learn a great deal working on such a project – what a marvellous opportunity he was offering me.

'Sort of. We'll see how it turns out. Some of the people I've worked with are still alive. We'll have to change names, and places, I suppose.'

'We'll become masters of disguise.'

'That's good. All the great truths are disguised. After all, the material world is at best a mask for the Spiritual World. I think that's why Michael Juste kept a bust of himself in the shop.'

'As a disguise?'

'He was externalizing his mask. It is best to keep the mask on the outside. If the mask slips into the inside, then it can become dangerous.'

I knew what he meant. One should not believe the outer lies. Masks were lies of a sort. 'There is a point where imagination not only masks reality, but presents it more vividly.'

He laughed, nodding his head. 'Where I come from, we call that art. Did you ever visit Najera, in La Rioja?' he asked.

'The monastery of Santa-Maria-la-Real?'

'Yes. There's a 15th-century carving of a fool on one of the stalls.'

I remembered the carving. 'He's blowing a flute, isn't he?'

'Yes. Like the Fool of the Tarot cards, he has a dog at his feet. Two dogs, in fact – but only one is barking at him. What is important, however, is the clothing he wears.'

'He has a foolscap, I think?'

'Yes. But his robe is the curious thing. He wears a robe which is so designed as to fall open at both front and back. In this way, his private parts are always visible. This is the *naked Fool*.

'The image has a long ancestry. His nakedness is a sign that the true Fool is prepared to show those things which others prefer to hide. Those Fools who show the way to that higher vision arising from initiation are often seen by the Sleepers as foolish.'

(The Sleepers are those who have not elected to follow a spiritual path. They are content with the realm of appearances, and want only to be left alone, to sleep.)

'There's a great deal to be learned from these mediaeval images of the Fool. The mediaeval *Feast of the Fool* was of profound importance simply because it had esoteric undertones. Of course, you'll learn more about this, if we do a book together.'

'A book about the naked Mark Hedsel?'

He laughed. 'Partly naked – that is to say, a Fool, transformed by *imag*ination.' He emphasized the *image* of the last word.

11

*Drawing of bench-end at Najera, showing the naked Fool,
with open cloak and three-pronged hat.*

There was a brief silence.

'Images,' he muttered, reflectively. 'Did you know that some Egyptian artists who cut hieroglyphics into the temple walls couldn't read them?

'That is really extraordinary.'

'The priests called their chisels *mer*, but the same sound also meant "death". Isn't this a mystery? It's a recognition that for something to show forth as an image – an illumination of an idea – something else has to die.'[24]

He shrugged, yet I could see that he was leading to the central principle of the arcane method – to the notion of *fission*, the fundamental process in initiation, which was so important to the Way of the Fool.

'Perhaps,' he continued, 'the sculptors who used the Egyptian *mer* didn't even know of its inner meaning. Their job was to ensure merely that they conformed to the prescribed canons of art: they knew the rules of disguise, but they didn't know what they were masking. They had no concept of the archetypes – what their priests called *neters* – they evoked.[25] With each glyph they carved, they called down spiritual agencies to inhabit material form: they worked magic, yet they did not know it.' He looked at me intently. 'Surely,' he said, 'that is an activity fit for fools?'

'Not just for fools,' I said. 'Aren't we all evoking archetypes – primal ideas – we don't fully understand?'

'Exactly. That is *exactly* what I mean. A man or woman's life reveals the archetypes they have followed. That's why the Fool is prepared to go through life naked to the world, knowing that the lower is nothing more than a reflection of the higher.'

Mark Hedsel died in 1997, before we had completed this work.[26]

There is a tendency for occult texts to romanticize the deaths of initiates and teachers. Reports that the Comte de Saint-Germain lived, with little physical change, well into his 130th year, is typical of this kind of literature.[27]

The death of an initiate is generally quite different from the death of one who has not been initiated. The true initiate has no need to spend years of purgation on the spiritual plane, and is empowered to return fairly quickly to the material world, in a new physical body. It is probably in this that the supposed antiquity of initiates – not to mention the biblical Patriarchs such as Noah – lies. Whilst it is probably not the case that the Comte de Saint-Germain was seen in Europe during a sequence of over a century, it is more likely true that, during this period, the Comte lived, with total memory recall of his previous incarnations, in at least two different embodiments.

To a limited extent, certain alchemical processes can arrest the degeneration of the physical body: it was a fair commonplace for mediaeval alchemists to live well over twice the normal life-span of their contemporaries.[28] However, one has to ask, Why should an initiate choose either to arrest degeneration, or to live much beyond the allotted time-span, unless he or she had a particular undertaking to complete? No one can study the arcane sciences for very long without realizing that the lower world is a reflection of the higher world, and that the human frame has been blessed with rhythms, natural periodicities and climacterics which are found in the cosmos – even expressed in the movements of the planets and stars. In so far as an initiate elects to extend a physical life, he or she may be prepared to strain these cosmic rhythms.

But great age is not always a blessing. Given the rapidity with which the physical body degenerates after a certain period of time, we can imagine that few would elect to live much beyond the normal allotted span.

I make these observations mainly to make it clear that Mark Hedsel is indeed dead – which is to say that he has passed from the physical plane of our familiar experience. I was with him to the very end, arranged the cremation and personally disposed of the ashes If anyone seeks his true memorial, or even the resting place of that inert dust which the alchemists called the *caput mortuum* (or death's head)[29] then they need only look around the interior entrance to the monastery of Sagrada di San Michele, near Susa, in Italy.

This stepped incline is called the Staircase of the Dead – not merely because it is dark, and because there are tombs at the bottom, but because all those who climb towards the zodiacal arch at the top are deemed to be the sleeping dead. It is only when they have passed through the arch of constellation images at the top, and have stepped into the light-filled courtyard, that they may be regarded as having entered the realm of the living. Of course, this transition is entirely symbolic, yet it is representative of an event which, even after 6,000 years, is still shrouded in mystery. It is symbolic of initiation.

No more fitting tomb – the so-called 'resting place' – could be envisaged for Mark Hedsel. While he did not personally place that richly symbolic arch at the top of the stairway, he had, in a previous lifetime, established its arcane zodiacal patterns. During an incarnation of the 12th century, he oversaw the sculpting of the figures on the arch.[30] The scattering of the dust upon those stairs was more than a symbolic disposal of a single lifetime – it was the recognition that an entire cycle of endeavour had come to an end. It was my conclusion that Mark Hedsel belonged far more to the 12th century than to the modern era, and it was fitting that this simple ash burial should memorialize the dedication of at least two lifetimes, devoted, in their different ways, to the study and dissemination of arcane knowledge.

This commentary on the seeming-end of an initiate leads almost naturally into reflections on the nature of initiation itself. There are very many different levels of initiation, so when we say that a person is an initiate, we are in danger of being confusing rather than informative. The very word initiate begs questions such as, 'initiate of which School?', and 'initiate to what degree, or grade?'

In the past, it was sufficient for a man to be initiated into one of the most ancient of the Greek Mysteries, of the corn goddess Demeter, at Eleusis, for him to be regarded by others with awe, for it was a mark that his being had changed, and that his knowledge of spiritual things had been extended. In modern times, the meaning of the word initiation has changed so fundamentally that whole 'esoteric schools' have been invented by occult-crazed individuals, or by others desirous of a tem-poral power, with grades of initiation which, high-sounding as they may have been, had and have no real value.[31] By the beginning of the 20th century, certain initiate grades appear to have been handed out like so many proficiency certificates, almost for the asking. When Dr R. W. Felkin (who had been initiated into very high-sounding levels within the Hermetic Order of the Golden Dawn) went to Germany in the early part of the 20th century in search of Teachers he believed had higher knowledge, he met with a number of people who were reluctant to give him information 'because he was not a Mason'. To satisfy their demands, he immediately sought initiation as a Freemason in an Edinburgh Lodge.[32] This play with the status of 'initiation', merely as a conferred title, has little or nothing to do with serious hermeticism. The true initiate carries his or her initiation within his or her being, and it is the level of being and knowledge which is the true arbiter of initiation.

Mark Hedsel made no bones about the way of initiation he followed: his was the *Way of the Fool*, a way which was externalized to some extent in the secret designs of the 22 atout (picture cards based on secret symbols) of the traditional Tarot cards, used in popular divination. Mark was initiated into a way leading into a stream of knowledge which is so different from ordinary knowledge that those who follow it are in constant danger of being misunderstood. With a slip of the tongue, or by an inappropriate action, they may appear a fool.[33]

As Mark Hedsel makes very evident in the following text, the Way of the Fool is intimately connected with the inner development of the human Ego (see page 21). The nourishing of the Ego is a perilous affair, and there are few on the path of such development who do not fall, from time to time.

'Mark, you have said that this development of the Ego consciousness was very much in evidence among artists – did the new stirrings of Ego begin in Florence, in the 15th century?'

He smiled, and I wondered if this was the question he had been anticipating.

'Earlier by several centuries, David. You see, such Spiritual developments, and changes in human psyche, are usually experienced first by poets or musicians, long before they are felt by others. Visual artists, for all their vision, are more Earth-bound than poets or musicians: poets have antennae for such things. In a manner of speaking, poets are "gatherers of the wind".[34] When a Spiritual change is in the air, it is generally the poets who sense this first, and give expression to it in poems or songs. Poets are sensitive dreamers. All artists, whether they be poets, painters or musicians, *dream* their images, before they encapsulate them into works of art, but the poet dreams more deeply.

'So, the true poets are the real visionaries, the true recipients of Spiritual developments, and if we look into European literature we shall find the earliest signs of the wise Fool cropping up among the wandering scholar-poets and troubadours, the singing-poets of Southern France, which in those days was rampant with heresy.'

'Then,' I said, 'this must take the Way of the Fool some way back into the 11th century?'

'Perhaps as far back as that – it is not a subject I have studied in any depth – but the poetry of the early 13th-century Monk of Orlac seems to be the earliest to develop the idea of the wise fool with any real conviction.[35] There is the taste of madness in his verse which can be easily taken for insanity by those who do not *know*, who are not informed by the esoteric vision.

'This implies either that his work was too full of piety for ordinary people, or that he was writing in the Green Language – the secret language of the esotericists.[36] In one of his verses, about a fellow poet, the Monk wrote, "in his entire life he's sung nothing but a few crazy words that no one understands". This fellow poet was Arnaut Daniel, who famously claimed to have hunted the hare with the ox, and swum against the rising tide . . .[37]

'Of course, very little of this makes much sense in ordinary terms. Yet, the fact is that the Monk of Orlac and Arnaut Daniel were brothers on the Path – the Monk knew very well what Arnaut had meant when he said that he could swim against the tide, and hunt with the ox.

'What we find so interesting about the work of this Monk is that he, like so many other poets of the times, insisted that no one could really understand what he or his associates were writing about.

'Now, it is not uncommon for poets to grumble about not being understood – but in the case of the Monk of Orlac and his companions, the issue is different. Normally, if you hear a poet complaining that no

The wandering fool: titlepage illustration from Rabelais' Gargantua, 1532.

one understands his verse, you can offer a fairly brutal response: you might be inclined to say, "Then write more clearly!" – or something to that effect. But you could not say such a thing to these poets of Provence with any real justice, for they were attempting to write poetry from an entirely new standpoint. They could not be understood because they had developed Spiritual organs which permitted them a vision well beyond the level of understanding of those around them.'

He cleared his throat. 'I quote from memory, but one of these poets wrote: "And when, in the city of Earth, which is full of madmen, God spared one man, the others considered him to be mad. They maltreated him because his wisdom was not theirs – for to them, the spirit of God is folly . . ."[38]

'These may appear to be mad-seeming words – yet to the experienced hermeticist, they are a sign that the individual who speaks them is already on the way to developing a strong Ego. Such a person has already taken the first stumbling steps towards the Path of the Fool.

'The tradition of the wise Fool – or the initiate Fool – runs strongly through mediaeval French literature, and culminates in the greatest fooler of them all – the 16th-century joker, François Rabelais.[39] Rabelais was really writing from a troubadour tradition, full of wit and humour, knowing that few of his readers would be able to follow him as he capered around the more profound levels of meaning.[40] Rabelais did not hide his subject – which was initiation – but he did hide its mysteries and teachings in magnificent displays of Green Language: behind his *bavard* joking, he kept his silence.[41] Rabelais' genius is such that his work is worth reading on an ordinary level, even when the deeper levels remain hidden. This is true poetic fooling. It is no accident that the first edition of Rabelais' fooling account of initiation, published in 1532, had on the title-page a woodcut of a Fool (see page 17).

'One cannot look upon this interesting image without recalling a more sophisticated version. This is the Fool painted by Hieronymus Bosch in a number of versions (plate 3).[42] Bosch disguised his fool in Christian clothing, of course: he included him in such themes as *The Prodigal Son*,[43] but one who is familiar with the spirit of the early 16th century will interpret the figure as a representation of the human being labouring under the challenge of a new development of the Ego. In fact, Bosch's picture has been called "The Fool" in the past, and there are many other pictures by this great artist in which the theme of the Fool is developed.[44] The reasons for this will become evident later, but I simply wanted to show how the word-images of poetry eventually become fixed as representations or symbols in painting.

'The kind of *wise fooling* which Rabelais and Bosch delighted in really began as the true art of the troubadours.'

I decided to return to an earlier point he had made.

'Is there a reason – I mean a cosmological reason – why the poet should be so endowed with sensitivity?'

'Yes. The poet speaks with words. That may sound like a truism, but the truth is that there are mysteries in words. It is no accident that the greatest mystery of all, the *Logos*, may be translated as meaning "Word". When they speak with new words, and new word forms, no one can understand them – *this is what the troubadours recognized*. Before a society can become receptive to a new idea, a new vocabulary must be created. The old vocabularies can speak only of the old things: they are like rusty railway tracks which run always in the same direction. A new vocabulary is required for new things, for new directions. The true poet finds it very hard to speak to his contemporaries, as he is using and forging a language which will be fully understood only by future generations . . .'

The Way of the Fool is no easy way, for it involves a balancing act, in which the Fool may stumble and become a fool. It is a cunning way, a way of strange knowledge. It is 'the Way that Is Not a Way' – 'the Way that Cannot Be Named'. Such titles alone should alert us to the ignorance of this Way, save among esotericists. Perhaps, when the ecclesiastical authorities attempted to root out the *Festum Fatuorum*, the Feast of Fools, in the 15th century, they succeeded in driving underground any esoteric groups linked with the Way of the Fool.[45] Records are sparse, save in the hints and guesses left in the arcane literature and traditions – some samples of which we shall examine. This sparseness of records alone would suggest that, before attempting to follow Mark Hedsel's account of his journey along so strange a path, we should make some attempt to examine in more detail the background to the esoteric Path he followed. For this reason, before turning to Mark Hedsel's remarkable book, I offer a brief survey of what the Way of the Fool involves.

The Way of the Fool

> . . . but we will speak only of those things which are difficult, and not to be grasped by the senses, but, indeed, which are almost contrary to the evidence of the senses.
>
> (Paracelsus, *Archidoxi Magica*, from *The Works of Paracelus* vol. I, p.117)

The Way of the Fool is the way of the independent traveller on the Path of initiation. Such a traveller may study under a variety of Masters, yet will strive always to preserve his or her own identity, and rarely undertakes vows of silence which will bind his or her being to a particular school or teaching. The fact that this travelling Fool is on a *Path* is meant to reflect that he or she is following the way of experience, which in ancient Greek was termed *pathein*.[1]

The Path of the Fool is the way of the developing Ego.[2] In esotericism, the Ego is the Self. This Self is a droplet of the Universal Mind, or Godhead. The Sanskrit term, *manas*, which may be translated as 'the immortal individual', as much as 'higher mind', is the equivalent of the real Ego. It is that droplet of the Godhead which has sought experience through involvement with matter. This minute particle of the Godhead is directed into matter in order to perceive Itself, or to gain experience in the realm of Its own creation.

Because it holds this direct connection with the Godhead, the fully developed Ego is indestructible. However, through the effects of incarnation, and the consequent darkening through involvement in matter, the human Ego does not remain omniscient, like its Godhead source. In this sense – in that its cosmic knowledge is limited by the 'hooding' mask of selfhood – the Ego rarely works with its full spiritual potential. From incarnation to incarnation the Ego dwells in what must be termed spiritual darkness in comparison with the light of the spiritual planes. Even so, it is

20

possible for the Ego, through is own efforts, to regain its former full potential, and to remove this darkening selfhood from its eyes.

While in life – chained to a physical body – the Ego must work into matter through three organs, or 'bodies', called in esotericism the Astral, the Etheric and the Physical, of which we shall learn more shortly.[3] These bodies are controlled by the human *Ego*, which the hermetic literature describes as sweeping down from the Spiritual World like a great bird – a pelican, phoenix or swan – to dwell in flesh on the material realm. The bird seems to be a curious one, for it has three wings rather than the usual pair.

The Ego is not entirely alone when it is cast adrift from the higher Spiritual world. It is accompanied by three higher Spiritual bodies, invisible to ordinary vision. Like the goddess Venus, the Ego is attended by three Graces, a triad of Spiritual beings, who weave a stately dance around her. In these three beings, we trace the three higher Spiritual companions of the new-born Ego: in modern esoteric literature, these are called the Atman, Buddhi and Manas.

The Ego is pulled to the Earth realm by three lower bodies. These both cushion it from, and link it with, the material world.

This image of the Ego as being fed by Spiritual powers, and yet immersed in matter, is not an easy one to grasp. The synopsis in Table 1 may make the relationship clearer.

TABLE 1 – THE SEVEN BODIES OF MAN

ATMAN BUDDHI MANAS	Spiritual bodies not yet adequately developed by non-initiates. Still embryonic in ordinary man.
EGO	The sacred SELF. It is this invisible body that most modern Westerners are now developing. This is the seat of control over the Will.
ASTRAL[4]	The Spiritual body of emotions, desires etc.
ETHERIC[5]	The Spiritual body of memory. It maintains the physical in cellular activity, and transmits emotions and desires to the physical.
PHYSICAL[6]	The only visible body in man. By nature (that is, when divorced from the etheric) it enters the state of death, and is in molecular activity. During life it is maintained in cellular activity, through its immersion in the Etheric.

The diagram presupposes that the Ego is itself a reflecting glass – a sort of mirror of potential – so that the Astral below it is reflected in the Manas above: the Physical is reflected in the highest Atman. This mirror image sets out the future development of mankind: for example, it is through the development of the Spiritual potential in the Atman that the physical will be redeemed.[7] Sometimes, Atman is 'Atma'.

The physical is the only body among the seven which is visible to ordinary sight. While the lower three to some extent interpenetrate each other, the Ego is located (in so far as it is active in space and time) more around the head. The three higher bodies, on which mankind will work in future ages, are in an embryonic state, and are best conceived of as existing above the head. However, it is misleading to locate them in space and time.

To some extent, we all have the illusion that we understand what the physical is, even though the initiate is inclined to regard it as the great mystery.[8] However, the Etheric, Astral and Ego will certainly present difficulties to those unfamiliar with modern arcane thought, and I shall attempt to look at these in the light of the Way of the Fool.

The Fool card of the Major Arcana, from a modern version
based on a traditional Marseilles deck of c. 1790.

22

The most enduring arcane image of this wandering Fool is that found on the early Tarot cards, which appeared in Europe during the 15th century. Although used at first as a card game, the Tarot was adopted fairly soon for the purpose of divination.[9] The most learned of esotericists have recognized that the Tarot incorporates a rich system of esoteric ideas, and was promulgated by an unknown arcane Brotherhood. The Fool card is replete with symbols bearing upon the Way of the Fool. It shows a bearded man wearing the cap and bells of the traditional jester. He is carrying on his right shoulder a stick, upon the end of which has been tied a bag. Usually, the progress of the Fool is hampered by an animal (in some images it is a dog, in others a cat) which claws at his legs or clothes. As we shall see, this curious symbolism throws light on the hermetic tradition of initiation which were practised in the temples of ancient Egypt.

The Ego is symbolized by the face itself, which is covered in the foolscap – the three 'horns and bells' – traditionally worn by the Fool. The three 'horns' are not intended to link the Fool with the Moon, as has been suggested,[10] but to show how the human Ego is bathed in the effulgency of the three higher, and as yet undeveloped, Spiritual bodies of Atman, Buddhi and Manas.

This hint of spirituality is also seen in the upward gaze of the Fool. The beard may pull his face down into the lower animal realm of the Astral, but his eyes (wherein the soul is discerned, and where the pupil that seeks instruction sits), look upwards to the heavens. The scroll-like extension to the headgear, which ends in a rounded finial, is in contrary movement to the sweep of the beard. The beard pulls down into hirsute animality, while the finial pulls upwards towards the heavens: this is the archetypal duality which lies behind most arcane thought. One can almost imagine the finial as a representative of the secret third eye, searching the Spiritual realms above.[11]

The unredeemed part of man – the dark shadow, as it is sometimes called – is undoubtedly in the sack over the Fool's back. Mark Hedsel sometimes referred to the contents of the sack as accumulated *karma*, or Spiritual debt and/or credit.[12] It contains the *dark matter* with which one on the Path must deal, at some time or another. This dark matter is accumulated lifetime after lifetime, and contrasts with the purity of the *prima materia*, or pristine Spiritual matter which is the soul's birthright.

The animal was widely adopted in mediaeval art as symbolic of the Astral, and this dog (or cat), which pursues and attacks the fool, is no exception. It is that *Astral* element in the Fool which has remained untamed. Because it has not been tamed, or integrated into his soul, it has an independent existence – it is a sort of shadow being, a reminder of the Astral creature which the poet Dante meets when he begins to walk the Path of his own initiation (see page 137). Since the Astral is the source of emotions, it is also the source of motion: in life it is particularly difficult to control the inner manifestation of the Astral in emotions, and its outer manifestations in movement. This e-*motion*, or motion outwards, is expressed in the aggressive action of the animal.

In his or her early development, the neophyte is advised to learn external control of the tendency to give immediate expression to emotions, and, indeed, the emotions themselves. When one begins to tread an esoteric Path, the emotions should become tools for experiencing the world, rather than the source of ensnarement, with the power to delude or flood over the soul. By dint of effort, the neophyte learns gradually to control this inner animal. Reference to Table 1 indicates that one purpose of such control is to so transform the Astral that it becomes Manas.

The sticks carried by the Fool represent the Etheric body of the Fool. This symbolism is sustained by the fact that sticks are cut from trees: according to the arcane tradition, the vegetative life of trees and plants is supported by the Etheric energies. This is why one of the terms for Etheric, used in mediaeval hermetic thought, was *ens vegetabilis* – or the 'vegetable essence'.[13]

In case it might be thought that this interpretation of the Fool card may have been stretched too far, it may be instructive to glance at a 17th-century alchemical engraving illustrating the standard arcane symbolism relating to the Astral and Etheric (opposite). The astral, or *animalis*, is represented by the human being, who is connected by a 'life-line' to the cosmos. This human being incorporates the Astral body of feelings, the Etheric life body and the physical body.

The Etheric, or *vegetabilis*, is symbolized by a flowering plant. This plant does not possess the astral body of feelings, but it does have the Etheric life body, which maintains the physical existence of the plant.

The physical, or *mineralis*, body is represented by a mountain – a block of earth, or rock. To show that this is not mere inert matter, the artist has covered it with the sigils for the seven planets: in this way, he intimates that all Spiritual possibilities exist in potential, buried within this Earthly matter. In such a context, the number seven usually indicates a connection with the traditional seven planets.

This image, from a major work by the alchemist Becher, illustrates clearly the nature of the Etheric. The Etheric life-force of plants pulls the Four Elements of matter into a form: however, as the plants have no

The alchemical 'Triad of Nature' – Mineral, Etheric and Astral. From the titlepage of J.J. Becher's Mille Hypotheses Chymicae, *1668.*

significant contact with the Astral plane, they do not become entangled with the emotional life which is the keynote of the Astral.

In Latin, the stick is *virga* – a sound close enough to virgin, and even Virgin, to suggest another role of the stick as a fertilizer of ideas. Mark Hedsel emphasized that the graphic etymology of the sticks may be traced to the Egyptian goddess *Maat*,[14] reminding us that a French name for the Fool is *mat*.

The *physical* body is, of course, the body of the Fool himself: it is sometimes called the *ass*, or *donkey*, perhaps to suggest that it is controlled by a rider – which is, of course, the Ego. The simplicity of this symbolism should not blind us to the fact that, in the hermetic lore, the physical body is one of the great Mysteries, whose true Spiritual nature has scarcely been explored.[15] Within the hermetic literature, the physical body is sometimes referred to as 'condensed wisdom'. In the card design, the body is distinguished from the head – the Spiritual thinking part – by the symbolic device of the stick, which cuts off the head from the lower body. In accordance with hermetic symbolism, the body is clothed: the clothing is itself merely the symbol of the physical elements which both enfold and reveal the inner form. The truth of this is expressed in the tear in the right leg of the Fool, for through the torn clothing we can see the skin, a reminder of the human being behind the Fool's disguise.[16] We may see a similar tear in the picture of the Fool in Bosch's picture of a wandering fool (plate 3). In these images, the physical is masked by the clothing, recalling the mediaeval *Festum Fatuorum*, or *Feast of Fools*, in which face-masks were worn even by priests.

According to Mark Hedsel, the name *ass*, which is one of the names given to the body in the Way of the Fool, is intended to recall the Feast of Fools.[17] Mark pointed out that, in the legends attached to the Christian Mysteries, the ass had been redeemed because it carried Christ in triumph into Jerusalem. As a sign of this redemption, Christ had left upon its shoulders a dark cross. This is the esoteric parable on the idea that our physical body, made from the Four Elements, is also the fourfold cross we must bear.

Even the pagan esoteric literature was well prepared to see the ass as a Mystery-symbol – as the creature from whom the high initiate might be born. In the most famous initiation-tale which has survived from the ancient world, the symbolism of the ass is given a sophisticated and dramatic form. In *The Golden Ass* of Apuleius, the hero, Lucius, is transformed into an ass because he dabbles in magic.[18] His original purpose, in illegally borrowing and using the unguents of an enchantress, Pamphile, had certainly not been to change himself into an ass, but to acquire the power to fly. As soon as his misuse of magic had transformed him into the ass shape, this ambition changed radically, and his greatest desire was to become human again.

After many degrading and dramatic adventures as an ass, Lucius realizes that the only help he will get is from the Spiritual realm. Towards the end of the book, while still imprisoned in the body of the donkey, Lucius awakes at that 'most secret time', when the Moon is strong in the skies. He decides to pray for liberation from his bestial form, naming the Moon goddess Isis with her many secret names. His prayer is efficacious. The goddess appears to him in a dream or vision. In the middle of her forehead is a mirror-like Moon which emits its own light. Only her cloak is utterly dark, and obscuring, yet upon her dress can be seen the stars and the Moon at its full. In the manner of the Egyptian goddess, Isis, and the Egyptian initiation priests, she carries a magical sistrum.[19] The visionary lady tells Lucius that she has come to his aid. The ass awakes from the vision to find himself in the midst of an initiation processional, which, in certain details, reminds one of the later mediaeval processions of the Feast of the Fools – save that this one was designed to serve the ancient Mysteries of Isis, rather than that of Christ.

Lucius has known from the very beginning of his affliction that if only he could eat a rose, then he would return to his human condition. Now, an initiate priest in the processional (prepared for such action by the goddess) holds towards the ass a bunch of roses. The Golden Ass, rich with all the knowledge and suffering he has gained through his bestial servitude, eats the roses, and is transformed, as in a miracle, back into the higher man.[20]

Caught in the sheer wonder and mystery of this longed-for transformation, Lucius stands still, and says nothing. He knows no words which could express his joy, nor even words which will thank the goddess for her bounty. Here, direct from the ancient Mystery-lore, we have a recognition that words are designed only for the ordinary realm, and play little part in the supreme Mysteries of spirit.

If the ancients went to such lengths to deal with the arcane significance of the body, we might ask if they tried to represent in a similar distinctive manner the higher, invisible bodies.

If we contemplate the sevenfold structure of Table 1 (see page 21), we should be able to trace in it a different set of names and images, proposed in ancient times.

It is not accidental that the ancients should liken the human Ego to the goddess Venus, and the higher ternary to the three Graces, for this mythology was linked with the higher being of man (Table 2). The Greek names for the Graces have received much attention in esoteric literature, and it is evident that these conceal great wisdom. The Italian scholar, Ficino – an esotericist who was associated with many great Italian artists who gave the Renaissance its distinctive feature[21] – not only translated their names, approximately as given in this list, but linked them to cosmic principles:

TABLE 2 – THE HIGHER BODIES IN ONE ANCIENT SYSTEM

HIGHER TRIAD	ATMAN	Euphrosynes	The Grace, 'Joyful', belonging to the starry world
	BUDDHI	Aglaia	The Grace, 'Splendour', belonging to the solar sphere
	MANAS	Thaliae	The Grace, 'Green and Fresh' belonging to the seeds of music
	EGO	Venus	The goddess of beauty

Ficino's esoteric writings had a deep impresssion on the Italian artist, Botticelli. It is therefore not surprising that the 'Venusian' symbolism hinted at in Table 2 may be seen in a new way by linking it directly with the two great Botticelli masterpieces, *The Birth of Venus* and the *Primavera*, both of which depict the goddess Venus treading lightly upon the Earth.[22] Table 3 sets down the correspondences with the realm of the physical world:

TABLE 3 – SYMBOLS OF THE LOWER BODIES

	ASTRAL	Air	Wind-blown tresses
LOWER TRIAD	ETHERIC	Water	Waves from which she is born
	PHYSICAL	Earth	The sand, or ground.

The image of wind-blown tresses recalls the fact that the Astral body is the body of desire: it is constantly in motion, as it seeks to reach after the object of its desire. This e-motional urgency is expressed in the motion of the tresses in the wind. In contrast, the Etheric body expresses itself through rhythms and regular patterns: hence, the rhythmic lapping of waves upon the sea-shore is a pertinent symbol for this invisible body.

An aim of meditation is to withdraw the Ego from the lower levels, where desire operates, and float free of the hypnotizing power of the material realm. In this way, the Ego can float as though on the surface of an entirely still lake. In this calm surface, the Ego may reflect the heavens above, and thus receive perfectly the effulgency of that Godhead of which it was part. In the Way of the Fool, this form of meditation is a prelude to looking into the secrets of Nature.

Now, one of the things which the Way of the Fool teaches is that if one wishes to remain in contact with the Godhead, desire (*kama*) is not in itself desirable. It is however eminently desirable – and even essential – for one wishing to gain experience of the material realm. Most Eastern philosophies all too readily teach an initiation of retreat – of flight back to spirit – as part of the cleansing of *kama*, or entanglement. In the Christian religion, such a way of flight is called the *Via Negativa*, or Negative Way. The Way of the Fool turns this idea around, and posits that the whole purpose of having a physical body (of 'riding an ass' or 'being an ass') is not to entertain notions of such a flight from the physical plane, but to use that body for gaining experience and knowledge.

The Way of the Fool is a sort of balancing act on a tightrope. While the

Fool has no wish to lose contact with his higher Self, he or she still wishes to gain experience of life: the Fool is pulled first this way, and then the next. Through such garnering of knowledge, he or she not only enriches the Ego, but also satisfies the need of the Godhead (of which the Ego is part) to explore the material plane. On the other hand, the Fool has no wish to gain experience of *superficial* life. His or her aim is always to pierce behind the surface, to penetrate the illusion of things, and to tap the reality hidden behind the snaring web of illusion. The Fool knows that the material plane, which so many people assume is the ultimate reality, is the most illusory of all things – a *maya* or shadow play.[23] We may trace in this belief an underlying conflict of the one who has elected to follow the Path of the Fool: he or she wishes to explore the material world in the full knowledge that the material world is a minefield of unrealities.

The ideal of the searching Fool is thinly disguised in many works of art and in a considerable body of literature which has developed since the 16th century. Very often, the theme of such art and literature dwells upon the uncertainty of the Ego, and upon the reluctance of the Ego to descend completely into the material realm – as the Way of the Fool demands.

This uncertainty and insecurity of the Ego in regard to thinking, feeling and willing is nowhere more clearly set down than in the portrayal of Hamlet, in Shakespeare's play. Although Shakespeare handled with incredible insight the nature of the Fool in several of his plays,[24] it is *Hamlet* which most clearly reflects the arcane meaning of the Ego. Hamlet's developing Ego is not strong enough to disentangle itself from the sense of death which is the inevitable consequence of entanglement in matter. Few heroes (if Prince Hamlet may be termed a hero at all) have recognized so completely the death-power of human thinking as to meditate upon a skull, contemplating the advantages and disadvantages of suicide. Few heroes have held such an insecure relationship to their beloved one, in the realm of feeling, as to drive her to distraction and suicide. Few heroes have descended so deeply into matter as to leap into an open grave; and few heroes have been so confused in their actions that they have killed an innocent man by running a sword through an arras – which was Shakespeare's symbol for the veil which, in the secret literature, hides the goddess Isis.[25] It seems that Shakespeare was intent upon portraying the breakdown of the normal human categories under the impact experienced by the Ego when it has been brought too deeply into matter. This confusion explains why the Prince of Denmark may be seen as both a genius and a Fool.

The play, *Hamlet*, is a study of the human spirit under the buffeting of an Ego which is not mature, and which feels it has lost contact with the Godhead. In this sense, Prince Hamlet is almost a child, and it was perceptive of Goethe to observe, in this character of the Prince, the image of a person on whom had been placed a task beyond his capability.[26]

Hamlet, like many esoteric works, was prophetic of the future development of Man. In esoteric terms, the period beginning the Renaissance in Italy, and the Elizabethan Age in England, marked a steady, if sometimes dramatic, growth of the human Ego. The esoteric School which directed the conditions for this growth was under the tutelage of the Medici family of 15th- and 16th-century Florence. In England, at that same time, the intensification of Ego, and its corresponding sense of separation from the Spiritual world, was so powerful that it encouraged one of the rulers of that time, Henry VIII, to break away from Papal authority. In this way, and perhaps unwittingly, he established a religion which envisaged a different relation between the human Ego and God from that taught by the Catholic Church.

In the numerological magic which lies behind the Tarot designs, the Fool card is generally associated with the zero. Some arcanists also link it with the *aleph*, which is the first letter of the Hebraic alphabet. This may seem to be something of a contradiction, for, in Hebraic numerology, the *aleph* is normally accorded the number one.[27] Indeed, some arcanists have linked the first card – the Juggler – with the *aleph* (opposite).

This seeming-conflict between the zero and the one is actually an intimate reflection on the nature of the Fool. The figure one – which stands alone and upright in the face of all other numbers – is clearly an excellent symbol for the Ego. There may be little doubt that the association between the numeral one and the Fool was intended to echo the letter I, which, in English, denotes the Ego. Only the possessor of an Ego can say *I* to that Ego. The Ego always stands alone in the face of what it is experiencing. It is the sole observer of the puppet play enacted before it. Perhaps it is this conflict between the circle of the zero and the number one (1) which explains the curious meditation figures (see Appendix page 355) – combinations of circles and straight lines – which Mark Hedsel presented to me shortly before his death.

With these considerations of the zero and the one, we reach into the Spiritual paradox of the Fool. This paradox is that the Fool, and the Ego itself, are *at once a zero and a one*. They each represent something which seems to be without foundation – a single thing severed from the whole – and yet which seems, at the same time, to be a complete unity, a unique

The Juggler card, from an Italian tarot deck of the mid-19th century. Note the Hebrew letter aleph (top right), which is echoed in the posture of his arms.

individuality. This conflict between not-being and being is one of the underlying themes of Hamlet's famous soliloquy, beginning, 'To be or not to be . . .'[28]

The stick carried by the Fool is also a symbol of the upright I, and thus of the Ego. The stick over the right shoulder of the Fool (see page 22) is weighed down by a bag which may be seen as another *zero* form – a circle. Thus, the stick and bag represent the altercation between being and nothingness which characterizes the human sense of Ego. 'Now I am this, now I am that' is the state of all humans who have not yet sufficiently developed their Egos to become their own man or woman. There is deep significance in the fact that the great early 16th-century occultist, Paracelsus, who knowingly stood at the very beginning of the period marking the development of the Ego, should have adopted publicly a Latin motto which translates, 'Let no man who can belong to himself belong to another.' This is the tutelary call of the nascent Ego.[29]

The divinatory system of cartomancy, or taromancy, was first developed in the south of Europe. The name *Fool* on the first Tarot card is a translation either of the French word *Le Mat*, or the equivalent Italian, *Il Matto*.[30] This derivation is not without significance, as the root *ma* is one of the important Sanskrit terms relating to *ma*tter, which participates in several important esoteric terms, such as *maya*.[31] This etymology has connotations that point to the pathway of the Fool, for this is 'the Way Down'. It is the way of descent into, or contemplation of, 'matter', through which one accumulates the dark matter of karma.

The development of the Ego has led to a new feeling for individual freedom, from both religious and political structures and strictures. As Mark Hedsel made clear, this burgeoning sense of freedom was felt strongly among poets and artists, who are usually particularly sensitive to Spiritual changes. Those artists who were fortunate enough to belong to esoteric Schools – where initiation was studied – began to create images which, if they did not serve the Schools themselves, became individual-istic to a level which would have been quite impossible in the heyday of Byzantine or late mediaeval Church art. When artists began to sign works of art, they were showing a concern no longer merely for the glory of God, or their patron, but for their own personal Egos. Through a signature or personal mark, the Ego recognizes that a deed – an act of Will – will continue after its lifetime or embodiment.

Jan van Eyck's famous lengthy signature on his painting of the wedding of Jan Arnolfini, now in the National Gallery, London, is not merely a signature to the picture, but a record of the artist's role as witness to the wedding, recording that 'I was here'.[32] However, not all stamps of the Ego were so elaborate, and not all were in the form of signatures. Some artists adopted personalized symbols as Ego-marks. For example, the 16th-century Flemish artist, Herri met de Bles, who was certainly involved in an esoteric group,[33] adopted a much older type of 'signature', in using an owl as his personal symbol. However, this owl was far more than merely the equivalent of his signature – it was also a symbol of the wisdom of the higher Self. As we shall see, it was a reflection of the same avian spirit which Mark Hedsel encountered in a deep experience in Ferrara. The 16th-century German alchemist, Heinrich Khunrath, used the device of an owl as a vignette in one of his books: this owl wore spectacles to symbolize its higher vision, and it carried in its claws a pair of torches. Alongside the bird were two burning candles. The motto beneath dwelled on this excess of light: 'What is the use of torches, lights and eyeglasses, if people will not see.'[34] The *Noctua*, or night-owl, was sacred to Minerva, Greek goddess of wisdom. Khunrath clearly felt that the arcane wisdom, with which he was familiar through his involvement with alchemy and Rosicrucianism, should be brought from the darkness of night into the light of day. Yet, as his motto indicates, he felt despair that, even when this hidden wisdom had been revealed, there were still many people who could not see it.

The nature and emphasis of initiation disciplines vary from School to School, yet, traditionally, the two major divisions in School methods arise from whether the teacher instructs by means of pictures and symbols, or by means of oral methods. In the earliest hermetic Egyptian literature which has survived into modern times, mainly in the Greek language, the two major divisions were called the *Epoptic* method, and the *Mystes* method, respectively. Some of the ancient Schools combined the two. For example, in the Eleusian cult of Demeter, widely popular in ancient Greece, the Mystes were initiated in the Lesser Mysteries, while the Epopts were initiated in the Greater Mysteries. Even in such combined systems, however, the two methods were seen as being so different that individuals were required to allow at least five years between the two initiations.

The *Epoptic* method taught by means of symbols and images while the *Mystes* method generally taught orally, with instructions given by the Master, sometimes in dialogue form. Within these two great methods, the various Paths ran in many directions, even though their purposes were the same – the perfecting of man, and the leading of the 'natural' man by ever ascending degrees to the state where he became a 'Spiritual' man.

One surviving document which points to the power of the ancient epoptic method is the mysterious *Book of Dzyan* which H. P. Blavatsky, the 19th-century esotericist, claimed was the inspirational basis for her masterwork on arcane lore, *The Secret Doctrine*.[35] However, this ancient, wordless book of images to which she refers is claimed to be far more than merely a collection of symbols. The esotericist G. S. Arundale, who constructed an entire meditative discipline around his familiarity with the text, informed his readers that the book was so 'magnetized' that anyone who contemplated the images was afforded insights of the most profound kind.[36] A person who follows a Path in modern times may have a similar epoptic relation to ancient symbols by meditating upon them, and this was certainly one of the meditative practices followed by Mark Hedsel (see Appendix, on page 355).[37] Certain symbols do have the undeniable capability of 'speaking' a language which cannot be equated in any way with the oral or written forms of language, and which cannot be translated. Symbols can bypass the thinking mechanism of the brain (which is accustomed to dealing with words), and work directly upon the soul. This is precisely how the epoptic method of initiation works. Certain forms of art were, in the past, designed precisely with this type of symbolism in mind.

In modern times it is the oral tradition of the *Mystes* which predominates in most arcane Schools. The five centuries which have passed since the introduction of printing into Europe have ensured an almost hypnotic reliance upon the power of words. With this hypnotically induced reliance has gone much of the old power to read the inner contents of pictures and symbols, save in a purely interpretational and analytical sense. This degeneration of a natural faculty of the soul has influenced the arcane Schools just as much as it has influenced ordinary life and thought. It has, indeed, encouraged some Schools to emphasize the need to develop a feeling for the power of symbols, and the ancient epoptic way, through what may be described as 'meditative looking'. This training of vision is based on the demonstrable truth that there is a faculty in man (a faculty which is presently deeply hidden) that can hear the speech of Nature.

The Way of the Fool is distinguished from the ordinary path of life, from ordinary conduct, by its commitment both to the search into Secret Knowledge, and by its 'meditative looking'. This is the great secret, and perhaps the only secret of the Way. The Way of the Fool is essentially the way of experience, by which the realm of matter is entered into and contemplated deeply, with a view to wresting from matter its hidden secrets.

There is a close parallel between certain impulses within the Way of the Fool, and the secret way of Rosicrucianism.[38] As Mark Hedsel makes quite clear, the Rosicrucians of late mediaeval Europe took it as their main task to ensure that the developing Ego would find a relationship with Christ by way of a clearly marked path of esoteric Christianity.[39]

In the view of most historians, Rosicrucianism itself did not appear in historical annals until the 17th century, as a result of which it was never persecuted as being heretical. However, its roots may be traced back (indeed, have been traced back) to the 14th century.[40] Many of the tracts and symbols published by the Rosicrucians were of an alchemical nature. This was inevitable, as there are very interesting parallels between the methods of Rosicrucianism and the spiritual aspirations behind Alchemy.[41]

Rosicrucianism was originally an esoteric Christian School which recognized that the same resurrectional life promised by Christ was also promised of Nature. The parallel between Man and Nature was recognized by the Rosicrucians, which is why, in their alchemical symbolism, Nature and Man was classified by a related triplicity of 'natural substances': *Salt, Mercury* and *Sulphur*, corresponding to Thinking, Feeling and Willing.[42]

Rosicrucianism, for all its Christian content, has its own roots in the hermeticism of the ancient Greeks, which (as we shall see) was itself Egyptian in origin.[43] When the scholar, Parthey, who specialized in hermetic lore, investigated the education of over 40 leading ancient Greek philosophers, writers and statesmen, he noted that all of them had studied under Egyptian teachers. For example, Plato had been a pupil of Sechnuphis, Pythagoras of Oenuphis, Eudoxus of Chonuphis, and so on.[44] These philosophers had studied in the hermetic Schools of Egypt – mainly in the secret Schools of Isis and Osiris.[45]

The study of the ancient hermetic texts, which had been one of the personal preoccupations of Mark Hedsel, reveals a seamless connection between the esoteric lore of ancient Egypt and the secret traditions and speculative philosophy of the Greeks. In its diversified classical forms – which included Gnosticism,[46] Alchemy and Astrology – it passed to Europe by means of Arabic learning, mainly through the great ninth-century astrological and alchemical schools of Baghdad. This same lore was then Europeanized and re-Christianized by the Rosicrucians. In this way has been preserved a living connection between the esoteric lore of ancient Egypt and modern hermeticism.

Man has changed since the times of ancient Greece, and he has changed even more since the times of ancient Egypt. The Schools have also developed, in order to accommodate these changes. Hermetic lore is very complex. Within its brief are found such diverse themes as reincarnation, astrology and karma, planetary spheres of descent, union with God and even many of the practical mental disciplines mentioned by Hedsel. The extraordinary fact is that these themes – and indeed all the important themes studied by modern occultists and hermeticists – are found in the earliest surviving Egyptian hermetic texts.[47] The connection between modern hermetic thought and the Egyptian mystery wisdom is very strong. It is so strong that I might claim the arcane literature of the past 2,000 years is nothing more than a series of footnotes to the ancient hermetic literature, examined in the light of the Resurrectional message of Christ, which laid the foundation for the New Mystery Wisdom of Christianity.

Are there any qualifications required for entering upon a Path? As we have pointed out, the way of the Path is not the same as the way of life, and qualifications for entry to a School are not at all like qualifications in life. Those who are in charge of the esoteric Schools know all too well that the secret of all mankind lies in the Will. They recognize that if a person wills to set out on a Path, then no School can possibly obstruct or deflect that person.

In theory, each School raises its own demands and preliminary qualifications. Generally, a willingness to be open-minded, experimental and committed is expected, if not always demanded. Some Schools insist that the neophyte should have a developed morality, since morality is not so much a badge of achievement in sweetness and light as an essential tool of investigation. Immorality – following the baser human instincts and impulses – leads to Spiritual blindness, and just as those who are blind in life cannot see the wonders around them, so the immoral cannot see on the Spiritual plane.

It is true that no one can develop very far without refining the inner moral world, and redeeming the darkness within. However, the Way of the Fool does not itself appear to make such an initial demand on the neophyte. Normally, demands on morality will arise later – not from outer commands, but from within the neophyte himself: this is one of the mysteries of the Way of the Fool. As the Fool progresses along the Way, the darker things begin to fall off. He or she may, for example, stop eating meat, drinking alcohol, or smoking . . . Generally, these decisions arise not so much from a show of willpower, but as an indication of a reluctance to engage in activities that seem to impede the meditations and exercises which lead to spiritual development.

What does one learn in these Schools, which so mysteriously make themselves available, and offer to teach what most people would regard as incomprehensible secrets? In brief – one learns about the Spiritual World which is a closed secret to ordinary vision. This, indeed, is the sole Mystery in which one is schooled. It is as simple as that.

However, in another way it is *not* quite as simple as that, for the Spiritual World is vast. The Spiritual World lies spread out in another realm beyond the world material, its invisible power interpenetrating and entirely sustaining this latter. In one respect – and perhaps only in one respect – esoteric knowledge is like ordinary knowledge: the more one knows, the further one sees, and the more one perceives just how vast and beyond comprehension is the reservoir of knowledge. Given this painful insight, the question which lies at the basis of all initiation dawns on the neophyte – how can a mere seed of a human brain hope to encompass this limitless creative wisdom? And, as is often the case on the Path, with the formulation of the heart-felt question comes the answer: the human brain can acquire this wisdom because it was fashioned from that same wisdom itself. The grey matter of the brain is actually the veil of the Spiritual substance of the stars.

It is said that only one who is fully healed may gaze upon the last Mystery with impunity. That 'undiscover'd country from whose bourn no traveller returns' is the Spiritual World beyond, from which, as Hamlet opines, ordinary men do not return.[48] However, it is a bourn from which those initiated at the highest levels may return at will, if they are willing to don the mask of time which incarnation offers, and mix with other humans.

The Way of the Fool makes use of a language, and repertoire of terms, which requires some explanation. Almost all esoteric systems have developed one form or other of what is called 'The Language of the Birds', or the 'Green Language', as a means of communication.[49] This is an arcane tongue which permits initiates, and those on the Path, to communicate secrets to one another in a form which is incomprehensible to those not versed in the language. Mark Hedsel discusses the nature of this language at several points in his text (see for example page 56). In addition to using this esoteric language, the Way of the Fool makes extensive use of a wide range of specialist arcane terms (all of which are explained in the text or in notes). The Way of the Fool is an ancient way: Mark Hedsel has no difficulty in tracing its historical records to roots in the mediaeval period. In view of this, it is surprising to find Mark Hedsel using certain arcane terms which only came into use in Europe during the late 19th century: his use of the Sanskrit, *Atman*, *Buddhi* and *Manas*, in Table 1 (page 21), is an example. A glance at recent history will help to explain this seeming contradiction.

All genuine esoteric teachings point to traditions that describe different physical forms in which mankind dwelled in earlier times. Some of the arcane literature which deals with these early conditions of pre-history seems to be well over 5,000, or even 6,000 years old, and is in a language scarcely known to philologists, called *Senzar*.[50]

This early language describes human forms which were quite unlike the present ones. The earliest human forms had no power to descend completely to the Earth at all.[51] Later on, these forms did float down to what was then the Earth, but even these were scarcely material. Later still, human beings took bodies which were suitable for swimming in water, and, subsequently, bodies which resembled animals. Only in comparatively recent times – before the Atlantean epoch – did the intelligent biped develop into the outer image with which we are familiar.

Connected with the story of the early, gradual descent into material bodies are two lands which we now call Lemuria and Atlantis. Each of these lost continents has gained considerable fame in the past century due to the attention paid to them by 19th-century British and American arcanists.[52] A vast literature has been constructed around these two continents, and around lore pertaining to them and even earlier continents. In spite of this literature, they remain misty to our vision, and it seems to be the last poor fragments of a once-mighty Atlantis which emerged into our own history only at the point, perhaps 12,000 years ago, when it was on the edge of collapse.[53] Atlantis remains for us a mythological shade to which much of the esoteric traditions that emerge from Tibet, India and Egypt may well be traced. The sad truth is that most of the arcane-seeming literature which deals with these historically remote continents reflects more the inventive mind of its authors than any actual Atlantean reality. Civilizations certainly existed on Atlantis, yet their true histories are still hidden in the secret archives.[54]

However, one reported detail in the popular account of Atlantean history which is undoubtedly true is the story of what happened prior to the catastrophic end of this great continent. This account was regarded by the Greek philosopher Plato as ancient, even when he mentioned it in the early part of the fifth century BC.[55] In modern arcane literature, the events which preceded the end of Atlantis are called the 'guided migrations'.

When it was clear to the Spiritual leaders of Atlantis that their continent was to sink in a final cataclysm, the teachers in the Mystery Schools gathered together a great number of their pupils, and began a slow and arduous journey from the stricken continent to the East. To the north-east lay what was to become the British Isles and the Franco-Spanish land mass. To the south-east lay the vast continent of Africa.

Guided by their initiate Teachers, these groups finally reached the Nile valley, which, far more fertile than it is today, was a black land lush with vegetal greenery. There they settled, and established the framework of what would eventually become the great civilization of Egypt.

Two other migrations had taken place from Atlantis in earlier times, before the final catastrophe; one to north India, the other to Egypt.[56] This meant that even before the Egyptian civilization was established, there were already initiate-based cultures in other parts of the world. Perhaps the more important of these was that which had been established to the north – partly in what is now called Tibet, partly in Nepal, and spreading into northern India, and into China.

From an esoteric point of view, the migrant offshoots from Atlantis –

that which settled Tibet and north India, and that which settled Egypt – were very different. With the passage of time, these differences became even more pronounced, for, in order to adapt to different localities and Spiritual needs, the Teachers who controlled them established entirely different Spiritual systems and methods of initiation.

At various times, there were meetings and fructifications between the Egyptian and Indian cultures, but these remained peripheral to the general drift of the esoteric history of these great civilizations. The Indo-Tibetan system began to dominate the East, while the Egyptian system began to dominate the West. Even up to recent times, it is the arcane tradition and esoteric lore that was handed down from ancient Egypt which has remained of enduring interest to the West.

Until comparatively recently, virtually every arcane system in practical use in the West was derived, ultimately, from the secret Schools of Egypt. The hermetic Mysteries of Isis and Osiris which had flourished in Egypt; the ancient Greek Mysteries of Asclepius at Cos, of Apollo at Delphi, of the *kore* (maiden) at Eleusis, which flourished in Greece and Rome; the Christian Mysteries of the Palestinian Jews, nourished by the Essenes, and the Gnostics; the hermetic Mysteries of alchemy and astrology which flourished during the Arabic Caliphate of Baghdad, in the eighth and ninth centuries, and which were eventually handed on to mediaeval Europe; the Mysteries of 15th-century Rosicrucianism which revitalized the Christian message – all these traced their origins and initiation techniques back to ancient Egypt. There were many rivers and streams, but only one source.[57]

Unfortunately, in recent years, this single source, which has enriched the Western schools for so many centuries, has been breached. In the past 120 years, modern esoteric thought has both suffered and benefited from an invasion of Sanskrit terms and Oriental ideas. This modern invasion was chiefly a consequence of the activities of the Theosophists, who introduced many Oriental ideas and terms into European thought towards the end of the 19th century.[58] These ideas and terminologies were undoubtedly well adapted for those of an Oriental nature, involved in Eastern disciplines, yet have not always proved to be quite so beneficial for those following a Western discipline. The Western tradition of initiation has always – even in pre-Christian Mystery Schools – been ultimately directed towards a Christian outlook. The Oriental tradition of initiation, for all its deep wisdom, recognized nothing of the role of Christ. With this lack of the Christian impulse, the Oriental esotericism cannot be of value to the development of Western esotericism.

Of course, in the distant past, there had been earlier importations of

Oriental terms, which entered the West largely by way of the secret Schools. Many of these terms appear to have been Sanskrit in origin – and may have been a result of trade between the two great civilizations of East and West, about 5,000 years ago. Among such imported words were many that were evidently once esoteric. For example, the Sanskrit esoteric term *Dyaus pitar* is still used in a slightly disguised form in most European languages, and, in a suitable symbolic form, in all modern horoscopes. This pair of words came, by way of the Greek version *Diou-pater*, then through the Latin *Juppiter*, into our modern form, *Jupiter*. A later version of the name, *Jove*, gave us such English words as jovial, and even entered the French and Italian day-name for the 'day of Jupiter' (our own Thursday, or Thor's day), their *Jeudi* and *Giovedi*, respectively. This development is merely a sample of a whole vocabulary of words which were once specialist terms in the Mystery Centres, and later demoted by exoteric use. It is with good reason that the philologist, Owen Barfield, points out that the English words *diurnal, diary, dial* and *divine* have a similar and communal origin, derived from a Sanskrit word for God.[59]

Now, while these survivals do reveal an earlier contact between ancient Greece and the northern Mystery Centres of Tibet and India, they are exceptional. Modern esoteric research into arcane lore reveals that the majority of words previously used in Mystery Centres may be traced not to India (the Indo-European root language), but to Egypt. This truth was so deeply felt by the 19th-century esoteric scholar, Gerald Massey, that he attempted to trace a very large number of English words to Egyptian origins.[60] Perhaps parts of Massey's book are slightly obsessive, yet his two volumes of etymology still make a most fascinating read for one interested in esoteric thought: many of his observations are based on the most profound insights. One of his theses is that the once-communal language of the Atlanteans was carried into the ancient roots of both Sanskrit and Egyptian. He argues that, in view of these findings, it is foolish to trace so many Greek words to Sanskrit, when one might just as easily trace them to the Egyptian.

Among the many examples which Massey examined in this connection is the Greek word that gave us our own word *sceptic*. Philologists tell us that the word is from the Greek *skeptikos*, 'one who examines'. This, it is usually argued by scholars fond of the Sanskrit theory of philology, is from the Sanskrit *spashta*, meaning 'manifest'. However, as Massey points out, it is far more reasonable to trace the Greek to the Egyptian word *skeb* which means 'to reflect'. Furthermore, the ancient Egyptian *Sep* was 'a judge', while a *tek* was 'a thing which had been hidden'. From this we can infer that a *Sep tek* was one who made judgements on hidden things, suggesting that the meaning, if not the sound, of sceptic has changed little in 5,000 years. Massey's philology does give us cause to question the accepted notion that such words as *sceptic* and *spectre* (another popular modern word which came down from Mystery Centres) were Latin renderings of Greek Epicurean terms, for it is clear that they were Egyptian, and predate the Greeks by many centuries.[61]

Several occultists of the early 20th century realized the dangers implicit in the orientalizing tendency of Theosophy, and opted to speak out. Among these was the remarkable esotericist Rudolf Steiner, who had familiarized himself in a very deep way with the Western hermetic tradition, and in particular with Rosicrucian thought.[62] He saw quite clearly that the development of Western esotericism was linked with Christ. Furthermore, he recognized that this connection could not be brought to any useful expression in Theosophy and its offshoots, for their models and archetypes were essentially Oriental, and were not published with the idea of Christ in mind.

Steiner recognized that only one living esoteric stream in the West had succeeded in maintaining a healthy relationship with Christ. This was the system of initiation developed by the Rosicrucians. Steiner was among the first to recognize that Rosicrucianism had been developed mainly to cope with the Spiritual changes which would become commonplace after the 16th century, when a new feeling for the Ego would become developed in Europe.[63]

One consequence of all the historical factors we have just examined is (as Mark Hedsel admits), that it often proves difficult to given an account of modern initiation systems without recourse to Theosophical terms. The Way of the Fool, which is especially interested in the Spiritual nature of language, is keen always to adopt new words and ideas, but (like many other Western Schools) has learned to be suspicious of the Oriental dictionaries, if only on the grounds that the Eastern system of initiation is so profoundly different from the Western. In consequence, Mark Hedsel has tried to extend and redefine some of the specialist Theosophical terms, giving an explanation of many in a form which I have tried to incorporate into the Bibliographic Notes at the end of this book. However, this attempt to incorporate widely used terms into the language of the Fool should not disguise the truth that those words frequently refer to models which are foreign to the modern view of things.

Mark Hedsel did not believe that the Theosophical system has provided a satisfactory terminology to aid the development of Western man, yet he was eminently a practical person. He recognized that most of the esoteric terms in use in the West today are in themselves derived from the stream of Theosophy. Had the Theosophical influence not been so pervasive, he would have elected to use the Graeco–Latin terms, as preserved by such great Rosicrucians as Paracelsus – if only because most of these terms carry us back to the Egyptian hermetic sources which nourished modern esoteric lore.[64]

It is curious that esotericism – which prides itself on its silence – seems to be so beleaguered by words. The need to preserve silence about the esoteric truths has always been an important theme in esoteric Schools, and in the art-forms such Schools have encouraged and supported. Round about 1520, the Flemish artist, Quentin Metsys, painted a most remarkable picture, now entitled (though without any real justification) *Allegory of Folly*. The picture depicts a foolish-looking man, wearing on his head – seemingly as an extension of his hat – a cock's head. He is literally wearing a cockscomb, the traditional symbol of the Fool.

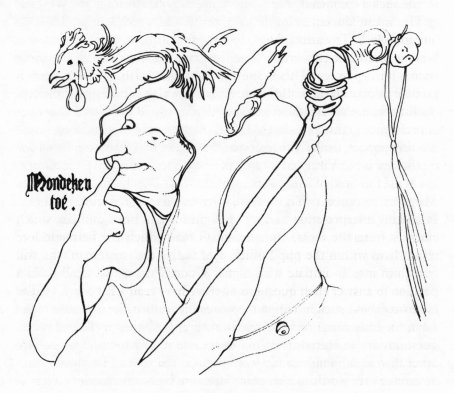

Drawing based on Quentin Metsys, Allegory of Folly, *(c. 1520) which deals with the initiation theme of potential spiritual growth, and the need for silence.*

Alongside the cock, but still projecting from the hat, are two large feathers. The man carries in his left arm a long stick, the top of which appears to be transforming into a mannikin. This small creature is bare-bottomed, and his head is twisted around to be almost frontal to the picture. Around his neck is what appears to be a necklace of fronds. We need not examine this picture in detail here: it is quite evident that, far from being an *Allegory of Folly*, the painting is constructed around an arcane theme pertaining to silence. In other words, this picture has been painted with initiates in mind. This is confirmed by several details within the image which would remain inexplicable save in terms of initiation symbolism.

The man may well *look* foolish, with his great aquiline nose, and foolish grin, yet he knows something concerning which he must not speak . . . This is confirmed by a black-letter inscription on the picture. Alongside the lips of the man (which are pressed closed with the index finger of his right hand) are the Flemish words *Mondeken toe*, which mean 'keep your mouth [trap] shut'. What does this Fool know which merits such a command, straight from the Mystery lore?

The mannikin emerging from the top of the stick is redolent of initiation lore. Towards its top, the wooden shaft of the stick seems to become plastic, or rubberoid. It appears that the mannikin is struggling from a birth-passage. This notion, of the virgin birth of a little man, is probably a play on the Latin for stick, *virga*, which is here giving birth to the little man. Perhaps the fronded necklace around the mannikin's neck is a reference to the corn-dolly. This is the mannikin's badge of office: he is a tiny poppet, or dolly, born from the stellar Virgo, who in the stellar mythology is the Virgin corn-goddess.[65]

On the forehead of Metsys' man, carefully located between the eyes, is a large excrescence: could this be a reference to a burgeoning third eye? Is it taking interpretation too far to link the birth of this mannikin, which emerges from the *virga*, with the small man which the hermetic lore insists lives within the pupil of the eye? Is this the small man who will transform into an initiate with higher vision? Perhaps we shall be in a position to answer such questions after we have read what Mark Hedsel has to say about such initiation themes as the feather, the cockscomb, the *Ishon* (or little man) and the transforming stick, the *virga*. Until such questions are answered, it will be as well to regard the picture as little other than an admonishment, warning the Fool to hold his tongue, and be careful with words, which point always to the mystery of the Logos.

* * *

'There is such a thing as magic.' It was one of the first things that Mark Hedsel said to me shortly after we had started working on the book. 'There is such a thing as magic,' he said, 'but it has been misunderstood.'

I looked at him inquiringly, in the hope that he would develop such a tantalizing theme.

'Most people think of magic as the subverting of natural laws,' he continued. 'However, real magic does not subvert anything. Magic is merely the result of directing the creative activity of the Spiritual world into the material plane. Those who know the rules for inviting such Spiritual intervention are called magicians.[66] Magic is concerned far more with knowledge than power: only the Black Magician will concern himself or herself with power.'

He smiled ironically. 'Yet do not think that all those who *call* themselves magicians have the power to command Spiritual intervention.'

I asked, 'If magic is, as you say, a matter of directing the activity of the Spiritual world, then, surely, when a gardener grows a flower in his garden, he is practising magic?'

'Most certainly. As one modern cabbalist has observed, every time we make a decent cup of tea, we are successfully invoking the Four Elements.[67] But consider carefully: you regard the flowering of a plant as a "natural thing" and assume that the flowering follows natural laws. This is a quite reasonable assumption – yet, in making such an assumption, we tend to forget that, in truth, we do not know what these natural laws are. All we see in the growth and flowering of a plant is an unfolding and developing on the material plane. Surely, this unfolding is the manifestation of something beyond the portal of our senses?

'We do not, with ordinary science at least, know what power pulls a seed into growth, lifts it to the surface of the Earth, and allows it to flower in such a combination of grace and colour. Did that grace of intense colour come from the black earth? we might ask in some surprise. In fact, we do not understand what a flower is. We have been misled in modern times by science: we tend to think that we have understood it when we have merely described a process of germination, rooting, growth and flowering. In truth, while we might be able to describe with some degree of accuracy, we do not understand. We are all too easily fooled by the outer manifestation, and forget the power of the invisible. If we could really understand what a flower is, then we would be able to understand the working of the Etheric, and we would have that Spiritual vision which marks the early stage of genuine initiation.

'Take, for example, that stage which we call "flowering". The ordinary view of the plant is that the flower itself marks the final development of the plant's life, yet this is not quite true. When the life of the plant is examined in the light of esoteric thought, other developments are observed taking the life of the plant further. For example, there is a sense in which the bee is a continuation of the flower, in which case the nectar of the flower can be seen as a higher development of the plant: as Goethe himself observed, it is surely no accident that the butterfly looks like certain flower-petals in flight. If you look at the flower and the butterfly with creative imagination, you will see the latter as a higher stage of development – of evolution, if you like – of the plant. Just so (and perhaps more directly perceptibly) the scent of the plant is a higher stage of plant life – a level of Spiritual development beyond the flower . . . In this higher sense, the flower, while still rooted in the earth, fills far more than the space of the garden.'

'In recent times, we have killed any feeling for the intervention of the Spiritual – for what we might call the magical – with our words and attitudes. We may readily admit that we do not know what magic is, but we cannot bring ourselves to admit that we do not really know what Nature is. The outer forms of Nature may be described, but it is only when the inner powers are perceived that Nature may be understood.'

I write here about magic, yet we are really dealing with the secrets of initiation, which is one form of magic. I should make myself quite clear. The Path of initiation, in its simplest form, consists of a series of techniques for speeding up ordinary human development. To an outsider, such a development may appear to be *magical*. Yet, in truth, it is in accord with the laws of chemistry and physics. If all goes well with the evolution of the Earth, in a distant future a great many people will entirely Spiritualize their bodies, and develop faculties and abilities which would now appear short of miraculous. The one on the Path of initiation is merely seeking to speed up this normal development, to attain these developed faculties and abilities more quickly.

We do not have to go in search of the miraculous, for it is all around us. Beyond the confines of the world we call our own is an invisible world, which pours into it influences and benefits without which we could not continue to exist for even a second. The Church, esoteric bodies and individual magicians continually entreat this world to pour Spiritual bounties in their own direction, to support their own specific undertakings and aspirations: this is prayer. This is the basis of the activity we call magic. The successful practice of magic is merely the use of special techniques to obtain Spiritual benefits from the higher realm.

Originally, the Christian Church was privy to the secrets of human evolution, and guardian of this knowledge, transmitted from the ancient Mystery Wisdom of Egypt and Greece, and merged with the new Mystery Wisdom of Christ. The early Church recognized that one of the factors in the Mystery of Christ was that He literally enacted upon Earth what was to become, in a distant period, the birthright of all good men and women. Traces of this esoteric teaching are still contained in many of the words used in the various sects of the Christian Church. For example, the term 'resurrectional body of Christ' was, in the Mystery Centres, *Augoeideian*, which meant 'body of rays'. This arcane was expressed in mediaeval art as an aura of radiations round the body of Christ. It would be unrealistic to imagine that the Church politic has been a trusted or efficient guardian of this ancient esoteric wisdom. The esoteric purpose behind the Mystery of Christ has, to some extent, been more accurately preserved within the various so-called 'heretical' bodies which were misunderstood by the Church, and persecuted. The persecutions which began in the 13th century, and turned into the hideous visage of the Catholic Inquisition, were a systematic attempt to stamp out the vestiges of the secret knowledge which survived in the 'heretical' groups such as the Gnostics, the Albigensians and the Templars.[68] The Church had forgotten that there is, inbuilt into certain souls, a wish to speed up their personal Spiritual development, in a direction which is no longer served by the Church.

The neophyte enters a Path – such as the Way of the Fool – which is essentially concerned with speeding up natural development. This notion of speeding up Nature is practicable only within a framework of a belief in reincarnation; the idea of rebirth from lifetime to lifetime lies at the root of all Mystery Wisdom. In the normal way of things, certain remarkable powers of vision will come to a person quite naturally over a period of many lifetimes. This development takes place in what we might call the School of Life, and involves no special esoteric training, discipline or knowledge. However, the same growth of vision may be earned by a special Schooling within the space of only one or two lifetimes.

The techniques for such speeded-up development – the techniques of initiation – are, of course, very ancient and well tried, yet there are still dangers involved in the speeding up of Nature. For example, under certain conditions, the developing Ego begins to think of itself as being somehow different, somehow supra-human. When this occurs, the one on the Path can easily degenerate under that disease of the soul which we call Egoism. This is a self-centred illusionism fostered by the demons, which, as Mark Hedsel's narrative makes quite clear, are always anxious to deflect humans from a Path of Spiritual development.

In modern esotericism, it is taught that within all human beings there dwell uninvited Spiritual beings. These beings have been given very many different names in different stages of history, but the mediaeval Christian Church categorized them under the general heading of demons. In modern esoteric lore they are sometimes called *shadows* or *doubles.* The word double, which has, to some extent, been commercialized in the German *dopplegänger,* is an excellent term, however. The double is a sort of dark double which so closely resembles its host that it may, when seen as a separate entity, be taken as that host itself.

However, in other respects, this 'double-goer' is quite different from its host. The healthy human being – what we have here called the 'host' – is usually full of creative energies, capable of happiness. He or she may be warm with other people and keen to help others. These are, indeed, the very qualities which one seeks to develop when on the Path – especially towards those others who accompany one on the Path. Unfortunately, the dark double has none of these important human qualities. It has no human warmth or joy, simply because it is not human. In effect, this shadow being is a remnant of a much older stream of human development, and is now something of an interloper in human life: it is almost parasitic. This double is an intruder within the human being it inhabits.

The point is that the sick human Ego is itself isolated and cold – it does not show a warm and lively interest in other people. This makes it a particularly useful tool for the dark double. The double is intensely intelligent, yet it lacks all human warmth: like everything else in the cosmos, it seeks out that which reflects its own nature.

The methods and techniques which have been designed in esoteric circles to cope with this dark double are themselves highly evolved, and no Adept would feel free to discuss them openly. Our purpose is not to discuss such techniques, but to point to the existence of the double, and indicate something of its role in the life of humans.

It is almost inevitable that one who has entered the Path of development will encounter this double within himself or herself. The encounter is rarely a pleasant one, as Mark Hedsel's account makes quite clear.

When I first read Mark Hedsel's draft of his book, it was this question of the double which I found the most difficult thing to understand. Even so,

I recognized that it was of great importance, and I resolved to ask him to explain his experience more fully.

'I understand your question. Even one who has had a direct experience of the double cannot understand it all that well, either. When I first encountered the double I was utterly shocked. It was rather like looking in a mirror and seeing not one's own reflection, but that of a dark monster which aped one's own external appearance and actions. It was a low-grade simian copy of myself. This double spoke with a simulacrum of my own voice, yet it was cold and aloof – totally egotistical, and totally lacking in interest in other human beings. It seemed that there was another person inside me, who was prepared to talk and make judgements on my behalf. What was perhaps most surprising was the extreme negativity of this being, its almost pathological hatred of any joy or warmth.

'As my understanding of the creature grew, I began to understand why the esoteric literature could describe it as being both natural and unnatural. It is natural in so far as we all have a double indwelling; it is unnatural in so far as it is a leech, a drain on energy, rather than an invited guest. It is natural in so far as it participates in our life; it is unnatural in that it is not in the least interested in our Spiritual well-being or personal destiny.

'My own taste of this inner being was akin to a feeling that I had living within me a desiccated old scholar, who had an unaccountable dislike of the world around, yet who could take over my life almost at will. Whilst its voice was dry and even whiny, the intelligence it displayed was quite extraordinary: it was far more clever in the manipulation of words and ideas than I would ever be. The dead old scholar was very clever and inventive, but not in the slightest way creative.

'Curiously, it was this very glimpse of the inner coldness which led me to see that the secret of life rests in what I can only call "creative joy". I was reminded that William Blake had perceived his own inner double – what he called his *spectre* – but he also saw that the inner spirit of man should be given over to the expression of eternal joy.[69] It is in this that the Path of the Rosicrucian (which was that followed by Blake) and the Path of the Fool seem to meet: they both see the inner Darkness as a double, and the inner Light as creative energy.

'This vision of the double, and the realization that there seemed to be no way of shrugging this monster off from my own being, was terrible. Afterwards, while reflecting upon this creature, I realized just how inappropriate was the word *shadow* or even *double,* for the creature who dwelled within us was really more substantial than a shadow, and far too remote from humanity to be a human double. A more fitting term would be *deadman*.

'It is a most distressing stage on the Path when one realizes that one is accompanied always and everywhere by a *deadman*, a clever deadman, anxious to usurp one's own being.'

He laughed. 'But I have at least pointed to the antidote, which is creative joy ... Furthermore, the problem is that the deadman is essential. You see, David, the Fool has to get rid of the deadman before he can climb into Heaven. It is the process which the esotericists call *fission* (or separation of the light and dark): for development, the dark must give way to the light, yet before that is possible, they must separate. Only then is fission possible.'[70]

Almost as soon as he had finished speaking, Mark seemed to lose interest in the theme of the deadman, as though it were better left undeveloped. He was pensive, and when he spoke again there was a new edge of seriousness in his voice.

'When you consider the number of times initiates have broken the silence, it may seem surprising that there are any secrets to tell.'

'You mean Plutarch and Apuleius?'[71] I suggested

'Yes – and Rabelais and Saint-Germain . . .'[72]

I nodded to show that I followed, yet I found myself wondering what he was driving at.

'But all these revelations have one thing in common . . .'

'Which is?'

'They only go so far. They do not seem to reach into the essence of initiation. Their accounts become stories, entertainments. For sure, they are filled with symbolism, insights and wit, yet they remain merely stories, bordering on myth. For some reason, they cannot reach into the truth. They describe only the outer events, the rituals – perhaps what they felt as human beings during the experience of the Mysteries . . . These authors could never tell what they learned about the Secret of Secrets – they never could reveal what really gripped them, stripped them, and led them naked into that splendour beyond.'

He laughed. 'Remember – when Lucius the ass is suddenly transformed back into human form, he has no words. The darkness of the ass has dropped away, and Lucius [whose name means 'light-filled'] is free of the darkness has become human, dwelling in the spiritual. Now – having been there myself – I understand why Lucius should have been rendered speechless. There are no words for the higher experiences – only symbols. There *is* a limit to what one can say with words. Once you step beyond the boundary of the ordinary, and wish to communicate what you have seen, then you have to speak in poetry or symbols.

'Yet even the poetic frenzy will only take you so far. As you continue on the visionary Path, even the rules of art begin to break down. You might, like Dante, make flights of poetic symbolism so sublime that they have the power to carry even the most obtuse reader beyond the familiar, into the Spiritual.[73] Or you might, like Rabelais, throw yourself into a buffoon's burlesque, fooling your way with an arcane language which few even recognize as arcane. You might even, like Mozart, break into music so exquisite that its beams of sunlight touch levels where few men have ever been . . .[74] Yet, in spite of this, there is a point beyond which art cannot go.'

We had been sitting side by side at the desk, the manuscript before us. Now, I turned to search his eyes, trying to seek an explanation. He seemed to speak reluctantly, and when he did, it was slowly.

'The truth I now recognize. It is more than merely a matter of words that holds one back . . . It is more even than a failure of art . . .'

He paused again, and then his face broke into a delightful smile.

'Yes – I know what it is. Cunning old Rabelais touched upon the truth – Rabelais, who had taken the Way of the Fool to the extreme, and was so accustomed to fooling around that he could deal with important things only with his old power of joking.[75] He summed up the problem. He revealed the nature of the shadow which falls over an initiate when he or she tries to speak.'

His eyes finally met mine.

'Rabelais, fearful that he might unwittingly reveal hidden secrets, said: "This Story would seem pleasant enough, were we not to have always the Fear of God before our Eyes." '[76]

Chapter One

> He who has passed through the innermost portal becomes
> somwhat different from other men: he is full of bliss, joy,
> and peace.
>
> (J.A. Comenius, *The Labyrinth of the World and the
> Paradise of the Heart*, Lutzom ed., 1905, p.215)

In a learned and amusing book on Irish saints, Hubert Butler tells a story
of St Odran of Iona that hides an initiation parable.[1] When St Columba
decided to build a church, he found that the chosen site was infested with
demons. He discovered that these creatures could be driven away only if
a holy man were buried alive on the spot. St Odran volunteered for this
honour, and was duly entombed. After three days, St Columba decided
to dig St Odran up, and ask for news of Heaven. The latter declared that
there is no wonder in Death, and Hell is not as is reported. On hearing
this, Columba cried out, 'Earth again upon the mouth of Odran, that he
may blab no more.'

Odran had discovered the secret which no one would believe, and was
silenced for his pains. From his own point of view, St Columba was wise
to silence St Odran, for if Death and the Afterlife are not as reported,
then much of the teaching of the Church is incorrect. In the larger
context of initiation, the story is of interest because the fact is that those
who have journeyed into the other world – the Spiritual world – usually
return with insights which are scarcely credible to those who have not
made such a voyage. The world may be said to be divided into those who
have seen, and who have returned, and those who have not seen at all.

In Papua New Guinea, there is a delightful pidgin-English phrase, *ples
daun*. It means 'down here place', and it refers to the Earth, the planet on
which we humans live. It is, quite literally, the place down here.[2] As we

51

write, we savour this delightful pidgin, because we are in the happy position of being able to distinguish the difference between this *ples daun*, and the higher world – that Spiritual world which is our true home. The ancient Indian masters called the lower world *maya*, or 'illusion': the Sanskrit word suggested that the familiar, or *ples daun*, is nothing more than a shadow play, enacted by puppets on strings – an illusion, or delusion, of the human senses.[3]

The Mysteries are so intimately concerned with the other world that it is difficult to speak or write about them with ordinary words. After all, ordinary words were designed for communication and commerce in the material realm. Fortunately, there is another language which is designed to deal with higher matters – though it is not one with which the majority of people are familiar. 'There is', said that initiate of initiates, the Egyptian Hermes Trismegistus, 'an ineffable and sacred speech, the relation of which exceeds the measure of man's ability'.[4] It is recognition of this truth of the existence of a deeper secret language, rather than any mere longing for secrecy, which guides initiates to observe silence about the higher things, about the Mysteries which they have seen (plate 4).

Usually, when an initiate is asked about initiation, he or she wisely says nothing. If they do elect to talk, then it is in poetic terms, or in mythologies, for the higher world lends itself to illuminating commentary only when approached artistically, and through the pictures which are natural to poetry. The secret language is a creative language of pictures.

The difference between those who have seen that, or a similar, vision and those who have not is considerable, and the Schools who control such things have always attempted to regulate intellectual commerce between the two different groups. It is not healthy for the recipient if those who have seen beyond the veil speak too openly to those who have not. Silence is usually adjured of those who have seen and returned, through the good offices of initiation, because great confusion can be spread by blabbing to those who are unlikely to understand this greater vision.

This concern for silence explains why, until modern times, virtually every individual who sought initiation had to promise in advance that he or she would not reveal any of the Mysteries they were taught. Some promised that, should they speak out, either with intent or in error, they would, for example, submit to having their tongues pulled out with white-hot pincers. Such promises are not made lightly by men and women who understand the symbolism in their vow.

We were never required to make such a promise; even so, we find ourselves reluctant to speak about what we know. We have no fear of white-hot pincers, or of what they symbolize: our fear is that, if we do not choose our words with sufficient care, we might mislead those who read them. We cannot reveal all we have learned, for the speech required to describe the Mysteries is not like the speech of ordinary men. Yet, what we may speak about with impunity will thrown a beam of light on many things which, for the majority of people, have remained in darkness.

The image of a beam of light is a good one, for it reminds us of the two-edged sword which is said to guard the way back to Eden. In the 17th century, the great mystic Jakob Boehme called such a light the *schrack*, 'the lightning flash'.[5] It was that galvanizing illumination which would follow on a decision to act. In the Boehmian lore, the *schrack* was the beamed energy of Mars, which was a dual planet, with positive and negative aspects.[6] The *schrack* was a flash which could either illumine or burn, and, under certain circumstances, even destroy.

The time is right for such illumination, or burning. It has been recognized by esotericists for a very long time that, as the 20th century reached its troubled end, many of the ancient secrets would have to be revealed. Even as we write, some of the esoteric schools are investigating, preserving and teaching some of the ancient Mysteries which would otherwise be lost in the face of changes which are to come. The metaphor of ark-building comes to mind.

The secret knowledge is protected. The ancient Egyptians – or perhaps the Greeks who studied their hermetic lore – claimed that the great secret could be found in the story of the resurrection of Osiris (plate 4) by the magic of his wife, the goddess Isis. Her temple image was clothed in veils, and it was forbidden any neophyte to lift these.[7] The seven veils of Isis were protected by the seven magical seals. At each stage, a magical name must be pronounced to protect the one who dares such sacrilege. The modern archaeologists who remove the wrappings from ancient Egyptian mummies still find tiny scarab beetles hidden in the bandage folds, and wonder at the superstitions of the ancients. What few archaeologists realize is that these scarabs are the outer signs of still-powerful, yet invisible charms.

There is a tradition in the Arcane Schools that each person who reaches the first level of initiation is given a name. That special name existed before he or she was initiated – even before he or she came to Earth – but, at this early stage of his or her journey into esoteric lore, the secret name is revealed. The use of these names, and even how they are introduced to the neophyte, varies from School to School. Some Schools forbid the speaking of the name, as a holy thing: their aim is to preserve the vibration intact, that it may gather power. In such cases, the name remains known only to the Teacher and the neophyte. Other Schools allow the Teacher to reveal it to the other *chelae*, or students, at the appropriate time. The time must be right, and well chosen, for the vibration of a name is influenced by space and time, and may, in turn, influence space and time. If the name is pronounced or heard in the wrong way, it can be misunderstood, or received in the wrong way. A stillborn name will have no power: it will neither heal nor guide.

The naming of names is an important magical ritual in the Mysteries, and is undertaken with the same ritualistic care as the ceremony of putting in the eye of the Buddha, practised in some Eastern countries.[8] The sounding of the name is calculated to bring that name into the light of day – into the familiar world of the senses – and establish in the one named a particular quality of life, or a particular mode of searching. When our Teacher in Paris revealed to us our own name – our secret name – we could not understand it. After revealing the name, he told us to go away and reflect upon its sound.

The secret name which, at that time, embarrassed us, was *Idiot*, yet our Teacher, who was from a Slavonic country, spoke in a guttural tongue and the word sounded both exotic and acceptable.

'You must not forget that your inner resonance is your name. It is the name you carry within yourself. Your inner name, Mark, is *Idiot*. You must meditate upon this name. You must discover its inner meaning. Only in such a way can you discover your own path. The path of the Idiot is a very special one, and very ancient.'

Some years passed before we began to understand the meaning of that strange name. Even more years would pass before we saw how the word permeated our being so deeply that it marked the destiny which was to unfold during our present lifetime.

Perhaps we should tell the story as it happened.

We had been studying for some months in a School in the Rochechouart area of Paris. Our Master was of Slavonic origin, but the meetings were generally held in French. The method of teaching (as in most modern Schools) involved the systematic development of the three Spiritual divisions of Man – the Etheric, Astral and Ego – by special exercises. Once a week we had a meeting during which we could discuss any questions which seemed to relate to esotericism, and to our exercises. For some time, the group had been studying the Green Language (the ancient language of the alchemists and occultists), which involved a complex play with the sounds and associations of words.

We had asked our Master a question about a Green Language word used by the alchemist Fulcanelli, in his all-too-brief mention of the Feast of the Fools which, in late mediaeval times, was held annually in France, and other parts of Europe.[9] This alchemist was one of the first lone occultists to explore in depth many of the secret and esoteric words and images of his mediaeval confrères. The published results of this exploration galvanized the esoteric fraternities of the first half of the 20th century to an extent that it is often difficult to discuss certain hermetic beliefs without reference to Fulcanelli. We phrased our question carefully.

'In his book on the secret of the cathedrals, Fulcanelli emphasized that the ass which served in the *Feast of Fools* had once trodden upon the streets of Jerusalem. He said that it had walked the streets with its *sabot*. I know that *sabot* means both hoof and wooden shoe – but I wonder if there is some arcane meaning in the word which will throw more light on the Feast of Fools?'

He nodded. 'Yes, *sabot* is a most interesting word. But to understand its hidden meaning, you must understand also the secrets in that pagan replay of the ass's entrance into Jerusalem, and the secret meaning in the ass itself. In the anarchic Feast of Fools, which is sometimes called the *Feast of the Donkey*, the ass is led through the portals of a church, or cathedral, into the nave, in a bawdy imitation of the entry into Jerusalem.[10] In the prayers and blasphemies which follow, in the place of the *Amen*, the folk present bray like asses. This might seem like sacrilege – even bearing in mind that mockery and lewdness was the order of the day during the Feast of Fools. Even so, we must ask, Did this sacrilege have an arcane significance?

'In Hebrew, the male ass is called the *hamor*, the she-ass *athon*. When, in the Bible, Zechariah prophesies that the Lord will come riding on an ass (a prophecy fulfilled in the entry into Jerusalem), he uses the word *athon*.[11] This is usually taken as a sign of meekness – of how Christ was reluctant to appear in the guise of a king. However, there are other ways of looking at this story. Since there was a proscription in Israel against riding horses (a proscription seemingly broken by Solomon), the ass had a different status from that of modern times: it was certainly not a lowly creature, but was used even by kings and wealthy men and women. Indeed, from *athon* is derived the plural *athona*, which always indicated someone who was mighty or rich. No doubt this explains some of the excitement felt by alchemists (many of whom read Hebrew as a necessary qualification to their art) at the story of the ass, for *athona* is (in Green Language terms) too close to the alchemical *athanor* not to arouse interest. The *athanor* was a self-feeding furnace, used by alchemists to maintain a steady temperature. Not surprisingly, alchemical images of

Saturn, or of solar 'kings' (words which denote initiate grades), sitting on ovens, are found in the alchemical works.

'The meaning of the Hebrew word which gave us "Jerusalem" has always been disputed by scholars. However, in the secret language of the Cabbala – the esoteric law of the Jews – it means "Foundation of Peace".[12] This throws some light on the importance accorded the Temple of Solomon, which was supposed to have been originally located in Jerusalem. When, in the *Festum Fatuorum*, or Feast of Fools, the donkey (sometimes it was an ass) was ridden through the archway of a church or cathedral, this was regarded as the equivalent of riding into Jerusalem, into peace. But this donkey, which carries (may we say it?) an *imitation of Christ* on its back, had hooves. As you say, in French, these are *sabots*. Fulcanelli is quite right to trace the *sabot* to both *Saba* and *Caba*.[13] I shall glance at the former in a moment, but I should observe immediately that *Caba* is linked with the mystery of the *Caballa*, the esoteric tradition of the Jews.

'The Land of Sheba – in French, *Saba* – is actually the land Sheba, the country of the Sabeans.[14] The Sabeans of Persia were famous as magician-astrologers. The name was important enough to be adopted by the mediaeval magicians as a word of power, and it is often found inscribed in magical sigils and spells (below). This "magical power" idea is continued into the mythology of the mediaeval times, for in *The Golden Legends*, the Queen of Sheba, through the power of her magical prevision, recognizes that a piece of wood which was used as a bridge across a river was the Cross of Christ.[15] Be that as it may, the Sabeans

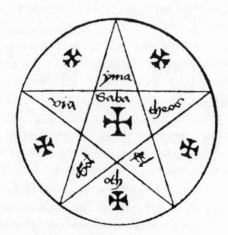

Detail of five-pointed star (pentagram) from a 16th century magical text.
The magical word in the centre reads, Saba.

56

were famous magicians, and the French word *Saba* which is used to denote them is very close to *sabot*, or clogs.

'What is more important, *Saba* is very close to *sabbat*, used to denote the meetings of the witches.[16] Even today, the French expression *faire un sabbat* means "to cause an uproar or tumult". With such expressions, we are getting very close to the exuberant spirit behind the Feast of Fools.

'We are now touching upon one of the great secrets of the mediaeval era. The mockery of the Church – expressed in stone in such sculptural details as the donkey dressed as a priest or more ephemerally in the annual *Feast of the Donkey*, as the Feast of Fools was sometimes called – is more than mere mockery. There were always initiates, working quietly within the Schools, who realized that the Church had strayed from its esoteric purpose, and had become a bureaucracy on the lines of the Roman Imperia. These initiates organized, or caused to develop, such underground symbols as the ass or donkey to attack the complacency of the Church. By such means, the noise of the *saba* was brought into the holy portals of the symbolic Jerusalem, which should be a place of peace, in order to indicate that the mismanagement was recognized, and understood. The question raised by this anarchic festivity was, Who is the Fool? Is it the donkey who carried Christ. Or the Church, who has *ceased* to carry Christ?

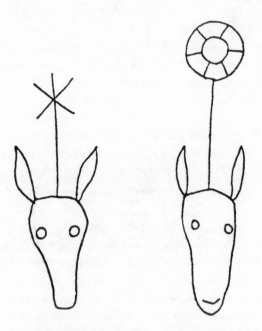

The sanctified ass – drawings of medieval papermarks, from Harold Bayley's The Lost Language of Symbolism, *1907.*

'One of the most remarkable iconographic survivals from this period when the Feast of Fools was so dominant are water-marks showing the donkey or ass. Between their great ears were six-pointed stars (see previous page). According to the specialist in such marks – Harold Bayley – the water-marks were part of a hidden language of esoteric groups which were persecuted by the Church. Bayley insisted this simple water-mark is an image of the glorified ass, the initiated ass. This is the ass that carried Moses back to Egypt, and Christ into Jerusalem.

'You see – even the water-marks indicate that there is such an asinine Way of initiation – the *Way of the Fool*.[17] The Way of the Ass, or the Way of the Fool, is guided by a star.

'Among these arcane watermarks is a series showing the image of a man's head. A bandage which previously covered his eye has been removed, and he is looking upwards in wonder. Harold Bayley was right

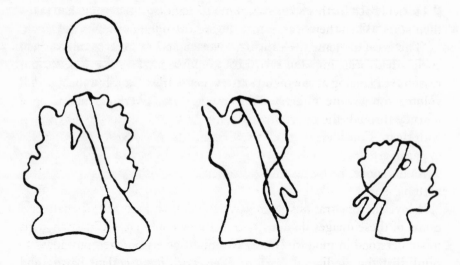

The cosmic vision, consequent to removal of the blindfold. Drawings of mediaeval papermarks, from Harold Bayley's The Lost Language of Symbolism, *1907.*

to equate this simple image with the words of the mystic Eckartshausen: there is "but One who is able to open our inner eyes, so that we may behold the Truth . . ." It is through this One that "the hoodwink of ignorance falls from our eyes . . ."[18]

'You see, Mark: it is the Fool who knows that he is being hoodwinked. It is the Fool who sets out on the Path to seek liberation from this state. In the end, it is the Fool who will have that blindfold removed from his inner eyes.

'No doubt, Mark, it will interest you to learn that the Greek origins of the word *Idiot* are linked with this idea of removing blindfolds.'

It was snowing in Paris. The leaden glare of the sky and the delicate swirls of flakes contrived to throw a soft luminescence into the room, but it was darker than usual, and the room felt more intimate, perhaps because the sound of the traffic was deadened.

Our Master was already in the room, as the group began to file in. We were among the first to enter, and chose to sit on the third row – not too near, and not too far away. On the small table to the side of his chair was a book. Our Master must have seen us looking at it, craning our head to read the title on the spine.

'Witkowski,' he said, reaching over and tapping the binding. 'Witkowski's pictorial travelogue through the pagan art of mediaeval churches.'[19]

He held back further words until the remainder of the group had taken their seats. When there was silence, he indicated the book with a flourish.

'The great alchemist, Fulcanelli – to whom I've referred more than once – had been impressed by this book; and that alone is sufficient reason for glancing at the pictures it contains. It's certainly a most useful volume for anyone interested in strange lore. Everyone intent on a journey through the churches and cathedrals of France should carry it with them. Considering its Christian contexts, it's a most original guide to pagan art.'

As his spoke, he began to flick through the old book, his face radiant with pleasure.

'I love the illustrations. Simple engravings, but so full of challenge. Some of these images demonstrate just how completely Christian art is misunderstood in modern times. We might be encouraged nowadays to think that the mediaeval *Feast of Fools*, with its attendant bawdy and chaos, was an exceptional throwback to an old Roman festival – a mere embarrassment to the Church, an inexplicable island of pagan celebration in the midst of an otherwise Christian land – but this was not the case at all. The profane imagery which Witkowski has collected from European churches or cathedrals indicates that the spirit which lay behind the Feast was intensely alive in the mediaeval world.[20] The *Feast of the Ass* stemmed from a powerful life-force – a primal joy – which has been almost vitiated in modern times, but which still survives, to some extent, in art.

'The ancients approached art in a very different way from us. They did not approach art with their intellects at all. They recognized, with a

Spiritual profundity we can scarcely comprehend, that true art offered an entry into the Spiritual world. Even in modern times, highly Spiritual individuals still have a feeling for this: Picasso is reported to have said that some of the great masterpieces he had purchased, and kept in his studio, were so powerful that he had to cover them with cloth. This is the right approach to art. Our galleries should be places of meditation, rather than cacophonous meeting places, for true art stands sentinel to the higher world.'

Marilyn, a woman in the front row, posed a question: 'In view of what you say, about art pertaining more to our emotions than to our intellect, then our appreciation of art must be connected with our Astral faculties?'

'Yes, that is true. The question is – what part of you do you use to appreciate a work of art? If you look only with your physical eyes, you will see nothing of value. It is easier to understand what I mean if we take music as a standard. If you listen to a great work of music – to Beethoven's *Triple Concerto*, for example – only with your ears, you will hear hardly anything. You must listen to music with the entire physical body. The body must remain perfectly still, for then the body becomes a sounding board for the Aetheric and Astral bodies. Only when there is a unison between the three bodies is it possible to begin to appreciate music.

'Well, this rule of listening applies also to art. In meditation, it is slightly more difficult to discount the body when contemplating a picture than it is when one listens to music.'

Marilyn spoke again: 'Is this meditative approach linked with the aesthetic experience?'

'Yes. Indeed, it is the source of our true experience of beauty. The aesthetic experience involves a separation in the soul – a fission of sorts. The aesthetic experience is the temporary dislocation of the Astral from the Aetheric – it is an entirely Spiritual experience, legitimately born of contact with secret elements within works of art. Even in the early part of the 19th century, the esotericist Goethe was aware of this magical element in art: this is why he recognized that one should not talk about a picture or sculpture unless one was in the presence of that work.[21] Without the work, there could be no aesthetic experience, and one would be in a position of talking only about the dead element – that is, about the physical picture without thought of its interaction on the Aetheric and Astral planes. This is one reason why art history of modern times is so dead and meaningless. It is dealing with physical art, and not with the living Etheric and Astral which is the true magic element in art.'

Maria, a particularly attractive young woman, who was sitting several rows behind us, asked a question: 'You have spoken several times about occult blinds, yet I am still not sure what you mean by occult blinds in relation to art. I know what occult blinds are, but I cannot see how they can be used in art. After all – you see a work of art for what it is. I fail to understand how what you see may also be a blind for something you cannot see.'

'Well, Maria, let us look at a couple of examples of superior mediaeval sculptures, to see if we can resolve this issue for you.'

He reached for Witkowski's book, and opened it to a double page with three illustrations.

'Pass these pictures around, and examine them, as I talk.'

He leaned forward, and handed the book to a girl in the front row.

'The wood-engraving to the left represents a sculpture in a mediaeval porch.[22] It shows a nude sinner being attacked by toad-like creatures and snakes. She is in the grasp of a demon. The detail to the right is from the same porch of the church of St Pierre, in Moissac in southern France: it shows a couple of sinners with demons on their backs.

'Now the casual observer will see in these sculptures a parable – they will see that the sinners are being punished in Hell or Purgatory. They are visual exhortations to renounce sin.

 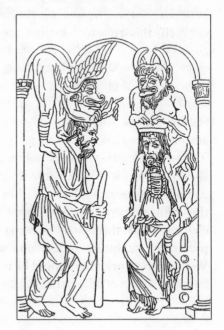

Wood engraving of demon grasping a woman, from the West front of Saint-Pierre, Moissac. 14th century, after Witkowski.

Wood engraving of demons riding on the back of a beggar and a miser. From the West front of Saint-Pierre, Moissac. 14th century, after Witkowski.

'The first thing we must realize is that the sculptors were not, as we might imagine, portraying a future state in Hell or Purgatory. The images are portrayals of ordinary human beings – *of ordinary sinners in life*. The woman attacked by reptiles, is a libertine. This is why her private parts and breasts are receiving such attention from the monster-toads, and why the demon who grasps her is being so sexually explicit with the snake.[23]

'The pair carrying demons piggy-back are intended to reveal the sin of Avarice: the seated figure, clutching his money-bags, is a miser, refusing to give alms to the beggar.

'However, these people are *not* in Hell: they are portrayals of Etheric and Astral forms. They reveal people as they would be seen by someone with developed clairvoyant vision, able to perceive on the Spiritual planes. They are symbolic forms of the Etheric and Astral bodies. A true clairvoyant would be able to *see* those hideous reptiles, and those possessing demons.

'The naked woman is not in Hell. She is depicted as a living being – but it is not her physical body which is being portrayed. It is her Etheric body. The truth is that, as a consequence of her predisposition to sin in a particular way, the soul of the libertine woman is constantly being devoured by monstrous forms. No matter how beautiful or alluring her physical body may be, her Etheric body is – as an immediate consequence of sin – darkened by demonic forms which devour her. I repeat – this is not a picture of punishment in Hell, but of an unhealthy Etheric body, in life. Such a body is distinctly in need of cleansing, of healing. Such a picture explains why Paracelsus could call the Etheric the "body of poisons".[24]

'The woman is portrayed nude, perhaps because this more forcefully illustrates her sin of concupiscence. However, there is another reason for this nudity – which contrasts forcefully with the fact that the men are clothed. The nudity reflects that she has been divested of her physical body. The nakedness of her body is intended as an indication that it is her Etheric body only – what the Moissac artists would have described as the *ens veneni*, or the *vegetabilis*.[25] This explains why she is lifting her arms, grasping at her hair. *This is the gesture of the Etheric soul.*[26] The same gesture is found in the Christian images painted and scratched on the walls of the catacombs, in Rome (see top figure on page 262), and has been called the "orans", or praying gesture. In fact, such images are derived from the Egyptian hieroglyphic for the *ka*:

62

'These hints leave us in no doubt that the sinning woman is alive, and that we are being privileged to look into the state of her Etheric body. This, Maria, is an example of the use of an occult blind.

'Now, turn your attention to the second engraving of the Moissac sculpture (see page 61). The person gifted with clairvoyant vision will see the beggar approaching the miser on the Astral plane. He will see the demons directing this transaction: the demons are, so to speak, bypassing the Ego of the men. This is no human transaction, but a demonic one. The demons sit above the heads of the men to show that they are gripping on to their Egos. Do not forget that our word possession is derived from a Latin word meaning literally "sitting on".[26] When, in the Lord's Prayer, we ask not to be led into temptation, we are requesting that we find sufficient strength within our Ego to resist the darkness constantly been laid upon our Astral bodies by demons, and other temptations.

'Now, in contrast to the nakedness of the libertine woman, the miser and the beggar are clothed. This may be explained in terms of the need to indicate their ranks – the beggar is in torn clothing, with only one trouser leg. We may judge from the clothing of the seated man that he is a person of some substance. However, there is another reason why the pair are clothed: this covering indicates that they are being depicted on the next level up from the Etheric – that is, on the Astral plane – on what in the days when this sculpture was made would have been called the *animalis*, or the *ens astrale*.

'We may have little doubt that the clothing is meant as a kind of Astral mask, for neither man wears shoes. This is an arcane technique for showing that neither is standing on the physical Earth. The most "Earthy" element in this portrayal is the heavy money-bag: this appears to be tied around his neck, as a punishment, weighing down his soul. This money-bag performs the same symbolizing function as the bag over the shoulder of the Fool in the Tarot card (see page 22).

'The demons who "possess" the couple are Astral beings: the wings of the one on the left indicate that it can "fly" on the Astral planes. The horns of the other, crescent in form, remind us that the demons are linked with the Moon. However, just as the woman does not know that her Etheric body is being devoured by monstrous forms, so the miser does not know that his Astral body is being weighed down by his riches, and by the demon which grips its legs around his neck. This is not so much symbolism as a direct portrayal of what can be perceived on the Spiritual plane, by those with eyes to see.'

He reached once more for the book.

'In fact, in this same wonderful book by Witkowski, there is a picture which is a sort of homily upon the nature of esotericism and occult blinds.

'On page 181. . . .' – he flicked back the pages, and once again handed the open book to a person on the front row, to look at and hand around – 'you will find a most interesting engraving. It is from a miniature in the French National Library, and depicts an event at a baptism.[27] Some scholars insist that it shows St John baptizing Mary Magdalene – but this

Baptism, or initiation, scene. Wood engraving from mediaeval manuscript,
after Witkowski.

is not a really important issue. In the early centuries, baptism involved total immersion, which is why the nude woman is standing in such a huge vat.[28] The waves of water on the floor are not pouring from the vat, as you might expect – they are there merely to indicate that St John the Baptist is symbolically standing in the River Jordan. This scene shows the lady with her arms raised, in precisely the same Etheric gesture we noted a little earlier. St John is shown reading from a book – possibly he is reading the baptismal rites – while he touches the woman's bowed head with his right hand. This, as I might hardly point out, is an initiation scene.

'See how the peace and decorum of this initiation contrasts with the tumult outside the baptistry! There, seven men fight among themselves to peer through holes and crannies in the fabric of the baptistry: they are not interested in initiation, but in catching a glimpse of the naked woman. One of these men is so excited, he is fainting: another seems to be driven mad because he cannot reach the building to peer in. They are deeply caught up in their own Astral emotions.

'If the decorous scene inside the baptistry is one of initiation, the chaos on the outside is surely a portrayal of the ordinary madness of the familiar world. These men cannot understand the Spiritual nature of the event. They see only the naked breasts of the woman: it is as though they look upon the naked form of Isis, but miss her inner meaning.

'This picture is a quite astounding portrayal of the relationship which the Mysteries have with the ordinary world. There is a sense in which the initiation is not hidden at all. It is true that the door of the baptistry is closed, as it should be. In spite of the tumult outside, the highly charged ritual continues. One has the feeling that it is taking place in a different space and time to that occupied by the men outside. This is a perfect analogy of the truth of initiation. It does belong to a different space and time to that experienced in the ordinary, familiar world. Not only do the occupants of the ordinary world fail to recognize what initiation is – they fail even to recognize initiates when they see them.

'The seven men cannot see what is really going on. They are deflected by the occult blind – the naked breasts and body of the woman, which suck the men down into the Astral level. They are blinded by the intense, passion-filled excitement generated from their own Astral bodies. Each man is blinded by himself – by what is probably intended to be one or other of the seven deadly sins, which arise from the Astral body. If they could move into a different part of themselves – into a higher part – the Astral scales would fall from their eyes, and they would realize that they are gazing on a Mystery – upon initiation.

'In just such a way did those in the Feast of Fools see only a donkey or ass being led, braying sacrilegiously, into a church. They did not see the wisdom hidden behind the veil of symbols. If those who played the ass in the Feast of Fools could stand back for a moment, and catch hold of their own inner peace . . . if they could only move into a different part of themselves, then they would realize that they were witnessing a profound Mystery.'

Perhaps it *is* idiotic to undertake to speak of the Mysteries. Perhaps it is foolish, yet one should recall that the roots of the word *Idiot* reach back, by way of Greek etymology, to the *eidos*, or Platonic forms which lie behind the phenomenal world, and even further back into the Moonlight of Sanskrit, which surfaced in Roman times in the Etruscan *Idus*, now remembered only as a system of dating.[29] In ancient times there was a deeper wisdom about such things, for it was recognized that ideas proceeded as a subtle light from the Spiritual realm, and could not find a seeding in the mind of every human being. It was recognized that someone had to take the foolish risk of being prepared to explain such ideas to others.

In the tremulous final section of Apuleius' tale of the *Golden Ass*, it is at the full Moon that Lucius – weary of passing his days in the shape of an ass – decided to pray to the veiled goddess Isis. It was the prayer which finally released him from the asinine form, and transformed him back to the shape of man. Suddenly changed, he found himself in the midst of a processional dedicated to the glory of Isis: the procession of men and women wound its way to perform the rituals of initiation into the Isiac Mysteries. Thus, Apuleius wove a sermon into his tale: the ass who had been forced to play the fool was led by the light of Isis into a higher part of himself, whence he was able to throw off his bestial bondage. Lucius recognized that he would never find sufficient praise for such a boon – 'not even if I had a thousand mouths and as many tongues, and could continue such praise for ever'.[30]

The worship of this Egyptian goddess was established in Greece as early as the fourth century BC, and she remained the most important of those other Egyptian gods and goddesses – such as Sarapis and Anubis – to whom the Greeks and Romans raised temples. The Mysteries of Isis survive in the hermetic literature, in the myths about her virginity, and in the mythologies attached to her son, Horus. Some of the Egyptian images which show her holding Horus against her breast (figure opposite), or on her knees are almost identical to the later images and statuettes of the Virgin Mother of Jesus. This is perhaps not surprising, as the Isiac Mysteries were enacted in preparation for the coming of Christ, and the new Mysteries of Christianity.

Because of Isis' connection with the Nile, water was always an important element in her worship. A Temple of Isis at Pompeii – preserved for many centuries in volcanic dust from the eruption of Vesuvius – still displays a cistern which was filled regularly with the waters of the Nile. Her most important festival among the Greeks was the *Ploiaphesia*, which marked the commencement of navigation.[31] Was not the floor of the Church over which this Virgin was protectress called the *nave*, a word which reminds us of our own word 'navigation'? Thus, the Virgin of the pre-Christian world was linked with water, just like the Virgin of the Christians.

Isis, with the ast (throne) head-dress, suckling the Horus child. Wood engraving,
from J.N. Lockyer, The Dawn of Astronomy, *1894.*

As his fascinating account of initiation continues, Lucius the former
ass indicates that, after sloughing off this dark form, he was eventually
initiated into all three grades of the Isis Mysteries, and reached a high
rank in the esoteric college of *Pastophores*. Apuleius tells us that he
entered the Isis cult on the day before the festival of the *Ploiaphesia*, and
offers a detailed description of what took place during the festivities,
revealing certain of the forbidden Mysteries. In his account of his
initiation, he mentions that he approached within the temple the confines
of death: this 'second death' is a classical stage in the process of initiation
(plate 4).[32]

In an ecstatic culmination of his experience he was allowed to
experience what has been called, in esoteric literature, *the midnight Sun*.
Lucius records, with some awe, that 'in the inner recesses of the temple
. . . at midnight, I saw the sun gleaming with a full bright light, and I saw
the infernal gods and the supernal gods, and I approached them face to
face'.[33]

This journey into the Spiritual world touches on the very highest level
of initiation, yet Lucius admits that he was, at that time, permitted other

remarkable visions and revelations concerning which he was forbidden to speak in public.

Had Apuleius really lifted the veil of Isis, we wonder?

The veil of Isis seems almost to have been a literary invention. The idea that she was veiled was a symbolic way of saying that she was a goddess of the Mysteries, who protected secrets which could not be seen by everyone, and which should be divulged by none. Only those initiated in her rites might lift the veil of Isis. However, even this famous veil seems to be little more than a prudish misunderstanding of the Greek word *peplos*, which, in the context of the inscription on the statue of the goddess, meant 'clothing'. The original warning was partly sexual, as might be expected of a beautiful goddess: no man might gaze upon her nakedness with impunity.[34] Is even the midnight Sun, a symbol of the Christ – the new Horus sun-god – then hidden from the eyes of all but initiates?

What other symbols disguise this powerful goddess? In mediaeval myths we hear of the unicorn. The creature was so shy that it would scarcely dare approach human kind, which it saw as a company of strangers, remote from the stellar light. The unicorn marvelled at all it saw in the world, yet was drawn to the sight of a spotless virgin, who sat on a grassy hill. The virgin, beautiful beyond all compare, was guarded on all sides by soldiers with drawn swords. While it is true that, in secret, the soldiers desired the virgin, their swords were directed outwards in her defence, for this was their sworn role, as servants of Mars. The unicorn crept forward, and knelt before the virgin, whom it had recognized as the Queen of the Sky, as the Heavenly Virgin, clothed in stars, holding the wheat sheaves which would replenish the dying earth. Thus it was that when the unicorn laid its single horn upon the lap of the Isis Virgin in love, it consummated all that the soldiers had secretly desired, yet had feared, to do.

The symbolism in the myth is almost transparent – so transparent that we hardly need point to it. The swords of the soldiers were held in their hands to ward off the outer world, while the sword of the unicorn had grown from its own head. The single horn had been seeded by the imaginative faculties.

It is perhaps no great wonder that the unicorn, the Isis Virgin in her many forms and the guardian soldiers are found in so many images in the pages of mediaeval alchemical books – and even in popular Christian prints (plate 5). One historian found well over 1,000 examples of the unicorn used as a water-mark symbol in late mediaeval times, at a time when such symbols were representative of hermetic groups.[35]

The unicorn water-marks – like the more famous foolscap water-

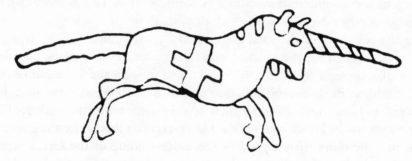

The sacred unicorn. Drawing of a medieval papermark,
from Harold Bayley's The Lost Language of Symbolism, *1907.*

marks – could be seen only by those few who held their documents up to
the light. This was part of the arcane significance of the water-mark, for
it hid the truth that the Light of Christ could reveal all secrets. Such
hiding of secrets was a commonplace in mediaeval times. Even the
alchemists, who wrote and published so many thousands of texts to
elucidate their art, rarely spoke openly of the Mysteries of Isis in their
secret science. They couched their secrets in codes, sigils and cyphers
which could be understood only by their fellows. They never revealed
the secrets of their art to the circle of strangers – those with the
unsheathed swords.

To those who have not been initiated, the writings and diagrams of the
alchemists are so many dead letters. Like all initiates before them, the
alchemists have kept their silence and their counsel. The vast outpouring

The 13th century nave dancing ground (sometimes called a maze)
in Chartres Cathedral.

of alchemical publications was never intended to enlighten the non-initiates: they were written and published for the few. Just as the cathedrals and churches had an external forecourt, or a narthex, to keep the uninitiated on the outside, and 'choirs' or sacred zodiacs, or even circular dancing grounds, reserved for the initiated (opposite page, bottom), so the laboratories had areas where would-be alchemists might stand.[36] These were places of Air – places where one had to listen, or to read words, and study the preliminary secrets dispensed by the element of Air. Only later, after this preliminary baptism of Air, was the neophyte allowed to become a **Zelator**, and stand before the Fire, and even be permitted to see that Secret Fire of the hidden sun.[37]

Before that higher vision was possible, however, he or she would have to recognize the inner alchemy, which is the search for the *prima materia*, or 'first matter', upon which the process of initiation depends.[38] The first matter is a rebus for the 'prima mater' (the first mother), which was a form of Isis.

Isis, her garment ripped to show her thigh, and thus to hint that she is newly denuded – her secrets divulged – appears as a detail in an alchemical book which offers to reveal the *Secret of All Secrets* to

Allegory of the lifted veil – Isis, with her flesh revealed. Detail from the title page of Michael Mier's Arcana Arcanissima, *1614.*

70

mankind. Many of the designs on this page hide the secret of alchemy, which the German Rosicrucian, Michael Maier, described with some accuracy as *aureum animi et Corporis medicamentum* ('the golden medicine of body and soul'). But a person unlearned in the secret lore would not know what to make of these crude figures, that tell in curious images the whole story of the spagyric, or alchemical, art.[39]

What distinguishes the one who has gazed upon the naked Isis by way of initiation? In sloughing off the *dark matter* (which is sometimes called the *black matter*) he can gaze upon the 'prima mater' – that Isis who is the *white matter*. He is said to have escaped the dark side of his own being, the *dark matter* which holds him in the land of the Sleepers. The Sleepers are the human slaves of the Moon goddess, Selene.[40] One makes the choice: either one sleeps to Selene, or awakes to Isis. In one of the most beautiful engravings of an alchemical laboratory which has survived from the 16th century, the initiate is reminded by way of a Latin motto that he, above all other men, must be prepared to be vigilant: he must remain awake, even while in ordinary slumber.[41] In this injunction lies the whole secret of initiation, for it is a command insisting that the initiate must remain free of the soporific influence of the dark Moon (see page 197). The true initiate-alchemist must not fall back into being one of the multitude of Sleepers.

But, to return to the *ples daun*. We have struggled through the first sleep (there are many grades of sleep) and have reached a stage where we could see the difference between the material world and the Spiritual world which hovers above it, and which, indeed, bestows life upon the former. It was not always so. There was a time when we confused the lower and the higher: rather foolishly, we confused the imprinting with the print. Then, later, as our understanding grew, we began to see the lower as a product of the higher – as its plaything. We perceived the higher as a place outside time – eternal, in its original Greek sense – with the lower enmeshed in time, or in what the Oriental mystics, versed in the secret power of sounds, called *maya*. We found confirmation of this relationship in the old occult books, and saw it as a truth expressed in arcane diagrams hidden by occult blinds. We saw it perfectly represented in the arcane engravings of the 18th-century divine and mystic, William Law, who represented the familiar world of our senses as an *Outworld*, subtended from the Spiritual (plate 6). In his diagrams, the higher trinity of Spirit projects downwards the duality of darkness and light, and from these opposite polarities was made the Outworld in which we dwell.[42] The diagram showed the creation of Spirit and matter (which Law wisely represented in alchemical terms as a dark matter), the latter a symbol of the *ples daun*.

With William Law's avid reader, the occultist William Blake, we delighted in this term, Outworld. This was the *ples daun*. When we first encountered it, the word caught a whiff of the alien feeling of the material world realm, which hung, as it were on puppet strings, from the Spiritual – perhaps as little more than a projection of fragile human senses. That Outworld was a remote place, a darkling plain, where the Spirit felt strangely debased and lonely.

Then, one day, what we had longed for during so many years happened. It happened, and turned upside down all we thought we knew. We were vouchsafed an experience which challenged our entrenched belief about the nature of reality. After this experience, we saw that Spirit and matter were not dualities, but different aspects of Spirit. Afterwards, we saw that the way down and the way up are the same, as the great hermetic teacher, Hermes Trismegistus, had insisted.[43] Just as Apuleius could remember exactly when and where he awoke from his nightmare of the ass, we also could remember our own awakening – in a garage to the south of Ferrara, in 1961.

It began in a remote and gaunt building which overlooks the Val di Susa, in north-western Italy.

The Sagrada di San Michele is a ruinous survival from a long-lost monastic past. It was built on a hill-top, and is itself almost an imitation of that mountainous ascent, for the stairs of the inner entrance, which lead to the upper courtyards and church, are very steep. The climb to the first courtyard is by way of a flight of steps called the *Scala dei Morti*, the Staircase of the Dead. There are tombs near the bottom, but at the top is an archway set with images of the stars: the stairs are a parable of a Spiritual ascent from Earthly death to stellar life. The symbolism is simple and perfect, yet it was not quite the symbolism intended by the architects. The archway was translated to this place some centuries after the monastery was built: it was carried, stone by stone, from the baptistry, which had once been outside the monastic enclave, and which is now all but destroyed.

The bas-relief images of the stars, through which one must pass to gain access to the monastery, are among the most fascinating in Europe. They probably date back to the 11th century, and show signs of being derived from Arabic astrological lore.[44] Sagrada di San Michele is a strange place, for it is a survival of that time when Islam and Christendom and the pagan world of Antiquity met, in a brief moment before Europe was once again engulfed in its usual pattern of fratricide and war. Here, a fortress monastery commemorated the coming together of two different religious ideals: within decades of its completion, other and more stern fortresses would sound to the clash of arms between these warring religions, as the might of Islam began to threaten and partly engulf mediaeval Christendom.

To the left of the portal are 11 images of the zodiacal constellations. There are 11, rather than the statutory 12, because Scorpius and Libra are merged as one, in the image of a scorpion grasping in its *chelae*, or claws, the balance of Libra (plate 7). In this form, the ancient Greek images of the zodiac were manumitted from the writings of the Alexandrian-Roman astronomer, Ptolemy, to the architects of the first Romanesque cathedrals.

To the right of the portal are 15 images of the constellations. Most of them are named on the marble in a lapidary script[45] As sculptural images, these may well be unique in European lapidary art. Perhaps the architect had them copied from an Arabic edition of the *Phaenomena* – a poem about the constellations – of the third-century BC poet, Aratus. The original manuscript prototype drawings seem to be lost, but there is no doubt that these bas-reliefs may be traced back into the loam of classical antiquity.

We had visited Sagrada di San Michele several times to study its arcane message. Indeed, we suspect that our friends had begun to think of it as our obsession. Why, they would ask, do you spend so much of your time working on a handful of 12th-century images? At that time, we could not answer. During our visits to the Sagrada we rarely met anyone with whom we could discuss the arcane symbols, or the esoteric ideas they embodied. Sometimes, to our delight, Italian families would gather on the knoll beneath the monastery, and hold rowdy picnics. A few would even make their way up the Staircase of the Dead, and wander around the vast church above. However, few seemed to be interested in the cosmic images of the archway, and none I met ever had the slightest intimation of the challenge they offered. This was not surprising: the symbols were designed by a Masonic Mystery School, and exhibited an arcane know-ledge which removed them from the understanding even of scholars.

On the last Wednesday of April, 1961,[46] we had agreed to give a lecture to a group of American art-history students. Our talk centred on the arcane significance of the astrological images, but we tied this account up with a brief history of zodiacal and constellational symbolism from classical times, through to the mediaeval period.

At the end of the lecture, two post-graduate students – Rachel and Christobel – approached us and asked if we knew of anything in Verona which had similar arcane significance. They told us that they planned to spent a couple of study weeks in that city in the first half of the following month. We told them a little about the esoteric content of the bronze doors of the basilica of San Zeno, and said that if they cared to meet us in the afternoon of Tuesday 5 September, outside San Zeno, then we would explain to them something of the mystery behind these beautiful bronze reliefs. We suggested that they might also like to spend a day in Padua, looking at the zodiacal frescos in the great hall of the Salone, and a day in Venice, examining the planetary and zodiacal images on the capitals on the exterior of the Doge's palace.

All these events were happening in the Outworld, as part of our non-secret life. They were, so to speak, part of the shadows cast by the strong light in which we lived. Yet, at that time, the inner world was in a turmoil. We had put a great deal of our time into the study of the astrological images in the Sagrada, but we could find no answers to the important questions which they raised in our soul. We could not find out why, or for what purpose, these images had been carved, and why they were not all absorbed into the artistic repertoire of Romanesque architecture. These images of the constellations were not found in other monasteries, churches or cathedrals: they seemed to be unique to the Sagrada.

No Romanesque architect seems to have seen the arcane implications in these images of the stars, and, as a consequence, these constellation images seem to have been lost to the stonemasons of the West. Few, if any, European specialists had studied these images, and there was a dearth of scholarly material dealing with them. The only possible clue we had to the reasons why the masons had made use of the Sagrada constellation images was a tantalizing manuscript in a secret code.

In our search for the origins of these images, we had found, hidden in the archives of the Vatican Library, a single manuscript which seemed to illuminate our search. It was a document which confirmed the name of the sculptor as Nicholas.[47] This was a common enough name in the 12th century, and it had proved impossible to link it with any well-known sculptor or astrologer of that name. Even so, it was clear to us that this Nicholas had been an initiate, for the whole arrangement of the cosmic images – albeit no longer in their original setting – was redolent with esoteric symbolism and power. Yet, for all our research, the identity of this person remained a mystery.[48] It was the key to his identity which obsessed us now.

Even the one thing which we suspected Nicholas had written

remained a mystery. In the manuscript which confirmed his name was a long and enigmatic sentence in mediaeval dog–Latin, which we could just about read, yet not grasp its inner meaning. The text seemed to encode something which defied our understanding.[49] We had to trace the literary sources on which the more readable sections were based. Until we had access to these, the code would remain an enigma – and with it, the identity of Nicholas.

On that day in the Sagrada, we had reached a crisis point. To this moment, we can recall the feeling in our soul when we sat upon the wall of the upper courtyard of the Sagrada, looking out over the Val di Susa. We gripped our arms around our legs, and contemplated the magnificent panorama of the Val di Susa which lay before us. Then we opened our hearts to the Spiritual world. We explained that we could no longer solve the problem of the Nicholas code without help. We had tried all the paths we knew, and felt that all we could do now was to hand the problem over to the angels. If we were to proceed further, we would need help. If no help were forthcoming, we would have to leave the mystery of the Sagrada behind, unsolved.

Almost immediately, Rachel and Christobel approached us, and asked if we knew anything about the sacred doors of San Zeno, in Verona.

When we parked our car in the square outside San Zeno, that Tuesday afternoon, Rachel and Christobel were standing beside one of the marble lions which guard the porch of the church. We were surprised, for we had made the tentative rendezvous over a fortnight earlier, and many things can deflect travellers through the beauties of northern Italy. Soon we stood inside the porch examining the beautiful bronze panels on the doors.[50] It was a warm afternoon, coloured by that genial indolence which pervades most church squares in Italy, yet, behind the indolence, we could feel an air of expectation, as though something of importance was going to happen.

For a while, the three of us looked at the panels in silence. Sunlight fell on them, picking out the reliefs with contrasting shadows.

'When were they made?' Christobel asked.

'Some panels are 12th-century, some 13th.'

'The same age as the Sagrada di San Michele?'

'Same period. Perhaps the Sagrada is a little earlier.'

'Is there anything astrological about them?' asked Rachel.

'Not in an obvious way,' we said, 'but what do you make of that?' We pointed at a panel.

'An acrobat?'

'No, not exactly. That is Salome, dancing.' We could see why Rachel had said acrobat. In her anxiety to please Herod, Salome had contorted her back into a circle. Her hand grasped for her own foot, and pulled it in towards her head. It was almost literally a round dance (plate 8). 'See how her head almost touches her feet. That is astrology. At least, it's mediaeval astrology.'

'Why?' Rachel sounded doubtful.

'Every part of the human being is linked with some part of the cosmos.'

We wished we had a mediaeval image of the zodiacal man to show the zodiacal rulerships, as we ran through the sequence: 'The head is ruled

The 'zodiac-man' – the rulership of the twelve signs of the zodiac over the human body. At the head is Aries, at the feet Pisces. Late 15th century woodcut.

by Aries, the throat by Taurus . . . the feet by Pisces. You see, then, that the head and the feet were linked with the two extremes of the zodiac. In the zodiac circle they touch – the feet of Pisces meet the head of Aries. Salome is imitating the zodiac, by bringing together the past of Aries and the future of Pisces.[51] In early Christian days there were such things as sacred dances, in which the dancers tried to link their bodies with the planetary movements. That is true astrology.'[52]

'Salome looks like a fish,' said Christobel.

'Yes, that is part of the symbolism. In a sense, she *is* a fish. Look.' We pointed to the right of the panel. 'There is Salome, again,[53] carrying the severed head of John the Baptist. She is the fish of Pisces, and St John is the head of Aries. Again, cosmic symbolism.'

'There are fishes on several panels,' observed Rachel. 'Look – even in the leaves.' Some panels were almost abstract patterns of tree leaves and branches, in which were hidden birds and fishes.

'Yes,' we nodded, smiling. There were two fish beneath two birds, forming a cross. 'You might imagine fishes in trees are great wonders – a parallel to the wonder of the biblical stories – yet the symbolism points to something beyond mere wonder. The leaves and branches are a mediaeval symbol for what we now call the Etheric.[54] The sculptors who made the door would probably have called it the *quintessentia*.'[55]

'The fifth element?'

'Yes. The invisible element which keeps the other four in union, without which there would be an endless discord in the pact of things.' We realized that we had fallen into quoting poetry.[56]

'The same quintessence you told us about at the Staircase of the Dead?' asked Rachel.

'Precisely the same.[57] In fact, if you look closely, you'll see that the whole of that panel is an allegory on the fifth element. The birds represent the Air element, the fishes the Water, the plants represent the Earth, and the flame-like orifice between the birds and the fishes represents Fire.[58] In the middle of the Fire are the cosmic radiations of the fifth element.'

Rachel grimaced. 'And there was I, under the impression that all I needed to understand Christian art was a good knowledge of the Bible.'

We laughed, more at the comical grimace than at her dawning realization. 'Yet the Bible has levels of symbolism which have not yet been fully explored.' Thoughts of just how complex this imagery was slipped through our mind, but we had no wish to make things too complicated for the girls. Perhaps we should explain one or two of the non-biblical images, however.

'In fact, not all the bronzes are biblical – some designs are based on the *Golden Legend*. This was a collection of myths, legends and half-truth lives of the Saints, put into manuscript form by Jacques de Voragine about the time these doors were made. For example, the panel which shows San Zeno fishing is from a tale in the *Golden Legend*.'

'At least the symbolism is still healthily Christian,' observed Christobel. A committed Christian, she had clearly been uneasy at the pagan imagery in the Sagrada.

'If you're interested in Christian symbolism, just look at that Crucifixion panel. See how the Sun radiates outwards. The head in the centre of that circle is Michael, the archangel of the Sun.'

'And who is the angel above the Moon?' she asked. The winged figure was standing in the upturned crescent of the Moon, as though it were a boat (plate 9).

'Gabriel – the archangel of the Moon. The Moon is above the left hand of Christ, while the Sun is above His right hand. The boat-like Moon is a symbol of the Waters, while the Sun is a symbol of Fire. These are the two opposite forces in the cosmos: in the mediaeval view of things, Fire rises, while Water descends. Yet the Christian mystery depends on the "miracle" by which Fire descends. See how a part of the Sun's light – in the form of a wing – breaks away, and pours into the crown of Christ. This shows that Christ, although crucified and dead, is still alive. He is alive in the Quintessence.'

'As I remember,' said Christobel, 'there was an eclipse at the Crucifixion.'

'Well, darkness flowed over the face of the earth because the Sun had gone out – or at least *something* had happened.[59] At any event, artists have always shown an interest in the symbolism behind the meeting of Sun and Moon – especially when painting the Crucifixion. In this panel, the Light returns in the higher body of Christ. The zodiac-Sun pours light into the crucified Christ, that, through Him, the Light may be made available to humanity. You can link this with the symbolism of Aries and Pisces, which we saw in the Salome panel. Here, light pours into the head of Christ, and the two men touch the feet of Christ with their own feet. Once again, it is an allegory of Aries and Pisces. In strictly Christian terms, it is a commentary on the first verses of the Gospel of St John.'

'And the men alongside Christ? One holds an instrument of torture. Who is he?'

'That is Nicodemus. The thing in his hand is a pair of pincers. He will use them to pull the nails from Christ's hands.'

'And the other man with his arms around Christ?'

'That is Joseph of Arimathea, who will carry the body of Christ for burial. Joseph is supposed to have brought the Grail to England, and buried it in Glastonbury. See – his foot is touching the feet of Christ. This is Pisces again. The sculptor wanted to show that Arimathea had become a fisher of men, under the guidance of a Fish. Centuries after this door was carved, William Blake wrote poems about Joseph of Arimathea, and drew imaginative portraits of him (opposite). Blake was interested in hidden symbolism, and he perceived very deep meaning in the story of the burial of Christ.[60] Blake believed that Joseph had been a secret disciple of Christ, and had journeyed to England, carrying the Grail. He had buried it in a hill, just as he had once buried the body of Christ in a rock tomb.'

Detail of engraving by William Blake after Salviati, called by Blake
'Joseph of Arimathea'. Note the Mithraic cap.

The two girls examined the doors with a new interest. Rachel started to count the number of radiations on the Sun. She would find that there were 88 – similar to the flames around the fire-ring of the Lord of the Dance, Siva.[61] Christobel was counting the many fishes on the various panels. We stood back and watched them. It was fascinating to see how an esoteric work could radiate its influence and arcane symbolism down the centuries.

As we had been talking, we had observed a sunburned, lanky man with a friendly smile, dressed in shorts and an open-necked check shirt, who had been hovering near enough to catch our words. He was carrying a large haversack, on which was stitched a cotton image of the stars and stripes. We wondered if he knew that the flag was a secret symbol, the stripes representing the *ples daun* and the white stars the Heavens. Did he know that the five-pointed star on his flag was also on the doors in front of us, as the star of Bethlehem, and that the same star was a sacred hieroglyphic from Egypt?[62]

The man hovered on the bottom steps of the porch for a moment or so, and then, turning abruptly, he walked northwards, and was soon lost to sight.

Christobel brought our attention back to the doors. She was pointing towards the panel which showed a bearded figure riding an ass (plate 10).

'Is that Christ entering Jerusalem?'

'Well, it looks very like the Entry, but it's really an image of Moses, returning to Egypt to seek his brothers. The stick he carries is the magic wand he used to work the miracles before Pharoah.'[63]

She peered closely at the panel. 'There's nothing written on the scroll he holds.'

'That's quite true, but in the 12th century the onlookers would have taken for granted that this Entry into Egypt was meant to be prophetic of the later Entry into Jerusalem, which also took place on the back of an ass.'

She nodded. 'Is this an initiation image?'

'For those who *know*, yes. The Entry into Jerusalem is a returning home. So, in a sense, was the return to Egypt: in the arcane tradition, Western esotericism was a result of the fusion of Jewish and Egyptian ideas. This fusion is "prophesied" by Moses returning to Egypt. There is also another level of meaning, touching on redemption. While Christ is in no need of Spiritual redemption, the ass which carries Him is transformed by his contact with Christ. Jerusalem is the symbol of the Spiritual world, the doors of which may be entered by initiates. Even the foolish ass cannot pass through such sacred doors without being touched by the Spirit.'

Christobel was silent for a while, then remarked: 'We tend to forget that Christianity was born from a union of ancient Jewish and Egyptian beliefs.'

We permitted the silence such a perceptive observation deserved, and merely nodded.

'Are the San Zeno doors unique as examples of esoteric art in Verona?' she asked.

We pondered for a moment or two, and then smiled, as the image of another ass nearby floated into our mind.

'I could set you a puzzle.'

She nodded, eagerly. 'Like the oracles?'

'Precisely. In the old baptistry, now called San Giovanni in Fonte, alongside the Verona Duomo, is a monolithic octagonal baptistry. Some of it may have been carved by the sculptor, Brioloto, who was active between 1189 and 1220, and who did the marble work on the façade of San Zeno. Each of the eight sides is carved with a Christian image. One side – almost facing on to the door – shows Christ on the ass, making His entry into Jerusalem . . . When you go into the church, look at the hanging arch above the head of the ass. The arch has been changed – it is unique among all the 40 hanging arches on the baptismal font. My puzzle is, *why?* Why should Brioloto have carved on the hanging arch above the head of the ass a cat holding a mouse in its teeth?'[64]

My question intrigued them, and a few minutes later, Rachel and Christobel had shouldered their backpacks, and were making their way down via Procopo, towards San Giovanni. It would be unlikely that we would meet them again. They had decided to follow our suggestion, and, later that day, were going to Venice to study the astrological mysteries on the façade of the Doge's palace.

Perhaps they would never realize that they had been used as agents by the Spiritual world to bring that man in an open-necked check shirt to us. Just as the hanging arch played cat and mouse with the head of the ass, so the Spiritual world was playing cat and mouse with us.

Like the two girls, we had to leave Verona. We climbed back into our car, intending to drive to Ferrara, where we wanted to examine once again the most impressive of the early Renaissance astrological frescos in Italy.

From via Scandiana, we entered through what must the least imposing doorway in any Italian palazzo into the Schifanoia Palace.[65] It was unbelievable to me that such a modest entrance could lead into such a treasure as the frescos of *The Months*. Like so many of the arcane images of Italy, *The Months* are misnamed, for the pictures are not of the months at all. They are studies of the three interpenetrating worlds of matter, soul and spirit, unified under an obscure astrological theme.[66] Unfortunately, not all these frescos have survived, but those which have are grouped in threes on the four walls. Each 'month' is further divided into three registers, the upper depicting the pagan gods, the middle astrological imagery, and the lower scenes from the lives of contemporaries of the artist in charge of the programme, Francesco del Cossa.[67]

While the name 'Months' is entirely inappropriate, it is the theme of the middle register which partly explains the name of the room – *La sala di Mesi* – as this furnishes the arcane programme in terms of the 12 zodiacal signs, which are – in the popular mind – linked with months. This central register is further divided into three unmarked verticals. Such a division has allowed the artist to use the register to represent what he would have considered to be the ancient Egyptian method of 'decanates'[68] in which each arc of the zodiac was divided into three equal sections. Each of these sections was accorded an image. This system of dividing the signs of the zodiac survived into mediaeval astrology, in which the divisions were sometimes called 'faces',[69] and sometimes 'decans'. There were several traditions which determined the planetary rulerships over these three divisions, but these do not concern us here.[70] In every case, three distinctive images were apportioned as symbols of these divisions. Examples of these may be seen in the three images which represent the three 'faces' of Pisces. It was images derived from this decan tradition which del Cossa set over the zodiacal register of his frescos.

Prima facies pifciū eſt ſaturni z eſt anxietatis.cogitationū multarū:itinerū mutandi ſe de loco ad locū inqrendi ſubſtantiam et victum.

Secuuda facies eiꞁ iouis z eſt ap reciandi ſe multū: voluntatis alte:petēdi ac intromittendi ſe derebus magnis z altis.

Tercia facies eſt martis:et eſt fornicationis z amplexa tionis:magne delectationis cum mulieribus z diligendi quietes.

Threefold division of a zodiacal sign into decans of 10 degree arcs. Each decan (in the text called a 'face') is accorded a special reading. Woodcut of 1490.

The 'month' on which we had fixed our attention was dedicated nominally to March. The central register therefore portrays the Ram of Aries. To the back and front of this running Ram are two decanate images, and, over the top of its back, the third (plate 11).

The topmost register shows a complex scene from mythology, centred upon Minerva in her chariot – she is one of the 12 Olympian gods and goddesses. Minerva, besides being a goddess of Wisdom, was also warlike, and it is probably this strain of Martian bellicosity which has linked her with Aries, itself ruled by the planet Mars.

The lowest register depicts the world of Man. Here the 15th-century Duke Borso dispenses justice (one of the activities associated with Aries). To the left, he is riding off to the hunt, with hounds and falcons: hunting is the delight of Mars and Aries.

Because the lowest register of the fresco is within easy reach, it has suffered the most damage. In a lowpoint of Ferrarese history, the Palazzo had been used as a tobacco warehouse, and although the frescos had been covered in plaster layers, and whitewashed over, this did not protect the surface from accidents and the constant rubbing consequent to daily use.

This same triple arrangement was maintained in the area depicting September – properly the sign Libra, with its decanates. The mythological register was of more immediate interest to us, however, for the god in the chariot is Vulcan, who introduced mankind to Alchemy. His chariot is drawn by monkeys, and we found ourselves wondering if the artists would have known that this association went back to the hermetic literature of Thoth, as a monkey-faced god.[71] To the right are the physical alchemists, beating iron – perhaps a reference to the name *Ferrara*, the place where iron is worked.[72] To the right of Vulcan's chariot are a pair of what appear to be sleepers, decorously wrapped in a sheet which might be taken for a shroud, were it not silver (plate 12). The couple are far from being asleep, however. They are lovers, creating a civilization through their passion. The nymph Ilia has left her beautiful blue and white dress neatly displayed by the bed, while Mars, with less respect for material things, has merely dropped his armour on the floor. They are divested of clothing (that is, of the physical body) to show that they are in the higher Spiritual world. Mars, being a god, will have no need to descend to the lower levels of the *ples daun*, until he once again feels the urge to delight in female flesh. Ilia, being human, will have to go back down to terra firma, however, and there she will be punished for this sin by death.

The secret of this couple of lovers is shown on the other side of Vulcan's chariot. In the sky (which is to say, once again, in the Spiritual domain) hovers a shield. It looks like a doorway into space: on it is painted the she-wolf suckling the twins Romulus and Remus, the former of whom would become the legendary founder of Rome. The beautiful nymph on the bed is conceiving these twins now, under the experienced guidance of Mars. In this bed of silver, Ilia will become the mother of the founders of Rome, Romulus and Remus.

In keeping with the theme of the fresco, this conception is a Spiritual alchemy – the birth of spirit, balancing the more material alchemy of the metal-workers on the far side of the chariot. Even the silver covering over the lovers reveals its symbolism, for it is the silver of the stars, rather than of the metal. Ilia had once been a vestal virgin, which meant that she was denied carnal knowledge. Like Vulcan, she had served at an esoteric fire.[73] The mythology insists that after the birth of the twins, out of wedlock, her brother Amulius threw her and her children in the River Tiber. The twins were miraculously saved, but Ilia was drowned.

The metal-workers to the right are beating iron on an anvil. What is the thing upon which the anvil rests, however? It looks like a black stone. Almost certainly it is the *niger lapis* with which the tomb of Rome's founder is connected. Should we be surprised that such a black stone figures in alchemical symbolism? Does it mark death, or that fission of which death is merely a sign – the return of spirit to the Spiritual realms? Meanwhile, Vulcan pulled by a pair of monkeys, and guarded by a bevy of monkeys (seven in all),[74] looks down at this plethora of symbols derived from his fire-art.

We had stepped fairly close to the painted wall to examine more intently the portraits of the Duke's companions, in the bottom register. Suddenly, from the corner of our eye, we caught a glimpse of the American we had seen on the steps of San Zeno, in Verona. He was minus the distinguishing backpack, but we would have known that open smile anywhere. Our eyes met in recognition. He gestured around at the walls with his right hand. There was a trace of humour in his eyes, as he remarked laconically, 'No one could get bored, here!'

We smiled back to show that we had understood the joke.[75]

He took a few paces towards us, and touched our arm. 'That was a fantastic talk you gave in Verona. I've never heard anyone speak in public about arcane symbolism before.' He smiled confidently, not for one moment doubting that anyone would wish to converse with him, then held out his hand. 'Richard Dayton.'

We shook hands. Although he kept his eyes intently on ours, there was no secret symbolism in the gesture.

'You are interested in such things?' we asked.

'Let me say that when I tell people what my academic work is, they usually go away.'

'Try us,' we suggested.

'I'm a university professor. Cologne University. I work in mediaeval codes.'

Involuntarily, we glanced up at Vulcan, master of the hermetic arts. Was this the response to our prayer in Sagrada di San Michele? we wondered. It was less than a month since we had put the question to the Spiritual world, yet it seemed that already the angels were offering a solution. We said, 'I think we should talk.'

'It will be a pleasure. Ferrara seems to have secret things in its very bones.'[76]

Richard Dayton spent many hours with us over the weekend. It was a delight to be in his presence, and his knowledge of mediaeval literature and arcane sigils was formidable. Naturally, we showed him a copy of the code of Nicholas, and, after studying it for an hour or so, he admitted himself baffled.

He asked if we had tried applying the codes favoured by Joachim di Fiore, that great 12th-century monk, who was fond of veiling mystical truths in numbers, letters and secret words.[77] We nodded. We had tried the keys of seven and three, as well as the interchanging of the Greek letters which marked the beginning and end of the alphabet, the *alpha* and *omega*. All our efforts had been to no avail. We were now convinced that our own mysterious text would not give way to such studied mediaeval manipulations.

We had a last meal together outside a restaurant in the Piazza Castello, where we could look out on to the trees and flowers of the gardens. During the meal he mentioned that one of the sigils in the code, which was clearly a form of the letter M, was identical to one in a Latin line on the tympanum of the duomo of Verona. He drew the letter-form in my notebook: ℺ According to the unwritten rules of codification, the M would be interchangeable for the constellation or zodiacal sign, Leo.[78]

'There is one other thing,' mused Richard. 'The first three words of the code seem strangely familiar.'

'Tenth or eleventh century?' we asked, knowing the date would be crucial.

'Tenth, I suspect. I seem to remember them from Helen Waddell's collection of lyrics.' He began to quote the Latin, strange in an American accent:

'Ego fui sola in sylva, Et dilexi loca secreta . . .'. Then he fell back into a less poetic diction, and translated the Latin: 'I have been alone in the woods and have loved the hidden places . . .'[79]

'There are the opening words of the code!'

'Precisely.' He looked very pleased with himself, and smiled.

'Hidden places . . .' we mused. 'An excellent way to begin a code.'

'If it is a quotation, then it might suggest that the entire text is built up from quotations.'

'I suspect that's why the three words are there. They are the sign of how the Latin is to be approached.'

'It doesn't take you much further, but at least you've gone *somewhere*.'

We could not believe how blind we had been, and how much time we had wasted applying mediaeval numerological codes, and alphabetical transferences. The idea that the entire script should be broken into separate sections was now quite evident from those first three Latin words.[80]

'Seven lines might even relate to seven planets,' we suggested.

Richard nodded. 'That would make particular sense if the code deals with zodiacal signs and constellations.'

'It would,' we agreed.

Later, when we had said goodbye to Richard, and returned to the hotel room, we found it impossible to sleep. The three words played leapfrog in our mind: we seemed, at last, to have a clue, however remote.

The following morning, which was Friday 22 September, we left Ferrara shortly after sunrise. We had to drive back to England, where we had several appointments, and needed to be back in London within three days. As we reached the outskirts of Ferrara and turned on to the main road which leads to the autostrada, our car broke down. We were surprised, for it had been serviced a few weeks earlier in Florence, and, for all its age, usually gave no trouble. We pushed it to the side of the road, and asked a passer-by if there was a garage nearby. The man jerked his hand over the wall against which we stood.

'By far the best place to break down in Ferrara,' he laughed. 'Old Faccetti will look after you. Faccetti is a magician in metal.'

Of the many thousands of men who had been initiated into the Mysteries which proliferated in ancient Rome, two, whose names have survived in historical documents, stand out for what they said about initiation. They were both qualified to speak on the subject, for they were initiates of high grade. That, however, seems to have been the only thing they had in common, for, in almost every other respect, they represented the two extremes of Roman life, during those fascinating early centuries, when the new Mystery Wisdom of Christ was flowing into the ancient Mystery Wisdom which had served the pagan schools. One was Vettius Valens, the other Flavius Claudius.

Valens was an astrologer of the first century AD. Among the birth charts which he cast, and which have survived the ravages of the centuries, are some of the earliest personal horoscopes known to the West. Beyond that quirk of history, he was otherwise of mediocre achievement. Even so, it was his destiny as an initiate to transmit certain forms of horoscopy to the West.[81]

In total contrast, Flavius Claudius was at one time the most important figure in the Roman world, deeply involved in the forging of events which still reverberate in our own modern world. In 355 AD, Constantius II called him from Athens, where he was studying pagan philosophy, to service in the West. On his arrival in Rome, he was put in charge of the troublesome outflung regions of Britain and Gaul, where he went to live. Eventually, by his austere personality and courageous examples, he so won over the soldiers under his command that he was proclaimed by them Augustus. Almost against his own wishes – and no doubt following the requirements of the arcane Schools – he became the most influential person in the ancient world. His subsequent history need not concern us here. The fact that he is better known as 'Julian the Apostate' tells its own story – of how his instinctive paganism led him to introduce an anti-Christian movement into Rome, at a time when the message of Christ had already taken root in the ancient world.

What, then – besides the fact that both were initiates – draws the minor astrologer Vettius Valens to Julian the Apostate? It is their identical attitude towards the initiation mysteries. Little of what Vettius Valens wrote has survived. However, in one letter, he lamented that he did not live in former times, when the initiates occupied themselves with the sacred science of astrology. It was, in his own words, a time 'when the clear Aether spake face to face with them, without disguise, without holding back aught, in answer to their deep scrutiny of holy things'.[82]

Julian the Apostate was a writer of great talent, and, in contrast to Vettius Valens, he left an enormous literature, a great deal of which has survived. Among his notes are his comments on astrology, which echo almost precisely the sentiments of Vettius Valens. Julian distingushed two types of astrology. There is that type which 'makes plausible hypotheses from the harmonies they observe in the visible spheres', and which we would deduce as being practical astrology. On the other hand, Julian points out that there was the astrology of the Mysteries. This was the astrology 'taught by the gods or might daemons'. The same secret astrology which Vettius Valens had linked with the Aether was being associated by Julian with the gods, who dwelled in the Aether.[83]

The Ether, which the later philosophers sometimes called the Quintessence, is no febrile imagination of the schools. The Ether exists all around, even today. Leonardo's enigmatic chalk drawing of the women and children in the National Gallery, in London, with the erroneous official title *The Virgin and Child with St Anne and St John the Baptist*, is still swathed in the Ether, as is the gallery itself, and the red bus which lumbers past in the street below the gallery, and the polluted skies above. The Ether is all around, yet it is not seen by all men and women.

A peculiar development of vision is usually required to see these dancing lights and pinprick explosions which have their origin in the sparkling sunlight.

There are no suitable earth-words to describe the Ether. The ancient Indian artists evolved graphic forms to represent each of the four elements of Fire, Earth, Air and Water, wisely symbolizing the Ether as a mere circle. Sometimes, they put in specks, to show that the circle was full:

When the circle was an empty zero, one could not be sure whether the Ether was in that small confining circumference, or in the entire cosmos outside that space. Those who originated that sigil would have known that even the circumference line was an illusion, a part of illusory *maya*, for the Ether cannot be contained or circumscribed.[84]

We had seen the Ether many times before. The sight of this moving light, for which there are really no equivalent earth-words, is not rare. Many of those on the path have access to this lovely vision. However, only in exceptional circumstances can non-initiates see it.

We were familiar with the Ether, yet its magical power seemed somehow more beautiful than usual, playing over the engine of an old sports car. Old Faccetti had welcomed the broken car, for he had a fondness for old vehicles. Our respect for his competence grew as he opened the bonnet: he knew precisely where to press the hidden release-catch, and where to cushion the metal stay. We could see that the car was in good hands.

The vibrations of the Ether had began quite gently, but increased rapidly. We recognized that we were standing at a point in space and time when a doorway into the Spiritual was being opened. The Ether rarely came unbidden into our sight. No man may open this door of his own volition, so we knew that something of importance was about to happen.

The old mechanic reached into the engine, and pulled off the broken head of the carburettor. In a guttural Italian we could hardly understand, he said, 'This is the culprit. It is gone, finished.'

He used the Italian word *rota*, which amused us: here we were, on the edge of the Ether, and an Italian was using a secret word from the mysteries, a word which some scholars claim is an anagram for *tarot*.

'It will take some days,' he continued. 'Perhaps we have to send to England. Your machine is not new, and it is English.' He was being polite, not ironic. The *macchina* was far from new.

Chapter One

We did not have several days to spend in Ferrara. We needed to have the car repaired immediately. The Etheric forms were dancing around the engine in such profusion that we were encouraged to feel very wise. To this day, we do not know how we knew about the powder, for we had never been in the mechanic's workshop. Perhaps the Etheric was telling us. Or perhaps it was Minerva, looking down over that alchemical symbol of the golden Ram.

'No, there is no need to go to England for this . . . On the shelf in your garage . . . The third shelf from the bottom . . . On the shelf is a special powder. You can use it to stick the carburettor.'

'What powder? In any case, powder will not work. That is stupid.' Once again, with *sciocco*, he strayed unawares into the language of the Philosophers, for the word means 'fool'.

'I promise you – it *will* work.' Perhaps there was something in the tone of our voice – some magic. Then that man, who carried in his little finger more knowledge of engines than we would ever carry in our whole body, went off to his garage workshop, and returned a few minutes later smiling.

'It will not work,' he said, holding the cataloy powder up, and shaking it towards us. 'It will certainly not work.'

By now, the lights were dancing so intensely that we moved away from the car, leaving the man to work his own private incantations. We sat on an upturned chassis at the back of the yard, and took out our notebook. Then, with the lights dancing like Blake's fairies around the end of our pencil, we sketched down the correct decoding for the ancient script of Nicholas.[85]

A silence had fallen over that light-filled yard, though the noises of busy suburban streets were all around.

'So, this code has kept its silence for 800 years?' we mused. Then, almost tremulously, we asked silently a question which had never before entered our head. It had never entered our head before because we knew there are some questions which have no answers on the material plane.

'Who was Nicholas?' we asked the Silence.

Then, for the first time in our life, we heard the voice of that Higher Being. It was not like any voice one hears on earth, for it was filled with a serene wisdom, a certainty which is inappropriate on the earth plane. Whatever that voice said would be true. We had read in Indian literature of the fabled hansa bird (it is said that the song of the *hansa bird*, which is one of ineffable beauty, can be heard by humans at important times in their Spiritual lives), and now we could feel the brush of its wings.[86]

'Who was Nicholas?' we had asked. And back came the answer we would never have expected, but which we knew, from the undeniable authority in the voice, must be true.

'You were,' said the voice. '*You were Nicholas . . .*'

For a long time – if one can place such an experience in time – we sat silent, with the swirling and bursting of explosions of light around us. The visions given to us were undeniable, and enriching: undoubtedly, they would change our life. Eventually, we bent our head in acceptance, realizing that it could not have been otherwise . . .

Afterwards, the Higher Voice told us other things – these things were not given as answers to questions, for we had no questions in the face of this extraordinary wisdom. Some things told to us during that moment – in the moment that T. S. Eliot called the timeless moment – changed our life, yet have no relevance to our present tale.[87]

The voice withdrew without greeting, even without the expected triple *Vale*.[88] The dance of lights gathered into a mist, like a dew – which we recognized as the magical *Ros* of the alchemists, which was also a rose, glittering from the heart of light.[89] Through the thin mist of dancing light shone the copper-brown eyes of the mechanic, laughing down at us.

'It worked! I would never believe it. The powder worked.'

'You are a good mechanic,' we said, trying to concentrate once more on the Earth. Did he know that he was an alchemist, participating in a transformation of soul? we wondered.

Faccetti was right. The powder had worked. Instead of taking days or weeks for the repair, it had become an alchemical operation lasting only hours, with the magistry of the magical powder *azoth*.[90] After we had backed out of the garage, into the street, the first thing we did was reach beneath the dashboard for the Ephemeris, which listed the planetary positions for the day. We skimmed our eyes down the tables, and almost chuckled to ourselves. Needless to say, the cosmos had reflected our Earthly experience. The Moon, which governs travel and mutations, was in opposition to direful Uranus: it was exactly on the lunar position of our own natal chart.

We drove back to England as though the old man had given the car wings. During that drive, we were able to shake off from our minds the obsession with the code of Sagrada di San Michele, and find a new point of inner balance from which to face other esoteric challenges.

Chapter Two

Even the passion that I revealed to thee and the others in the round dance, I would have it called a mystery.

(Christ speaking to John after the Passion. From 'The Acts of St John, Chapters 94–102', translated by Max Pulver in his article, ' "Jesus" Round Dance and Crucifixion According to the Acts of St John'. *The Mysteries. Papers from the Eranos Yearbooks*, Bollingen Series XXX.2, 1971 ed., p. 182.)

The Greeks myths tell how, after he had killed the Minotaur on Crete, Theseus sailed to the sacred island of Delos, with his new lover Ariadne and some of the Athenian youths and virgins he had rescued. On reaching terra firma, he and his companions are said to have joined together in a maze-like dance, imitating in their pathways the intricate windings of the labyrinth from which they had escaped.[1] Was this dance an expression of exuberant joy, a celebration of their escape, or was it a sign of the esoteric background to the tale of the labyrinth?

Plutarch, who recounts the story, calls it the crane-dance, using the Greek word *geranos* to describe it.[2] The word, which means 'crane', is usually explained as referring to a dance which resembles the movement of cranes. However, the maze-dance described by Plutarch does not appear to be at all like that of a bird.

Now, Plutarch was a self-confessed initiate (see page 260), and was therefore accustomed to using occult blinds to mislead the uninitiated and disguise his truths. Is it possible that there is some other meaning in *geranos*, which the interpreters of Plutarch have overlooked? Such a suggestion is reasonable, as the Greek word *geraneion* denoted an alchemical substance.[3]

In fact, we do not have to comb through alchemical documents to find a clue to a more apposite meaning in the term 'crane-dance'. The Greek word, besides referring to what ornithologists call the *Grus cinerea*, or crane, also denoted an ordinary crane which could be used to lift things – a mechanical lever.[4] Is it not possible that those who danced at Delos, to mark their escape from the Minotaur, were dancing in a way that would allow them to be lifted from their physical bodies, towards the stars?

The question is not at all inappropriate, considering that this is the chief purpose of certain sacred dances – as is clear from the Sufi whirling dervishes, who dance to become one with God, and find an inner stillness. As we shall learn, there were, in ancient times, esoteric schools of dance in Italy, long before the Sufis established their dance patterns.

The complex patterns of the true dancer are perhaps recognition of this cosmic movement – of what the ancient Indian Brahmins called the *Dance of Siva*, this god being the representation of the generative powers, in the Vedic religions. The disciples of the initiate Pythagoras saw dance as an attempt to replicate the movements of the planets and stars: they might have claimed the same object of true meditation.[5]

In what has been described as 'the rarest of occult manuscripts'[6] is an account of a body-free movement through space. The candidate seeking initiation records how he was allowed to leave the surface of the Earth for a short while. At first, he was lifted upwards by an invisible guide. So high did he travel that the Earth seemed little more than a vague cloud. 'I had,' he recalls, 'been lifted to an immense height. My invisible guide abandoned me and I descended once more. For a long time I rolled through space . . .'[7] Once again, he is lifted by his guide, until he is travelling an immeasurable distance beyond the Earth. 'I saw globes spinning around me and earths gravitate towards my feet . . .' For all the fear he had felt, the experience recounted by this neophyte was not so much a trial as a foretaste of what is nowadays called Astral Travel – a journey into the starry world of Spiritual realms.

This description of Astral Travel – of a journey to the stars – is by no means uncommon in esoteric literature. Could we trace in such descriptions of being lifted by an invisible guide a confirmation of our proposed esoteric meaning of the term 'crane-dance'? There is no doubt whatsoever that in writing about this Astral Travel, the author (who might have been the Comte de Saint-Germain) was convinced that he was telling the story of a crane-dance. Each chapter of this remarkable book is prefaced by an esoteric image. The image which prefaces this story of the flight into the heavens contains three objects and four blocks of secret codes (opposite).[8] One of the objects is an antique altar, its flames burning upward. The second is a candlestick, the base of which is made from two interlacing bronze snakes, supporting a single candle.

The third is a crane, in flight. Just as the flames of altar and candle lift the Soul of Light upwards, so will the crane.[9]

The crane, the candle and the altar. Plate from
The Most Holy Trinosophia – *probably late 18th century.*

Our thesis is that when we enter deeply into meditation, be it through stillness or through dance, then we are 'craned' upward by invisible forces into the Spiritual realm. We live upon a planet which is in perpetual dance. The choreography of the dance is still a secret, even to astronomers, for while it is true that the Earth dances in a circle around the Sun, it also wobbles, and its solar centre is far from being fixed in cosmic terms. Who may describe with any precision the actual trajectory of such a complicated movement? We are ourselves part of the cosmos, part of the Earth, and part of this cosmic trajectory and dance. Those who attempt to seek stillness within themselves, and hope through such stillness to reach into the Spiritual world, are already in motion, by virtue of being denizens of the Earth. Whatever the intentions of the meditator, all meditation is conducted in dance.

The stuff of the world is an image reflected on the calm surface of a pool. Without the surface, where water and air seem to meet, there would be no reflection, and there is only the reflection. The best hope for the growing soul amidst this illusion lies in meditation, in the strengthening of the mind. This fixity amidst the whirling fire-circle in which the god Siva dances[10] is the silence at the heart-throb of nature. The hope lies, as T. S. Eliot put it, 'at the still point of the turning world'.[11]

The threats to the inner silence which is born of meditation are from within and without: sometimes they are like the lapping of gentle waves upon the shore, at others, like mighty storms crashing on the shingle. Just as the healthy man who has done wrong will have periodic attacks of guilt, as connected memories surface, so all men immersed in life will have attacks of bad karma. Both the inner and outer attacks (which the wise men of the East call *vasanas*) arise from past karma.[12] These *vasanas* rise in the mind, one after the other. They are, as the Sanskrit literature tells us, like waves upon the sands. The early Christian monks were less poetic than the Indian yogins, and perhaps more given to theriomorphic imagery: they saw the sea waves as hordes of monstrous beasts and demons distracting the mind with delirious images, masking the seven deadly sins.

What is the nature of this crane-dance of life, in which we are lapped by waves of karma? In effect, the outer dance – whether it lifts us to the Heavens, or merely leaves us whirling in space – depends upon another dance. This is the inner dance of the blood. The circulation of the blood is the thing which measures our inner dance: it is an inner sea, the waves of which are also like the *vasanas*, measuring inexorably the ebb and flow of karmic imperatives.

With the word blood, we reach at the beginning of things. We are born into the world in blood and tears, and all too often we leave the world in blood and tears. There is probably no need for a gloss on such a statement: in a very real sense, its meaning is self-evident. Even so, there is an esoteric content that needs some clarification.

The blood, which Goethe extolled as the most sacred of fluids, transmits not merely that ancient figment, heredity, and that modern figment, the genes, but that non-figment karma – the accumulated debt of sins which shape our lives.[13] The secret Schools teach that, for our karma to unfold, and for the debt to be wiped away, we must enter into the stream of humanity, and dip for a while into a blood-line: we must submit to the changing body which is subject to the multiplicity of mutations offered by the Earth. This esoteric tradition that the body and the blood are linked with redemption is hinted at in the old Gnostic texts, which speculate that the name Adam meant both 'red' and 'earth', and that from the earth, through the Mysteries, the human 'light' might be born.[14] It is this etymology which explains why one sacred text could interpret the name Adam as meaning 'virgin earth', 'earth the colour of blood', 'earth red as fire', and so on.[15]

Our blood and tears are, like the sweat of our brow, the liquids we spill to redeem our *karma* whilst dwelling in the body.[16] In the alchemical literature, blood is red, and tears are white. For the moment, however, we shall not concern ourselves with blood, but with the Mystery of tears.

Tears contain salt, which is one of the high Mysteries of alchemy. In the arcane texts, salt is the residue of fire, just as salt tears are a residue of an inner emotional burning.[17]

Salt is one of the *Three Principles* in alchemy, and is reflected in cosmos and man. We shall have reason to examine this mystic triad of Salt, Mercury and Sulphur at a later point (see page 140). For the moment, however, we should observe that for all it seems to be an inert white powder, salt is one of the great Mysteries and symbols of initiation. In the alchemical tradition, salt symbolized a sacred covenant which might never be broken, such as the covenant entered into by a new initiate with his school or master. The covenant of salt in the Old Testament may have a different meaning to that usually inferred.[18] The New Testament is less evasive about salt, for in Matthew, the initiated elect are the Salt of the Earth. With the passage of time, and under the imperative of political correctness, this rank of salthood had been demoted, and those who are now described as being the salt of the Earth are usually little more than simple peasants.[19] In earlier days, however, the elect would sit in the place of distinction 'above the salt', for they had conquered the salt within themselves. For what other reason was the *salinum*, or salt cellar, important in mediaeval gatherings around the table?[20]

Of course, scholars might argue that in this play with the word *sal* we deal with linguistic traces from different etymologies. However, the fact is that in the earliest known Latin literature, *Sal*, besides denoting common salt, also meant 'cunning' and 'wit'. A good Fool was always a salty Fool, worth his salt. His salary was paid in recognition of his worth, and he was, in truth, no fool in the ordinary sense of the word.

In several alchemical treatises, the 15th-century master Paracelsus gives a formula for making the *Water of Salt*, which is nothing more than a thinly disguised reference to initiation.[21] Paracelsus advises us to 'distil a sufficient number of times till the salt shall depart from it'. This, he tells us, will take place quickly, for salt 'does not penetrate the interior nature'. When the salt has gone, 'then the gold will be found in the liquid'. This is almost a summary of the process of initiation – the removal of the dross (which does not penetrate the interior nature), and the retrieval of the sacred, hidden within. On examination, we find that the formula does not make for Paracelsus, or for us, a *Water of Salt*, but a Water bereft of Salt, which is to say, an initiate who can no longer cry. 'Before the eyes can see they must be incapable of tears', reads the arcane text.[22]

The alchemists would sometimes symbolize salt with the most simple of all sigils – a tiny square, or rectangle □. Was this an attempt to delineate the Mysteries of the Four Elements in the four lines which described an empty space – like the space between air and water – or was it an attempt to draw a coffin? That learned collector of curious ideas, the Reverend Brewer (who knew nothing at all about secret knowledge), reminds us that it is still not uncommon to put salt into coffins.[23]

Is salt related in some way with death? Another sigil for salt – widely used in Rosicrucian alchemical groups – was a circle with a horizontal cross-line. This widely used sigil ⊖ was derived from the capital letter, the *theta*, of the Greek *Thanatos* which meant 'death'.[24]

In a number of alchemical texts, salt represents the thought-process in man, which is a process of death. Salt is the residue of the Spiritual activity which takes place in the head. Salt, as an alchemical triad, is in the dross left over when life has fled, it is the skull, the death's head: it is the white powder left behind when the gold is extracted. *It is the ash of thought*.

When the head – or its Spiritual activity, which we call thinking – reaches a point where it can no longer understand, when it reaches a point where the order in the universe seems to break down, at that moment, the head issues salt tears.

Why should human thinking – that process which has produced our much-vaunted civilization of surface rationalism – be linked in arcane circles with death? Surely, in modern times, we should argue that human thinking is our salvation, the process which will lead us to the promised land? Needless to say, any initiate worth his inner salt would challenge such a view. The author of *A Discourse of Fire and Salt* makes it clear that there is a mystical interchange between the two. For this Adept, there are two Salts – one is born of the activity of Fire, while another is the Salt which remains after the burning, itself 'a potential Fire'.[25] In this perpetual interaction of Fire and Salt, which lies at the basis of the phenomenal world, Salt represents the inert state of Death. Yet no alchemist would ever say that a thing can die in the sense of being perpetually excluded from life. Death is an interlude between lifetimes.

There was the salt of true thinking, untouched by the taint of death. In ancient times, the inventions of the clever mind were also salty. The *salse* tales of the clever Roman poets were witty and facetious.[26] No doubt their poems came leaping from the mind, following the verb *salere*, 'to bound', 'to spring', which gives us the noun *saltator*, 'leaper', for it was recognized that ideas leapt down from the Spiritual into the receptive minds of poets. A word which sounds so similar to the name of the simple condiment suggests to us a deep meaning. It points to many a mystery in the ancient world. It points, for example, to the *Salii*, the splendidly garbed Leapers, the dancers in air, who formed one of the many special colleges of priests at Rome. What little we know of this mysterious group is that they chanted and spoke in an unintelligible language, that they dedicated themselves to Mars, and were an esoteric brotherhood.[27]

As most of the relevant records have been lost, history is silent about the real importance of this esoteric body of 12, and only mythology is likely to provide an answer to questions as to their function. Mythology tells how a shield fell from heaven (remember that verb for falling, *salio*), and it was predicted that wherever this was kept in safety, that city would dominate the rest of the world. To hide this valuable shield, Numa – the seventh-century BC king of Rome – wisely had 11 copies made, so that no one would be able to distinguish the true one. He appointed 12 priests from the ranks of the patricians as guardians. These were guarding, by proxy, the future of the city and their city's imperium. Evidently, the mysterious shield from Heaven was a version of the secret Palladium, which also stayed in Rome for an age.[28] The shield was called the aegis, and was worn by Minerva, the goddess of wisdom, whose emblem was the wise owl.

If ever there was an initiation myth, then this is one. Not only are the 12 dancers of the Salii chosen to guard a gift from Heaven, but they are the ones who know which of the 12 shields is the genuine one. Their unintelligible tongue was the Language of the Birds – the secret language of esotericism[29] – and their leaping was a sacred form of dance.

The area of Rochechouart, where we studied, in Paris, is of fairly recent origin. In the century which saw that massive social experiment called the French Revolution, the area was still largely fields and market gardens, served with village taverns selling a wine which made you jump, even before it made you drunk.[30] The name was lent to the area, and later to the street and boulevard, by Marguerite de Rochechouart, who had been the Abbess of Montmartre up to 1727. The first modernistic 'development' to encroach on the peasant greenery had been at the instigation of Napoleon, who established the huge abbatoir, later replaced by the less sanguinary College Rollin. The ruins of Marguerite's abbey had been set aside for development for decades, yet it was not until 1875 that the foundation stone of Sacre-Coeur was laid. By then, the gardens and markets had been so thoroughly built over that parts of it were already in that pleasant state of decay beloved of artists. The boulevard once housed *Le Chat Noir*, still remembered by art-lovers for the lithographed posters of such artists as Toulouse-Lautrec, who frequented the tavern, and by esotericists because of the ancient magic in the name (see page 133).

When we first came to this part of Paris, in the 1950s, we did not think of Lautrec, nor of the abbess' namesake, but of the most famous alchemists of the present century. It was in the rooms of the artist Jean-Julien Champagne, in rue de Rochechouart, that the mysterious esotericist, Fulcanelli, seems to have emerged into history. His remarkable book on the hermetic coding of the cathedrals of France, which broke some of the hermetic silence concerning alchemy, was published in 1926.[31]

We had read the book several times, but at that point in our life, we had not made any especially deep studies of the sites he discussed. The main contribution the book made to our own life of esotericism is that it afforded us our first glimpse into the existence of the Green Language, the secret language of esotericism. Fulcanelli remains a secret, but he is probably more of a secret than even bibliophiles and esoteric historians realize. Fulcanelli's closest disciple, Eugène Canseliet, who wrote the preface for this work, claimed him as Master, yet admitted that Fulcanelli himself had disappeared from his group of hermeticists some years earlier.[32]

Three years after his first, another book by Fulcanelli appeared, as though to prove that he was still alive, and still a master in esoteric lore.[33] He was alive, yet his identity remained a mystery. In 1929, at the publication of his second book, Fulcanelli must have been at least 50 years of age: to judge from contemporaneous references, he was much older. One might, therefore, imagine our confusion when, in 1978, an esotericist we met in Italy told us that he was a personal friend of Fulcanelli, who was then living near Florence and still interested in alchemy (see page 303ff). Perhaps there was nothing strange in the idea of an alchemist, who seems to have mastered the Great Secret, living so many years beyond the alloted span. After all, one of the names for the mysterious Stone of the Philosophers was *aquae juventis*, 'the Waters of Youth', better known as the *aqua vitae*, 'Water of Life'.

In those early days we were innocent. We did not even suspect that the whole cosmos is designed to instruct – that the whole of life is a process of Schooling. We took things for granted, and it seemed quite natural that the place where we first began to study under a master should be in Boulevard de Rochechouart, redolent with the ancient esotericism which flowed through the veins of the elusive Fulcanelli.

In the Parisian autumn of 1956, the leaves were vibrating the terraced gardens of the Sacre-Coeur with reds, orange and yellows, yet, so near to the end of the terrible occupation by the Nazis, Paris seemed bathed in endless spring.

In the basement of the house, the whole group was involved in the more intense vibrations of a temple dance imported to Europe from Tibet, China and Nepal. We had first seen these steps practised by a serious, shaven-headed boy of six or seven, near Kathmandu, in Nepal.[34] The interpreter had called it the *Thatrug*, which, he told us, meant 'Dance of the Directions'.[35] At the time, the dance had seemed easy, yet this was only because we had not learned its dark secret. We did not know that with each mastery of one direction, a new element was introduced, so that the dance became a terrible odyssey of learning, a frightful endless exercise in the unremitting concentration of attention.

We had practised this dance for some months, yet always with difficulty. While we found it possible to relate the feet, hands, head and spine in the patterns determined by the complicated piano music, we could go no further. We found it impossible to bring the gestures into relationship with the complex series of mantras of Sanskrit words, which were to be repeated in various codified orders, to fit the movements of the body.

Of course, the words of the mantras were said in silence. This had surprised us at first, until we learned from those in similar dance circles, but more advanced on the Path, that it was our Master's practice to listen to the inner words of each person as they danced.

Our personal struggle seemed hopeless. It must have been evident to the Teacher that we would never learn the *Thatrug*. As we danced, his eye rested on our own two feet as they did the out-of-synchronization shuffles to the sequence of inner words. His face remained impassive, yet the time eventually came when he had no alternative but to motion us to stop, and stand aside. This was humiliation. To be singled out in such a way was a sign of failure. At the very best, it could mean that one's efforts were distracting the others from their necessary inner activity.

For once, the Teacher did not motion us to sit on the cushions which were scattered at the far end of the room, behind the dancers. He held up the back of his hand towards us, and crooked his fingers once, signing that we should stand alongside him.

In one of the apocryphal Christian books, the *Acts of St John*, we learn that on his final day Christ danced a sacred round with his 12 disciples. As the time of death approached, his disciples fled. 'We fled like the lost or like nightwalkers, one this way, one that way.' Even John – the initiated among the disciples – tells how he could not bear the suffering on the cross, and fled to the Mount of Olives to mourn. Then, as he stayed on the Mount, darkness descended on the whole earth at the sixth hour.[36]

John had no doubt that he had fled the death of his Master of his own volition. He had no doubt that it was his own decision to climb the Mount of Olives, to mourn his loss. However, when the living Christ appeared to him in the middle of the cave, and illumined it by the presence of his transformed body, which radiated light, John learned otherwise. Christ explained that it was *He* who had secretly caused John to go up the Mount of Olives. Christ had done this 'that thou mightest hear what the disciple must learn from his master and man from God'.[37] The dancing with Christ, and the fleeing and the climbing had been a kind of *maya* – at best a sleepwalk; they had happened, yet they had not been done of his own volition. John was in the secret power of his Teacher, who could see what His disciple still needed to learn.

The story, which is told in an apocryphal text that seems to have been rejected by the Church fathers because of its *docetism* – the notion that the body of Christ was not real – is an accurate account of what may happen in the Schools.[38] The student cannot always understand the mind or manipulative power of those of higher initiation: the student does not always read aright the intentions of the Master.

In just such a way, we failed to understand the true purpose of our Master in rue de Rochechouart.

We stood alongside our Master, and lifted our face to the dancers. We had practised the *Thatrug* – that easy dance of the Nepalese child – for weeks, but we had never seen it being done by the others. Even in a group, where one is expected to merge Ego and become as one with the others, the Spiritual activity of such an exercise drives the Ego deeply into the physical body.[39] Now, we watched the dance in amazement. Even as we watched, things changed. Everything seemed intensified – so Spiritual that the physical bodies scarcely seemed real, yet they themselves were lord of the dance. Was this vision a hint as to why Kali of the dance sometimes had five heads, each marked with a third eye of higher vision, and a multitude of arms? Kali was a Spiritual being who would never be seen on Earth, yet somehow his energy was present in the dancers, so immanent in their suffering that we could imagine the many strained faces and arms of the dancers merging into one single figure of this terrible god.

The smell of human sweat which usually permeated the room evaporated. Now that we were freed of the imperative to obey the notes by making a corresponding movement, the music took on an exquisite beauty. There seemed to be soft colours hovering around the line of people.

They were by no means *ordinary* people, yet when I first began to work among them, and get to know their foibles, I was struck by how ordinary they seemed. Their occupations were ordinary, and their outer lives seemed ordinary. One, who was now rumoured to have been a leader in the French Resistance, ran a *tabac*. Another was an architect, and yet another a probationer in a firm of solicitors. Two of the girls earned their living as nurses, and at least half a dozen were students in various departments of the Sorbonne. Although we were in France, only two or three were French. There were two Englishwomen, three Americans, a Pole and two Spaniards. The others were immigrants, mainly from Slavic countries, the tragic flotsam and jetsam of the war years. There were no Germans among the dancers. The Second World War had left its wounds, and there was still an open hostility against the Germans in Paris. Our own French was heavily accented, and the shop keepers would sometimes ensure that we were not Germanic before serving us – sometimes staring into our face with impudent rudeness, or even asking us directly.

Among the more immediately interesting people in the group of dancers was a young girl who was stunningly beautiful, and always dressed with that simple-seeming casual grace which is so much a part of the French mystique. How a beautiful Jewish girl had survived the war years in France, we will never understand.

What swept us away in amazement as we watched that dance was that we could scarcely distinguish the lovely Jewish girl from the others. The faces of all the dancers were so transformed by inner light – illumined by the *phos* (light) mentioned in the ancient hermetic texts – that they each seemed very beautiful. These faces seemed stamped anew by Spirit. We were astonished that Spiritual effort could so transform the physical body that it could change its appearance beyond all recognition.

As we watched their dance, we perceived the reason why the alchemists could say that the human frame divine was an *athanor*. The Arabic word is usually translated as meaning furnace, yet this is insufficient as a translation. What is special about the alchemical *athanor* is that it has a self-feeding system, designed to maintain its own heat. This is what we saw in those people – that they were being transformed by a Spiritual heat which was self-engendered: they were, to misuse a word from Theosophy, the sweat-born.[40] One has heard before the phrase 'radiant with beauty', but until one has seen such sweat-born transformation, one does not know the true meaning of the phrase. Was there some hint in this physical transformation as to why the disciples had not recognized the risen Christ?

'Turn,' said the Teacher. He was not looking in our direction, yet we knew that he was speaking to us.

We hesitated, for we did not quite understand.

'Turn to the wall. Behind.' He spoke almost curtly.

We swung on our heels away from that radiance to face the wall, like some delinquent. Why had the Teacher wished us to look away? Was this some form of punishment, another humiliation, a further imposition?

'Now listen,' he whispered, gruffly.

We listened, but we were not sure what we were supposed to listen to. Was it the thud of bare feet falling on the wooden floor? Was it the music? We tried to listen. We noticed for the first time that the room echoed. People who have not tried such exercises do not realize how very hard it is to listen in the right way. For one thing, the auditory tapestry is so rich that one adapts easily into making unconscious selections. For another, the listener easily becomes preoccupied with the activity of listening, and forgets to listen. Even when one is on the Path of Initiation, the inner voices rehearse and interrupt, deflect from the real.

As we faced the wall, and struggled with our inner attention, a strange thing began to happen: one of the notes in the music began to stand out from all the others. It was as though there was a music within the music. It was as though someone in the distance was playing a drum, and the extra rhythm had no relation to the music in the room. This deeper note-beat (we cannot think of a better word) became so insistent that we began to hear only this. We seemed like an embryo enmeshed in the music of the spheres, listening only to our own heart-beat. As we listened, a picture flooded into our mind. It was a picture of a vast palace, with many gateways. For some reason I thought of the *Epic of Gilgamesh* – an early Babylonian epic with esoteric overtones – and the description of the hero's heart-beat, as he descended the dark stairs into the realm of shades, in search of his friend.[41]

It was at that moment that we began to cry salt tears. There was no sorrow. No sadness. Only tears, welling from our eyes. It was as though someone else was crying, for we had no wish to cry. Each time the note was struck on the piano, tears came. The tears had nothing to do with grief, or with memory: they were being evoked only by that single musical note. We could hear the rich music to which the others danced, yet the single note extracted itself from this, and formed its own rhythm, to which we cried.

In alchemical terms, we were experiencing fission, that separation and moving of the light away from rejected darkness, figured in the contrast between the upward-striving flame and the candle. We were depositing salt, because a golden flame was rising in our soul. We were experiencing the separating of the higher from the lower. When fission takes place, the higher rises like a flame, while the lower falls to the centre of the Earth, a salty reject.

Under the impress of tears, we had closed our eyes, and did not open them even when the music had stopped. Eventually, the dancers left the room. We listened to their feet sliding over the polished wood, and relief flooded through us, for our humiliation was over. We remained standing with our back to the room and to our Teacher, who was seated as before. With the end of the music, our crying had come to an end.

'You had tears?' asked the Teacher, inviting us to sit on the cushions.

The question had been rhetorical, but we nodded.

'When the outer note corresponds to the inner note, then there are always tears. That is the law.' Infuriating as such a gnomic statement might be, it was a characteristic of the way our Master taught.

He was silent for a long time. At length, he rested his eyes on ours, quizzically open.

'Of what epic did you think?'

'Of Gilgamesh. Of the *Epic of Gilgamesh*,' we said quickly, to hide our surprise. Perhaps it was not surprising, for, in this ancient Babylonian epic, the great King Gilgamesh had also entered a Path, in search of meaning.

He nodded once more. Then he spoke, his voice characteristically lending strange emphasis to unexpected words, as though by such emphatic loading he intended a meaning beyond the ordinary. Sometimes he spoke in French, sometimes in a disjointed English. His German and Italian were excellent, yet we never heard him speak in the former, and only rarely in the latter.

'In the days of Gilgamesh, before the king had discovered the pain of Ishtar, he had sacred rooms built in the palace at Erech. He had the portal of the third palace hall so designed that when any person walked through it, they would begin to cry. The Babylonians called that gate *Bilu-sha-ziri*.[42] This is a name you must remember. The gate had no need of guardians, for its purpose was not to bar or prevent entry, but to reveal. All men of inner substance who visited the Lord of the World – be he ambassador or slave – would cry tears before entering the presence. That gate of *Bilu* had the power to call up tears by art.'

We knew that our own had not been ordinary tears.

'Your direction is not with this dance, nor with music, nor even with this place. The dance is nothing to you, now. But you must try to remember the doors. There were two doors, one for the inner sound, the other for the outer.'

Although he spoke slowly, we found it hard to follow his sentences. He fell into a silence which suggested that he had finished speaking, but then he took up his thread again, this time in English.

'You permit these things to mill – that is the English I think – to mill around your head. You are typically English. It is the English who brought this type of thinking to the world. Soon, that will be over – the need for such thinking.' He broke into Italian, to make a semantic point, as the Italian for head is *testa*. 'The head can offer no testament to these things you follow, these things you seek. The tears come only for those who still do not understand. They are the test of understanding. You must learn to escape the head with these things. *You think too much in this way*. Learn to look more. Shake your head free, and look. Look at the source of sound. Look at the ear. If you look at the ear, you will see why there were two doors at Erech. Is the ear an entry or a gauze – a veil? Does it filter or does it block? There is a greater Mystery in the veil than is generally realized, Mark, and it is one of the Mysteries you will have to explore. For the moment, I can only tell you that the veil which looks like delicate white lace is made of salt.'

In the Egyptian myths, the human-headed god Ptah is said to have created the world from dark clay. Ptah was from the ancient Mystery Centre of Memphis, which in the ancient tongue was called *Hi Ku Ptah*. This ancient Egyptian phrase meant 'the Home of Ptah'. The Greeks lisped this Egyptian as 'Aegyptos', and from this imperfect pronunciation modern Europeans have derived the European name for Egypt.

In the recesses of the great temple at Abu Simbel, one still finds an image of Ptah. During the 20 days after 10 February, and for the same period after 10 October, the sun strikes deep into the darkness of the funerary chamber. Its solar rays gild the stone deities in the chamber. Only three images are bathed in this warm shower of gold. The fourth image, that of Ptah, is scarcely touched, leaving the statue in the dark wilderness during those 40 days of light. Ptah is veiled in darkness, destined to remain perpetually in the shade, as befits a funerary god. It seems that according to the Egyptian mythology, the world was created by a god of shadows.

In Western creation myths, such darkness is represented by a snake. This serpent of Paradise was at first merely a cunning serpent, but later it was called the Devil, and Satan.[43] Earlier than the Christian stories was another garden-serpent: this was *Ladon*, who in the Greek mythology was the serpent-guardian of the apples.[44] This serpent was not concerned with temptation, nor with the fall or rise of humanity: his function was simply that of guardian.

The later alchemists, schooled in hidden meanings, recognized the true identity of Ladon. He was the *snake within* – the guardian of the inner riches. The tree guarded by this snake was inside man. In so far as this mystic tree, which bore the mystic apples, had a physical form, it was the serpentine spine, with its vertebrate trunk, and ramifications of nervous branches reaching into the cranium. The magnificent fruit of

'The dragon destroys the woman, the woman destroys the dragon.'
The final engraving to Michael Maier's Atalanta Fugiens *(1618).*

this tree was the human brain, and its flower was called the Crown chakra.[45] The alchemists knew that the snake wound its sinuous form around the spine inside the human frame, yet they often portrayed it on the outside, to reveal its terrible power.

There is something splendid in the Greek mythology, for one has the feeling that the mythologizers sided with the dragon-snake: it was, after all, a guardian of the magical apples, a symbol of the Secret Wisdom which some men and women seek. This spinal fruit may have been called an apple in the Hesperides myth, yet it was really a *golden* apple. Just so, the fruit of the tree of Eden was later called an apple, though the name used to describe it in Latin – *malus* – was a double-entendre, designating both 'fruit' and 'evil'. The double imaging often merged, and the fruited tree was seen as the human being, infested with evil, as a consequence of the Fall engineered by the Serpent.[46]

In the Greek myths, the serpent-guardian was tended by three humans, also linked with darkness. Even in Greece, at the beginning of our Western civilization, when life was fresh, and it was delightful to live in a human body, the *Daughters of Light* – the Golden Daughters of Evening – were born of darkness. The three Hesperides,[47] who were also guardians of the golden apples, were born of Erebus and Night. Some claim they were born of the union between the dark goddess Ceto and her brother, the sea-monster Phorcys, who also fathered the terrible Gorgons. In either version of the myth, the fathers were gods of darkness, or, in modern parlance, demons. Erebus, which means 'darkness' in the Greek language, was that dark inter-space through which shades of the newly dead must pass on their way to Hades. It was to Phorcys that Plato pointed, in his *Timaeus*, as the one responsible for inserting human souls into matter, producing for them the 'sensible natures'. Phorcys was the being who forced mankind down the well-rope which dangled into the murky darkness of the Earth.

The 17th-century alchemist, Michael Maier, chose to ignore the darkness implicit in the story of the Hesperides. He elected rather to write of the three Hesperides as though they were the daughters of Zeus and the mortal Themis, and he laid their secret garden to the West – perhaps in memory of the fabled lands of Atlantis.[48] In his arcane book, *Atalanta Fugiens*,[49] he named them Aegle, Arethusa and Hespertusa (plate 13).

Maier was interested in the destiny of the stolen golden apples, once they had come to Earth, for he saw them as the seedings of Spiritual wisdom. The apples were Ideals become ideas in the world of man. The fact that the myth describes them as apples is perhaps less important than that they were three, the sacred number of alchemy, a reference to the Three Principles of Salt, Mercury and Sulphur.[50]

After Hercules had killed the serpent Ladon, he gave the stolen apples to Venus, who used them for one of her more devious plans. The beautiful Atalanta had to marry whichever suitor should beat her in a race. Among the racing suitors was Hippomenes, in whom Atalanta had shown little or no interest. Now – perhaps to weave trouble for mortals – Venus gave the young Hippomenes the three golden apples of the Hesperides, and told him to throw these in front of the racing Atalanta. Because the fleet beauty stopped to collect each apple as it dropped, she lost the race. Hippomenes won, and claimed the reluctant Atalanta as his bride.

Although manipulated to this finale by the gods, the story did not end in marriage, for Hippomenes could not resist his dark demon of desire, which lurks in even the best of us. In his urgency to consummate his lust, he carried Atalanta into a temple. There, he enjoyed her body against the altar, in contravention of the most sacred rules.

How Hippomenes had hoped not to offend the mother of the gods with the most dire consequences, no one has explained. Equally, the reason why the goddess should punish his victim with the same severity as she punished him has also never been explained – it remains one of the tantalizing questions in Greek mythology. At all events, sinner and sinned against were turned into lions.

The engravings to Maier's *Atalanta* book are among the finest of all alchemical pictures. It is evident that Maier strips from the ancient mythology much of the original significance, which was related to dualism, and the age-old conflict of male and female. We need not concern ourselves with how Maier twists the mythology, and translates its meanings to suit his own purposes. What is important is that the last plate of the series shows the serpent dragon wrapped around the woman who, according to the inscription, is Venus (see figure on page 105). As we have seen, this is the dark snake within, constricting the *phos*, the inner light of the Ego.

It was Venus who had interceded on behalf of Hippomenes, and who had consequently connived in the subsequent history – perhaps, it is rumoured, even in the rape of Atalanta in the holy place. It is Venus who is finally restricted by the snake, a detail of the story which reminds us of the encounter between the serpent and Eve. What message may an esotericist read into this complicated tale?[51]

The title-page to Maier's alchemical book, *Atalanta Fugiens*, which is subtitled 'New Emblems, concering the alchemical secrets of nature', tells this delightful myth on its border in a series of vignettes, set in a garden (plate 13).[52]

As Maier's title-page reveals, the killing of Ladon, and the primal theft of the golden apples, had been done by a man who wore a lion's skin. Was this a version of the eternal esoteric truth that the outside will perforce become the inside? In esotericism, this reversal is sometimes expressed in the dictum that moral beauty – the inner beauty, or inner light – in one lifetime becomes outer physical beauty in the next. This is an expression of the first law of reincarnation, reminding us that the story of Atalanta is partly the tale of descent into matter, which is the downward pathway of reincarnation.[53] It would seem inevitable that what one surrounds oneself with in one lifetime will become the inner in the next: that one who wears a lion skin as an outer emblem would, in consequence, take on the innards of a lion.

Michael Maier's set of 50 emblems in *Atalanta Fugiens* is the most esoteric of all those published by the arcane printing house of de Bry in the early 17th century. Every emblem and text is replete with arcane messages, and Maier is right to tell his readers that the book has been designed not merely to be read, but also to serve as a focus for meditation.

It is perhaps not surprising that the alchemist, Jean d'Espagnet, should have praised the *Emblemata*, because 'they depict with sufficient clarity for clairvoyant eyes' the secrets of the Great Work, which is alchemy.[54] In the text, Maier himself admits that he had designed the work to be available for the senses of special people. What is important is the link he draws, in secret emblems, between this higher knowledge and the three apples which are the nominal subject of his alchemical discourse.

There were three golden apples retrieved by Hercules, and gifted to Venus. This triad is symbolic of the sacred treasures of knowledge stolen from the serpent. It is a moot point whether they represent the upper triad (now called Atman, Buddhi and Manas – see Table 1, page 21) or the lower triad of Astral, Etheric and Physical. Inevitably, there are three golden apples in each of the continuous narrations on the title page of Maier's book. This should lead us to suspect that there must be three modes of apprehending this treasured knowledge.

This suspicion is well founded, for, as Maier tells us on his title page, the book is 'designed in part for the eyes and intellect . . . and for the ears'.[55] The book was intended to serve a triad of senses:

The eyes can see the arcane designs.

The intellect can follow the Latin maxims and mottos (which by no means merely parallel the text).

The ears can follow the music.

It is with this third part of the design that we reach into something quite extraordinary – possibly even unique – in an alchemical text. In the 1617 edition of his alchemical book, Maier has included music to be sung!

The music was set out in 50 musical fugues in late mediaeval notation.[56] This explains another link with the three guardian women, the Hesperides, for they were renowned for their musical accomplishment, for their sweet voices in song.

The musical fugue is partly chosen to match the title, for *Atalanta Fugiens* means 'Fleeing Atalanta', and the word fugue is from the Italian *fugare*, meaning 'to put to flight'. For similar 'design' purposes, Maier divides the 50 fugues into three parts, to mirror the three Hesperides whose three apples are involved in the flight.

We have in these triads, as in the three organs of perception, a hint of the three titles he has taken from the Schools. They are Eyes, Intellect and Ears. These are of course the eyes which see beyond, the intellect which penetrates beyond, and the ears which hear beyond. They each penetrate beyond the normal, into the Spiritual realms. They are the organs of perception which can pierce through the veils of Isis.

The triad of perceptions is reflected in the opening of the book. The first (sight) is in the title-page. In this, we may study with our eyes the picture-story of Atalanta, and the descent of the pair into the body of lions. The tale is told in continuous representation, and, so that our eyes should not be deceived, the names of all the participants are written alongside their forms. Only the names of the rapist and the raped are omitted, for these two are in the temple, in the sacred place where the silence may not be broken, and names must not be muttered.

The second of the triad (intellect) is in the portrait of Maier, for in the unravelling of this we must use our intellect (plate 14). To understand this image, we must work out the meanings of the unlettered symbols, as well as the abbreviations and meanings in the Latin below. Nothing is spelled out for us, and all is in riddle. It is in this context that the year of his life becomes important. The inscription alongside tells us that Maier is in *Aestatis Suae* 49 – his 49th year. In that year, the septenary of the seventh planet, Saturn, is completed.[57] Saturn is the planet ruling intellect. In his right hand, Maier (every bit a scholar) holds a book. He is marking his place in the text with the index finger, and thrusting out the middle. In palmistry, this is the finger of Saturn, which rules intellect, and thought.

The third of the triad (hearing) is in the first emblem which follows the portrait. It is a homily on music. The head and arms of the man, which the modern reader may interpret as bursting with flames, actually stream air-eddies, for the figure personifies the Wind. In the stomach of this Wind-man is an embryo.

'The Wind has carried it in his stomach'. The first in the sequence of engravings to Michael Maier's Atalanta Fugiens *(1618).*

This embryo is the fledgling initiate listening to the music of the spheres, its shape, like the shape of all embryos, similar to that of an ear listening. Perhaps in this case the embryo listens to the musical version of Maier's verses, printed in notation on the opposite page? The connection is not mere fantasy, for it is designed into the very structure of the book. When the book is closed, the pages meet, and the Latin words, *Embryo vento* ('the embryo in the stomach'), literally lie flat on the embryo in the stomach of the Wind. The music touches the ear-shape of this nascent Son of Man, just as the planetary music of the spheres plays unheard in the ears of all men and women on Earth, who are, by definition, preparing for initiation.[58]

In such graphics did the alchemists hide their secrets, and in this particular set of engravings did Michael Maier hide from all but initiates his three gifts from the Schools. The secrets were guarded, much as the apples were guarded by Ladon, the wise snake.

It is no accident that the second plate in the series shows the child, no longer an ear-shaped embryo, being suckled by the mighty breasts of the *Anima Mundi*.[59] As if to drive home the analogy, we see alongside Romulus and Remus being suckled by the wolf, and Amaltheia's goat suckling the god-child, Zeus.[60]

'His Nurse is the Earth'. The second in the sequence of engravings
to Michael Maier's Atalanta Fugiens *(1618).*

We should not pass by this second emblem, which hints at the Secret Magnesia of the Wise,[61] without reflecting upon two details. When the child Zeus had finished sucking of the goat, he broke off one of its horns in gratitude, and invested it with the magical power of granting its possessor all his dreams. Here we find the origin of the legend of the cornucopia. As in the fairy stories, a dream come true sounds a marvellous reward; yet, in the sequel tales, dreams come true are not always to be desired. One must be careful of what one dreams.[62]

The posture of the Earth-woman is symbolic. Her right hand, emblematic of the right-hand path, presses the child to her breast, the source of her milk. Her left hand, emblematic of the left-hand path, points down to the wolf, which, for all it suckled the two children who will found Rome, is still a beast, still a symbol of a darkness so dark that it has not yet started to slouch towards Bethlehem to be born.[63]

Between these two extremes of man's potential development – between the goat that fed the pater of the gods, and the wolf that suckled the pater of Rome – stands the milk-mother which the alchemists call *Magnesia*.[64] The embryo of the previous emblem is now born into the world, and suckles at this ungainly mater. 'The Earth is its nurse', announces the Latin text in a sly (yet typically alchemical) allusion to the famous Emerald Tablet of early alchemy.[65]

The unspoken mystery we face in the picture is, what is the liquid this child drinks from that breast? If we can answer this question, we are on the road to understanding the nature of initiation.

The alchemical texts will assure you that the liquid which squirts from the breasts of Magnesia is not milk. It is the *lac Virginis*, or Virgin's milk, which is asexual and watery, and as white as salt.[66] This is the *hermetic water* which, as Fulcanelli reminds us, does not wet human hands. This milk of the Magnesia is perhaps somewhat like the metallic mercury, in that it does not wet hands, yet it is something altogether more ethereal. It is the priceless water which spurts from the fountain of *Holmat*.[67] It is the precious liquid which spurts from the sides of the crucified Christ, to the touch of the lance of Longinus. It is probably also the precious liquid in the fountain of the Garden of Eden (plate 5). This sacred liquid was never milk, even when it spurted from the breasts of an oceanic woman (opposite). It was the life-saving water of the alchemical fountain, the ever-running sacrifice of those initiates who pool their saltless tears for the good of the world.

In alchemy, the salt tears are merely the sign that the brain is frustrated: the flames of desire have reduced matter to its constituent salt. Our mortal tears are signal that the mind cannot understand. This is why it is said that the true initiate has no tears – not because he or she cannot suffer, but because he or she understands everything, and such a mind will have no frustration, no need for tears. In this simple truth lies the first secret of initiation.

It seems that in our end is our beginning. We come into the world material in blood and tears, and we are born into the Spiritual world in red blood and white tears. Yet, the end is always different from the beginning. At this ending, we do not take with us the encumbrances of the Earth, the dross *matter*, but those Spiritual things which we have made our own, those invisible things we have attracted, magnet-like, to ourselves. Thus, the same words disguise different things, and the liquids which mark the beginning are not those which mark the ending.

The Magnesia squirting her sacred milk into the sea, symbol of the soul.
Plate from J.D. Mylius, Philosophia Reformata *1622.*

The manuscripts and books of the alchemists tell us that the blood and water of the virgin *mater* are purified, and that one of the names for this purified alchemical woman is Magnesia. She is the magnet-woman who draws to her for nourishment those Sons of Man who do not find the world material sufficient, and wish to become Sons of God, or initiates.

Everything will change for the neophyte who suckles at the breast of this *Alba Mater*[68] who is Magnesia, for the vision she offers is the vision the neophyte seeks – the first insight into the Spiritual world. When that vision is revealed, and the first part of his or her journey comes to an end, everything will change. Everything will change in a twinkling of a eye, just as, in the pre-Christian Mysteries, everything changed after the dance to Eleusis, to witness the Great Mystery of the Earth-goddess, Demeter, who was the Magnesia of the ancient world.

In June, 1613, when the newly married Princess Elizabeth, daughter of James I of England, arrived at Heidelberg Castle, she was welcomed by several days of pageants devised by some of the cleverest men in Europe. Numerous triumphal chariots, filled with mythological figures, rolled by, each one stunning in opulence and redolent of the arcane symbolism beloved of the Renaissance.[69]

Her new and youthful husband, Frederick V, Elector Palatine, participated in the pageant, appearing masked among the most impressive of these huge floats. He was arrayed as Jason, sailing the good ship *Argo* with a crew of 50 argonauts in search of the Golden Fleece.

The role came almost as second nature to Frederick. This intelligent and sensitive man was certainly a Rosicrucian[70] and as aware as Maier of the arcane significance of the story of the Argonauts which lay behind the alchemist's account of *Atalanta Fugiens* . . .

In fact, while it was a natural role for the Elector to play the Argonaut, there was an even more important reason why the idea of the pageant ship should have been mooted by the organizers of this royal pageant. The *Argo* was a reference to the Order of the Golden Fleece, of which Frederick was a member. The esoteric element in the symbolism of a Golden Fleece, which had been so evident to the alchemists who sought for the inner gold, had been incorporated in the symbolism of this order. The possession of the Golden Fleece was seen as a step in ensuring the right conduct of knightly power. The Order of the Golden Fleece had been, in origin, an esoteric group charged partly with the maintenance of morality in the knightly classes, and partly with influencing the politics of Europe.[71]

The Golden Fleece of the myth was a particular fleece – certainly the most famous fleece in the ancient world – with a magical power which could be fully understood only by those capable of piercing into the hidden meanings of the myths. However, in ancient times, even the more ordinary fleeces were perceived as possessing tremendous magical power. The fleeces used in the early Greek agrarian rites were believed to have the power not only to drive away evil, but also to free from all uncleanliness and evil influences anyone who touched them.[72] Such fleeces, used in healing and magic, were always those taken from sacrificed animals, which means that they had been dedicated to the gods.

The fact that such a fleece was 'owned by the gods' goes a long way to explaining the esoteric background to the mythology of the Fleece. Like the philosopher's stone, it was a health-giver and protector, as well as something of inestimable Spiritual value. Such considerations explain why an esoteric body charged with maintaining morality, or inner cleanliness, should choose a fleece as its chief emblem. It was *golden* because it was a Spiritual fleece, the object of desire of all those alchemists who were prepared to imitate the voyage of the *Argo*, and be courageous enough to slay the dragon Ladon among the trees.

In the first two decades of the 17th century, the castle at Heidelberg became justly famed as a centre of Rosicrucianism and esoteric culture, yet it was its magnificent gardens which had attracted the most enduring attention.[73] The gardens at Heidelberg were constructed on a level of ground blasted out of the mountain top by explosives, under the direction of the engineer, Salomon de Caus. The achievement was esteemed as the eighth wonder of the world.[74] These gardens were more than floral displays – they were exhibition areas, renowned for their mechanical contrivances, such as moving metal gods, speaking automata, and a variety of impressive magical gadgets. Perhaps on display was a version of Hero's mechanical horse, which could be beheaded, and yet continue to drink water through its mouth, unperturbed.[75] This combination of losing the head, yet remaining endowed with the mystic ability to take in the waters of life, was a play on the mystery of Aries and Pisces (see page 278).[76]

Images of gardens, usually set with mechanical fountains and figures which look very much like statues, proliferate in 17th-century alchemical books,[77] and one wonders to what extent this was a result of the influence of Salomon de Caus' gardens at Heidelberg. There is one fascinating plate, from an alchemical work by the Tyrolese alchemist, Steffan Michelspacher, which depicts the Philosopher's Mountain, the top of which has been levelled off to accommodate a statue of the hermetic Mercury, with star and caduceus in either hand.[78]

Underlying this rich outer display of intellectual brilliance lay the early attempts of the Rosicrucians to (as they put it) 'bring out into the light of day' their new programme of esoteric development. Towards this end, they had chosen the ways of alchemy and astrology as a rightful path towards Christian enlightenment.

While the men of the past could elect to touch a Golden Fleece to find cure of soul, the Rosicrucians would shortly be offering the touch of Christ's hand – the hand of the Fisher King, in the emblem of the two fishes – and the single fish – symbolizing the Age of Pisces.

We had travelled to Heidelberg following our plan to retrace the footsteps of such alchemists as Maier – looking at the remains of the towns and libraries where he had lived and studied.

Like the youthful Elizabeth, we stopped first at Oppenheim where some of the greatest occult books of the 17th century had been published. It was while at Oppenheim that we met Adriano Luksch, a specialist in mediaeval horology.[79] After some conversation with him, we decided to abandon our intended itinerary for what we hoped would prove a more instructive journey. We planned, after visiting Heidelberg Castle, to continue east, towards what was then Czechoslovakia, and meet up with Adriano in Prague, where he lived. This decision was taken in the light of the knowledge that my new companion was a specialist in the mediaeval zodiacal clock in the Old Town Hall complex in Prague. We were keen to learn from such a man, in this area of specialization. In any case, a journey to Prague appealed to us, as we had always wanted to see the so-called Golden Lane – the row of alchemical houses on the walls of Prague Castle – and to pay respects at the tomb of the astrologer-alchemist, Tycho Brahe, who had been buried in that city.

Heidelberg is one of those cities which has been accorded the rulership of Virgo.[80] It had intrigued us that on the day we arrived in the city, in April, 1958, the planet Pluto should be in the first few minutes of this sign, just on the point of falling back into Leo. With dark Pluto, the god of the ancient Underworld, poised in this Earth sign (and in a degree which was emphatic in our own chart), we might have expected something extraordinary to happen. We might reasonably anticipate some welling up of hidden material from the past.

However, if this had been our expectation, we were disappointed. Nothing untoward happened, and our stay in Heidelberg was delightfully without incident. For a few days, we busied ourselves in the city, taking lodgings in a small hotel near the university library. We had appointments with one or two people, and we were anxious to undertake a little research in the university library – as a consequence of which it was not until early morning on the following Thursday that we were free to visit the castle itself, towering above the River Neckar.

We were the first to arrive at the great metal gates that Thursday morning, and the areas on either side of the gate were empty of people. We rang the bell (as the janitor had said we should, when we had telephoned), and waited patiently for him to open up. Although it was early in the year, there had been a magnificent sunrise, and now, as we walked through the inner wall-gates into the great courtyard, it seemed that molten gold had been poured on to the red sandstone of the castle, as the rays of the sun warmed it.[81] The golden glow immediately called to mind those images of the past when Frederick's gilded *Argo* had seemed to float on dry land in this same yard, announcing in secret symbolism the mysteries of the stellar Ram.

We had little time to watch this solar play on the planetary and mythological figures on the huge façade, for we had made an appointment to see the one room in the castle about which we had read so much in late mediaeval tracts. We had come to see the old alchemical laboratory, which had been especially constructed inside the castle, in late mediaeval times. As we walked across the cobbled square we were tempted to linger, but the semi-discreet coughs of the janitor told us that there was little time to waste. Perhaps it was not strictly legal for us to be there; perhaps the curator of the Castle museum knew nothing of this visit.

As the janitor shuffled ahead of us, down the stairs, unlocking doors as he went, he had the appearance of a mediaeval turnkey, in his long military-style coat and with his heavy bunch of keys chained to his leather belt, yet he had none of the inner joy one feels in the mediaeval art and literature, and his eyes did not respond to the excitement in our own. He was locked up somewhere in the troubles of his own life, a dour fellow seemingly unresponsive to the ancient beauty around him. Even when we had greeted him with an observation on how beautiful the early sunlight was, he had merely grunted, and he took the offered *Trinkgeld* without any demonstration of pleasure, almost furtively.

We had hoped that we would be able to wander around in the circular space, below the stone-built dome, but this dour fellow had other ideas. It was *verboten* to go beyond the restrictive notice. A man of less Teutonic aspect might have permitted a scholar to leap over this fragile guard, but we realized there would be little point in even suggesting such an infringement of the rules. In Germany, rules are rarely made to be broken. He had reason on his side, for our access was restricted by a temporary fencing that had been constructed at the bottom of the stairway leading into the circular floorspace.

Two of the 16th-century fireplaces were still intact, as was a metal furnace, an athanor, of indeterminate age.[82] There were a number of fixed stone tables curved against the walls which circled the room. Above were shelves with alembics, retorts, Wolff flasks, and all the retainers useful to the alchemist and apothecary. As our eyes ran over these ancient jars, we could not push back the strange sensation that the athanor should not be there.

There was something nagging at the back of our mind. We had a distinct feeling that this old circular room had changed. We had seen 16th-century engravings in the university library, but we could not put our finger on precisely what *had* changed. We realized that a major restructuring was very unlikely, as the design was simplicity itself, and the unplastered stone walls must have been very close to the original state – unless, of course, they had originally been painted with frescos which had been lost with the passing of time. Even the name had been changed, for it was now the *Apothekerturm*, the apothecary's tower.

The huge space beneath the retort-shaped ceiling was void of any feeling – any spirits which might have lingered on with the departure of the last alchemists must have fled long ago. We were just about to turn away, and mount the stairs leading back into the courtyard, when our attention was taken by the walls.

It was as though one could see through them – or rather *into* them – into their living essence: the stone was a living, vibrating entity. The walls were not *veils*, in the sense that they were insubstantial enough for one to brush them aside, or see through them – yet they were no longer solid. The walls were somehow less substantial than the beehive shape they defined in the laboratory.

We seemed to be on the edge of contacting something buried deeply within ourself, but the janitor was already making signs that we should leave. Once we turned our back on the walls, to climb the stairs, the strange feeling instantly evaporated, and we returned to that level of being which is usually called reality.

The sun was still bright as we regained the courtyard. We decided to take advantage of this unexpected early warmth, and walk through the famous castle gardens.[83] This eighth wonder of the world, with its lawns and rare flowers, its mechanical wonders, complicated mazes, hydraulic fountains and toys, had been totally destroyed later in the 17th century during the Thirty Years War, which began shortly after Frederick and Elizabeth were married, and expelled from Heidelberg. We did not expect to catch even a whiff of the Rosicrucian past as we strolled over the rough lawns. However, partly hidden in the shrubbery was a lifesize bust of Goethe, on a plinth. Almost as soon as we saw it, we recalled that this great man had found these gardens agreeable, and had passed long periods of meditation seated near the place where the bust had been placed. We saw this simple bust as a clue to the continuity of the Rosicrucian tradition in Europe. For all the destruction which followed 1622, this garden was still a remarkable achievement, for it had been wrested from the Earth: it was, so to speak, a Philosopher's Mountain excavated by a Rosicrucianist who must have known the extraordinary Simon Studion. This Simon Studion had, through a remarkable study of prophecies, continued into the 17th century the Rosicrucian tendencies of earlier esotericists whose ideas had been hidden in the literature of such secret initiate groups as the Joachimites, in a chain with neatly forged connecting links.[84] In this place the Rosicrucianism of the invisible Schools is linked with Simon Studion, who is, in turn, linked with Salomon de Caus, who is further linked with Goethe, who is linked with 20th-century Rosicrucianism by more chains than can be described simply.

The mysterious gardens had lasted only a few years, yet they still formed a material essence for the golden chain which links together the secret brotherhoods. The remote past of the Rosicrucians was preserved on a flat hill top, where it merged with the future esotericism nurtured by Goethe. The greatest student of Goethe had been Rudolf Steiner, who, in the early 20th century, openly proclaimed the merits of esoteric Rosicrucianism.[85]

Was this chain of reasoning – this vision of the continuity in the secret Schools – leading us in some way to understand those misgivings, and half-digested feelings, we had experienced in the alchemical laboratory?

The furnace had been inside the laboratory. Now, we suddenly recalled that when he was designing his magnificent Goetheanum, the centre for Anthroposophy[86] at Dornach, Rudolf Steiner had insisted that, for entirely Spiritual reasons, the furnace which would heat the place should be sited some distance away from the main building, and certainly not inside it.[87]

What were we to derive from this chains of connections? Did we see the laboratory of Heidelberg, which was an image of man according to the ancient alchemists, as a prototype for the Goetheanum? Or, indeed, did we sense the Goetheanum as a flowering in wood – and later, in concrete – of the Rosicrucian spirit, born again in Heidelberg in the early 17th century?

We sat upon a nearside bench, on this man-made level on the hill overlooking the River Neckar, and began to meditate.

Almost immediately, meditation pictures began to arise in our mind's eye. We saw in image the walls of the alchemical laboratory we had just visited. This time, in the burning glass of our mind, they were pulsating with life. But it was not the life itself, or the unnatural pulsations of stone, which caught our attention, so much as the feeling of something else behind it – something we could not quite catch. The physical form was dissolving under the impress of the Spiritual which lay behind it. This feeling of something hidden, about to be released into the light of day, remained with us for the remainder of our stay in Heidelberg. We wondered, even as we were leaving the gardens, Was this the unique stamp of Pluto (that ruler of hidden things) we had sensed in the air when we first arrived in the city?

The journey eastwards to Czechoslovakia did not prove as easy as we had imagined. The bureaucracy at the border control delayed us, and we did not reach Prague until the end of April.

On the last Sunday of the month, prior to arriving at Prague, we called at Karlstejn, which had once been the stronghold of the last initiated ruler in Europe, the remarkable Charles IV (1316–1378).[88] At Karlstejn, Charles kept the vast riches of the imperial insignia, and a number of relics which were believed to have 'witnessed' the death and Resurrection of Christ. Later, he added to this invaluable collection the Imperial coronation jewels.

In those days, there was little Western tourism in the country, and there was an air of desolation through the lands which had once been Bohemia. Nearby Prague was undoubtedly still an intellectual and artistic centre, but most of the creative work was being done almost in spite of the prevailing political conditions and politics, in homes and secret gatherings. Karlstejn, in spite of its former grandeur, seemed somehow without spirit. We wandered around the huge castle alone – save, of course, for the obligatory guide, Fraulein Fischer, who was anxious to practise her English, because, as she put it, 'English is the language of the future.'

The same air of desolation which hung over the countryside hovered in most of the great rooms of the palace, which were in a state of disrepair. There was, however, one room where the sadness of desolation was pierced by what we can describe as an inner integral light. This was in the private oratory known as St Catherine's Chapel.[89]

For almost seven centuries, the walls of this small oratory have been lined with polished semi-precious stones, but it is said that in Charles' day colourful frescos covered every surface.[90] One picture which Charles would have known still survives in a niche above the altar: it shows the child Jesus in the arms of the Virgin. The holy figures are large in proportion to the Emperor and his wife Anna who kneel on either side, but Jesus is leaning over to touch Charles' hand.[91]

The fresco was in a bad state of repair, yet, perhaps because it was set back in a niche, it helped give the impression that all the later lapidary additions to the walls – the encrustations of polished stones, and so on – were merely added as a sort of protective overcoat to guard the secret symbols of the original frescos. The whole surface of wall seemed to pulsate with a life which emanated from within. We were experiencing that same lapidary power which we had observed in the walls of the Heidelberg laboratory. It remained with us for a few moments, but, once again, we felt it unwise to indulge too freely in meditation in the presence of a guide.

The Great Tower may be approached only by means of a wooden bridge from the Mary Tower. This security measure seems to have been instituted by Charles himself, and we wondered to what extent it was an attempt to introduce the Nordic mythology of the bridge of Bifrost, which connected the outside world with Asgard, the city of the Aesir, where dwelled the entourage of the god Odin.[92]

In this Great Tower is what used to be one of the most sacred rooms in Europe. This is the Holy Rood Chapel, on the second floor, where Charles kept the sacred relics and the rich imperial jewellery. When we entered, the chapel was entirely empty, but, even in the half-light, the sight which met our eyes was splendid. As in the Catherine Chapel, the walls had been decorated with polished semi-precious stones, such as quartz, jasper and amethyst, set in gilded stucco. The larger of the inset stones (possibly in red chalcedony) were arranged to form a series of crosses.

The simple cross-vaulting offered four large arched wall spaces, which were richly covered in paintings, mainly of ecclesiastical personalities. Like the frescoed images of Egyptian gods and goddesses, these ecclesiastical figures were also image-guardians. The Egyptian deities had guarded the way to the treasures of Heaven, threatening the pit of postmortem punishment for those who failed their searching scrutiny, but these Church dignitaries guarded a more Earthly treasure. *Or did they?* Was there some greater secret at Karlstejn than is generally recognized?

Surely Charles IV, who was an initiate of a very high standing, would have conducted esoteric gatherings in this palace? Was this the *real* secret of Karlstejn, the very name of which means 'Stone of Charles'? Was this stone of Charles[93] the secret stone of the alchemists, the Philosopher's Stone? Why else decorate the walls with stones which, according to all the mediaeval lapidaries, were known to heal and redeem? As a matter of fact, the stones which we could identify – the varieties of quartz, the jasper and the amethyst, were all magical stones mentioned in the biblical *Revelation* as composing the walls of the Holy City.[94] This would suggest that the architects were attempting to equate this treasury with Heaven itself.

Even the massive vaulting which soared into space was moulded and decorated into a celestial motive. The entire surface, part stonework and part gesso, was richly gilded, and set with small reflective star-shaped glass, designed to pick up the candle light with which the chapel would have been illumined. This flicker of pinpoint lights was meant to symbolize the starry realm, the true home of the initiate.

To judge from surviving records, it is quite certain that some of the treasures were kept in a secret space within the chapel.[95] This Secret of Secrets was approached by a doorway, beneath the altar, which was walled up in the 19th century. Prior to this, in the third decade of that century, when the secret room of the treasury was being cleaned out, a crocodile's skull was found. This skull has been dismissed as one of the curiosities which the emperor brought back from his travels, but there is surely a much deeper symbolism in the idea of placing the skull of a crocodile in the secret part of a chapel which proclaims creation.[96] In the hermetic literature, the descent of the soul had been described, and symbols accorded to it, as it fell into physical incarnation. At first it was called the *golden hawk*, for it is linked with the Egyptian god Horus, whose symbol is the hawk. From this splendid divine semblance (and after passing into the realm of Time), the soul assumed the form of the *golden lily*, sometimes called the 'lily of light'. Later still, the soul passed into the pre-conception state, in the form of the sacred serpent, the *uraeus*, explained in the sacred texts as the 'Soul of the Earth'. Finally, as the hermetic texts tells us, the soul assumed the semblance of a *crocodile*, for in being born it took on the passions communal to humanity.[97]

Perhaps the crocodile skull had been an integral part of the magic which permeated the construction of this chapel. Perhaps the skull was an Egyptian seed buried in the underground part of the chapel – a memorial of the origins of the Rosicrucian schools which were to flourish in Europe, and which were born of hermetic wisdom.

As we meditated on this model of the cosmos, we had exactly the same feeling as that which washed over us when we gazed into the St Catherine Chapel – once again the walls were alive. This time, however, the feeling was more intense and vivid. Our mind, ever anxious to explain such feelings, rushed in with accounts of the elemental spirits[98] which would be the guardians of the stones – placed there at the command of magicians – and of the old stories of how mediaeval artists could paint pictures which could heal and speak.

We reached Prague before lunchtime on the following day, which was Monday, and made our way to a café in the Market Square, where we had agreed to meet Adriano Luksch.

Before settling down to wait for him, we had stepped into the nearby Tyn church to pay our respects in front of the beautifully carved memorial tomb of the Danish alchemist-astronomer, Tycho Brahe.[99] The zodiacal clock had also beckoned, and while we did examine it for a few brief minutes, we chose to await the expert, and learn as we looked.

Rarely can one sit outside a café and see such a diverse panorama of history encapsulated in stone as in this Market Square. Every building seemed to breathe an atmosphere of its own period. The Old Town Hall

– the houses behind it still unrepaired after the German bombing during the Second World War – dominated the scene. To our left was a house in which Mozart had lived, while across the square were the great towers of such churches as the baroque St Nicholas, and the 15th-century Tyn. Directly ahead of us was the art nouveau monument to Jan Hus, the Bohemian religious reformer, who was burned alive for heresy in Germany, still singing the *Kyrie Eleison*, even as the flames ate into his flesh.

There was a sense in which Charles IV had brought Prague to life. As soon as he ascended to the Bohemian throne, after the death of his father at the battle of Crécy in 1346, the first thing he did was to establish a university in the city – one of the first such centres of learning north of the Alps. As an initiate who was charged with preparing the life of the north for the spread of esoteric Christianity, he recognized that the key to such expansion lay in education.

We were reflecting on the little history of Prague we knew, when Adriano arrived, wringing his hands humorously, in sign of apology for being so late. However, the planet Mercury would be retrograde for at least another 24 hours, and we were not expecting punctuality from anyone.

He lit a cheroot. 'Have you been up to see the famous Golden Lane?' he asked.

'I've been in Prague for less than an hour. I saw the Brahe memorial, and I glanced at the clock . . .'

He interupted us with a shrug. 'That, I'm afraid, is what most people do – they merely glance at it – but you and I will really look at it. Every single symbol.'

Twenty minutes later, we were standing before the huge clock tower. The horlogium was probably even larger than the 16th-century clock inside the cathedral at Strasbourg, which was certainly more ornate and more complex than this,[100] yet there were things which both had in common. Both had two great dials – one to tell earth time (plate 15), the other to tell the time by the stars (plate 16). They both had processional automata, displaying the diurnal order of the planets. Today being Monday, Luna could be seen, riding her chariot, the silver crescent on her head.

'Adriano, what is that golden castle in the centre of the lower dial?' we asked. The lower face was a ground of pure gold, inset with small painted roundels of the activities of the 12 months and the 12 zodiacal signs.[101] In the very centre was a castle, with three towers.

'It is Prague. Some say it is a stylized representation of Peter Parler's

The triple-towered city at the centre of the lower zodiacal clock-face in Prague.
Some say that it represents the Charles Bridge, while others say it represents Prague itself.

bridge gate, which he built for Charles IV over the Vltava. Similar images are found in numerous heraldic devices through the city.'

This was our first disppointment, for we knew he was wrong. Adriano was offering us only the official explanations. We knew that the central golden castle was meant to represent Jerusalem, or the Holy City. This golden circle was surrounded by the concentrics of the zodiac and the image of serial Time (the monthly seasons). The golden castle was at the centre of the cosmic world, while Prague was not. In contrast, Jerusalem, or the City of God, was at the centre of the cosmos, according to the mediaeval view of things. The three towers of the castle were symbolic of the Trinity. The portcullis on the gate was lifted to show that this castle could be entered by anyone. The City of God lay at the centre of all human activity, and this is what the turreted city must represent – it must be archetypal.[102] The outer periphery was a white band on which was painted in a beautiful script the 365 festivals of the year. A winged figure held a pointer towards the top marker, which indicated the feast to be observed on that day. We could not remember what festival would be celebrated on 28 April, nor could we read the script at this distance.[103]

'What do you make of the winged figure?'

'The angel? He is pointing out the days – the ecclesiastical calendar.'

Once again, a twinge of disappointment. The figure was the Archangel Michael, as his sword and buckler made clear.

'And the man opposite?'

'He is an Arabian astronomer,' said Adriano. 'You can see his telescope. Much of the astronomy used in the building of this clock came from the astronomers of Baghdad.'

This was true, but already we had realized that there would be no point in asking Adriano about the two figures beneath the clock, for these were esoteric images. They were bas-relief images, cut into the stonework, depicting two sleeping men. One was slumped forward completely asleep, the other was supporting his head on his arm, eyes closed. *These were the Sleepers.* They represented ordinary humanity, sleeping, and unware of the golden cosmic mysteries above them, in the golden clockface. Would they perhaps wake to the cosmic wonders above them before they died?

'I have obtained permission to go into the building,' he said almost casually. 'We can examine the mechanism on the inside, if you wish.'

We eagerly accepted his invitation, and spent a couple of hours listening to an intriguing account of how the complex mechanisms worked. This was the *real* expertise of Adriano Luksch.

In the evening, we attended an opera at the *Stavovske divadlo*, where Mozart's *Don Giovanni* had first been performed.[104] Afterwards, we wandered the streets of the Old Town, over the bridge built by Charles IV, and up to the cathedral of St Vitus. As we sauntered along, we looked at the mediaeval symbols on the ancient buildings. Why did images of golden fish predominate in this city, ruled by Leo? Prague was a Leo city set in a Leo country.[105] For a while, we troubled to count the number of images we found of the three-towered castle, but there were so many, we soon gave up.

Perhaps Adriano was right, and it was foolish of us to read cosmic symbolism into the centre of the clock. Could the image of the triple-towered castle represent both the City of God and Prague, depending upon the context in which they appeared? Did the mediaeval artists believe that Prague was a City of God?

At daybreak on the following morning, we returned alone to look at the clock, and to meditate upon it without distraction. We could see that the Moon was newly in Virgo, for the upper face had a clock-hand distinguished by a great silver ball near the end of the pointer: this pointer indicating the diurnally rapid movement of the Moon against the zodiac. The other pointer indicated that the Moon was in the harmonious relationship of trine with the Sun, set in the Earth-sign Taurus.

Once again, we let our eyes drop to the face of the lower clock, to the still centre of the Spiritual world. On this were the beautiful roundels and zodiacal figures painted by Josef Manes. Our eyes fell on the distinctive image of Capricorn. Why was Capricorn the goat carrying a young child? We had never seen this in a zodiacal image before. The more usual image of Capricorn was a goat-fish, and the oriental image had been a crocodile, called the *makara*. The *makara* goat-fish crocodile had been one of the initiate instructors of mankind.[106] Was this an embryonic child, carried on the back of a celestial god, who represented the Earth? Was this Capricorn carrying the child he was to instruct? Could it be that this child was the newly wakened soul of those Sleepers below?

It was as we stood, ruminating on these individual symbols, that the strange feelings which had troubled us in Heidelberg and Karlstejn began to return. The whole golden surface of the lower clock began to vibrate, as though operated by some delicate mechanism behind. The clock, and the bas-relief images around it, the tower itself, and the whole of Prague was alive. Then, suddenly, it was as though we could feel our soul being sucked into this golden circle, into the centre, towards the open gateway beneath the portcullis. At that moment, we knew what this vibrating veil around us was. It was the first veil of Isis – the dark one, which no ordinary man might lift. This veil of nature had suddenly changed: it had become for us what Plutarch had called 'that smooth pure raiment that does not weigh upon the watcher' – the veil that had no substance or mass.[107]

Then, as this realization that all around us was the unlifted veil of Isis dawned upon us, we began to understand what had lain behind our earlier feelings, in Heidelberg and Karlstejn. Now it was clear, for we knew that when we looked upon this clock, and at its City of God centre, *we were remembering*.

How, indeed, had we known that the three-towered castle was an image of the City of God? Perhaps indeed there *had* been a three-towered castle with a portcullis in Prague in earlier days, and perhaps Adriano had been right in describing this as a symbol of Prague. Yet we *knew* that it was an image not of any Earthly city, but of the celestial City of God. How could we know such things, unless we were linked directly with the archetypal plane ourselves?

This was an important question, yet all too rarely do we stop to question why we know, and even what we know. There is the knowing from books, from other people, from experience . . . All this is true, yet there is also another kind of knowing which is free from this scrambling about on the time-infested material plane. Plato had called this type of knowledge *amamnesis*, or recollection.[108] Where the soul had existed before was perhaps immaterial – what was important was that we had within us a faculty of soul which could remember. We might be remembering from previous lifetimes, or from a time when our soul was witnessing, body-free in the Spiritual world, the making of history. What was important to us was that we had seen within ourselves a golden hoard of wisdom, guarded by a dragon, a Ladon, which later men had called a veil.

At that time, we were still working in the Parisian School. We call it the Parisian School, even though by this time it had been moved from Paris further south, in the Loire Valley. When, after our long journey through Bohemia, we returned, we drove down to Bellegarde and raised the matter of our experiences with our Master.

He examined our face for a moment or two, and smiled slowly before beginning to speak.

His face broke into a huge smile. 'Most of all, I like your story of the Sleepers, Mark. Those sleepers below look up at those sleepers above, and wonder why they are shown sleeping . . . It is ironic, *n'est-ce pas?*'

He became serious again. 'What I must say, Mark, is that your walls moved *because you are just beginning to grow wings*. It is not natural at this stage for men and women to grow wings – yet all esoteric work is against nature, and you are beginning to feel what it is like to grow wings . . . You may never learn to dance properly, Mark – but it is quite possible that you will learn to fly.'

We smiled weakly to acknowledge his joke.

'You must nurture such experiences. All these books you read, and all this talk you indulge in – all your cleverness – will not help you grow wings, Mark. You must learn to listen and watch. This is what the moving walls are telling you.'

Once again, he smiled, but now there was a new softness in his voice. Before, when he spoke to us, we had always sensed an element of mockery, as if he was of the opinion that we were not yet ready to be in a School. This tone had now disappeared from his voice.

'You are still young, and have a long way to go. From what you describe, I see that you are being led by your own inner promptings. You have, so to speak, an inner ear for things.' He flicked his finger ends together rapidly over his own ear, as though to give some resonance to his words.

'That is a very special Way. You will have to develop it further. You will have to learn how to hear yourself – to touch the things inside. This is an art which no one can teach you. Few people listen to their inner self any more. You are choosing a lonely way.'

As he spoke, he ran his index finger under his chin, as though searching for the proper words. He was speaking in French, which was not his natural language.

'Now, among the early experiences of one who set out on the Path of the Fool is one akin to the experiences you have described.' He looked at us wide-eyed, in an almost humorous manner, which was one of his characteristic ways of asking a question. 'The material world was dissolving?'

'The walls, the clock face . . . Yes.'

'And you learned things from this dissolving of form?'

'I learned a great deal.' We said this with some emphasis. 'I learned about the veil of Isis, the *peplos*.'

'Do not forget, Mark, that there are more veils than one. The peplos is merely the dark outer veil – the occult blind for those who do not know about such things.' His voice changed, and took on a solicitous quality. 'But you did not feel insecure? When the walls dissolved, you did not feel insecure?'

'No. Not in the least.'

'That is a good sign, Mark. You saw truth. Nature – the world of phenomena – is a veil for Spiritual activity, and it is as well to realize this early on in your esoteric development. Yet such an experience, while essential in the early stages of development, should not lead you to think that the world down here is unreal. All that you were being shown is that the world down here is not quite what you had imagined it to be.' He broke into English, which was not as good as his French, and was strangely guttural with the hint of a Slavonic accent. 'The world down here is a veil. It is such a transparent veil that it is possible to gain – to acquire – the power to see through the Earth itself. To the other side. Right through.'

'The midnight Sun,' we ventured, in French. Somehow, the French, *le soleil de minuit*, did not sound as strong as the English, and we wondered if he would know what we meant.

'Ze Zun of ze midnight,' he replied in English, with sly humour, mocking his own accent. 'Yes that is how insubstantial is the material world. The wise men of old rightly called it a veil, for a veil is a flimsy thing. I think that, in English, some joke and call it a vale of tears. There is a truth in such word-games, for the ancient Egyptians saw the veil of Isis as so many tears, streaming downwards from the skies.' He fell back into French. 'Yet, tears or not, this veil of the world is very real. Only one who wishes not to turn his back on this veil, and who is prepared to walk towards it with resolution, will be able to find his Way in modern times. The veil has no tongue, yet it has words. If you listen intently enough, and catch those words, you will learn extraordinary things.'

Once more, there was a silence as he pondered. From outside floated the sound of piano music from the dance hall. It was foolish to ask if such mechanical sounds also had speech: music *was* higher speech.

'While the experience is fairly common with young people on the Path, it is rarely quite so dramatic as in your case. You say that you experienced it three times, and each time, it grew stronger?'

128

'Yes.' The last experience of dissolving, in Prague, had been so intense that we had felt as though we were being sucked into the golden clockface.

He slid his finger over his chin once more, and then asked, 'This alchemical laboratory at Heidelberg – it is below ground?'

We were surprised by the question. 'Yes.'

'And the clocks at Prague towered over your head?'

'Yes.'

'I imagine that the clockface must have been circular, but I must ask if the laboratory was designed to a circular ground-plan?'

'It was.'

'Then you see, it was working on three levels – through your willing, feeling and thinking. In the first instance, your feet were touching a circle as the veil shifted. In the final experience, your face was turned upwards towards another circle. These things are important. Architecture works into our Spiritual bodies in curious ways. You see, a part of our Spiritual being *imitates* everything we confront. When we see a symbol, we imitate that symbol. This is one way the not-so-clever – the ones who are not immersed in that intellectualism which is so popular nowadays – feed their spirit. They do not understand with their consciousness the voices of the symbols, but their bodies drink in the power of that noiseless sound. Christianity is for everyone – not just for clever people. Cleverness can so easily get in the way of true understanding.'

He seemed to be reflecting on what he had said. 'I used the word *imitation*. However, imitation is not quite the right word. But, if I were to give you the word from the hermetic wisdom, you would not understand it, yet. However, the word is not important: one imitates external forms, trying to assimilate them into one's being. This imitation can lead to major inner tensions which are resolved either by tears, or by an opening into the Spiritual world.'

'I could feel tears behind the experience – welling up.'

'Yes, that is normal. Quite normal.'

There was a long silence. Eventually, he smiled, and observed, 'Tears are normal in such circumstances, Mark, yet what you experienced was not at all common. You must be grateful. The nature of the dark veil is not always seen with such clarity.'

'Thank you. I will remember that.'

'You know, Mark, there are mediaeval churches in Europe designed to work precisely upon these three levels in man. The crypt works upon the Will, the aisle upon the Emotions, and the raised altar (or, in some cases, the images above the altar) on the Thinking. Keep your eye open for such buildings – if they are not themselves intended as places of Christian initiation, they are architecturally based on such designs. By kneeling in such a place – by walking through such a place – a man or a woman can contact hidden parts within themselves.'

Once again the wide-eyed look of inquiry.

'Have you read Goethe?' He asked the question in such a way as to imply a deeper meaning than usual in it.

'Not much. His *Italian Journey* . . .'

'A man in your position should read Goethe. Everyone on the Path should read Goethe. You should carry paperback Goethes in all your pockets, Mark. That man was almost two centuries ahead of his time, and knew better than anyone that the approach to Nature should be artistic, yet rooted in attention to facts. Goethe said something which you could be well advised to take as your personal motto. He said, "While the true is Godlike, it does not appear directly. We must divine its reality from its manifestations." '

He smiled at us once more, revealing the weasel-like appearance of his eyes. He was a small man, clean shaven, with intense eyes set in a thin face which, in spite of all we knew about his inner powers, always reminded us of a weasel. (If Leonardo da Vinci had been able to paint his portrait, then it would have looked something like the ermine-eyed Cecilia Gallerani. She had been the mistress of Ludovico of Milan, and seems to have disliked Leonardo for the comparison he made between her own face and that of the ermine in her hands.)[109] He smiled, and then rose from his cushions.

He rose. It would not be accurate to say that he stood up. Our Teacher's energy was extraordinary, and this explains why one has to say that he had risen. One moment he was sitting cross-legged on the cushions, and the next he was standing upright in front of the cushions, as though there had been no spatial disturbance.

Later in life, we saw old men make this same grace-filled rising as they left their cushions in the Arabic *diwanirs*,[110] and it was only then that we realized where he must have learned the art.

He had risen, and before turning, he made a little bow to us, perhaps in mockery of a Middle-Eastern *salaam*. Then he turned, and walked away without looking back.[111]

Chapter Three

For all that meets the bodily sense I deem
Symbolical, one mightly alphabet
For infant minds: and we in this low world
Placed with our backs to bright Reality,
That we may learn with young unwounded ken
The substance from the shadow.

(Coleridge, 'The Destiny of Nations'.)

The historian Dollinger said that if he were asked to name the most evil day in the history of the world, then it would be 13 October 1307. This was the day on which Philip the Fair of France ordered the arrest of the French Templars.[1]

Dollinger is right to see this as a crisis date in the history of the world, for it marked an outrageous attempt by those who should have known better to destroy an esoteric order.[2] Dollinger may well have been under the impression that this mass arrest, and the final extirpation of the Order of Templars, destroyed the important esoteric undertaking which it had been entrusted to accomplish. However, there is a sense in which the esoteric work of the Templars did not come to an end with their murder. Whilst it is true that the history of esoteric movements was never the same after the destruction of the Templars by the French king, some of the Knights escaped to Germany and England where their brothers were more secure, and less in danger from the Inquisition.[3] The Templars' secret programme of reform went underground, in the best style of persecuted occult streams. This probably explains why Rosicrucianism – the next important phase of esoteric development – emerged in Germany, and was established in England, long before it was established in France. Even so, Dollinger is quite right to see the events of 1307 in terms of a world crisis, reflected in the destiny of an esoteric movement.

131

Our impression is that every person who undertakes Spiritual development leading to initiation must, at some point or another, encounter a crisis equivalent to that of 1307. Such an encounter marks a sort of crossroads, when the would-be initiate will, as a result of persecution or a mistake, either go underground or change his or her direction.

Our own 'evil day' was encountered in Italy, in the 1960s.

In the opening Canto of his *Purgatorio*, the poet Dante tells how as he made his way towards Hell he was confronted by an unidentified animal, *una lonza*.[4] The creature neither threatened him nor impeded his passage. Its appearance was not adequately accounted for in the poem, and the reason why Dante mentioned it at all is something of a mystery in terms of ordinary symbolism. The usual literary 'explanation' for this creature is that it is a panther, which symbolizes 'pleasure or luxury'. The esotericist knows different, however. The creature is a symbol of what has been called in relatively modern times the 'Dweller on the Threshold'.[5] It is a Spiritual entity which must be passed by all mortals who wish to enter into the Spiritual realms of Hell and Purgatory.[6] It neither threatened nor impeded Dante because, in his visionary poem, he had the privilege of travelling in the Spiritual spheres with his body intact, and with a promise that he would come to no harm. Unlike all the other entities he encountered in the Spiritual realms beyond – angels, defunct humans and demons – his own body cast a shadow.[7] This shadow marked the poet out as an interloper in the Spiritual world – as someone who had penetrated into the higher realms to which he was not normally allowed access. He was, in a word, an initiate sky-walker. This is the reason why he was permitted to pass the guardianship of the *lonza*, which wandered around in that threshold between the material Earth and the Spiritual realms, as a guardian of the Threshold.

The term 'Dweller on the Threshold' is comparatively modern, but the demonic entities denoted by the phrase are as old as mankind. The Dweller is a sort of demonic buffer between the two worlds: it is there as a guardian to prevent the unprepared from entering into a realm which they would not be able to bear, without special protection.

Being ancient, these demonic guardians have very many different names in the esoteric tradition, and certain of the strange monsters depicted by the early alchemists pertain to this guardian (plate 17).[8] We shall use the modern phrase here mainly because it does convey more completely something of the nature of the Spiritual experience, which the alchemists demonized or rendered in arcane words and images. Dante's quiescent panther may appear to have been no fearsome thing, though the arcanist will recognize in the word *lonza* a depth of infernal meaning.[9]

Because the Spiritual world had allowed the poet Dante to enter into Heaven, Hell and Purgatory, he was not required to pass the usual *test*. Normally, when an initiate sets out to penetrate into the next higher realm, to gain knowledge through looking directly upon the hidden secrets, he or she must pass a test. The process of initiation has prepared that person for the test, so that he or she can continue on the exploration without undue hindrance. One presumes that had another person (other than Dante) found themselves in that dark wood, faced with the *lonza*, then they would have been attacked, and driven away from the entrance to the higher world beyond. The test is an integral part of the process of initiation, and echoes of it are still from in the numerous so-called initiation processes of primitive tribes. The tests of the more advanced initiation centres are usually represented in terms of encounters with demonic entities. Among the most well-documented of sophisticated initiation tests is that involved with the encounter with the Dweller.

In modern literature, the esoteric truths behind the Dwellers have been developed with real artistic genius by the occult artist poet, Austin Osman Spare. Spare pluralized the Dweller, and made of it *Dwellers on the Threshold*. He represented these entities in drawings, words and diagrams, and it is clear that he regarded them as guardians between this and the next world. Taking a cue from the occult tradition, he showed these creatures as a sort of window in the mind, separating ordinary consciousness from the Spiritual realm beyond. In one of a series of drawings, which Spare wisely associated with Dante's *Inferno*, the dwellers are portrayed in a window, and the representative of ordinary human consciousness is sitting in a chair, with demonic black cat entities around him (plate 18).[10] Earlier in the work, Spare had written a message which is clear to any sky-walker in the Spiritual realms:[11]

> I sent my soul through the invisible,
> Some letter of that after life to spell:
> And by and by my soul return'd to me,
> And answer'd I myself am Heaven and Hell.[12]

For both Blake and Spare, penetrating the veil of the Dweller, or the - Monsters, leads to a new assessment of the self. Beyond the threshold, the illusions which pin the ego to Time and Space are shattered. It is very unlikely that anyone would pass through the threshold without being changed.

The sense of Spiritual separation, which is the hallmark of ordinary existence, has boundaries which disappear in the Higher Realms. On the higher plane, the distinction between the outer and the inner is no longer clear.

Spare, like Dante, was steeped in mythology. This accounts for why so many of his pictures are arcane reflections on ancient mythological truths. In one of his writings, he developed the ancient Greeks' image of the butterfly, which he recognized was a symbol of the human soul, caught in the spirals of reincarnation. He used the butterfly to point to the blurring of the boundaries between the realm of ordinary existence and the Higher Realm which may be encountered by the initiate, when he or she moves from one world to the next. During this movement, the distinction between self and others – between what is out there, and what is inside oneself – becomes blurred. Spare realized that the distinction between the inner and the outer worlds, which we have as a normal experience of life, is something of an illusion. He wrote:

If you hurt the Butterfly you hurt yourself, but your belief that you don't hurt yourself protects you from hurt – for a time![13]

Of course, that *time* to which he refers is the moment of death.

If we can struggle beyond the veil of the *Dwellers*, by means of initiation, or if we find ourself suddenly passed through the veil, as a result of death, then we are confronted with all the deeds we did in life. What we did as outer things now confront us as inner experiences. After death, we are presented with – as though reflected in a magical glass – images of all our earthly deeds: all the hurts we have done to the butterfly (and, indeed, to all creatures) will come back to haunt us. Fairly soon after death, one begins to feel the pain one has caused others.

Once we have passed through the threshold, the hurts we did to others become our own hurt. Through this soul-pain, one is able partly to redeem the act of cruelty. It is a cosmic truth that the hurter must become the hurt. Initiates recognize this as the secret of Purgatory, for the state of Purgatory is nothing more than the unfolding, on the Spiritual plane, of the reality of all those deeds we enacted on Earth. In this plane beyond the Dwellers, there is no more illusion: we will see ourself as others saw us, as others endured us.

Under what circumstances do we follow in the footsteps of Dante, and encounter the Dweller? Under normal circumstances, the human passes beyond the Dweller on the Threshold only after death. This is the proper and normal experience of Purgatory, which is an unfolding of something already latent within the deceased human – latent in shadow because it was created by him or her.

Under extraordinary circumstances, the human passes beyond the Dweller as a consequence of initiation. It is not possible to reach the higher levels of initiation without experiencing the Dweller. It is not possible to dwell in the Higher Light without being cleansed.

This idea of cleansing was expressed in ancient times by means of a very basic symbolism, taken from a plant, called the *moly*. In classical mythology, the black root of the sacred *moly* plant had to be cut away, to leave behind the valuable white flower. The black root was human sin, and the white flower was the human soul, or spirit. The symbolism indicates that the spirit had to lose its darkness to proceed into higher realms. The name, *moly*, survived in a magical context, but its original cleansing property seems to have been forgotten.[14] However, the idea that the soul is a flower, and that its roots are gripped in dark earth, is a wonderful archetype, as it expresses perfectly the idea of the human condition: the roots nourish, yet they hold the soul close to the Earth.

When we are uprooted – when the illusions surrounding ordinary life are pulled away, at death, or at higher initiation – the inner monsters are revealed as being also on the outside. It is indeed a terrible experience to discover, at these crisis points of enlightenment, that all one's deeds, innermost thoughts and desires have external embodiments. This is indeed a foretaste of hell and purgatory.

During such research, while concentrating on the mediaeval con-stellation images at the top of the Staircase of the Dead, in Sagra di San Michele, we found ourselves attracted to the meaning in one image in particular. This was a bas-relief of the horse-man Centaurus, holding what appears to be a rabbit or hare in his hand (plate 19). Subsequent research showed that this mediaeval hare has a curious and unfortunate ancestry: in spite of being portrayed as a helpless rabbit, in the mediaeval star-lore it was called *Bestia*, or The Beast.[15] The creature was disguised, for subsequent investigation revealed to us that the form of the timid rabbit was a mask for a spirit of powerful depravity.

The *inner beast* is one of many names given to the creature which lurks, in a variety of guises, within everyone. It is, literally, the monster within – that dark part of the human soul which is in need of redemption. In terms of the astrological theories which apportion metals to the planets, the inner beast is the weight of lead which every person carries, somewhere in the soul.[16]

In the hermetic and alchemical tradition, each of the seven planets is associated with a metal – the Sun rules gold, the Moon silver, and so on. The cold and distant planet, Saturn, rules over lead, and hermetically speaking it is this heavy metal which the Fool carries in the bag slung over his stick (see figure on page 22). On one level of symbolism, this lead is the dead-weight of karma which must be redeemed, by the alchemical process of initiation. This hermetic Fool, with bag and stick, has an excellent pedigree, for the Shepherd or Pastoral Hermas of the ancient hermetic texts carries a wallet on his shoulder and a staff in his hands.[17]

The *inner beast* of modern esotericism has been 'personified' or 'spiritualized'. Rightly or wrongly, it has been called the 'Dweller on the Threshold'.[18] This Dweller is a reminder of the karmic debts which have to be repaid, of the darkness which must yet be woven into light, to make of the red-man Adam (see page 94) a creature of light – what the ancient hermeticists called the *phos*.[19] Like most wild predators, this inner beast must be confronted, and wherever possible brought into the light of day. In the light, most dark monsters evaporate, or lose some of their powers.

The true horror of the Bestia is that it dwells in each of us. This is why the Path of initiation leads inevitably to the hunting of the Beast within. A confrontation with the monster is inevitable for one who has set out on a Path. At some time or another in the life of the neophyte on the Path, the Beast within must be faced. If it is not faced, then the Beast will emerge and confront the neophyte. This esoteric truth is expressed to perfection in the ancient mythology of Theseus and the Minotaur. The monster (which was created by the sin of an unlawful human sexual encounter)[20] is imprisoned in a labyrinth. The labyrinth, with its winding corridors, is an image of the sausage-like brain within the cranium of man. In these corridors of the brain there roams a Minotaur which we must face with the courage of Theseus. When the dark beast is tackled on the inside of the labyrinth – within the secret places of the mind – the conflict which results is that which in religious disciplines is called the Dark Night of the Soul.[21] When the creature comes ravaging from without, through the tunnels of *maya*, then it is called the Testing.

In art, the dark creature is usually pictured as a slothful coiling monster. Its image is found nowadays on a thousand war memorials to those two upsurgings of the Bestia which we call the World Wars. Many of these portray the creature as a dragon, trampled underfoot by an armoured St George. This ancient image speaks volumes, for the monster is truly a kind of dinosaur, in part a remnant of the ancient worlds in which human beings evolved sufficiently to take on physical bodies, in remote lifetimes.[22] It is a throwback to our own antiquity – to unresolved and unredeemed histories in our own past lives. Just as its ancestry is ancient, so is its mythology, for it was already clearly defined in Assyrian literature, as the water-monster *Tiamat*.[23] The monster born of Pasiphae was fathered by a bull sent by Poseidon: this god was ruler of the sea – that universal symbol of the human soul.

The idea of there being an attendant monster within man and woman is very ancient: the inner sea-monster Leviathan, about whom Blake wrote with such passion, is probably even more ancient than the Tiamat mythology. When the Egyptian Anubis weighs the heart of the deceased against the *maat*, or feather of truth, shortly after death, he is accompanied by the monster Amemit, 'the devourer'. The implication for anyone contemplating such imagery is very clear: this creature is the dark side, which wishes to devour its own.

William Blake had been a master-hunter and exposer of this Bestia, the inner beast – of what he called the Spectre.[24] The horoscope of William Blake is such that it places considerable influence precisely upon that part of the skies called Bestia.[25] No good astrologer would be surprised to find that the issues with which Blake dealt in his poetry are revealed within his chart. It could not be otherwise, for, if the inner is always a reflection of the outer, then the birth, which occurs always at the centre of the cosmos, must reflect the great circle of the zodiac on the periphery.[26] This is true not only of men of genius, such as Blake, but even of those lives which may appear, to the uninitiated, to be vacuous or without obvious creative import. That these human issues of personal destiny should be reflected in the ancient patterns of the stars is not at all surprising, for if we are not periodically reborn from the stars, then whence do we come?

Blake was a Rosicrucian initiate, deeply involved in the study of the greatest of all Rosicrucian writers, the German mystic and shoemaker, Jakob Boehme, who had a considerable knowledge of astrology.[27] Blake had also studied astrology – sufficiently to be able to converse intelligently with that unconventional and influential English artist-astrologer, John Varley.[28] All this suggests that it is very unlikely that Blake was unaware of the influence of the Beast in his own chart and life. Indeed, in one poem he comes very close to identifying the outer manifestation of the dual creature by name.

> My Spectre around me night and day
> Like a wild beast guards my way:
> My Emanations from within
> Weeps incessantly for my sin.[29]

The implications of this dual Spectre and Emanation became more clear to us when we examined the astrological tradition concerning the origin of its celestial counterpart, the Bestia of the heavens. According to star-lore legends, the bloodthirsty King Lycaon of Arcadia once sacrificed a child on an altar; because he had not successfully undergone fission, he still enacted externally within him his own unredeemed darkness. On another occasion, he tried to induce the god Zeus to eat human flesh. The first deed resulted in his being turned into the Bestia at his death, while the second deed resulted in the Deluge, which almost brought to an end the race of men. We see, then, that the part of the skies occupied by *Bestia* has an influence which is linked with murder by a cosmic villain. We see also in this tale the beginnings of that great truth which Blake recognized – that the Beast is a dual creature; the deed of Lycaon brought death to an individual, and threatened even to overwhelm the entire world.[30]

Of course, it is one thing to write dispassionately about the monster within, hiding behind the extraordinary poetic vision of Blake. It is a very different thing to describe in poetic literature the pain attendant upon the stirring of such a creature in a private life, when the monster appears on the outside, in the outer form of the Spectre. Escaped from the labyrinth brain, it advances like the Leviathan seen by William Blake in a vision, 'with all the fury of a Spiritual existence'.[31] When such a monster appears, the events which follow are often dramatic, and the very stuff of personal tragedy.

In some ways, William Blake represents the human spirit which saw through the temptations of the materialism that developed in England (and later in Europe) as a consequence of the Industrial Revolution. While the majority of men were led down into a more intimate relationship with matter (which the esotericists have called *maya*), William Blake remained as a sentinel to the primacy of Spirit, reminding those around him of the visionary Higher World, with which he was so intimate.

If we look into the history of England prior to the emergence of the Romantic Movement, we see two important leaders of that movement which took Mankind into the materialism which Blake found so repugnant. These were the politican and essay-writer, Francis Bacon, and the chemist, Robert Boyle. It was Bacon who laid the foundations for what was to develop in Western civilization as materialism. His disciple, Boyle, strove to introduce in the stream of science an approach to nature which was essentially experimental and inductive. He recognized that part of this process would involve the questioning, and even the ridiculing, of early alchemical ideas.

We owe the most intelligent survey of the previous life of Bacon to the Spiritual researches of Rudolf Steiner. In a series of remarkable lectures, delivered in 1924, the year before he died, Steiner revealed that Francis Bacon had lived in a previous embodiment in ninth-century Baghdad.[32] The wisdom Bacon imbibed in this intellectually brilliant Islamic centre (where alchemy and astrology were studied with a precision and depth rarely seen in the world) was transmitted into a later incarnation, in 16th-century England. Steiner indicates that in the Baghdad incarnation, Bacon was none other than the remarkable Haroun al Raschid, the very pivot of Islamic brilliance at that time.

Haroun's important position in regard to the sciences, arts and literature of the time enabled him to gain an almost encyclopaedic grasp of contemporary learning. The learning of that time – especially that connected with alchemy – was already beginning to free itself from the shackles of pure speculation. It was, indeed, becoming purposive – experiments with Nature were being conducted to see what secrets and powers Nature would reveal. In this intellectual urge, to seek in Nature certain practical utilities (which is now the guiding power behind modern scientific research), Steiner traces the beginnings of what was later called materialism.

Robert Boyle, Bacon's heir, was one of the founder members of the Royal Society, the oldest scientific society in Britain, which was instituted in 1660. In fact, Boyle also belonged to that small group of people who had met together regularly over a period of about 15 years prior to 1660, and whose meetings led to the formal foundation. Boyle, like the 17th-century reformer and Rosicrucian, Comenius,[33] had referred to this earlier group as an 'Invisible College'. This phrase indicates that the roots of the Society lay in the Rosicrucian endeavours of the first half of that century.

Robert Boyle is of great importance to our study of the development of materialism in the West. It has become our conviction that this was mainly because he was the individual who – working from impulses initiated in a previous incarnation – put the experimental method proposed by Francis Bacon into practice, with such profound conviction. In exoteric history, Robert Boyle is recognized as a polymath, whose arcane leanings led him to study Hebrew, Greek, Chaldean and Syriac. He is rightly honoured with modernizing the word 'chemistry', and divesting it of its *Paracelsian* (which is to say, esoteric) associations.

Our own particular interest lay in Boyle's emotional attitude to alchemy. Boyle could see that alchemy was concerned with Spiritual matters – that it was the arcane science of the soul. In that respect, alchemy obscured the science of the investigation of matter which he favoured – what was later called 'mechanical philosophy',[34] to distinguish it from Spiritual philosophy. Boyle firmly believed that the new experimental science could rest upon sound principles only if it concerned itself with things which could be measured, perceived and weighed. In this last belief, we can trace the whole story of modern science, up to its most moribund period.

There was a great deal in Boyle's thinking which supported the alchemical approach to nature.[35] For example, it is certain that he did not believe (as so many modern scientists and historians of alchemy seem to believe) that the arcane Three Principles were material things. He knew that Salt represented the principle of Thinking, that Sulphur represented the principle of Will, and that Mercury was the reconciler of these opposites. Yet, as we read the tortuous writings of Boyle, it becomes evident that he did misrepresent the intentions behind alchemy, and did this knowingly. Some of Boyle's writings are not all that different from those of contemporary occultists, herbalists and quacks. Even so, in his enthusiasm for a materialist explanation for things, Boyle often overlooked the Spiritual implications of his work. We may see this, for example, in his experiments with air. Boyle's proposition that 'Sound . . . consists in an undulating motion of the air' is on the edge of the modern scientific approach to nature, yet it misses the very element which intrigued the more perceptive alchemists – namely, that sound is not, *per se*, an undulating motion in the air, but a psycho-Spiritual experience in the soul of man.

Boyle's attitude to alchemy, and to the Spiritual realm, is evident even in the terms he used, such as 'effluvia', 'chemical affinity' and 'Pestilential steams'. For all these were beginning to gain acceptance in his day, they really seem to be nothing more than new terms to disguise the old theory of 'sympathies'.[35] This new vocabulary, which rejected the ancient structures that had vitalized alchemical researches, was designed to lead to a new type of science. Boyle's friend, the author Daniel Sennert, wrote a report on how the venom of certain spiders was so powerful that it could pass (by the process of 'effluvia') through the leather soles of those who stepped upon them. In turn, Boyle claimed that wounded animals could so impregnate the air with invisible 'effluvia' that dogs pursuing them would be poisoned.[36] Of course, such things had been observed and explained in the early occult amuletic literature, where the theory of sympathies was deeply entrenched: what was new in Sennert and Boyle's accounts were the vocabularies.

Aware that new vocabularies were vital if a new materialistic science was to develop, Boyle used new terminologies wherever possible. Yet, in spite of the depth of his Bacon-derived scientific outlook, he could not throw off entirely the old Spiritual outlook. Indeed, in his books, Boyle offered 'cures' which are in no way different from the sympathetic magic of the earlier writers. For example, he claimed that a dog bitten by a mad dog could be cured with star-plantain – but the curative virtue he described in this recipe seems to be derived from the numerology (or numerological progression) in which the herb is dispensed.[37] Whatever the value of the specific, its curative power lay in occult virtues.

The invisible sympathies (or virtues) tied in union the Great Chain of Being which stretched from God to man and was itself a Spiritual and invisible chain.[38] When the Spiritual element was removed, the chain was broken. The world left dangling without the support of spirit could no longer be visualized as a unison, but as an aggregate of entities which, while they might sometimes exhibit chemical affinities, were not united in a Spiritual purpose. This direction of thinking, which we now see spread around in the outer world, is what we call 'materialism'.

It is quite clear that the work of many of the contemporaries of Boyle led to the final bifurcation between 'alchemy' and 'chemistry'. Within a surprisingly few years, chemistry became a search into matter itself, rather than a search for any secret of Spiritual transmutation, which had been one purpose behind earlier forms of alchemy. The word *chemist*, or *chymist*, was for a while used contemptuously, as the equivalent of alchemist, until Boyle published, in 1661, his influential *The Sceptical Chymist*.

All these streams – which represent a flight from Spirit – seemed to come together in the life and work of Boyle, which is why we developed such an interest in him. However, our researches into Boyle, on an arcane level, were hampered in a most curious way.

There are certain people whose lifetimes present inexplicable difficulties to the occultist who sets out to seek their previous incarnations. Sometimes, only vague indications can be gained as to the time and place in which a previous lifetime took place. The technical difficulty is mentioned in this context only because it applied to our study of Boyle. We could intuit that the attitudes of Robert Boyle, like those of his great mentor, Francis Bacon, could be traced back to ninth-century Baghdad. However, while Bacon's previous life, as the remarkable Haroun al Raschid, has been well documented, we could not identify the individuality who eventually became Robert Boyle.

We had struggled for some time with the question of Boyle's identity in his previous lifetime under the Baghdad Caliphate. It was evident to us that he must have been associated with, if not directly connected with, the Baghdad court which Haroun al Raschid controlled. However, we could not, through our own efforts, contact this past stream of history. Boyle's previous lifetime remained inaccessible to us.

Fortunately, we had heard of a remarkable Italian who had developed his clairvoyant abilities to a very high degree. After discussing the issue with our Teacher, we decided to approach this individual – who at that time lived near the old university in Bergamo – to see if he could help.

This man, whom we shall call Muscos,[39] began by making some unsolicited remarks about our own Spiritual bodies. He described for us their colours, and indicated how they were changing. In particular he was interested in a dark reddish band around the stomach area.

'You are still struggling with . . .'

'A moral issue . . .' we put in quickly. The contrast between the effort we had put into this moral issue, and the poor results which we had obtained, was already a source of embarrassment to ourselves.[40]

'Just so. But such colours are mere coloratura.[41] Soon they will be like *pentimenti*, brushed over and eradicated by the superior artist. Your painting is moving towards a new style. Soon, you will be able to say of this thing, "it has vanished for ever".' He had used the Italian, *egli spari*, which really means 'vanished from sight' – a curious phrase for something which was quite invisible for ordinary men. It was as though he was anxious to reveal the strangeness of his own position.

We had been deeply impressed by his vision. It was a clear vision, yet one he could translate with facility into ordinary words. He was a man of outstanding ability, and I asked him, 'Why do you not undertake to be a Teacher yourself?'

'I think that I can be of more service in the present times by working on a lower level.' He was being matter-of-fact, rather than modest.

We raised our eyebrows. This was certainly no low level on which we found ourselves at the moment.

'The present situation is different. You have come to me for information – for an answer to your questions. That is of deep interest to me, yet it is a rare thing. The majority of people do not come to me because they recognize a Master, but because they have problems. Life problems.'

'A bulldozer to crack a nut?' we asked. The Italian *agripista* is somehow more fitting than the English suggests.

Muscos chuckled at the metaphor. 'You are too kind. But yes, you are right – I suppose that I am something of an *agripista* running over nuts.'

Even before calling on Muscos, we had suspected that there would be no need to spell out the purpose of our visit: he would be able to see precisely why we had called upon him.

He stared at me for some while, yet his vision was inward, and it was as though the bright lights of his eyes were dimmed. He was incredibly still, unbreathing like the statue of a Buddha. After a moment or two, he spoke.

'Now that I put my attention on your question, I can understand why you do not find it easy to establish a precise connection between Boyle and the Baghdad court. It is possible that you are looking at the wrong area, and perhaps even slightly towards the wrong time.[42] As I look myself, the name of the great Alkindi seems to crop up.' He laughed, almost self-deprecatingly, and we observed that his eyes were once again outward-seeing. 'Fortunately, I do not have to look into the *Stream* for everything. The Milk and the Sacred Waters do not meet, save in this silver river.'

He was speaking our own language. We knew exactly what he meant. His almost casual use of the word 'Stream' sent shivers up my spine. The *Virgin Sea* was a term no longer used in esotericism, but one which we had encountered often enough in our studies of Paracelsus.[43] The idea of this nourishing fount of virginal wisdom was expressed in some of the most curious alchemical images of the 17th century (see figure on page 113). The white milk of the Virgin, the *lac virginis*, was the white light of the stars, transmuted into wisdom as it flows down to the Earth plane. Did Muscos see so clearly into our soul that he could perceive even this unimportant footnote of interest? Or was there a living connection tying Muscos to that most errant Fool of all Fools, Paracelsus? Were we indeed on the same Path, with the man before me so advanced that I could not recognize a brother?

'As it is,' Muscos continued, 'I happen to remember that Alkindi, immersed as he was in Arabic astrological and magical lore, held one view which was not at all popular in Baghdad in the ninth century.'

'That relating to alchemy?'

'Ah, you know!' Muscos laughed, and then added, 'Of course you know!' He smiled acknowledgement of his error, before continuing. 'Alkindi argued that the art of alchemy was deceptive. He insisted that transmutation was not possible. A strange belief at that time! It meant that Alkindi was rejecting the transforming power of the Quintessence.'

We nodded. It had been something we had never really understood.

Muscos spoke again, yet there was still humour in his voice. 'Now, there, with your Alkindi, we see another bulldozer at work – a threat to those around. He was challenging prejudices – never a popular occupation, in any place or time. Can you remember the title of his book on alchemy?'

'*The Deceits of the Alchemists*?' we suggested.

'Quite. Cannot you see your Mr Boyle here?'

We considered his words, but could make no leap from the Caliphate to 17th-century England.

'Don't you *see*,' he insisted, 'Boyle wrote a book called *The Sceptical Chymist*? It is too close to pass by unnoticed in a chain of lifetimes!'

Immediately, everything fell into place. We instantly perceived other, less obvious, connections between the two men. 'So you suggest that Alkindi's view of alchemy, though expressed in very different terms, resurfaced in the writings of Boyle?' We were restating the obvious, for already we had been enlightened by this remarkable man. Everything had been made clear to the consciousness soul, reflected from the surface of that eternal River.

'It seems so, doesn't it?'

It had been a long time since we had glanced at Alkindi's work, yet we recalled that it did suggest certain themes in Boyle's seminal work. The idea that alchemy was an invalid art was one of the conclusions to which Boyle came, and was one of the driving forces in his early experimental work.

'The comparison makes sense,' Muscos said. 'Boyle's criticism – like that of Alkindi – was rooted in what can only be called a one-sided view of the Art. In his embodiment as both Arab and Englishman, he never appears to have taken into account the Spiritual side of alchemy. His was a sort of controlled conspiracy of silence.'

Muscos was right. Clearly, it had been the destiny of Boyle to ignore, or push aside, the Spiritual side of alchemy. He needed to do this if he was to redraw its theories of matter, in order to lead the world towards materialism. The truth is that had not Bacon in the 16th century, and such disciples as Boyle in the next century, led science towards materialism, then the Industrial Revolution would never have developed in England when it did.

'If' – and with that word, Muscos slid his eyes upwards to meet mine in that gesture beloved by many Teachers – 'the subject interests you, then you might like to glance at the history of Ragley Hall in Warwickshire, which under the guidance of Lady Conway was the most important esoteric centre in England; and that other unsung genius of the times, van Helmont.'[44]

In such a way do the truly wise throw out suggestions which lead to years of research. At that time, however, we had no sense of how great an undertaking he was proposing when he mentioned the Rosicrucian, van Helmont, who was to become the next obsession to take our mind, once the problem of Boyle had been set aside.

As we left Muscos, we were in a state of elation. We found ourselves walking in the intense sunlight of the great square of the Piazza Vecchia, of the *alta citta*, staring down at the combinations of sphinxes, lions and camel-headed serpents that protected the water fountains. These were not inappropriate symbols in view of our previous conversation with Muscos. They were symbols of inner Man, spread out around the water which wells up from the Earth – the water of earth wisdom. The sphinxes symbolized human thinking, the lions symbolized human feeling, and the camel-headed serpents, with their thick bodies woven around the stone pillars, were the Will in Man. These stone figures were carved at a time when the alchemical Three Principles were still alive in the minds of most men and women. The statuary of the fountains would have held few mysteries for most people in the 17th century.[45]

It was midday, and the sun was very intense. We sought the protective shadows of the undercroft of the Palazzo del Podesta, where the huge zodiacal calendarium lay in the shadows, the beautifully incised sigils for the zodiacal signs at our feet.[46] Those wise men who had designed the *alta citta* of Bergamo had implanted a fountain which symbolized wisdom from the earth, and an horlogium which symbolized wisdom from the stars. Was this why the marble calibration-scale was white, like milk?

Our mind was filled with excitement. Muscos' remarkable insights had confirmed some of our own suspicions about the development of science in England. Boyle's attitude to the arcane had been a curious one, and, for all that he had been claimed as a Rosicrucian, his esoteric adherences had not been at all clear. There could be no doubt that Boyle had close contact with many individuals who were involved in a powerful esoteric school, which was linked with the Rosicrucian impulse.

There was no seating in the undercroft, so we decided to find a chair in the Capella Colleoni, the inner peace of which so contrasted with its coruscation of confusing marble forms.[47] The chapel was empty, and we sat on a wicker-based chair by the altar steps, to think. The three statues of Bartolomeo Manni looked down upon us, from between the two twisted columns which represented the Temple of Solomon.[48] What was the relationship between these twisted Masonic columns of *Jachin* and *Boaz* and the vertically twisting serpents guarding the fountain in the old square outside? Did they indeed represent the mystery of the bisexuality of the Ineffable, of God, as some scholars believed?[49] Or were they relics of the time when gods always went in pairs – Isis and Osiris, Astoreth and Baal, and so on?[50] The twisting serpents were certainly bisexual in themselves, and could not be representative of male and female. The human Will – the yellow Sulphur of the alchemists – unlike human thinking or feeling, was as yet bisexual, or androgyne.[51]

We turned our attention away from these outer symbols, and cast our mind over the conversation with Muscos. Our thinking was clearer, now. What we had learned about Boyle, and his previous lifetime, clarified our understanding of that descent into darkness which we call the Industrial Revolution. Like all historically important movements, it had been planned centuries before it occurred, and was an outcome of the activity of those Schools that oversee the development of historical periods. Now, the whole issue of materialism was clear to us: it was one involving the separation of two impulses – one towards darkness, the other towards light. The darker materialism was a prelude to a particular view – a scientific view – of Nature as bereft of Spirit. The light side of this (that is, the light which sparked from this fission) developed the Rosicrucian impulse, and its related Romantic Movement, which viewed Nature in terms of Spirit.

One Wednesday – it was 15 February 1961 – as the group was breaking up after a meeting in Bellegarde, our Master motioned for us to remain behind, indicating that he wanted to talk with us alone. We remember the date precisely because it was on this day that Melita first joined the circle. Normally, we would have been delighted by being marked out for such a distinction as a private interview with our Master. However, on this occasion, we felt almost cheated, for our first sight of Melita had been something akin to a thunderclap in our soul.

Among the great initiate wisdom which has proceded from ancient China is the literature attached to the 'Book of Change', the *I Ching*. In modern times, this book has been demoted to a rather low level, mainly to satisfy egocentric divinatory practices, yet it is still one of the most remarkable initiation systems in the world. A correct use of the triagrams and hexagrams of the *I Ching* will allow a person to examine all the mayic phenomena of the ever-changing world.

The book studies the phenomena of the created world, and attempts to trace in it the interactions of archetypes. Some scholars claim that there are eight archetypes in operation, but others argue that there are 64. Yet others, studying the permutations to which the 64 figures of the book may be subjected, claim that there are a myriad archetypes.

Among the basic 64 archetypal figures, or hexagrams, is one which deals with *Inner Truth*.[52] The Chinese character which denotes truth is an archaic picture of a bird resting its protective claws on the head of a newly hatched young. The ancient sages pictured truth as a delicate thing, egg-born, and in perpetual need of protection. On one level, the hexagram deals, stage by stage, with the consequences of inner truth and sincerity, as it pertains to the familiar world. On a deeper level the hexagram deals with the consequences of love, for love itself is nothing more than the recognition in another person of the truth within his or her soul.

In the cosmic conditions set out in the hexagram, it is made quite clear that under certain circumstances love can lead to distress of soul. The Chinese text tells how a man (though it could just as well be a woman) who has not fully grasped the cosmic nature of love may elect to make of the soul he has perceived a love-object. Thus is love and possession confused. When such a deed is done – when the lover seeks to bind to himself a love – then is his soul plunged into a state of unbalance. 'Now he beats upon the drum: now he no longer beats the drum. Now he laughs, now he cries,' says the Chinese text. On seeing and binding to himself his beloved – his anima – such a man will change immediately, for he will no longer be able to determine who is the lover and whom the beloved, who the pursuer and whom pursued. This, the text of the *I Ching* suggests, is a condition of human love, and it depends upon the souls of those involved as to whether they regard love as the greatest of all joys, or as an affliction.

The text of this hexagram came to mind, almost like a steadying star in the maelstrom of our soul, as we looked upon Melita. She was astoundingly beautiful, and seemed to be filled with an inner light so strong that it was almost visible. From that first moment, we wanted to talk with her, to greet her like some long lost friend. Behind this innocent joy, there was also a powerful sexual attraction. As we sat on that wooden chair, listening to the questions and answers, we could almost feel the presence of Melita radiating an effulgence from behind us. We were experiencing, for the first time in our life, something of the conflict between sulphur and salt which lies in the being of all men and women (see page 140).

After our Master had gestured towards us, Melita left with all the others. We had no opportunity to introduce ourselves. For the remaining days until the next meeting, we found ourselves living almost in a daze of unaccountable dream-like yearnings to be near her.

When the room was empty, and we had prepared tea, our Master turned to a question we had raised earlier. It touched upon the word which he had identified as being our own – the name *Idiot*.

He observed, 'You do not have to look far in the esoteric literature to see how often the arcanists use the word *idiot* to cover hidden issues. What may be understood by those not involved in esotericism to be foolish is often a cover for higher wisdom.[53] This is one reason why Sebastian Brandt's book, *Ship of Fools,* was so popular in the late 15th century – and for years afterwards – because it hid many deeper truths about the idiotic in man.'[54]

The Fool as a blind–man, stepping from the grave, and feeling his way with the aid of two sticks. From the 1493 edition of S. Brandt The Ship of Fools.

'I thought that *Ship of Fools* was satirical?'

'Yes, but satirical of what? It was satirical of society – not of foolishness. In fact, Brandt's book was merely the flowering of a considerable tradition. He was influenced by Nigel Wireker's *Mirror of Fools,* which had been widely circulated in manuscript in the 12th century. Brandt paid more attention to the sensuality and riot inherent in the nature of the Fool: almost certainly he was influenced in this by the established riot of the *Feast of Fools.* All these things must be seen in context – the idea of the rebellious fool in Brandt, and in related language, mirrors a reaction against the Church. By the time Brandt produced his book at the end of the 15th century, there was already tremendous support for the idea of the Reformation, and for a breakaway from the Church. This literature can only be understood in its esoteric nature in terms of the growth of the human Ego, which would, of necessity, result in a breakaway from ecclesiastical conventions. The youthful Ego is foolish. But the question is, What is foolishness, and what is it to be wise? The flower may be wise in matters of light, but the root is wise in matters of the Earth. Do you see my drift?'

'The Fool is rooted in the dark earth?'

'Perhaps it is merely an accident that the land of Egypt was once called the "Black Earth"?'

We nodded. It was clear that the issue of the Fool in esotericism was more complex than we had suspected. There was no doubt that the image of the Fool in the Tarot series was portraying a wise Fool. Was this true also of such literature as the *Ship of Fools*?

'Brandt's account of the world of Fools was very little to do with a ship at all – even the image of the ship seems to have been something of an afterthought. There is no accident in this, for in such a context the ship was a symbol of the Church (remember the double meaning of the word *nave*?). In fact Brandt was writing of the world of *Narragonia*: the Strasbourg edition of his book, pirated in 1494, is actually entitled *The New Ship of Narragonia*.[55] The word is the German equivalent of 'Land of Fools'. Here we touch on a very well-established mediaeval tradition, for the Land of Fools had been called *Shluraffenland* in Germany . . .'

'The *Cockayne* of English poetry?' Things were falling into place.

'Exactly, Mark. What was Cockayne?'

'A fairytale land, where one led an idle and luxurious life. Houses were made of barley-sugar, the streets paved with exquisite pastries . . .'

'Exactly so. The streets were paved with the *kuchen*, or cakes, which gave the word *Cockayne*.' The name is as good an equivalent of the Astral Plane as you are likely to find in ordinary literature. In the fairy stories you can read of children, lost in a wood, who come across strange houses made of cookies: such children are being faced with the Astral, where they will be in danger, simply because they do not know enough to deal with that realm. The witch in such stories is a guardian of the Threshold.'

'So the Fool follows the way which leads to the Astral?'

'To the *Spiritual*,' he corrected us. 'Think carefully about the French version of the Way of the Fool: it is *La Voie du Mat*. Think carefully, and tell me where you have heard such words before.'

'*Mat* is in *maya*, and in *matter*?'

'That will do for the moment – though there are other connections far more pregnant. Why *maya*, and why *matter*? Because the Great *Mater*, the Great Mother, brings material form into the world. It is no accident that these words with such different meanings have a communal origin, in the Sanskrit *ma*. The Fool, the *Mat*, is the one who will *mate* with the *mater* to produce *matter* . . .'

He took the teacup between both hands, and sipped. He seemed to be thinking very deeply about something. After a while, he returned to the same theme.

'The Fool is the one who looks through this material illusion – the *mat* sees through *mat*ter, so to speak. This makes him one who is prepared to suffer. Only a Fool would be prepared to suffer. I do not have in mind merely that the Fool is prepared – or at least, should be prepared – to jump into the unknown, into the great void, perhaps even into the mouth of a waiting crocodile.' He was thinking of a particular Tarot design of the Fool card. 'No, he is also prepared to suffer patiently. He is shown carrying a heavy weight upon his straight stick. Do you see what I mean? A *straight stick*. What does that mean? Why should a Fool carry a weight on the end of a straight stick? And what is in that heavy bag, tied to the stick?' He held up his hand, grinning. 'Do not try to answer. I am not interested in hearing you display book learning. Think about it. What is in *your* heavy bag, Mark? If you think about that stick and its bag, you will soon see that the Way of the Fool does not extend very far without pain, for the Fool is one who has elected to struggle with matter. A whole truth is built into that curious image of the Fool. Consider once again that strange foolscap. We have talked about it together before, but now we should talk about it again, for things will soon change for you.'

We nodded, though, of course, we did not really know what he meant. What changes were ahead?

'The cap is three-pronged. In truth, the threefold cap is the three-pronged *shin* of the Hebrew alphabet.' He drew the letter in the air: **ש** 'You know the letter *shin*?'

We nodded.

'The early Hebraic scholars used what they called the "three flames" of *shin* to represent the highermost trinity in the Sephirothic Tree. This meant that the triple *shin* sat on top of the tree, just as the human head sits on top of the spine.[57] Any esotericist who wished to portray the true wanderer on the Path would be compelled to fit the man with a triple crown. This could be the triple crown of the Pope, set with jewels, as symbol of the Roman imperium which had taken on the vestments symbolic of initiation. On the other hand, it could be the triple cap of the Fool, set with finial bells that would tinkle to remind him of the everpresent unheard music of the spheres. In this context, the triad of *shin* might be called the Atman, Buddhi and Manas, but whatever names you ascribe them, it is clear that the Fool must wear that triple cap with care.

'*Shin* means "spirit", and its number is 300. Eliphas Levi, that stupid defrocked priest who drew a link between the Fool card and *aleph*, revealed his ignorance and misled a whole generation, for the number of aleph is one.[57] The Fool of esotericism recognizes the value of the Spiritual, and will sacrifice anything to obtain ingress to its upper realms, guarded so well by the three flames of *shin*. This is the reason why he elects to wear the cap. It is a sign that he is prepared to suffer the three flames, which echo the three wounds of Christ.

'In truth, this *shin* is symbol of a way of *pathein*, the path of suffering. You see, then, young Mark – pain is also a Way. It is sometimes called the Triple Way. The dog Cerberus was three-headed, and guarded the gates to the flames of Hell. And, while we touch on classical mythology . . . I must ask, do you think that Odysseus would have started such a voyage without thought that he and his companions would be hurt?'

He slid an atout from a pack of cards, and passed it to us. It was an image of the Fool of the Tarot pack. At the base was the word *le Fou*, the old French for Fool. Alongside it was the Hebrew *shin*.

'Besides meaning "fool", *mat* means mast. Those who could not stand the song of the siren – who knew that it would bring only suffering and death – were tied to the mast, that they could hear the song without losing their minds. The Fool, like Odysseus, is cunning and listens to that song, for he is bound tightly to his own mast.[58] There is one meaning to the straight stick you carry over your shoulder.

'Look at this card carefully. It was designed by a late 19th-century symbolist, Oswald Wirth. Later, the same card was reworked to show the Fool walking towards a precipice (plate 20). In some popular cards – in those designed by occultists with a penchant for the dramatization of esoteric matters – the precipice is turned into a lake, and in the waters is a crocodile – the *makara* of the esoteric tradition – its open jaws yawning up towards the Fool.[59] This is why in some esoteric systems the Way of the Fool is also called the Way of Suffering. The jester of the French courts was the one who gested. The *gest* was a deed well done: long before it became an epic well sung, it lay in gestation. The *gest*, which was a deed of prowess, and the idle-seeming chatter of the jester are etymologically linked.'[60]

He slipped the card back among the others.

'Anyone who elects to speed up evolution – to increase the rate of natural development – may save lifetimes, but in so doing they must inevitably concentrate the potential for pain. Suffering is also a way of learning, as you should know from the stories of the martyrs and the saints. This is why you should read the story of Odysseus with respect. He knew of the dangers he would face, and he knew of the suffering which would come to him and his companions. If you should have any doubts that this ancient Greek text was esoteric, then recall that those on the Odyssey were called the *Nostoi*. This word, in a misunderstood context, has become an integral secret term of the alchemists.'[61]

He nodded to show that the interview was at an end, and as he did so, dealt a card from the pack. It was the Pope card, with its triple crown. 'Pay attention to these things: the upper *shin* can mean very different things: it may be a symbol of power, or a sign of wisdom, depending upon how it is used.'

We were apprehensive when we left. Was the Master saying that the time had come for him to fling at us a taste of suffering? Would we be prepared for such a testing? We had seen our Master do this with others. An appropriate word, and a man or a woman could be reduced to a wreck. Afterwards, those destroyed in this way could elect to leave the group, or remain, but either way, these people would be fundamentally changed. While the destroying was an art which could be practised without danger by an initiate of the highest level, the rebuilding and remoulding seemed to demand even more understanding and knowledge.

However, as the days slipped by, our Master did not dispense towards us any suffering, and the question which began to burn in our soul was 'Why not us?' We would gather together our faults – our unredeemed features – and see how the worst of these was impossible to control. The Master had christened all our central sins – all the sins of members of the circle – as unredeemed features.[62] It is possible, he had said, to deal with most defects within the inner being: with attention, discipline and meditation, most things could be healed. Yet there remained always the core – that inner failing or sin which was beyond personal redemption, and required for its healing a grace.

We found in practice the terrible confirmation of this truth we had learned in theory, from our reading, and from our Master. We found that no amount of work, no amount of prayer, no supplications, could change this central sin. It coloured everything we did, it accompanied us, everywhere we went, like the shadow being it was. The more we tried to correct it, the more it asserted its supremacy. The more we studied it, the more it seemed to be empowered by our attention. It took on a life of its own, becoming like a monster out of control. It danced in front of us, in mockery of our aspirations, and we knew that we were catching glimpses of that monstrous 'Dweller on the Threshold'. It was perhaps no accident that the inventor of this term belonged to the identical literary tradition as the one who invented our modern Prometheus, Frankenstein.[63]

152

We recognized that there was only one cure for this sin: it had to be burned away in the open. Yet, our Master still elected not to make our sin public. It seemed that he did not wish to cauterize us, yet.

In retrospect, it is easy to see innocent we were, and how learned was our Master. We did not see that such a cauterizing could be self-administered, and, as he had intimated, life itself is as much a Teacher as any Master. We did not see that some sin is so deep-set that only the Self has sufficient wisdom to draw its unsuspecting victim to the cauterizing flames.

Some weeks would pass before we saw what our Master foresaw. During that time, we continued our research into the reincarnations of those who brought about the Industrial Revolution in England – thus leading Mankind into its deepest relationship with matter.

Early in 1961, our Teacher had moved his school from rue de Rochechouart. He had gone to live near Bellegarde, to the north of the Loire Valley, and the students in our group would go down to see him at least twice a week. As it happened, Melita already lived in Orléans, and we began to stay overnight in her flat. It was never easy to get to Bellegarde, and we guessed that the move was partly prompted by our Master's wish to make things more difficult for us.

From time to time, others who attended the meetings would come back to Melita's flat, to talk, or even read together books suggested by our Master. On some rare occasions, those we called 'the Higher-Astrals' would drop in. These were the more advanced pupils who studied under our Master, and who had been with him for a much longer time. Among these was a somewhat flamboyant Italian named Rafaelo Cansale.

Rafaelo was a much older man – perhaps 25 years older than us – who seemed not only very wealthy, but something of an aristocrat. He was always impeccably dressed, and he intimated that this was necessary because of his standing in life. He told us that he worked for an established Parisian firm of public relation consultants, and certainly had what appeared to be an inexhaustible expense account. The huge Jaguar he parked outside the road in the poorer distict of Orléans always looked out of place, yet he never showed the slightest sign of snobbishness. Sometimes, when the spirit took him, he would pile whomsoever was in the flat into his car, and drive into the centre of Orléans, where we would eat at his expense in gourmet restaurants. It seemed strange that a person on an initiate Path should be so conversant with wines, and prepared to drink so freely, because our Master had advised us not to take alcohol.

Our friendship with Rafaelo flowered. We felt proud that someone so advanced in the ways of esoteric development was prepared to spend so much time with us. He was immensely knowledgeable concerning esoteric matters, and the conversations which flowed around our meetings were of the highest order.

Meanwhile, the unexpected happened, as it always does. We fell in love with Melita. We took every opportunity to see her, and to be near to her, even to the point of undertaking extra duties if this meant there was a chance of our meeting with her. We had become entranced by her. Those who have been in love will understand this word, entranced, while those who have not been so fortunate will not understand it, for love is an experience beyond description.

How completely, and with what extraordinary wisdom, we choose our united pathway. When it comes to destiny, we are as surefooted as goats. We forget the myths, which are stars to guide those stranded on the Earth plane. Odysseus had no imperative to land upon the shores of Aeaea, no need to ask directions of Circe, other than the imperative of destiny.[64] Just so, when we reach out to pull towards us our archetype of love.

Yet, when two souls meet, with their horoscopes so arranged in Earthly time and cosmic place that the Moon of the woman is on the same degree as the Sun of the man, then there is no alternative but for them to draw together, and marry. To marry, as the cabbalistic lore insists, requires that man and woman look upon each other face to face, so that no other gaze can weave its eyebeams between the two. The whole cosmos conspires to bring two lovers together. Because of the grandeur of this conspiracy, if an end is to be made of love; if the two are to be dragged apart; if the archeteypes are to be wrenched from their places in Heaven – then, such a deed must be done by the gods. This is why the marriage ceremony warns the congregation that the Heaven-wrought union they have witnessed should not be pulled asunder by man.

We were married one Monday in 1961, when the Sun was on her own Scorpionic ascendant of 21 degrees. Melita, who could, in our estimation, have chosen any man, because of her beauty and grace, bound herself to us. We neither of us at that time knew that, on occasions, even the stars weep. Later – many years later – when friends talked with us about these things which had happened to people now old, they asked us if we had known what would happen. And, truthfully, we answered, Yes.

Look at these images of 35 years ago, stained in visual purple. There is Melita. She is walking across the Luxembourg Gardens with a young man, stepping on the lengthened shadows of tree branches. It is so early in spring that the branches of the trees are almost bare, and Melita is so well versed in arcane lore to know that bare or leaved, they are symbols of the Sephirothic Tree, each branch bearing ten branches, each branch of which bears a further ten branches, ad infinitum. She is dressed in Tom Sawyer clothes – tight trousers, ragged around the knees, a shirt wrapped tightly over her breasts, leaving her naked at the midriff. On her head, she wears a straw coolie hat, curving to a single point. She is so lovely that the two old gardeners stop their work, and lean on their sticks, to watch in admiration as she walks through their park. The young man alongide her looks a little too severe, but the girl is full of happiness.

'Listen,' she cried, as we crossed the Luxembourg Gardens. The early Sun was scattering long shadows of branches across the grass. 'Listen – the shadows snap as we tread on them.'

Circe herself could not have bewitched a seagoing man so completely. And yet here was a woman who was prepared to share our life of Spirit. She had come to our Teacher in search of meaning, and even the promise we found in each other was not sufficient to slake the inner hunger of our souls. We were the true *nostoi* on the sea's waves. We remained, and we worked, and we meditated, and we tried to reach the levels of initiation which beckoned.

Melita. Even forty years later, as we write about her, dictating these words to a friend, our voice quivers. We remember her beauty, her grace of form, and her independence of spirit. Now, because time has passed, and imaginations have been pushed aside, we can thank Melita for what she came to teach us. Long ago, we forgot the pain she brought.

Two months after we were married, in the first week of January of 1962, the Master decided, for reasons which were never revealed to us, to move once again – this time to Italy. He set up his teaching centre in an old villa below Castello di Belcaro, outside Siena, yet elected to live in a small flat in via Banchi di Sopra, in the city itself.[65] After a short delay, we both followed him, renting a small house which had once served a vineyard, on the slopes below the walled hill town of Montereggioni. Melita took a job as a translator for a travel firm in Siena, and we continued our research into esoteric thought, taking advantage of the excellent libraries in Florence. We earned our living as a translator, writing occasional journalistic pieces.

Rafaelo would come fortnightly to the meetings, rather than twice a week. His work in France did not permit him to give up his Parisian home. Indeed, by this time, he had made it clear to us that his family had no inkling of his esoteric work, and would neither understand nor appreciate an enforced move from their penthouse flat in Paris to Siena.

Now, instead of driving the long distance, Rafaelo would usually fly to Pisa, and hire a car at the airport. Sometimes, when we were able, we would pick him up, and drive him to Siena. For reasons which were never made clear, he would not stay overnight with us in our small farmhouse, but would book into rather expensive hotels in Siena. He joked that because Dante had placed Montereggione in his Hell, a man of his social standing could not attract calumny by spending time there.[66]

Rafaelo seems to have developed a particularly close connection with our Master, for he began to spend a considerable amount of time in Siena and Belcaro, seemingly doing business on his behalf. He did not always let us know when he would be coming, and on at least two occasions, while alone in the city, we saw him in the Piazza del Campo, and Via di Citta, during periods when we had been led to believe he was still in Paris. The first time, we hurried down the great fan of the square to greet him, and were surprised to sense that he was not really pleased that we had accosted him. There was something in his manner which suggested that he was on School business, of great import to our Master, and could not be delayed. On the second occasion, remembering this somewhat frosty reception, we decided to ignore him. We watched as he sauntered along the Piccolomini delle Papesse, looking for all the world like a *capo di capi*, even down to the white shoes. Perhaps, once again, he was involved in some enterprise for our Master, and was best left alone.

There had been signs during the week. Almost prophetic signs. On the Monday, a frog – or a toad – had fallen from the innermost chimney ledge behind the 16th-century fireplace, and had landed on top of the immense stove. We thought frogs did not make such sounds, yet we seemed to hear the scream as the creature shrivelled into the hot metal. The entire top of the oven was covered in soot, and the stench of the burned flesh was unimaginable. Later, as we scraped off the black mass from the metal, a plea from some initiation myth rang through our mind: 'No more those flames. My fingertips are molten lead, my eyes are liquid gold, my soul the black soot of that ancient one. No longer baste me in those flames. Even the higher perfecting is not worth such pains as these.'[67] We scraped away the charred mass with a kitchen knife, and dropped the remains into the furnace. We wanted all traces of the accident to be removed by the time Melita returned home from work.

Because of the smell of burning flesh – so strange in a vegetarian kitchen – we could no longer remain in the house, so, opening all the windows and doors, we moved our books to the patio; there we tried to read, but could no longer pay attention. The death of the frog seemed to work into our soul-life like a dark premonition, and our imagination played around with the deeper meanings in an event which had, with such undisguised symbolism, left a sacrificial black mass on an oven.

The following day, while backing the car into the drive, Melita ran over a cat. In the evening, when we returned, she told us through her tears of how its back was broken, and how its smashed ribs stuck through the fur, like the sprockets of a broken umbrella. Yet the horror was that the poor creature was not dead. Melita could not bear to see it in such pain, or hear its mewing. Somehow, she managed to lift a huge stone from the rockery which bordered the driveway, and grasping it above her knees, clutching it against the fronts of her thighs, she waddled over to the mewling cat and dropped the heavy stone upon it. Only then did the piteous howling stop.

Melita cried all night. Strangely, she refused to allow us to comfort her, and, as the darkness slowly gave rise to dawn, we began to sense that she was not crying only for the crushed cat.

We had planned to drive to Siena that morning, to research in a private library, the owner of which had invited us to stay overnight. Now, however, with Melita in such a state, we felt that we should not do this, and so we went into our own workroom to lie down on the *chaise-longue*, to have a short sleep.

Melita must have imagined that we had gone to Siena, for when we awoke, the house was empty. At least, there was no one in the lower rooms. Then we realized what must have happened. Melita would have been tired after that awful night, and she would have stayed in bed. We crept up the stairs, and peered into the room. Our guess had been right – she was still sleeping.

We rang her office, to say that she would not be going in that day, and were surprised to learn that she had already cancelled. We went downstairs to make breakfast. As we ran water into the kettle, we remembered the cat, still half-interred beneath the rockery stone, and went out to attend to its burial. Melita's Fiat was parked where she had left it before the accident, and our own vehicle was still half through the gates, its back jutting out into the road. By the wheels of her car was the rockery stone she had dropped on the cat. Rivulets of blood had run along the crevices between the paving slabs of the drive, and were now congealed. As we lifted away the stone and pushed the crushed body towards the shrubbery our stomach heaved. We buried the body without ceremony in the soft earth.

We could not move Melita's car, for we could not find the keys. Since we could not bring our own car into the driveway, we drove it into a side-street, further along the road, where it would be safe. By means of such simple deeds Lachesis of the three Fates weaves destinies for the shears of Atropos.[68]

After breakfast, we returned to the workroom, and began to write. It rarely happened that we fell asleep as we worked, but, perhaps because the night had been too much for us, we found ourself beginning to doze. We took our book over to the *chaise-longue*, so that we could rest as we read, yet within a few minutes we were fast asleep.

We awoke to a feeling of intense cold. The central heating was not programmed to give warmth during the daytime, yet, even so, the room was unnaturally cold. We had the impression that it must be snowing outside. We glanced at our watch. It was three o'clock in the afternoon. Our legs were stiff with the ice cold, yet it was sunny outside in the late September day.

We went into the kitchen. Melita must have been up, for on the table was bread and cheese. There was also a half-filled wine glass. A wine glass – when Melita never drank wine? We looked out of the window. Melita had moved her Fiat. It was now parked in its usual position alongside the wall. We walked on to the patio, and saw that Rafaelo's hired Mercedes was in the driveway.

Almost certainly, they would be in the garden, by the lily pool, where we usually sat when he called upon us. We made a coffee, and strolled round to the garden to greet them. The seats by the shrubbery were empty.

They were not in the living room. Perhaps they had walked into the village to buy food for the night's meal? At that moment, we heard a sound, just a little like the mewling of a cat. Then, suddenly, as though from nowhere, an image of the soot, the screaming frog and the tufts of red-stained fur merged into a single image in our mind, and we *knew*. We ran upstairs and threw open the bedroom door. There they both were, together on the bed – white bodies naked, as in the Fire Sermon.[69]

As we looked down upon Melita and Rafaelo, we were shrivelling on the red-hot stove. And there was no release from the heat, and no escape from those inner flames.

Incongruously, Rafaelo snatched at the sheet, and covered the front of his body. Then he leapt out of the bed, and through the far door, slamming it behind him as he fled. It took us a moment or two to open the door, but as soon as we did, we saw him running down the stairs. Towards the bottom, he tripped upon the bed sheet, and fell into the newel post, badly gashing his forehead.

We pursued him, leaping down the stairs as though in aerial flight, yet somehow he was quicker, driven by the terrible sisters. The key had been in the lock on the outside of the door, and he had sufficient presence of mind to turn it. To continue pursuit, we had to run back through the house to the kitchen door. Now we were able to follow a trail of blood over the marble floor of the patio, towards the drive.

Perhaps he had left his keys in the ignition, for we heard the explosion of his engine and the crash of gears as he screeched away. We pursued no further. We turned the heavy key in the door of the kitchen, and made sure that the hall door was also still locked. We sat with our elbows on the kitchen table, and tried to regain our breath. On the table was a jar of autumnal flowers, their petals dropped, and motionless.[70]

Later, we went back to the bedroom. Melita was no longer in bed, but we did not expect her to be. We looked out of the window, to make sure that her car had gone. We collected together Rafaelo's clothes, and threw them as so much dirty laundry into a bedsheet. We carried them down to the kitchen, and, using a Stanley knife, cut them into pieces sufficiently small to feed them through the grilled door of the furnace. The smell of the burning fabric hung around the kitchen for several hours, recalling the stench of the blackened frog.

The phone disturbed our reverie. It was Melita to say that she was at the hospital with Rafaelo. She had told the doctors that he had slipped in the shower. Would we send a taxi to the hospital with his clothes? We put the phone down without answering.

We held our silence about what had happened. Questions were asked by the others, yet no one could explain why Rafaelo and Melita had been driving southwards on the *autostrada* in separate cars. Melita was behind his Mercedes, in the small Fiat. A farmer had broken the strict rules and had burned the stubble in one of his fields adjoining the motorway. The wind had suddenly freshened, and changed direction. The flames were quickly fanned out of control, and the smoke drifted into the path of the traffic, hanging in an impenetrable veil in front of a bridge. In the unexpected blackout, a lorry hit the side of the bridge and skewed over into the middle of the road.

As is usually the case on the Italian *autostradas*, everyone was driving too fast. Within seconds, 16 vehicles had piled into each other in the sightless fog. Melita's car had smashed into the back of Rafaelo's Mercedes, and the two cars slewed off the road into the ditch, landing on their roofs. She had been killed instantly. It took the firemen an hour to release Rafaelo. He survived in a coma for several days, dying without regaining consciousness.

In the morgue, we looked down upon Melita's ruined beauty almost without emotion. Her face had smashed into the wheel. Perhaps the last thing she had seen as she crashed forward was the three-spoked logo on the car in front. The symbolism of this triple destroyer chilled us. Our brain was being merciful – cancelling out a true perception of the world. We knew that this was only the body, and that Melita herself was watching, hands raised in astonishment. She was in need of special prayers and readings, yet we were so benumbed we could not find the inner strength for these things, until the next day.

Within the same month, we had left the house below Dante's Montereggione, and returned to England. It had not been our intention to leave our Master in this way – or in any way at all – but now we left him. Our heart, which had so recently been filled with joy, was little more than a broken vessel which, we imagined, could never again carry any emotion other than sorrow. Yet, as the years passed, and as time began to heal, we could not doubt that we had learned, and grown, and that our soul was the richer for what had passed between us near Siena. We knew now that our Master had been right: the *shin*-headed fool, who is designed to learn from suffering and pain, should wear his triple cap with care.

The art of the flame is the art of alchemy, yet does the alchemist hear the screams of the dross metals he burns? Is it true – as the arcane Schools teach – that the cosmos feels no human pain, and only holds in mind the splendour which is to come? Burned from our soul was all jealousy. How can a Fool be jealous, or consumed with pride, when such enlightenment as this has been bestowed? What fool, or *mat*, has the power to judge how the feather of *Maat* may fall in the underworld?[71]

For a long time after the experience of Montereggione, we were rootless. At length, we decided to leave behind the Old World, and explore the New: we travelled to the United States. It did not seem to be the right time to work with a Master, and we decided to begin a course of studies under a Spiritualist, with a view to exploring what some people have called the *Shadow Land*.[72]

We had heard from American friends of the remarkable English medium, Lady C., then practising in Boston, Massachusetts, who, because she had no need to earn her living through Spiritual communications, had decided to take on a few students. Her expressed aim was to lead them towards an understanding of this realm of Spirits.

At that time, we knew very little about Spiritualism itself. We had read a few of the works of the great American clairvoyant, Andrew Jackson Davis, and had even studied his warnings regarding the evil influences of the *diakka* – evil and egocentric beings that surround certain forms of mediumship.[73] However, we were completely unversed in these matters, and felt that our contact with such phenomena would not do us any harm.

After a brief interview with Lady C (to whom we were introduced by a friend), we were invited to join her circle, and conduct with her various 'experiments' at the fortnightly meetings in Boston.

By the early 1960s we were earning our living writing short articles – usually with an archaeological theme – intended mainly for publication in academic journals. Lady C is unlikely to have known about this activity from any actual reading of our published material, which dealt with highly specialist areas, but (as she told us) she could clearly see from our aura that we were involved in what she called 'a sort of journalism' Without waiting for us to confirm this, she laid down one condition if we were to work with her in 'psychic development': we should agree beforehand not to write about, or publish, any accounts of the incidents or Spiritual encounters we observed in her circles. We agreed.[74] This was a most interesting embargo, for, while our Master occasionally made it quite clear that certain things he told us should not be passed on to profane sources, there had never – up to that point – been any question of total silence being imposed upon us.

The house where the experiments with mediumship were conducted was not far from the old Episcopal Church, at the foot of Copp's Hill, near the cemetery in which the Mather family of witch-hunting fame lie interred.[75] It was rumoured in Lady C's circle that the early Spirit-photographer, William Mumler, had lived in the same house, a hundred years previously, and it was here that he had made the first pictures of a 'Spirit' – the image of his young cousin, who had been dead for 12 years. Whether this was true or not, Mumler *was* from Boston, and he certainly had contributed to making psychic photography famous, if only because of his trial for fraud in New York.[76]

The house seemed to be post-Mumler, but we liked the story for it seemed to link our own activities with a significant past. The entrance to the basement, which had presumably been the servant's entrance, was reached by steps which led down to the side-entrance, the door of which was hidden beneath the raised steps of the main portal. The well of this basement was dark, the door badly weathered, conveying the impression of being one of those doors 'through which harmless phantoms on their errands glide'.[77] We never visited the upper part of the house, and it was as though the activities in the lower part were kept quite separate from the living accommodation above. The heavy drape curtains in the basement rooms were always kept drawn, and in semi-sealed environment the smell of the fresh flowers (which, we were led to believe, was intended to attract beneficent spirits) was somewhat oppressive. We should have realized at the outset that this somnulent darkness could not be condusive to real Spiritual activity, but, at this stage, we had few doubts about the morality of what we were involving ourselves in.

While Lady C insisted on calling her undertakings 'experiments', it quickly became apparent that this was something of a misnomer. What she conducted were little more than ordinary seances, involving clairvoyance and clairaudience. So far as we could see, these seances were not directly meant to open one up to new discoveries, or even to be recorded in a scientific sense: they were experiments only in the sense used in mediaeval magical practices, and were little more than the ancient 'spirit raising'.[78]

There were around 15 people in Lady C's circle, each of whom had undertaken to open themselves to possible psychic development. Most of them were fairly old – no doubt familiar with the pain of bereavement, and anxious to make contact with their loved ones. For all the group was called 'a circle', we would sit in an ellipse: at one end of the ellipse was an ornately carved Victorian *chaise-longue*, used by Lady C as a sort of throne, from which she could command a clear view of the others in her group. The elliptical shape recalled the form of the egg, or even the embryo, and we could not help asking ourselves what would be hatched in this fecund darkness. We did not have to wait long for an answer.

In the group, it was commonplace for messages to be received from some unidentified 'Spiritual' source by Lady C, and passed on to those in the group for whom they were intended. While these messages were often of a deadening banality for those outside the exchange, they usually did have some significance for those involved. On the whole, they were messages of support, or encouragement, suggesting that the entities in the Spirit world were intimately concerned with the welfare of the living. They had no literary or philosophical importance.

On some occasions, Lady C would write down the messages. In those days, while the word *channelling* was sometimes used of such seance communications, the older mediumistic terminology was more popular, and it was recognized that there was essentially no difference between channelling and the earlier evoking of spirits. Lady C was mostly involved in what was generally called automatic writing.[79] Like many mediums, before and after her time, Lady C was in contact with an entity who identified himself with a particular name, and even intimated that he had been alive during the early Christian persecutions. We were too inexperienced at the time to realize just how dangerous this approach to the Spiritual realms can be.

Generally we found it difficult to determine whether the 'spirit' messages were, as Lady C claimed, from disincarnate entities at all. We recognized that, within the framework of arcane lore pertaining to reincarnation, it was quite impossible for such personalities as Cleophas, Philip the Apostle or Joan of Arc to be in contact with contemporary Europeans[80] – just as it would not have been possible for the spirits of Galen or Swedenborg to have conversed with the youthful Andrew Jackson Davis, as he had so fondly imagined.

It was only rarely that one of Lady C's messages was predictive in nature. However, on one occasion, a message which psychologists might call monitory[81] was received under her mediumship. A warning came through the medium advising one of the ladies present not to make a planned journey by air – as we recall, this was an internal flight to Texas. A couple of weeks later, the recipient of the message thanked Lady C for the message. The plane she had intended to catch had crashed, killing all those on board.

We ourselves received many messages which could be construed as coming from another realm. Lady C did appear to have an extraordinary ability to sense the appearances of one's deceased friends and relatives. In particular, we would receive messages from what Lady C maintained was our maternal grandfather. Lady C was not able to give his second name, but she did provide quite accurately his personal name, which happened to be the uncommon Sebastian. She described him as being of military bearing, always impeccably turned out, and in the service of the British Army – though, as she put it, 'working in a distant land'. In fact, our grandfather had been a high-ranking officer in the Indian army during the Raj, towards the end of the 19th century. We met him only one one or two occasions in our youth, when he was already an old man. We still have faded photographs of him taken in the heyday of the Raj, seated in the place of honour among the serried ranks of officers and men under his command.

But our deepest experience with Lady C was of a kind which led us to question the validity of what we were doing in this Boston group. During one fortnightly seance in the darkened room, Lady C unexpectedly went into a trance. This was not her usual method of making contact with the shadow-land. Normally, when she delivered messages, or gave us instructions to help in our psychic development, she appeared to be fully conscious. In this case, however, her head slumped forward, and she seemed to be in a deep sleep. We now began to see the purpose behind the *chaise-longue*, for when her head fell forward, one of her assistants moved quietly to her side, and supported her. Lady C began to talk, describing what must have been a clairaudient experience.

'I see a tall man walking into the room. He has a full beard. He comes by way of the door, yet I see from his gesture that he does not like doors. Doors lead into rooms, and this man does not like to be in rooms. He prefers to be free. This man loves the open countryside.'

She hesitated.

'No, he shakes his head at my words. He loves the open spaces. Yes. Now he is showing me the world he loves.'

After a few moments of silence, Lady C began to speak again.

'Yes, there is a ridge of sand. We climb the ridge together, and over the top we see yet more undulations of sand. This is the world he loves. He shows me that there are no rooms here. Only tents, in the distance.'

Slowly, Lady C's entire body was slumping forward, yet she continued to speak.

'Now he sits down on the floor in the centre of our circle. He takes off his hat. It is a strange hat. It is really a red scarf. I think I can see red lines on the scarf. He is folding it neatly into a square. Now he gets up, and carries the scarf. He takes it to . . .'

Lady C did not look look towards us, nor did she wake up, but she spoke our name.

'He stands in front of *you*, Mark. He does not say anything, but he smiles at you. He turns to me, and indicates that *you* will understand his actions. You will be the only one here to understand. Now he puts his finger to his lips, and slides the scarf on to your knee. He is trying to tell you something: but he will not pass the message on to me. He says that I will not understand. For a moment or two he looks down upon you. I can see that he is a friend.

'Now he fades away. The scarf on your knee has also faded away. There are still a few threads of ectoplasm[82] on your knee, but these are shrivelling. All I can tell you is that this man's name begins with E.'

We could not see the ectoplasm, but we certainly recognized the name beginning with E.

When Lady C awoke from this trance, she had no recollection of what had happened.

The story of Spiritualism is mainly that of deception, as any proficient account of the subject makes quite evident.[83] However, our own experience with Lady C convinced us that it is quite possible, at times, for mediums to perceive on a different plane, and to transmit what they see to others. We make this pronouncement based entirely on our own direct experience, and being fully aware that 99 per cent of the so-called Spiritualist phenomena is fraudulent. We also make this pronouncement fully aware that the 'different plane' to which we refer is not in any sense a higher plane, and certainly has nothing to do with the realm of the dead. From her account, we recognized the visitant was our friend, Ahmed, whom we had met in Baghdad, in the mid 1950s.

It had been our first visit to this city, and we had known no one. We had been surprised at how run-down and seedy this once-great city was in those days: the shadow of Hulaku the Mongol, who had put Baghdad to the sword in the 13th century, and who had turned the well-irrigated fertile land into bleak steppes, still seemed to hang over it. The only real beauty we discovered in the city was the superb Islamic architecture of the old mosques.

On our second day there, we had stopped to watch a man digging in the earth alongside one of the mosques. We had imagined that he was an archaeologist, for he dug with almost infinite care, from time to time brushing away the hard sand from around shards or pebbles. After a while, he looked up, and our eyes met. He nodded towards me, placed his soft brush on the edge of the walls, and climbed from the pit.

He was wearing the *kophia* which Lady C was to identify as a red scarf. Although the *kophia* is of intensely practical value as a protection against the sun and windstorms (which can throw slashes of sand with such ferocity that they cut the flesh) its deeper importance is more than merely practical or even sartorial. We suspect that only an Arab could give a full account of the subtle symbolism involved in the wearing of a *kophia*, and it is reasonable to assume that at one time it was a sign of grade in an esoteric School, descended to mere general wear, much as the distinctive Mithraic cap, the *liberia* or Phrygian cap, of the esoteric followers of Mithras had degenerated into the headgear of the French revolutionaries.[84]

'Let me take you for the best coffee in Baghdad,' the man said, almost casually, as though he had known me for a long time. His eyes were as intensely blue as the azure skies behind his head. 'My name is Ahmed, son of Mohammed Benawi,' he said, pressing his right hand over his heart, Arab style.

'I am Mark Hedsel.'

Although he spoke French, he must have sensed my accent

immediately. 'You would prefer to speak English?'

We nodded, and he fell into this language with extraordinary fluency.

'My father was Arabic, and worked as a aero mechanic at the British airstrip of Habbanyia. My mother is Italian, but she has wisely returned to Calabria. A strange mixture of blood and genes there, you will agree! I learned the English language from my father – may God rest his soul, My french was from France, for I studied engineering in Cairo and in Paris, at the Sorbonne.'

The black coffee, poured Arab-style from gracious copper pots through the spiky green leaves, was good, but it was clear that what attracted our new-found friend to the place was an ancient *flipper*,[85] which he consistently called *le flippeur*.

'You play the *flippeur* – the pin-ball machines?'

'Without grace,' we laughed, 'but with great enthusiasm.'

By European standards, the pin-ball machine was very primitive. Most of the light-bulbs behind the lurid militaristic picture were dead, yet in the hands of this man, the whole machinery could come alive, as he shook, persuaded and cajoled the huge ball-bearings to do his bidding in the maze of flashing electric lights, spiralled metal and pitfalls.

'You play superbly,' we acknowledged.

'A wasted youth, followed by wasted manhood,' he grunted, still pulling savagely at the spring-loaded handle. 'The alternative was becoming a poet. I chose to become an engineer.' Although Ahmed was perhaps only a year or so older than us, he was a gaunt, unkempt giant, whose heavy beard conspired to make him appear older than his years. 'And you?' he glanced towards us from the corners of his eyes. 'What brings you to Baghdad?'

'I was offered a lift on a convoy. But I wanted to see the mosques and the museum.'

'The people, too,' he suggested. 'The people here are fantastic. I am so fantastic that I will take you to see the mosque and the museum. Everyone who comes to Baghdad wants to see the battery.'

'The battery?'

'You do not know about the battery?' He pretended incredulity. 'You will know about the guardian monsters from Erech – the creatures with the magnificent wings and heads of a bearded man – you will know of the fish-man, and of the great statues of the kings.[86] But you do not know of the battery? If I could pull myself away from this most serious game, I would take you immediately to the museum and show you this famed wonder.[87] But the game must come first.'

As he manipulated the machine, we talked, exchanging stories from our life. His knowledge of Arabic literature and poetry was encyclopaedic, and it soon became evident that he had read a great deal of the esoteric literature, for he would occasionally quote from the original Persian of Rumi's *Mathnawi*, always translating it for us into English.

> It is the rain of God we weep.
> It is the lightning of God we laugh.[88]

Our sense that he had some contact with a School was strengthened when Ahmed told us stories from the life of the alchemist, Dhu'l-Nun, famed for his Foolish Wisdom.[89] The 'Treasure Story' Ahmed told us was a development on the ancient Arabic traditions of hidden treasure, which crops up in the popular tales of Aladdin, in the mystical terms beloved by the Sufi. The 'Treasure Story' tells how Dhu'l-Nun and some friends found a cache of gold and jewels, covered by a wooden board on which was inscribed the name of God, in Arabic. His friends took the gold and jewels, but Dhu'l-Nun asked only for the real treasure, which was the name of his Beloved God, that he could grasp. In reward for his having recognized the value of the treasures, God opened for Dhu'l-Nun the gates of wisdom. Dhu'l Nun's choice of the treasures might have seemed foolish to ordinary men, but to those who had knowledge of God, it was a choice indicative of great wisdom. Dhu'l-Nun had seen that the name of God was the only thing in the world at which it was worth grasping, for this would lift him to Heaven.[90]

Having told the tale, in a beautiful economy of English, Ahmed remarked that the story of Dhu'l-Nun's treasure symbolized poetry in action. We ourselves, however, recognized in the tale an account of initiation.

It was Ahmed's natural poesy which attracted him – the fact that whatever his religious calling he mingled every step through life with poetic vision. The prejudices of our times (inclined to grasp at the gold and jewels, rather than at the real treasure) would probably read this poetry as merely emerging from the genes: Ahmed was the burning soul of the Italian, merged with the natural asceticism of the Bedouin. However, we saw Ahmed in a different light – his love of the Sufi stories and poetry, alongside his silence about arcane matters, indicated that he was a man in Spiritual preparation, and we were finally persuaded us that he must belong to a Sufi sect which had commanded total silence relating to the Mysteries under every circumstance.[91]

Whatever his esoteric credentials, Ahmed had an immense love for life, and a profound mistrust of all normal values. He was, in fact, one of the most independent and free-thinking souls we have ever had the privilege to meet. We learned a great deal about human values from him, and, through our friendship, unexpectedly developed some degree of elegance with the pin-ball machines. At first, we had thought that this would be an immense waste of time, but Ahmed was a master of the game, and he showed us just what mastery could achieve. There was no possibility of our learning the game to his level. Our fingers were not sufficiently subtle to operate the flippers, and we did not feel, to the required hair-breadth delicacy, the point at which the shaking of the world's foundations would light the word TILT, and bring the game to an end. We could not approach his expertise, but at least, through his presence, we were left with a permanent aspiration. We observed that Ahmed's excitement was at the beginning of each movement of the ball. As he released the loaded spring, and watched the ball shoot into the space above the machine his face was always translucent, reminding us of the facial expressions of the whirling dervishes, at the fastest sweep of their gyrations.

We could sense that for Ahmed the game was a parable for life, which is the permanent avoidance of the final tilting. Ahmed himself became the ball, shot into the well of traps and springs. He was as free as the ball itself! for he belonged neither to Italy nor to Bahrain, where he had been born: like the balls he careered through the multifoliate lights and traps of the game, his direction impelled by some curious external impulse. For him, the game *was* life, and deadly serious: it had to be played with infinite care and mastery.

When playing the game, Ahmed always wore his *kophia* head-scarf, which would drop low over his forehead. On some occasions, while stooping over the glass top, the head-scarf would fall so low that he must have been blinded by the fabric, and reduced to playing by touch, rather than from vision.

'*Enkidu!*' We shouted at him one day, as we watched him play in this seeming blindness.[92] As he nodded to show that he understood, his headdress flopped even lower over his face, yet he refused to be deflected from the energetic game. Later, as we sipped coffee he said: 'Did you call me Enkidu because I had become a wild man?'

We nodded. Leaping about in front of the machine, with his fingers poised over the flippers, his whole body gyrating to move the table, he was a wild man of sorts.

'Did you ask yourself the question of the poets – Who moves the ball? And who moves the man?' His blue eyes pierced into our own.

Once again we nodded. 'You were the wild man. I think Enkidu is your secret name.'

We had shouted out the name without any real consciousness, yet it led to an extraordinary adventure. Delighted that he had discovered something we had in common, Ahmed sat with us for the whole of a day reading the *Epic of Gilgamesh*.[93] The night had closed in when he finished, but he was still charged with energetic excitement.

'Tomorrow,' he said, 'tomorrow, we visit Warka.'

'Warka?'

'Warka, my friend, is where ancient Erech once stood. Where Gilgamesh reigned. Where Gilgamesh met his wild-man, Enkidu.'

We set off before dawn, driving until the desert road became too rough, then taking to camels.

Ahmed strode through the hard sand leading the two camels with delight upon his face. We were not quite so happy, for whilst during the day there was a radiant heat with the night came the cold winds. We arrived at Warka well after dark. We couldn't see clearly as we stumbled into the rubble-filled trenches behind the temple, to find a place to sleep, and we were both fearful in case we disturbed snakes.

Ahmed took a thick piece of wood, and beat the loose sand around the edge of the trench.

'I cannot stand snakes. The desert is filled with them at night. Are all fears so irrational?'

We tried to sleep wrapped in our great-coats, hiding from the winds in the defile behind the platforms of the White Temple. Above us wheeled the same unmoving stars Gilgamesh had seen from his palaces of Sumer. The four great stellar markers he had seen were still in their ancient places, though now with different names.[94] It was too cold for us to sleep, and, to pass the time, Ahmed talked to us about the Arabic names for some of the stars, and some of the ancient legends. Sometimes, he would give their names first in Arabic and then in Persian.

'Isn't Orion called "The Giant" in Arabic?'

'*Al Jabbar*,'[95] he confirmed. 'For for some, that is the name. For poets, it is so named. *Al Jabba* certainly means "the Giant". I'm not surprised you should ask about this first: it certainly stands out in the skies. There is a psychic unity in the image: the picture of a belted giant is drawn by the stars, rather than by our imagination. The giant is held together by some force behind the stars – some hidden intensity. The Akkadians called it *Uruanna*, the Light of Heaven, yet the Arabs brought it down to Earth when they called it *Algebar*, "the giant".[96]

'Some 16th-century Europeans brought it even closer to the Earth. They imagined that the constellation was called the *Snake* in Arabic. They thought that it was *Al Shuja*, and this meant "serpent".'[97]

'It does mean "serpent". And I can understand such a confusion among Europeans, with no knowledge of Arabic. But the giant was really a god, and never a serpent. In Egyptian astrology, Orion was *Horus*, among the highest of the gods.'

This was true. In the zodiac at Denderah he was Horus in the boat, surrounded by stars. Even earlier, Orion had been called *Sahu*.[98]

'And the belt?' we asked.

'Orion's belt?'

We nodded.

'That is *Al Nijad*.[99] The three stars of the belt were supposed to be reflected on the Earth plane by the three pyramids at Gizah. What do you think of that?'

'An old idea, but not one that bears close examination.'[100]

'In any case, on such a night as this it would be more reasonable to talk about the colder stars of the north.' He pointed to the constellation of Ursa Major. 'That is *al Dubhe* – the Great Bear. But before the Arabs took this idea of the bear from the Greeks, the Phoenicians had called it *Parrasis*, which meant "fiducial", or guide-star. Perhaps it guided sailors. Perhaps it guided pyramid builders. Who knows?'

'The cold called *Dubhe* to your mind.'

'What do you mean?'

'Did you think of *Dubhe* because the ancients believed that it revolves round the frozen pole? The Pole star is unmoving because it is frozen in space and time?'[101]

He laughed.

'The Persians were wise, for they saw it as bier, carrying dead bodies. That is the true coldness, death. The bear is linked with death. Maulana tells the story of the bear that used to guard a man who had once saved it from a dragon. One day, the man fell asleep, and the bear watched over him, to ensure that he came to no harm. Flies began to buzz over the man, and the bear wafted them away with its great paw. The flies would keep returning, so the bear picked up a huge stone, and when the flies were buzzing over the man's face, he dropped it on the flies to kill them, smashing the man's skull.'[102]

'That is a good story. There's a sort of relic of the story in the Greek word for Arctic, for *ourcs* meant 'bear-guardian'. I know from my reading in astrology that the stars – the source of our life – are also killers.'

'We have an Arabic proverb: the befriended bear brings trouble.'

'That's true, for sure.' It was the Egyptian-born astrologer Ptolemy who had lead the Arabs into recognizing that some stars were killers. 'The idea's universal. You know, the bear was traced in the stars even by the North American Indians.[103] Could that be accident?'

Ahmed chuckled. 'Is there such a thing as accident?'

'Not in my philosophy. Just see how thick the veil is.'

'Ah – the veil with many names, the *uzur*.[104] What is the real? Look – you've just pointed to three stars set in the belt of a giant which would have been much the same in appearance in the days when Gilgamesh lived. Yet the middle star, *Alnilam*, moves at over 16 miles a second, and *Alnitak* at just over half that speed. *Per second*. Doesn't the distance alone reveal that everything is *maya* – illusion? If those stars are not a veil, nothing is.' We nodded. He continued: 'And, in that illusion, the Moon seems to move more quickly even than the stars! My forebears would located the Moon by its night-sign, the so-called *manzils*.[105] You see – tonight, the Moon is near *Al Fargh*, "the Water Bucket". For the early Arabs, this meant that it was not a time to make a voyage . . .'

'Yet we journeyed to this place . . .'

'Yes,' he laughed, 'and, and in consequence, we may freeze to death without our bear-skins: the water in our bucket is turning to ice. Yet we have free will: we can defy the Fates of the ancients: there may be no wisdom in such defiance, but at least there is dignity. In fact, in my horoscope, the Sun was on that star Fomalhaut – the one up there – set in the head of the Southern Fish. Its Arabic name reveals its position: it is from *Fum al Hut*, "Mouth of the Fish". It was one of the four Royal Stars in Persia, when the *Gilgamesh* epic was written. Once, I was quite proud of this link with my Sun, for the Fish is a symbol of the hidden wisdom, but then one day I discovered that the earlier Arabic name was *Al Difdi al Awwal*, which mean "the first frog", and I was no longer quite so sure about myself, or about my ancestry or destiny.'[106]

He made a croaking sound, and we laughed.

'Well, the frog of Western lore changes into a Prince . . .'

'A comforting thought but I'd rather be fish.'

Later, as the cold became too intense even to point bare fingers towards the stars, we snuggled more deeply into our coats. It was too cold to talk.

By midnight, the cold was so intense that even Ahmed gave in. He scrambled into the ruins behind the temple and liberated a canvas awning, which was protecting an area being dug by archaeologists. After he had beaten the canvas thoroughly, to make sure there were no snakes curled up inside it, we folded it over on the ground. Still wearing our great-coats, we climbed into the folds of the canvas, which at least helped keep of the searing wind. We could empathize with Enkidu and Gilgamesh in the cold wastes of Hell. There was a natural transition in our imagination from our own freezing condition to the cold misery of the Hell in which the two heroes had huddled, and we started talking of the *Epic of Gilgamesh*.

'Would you like to hear some of the Epic?' Ahmed asked.

'You know it off by heart?'

'Only a little. And then only in Arabic. It is an Arabic tradition to learn great poetry by heart.' He laughed ironically. 'Recitations help pass the nights in the desert!'

'Do you know the words of Sabitu?' we asked. 'The part where she advises Gilgamesh to abandon the Path and give up his search?'

'Unlike you,' said Ahmed, glancing towards us, a mist of breath hovering over the top of the upturned collar of his great-coat. Then he broke into an Arabic version of the Epic, which he translated, line by line. Even in this disjointed frame, it lost none of its vigour or beauty.

> Gilgamesh, wherefore hurry on this path?
> The Life you seek, you will not find.
> When gods in wisdom fashioned man,
> They moulded in that red loam Death,
> Kept back sweet Life for gods alone.
> Rejoice, and keep your belly filled,
> Let nights and days be merry.
> Let night on soft-fleshed virgins pass,
> Let days in joyous feasting while away.[107]

The sea-lady, Sabitu, was trying to persuade Gilgamesh to leave the dangerous path: he should remain content with ordinary human life . . . Yet Gilgamesh would not listen to her words. The great king Gilgamesh sought more – the gold and jewels so readily available to him, as the most powerful king on Earth, were of no value to him. He knew that unless he could circumvent death, then life itself could have no further joys for him. What joy could there be for any man who knew that everything ended in a finale of death? This is why, against all advice, he set out with Enkidu on that journey to the ends of the Earth – even to the Sea of Death – in search of the magical plant which, his magicians had told him, could alone bestow upon him eternal Life.

'Do you know the lines about the Plant of Life?'

'And about the snake,' he replied. 'The Plant and the snake are almost one and the same – quite inseparable. They are both symbols of the spine. One is dead, the other alive.'

'Which is dead, Ahmed – the Plant or the snake?'

'Ah – that is the question we must answer for ourselves. In the Bible, the snake issues words of beguilement and death, is that not so? Perhaps that is why I fear snakes. But just listen to these voices from my past.'

Once again he fell to reciting lines from the *Epic*:

> The plant which glows as bright as heaven
> On a clear and star-filled desert night,
> Its brightness confound to eyes of man,
> Is grasped in jaws of that black snake,
> Held fathoms neath the ocean of despair.

This was the inner ocean, which implied that the seeds of the plant were buried in man. Ahmed quoted more:

> Held in bitter waters known but to one –
> That man half-god, wild-eyed with loneliness
> That man half-god who longs for soothing death.

This wise man, standing alone at the End of the World, was *Utnapishtim*, who knew of the whereabouts of the Plant of Life, and also of the cunning snake which guarded it.

'Even with that knowledge, Utnapishtim did not find happiness,' we remarked.

'And he was one who had attained to eternal Life. What sadness there is in this *Epic*. It portrays a time in history when men were awaiting a redeemer.'

Ahmed's insight astonished us. The Redeemer would not come for almost 2,000 years, yet already men were desperate for His coming.

'Yes,' we murmured. 'That seems to me the message in the *Epic*. Without that message, then we are all lost. The *Epic of Gilgamesh* is the epic of every man and woman.'

'The idea of a redemption is the only thing which can alleviate the horror of that scene in Hell. Dhu'l-Nun's board inscribed with the name *Allah* was a life-raft.' Ahmed said this with his customary simplicity, yet we saw in his words just how deeply his soul longed for the Spirit.

The most heart-rending part of the *Epic* is when, after his friend Enkidu is killed, Gilgamesh descends to the Babylonian Hell, where the dead ate only ashes, and sat like tongueless crows in silence, to seek him out. He has no power to rescue his friend from Hell, but had gained the chance to see him for the last time. During the visit, Gilgamesh asks Enkidu to tell him about this dark realm of Spirits.

'My friend,' says Enkidu, 'I cannot tell thee about this dark world. I cannot tell thee. If I were to tell thee all, thou wouldst sit down and weep.'

To which Gilgamesh replies, 'Then let us sit down and weep together. For all my tears, I would fain learn about the land of Spirits.'

Almost evoked by our poetic theme, the first light of dawn began to break over the rim of the desert. Slowly, the light dissolved the monstrous forms of the temple, and within half an hour the red disc of the sun hung over the horizon, transforming the ruins into a sacred *bayt nuri*.[108] Almost immediately, the world around shivered at this promise of yet another furnace.

Ahmed was already up, his great-coat removed, as he did physical exercises to restore his circulation. He pulled his arms behind his head, clasped his hands on the back of his neck, and looked towards the disk of the sun which hung over the rim of the desert.

'You are right. I think that I am a wild man. No one has ever tamed the desert, and I am its child. The desert is the proper home of a wild man, for there is no *wasta* in its compass. The desert gives to no man.'[119] He gestured around, towards the other horizon.

'Even these aromatic coffee shops are too confining, unless they have within them the vast adventure of a pin-ball machine. You feel with the pin-ball that you are dealing with the stars, controlling with your own fingers the movements of metallic planets through the Heavens.' He grinned at me.

'Yes, the pin-ball is the net which captures the wild man, Enkidu.'

We laughed at the artistic development of the conceit, for in former times a name for karma was 'the net', but then we pulled him up short.

'No, Ahmed. Remember – it was not a net that captured Enkidu.'

He joined our laughter, for he saw our drift. 'You are right, my friend. No net would hold that giant wild man of the desert. It was a *woman* – a temple prostitute – that entrapped him. The captress was a slave girl of Ishtar, with her tent dances and lascivious enticements. Yet some say this was Ishtar herself, veiled as a slave-girl, and enamoured of Enkidu.[110] You called me Enkidu, yet *I* will not be captured by a woman, my friend. My life is too short. There is no room in my life for such darkness as a prison.'

We were struck by his last words. In truth, when I had called out the name *Enkidu*, I had been thinking of the wild man in a prison.

'When you played the *flippeur*, your face was all but covered by the folds of your *kophia*. I thought of Enkidu in the Underworld.'

He mused for a moment, and then observed, 'When Gilgamesh visits Enkidu in the darkness, his friend has still not lost his love and longing for the world above. In his agony of soul, he tells Gilgamesh to flee the darkness, and to enjoy Earthly life while he can. Ashes and frozen tears might be the unwelcome lot of the dead, but the living should flee such things, in search of life. Never forget,' he said seriously, 'that the *Epic* ends in sadness. Enkidu is left in the darkness of Hell. Utnapishtim remains in his loneliness. Gilgamesh does not keep the Plant of Life which he sought.'

Ahmed's *kophia* had been the veiled message in that darkened seance room. The unconscious Lady C had been quite right: we *were* the only one in the room who had understood.

We did not explain to Lady C the meaning behind this strange encounter in the seance, but we knew – or at least thought we knew – what it meant.

The full meaning revealed itself only a few weeks later.

Immediately after this dream-like encounter, we resolved to contact Ahmed, to see if he had had any similar curious sensations at the same time. Did he know what had happened in that Boston seance room? we wondered. Such a question would appeal to his sense of humour. In any case, he would know that certain dervish Masters were reputed to have the power of bilocation when in a state of estatic motion.[111]

That same night, we wrote a long letter, telling him what had happened, and making a few tentative suggestions as to what the vision might have meant. Was he advising us, we asked, to leave behind the darkened seance room, which was for him an equivalent of the Babylonian Underworld? Were we to give up these 'experiments' in darkness, where the entities might leap from their graves? If this had not been his message, could he himself throw any light upon the strange vision? Why had his visionary self taken off his *kophia*, and slipped it on to our knee? Was this some Arabic form of homage, which we knew nothing about?

As usual, we addressed the letter poste restante in Bahrain, where we had last been in touch with him. We knew that we might have to wait several months for a reply.

Three weeks later, we received a letter postmarked Safat, Kuwait. It had been addressed to us in London, whence it had been forwarded to the States. The envelope had been posted about a week before the strange encounter in the seance room.

The letter was from someone we did not know. The writer told us that Ahmed had crossed from Saudi to Kuwait, to work for a while in the developing oil fields of the southern desert – the Getty fields. A short while after arriving, he was bitten in the thigh by a poisonous snake and died two and a half days later. Following his last request, he had been buried in the desert.

The writer told us that among Ahmed's few possessions were some letters from us, and it was from the most recent of these that the man had taken our address to write with the bad news.

When the vision of Ahmed had appeared in the dark basement, he had been dead for several days. Now we understood that final gesture of the shade. It was not a warning to us, at all, but a sign that he had stopped wandering the desert like one of the ever-restless Bedouins. Surely, he had he shaken off his *kophia* to show that his head was, at last, open to the upper stars?

In a sense, the stars which so fascinated him, and the Earth-bound snakes he so feared, had their final say. It was the star *Fomalhaut*, set in the head of the Southern Fish, which had taken his life. This star was the *anaretic* – the killer – which brought death by means of a serpent bite.[112]

Chapter Four

Thus mankind came into being. Mankind was made from the
tears that sprang from my Eye.

(Song of the Egyptian god, Atum, from the fourth-century BC
creation myth in the *Bremner Rhind Papyrus*)

On 27 December 1666, John Frederick Helvetius, the physician to the
Prince of Orange, was approached in his alchemical study in The Hague
by an Adept, unknown to him, and never identified by historians.[1] The
meeting was to change Helvetius' life by leading him into a new
understanding of alchemy, as a result of which he wrote the alchemical
texts for which he is now famous in arcane circles.

In a later meeting, the stranger – whom Helvetius referred to as 'the
Artist Elias'[2] – gave the physician a tiny piece of the Philosopher's Stone,
by which he would be able to convert lead to gold. Helvetius objected that
the 'pale sulphur-coloured' substance was tiny: it was no larger than a
coriander seed, and seemed far too small to transform a large quantity of
lead.[3] The stranger promptly took back the seed, and, with a smile,
snipped it in two with his thumb nail. He handed the smaller of the
fragments back to Helvetius.

'Even now,' he said, 'it will be sufficient.' His words proved to be
correct, for, as Helvetius tells us, he used this fragment to transform
almost an ounce of lead into the finest gold.

The story is worth recalling because, like Helvetius, we have always
been amazed at how little Spiritual activity is required to obtain
extraordinary results. A seed-sized portion of the inner stone of Spiritual
effort will transform enormous amounts of the leaden inertia we all
encounter in our own souls. The Philosopher's Stone handed to
Helvetius was the yellow of sulphur, reminding us that the Will force in
Man – that force which can move mountains – is called by alchemists

Sulphur (see page 140). All through our life, we have been astonished at how little activity of Will is required to engender remarkable insights into that Spiritual realm which lies behind the veil of phenomena. Perhaps this is because the Spiritual realm is so generous with its bounty, so ready to give to those who are prepared to seek and receive.

As we shall see, even a single word, when spoken at the right time and in the right tone, can change for the good the life of an individual on the Path.

As with all important alchemical stories, there are meanings within meanings in this account of Helvetius' meeting with the mysterious Adept. Without doubt, the reason why Helvetius so carefully recorded the time and date of his meeting with the stranger was because of its astrological importance. In the 'forenoon' of that day, no fewer than five planets were in Capricorn, and Saturn (the ruler of lead, and the ruler of the alchemical process which transforms lead) was in the 'scholarly degree' of 21 Capricorn.[4] Helvetius seems to be of the opinion that the operation of alchemy, like the operations of true Will, involves the whole cosmos – that for true magic to work, the Heavens and Earth must be in accord.

The lesson such Adepts teach is the secret *Magistry* of the alchemical stone. The Teachers of this Mystery are called *Masters* (the modern university Masters degree, which has been so demoted of late, was originally a degree of initiation). The original Latin term for Master was not *Magister*, but *Magester*, and was thus linked with, if not actually cognate with, *Mage*, or 'magician'. What the archetypal Adept taught was, quite literally, the *magian lore* or *magic* – the laws pertaining to the Spiritual world. In the Bible, Christ is called 'Master', and in at least one section he is associated with the biblical Elias.[5] Was Helvetius weaving a parable about the transforming power of Christ, as the cosmic alchemist? This Artist Elias – or someone very much like him – is reported to have made contact with several alchemical seekers, and is clearly the living archetype of the Teacher. The story reminds us that there is a secret Elias, or Master, ready to approach all those who seriously long to find inner fulfilment and development.

These words, *magister* and *mage*, connoting their ancient meanings, are still used in certain secret societies. For example, in the rules and ordinances of the Rosicrucian Society of England, we find seven grades.[6] The two highest grades are *Magister Templi* (Master of the Temple) and *Magus*, the latter being merely the Latin for magician, or learned man. These titles or ranks are bestowed in recognition that the brethren have learned the Magistry of the secret teaching of the Rosicrucians – the secrets of the transforming of Saturn. We shall examine this tradition of Saturn, and its connections with Capricorn, in esoteric literature later (see page 275ff).

In a far more sophisticated treatment of the grades, preserved within the Masonic brotherhoods, a series of initiation titles, ranging from the *Apprentice* through to the *Secret Master*, the *Elu of the Fifteen*, and into the *Master of the Royal Secret*, have been listed, not only with the correct titles of the 32 grades of initiation indicated, but even with an account of some of their esoteric grounding.[7] Such titles and grades all serve to remind us that initiation is itself a series of initiations into lesser Mysteries, which eventually lead to an overview of the Greater Mystery.

Undoubtedly, the arcane background to such alchemical stories as the one told by Helvetius about his meeting with the *Adeptus* is of great interest for those on the Path. Meetings between those on the Path with such high Adepts are always fascinating for those intent on joining an esoteric group, or who have already entered a Way. Such an interest aside, however, we have another reason for quoting the story here, and this is related to the grain–like size of the transformative powder carried and used by the Adept. In alchemical terms, this seed relates to the idea of *potency*, which, in the arcane tradition, has a slightly different meaning to that usually expressed in ordinary language.[8] In alchemy, as in certain forms of arcane medicine which have developed from alchemy, a minute portion of a substance may be charged with a magical potency which seems almost to be inversely proportional to its size. A fragment of the secret stone no larger than half a coriander seed will transform almost an ounce of lead: this is in a proportion of about 1:1000. The stone must have been highly potent to work such magic, and the alchemist must have had considerable knowledge to know how to release such a power. This idea, of revealing hidden potency in minute quantities, seems to have been transferred from ancient alchemy to the more modern medical science of homoeopathy.

Homoeopathy, with its magic of the minimum dose,[9] was introduced into Western culture in the 18th century by the German, Samuel Hahnemann, who seems, like his more illustrious forebear, Paracelsus, to have followed his own Star (a name the latter used for personal destiny) in the face of all opposition. In the mid-18th century, medicine was dominated by leechdom and other forms of bloodletting.[10] With the development of a new materialistic chemistry from alchemy, and the emergence of a new science from the natural magic of mediaeval occultism, the time was right for a new approach to the Spiritual side of medicine, which might otherwise be lost under the welter of materialistic science. It was Hahnemann who had the genius to grasp the opportunity to develop this Spiritual side.

The theory underlying Hahnemann's homoeopathy is that illnesses may be successfully treated with doses of drugs which, when administered in sufficient quantity, would promote symptoms, or even pathological conditions, similar to those being treated. It is perfectly true that some early medical and alchemical literature – including certain passages in Paracelsus – does suggest ideas based on principles similar to those of homoeopathy.[11] For example, the 11th-century Arab physician, Avicenna, certainly taught that the perfect *magisterium* was one part in a thousand: it is therefore easy to leap to the conclusion that he was expressing an homoeopathic principle.[12] However, it is more likely that he was defining the *potentia* of the alchemical Stone – the remarkable fact revealed so dramatically to Helvetius by the unknown Adept.

In denying the existence of a true homoeopathy prior to Hahnemann, we are not for one moment denying that this great innovator did not have an awareness of the medical practices of the arcane traditions of Rosicrucians and alchemists. The truth is that Hahneman had a deep interest in esoteric lore and the arcane tradition. Hahnemann was a practising and initiated Mason, which meant that he would have had some considerable insight into hermetic lore. He had entered the Lodge at Hermannstadt in 1777 – almost certainly proposed by the influential Baron von Brukenthal, for whom he worked as librarian and physican. After his move to Leipzig, in 1817, he continued in the Craft, joining the *Lodge of Minerva of the Three Palms*, in that city.[13] In those days – of Masons such as Goethe, Schiller and Wieland – it would be impossible for a practising Mason not to be aware of certain secrets of the arcane alchemical and Rosicrucian tradition in medicine. Given this connection, Hahnemann would have been able to supplement his knowledge of Paracelsian and traditional medicine with some of the more secret streams which fed initiation lore in his Masonic School.[14]

The term *trituration*, which is now widely used to describe the production of homoeopathic products, was derived by Hahnemann from earlier pharmacological practices, such as were used by Paracelsus and other late-mediaeval doctors and herbalists. The word was used to denote the reduction of a substance to a very fine powder – especially it was used in that process by which 10 parts of drug or medical substance was reduced by the addition of 90 parts of liquid. Hahnemann's use of this word might lead us to suspect a connection between his method and the earlier mediaeval medicine, yet such a suspicion would be ill-founded. In fact, the triturations of homoeopathic products usually involve an altogether different order of reduction or dilution from that practised in early pharmacies.

The principle of homoeopathic trituration is simple, and we need only refer to Hahnemann's own notes to grasp the method practised even today. If a preparation from a plant, such as Monkshood, was intended, a mother tincture was produced by way of an alcoholic extract of the crushed plant. This was then diluted by nine parts of an alcohol-water mixture, to give the first decimal potency. This mixture was then diluted by a further nine parts of alcohol-water, to give the potency of a second decimal potency. After each dilution, the mixture was shaken strongly. The operation was repeated to give the required decimal potency.

After the third trituration, one would expect the original mother tincture of Monkshood to be so diluted as to have lost all its original power: there would be, at best, a molecule or so in a third or fourth trituration. Homoeopaths agree with this statistic, and some even point out that a third trituration is said to contain about a millionth part of the original drug. In terms of ordinary medical theory, a preparation of this kind would be regarded as being little more than a placebo. Surprisingly, this theory is confounded by actual practice. Under normal circumstances, the process of trituration would be imagined to weaken the power of a drug, whereas it actually increases its potency.

The homoeopath, Dr Molson, once organized the Brighton coastguards to continue triturating common salt – the *Natrum Muriaticum* of homoeopathy – to the point where the original substance was reduced far beyond the one-in-a-million of the third trituration. He found the resulting trituration 'almost explosive', and so powerful that he was afraid to administer it to patients.[15] The extraordinary fact is that, in terms of ordinary physics, homoeopathic trituration defies common sense.

Clearly, the power of a triturated drug lies in something which can neither be seen nor measured, save in relation to its effect on the sick person. It is this fact which explains why homoeopathy – which as a curative art is indisputably effective – has received such short shrift from the scientific and medical establishments, which have inherited a science and art rooted in the measurable.

Aware that the dramatic effects of trituration are beyond reason, some homoeopaths have adopted Hahnemann's own word, *potentization*, as a convenient alternative for trituration. The great homoeopath, J. T. Kent, seems to have been aware that the mere adopting of a word does not change the fundamental mystery of the minimum dose, when he wrote,

'If we follow along the line of potentization we lose the idea of power that is manifest to an uninitiated mind.'[16] When Hahnemann adopted the word *potency* to describe the power developed by trituration, he knew full well that it was an arcane term, used to denote a relationship between the realm of Spirit and the material world.[17]

Hahnemann's first book on homoeopathy, published in 1805, listed 26 remedies. Among these were Aconite (or Monkshood) and Belladonna, two poisons, which he showed, beyond a shadow of doubt, could be used beneficially in curative medicine, when triturated. What distinguished the work of Hahnemann from all previous medical practices was his systematic research, his method of 'proving' (or testing his attenuated drugs – usually on colleagues or friends, and always with their permission), to build up 'drug-pictures'. Hahnemann's phrase of 1810 – now so widely quoted in homoeopathic texts – was *similia similibus curentur* (let like be treated with like). This is strikingly similar to that used by the doyen of occult medicine, Paracelsus – *similia similibus curantur*, the more forthright, 'like is cured by like'.[18]

Of course, there is much evidence to show that Paracelsus, and doctors before him, did actually effect cures from the traces of 'like' substances in minute quantities in herbs, and so on. There is even some evidence to suggest that they understood the principles of how these cures worked. However, this 'sympathetic herbalism' does not appear to be related to the preparation by trituration proposed by Hahnemann. The important thing, in this context, is that the Paracelsian notion of 'like curing like' is rooted in the ancient hermetic principle of planetary, zodiacal and stellar signatures. The hermetic literature has always maintained that an illness can be cured by a medicament of the like 'signature'. Although all celestial phenomena rained their 'signatures' on Earth, these arcane signatures were usually expressed by alchemists, astrologers and doctors in terms of the seven planets. For example, it was maintained that preparations from the poisonous plant, Monkshood, could be used to cure certain malignancies of a Saturnine kind, purely on the grounds that the plant was ruled by the planet Saturn.

Again, in the herbal tradition, Mugwort was touched by the signature of the 'planet', the Moon. In ordinary medical preparations – as in popular witchcraft and other occult rites – it was used as an aid to releasing psychic consciousness, because of its well-established power to induce both prophetic dreams and astral projection, or sky-walking. Even those arcanists who were not given to seeking such psychic results recognized the lunar nature of Mugwort, and viewed dreams as imperfect memories of astral projections, largely forgotten on awaking.

They knew that a lunar plant, such as Mugwort, would help intensify not merely the power of dreaming, but even the post-sleep memory of dreaming.

The homoeopaths might play down the 'lunar signature', yet they could not help but record that their drug picture involved som-nambulism. They knew that an individual suffering from the condition would get up in the middle of the night and work, but, in the morning, rarely remember this. The classical name for Mugwort – Artemesia – was adopted by the homoeopaths for their own triturated preparation. However, even this was redolent with associations pertaining to sleep and dreams. In Greek mythology Artemesia was a Moon goddess, associated with Selene, and, as we shall see, it was this latter goddess who seduced the sleeping Endymion, and kept him in that dream-like condition of the Sleepers, which every one on the Path seeks to awake from.[19]

No matter how we tried, we could not shake off the darkness of Siena. No amount of meditation or inner adjustments seemed to free us from our inner demons. At last, however, we decided to return to the discipline of the Fool under the guidance of a Master. No sooner had we come to this decision than we heard of a remarkable Teacher in the United States, who was interested in the Way of the Fool. We wrote to this man, in New York, asking if it would be possible to study with him for a probationary period. Much to our surprise, he sent a response by return post. In this letter, written with a calligraphy which indicated that he was a scholar, he said that we would be welcome to study with him in New York for a probationary period of one year. At the end of that period, we would talk about what we both intended for the future.

It was our first visit to New York. There was an intense feeling of regeneration in the air. The Beatles, already emerging from their small cavern in Liverpool, would soon have their first success in the United States. In New York, the Philharmonic Hall had just opened to acoustics trouble. Andy Warhol had begun his first trashing of society with his Coca-Cola pictures. In the Heavens, John Glenn had just gone com-pletely round the Earth three times in his Mercury capsule. Preparations were in hand for the construction of a giant Unisphere,[20] a hollow sphere representing the Earth. As we watched the great hollow globe of the Unisphere being constructed, with the Earth overlaid on the lines of latitude and longitude, it pleased our symbolizing mind to perceive that, in the midst of New York, there was being constructed an image of the world as a hollow illusion.[21]

In the streets of New York, Paris and London, there was a feeling of sexual liberation in the air, and we recalled Isherwood's writings about his experience of pre-War Berlin: he said that he could tell from the alert glances of the girls in the streets of Berlin that a war was soon to come.

Our new Master soon proved to be entirely different from the one we had worked under in Paris and Siena. He was plump, jolly and expansive in his gestures: he sported a carefully cultivated goatee beard. The flamboyance in his manner suggested a past connection with the theatre, and because his eyes were creased with laughter lines, he gave the impression of being in a state of constant happiness. One of his characteristic gestures seemed designed to emphasize his bubbling humour: he would rest his thumb upon his chin, and flick his index finger rapidly over his lower lip. One had the feeling that he was pulling his face to mimic the laughter that was constantly welling up inside.

Our new Master was an intellectual, in the best sense of the word. He was an established and respected scholar in his own right – an author in a specialist area of history – working like so many esotericists under a pseudonym.[22] He was especially interested in the Spiritual implications of creative activity, and – perhaps because of this interest – was an established Goethean scholar.

The house in which we worked was also very different from the ones in France and Italy. We were never clear whether our Master rented the part of the house in which he lived, but we would gather in a large studio, which had galleries running alongside one part of the room, leaving one with the uneasy impression that we were waiting for musicians to materialize and play. The studio was in West 57th Street, and it was rumoured that it had once belonged to the American artist, Hassam, who painted canvases something in the manner of the French impressionist, Monet.[23]

We were very impressed by the Hassam canvases we saw in galleries.[24] His pictures were by no means servile copies of Monet, but had a lyrical quality of their own, and an underlying structure which seemed worthy more of Cézanne than Monet.[25] In researching Hassam, we began to realize just how many studios there had been in West 57th Street, which in the 1890s had housed many of the rich and famous: perhaps the tradition which linked Hassam with the studio might have been groundless.[26] Still it had been an artist's studio, and there was a distinct feeling of creativity and joy in the atmosphere, which corresponded closely with the exuberant style of our new Teacher. It seemed entirely fitting that a Teacher who was so thoroughly creative in attitude and manner should surround himself with a creative-seeming environment, steeped in cultural history.

The curious, yet entirely practical, lore of homoeopathy had mingled strangely with demon-lore in one response our new Teacher gave to a question about the Lower Way, sometimes mistakenly called the Forbidden Way, or (more correctly) the *Way of Set*. In the later Egyptian hermetic tradition, Set was lord of the powers of evil, and the Way of Set was that forbidden to all those who loved and followed the Light.

It took only a few weeks – and a deep Spiritual experience – for us to understand why our Master had elected to bring together the two quite different ideas of homoeopathy and the demons. When we did finally understand his words, we had yet another confirmation of just how profound was his perception of the needs of his pupils.

One of the group had asked a question about the initiatory Way of Set. This question had been sparked off by a startling piece of information that Ron Hubbard, the founder of Scientology, had been involved in a black-magical practice linked with the so-called 'Great Beast', Aleister Crowley.[27] The questioner, who was as new to the group as we were, had expressed some surprise that individuals should seek a Way of Darkness in the face of the evidence that the Ways of Light were not only less dangerous, but primal in initiation.

Our Master seemed to agree with this.

'It is a strange truth that in various parts of the world – but especially in Europe and North America, where the pressures on the growing Spiritual life of human beings are at their most intense – groups of people seek into the hidden demonic realms for answers to their soul questions.

'The Way of Darkness is deeply entrenched in the Western world, and many of its beliefs have become part and parcel of our civilization. The reasons for this are extremely complex. However, it is perhaps sufficient for me to say that one cannot be involved on the Path for very long without realizing that everything in the world must have its shadow-form. This is because the world is in balance, and the upper reflects the lower. Even our own initiatory method must have its dark counterpart, somewhere in the world. That there should be humans given over to the service of darkness is inevitable, simply because some elect to work with Light.

'The shadow-form of the true initiation schools is found in the various ways of *Set*. You probably know that one may trace all the initiation wisdom of Europe back to Egypt, and back to the archetypal written initiation documents of hermeticism,[28] or even to the so-called *Book of the Dead*. Just so, one may trace a parallel Egyptian school, which concerns itself with the dark side of the Spiritual world: in modern times this is called the Way of Set.'

He looked directly ahead, at one of the group.

'John, you have a question?'

'Yes, sir. How was it possible for a man of such intelligence and insight as Aleister Crowley to involve himself in practices which were ultimately of no evolutionary value to the world?'

'We should not under-estimate his intelligence, learning or Spiritual insights, but in essence, Crowley lacked the moral fibre necessary for a correct Spiritual development. Crowley's Ego was overbalanced – possibly due to a misuse of drugs – and he did the one thing which is forbidden any real magus – he manipulated people. In the White Schools it is utterly forbidden for a Teacher or an initiate of any grade to manipulate another human. As it happens, Crowley *did* believe that his own ideas would contribute to the evolution of the world. He just happened to be wrong. He did not know enough.[29]

'Aleister Crowley, for all his faults, was enormously learned in arcane literature. In some arcane circles, this kind of learning is called "head knowledge", because it is not brought into the other parts of the human being, and does not enter into that person's moral life.

'An example of this clever head knowledge may be seen in his choice of the name *Lam* which Crowley used of the so-called extraterrestrial being he encountered. The portrait which Crowley drew of this creature is well known, for it formed the frontispiece for one of his own works.[30]

'*Lam* is a curious name. Why did Crowley give this creature the name *Lam*? we might ask. Being an esotericist, Crowley realized that for a word to take Spiritual root in a culture, it would be necessary to unite within it both the skies and the Earth. After all, this is precisely what happens when a farmer plants seeds – in former times, it was recognized that farmers had to take into account far more than merely the seasons; one had to take into account the phases of the Moon, and even the constellations.

'To create this powerful union in his seed-word, Crowley adopted an Arabic letter which, according to certain arcane Arabic literature, united the Heavens with the Earth. This letter, *Lam*, is the fifth in an Arabic amuletic charm, based on the opening of the *Koran*, called the *Basmallah*.[31] Part of the overall significance of this choice is that the *Basmallah* is used, either as a spoken phrase, or as a written charm, to hold back the 19 guardians of Hell.[32] *Lam* is one of those "words of power" which are so highly respected by magicians, and which may be used by them to great effect.

'Crowley was aware of the need to choose a name which was linked both with the stars and with the Earth. Yet he also sought a formula – a Spiritual mechanism – which would keep back demons. This is of profound interest to us. Almost all black magical practices – when handled by the dark Adepts – attempt to make use of this triadic power. In effect, the name *Lam* – with its three European letters – is a triple invocation. As with the spells in the Egyptian *Book of the Dead*, it attempts to present a formula for restraining a certain class of demonic guardians, in order to allow the soul to pass through the secret passageways which run between the stars and the Earth.

'The word *Lam* appears to have been constructed by Crowley to serve exclusively the egotistical principles – self-serving principles – which lie at the root of black magic. This contrasts with the rituals of the Egyptian book, which is designed exclusively to serve the sacred purposes of initiation [plate 4].

'For all its unfortunate title, the collection of papyri which make up the so-called *Book of the Dead* are all concerned with life: the titles given to these documents by the ancient Egyptians all pointed to the initiatory ascent into Light. Indeed, one remarkable modern scholar has pointed out recently that the title used by the Egyptian scribes for their collection of initiation documents is *The Book of the Coming Forth by Day*.[33] Of course, in those days, books were rarely given titles, but this name does appear in a sort of colophon in the papyri.

'The Light initiation practices of ancient Egypt were balanced by a number of Dark initiation practices. These were linked with *Set*, the brother-husband of Nephthys. In Egyptian mythology, Set is said to have ruled over Upper Egypt, while his brother Horus ruled over Lower Egypt. In this archetypal rulership, we see the emergent dualism which coloured Egyptian initiation practices, and which (as a consequence) colours all modern Western esotericism. Among the many associations which will be of immediate interest to the student of esotericism is the fact that Set ruled over the circumpolar stars, and that he had a *pig* as his totem. There is a deep esoteric reason why the pig – itself regarded as a lunar creature – should also be linked with the pole stars.[34]

'*Set* is another word rendered in English as a three-letter word of power: it is the name of the representative of the Way of the Shadows. In Europe, and in the United States, there are still men and women of considerable learning and accomplishment who involve themselves in service of the rites of Set. There have always been such Schools, and all too often they are organized by individuals who are far from being harmoniously developed within themselves. All too often, such individuals, for all they are very clever, are morally deficient.'

He paused, and looked around the group, perhaps to indicate a slight change of direction.

'A few moments ago, I mentioned the connection between Set and the pig totem. One might imagine that this connection would explain why some religious sects regard the pig as being unclean. However, it is likely that the reasons why some groups looked askance at the pig were more than totemistic, and were connected with the fact that the pig is one of the few animals that *sweats*. We must bear in mind that the water which pigs sweat is a highly valuable commodity in the desert. It was probably bad economy to keep and breed animals which so freely used up the life-preserving water, so scarce in the desert. Most of the religious sects which regard the pig as being unclean originated in the desert.

'However, the issue is far deeper than mere economics. Indeed, it may even be this characteristic of the pig – the fact that it exudes water through its skin, as humans do – that led to the ancient link between *Set* and the pig. In the Egyptian mythology, the four sons of Horus (the god of Light) were linked with the mysteries of the canopic jars. These were four jars in which the organs of the dead were kept, after the body had been preserved and bound, according to the rites of mummification.[35] Now, the Egyptian initiates recognized that the Earthly had to have a stellar counterpart. The four gods of the canopic jars – that is to say, the stellar equivalents of the canopic jars – were located in the *Chariot of the Gods*, an Egyptian stellar constellation, to guard over the circumpolar stars which belonged to Set.[36] These four stars enclosed in the starry skies the stellar Set, in much the same way as the four canopic jars enclosed the inner organs of the deceased. The four guardian canopics, and the four guardian stars, are examples not merely of the way the initiation Schools would seek to reflect the Earthly and the cosmic in a single symbol. They are examples also of the interiorized and the exteriorized, of the Way In and the Way Out being the same – of breathing in being an essential part of breathing out, and so on. As you see, there are deep esoteric teachings in these alignments.

'Now, already you are all aware of the arcane teaching which insists that the inner must become the outer, the outer the inner. This arcane law lies at the basis of the mysteries of reincarnation, and of the Egyptian rites of mummification – but this need not concern us here. What is important within our theme is that the pig of *Set* is defined in terms of what it exudes – the precious water.

'In contrast, the Horus guardians are defined in terms of what they enclose – the organs. The pig of Set is a permanent transmitter of liquid from the inner organs to the outer world. The canopic guardians are permanent excluders, which prevent the organs from ever reaching out into the outer world. The symbolism of this is profound, and takes on many ramifications in Egyptian mythology and its occult dependencies.

'You may have heard that certain followers of Set were called the Red-eyed Ones. The Typhonians, or followers of Set, were said to be recognized by the redness of their eyes. Here, in this name, we have an example of exteriorization. The red of the body organs within the canopic jars may be seen as exuding from the eyes of the followers of Set. The canopic jars – the retainers of dead organs – were, so to speak, visualized as leaking. There are profound arcane truths to be perceived in this lore, which links the stars with both life and death.'

There was a silence, as our Master gathered his thoughts.

'But, to return to the original question, which was about why certain people seek to make contact with the demons. Those who seek to serve the demons are always morally deficient. Of course, even the White Schools investigated demonic powers, but the ones who directed such research were always initiates of a very high order, who knew what they were doing. In my opinion, Crowley did not know what he was doing.[37] The White Schools did at times use the Dark powers. They knew that without the Dark powers, there could be no Light. Dark and Light are interdependent. Evolution of mankind can only proceed into light if some humans fall back into darkness. You cannot have the Way Up without the Way Down. Had there been no White Schools that were prepared to make use of the demons, and the realm of Darkness, then there would have been no oracles such as the one Homer writes about on the Acheron [plate 21].[38]

'Besides serving as a divinatory centre for the public, such oracles were always involved with Schooling for initiation. However, their prime purpose in those days was not to afford contact between the demons and the profane. It was recognized that anyone who sought such contact would have to be specially prepared and protected. This wisdom appears to have been lost in many arcane circles, today, which is why Spiritualism has become such a dangerous undertaking.

'The rapid Way Down is more unsure, more beset with dangers, than the slow Way Up. Ask yourself, Why was the gate to Hell guarded by a dog? This was three-headed Cerberus, the dark shadow image of man, who, in his Spiritual being, is also triple. Man is body, soul and spirit, while the Hades dog is three-headed, with the tail of that serpent which led to Man's fall into matter [see next page].[39] It is no accident that the snake-tail hangs downwards, pointing always to the centre of the Earth. It is no accident that the psychopomp who guides the newly dead souls to Hell is often portrayed as being dog-headed. This dog-headed dark form is that of the Egyptian god Thoth, the Thrice-greatest, the guardian

Hercules restraining the three-headed dog guardian at the gates of Hades.
Woodengraving from F. Creuzer, Symbolik und Mythologie der Alten Voelker, *1819.*

of all initiation wisdom. The true seeker after knowledge will have no dealings with the three-headed dog which guards the dark world.

'Thoth was often portrayed in the Egyptian initiation documents as ape-headed [opposite]. Because he was the greatest of the gods in ancient magic, he suffered greatly at the hands of the early Christians. This explains why the monkey, derived from his image, was adopted as a demon in the very early days of Christianity.[40] There is a need to redeem the monkey which dwells within each of us, by turning it back into the god of wisdom. This redemption is not possible for one who continues to pander to, or feed, the monkey. The Way Down is not the same as the Way Up. Like mind-changing drug-taking, the Way Down is forbidden in the White Schools, for it can be fatal, and is almost always destructive.'

'Well, as I've told you before, any illegal entry into the Spiritual world may prove fatal. One cannot coerce the Spiritual: if one attempts to enter into the Light without preparation, one always faces the trials and dangers of Darkness. At the very least, an enforced entry into initiation will drive the illegal entrant insane. An intense preparation for such entry is required, and special organs must be developed, to pierce with safety the veil which separates the material from the Spiritual. There are certain

190

*Thoth as a monkey-god (baboon-god) presenting the remade Eye of the Moon
in the guise of the ibis- headed god of Hemopolis.*

demons that attempt to persuade Man otherwise – seek to induce him to
pass through the veil unprepared. *When this happens, the unprepared soul
cannot wholly return.* More and more, we will see the social fabric of the
world torn by souls who have entered the lower levels of the Astral Plane
by means of drugs, and have found they cannot properly return. This is
truly a Hell on Earth for such people, for they belong neither to this
world, nor to the other. With such a danger, why try, when there are
other ways – legitimate ways?'

Our Master had forbidden any of us to have any contact with drugs, on
threat of expulsion from the circle. He was not prepared to discuss the
reasons for his embargo, other than to say that drug abuse can damage the
Spiritual development for several lifetimes.

'Even the weaker narcotics and drugs in plants can have a deleterious
effect on the human soul and spirit: they are the seeds of Set – food for
the monkey-demon. Consider the poisonous plant Monkshood. One who
takes such a plant begins to fear the future, to fear death. At the same
time, they become convinced that they can predict the day – usually not
too far in the future – when they will die. However, as the wiccan
grimoires – the witchcraft notebooks – will tell you about Monkshood, a
usual consequence of taking the drug is that one becomes clairvoyant.
With the aid of this poison, one begins to live in the Spiritual world
before one is prepared for such a highly charged habitation. Such a
successful attempt to insert onself into a domain for which there has been
no special training means that the relationship with the physical plane is
loosened. Even if the person survives, it is often the case that the Spiritual
faculties are so weakened that the victim thinks that everything is a
dream. This again is the stamp of the higher world, for in truth – in

191

comparison with the intense richness of the higher realm – this ordinary world is something of a dream. If the poison is taken to excess, death sets in. It is a most intolerable death, and since it is self-administered, the pain does not end after the body has been left behind. The clairvoyancy which precedes such a death is merely a sign that the Spirit is already separating from the physical, and entering the Astral Plane. It is a characteristic of Monkshood that it gives one the impression of being released from the body, to a point where one may believe one has the ability to fly.

'The taking of the poison Monkshood is an example of one illegitimate way into the Spiritual world: however, if the entry is complete, and the entrant is not an initiate, then there is no return. This is one reason – one reason among many – why the Schools keep their secrets from the common herd. You can enter the Spiritual world in a split second, if you want. The problem is always that of finding a way back. Just so, you can enter the world of the demons, if you are not too worried about returning to the Earth. But' – he grimaced – 'I am reasonably confident that you would want to come back pretty quickly, if you caught sight of the demons.'

He paused, and perhaps because he was thinking of the dog which follows the Fool around in the Tarot card, he nodded towards us.

'Have you ever been attacked by a wild animal?' He must have known what our answer would be.

'A dog,' we replied, truthfully, 'a mad dog.'

'Yes, a savage dog can be frightening, yet a demon has a hundred times the savagery of a dog: it is without mercy, and has no fear of humans. So far as demons are concerned, humans are helpless victims, nothing more. I tell you, the most terrible pictures which have been given in the old grimoires are nothing – pale imitations – of the grotesque power and appearances of the demons. Imagine being in the grip of an entity which has no mercy, no feeling for the suffering of another.

'In fact, the merciless quality of the demons may be felt on the Earth plane, for this demonic power lies just beyond the threshold, in what the scientists might call the submolecular world, or sub-atomic. This is really the realm of the demons. What I am saying here has nothing to do with the *size* of demons, you understand. The *size* of demons is irrelevant: my point is merely that demons live beyond the threshold of our own familiar world. But, remember – the scientists know nothing about the lower worlds. They do not know that the lower world is just as much alive as the upper. What did Anthony Rusca say, "not so much as an hair's-breadth empty of demons in heaven, Earth, or waters, above or under the Earth".'[41]

It was within a few weeks of starting work with our new Master that he took us to a higher level of development by means of a single word. The word had a connotation of demonism about it, and, when we considered its effects later, we saw that its introduction into our psyche was akin to the power of a homoeopathic remedy of a millionth potency.

At the time, the whole group of students had gone to stay in a large country house, to the north of New York. Each month our Master would arrange a long weekend there, when we would each be assigned particular – and often peculiar – tasks. We had to meditate on stones or plants, and then speak of our observations to the assembled circle, later in the same evening, or dig in the garden, or general labouring. Whatever the task, the Master estimated more highly the attention we put into such activities than the end results. He insisted that creative activity was its own reward – while one may have useful consequences to creative work (such as a painting, a piece of music, poetry, or a beautiful garden), this 'result' was irrelevant: 'Creative activity is not only its own reward – it is also a sacrifice. You must learn not to expect anything beyond the joy of creativity, of the expenditure of creative energy.'[42]

On this particular occasion, we had spent the entire day clearing brambles from an old vegetable patch, with a view to planting potatoes, but, now that the sun had set, we were relaxing.

Our Master was standing in the kitchen, supervising the cooks (he was an excellent cook himself). Two rooms led off the kitchen. In one room, some of the other students were talking, their voices counterpointed against the strains of the finale of Alban Berg's arcane *Lyric Suite*, which was playing in the other room.[43]

As we walked past him, carrying logs for the fire, he glanced up and, seeing there was no one else within earshot, asked almost casually: 'What do you know of *Sassuwunnu*?'[44]

We had never heard the word before, yet the effect of its sound on our psyche was explosive. The remarkable thing is that, while we were not familiar with the word, we knew immediately what it meant. There was a rush of light within our being, and it was as though the outer world suddenly turned magenta, as if there had been a reversal from light to dark, and we were, for a millisecond, looking at a photographic negative. Another hue – perhaps one should say *light* – seemed to flash upwards from our middle region; yet, in a strange way it seemed to bypass our head. Our thinking was extremely calm – in total contrast to our emotional world, which was supercharged with excitement. It was our first experience of separation between the three coterminous activities in man, wherein the intellectual, the emotional and the visceral life of Will are clearly distinguished. The word had both thrown us and reintegrated us, within the instant.

We knew – how, we cannot say – that the word was of Mesopotamian origin, from a very remote period. Although we had never heard the word before (at least, in this lifetime, and perhaps for many lifetimes) we knew what it pertained to, and that it was vastly evil. The word had seemed to hit us, or resonate, in the upper part of the rib-cage, below the clavicals. We record this without, as yet, having found any explanation for this physiological fact.

The word evoked distinct pictures, or images that were somehow dark, redolent of cruelty, yet traces of highly personal memories. They seemed like images garnered from a former lifetime, flooding in from a very remote past. It is as though they had been ghosts – the *preta*, or hungry ghosts, of the Oriental world – which, until now, we had been unprepared to confront.[45]

The word stayed with us as a kind of inner reverberation. We must have made some response to our Master, and we must have gone about our business as before. This was surely the case, for, after we had tossed the logs on the fire, we went into the adjoining room to turn over the reel on which Berg's *Lyric Suite* was playing. We adjusted the dials of the tape machine, and even had a conversation with someone shortly afterwards. Yet, within that millisecond, something within us had changed. The word took us into an altogether different realm of Spiritual exploration and insight.

Even as we tossed the beech logs on to the fire, we knew that this was a significant act. We knew that every action – even the most casual-seeming – was redolent with importance. 'As something rises, so must something fall,' our Master would say from time to time, and here we were allowing the black-edged detritus of a once-living tree to fall on flames which immediately leapt upwards in a pyrotechnic display of white and red. *Every detail seemed important.* In the ring patterns of the sawn logs were the concentric records of annual weather and sun-spots, drawn by unknown Etheric powers and elemental agonies: it was an arboreal calendar of solar motions which had occurred long before we had been born. We were burning the past, as though in a sacrificial gesture. The beech tree, like all nature, had been given its form and growth by the Moon, its conceptual energy by the Sun. Now its form would be dissolved into black smoke, while its energy would be turned back into a weak imitation of that Spiritual heat whence it came. These realizations were instantaneous and had the feeling of truth: overlaying them was the assured knowledge that these logs were part of oneself, and that nothing could ever be sacrificed, for, as the Sanskrit texts insist, there is no giver, and nothing given.

We knew instinctively that the word had started us on a new journey. Perhaps insights gathered in a previous incarnation were being made available to us. One thing was clear, as the experience began to recede – that it was infinitely better to carry these verbal 'ghosts' in our consciousness than to allow them to work their darkness in the sub-conscious. Now our consciousness could burn them up with Spiritual activity, just as the flames had burned that clog calendar of past years. The events of Siena seemed remote, and we knew that we would not be troubled further by those ghosts.

As so often happens when a person moves to a higher level, and is offered the potential of further development, the demonic forces began to manifest themselves on the Astral Plane. In esotericism, this is recognized as the natural consequence of the *fission* which takes place at each stage of development.[46] This notion of the higher light trampling down the darker lunar element is often expressed in alchemical imagery as the image of a woman standing upon the Moon.

Alchemical image of the virginal Queen standing upon the lunar crescent. Detail from a late 16th century reworking of the 1550 edition of Rosarium Philosophorum.

This unwanted demonic activity which began afterwards to colour our soul life was deeply frightening, and the attendant experiences do not form a particularly savoury part of our story. It is perhaps sufficient to say that the attacks of these entities on the lower levels of the Astral became so savage that we felt inadequate to deal with them, and called on Christ to help us in His role as spiritual guide.[47] We scarcely need record that the response was both immediate and totally effective.

After the single word *Sassuwunnu* had changed our Spiritual direction, we found that our line of thinking had altered. For reasons which were not altogether clear to us, we were reluctant to ask questions of our Master when we all gathered together for discussions. It is as though we had been thrown upon our Self, and we felt that our inner struggle could be dealt with only through personal meditation, rather than through listening to the words of another, however wise these might be.

However, in addition to the changes brought about through that single word, there were also other changes in our questions. We became fascinated by the nature of the Moon, and with the other female planet, Venus. It was as though our attention had been drawn to the feminine side of Darkness and Light, as represented in the purgatorial side of the Moon, and the burning light of Venus. Our questions led our Master to some fascinating and unexpected observations about the lunar connections in ancient esoteric lore, and it was not surprising that the few questions we did put to our Master at that time concerned these planets.

'Do you know what the *third-day pig* is?' he asked in response to a question I had put to him about the Moon. Although our Master was looking directly at us, everyone shook their heads, as though he had directed the question to each of us personally. Perhaps the question had been rhetorical, for he continued almost immediately. 'The *three-day pig* is a phrase from the ancient Mysteries. Prior to the initiation held during the Greater Mysteries of the Boedromion at Eleusis, in Greece, there was what the Greeks called the *Halade Mystai*.[48] Early in the morning, the candidates for initiation would make their way to the sea, carrying young pigs, which they would wash and then sacrifice. The usual – we might even say the exoteric – explanation for this sacrifice is that they considered the blood of the pig to be especially pure, and much appreciated by the gods of the Underworld. They buried the killed pigs deep in the Earth, after the blood and slaughtered bodies had been dedicated to these infernal gods. Because the sacrifice was held on the third day of the Greater Mystery, such a creature was called the third-day pig.'

He raised his eyebrows, and smiled. 'Now, as with all Mysteries of initiation, the term is not quite correct – it is meant to hide something. It was not a third-day pig, but a two-and-a-half-day pig, as the sacrifices always took place in the morning. The fact that the rites were conducted near the sea should lend a clue to one aspect of this arcane symbolism, for the two-and-a-half day period is a lunar period. In two and a half days, the Moon completely traverses one sign of the zodiac: the period, cosmically speaking, is a 12th part of the month. Now, perhaps, you will begin to see something of the deeper significance of the third-day pig?'

Perhaps once again the question had been rhetorical. At all events, there was no sound from the circle.

'In a sense, the third-day pig is humanity – the liquid sweat of the Earth. Humanity is in thrall to the Moon – mankind is subject to the two-and-a-half-day rhythm, and to all other lunar periodicities.[49] In another sense, the third-day pig is the animal of *Set*, the reject darker side of Mankind – that *lucifuge* side, which does not strive towards the light.

'This truth is recognized both in the overt symbolism of the pig sacrifice, and in its deeper arcane implications. The initiation centres have always recognized that Mankind is in thrall to the Moon – that ordinary men and women are sleeping under the influence of the lunar powers. This is sometimes symbolized through the typical lunar symbols of the serpent – the Egyptian snake, *Apep* (plate 22), or the alchemical serpent, wrapped around the human form. It is usually portrayed as possessor of the spine of man or woman (see figure on page 105), yet which belongs to the Moon. This may account for the fact that serpents entwine in the hair of the Moon-goddess Hecate: one of the most widespread of beliefs is that certain snakes are the dead, returned to the Earth Plane. The snakes in the hair of Hecate are a sign of the extent to which the serpent still whispers imaginative words into the thinking of Mankind. These imaginative words are pictures derived from the Moon, the realm of imagination.

'In Greek mythology, we learn that Endymion – the archetypal human – is put into a hypnotic sleep by Selene, the Moon-goddess, in order that she can work her sexual will upon him. This story should remind us that, in esotericism, this physical death is equated to the Spiritual death of initiation – to that time when one is transposed to a Higher Realm of being. This "death" is the sacrifice which is no sacrifice. This, of course, is the mystical death.

'The symbolism of the three-day pig must now be evident. The creature is a surrogate for a sacrifice which is no sacrifice, as the loss is of no value in the face of that gained. In the remarkable alchemical scroll drawn up by the English alchemist George Ripley[50] in the 16th century, there is a reference to this initiation in the context of the sacred *Hermes Bird*[51] and the lunar dragon,[52] wherein he describes the Philosopher's Stone as that which has the power "to quicken the dead". This stone imparts the death of initiation, which is not death. He that is touched by it both dies and is quickened.

'Perhaps this explains why the highest initiation chamber in the Great Pyramid of Cheops has within it an open tomb, a lidless sarcophagus. In Greek, the original "sarcophagus" was a "flesh-eater" – the stone from which it was made was said to have such a caustic property that it would devour the flesh within 40 days. With the body eaten away, the Spirit was free to live again. It is the same symbol of regeneration as we see in the Christian Resurrection story of the cave, or burial chamber, visited by the three women – for this was an open tomb.[53] The open tomb was an initiation chamber, where the body could be placed while the priests performed initiation ceremonies on the Spirit (plate 4).

'What happens to our higher principle at this fission of porcine sacrifice is of direct account in the symbolism of the three-day pig. Just as in a sacrifice involving a burnt offering, where the flames go upwards, and the carbonized remains go downwards, so the sacrifice of the third-day pig is a fission of separation. Note this word, *fission*. One cannot go far in the hermetic studies without having formed a good idea of what Spiritual fission implies. In the Great Pyramid, one passageway leads downwards, towards the bowels of the Earth, the passage being cut into the living rock, and ending in the Well of Ordeals. Half-way down this passageway, another rises steeply upwards, towards the chambers of initiation, and ultimately to the lidless sarcophagus, which some have called the Open Tomb.

'On one level, then, the pig is symbol of the lower nature, which must be buried – or, more accurately, placed into the hands of the infernal hordes, to which it rightly belongs. Meanwhile, the initiated Spirit rises upwards on the *scalae* of perfection.[54] As you know, only the initiates sacrifice at the *Helade Mystai*, so we may presume that, at the symbolical death, it is only the lower part of the "pig" – the body and the blood – which is rendered unto the lower world. The higher world carries the Spirit to a higher realm, in the wonder of initiation. After the pig sacrifice, the neophytes return to the Telesterion at Eleusis, and continue with their inititation.

'You see, the three-day pig is a symbol of this rejected part, of the dark part pushed downwards after the separation which is the immediate consequence of initiation.'

'Why,' asked one of the young women in our circle, 'is the emphasis given to the three days? Surely, it is just another sacrifice, such as was common in pre–Christian rites?'

'You will find, as your studies progress, that the change from two and a half to three is no mere obfuscation, for the number three has deep meaning in relation to Spiritual fission.[55] The number three takes a great deal of its numerological significance from the idea of fission. You will recall that one of the inscriptions on the Temple of Apollo at Delphi was "Number is the law of the Cosmos". The number three represents the idea of fusion, wisdom, love and Spiritual expression. However, when you consider these things, remember that the three-day pig is really a two-and-a-half-day pig – it requires something else, something expressed only in the Mysteries concerning which we cannot speak openly – to bring it to the *completion* of three. The lunar number, of two and a half, is out of balance, whereas the three is balanced – one on either side of the one: 1 + 1 + 1. Given the lunar connection with this number, it is perhaps not surprising that the form for three may also be stripped down to a sigil which exhibits three points, conjoining two lunar crescents: ◡◡. Of course, these last two are linear balances, while the symbol for Libra is a vertical balance of three: ♎. The upper curvature represent the Sun, the lower rectilinear the Earth. The third element is the space between them. This arrangement, however, is vertical balance, relating the higher to the lower.

'This perfect balance of Libra is distinct from the lunar two-and-a-half-day period which marks out the "incomplete" human who is still subjected to the Moon. This is the still-sleeping human. Just as the three is a perfect balance, the three-day period is that of the initiate, who has sloughed off the pig: this is the complete man or woman, no longer sleeping, and no longer subjected to the imperative of the lunar periodicity. In a sense, it is the number of Resurrection, expressed in the Three Years of Christ's ministry, or the Three Days of Golgotha.

'Now you will see something of the extent to which the alchemical images which portray a woman standing on a lunar crescent (see figure on page 195) are intended to illustrate initiation processes. The woman, or soul, has risen to a point where she may stand in triumph over the two-and-a-half-day pig! Her balance on that unstable crescent is a sign that she has attained to the level of the three.'

He nodded to the most beautiful girl in the circle.'

'Caroline, you may not be aware of this, but your own name begins with the letter associated with the balance of the number three. Balance is a grace of spirit. This is why the horizon stone played such an important part in the Egyptian mysteries. The hieroglyphic depicts the meeting of Sun and Earth.'

He leaned forward, and sketched a diagram on the board.

'This symbol is the only hieroglyphic on the outer wall of the Great Pyramid. It is a primal power-sound. The name given to the pyramid was *Akhet Khufu*, which meant "horizon of Khufu" – this latter term was misunderstood by later Egyptologists, who turned it into the name Cheops. This pregnant symbol is located above the passageway which pierces into the rock foundations of the vast structure: ⌣ .'

'As a symbol, it survived into modern times. As you will have guessed, the horizon hieroglyphic is the source of our modern symbol for Libra, the cosmic balance, which now consists of three elements: ⌣ .'

When he had drawn the sigil, he ran the back of his pencil through the curvature of space which separated the solar disc from the horizon of Earth. 'The invisible space is just as important as the Sun and Earth. Do you see how even the most simple-seeming of the arcane symbols are steeped in hermetic antiquity?'

He laughed to himself, and, with his left hand resting against his beard, he flicked at his lower lip in some amusement. Perhaps he had realized that he was being carried by his own thoughts in a direction he had no wish to explore. He returned to his main theme. 'We should all look into the numerological significance of our names. Caroline, the C form we now use is the rounding of the Greek *gamma*, which is linked with the number three.'[56]

He cut the simple rectilinear form of the *gamma* in the air with his finger.

'Four *gammas* arranged in a circle with a communal centre make the swastika, the solar symbol. Numerologically, these four gammas total twelve, and echo the path of the Sun against the zodiac belt:

As a consequence, we recognize the C-form as being cut from the swastika, severed as it were from the Sun. On a far deeper level, the swastika is also a symbol of reincarnation, for the three and the one combine from lifetime to lifetime.[57] The important thing is that this solar number, because it is made up of multiples of three, is linked with higher initiation. The ordinary man and woman is linked only with the lower lunar number of two and a half, which cannot be used to construct a swastika.

'In the Buddhist symbolism, the swastika is usually in mirror-image, to suggest a movement against the Sun. This reversal is typical of a symbol pertaining to the Astral realm. However, if we return to the European swastika, we realize that a parallel level of symbolism is that the *gamma* was also a symbol for *Gaea*, the Earth goddess. Hence, the C is also cut from the Earth: this reflects what was once a historical cosmic reality, when the Moon was cut from the Earth.

'One can learn a great deal from meditating on the present alphabet, and its relationship to the ancient forms. The Greek *gamma* is an inner sacred sound – this is why the sound itself cuts. As you make the sound, you can feel the cut in your throat. The sound cuts the inner from the outer. There is magic power in such sounds: with sound alone it would be possible to destroy or create.'

He made another drawing in the air – an outlined *gamma*: $\sqrt{ }$. 'The Masonic 'square' is really a form of the *gamma* with all its numerological and arcane associations, which may be traced back to the Egyptian mysteries, where it is so holy that it is represented hieroglyphically as a throne. It is with the aid of the inner *gamma* that we discover our inner rectitude – that we remain square to the inner and outer worlds.[58] We do not want to degenerate into the arcane weaving which is now so popular in certain occult circles, but such associations are of great importance when we seek to reach into the minds of the ancients. You see, it is totally erroneous to believe that the ancients thought in the way we do. They were much more clever with their cosmic associations than we are, but this is because their thinking was more subtle, less weighted down by minerality. They could see Spiritual beings for which we now merely have the half-forgotten names. Imagine discussing with one of your companions whether a cabbage exists or not – for the ancients, this would be much the same as discussing whether the nine ranks of angels exist, or whether there were 42 inner judges. How can you argue about the existence of something you can perceive?

'Well, perhaps now you can see the link between the three-day pig and the Moon? On the lowest level of symbolism, the letter C is itself a crescent, the eternal symbol of the Moon. The form of the *gamma* is made from the junction of an horizon line with a vertical – the first pertains to the Earth, the other to the Spirit. This is a letter of fission, cutting between matter and Spirit. Just so does the Moon operate: yet this is the redeemed lunar quality, because it is a three: it is complete, and in harmonic balance.'

There was a long silence.

'But the *pig*. Let us glance once more at the symbolism of the famous three-day pig. We are the pig, awaiting sacrifice. We are in thrall to the Moon: we are all sleeping Endymions, who must render to the Moon that which bears the imprint of the Moon. Let us presume that the sacrifice of the three-day pig is symbolical of the *three days* . . .' – he emphasized the words to show that they had a much deeper meaning than might be at first apparent – '. . . that we spend in the sphere of the Moon after our death.[59] As you know, in traditional Christianity, this period is called Purgatory. In esotericism, it has other names, with which you will all be familiar. The three-day pig is a *symbol'* – he emphasized the word – 'of this period we must spend in Purgatory.

'If you reflect upon it, you will see that it is not a far-fetched symbolism. The pig, through its association with *Set*, is a creature of the Moon, and the period in Purgatory is a "blood sacrifice" in the sense that during that experience the sins of the blood – one might say the sweat of our blood sins – are washed away. In Purgatory, at great cost to ourselves, we sacrifice our sins. These entities – our sins – are devoured by the demons in what might be regarded as a blood-lust. We have clung to our sins throughout our lifetime, and letting them go is no easy matter: they must be *torn* away from us.

'Purgatory is a sort of cosmic clearing house – even a place of enforced learning – where the entities and dispositions born of sin find fulfilment and regeneration. Without the existence of such a cleansing house, the Spiritual atmosphere of the Earth would have been completely poisoned long ago.

'The skull-face of the Moon, glaring down with cratered eyes at the world, is a perpetual memorial to the inexorable consequences of human sin. It would be possible to point to vast documentary sources for this belief that the Moon is the cosmic centre of purgatory – it is indeed encapsulated in very many symbols in Christian doctrine and symbolism. On what may be the most obvious level, the very idea that demons have horns is probably a throw-back to the idea of the crescent of the Moon, their natural homeland: they are, so to speak, branded with the *C* of the crescent.

'You were quite right, Mark . . .' – much to our chagrin, he turned to us, making public private conversations we had had with him – '. . . to link the Moon with demonic assault, and with the dark realm of seances and atavistic clairvoyancy. The demonic beings love the dark. While it is true that the seance rooms are kept dark to enable amateur conjurors to perform without detection, it is also true that those Spiritual beings who work evil through such seances love the dark. They are *lucifuges*.[60] Just as they cannot understand the need for light, so they cannot understand human love.

'The ancients used darkness, not to contact the demons, but to contact the Higher Beings. One reason why the so-called air-shafts in the Great Pyramid are directed towards specific stars is to allow these stellar influences to pierce into the darkness where the initiations took place.[61]

'The ancients built their stone circles to enable them to use darkness for specific purposes. They knew that during an eclipse, when the Moon is thrown into darkness, the effect of the Moon is, to some extent, weakened. At such times, certain diabolical and evil influences which have been built up in the aura of the Earth can escape. It is as though a safety valve has been opened in the skies, pouring into the cosmos down the dark tunnel of the Black Moon, which hangs in the shadow of the Earth. This Black Moon – the Moon of snake-infested Hecate in the ancient mythology – is quite different from the Lighted Moon. In some of the ancient centres this Black Moon was even given a different name.[62]

'The Lighted Moon is, to some extent, Spiritually warmed by the Sun. One has to be attuned to cosmic realities to feel the difference between the Dark Moon and the full Moon. When the Sun is eclipsed by the Dark Moon, then it is not unusual for birds to drop from the skies in fear.[63] Great wisdom is shown in such fear. You must all try to experience an eclipse – solar or lunar – to catch a feeling of this cosmic reality. There is a frisson in the air, quite unlike anything which can be felt under normal circumstances. The primaeval terror of the Moon among the ancients was not entirely unrealistic: in those days, there was a different consciousness which allowed men to perceive cosmic realities that are now hidden from us. You will never understand why the ancient stone circles were built if you do not familiarize yourself with the Dark Moon.'

As our Master spoke, one of the group had been becoming increasingly worried. He would shuffle his feet and shake his head, when the convention during these talks was that we should remain as still as possible, on the principle that the body language should be under control, if only to aid clarity of thinking. After a while, the Master said, not unkindly:

'Philip – you want to make an observation?'

'Yes.' There was a trace of challenge in the tone of his voice. 'You speak of the Moon as the centre of Purgatory, yet in all the esoteric literature – from Egyptian to Dante – Purgatory is located in the centre of the Earth. How can you explain this contradiction?'

'Your question is a good one. To answer it fully, I will have to introduce a topic which I would have preferred to speak about much later. Undoubtedly, what I have to say will take us to the very edge of what is permissible in such gatherings as this – in a group where there are persons present who have not attained the highest level of initiation.'

The atmosphere was electric: one could almost feel the presence of all the others in that room, as if each were part of oneself. As we separated, and went about our business, the frisson of electrical charge did not dissipate. For the remainder of the week, it could be felt playing between our souls in even the most pedestrian of encounters. It was as though we were all waiting, on a higher level of ourselves, to learn this deeper secret of the Moon.

In former times, the house in New York in which our Master lived had been occupied by remarkable people. It seems that, in the early decades of the 20th century, several members of the hermetic society known as the Golden Dawn used to meet in the house for informal discussions, and perhaps even for rituals. For all the Golden Dawn was a European order, its arcane roots were buried in the United States, and this connection was probably reflected in the meetings which appear to have been held in the house.[64] At times, one could almost sense something of the rarified atmosphere of Annie Horniman,[65] of W. B. Yeats,[66] and even of those more involved in the darker side of the Astral realm, such as Crowley, all of whom appear to have had some contact with the house on one occasion or another. By the time the premises were being used by our Teacher, all such connections had been severed: the various magical orders born of the fragmentation of the Golden Dawn[67] had moved to other parts of the United States, Britain and the European Continent. We mention the early connections mainly to convey something of the atmosphere in the place, but also to prepare the background for the events leading up to a remarkable story relating to our Master in New York.

At that time, in order to be near our Master, we were living in a small room behind the studio. We did not pay rent, but undertook manual work and various other duties in lieu of payment. This allowed us to establish a more intimate and special relationship with him than is usually afforded between Zelator and Teacher. He was especially fond of Turkish coffee, and one of our early-morning duties was to prepare coffee with all the seriousness of a dervish ritual, and take this to his room. Although 40 years have elapsed since those days, we cannot smell the scent of this particular brand of coffee without recalling those days in New York.

On one occasion, our Master asked us to clean out the loft of the house. He did not explain the reason for this, but we learned later that he had decided to put in a retractable aluminium stairway to give access to the loft space. It seemed that he planned to turn it into a meditation room.

The task proved to be far more difficult than we had imagined at the outset, for there was no electricity in the loft, and no floor-boards on which to walk. In the end, to ensure the fragile joists were strong enough to carry a floor, we had to underpin each one with metal cables, and hang them from the roof beams. In the past, someone had bypassed this complex operation by laying over the joists a rough raft, made from a couple of doors. With the passage of time, these doors had become so piled over with clutter and rubbish that we were surprised the inadequate joists had not collapsed under the weight.

Whether our Master had in mind an intentional symbolism in this request to clear out an upper room, we shall never know. We had realized some considerable time ago that the main impediment to our Spiritual development lay in our untrained thinking, as much as in the accumulation of debris in our minds. Our Master could not have failed to have realized this, himself. However, though we lacked in intellectual insight, our imagination was highly receptive. It did not, at this stage, permit us to catch other than brief glimpses of things beyond the veil, yet it did enable us to sense things, as though they were just around the corner, already materialized on some plane inaccessible to the ordinary senses.

In that half-gloom of torch-light, we suddenly had the distinct impression that the horizontal doors were those over the vertical cell into which Vivien had enticed the magician Merlin to his death.[68] The doors seemed to lie over an opening into a pit – into the magical well or cellar of the Arthurian legends. Once a door was lifted, Merlin would descend, to remain entombed within for the rest of his days. What struck us most forceably about this initiation image was that the tomb was not entered in the normal way, but was designed for vertical descent, like the ancient initiation symbol of Libra. This thought – or, perhaps we should say, imaginative picture – came unbidden. The fact that the image was actually a powerful prevision was revealed to us only later.

Meanwhile, within a few minutes of attempting to transport an electric flex into the darkness of the loft, as a preliminary to clearing away the dirty rubbish, our face, hands and clothing had themselves become as necrotic as the supposedly dead Merlin. Was it possible that the Master had wanted to teach us something about the state of our thinking? Did he wish us to learn about that death-process of ordinary thought that takes place in the inaccessible loft which we call the brain? In those days, we searched for symbolism in every act and request of our Master.

The loft was strewn with ancient cobwebs and covered in a patina of a century's dust. The imported light from the single electricity bulb lent

very little illumination for our task. Even so, in the demi–light we discovered a considerable amount of bric-à-brac, and three small treasures.
Among the bric-à-brac were a number of Rosicrucian pectorals which
must have been used in rituals, a crumbling jenny-haniver, and a human
thigh-bone trumpet, with an exquisitely cast bell and mouthpiece in the
form of grotesque heads.[69] The treasures were of a higher quality. The
first was a personal grimoire, bound in black leather, with a pentagram
tooled in gold and silver on the back. The second was a wooden box of
glass plates, of the kind used by photographers in the final decades of the
19th century. The third was a typescript in Sanskrit-English, in what
appeared to be a parallel translation: it had been wrapped in an oil-skin,
for protection.

The wiccan grimoire appeared to be of the kind kept by the early
disciples of the writer on wiccan lore, Leland.[70] The name of the original
owner was given in the usual motto form, and later we were able to
identify him. Although he passed away some years ago, he is still
remembered because of his friendship with Crowley, and for his
authorship of two slim volumes on arcane lore. The signature of Crowley
which appears on the back fly-leaf, along with the *caput* sigil associated
with this magician, may be one of the many forgeries which were around
even during his lifetime.[71]

The second treasure, a pear-wood box, contained about 20 glass plates,
only half a dozen of which were not badly cracked. At first, we imagined
that they were portraits, the heads of the sitters characteristically stiff
because of the metal support used to accommodate the slow shutter speed
of the late 19th-century photographer. However, when we had cleaned
the plates, and examined them in the light of day, we found that they
were ghost photographs.

A text associated, however peripherally, with the 'Great Beast'
Crowley, and a collection of so-called ghost pictures were fairly dramatic
finds. However, as things turned out, it was the less dramatic bilingual
text which led to illumination. The manuscript had neither binding nor
title, and we presume that these had been torn away. The initials J.W.
pencilled on the first page gave us our first clue, and eventually we
satisfied ourselves that the typescript, in Sanskrit-English, was culled
from Sir John Woodroffe's *Sat-Cakra-Nipurana*, a study of the lotus
flower chakras, entitled in English *The Serpent Power*.[72] For some while
afterwards, this book became our favoured reading. It was, indeed, our
search through a published and complete version of this work which led
us to see something of the level on which a Master such as our own can
work.

We usually met with our Master in a formal study group on Thursdays. On the Wednesday, while still searching for the actual source of the fragments from the *Sat-Cakra-Nipurana*, we came across the photograph of Sir John Woodroffe which prefaced the early editions of the work, published in India.[73] In the fading picture, Woodroffe is standing near the base of the huge wheeled chariot of stone which is the temple at Konarak, in southern India.[74] We know now that above Woodroffe's head, yet not visible in the photograph, is a roof niche containing the blue-granite statue of the Sun-god Surya which is one of the wonders of India.[75]

In those early New York days, we had not yet been to Konarak, and we had no reason to think of that magnificent statue. Our thoughts – perhaps simplified by the cleansing of the loft – were far more elementary. Why, we asked ourself as we gazed at the picture, had the Indian, P. K. Dutta, photographed Sir John Woodroffe in profile? The pose looked so awkward, so ungainly.

Woodroffe did not wear the Indian clothing with any grace. Of course, this does not surprise us, nowadays. Since that time, we have travelled widely on the sub-continent, as well as in the Far East, and we have often observed Europeans dressed in a similar way to Woodroffe, draped in Indian cloth. In all this time, we have never met a European who has worn such Eastern clothes with grace. We know now why this is so. It is to do with the conflict between Astral and Etheric forces. The Indian sub-continent, and the Indian Spiritual life, is permeated with a grace of Astrality quite foreign to the West.[76]

Sir John Woodroffe was perhaps the greatest Sanskrit scholar of his day. In many ways he was a genius, yet even he could not wear Indian clothes in the way any Indian peasant can wear them. He looks awkward as he presents his profile to the camera. Why his profile? we wondered again. We pushed the question aside, as we began to search through Woodroffe's book for our half-remembered references to the *anahata chakra*, or the flaming flower which burned at the region of the heart.

The question about the profile, and the answer to the question, would come back to us in a most remarkable way.

It is sufficient to explain that the question we put to our Master was related to something that had begun to puzzle us as we read through Woodroffe's text.

Our Master had laughed at our question. Perhaps he was not surprised by it, for, a few weeks earlier, we had shown him the grimy manuscript we had found in his loft.

'Yes, you speak truly. Your words are exact and penetrating. But to what point? Your words, even though expressed as heart questions, are truthful. Your questions are rooted in truth. But look, my dear friend, what is the point of such questions? And what is the point of my answers?'

He turned his face away from us, to the larger group.

'Listen, for I am an old man, and the words of old men resonate like no other words. For all this age, I now know only one thing, and it is from this one thing that emerge the answers to all your questions. It is the thing to which all initiation leads. All I know now, after all this searching, is that the secret of everything is *love*.'

A profound silence settled over the room.

'There was nothing in the beginning but love. There was nothing during those years of struggle but love. And now, with the end in sight, I am blessed with the knowledge that there is nothing more than love, here and now, and in the world beyond. When, in the Egyptian myths, Atum created air and water, it was through love, and it was through love that he sought to unite with them once again. It was through love that he bound to his own forehead the third eye. It is through love that this Eye will grow once more on human beings. The purpose behind all initiation is the furtherance of love.'

On that Thursday evening, as the others filed out of the room, he nodded to us, and we walked over to him. We supposed that he wanted to discuss with us the loft, which was almost finished. We needed only to agree the colour of paint to be used on the walls which we had erected to hide the metal ties.

'Your questions must come from the heart, my friend.' It seemed merely to be an observation, so we nodded. '*Only from the heart*,' he insisted. As he finished his last sentence, he swung his face round to look down upon us with his steel-grey eyes. 'You must know that there is no time for questions which do not come from the heart?'

Once again we nodded, but in truth we did not catch his drift. He leaned forward and touched our forehead, just above the root of our nose.

'The *profile* . . .' he began. The word echoed through our soul, for this had been the true question we had carried in our heart when we contemplated the picture of Sir John Woodroffe. Why, we had asked ourselves, had he elected to be photographed in profile? '. . . the profile of a human being is a special thing for those with eyes to see. The profile reveals the karma to those who know about such things. If you look carefully at any face, you will see in the profile the story of past lifetimes.'

He paused, and smiled at us, his face radiant. Masters never have favourites among their pupils, yet, because we were living in his household, a special bond had developed between us.

'Why do you ask questions about husks, about words, when you have so many living questions in your mind? Your task now is to consider the profile, and determine what connection this bears to love. Consider, for example, why the Egyptians would paint the eyes in frontal appearance, even when they showed the face in profile. Why? Consider also the *uraeus* snake, which reveals its pent-up energies of striking only when viewed from the side. There is a profound mystery here. Think upon these things. The true man is seen from many places, and none is ever the same. Why is this so?

'In the Schools, there are signals and passwords linked with the eyes. The stroking of the eyebrow is one. Consider this only – for I do not wish to discuss with you the meaning of this gesture – consider this only, that it is a gesture which can have meaning only when the person making it is facing frontally on to you. It is not possible to make that symbolic gesture when viewed in profile. You must think about these things, for they are important. How could this not be otherwise, if the ancients elected to link the eyes with the Sun and the Moon? In a Spiritual sense, the man or woman of profile is not the same as the man or woman of frontal view. I repeat – consider these things, for they are of profound importance. I give you this knowledge beyond your years as a gift. You must carry these words until you have made them your own. Meanwhile, remember that the profile will speak more easily about the past than will the face turned towards you.'

He paused, and laughed one of his deep belly-laughs, rocking backwards and forwards in the lotus position. At such times, he reminded us of a daruma doll. It was a strange image to conjure, for he was a man of immense dignity and extraordinary grace of movement.

'From this, perhaps you will learn only to ask questions from the heart, my friend.'

As always, our Master was right, and all we could do was hang our head in shame at our mistake.

He laughed again, but his face was kindly. 'Mark – what I speak about may be found in Goethe. But I wish you to meditate on these things, and draw the truths out of your own soul. Only in such a way can these truths belong to you. Only in this way can you make them your own. A truth which is not your own is no truth at all.'

For a moment, we though that this was the end of our private meeting, but he smiled once again.

'And Goethe? Do you know his story of the snake?'[77]

We shook our head.

'It is a story about the profile and the frontal view. The green snake is the profile view, and the flower of the story may be seen from the front.'

We shook our head again to show that we did not grasp his point.

'No matter. You will understand later. In the story, the Golden King asks the Old Man, "How many secrets do you know?"

' "Three," said the Old Man.

' "And which of these is the most important?" inquired the Silver King.

' "The revealed," answered the Old Man, enigmatically.

' "Will you explain it to us?" asked the Brazen King.

' "When I have learned the fourth secret," was the answer . . .' Our Master nodded in approbation. 'Now you have before you another Old Man. But this one is more daring – perhaps more foolish. Perhaps I have been made foolish by the coffee your brew for me – like Ibsen with his *Peer Gynt* I have become reckless!'[78]

Once again he did his daruma belly laugh.

'Yet, whatever the cause, I am more foolish than that Old Man of Goethe, for I am prepared to reveal to you the fourth secret . . . *The fourth secret is love*. If you truly love, then you cannot ask the wrong questions. If you truly love, then the organs of growth, such as the Third Eye, will unfold in their own way. Love is itself a way of initiation. Love teaches one how to look at the world.'[79]

He reached forward, and with his finger drew a circle on the table top. As he leaned forward, his eyes were still peering on our face from under his deep eyebrows, inspecting us for response.

'The circle. What a mystery there is in a circle! The circle is magical because it includes and excludes at one and the same time. Here' – he tapped the top of the table with his index finger – 'it includes part of the table. It seems to exclude the other parts of the table, and the room in which the table stands, and the street in which is situated the house, and the city of which the street is part . . . Just so, indeed, even the planets, the stars and the cosmos are excluded also. Exactly as the line defines the contents of the circle, so it defines the contents of that which is beyond the circle, in the six directions of space. This is why the magical circle is so powerful, for the magician who *knows*.'

He emphasized the word 'knows', perhaps to link his words with the Greek-derived *gnosis*, which we sometimes used in group conversations.

'The magician who knows can select from the outer exclusion, and place within the including circle whatsoever he wishes. This is why the magician can protect himself from the demons, for they may not invade his prescribed thought-patterns. You cannot have a drawn circle divorced from the thought behind it.'

'Then every circle is a magical circle?' We phrased the question as though it were rhetorical.

'Precisely.' He seemed to be approving. 'Now, look at that circle. What do you see?'

'The table top.'

'That is good. The outer eye of the young man looks outward.'

He reached forward, and touched our forehead, just between the eyes. 'Now what do you see?'

The vision did not appear to be on the table, but in a circle drawn on the inside of our forehead in the place of the *ajna*.[80] Our words place the vision in space and time, yet the vision was not of space, and seemed already to transcend time. A vision is a vision, and there are no words to describe a vision, save perhaps as pale inadequacies. The circle seemed to have turned into tongues of fire, and to have sprouted wings. There were four huge wings on the upper periphery, yet which was the upper arc and which the lower was not clear, for there was nothing spatial about this burning circle. Seated on the outside of the circle, yet within an oval of flames, in what might have been a sacred niche (though once again, we wrongly place it in space), was a woman. Her form was white, as though it were coloured with the light of the full Moon, yet at the same time she was red. The redness – which seemed to vibrate – was graduated more towards the top of her body, at what we might call the head, save that this was scarcely human, as she had six faces. Each face had three eyes, the third eye being as clearly opened as the other two. Her six arms seemed to dance. Perhaps she was dancing, or perhaps juggling.

We could make out four objects which might have been in her hands, or might have been in the intense blue sky behind and above her hands. One of the objects was like a human skull. She made a gesture towards us, but we could not understand its meaning. Yet it seemed to us that these were made into separate things only by the limitations of our own understanding, for they were really the same things: each was the outer aspect of the other. With the vision of these juggled objects came the sound of their communal word, even though there was nothing auditory about the vision, but in certain higher states it is possible to have an auditory experience which has no parallel in the vibrations of the familiar world. The word was *Kala-kuta*, which we knew, from the sound, was the secret emissary of Death. The soundless word seemed to hover over the right-hand half of the inner circle, which had now taken the form of a petal.

Perhaps the woman was there for a long time. We do not know, as time had little relevance. She seemed to grow smaller until at last she remained something like a seed-form in the circle of our mind. We knew that the circle was 800,000,000 miles in expanse, and filled with the brightness of 10,000,000 suns. The woman had disappeared from our vision, yet we knew that she remained *in potentia* as a seed within the burning kernel. At the same time, rather than being merely at the centre of the circle, we had the distinct impression that she was also spread out on the periphery. The whole circle pulsed as though it were a beating heart, a living form awaiting to unfold.

The image became more personal. Throughout the vision, it was as though the space had always been divided into two clear halves, each as important as the other. Now one half seemed to represent the beginning, and the other the end. We were tempted to look for the letters alpha and omega, but such letters as we saw were not in any language we knew. Much to our surprise, instead of the beginning moving forward in time, the end began to move backwards, and the images we saw were from our own life. At first, we saw rapid reversed images of what was yet to come, and then, later, these merged with what had already happened. The merged images continued to project in reverse.

We write as though this was somehow a process of reversal in time, though the truth is more that the images were presented as in an instant, without time, for time had no place in this visionary world. Nor did death have any dominion. The repetition of death and lifetime picked out in the reversing mirror had not dominion over our soul. Both death and life served merely for clarification. It was through this clarification that the two petals began to form an unbroken chain.

Then we knew that one of the other objects in the juggling hands of the red-faced woman had been a rosary, and had we looked closely we would have seen each bead as a fiery circle divided into two, with a woman holding another skull and yet another rosary. The image redoubled, to make four such women, with four lunar-like skulls. As we saw the end merged into the embryonic form at the beginning, there remained still two divisions, or petals, each promissory of past and future.

But now, after all this endless circuit of time, the vision began to fade, and we were left with the circle, at first drawn in light upon the front of our skull, and then later in an imagined form on the table top.

'You saw it?' our Master asked.

'I saw it.'

'It was the *ajna* vision. A vision of the Third Eye. The Eye seeing itself.'

'And the woman who became four women?' we asked.

'The woman is *Hakini*.'[81]

He flicked his chin, reflectively, and his eyes met ours, to indicate the importance of what he had to say.

'When you contemplate the vision, remember that this is just the beginning. It is promise of what you may become. This is not the sky-walking of which one hears so much nowadays, but a walking in the light within.[82] You must understand that, for the true initiate, the two are the same. This is why the initiate may be called a bird-man, and why the language he uses is sometimes called the Language of the Birds.'

A few days later, our Master left us. He died in his room below the loft, its floor newly sprung on wire cable supports. Almost immediately, we had an insight into that curious image of Vivien and Merlin that had been conjured by the doors. Our wizard Master *had* been in the well – in the room beneath the loft – and was already on the point of death. What strange previsions are called forth from a Fool on the path.

Is the sting of death meant for those who die, or for those who remain behind? This was the question we would ask ourselves, after our Master had gone. In the mornings, our hand would reach for the copper pan on the stove, and we would recognize that our hands did not yet know that our Master was dead. Does each centre of our triple being work at different rates and with different memories? Is it true that what our mind apprehends in a second may take weeks for our feeling to assimilate, and even longer for our Will to take in?

Perhaps the poison in the sting is that so much remains behind, reminding one of what has been lost. Many of our Master's words still echoed in our mind, and his example still guided our footsteps – at least as an ideal if not as an actual practised reality. Sometimes, it was as though he spoke to us in secret from beyond the veil, so we could not be sure whether we remembered his words, or whether his words were being newly addressed by what we might only term psychic means. He seemed to live in our heart, and even in our head, in that incessant chatter which, we learn in the Schools, is the excrement of thought.

'Venus is called the planet of love, by those who do not know about the Mysteries,' he had said, starting us out on a long journey in search of arcane images. We knew that the esoteric Venus was the planet of inner light, and that love is itself an expression of this phosphorescence.[83] His concluding sentence on that day had puzzled us, however.

'After an eclipse of Venus, the soul must become a wanderer for a while. Venus is the inner flame: she finds it hard to bear the darkness of eclipse.' We had not understood then, but now we did, for we were living through such an eclipse.

The day after the *ajna* vision, he had discussed with us the arcane symbolism of the *uraeus* and the Third Eye in considerable detail: 'You will find in the modern occult books that the *ajna chakra* is linked with Neptune, yet scientists and astrologers have known about the planet for too short a time for all but the highest Adepts to know the significance of its working in the microcosm.[84] It is Venus which presently has rule over the chakra. Consider carefully the Egyptian mythology, which has Atum binding his Eye back to his forehead, and you will see what I mean.[85] He takes back his *Eye* through love. Through love, he attains to the higher vision. Yet, you must know that there is an old Venus, and a Venus to come. To understand the chakra, you must make old Venus your own. You must bring these things into your soul, to truly understand them. Perhaps, one day, you should go to Mexico. There are clues to such mysteries in these places still.'

Did we really have to travel to another world to find what we were looking for? Or were we merely trying to forget our personal loss?

In 1976, Luis Arochi showed that the *Castillo* pyramid at Chichen Itza in Mexico was so designed that, at the vernal and autumnal equinox, its ceremonial stairway was transformed into the image of a snake.[86] At the equinoxes, the projection of the Sun's beams through the steps of the pyramid throws seven isosceles triangles on to the vertical wall of the ceremonial steps. The result is the convincing light-image of a snake, which, with the movement of the Earth, seems to slither down the stairway. The head of this Castillo snake is more permanent than the transient light effects: it is carved in stone at the base of the pyramid. This serpent of conjoined light and stone slithers up the stairway in spring, and down in autumn.

Arochi showed that the shape of the serpent was based on the rattlesnake, *Crotolus*. In Mexico, and further south, the rattlesnake was often deified. Live snakes were kept in temples, and fed on the flesh of human sacrificial victims. The ghastly image of the Aztec goddess, Coatlicue, in the Anthropological Museum of Mexico City, can only be explained in terms of such sacrifices. Her name means 'Serpent'.

The astronomer Marian Hatch noted that one of the stars in the constellation *Draco* – the huge snake which slithers across the northern part of the skies in a sequence of 18 visible stars – had served as a fiducial, or guide-star, for the Mayans from 1800 BC and 500 AD.[87] At that time, it transited the meridian at midnight on the 23 May and 22 November every year, with a deviation of less than one degree. Hatch noticed that the pathway of this star corresponded with the pictures of serpents on the pages of one of the most remarkable codices to have come from pre-Columbian South America, the *Tro-Cortesianus Codex*.[88]

The snake – equivalent of the European draco – winding its way through the calendrical day-signs. Drawing based on two fold-sheets from the Mayan Tro-Cortesianus Codex.

In the illustrations for this Codex, the day signs of the Mayan calendar are presented in four columns, under which the body of the snake interweaves in a variety of five different positions. When the day signs and the snakes are read in combination, they provide, among other things, a perpetual calendar for a periodicity of 52 years. This period is half of a Venus cycle of 104: Samuel Block, the American architect who was the first to recognize the implications of the Codex, took it to be a Venus Calendar. The interaction of serpent and day signs permitted one to read the times when Venus appeared as a morning and evening star, and when it was involved in superior and inferior conjunctions with the Sun.[89]

When we came across these accounts of the Mayan and Aztec sky snakes, we were struck by the curious coincidence that the same dragon had been traced in the skies by the ancient astronomers and astrologers of Babylonia, Greece and Rome.[90] To this day, on the roof of the first-century AD Mithraic initiation cell, on the Italian island of Ponza, is a snake with much the same form as the Mayan star-calendar. Both snakes seem to wind a serpentine path through an arc which almost circles the northern pole-star.[91] In the Western initiation tradition, the serpent was part of the complex astrological symbolism of the Mithras cult.[92] Images often show the god Mithras – sometimes depicted standing in a zodiacal circle – killing a bull (plate 23). Around the feet of the bull, or prone on the floor alongside it, is a long snake. This same serpent curls through the centre of the heavens of the earliest star maps that have survived from the ancient world.

Antique constellation–map, supported by personifications of Sun and Moon.
At the centre the serpent winds its way around the two bears.

What really fascinated us about the connection between the ancient Mayan diagrams and the classical descriptions of the Western stars was that the draco tail of the Mayans ended on the *Pleiades*.[93] The Yucatec Mayan *Tzab* means the 'rattle of a rattlesnake', and also 'Pleiades'. Bearing in mind that the rattle of this snake is in the tail, we find it remarkable that in ancient times the Western astronomers of Greece located the tail of their Taurus, the Bull, precisely on the Pleiades.[94] The Mayan cult of the rattlesnake, with its tail on the Pleiades, and the Persian Mithraic cult of the Bull, with *its* tail on the Pleiades, seemed to meet in a most extraordinary way. Just what was the connection between the Middle East and South America in ancient times?[95]

To arrive at a satisfactory answer to this question, we must turn our attention away from a serpentine constellation to a planet. It seems that there were two images for Venus in pre-Columbian astronomy. The most elaborate was that of a winged disc:

Venus, portrayed as a circle, with a smaller circle at its centre, has four wings. In this form, it is portrayed in Mexican codices marking a number of significant planetary orientation positions for religious buildings. For example, it is often drawn framing the port-hole windows or door of a temple, or just rising between the V crenellations of a ball-court, or some similar architectural structure:

Such diagrams remind us that one function of the pyramids was to measure the risings and settings of Venus, and thus check the accuracy of one of the three calendrical systems which regulated the pre-Columbian civilization.

The similarity between this Mayan image, or sigil, for Venus and certain symbols in the Western world had fascinated us for a very long time.[96] We were not the first to note the similarity in its structure with certain of the ancient symbols for the Sun god, Ahura Mazdao of the ancient Chaldeans, which showed him as a disc with wings.

Detail of the winged Solar god, Ahuro Mazdao, from a Persian bas-relief.
Engraving from Coste, Perse Ancienne. *1883 ed.*

The image also reminded us of another winged disc of Egypt, which offered a further curious parallel with the Venus of the Mayans. The interesting thing about this was that it was directly linked with the serpent, at which we have already glanced, called the *uraeus* serpent by the later Greeks.

Even in modern times, the uraeus is not hard to locate in Egypt. It is perhaps one of the most frequently found of all ancient Egyptian symbols of godhead. This serpent-image is still preserved on the foreheads of the giant statues of Rameses II in the temples of ancient Thebes, and is especially notable on those in the temple of Luxor itself (plate 24). The uraeus is an image of a coiled serpent, its head poised forward, as though ready to strike. It is the transformed eye of the god Atum, in the form recounted in the ancient Creation myth.[97]

The uraeus, or cobra-symbol, on the crown, above the forehead of the pharaohs, or even on the forehead itself, is usually explained by Egyptian archaeologists as being symbolic of 'the solar disc' – whatever that may mean.[98] The meaning behind the cobra symbolism is transparent to those with higher knowledge. The uraeus represents an alert higher vision – the vision of the serpent initiate – ready (as it were) to strike outwards with the rapidity of the snake movement. It represents the alert, redeemed vision of the original eye, which belonged to the Creator – the developed Spiritual vision of the higher Spiritual world. The uraeus is the active serpent energy of higher clairvoyance – it is the vision which rightly belongs to the denizens of the stars. It is vision transformed into initiation wisdom by a searching Eye.

The placing of this serpentine eye between the ordinary eyes explains why it is sometimes called the 'Third Eye'. The fact that it is often located on the forehead of the Pharoahs is a direct reminder that the ancient kings were virtually gods, and thus representatives of the serpentine Eye of Atum. Because of the nature of the sacred hierarchies which dominated ancient Egypt, the Pharoahs were themselves high initiates: through their Spiritual heritage, they had the power of what we have seen the Oriental esotericists call the *ajna chakra* already developed.[99] Through this organ, they had access to direct vision of the Spiritual world. In such Pharoah initiates, the *ajna* was already awakened and active.

In some literature, this secret centre is described as a flower, or lotus, with 64 petals. Those who have developed the power to see these secret chakra centres on the human body describe them as being in movement. They are spinning discs of colour, so rapid in motion that their rays or petals are blurred, giving them the appearance of rotating flame.

In ancient times, the interface between the material and the physical worlds was the Egyptian hieroglyphic ◯ called *Ru*, drawn in a form which was called the *vesica piscis* by the early Christians.

When our Master had suggested that there was a connection between the Third Eye (the *Ru*, ◯, or place of entrance between the eyes), we had imagined that he was referring to the fact that the symbol for *Ru* seems to have been the origin of the Egyptian *Ankh* symbol ☥, which was in turn adopted as the symbol for Venus: ♀.

Since the hieroglyphic *Ru* meant 'birth passage', 'doorway' and 'vagina', it was held as a dual symbol – one could be born either into the material world, as in a physical birth, or into the Spiritual world, as in an initiation. The *Ru* allows entry into the Spiritual world, and ingress back into the material realm.

One might imagine that the secret eye of the Egyptians, which allows the initiate to peer into the Spiritual world, has disappeared from European art. However, this is not the case at all. As we might expect, because the secret eye touches upon the vision of initiation, the eye symbol has survived extensively in alchemical and Rosicrucian imagery. One masterpiece, painted about 1475, by Hieronymus Bosch, is constructed entirely around the mystery of the secret eye.[100] This oil-painting, now in the Prado, depicting the *Seven Deadly Sins* (plate 25), was one of the favourite paintings of Philip II of Spain, a morose and introverted king, who was steeped in esoteric and Neoplatonic learning.[101] The painting served him as a table-top, and it was kept by Philip in his own bedroom as a focus for meditation on the frailty of life.

This exquisitely painted table-top is square, its centre dominated by a huge circle, with small circular medallions in each corner. The outer concentric of the large circle is divided into seven segments, in each of which is depicted one of the seven deadly sins: Sloth, Anger, Avarice, Gluttony, Envy, Pride and Lust. In the four corners, which 'square the circle', are images of the Four Last Things. In the centre is an eye. However, this inner concentric is ambiguous, for besides looking like the iris of an eye, it appears also to be an aureole of splendid sun-rays. If we read it as an eye, then the inner circle is a pupil. In this pupil is an image of Christ, emerging from the tomb: it is a resurrectional image, an initiation image.

In fact, Bosch leaves us in no doubt that this huge circle is intended as a painting of an eye. Beneath the figure of Christ he has painted the Latin, 'Take care, take care, the Lord sees'.[102] Christ is looking out from this great eye, as though watching the sins of the World. Where have we already encountered this tiny man in the pupil of the eye?

In the ancient hermetic literature, the *Ishon* is the small man in the pupil of the eye (see page 345).[103] If we needed confirmation that Bosch is working in an arcane tradition, we do not need to study his grotesque symbolism of hellish-seeming figures – we need only cast our own eye over this Christianized *Ishon*, to see how profoundly involved the artist was in esoteric thought. When we do this, then Christ will be in the apple of our eye, with the seven deadly sins peripheral, on the outside of our being.

The Bosch eye is a graphic variant on the *Ru* eye of the ancient Egyptian symbolism, for *Ru* meant 'doorway', or 'secret entrance' – and Christ is also 'The Way'. Christ, like the *Ru*, is the entrance to the Spiritual world, the guide of the modern initiate. The resurrection of Christ, when He emerges in higher life from the tomb, radiating an aureole of light, is the enduring symbol of initiation. Bosch's painting implies that if we can circumnavigate our own Self (our own inner eye) and reject the seven deadly sins, then we can see the Christ in all his glory. We can be lifted to the higher life of Spirit ourselves. Bosch's painting is a rare *fission* image, for the seven-arced outer concentric represents the darkness in man – the seven sins – while the inner concentric represents the being of Light he may become. The painting is resurrectional, for the path to the inner Light is by way of the seven-fold struggle against sin. Bosch has been careful to encapsulate in each of these seven direful images a symbol of hope: each of the seven sins may be redeemed.[104]

The Vesica Piscis as an aureole in Christian Art, derived from the Egyptian ru. Drawing based on stained glass window in Burgos Cathedral, Spain.

The imagery of the *Ru* has survived into Christian art in several forms – but in order to illustrate something of the implications of the sexual connotations in the *Ru* (which, will be recalled, is also the vagina), we shall examine a modern painting of rare quality which incorporates two *Ru* symbols into its composition. The picture is a wash drawing, intended to illustrate a text on Egyptian mythology.[105] It shows the god Osiris in sexual union with the goddess Isis.

Even the title of Fay Pomerance's *Union of Isis with Osiris* (plate 26) implies a sexual theme. The picture is however more than a dramatic portrayal of sexual union – it is a representation of a cosmological conception, which relates to initiation. As we shall see, it incorporates two *Ru* symbols, which, among other things, symbolize eyes. The greater *Ru* in the picture represents the seeing eye of the gods, the lesser *Ru* represents the seeing eye of the human involved in initiation – he or she is the one who is being 'conceived' through this sexual activity of Isis and Osiris. As a result of this conception, the neophyte who was previously fragmented, or cut into 14 pieces (see below), is reconstituted, whole and complete: he or she becomes a healthy individual within the womb of the cosmos.

In Egyptian mythology, Isis conceives her son Horus through an incomplete sexual union with her brother-husband, Osiris. It is such a conception – sometimes described in the Egyptian literature as a *Virgin conception* – which the artist illustrates here. This conception of Horus in the womb of Isis takes place only when the goddess has managed to put back together the body of Osiris, which had been cut into 14 pieces by Set.

The tranquillity with which Isis receives the seed is contrasted with the tortured form of Osiris in the act of conception. It is a conception almost by proxy, for he can succeed in this act only from his Higher Being.

The artist has emphasized that this is a cosmic sexual deed by introducing the Egyptian *Ru* as a uniting energy between the goddess and the god. The top of the *Ru* swings over the shoulders of Isis, near the top of the picture, and sweeps down to unite with the shoulder blades of Osiris, as though the *Ru* were a pair of wings, lifting his wounded body towards Isis.

The body of Osiris has been newly constituted from the 14 parts of his own body. It would seem that, in consequence, his body is grotesquely deformed. However, this is not the case. In effect, he is portrayed as a god in *fission*, in separation, with the higher Light separating from the lower Darkness. It is this fission which accounts for the major dislocation of form in the picture. The arms of Osiris are lifted upwards, and transform into the upper parts of legs, to which are adjoined a torso. The radiant Sun seems to form his head, suggesting that the massive distortion of the arms is intended to portray Osiris stripping off his bodily skin, as one might a shirt. Osiris is in a state of fission, separating the higher Spiritual part from the lower. This is why he is depicted kneeling with his darker body on the Earth globe, yet merging his light body with the Sun.

Emerging partly from the Sun, yet transmitted from the sexual regions of this higher body, is a blast of light, which penetrates through the uniting shadowy *Ru* into a smaller *Ru*, which marks the open vagina, or womb, of Isis. If Osiris is presented as a being of Light, Isis is represented as a being of Darkness, save for the aureole around her head.

Her distinctive headgear is a reminder of the Egyptian symbolism, which usually portrays the goddess with a throne upon her head. This symbol is essentially a hieroglyphic which developed from the sound of her name. The Isiac imagery is actually more complex than first meets the eye, for the structure of her body is cleverly designed to reflect the form of a charm, the *thet*, which is usually called 'The Blood of Isis':

The form of this *thet* has puzzled Egyptologists, but it clearly combines the uterus and vagina with the ancient *ankh*, the so-called 'symbol of life'. When the structure of the *thet* is perceived in the drawing, it is clear that the radiant solar ejaculation from Osiris is entering the vagina area of Isis, while the 'arms' of the *thet* form the dark *Ru* which pulls Isis and Osiris together, with their heads as nodal points.

Isis is linked with his darker, lower body, for she is tied to it by the shadowy *Ru*. However, she receives the seed from his higher body.

One fascinating esoteric graphic device in this remarkable picture is that the number of rays emitting from the Sun is exactly 72. This is the sacred number of stellar precession, which we recognize as being linked with both the Sun and the human blood. This is no mere imposition of a meaningful numerology, for the 72 is mentioned in the Osiris legends. Before Osiris had been born, the monkey-headed god Thoth gambled with the Moon, to obtain from it a 72nd part of the day. He won the gamble, and eventually gained five whole days. It is likely that this part of the myth is an esoteric explanation of how the lunar calendar of 360 days (30 days of 12 months) was transformed into the solar calendar of 365 days: this solar calendar was said to begin at the time of the birth of Osiris, which perhaps explains the importance of the solar radiants in this remarkable picture by Fay Pomerance.

The eye, however disguised, serves as an entry into the higher world for ancient Egyptians, for a 16th-century artist, and for a painter of the

20th century. Is it possible that in this admixture of different myths and cultures, we could seek the organ which allowed us to see directly into the Spiritual world, and which in ancient times was linked with Venus, the planet of love?

The astrologers of Mesoamerica had recognized long before those of Europe that the solar cycle of Venus was 224.7 days, and that the sidereal cycle of Venus was 583.92 days. The so-called 'Venus period' of 104 years, which is actually a double cycle of 52 years, is a result of successful attempts to reconcile the solar, sacred and Venus calendars.[106] In the surviving codices, Venus is usually shown as a circle with wings: 🜨. Are the two pairs of wings a reference to this doubling of the actual cycle?

This pre-Conquest symbol for Venus had intrigued us for several years. Why should the disc be given wings? we wondered. The winged symbol linked with that for the Mesopotamian sun-being, Ahura Mazda (see bottom figure on page 217), and reminded us of images as far from the Mesoamerican world as the vast macrocosmic vision of the Abbess and esoteric Christian Hildegarde of Bingen.[107] The ancients of our Western culture had given the emissary of Venus wings. This ever-youthful female Cupid flew through the air dispensing the higher wisdom of love. Could this ancient Graeco–Mesopotamian idea of the love-bearer (a version of an earlier light-bearer, Lucifer as *Phosphoros*) have been transmitted in such a way as to form the extraordinary symbol for Venus in the South American astronomy? It was a far-fetched idea, and a ridiculous one. However, we had already begun to suspect that certain archetypal ideas do transcend history and manumission, and perhaps this was one of them. We could not believe, even for one moment, that the wings of the Venus symbol were even vaguely related to the wings of Cupid, yet we could not find ourself doubting the proposal of our Master that the Venus of the Mexican races was somehow linked with the sacred *ajna* chakra, located between the eyes.[108] If we took this to be true, then so many things began to fall into place.

We knew little about the Venus of the Aztecs and Mayans, and access to knowledge was restricted. We learned that the Peruvian name for Venus was *Chasca*, meaning 'curling hair'.[109] The word suggests that the rays of the female star are visualized as locks of hair. Could our wings or flames be hair, reminders of the Greek imagery which gave us the word 'comet'?

The 16th-century English initiate and Rosicrucian, Dr John Dee – perhaps the most learned man of his day – recorded how, in 1575, Queen Elizabeth I of England, along with her Privy Council and other members of the nobility, visited his house in Mortlake, close to London, in order to inspect his remarkable library.[110] The Queen was surprised to find that Dee's wife had just died, and so was reluctant to actually enter his house. However, she was impatient to see his scrying glass, and a crystal which Dee himself called 'my glass so famous'. This crystal, listed as 'Dr Dee's Shew Stone', is now in the British Museum, along with his other, most surprising magical instrument – an Aztec obsidian scrying glass which is now known to have come from South America. Both crystal and glass were used by Dee in his experiments with raising spirits. Dee did not appear to know much about the history of his obsidian mirror, but it has been shown that it is one used by Aztec or Mayan priests for gazing into futurity. Most surprisingly, this dark mirror was linked with the Venus of the pre-Columbians.

It seems that the Aztecs sometimes call Venus *Acatl*. This latter meant 'reed-day', and was the name of the day on which the Venus cycle began. The deity who presided over the reed-day, *Acatl*, was the chief god of the pantheon, *Tezcatlipoca*, whose name means 'Smoking Mirror'. Undoubtedly, his name is a reference to the obsidian mirrors used by magicians, for predictive purposes. *Tezcatlipoca* is supposed to read from his dark mirror all things which will happen in the world.[111] What is of immediate interest to us, however, is that the Venus of mediaeval astrology is often portrayed carrying a mirror – though the symbolism here is usually explained away in terms of feminine vanity, rather than in terms of predictive power. Some historians had suggested (quite wrongly, as it turns out) that the familiar Western sigil for Venus, ♀, which has now been usurped as a symbol for femininity, was merely a vestigial drawing of a mirror. The early form, in Graeco-Byzantine horoscopes – a sort of tailed circle ♀ – had certainly looked like a mirror, yet it had probably been nothing more than the first letter of the Greek *Phosphoros*, 'Light-bearer' – three letters so important in the initiation literature.[112] There is a much deeper mystery in the origin of this simple-seeming symbol than is generally realized.

What is the source of these strains of symbolism which seem to link together the ancient worlds, and which are intimately linked with the visionary eye between the eyes of ordinary men and women?

The landscape around the sacred site of the great pyramids of Teotihuican, near Mexico City, is dotted with rocks, some of which bear graffiti images of encircled crosses. Sometimes the circles are indented with cup-shapes, and sometimes the designs are marked with additional diameter lines, fainter than the primal cross:

These lines and cup-shapes are orientation markers, which correspond to planetary directions, such as the rising points of Sun, Moon and Venus, and even to the placings of temples and pyramids on the site itself. The encircled crosses, which we might, out of context, call Celtic Crosses, are so precisely orientated that it is still relatively easy to determine their specific orientations. For example, the cross near the processional avenue, to the west of the Temple of the Sun, is directed so that one of its cupped arcs (65 degrees to the east of astronomical north) exactly frames the body of the rising Sun, as it emerges over the side of the pyramid, at the summer solstice.[113] Other encircled crosses reveal far more than summer and winter solstices: they mark precisely the extreme settings of Sun and Moon, and the heliacal rising and setting of Venus.

In 1963, the archaeologist Bennyhoff located one of the more obscure of these markers on the hillside of Malinalli, in Colorado Chico. The marker was later discovered to be part of a system of ancient graffiti designed to reveal the secret and sacred orientations of the vast temple site of Teotihuican, which is a vast observatory for the study of Sun, Moon and Venus, and capable of measuring sightings of other planets, and certain stars.[114]

We had explored the area in the late 1960s, in company with a group of practising Rosicrucians, who had become interested in the question of the solar-lunar orientations of the Aztec temples. This particular group seemed to be well-informed about the Aztec and Mayan sites, and knew a little about the background to Mesoamerican astronomy. They were particularly anxious to study the orientations in the great temple complex at Monte Alban in Oaxaca where, we had discovered during a previous visit, were preserved not only the ancient Aztec observatory, but the actual viewing chamber, sunk into the steps of the pyramid, to enable the astrologer to observe orientations at the site.[115] We had been thrilled to involve ourselves in such an intimate exploration of ancient thought, looking down from the pyramid towards horizontal declivities which (were they restored) would offer precise sighting points. By standing in this chamber, with the vertical shaft behind us, we established for ourselves that the wedge-shapes of the pyramids, though in sad repair, would have been fiducials, or markers, for the settings of Sun, Moon and Venus. Our own suspicions – which were intuitions rooted in some experience of ancient astrological techniques – were confirmed in 1974, when astro-archaeologists demonstrated that identical orientations had been shown to be valid: it was recognized that the astronomer-priests of Chichen Itza had used similar viewing chambers to record heliacal risings of such stars as Canopus, Castor and Pollux.[116] Significantly, these same scholars came to the conclusion that asterisms such as the *Pleiades* could be observed at the same time as Venus transits.

It was the large slabs, laid along the retaining walls of a pyramid like so many disused grave-stones, with bas-reliefs of the 'dancers', which had first caught our attention in this amazing site of Monte Alban (plate 27). When we researched these enigmatic figures, we were intuiting their purposes, our intuition being based on the conviction that they were produced within initiation centres. We felt instictively that they were dancing to show that they had woken up to the Spiritual world – that they were no longer the Sleepers, but initiated to the Higher Realms. Their own Astral bodies were dancing to the new power of the seven chakras. Later we discovered that one or two other investigators had come to the same conclusion as ourselves – namely, that the hieroglyphics on their bodies represented the chakras.[117] The identity of the earlier settlers who had left behind these remarkable carvings is unknown, but to judge from their images, they seemed to be of a Negroid stock, with facial characteristics which remind us more of the Olmecs than the Aztecs.[118]

It was, however, not at Monte Alban, but at Teotihuican – a site which one would have imagined had been washed clean of antiquity by modern tourism and extensive 'restorations' – that we experienced once again at first hand the ineffable workings of the Spiritual world. It was at Teotihuican that we were permitted an insight into the wisdom of Goethe, who had once written that, for the Spiritual world to work creatively into one's life, all that is necessary is for us to commit ourselves wholeheartedly to a course of action. The key word, for Goethe, had been *commitment*, for it is the serenity of soul which arises from commitment that permits the secret world of Spirit to participate in our affairs. Our experience at Teotihuican, with our party of American Rosicrucians, was a supreme example of this truth.

The area of Colorado Chico in which the orientation graffiti had been found by Bennyhoff was not easily accessible. Among the group of Rosicrucians who were anxious to examine and explore these orientations, which were then not published,[119] but openly rumoured, were several elderly people. The group organizer therefore laid on a number of mules to carry these people over the rocky terrain. We made a picturesque group, as we set off at first light, the mules, as usual, moving far too slowly for our own impatient Leonine temperament. We found ourselves walking alongside an old lady from the United States, who, one would imagine, was not accustomed to riding anything less comfortable than a stretch limousine. As the string of loaded mules made its way towards the west, we chatted together.

'I'm from Boston,' Margaret told us, by way of introduction, 'but I have spent most of my life in San Jose, California. It was my 70th last month,' she continued. 'I decided that if I did not visit the pyramids this year, then I might not visit them at all.'

We walked alongside her mule, talking to her. It emerged that it had been her life-long ambition to visit the Mexican archaeological sites. Somehow, her life had been too occupied for her to make such a trip before. It was the quite normal story of a well-filled social life – marriage, children and grandchildren – delaying and even frustrating Spiritual aspirations. So, as she neared her 70th birthday, with its magical septenary, she sensed that she had reached the now-or-never stage. Accordingly, she had joined with her companions, most of whom were a decade or more younger than herself.

As our party reached the rocky outcroppings where the first examples of orientation graffiti were located, a curious thing happened. Very slowly, almost as though in slow-motion, Margaret slipped off her mule. Fortunately, as we were still walking alongside, we managed to break her fall, yet even so she did hit the ground with some force. Fortunately, she was more shocked than hurt. After a brief examination, it became clear to us that she was suffering from mild dehydration. The sun was not high, yet already it was very hot. With the help of others, we managed to get Margaret back on the mule, and then decided to take her back to the bus, where there was shade, and someone to look after her.

Our trip back was in silence. Once again, we walked alongside the mule, but this time we moved with more urgency. The sun rose ever higher, and the temperature began to soar. Then, within less than an hour, we arrived back at the bus. We put Margaret in the care of the driver – who happened by chance to be also from Boston – with instructions to allow her to sip water, and to stay in the air-conditioned interior.

As soon as we were satisfied that she was comfortable, we made our way back towards the rocks as rapidly as possible. We knew that it was unlikely that the party would be able to make much sense of the incised orientation lines without our own commentary, for the designs would come alive only when the intended orientations were pointed out. As we approached the area, we saw that the party had wandered off to the left, a considerable distance from the incised rocks we wished to show them.

To catch up with them, we deviated from the hard pathway, and began to make our way across the rubble and grass-tangled rocks, towards the south. On such minor deviations in life are the Mysteries based. If we had not left the pathway, and changed our direction to the south, then we would not have had one of the most remarkable experiences of our life.

The intense heat rayed a shivering miasma of undulating mirages over the landscape, making it seem unreal. After we had gone a few hundred yards, we saw two Mexican children playing among the rocks. As we reached the pair, the girl – who was perhaps about ten years old – suddenly stood up and began waving her arms towards us.

'Doctor, doctor,' she called in English. She had taken us to be an archaeologist. Gesticulating wildly, she ran over towards us, and placed in our hands what at first appeared to be a flat pebble. It was a shard. On it was incised the winged disc hieroglyphic for Venus:

We cannot remember much of what happened over the next few hours. Our first impulse – which we followed – was to push our hands into our pockets and give the girl all the money we were carrying.

We must have caught up with the party, and even given a practical demonstration of how several of the orientation lines worked. In fact, the sequence of events is still unclear in our memory, yet, as we walked from Colorado Chico, we can still recall one of the party asking why we were laughing.

Our response was only partly true.

'I was just considering what the Spanish soldiers and priests would have thought had they seen these graffiti of crosses – so like their familiar Celtic crosses.'[120]

Such a thought *had* passed through our mind earlier, as we talked to the group about how the incised cross, and its indented circle, orientated to the distant pyramids. Yet this was not the thought which amused us now.

We were laughing because our hand was still gripping tightly the extraordinary shard, which will remain with us until we die. We were laughing with joy at this reminder of how the cosmic beings use their infinite creativity to work into the world of Man. We had literally followed our Master's advice, and made the symbol of Venus our own.

If, at that moment, an Olmec artist had elected to carve an image of our Etheric body, replete with hieroglyphics for the chakras, then he would surely have portrayed us as a dancing man.

Chapter Five

O Egypt, Egypt! Of thy religious rites nothing will survive but fables which your children's children will not believe. Nothing telling of your piety will survive, other than words incised on stone.

(After the Latin quoted from Asclepius III. 25, in W. Scott, *Hermetica*, 1924, i, p.342, in the Waddell edition of *Manetho*, 1940)

The Greek philosopher Plato was himself an initiate, and had studied in the initiation Schools of Egypt.[1] This implies that many of the things he wrote must have been intended to be read, on their deepest levels of interpretation, in the light of initiation wisdom. Among the various sayings which he recorded as being directly from the ancient Mysteries was the phrase, 'Many are the Thyrsus-bearers, but few are the Mystes'.[2] The truth contained within this cryptic line is just as poignant today as it was in the time of Plato.

As we shall see, the Mystes are initiates in a particular form of Mystery lore. The Thyrsus-bearers are those who follow the Mysteries, as initiates. In the processionals which led to the Mystery Centres, the appellants, or the neophytes, carried the *thyrsus*, which was a staff wreathed in ivy or vine-leaves, and topped with a pine-cone. This wand was so important in ancient times that its presence in a work of art was a guarantee that the subject dealt either with initiation, or with one or other of the Mysteries.

The sacred thyrsus is very much in evidence in the ritual flagellation scene depicted in the first century BC fresco in the Villa of Mysteries at Pompeii.[3] The staff seems to hover in the air, behind the body of the naked female dancer, its pine-cone head over the top of the initiate who pulls back the robe of the kneeling girl, to bare her back for flagellation (plate 28). This fresco, which may be a copy of an Hellenistic original, portrays an incident from a Mysteries ritual which has not been identified.[4] Why the thyrsus should hover in the air has never been explained, though it might have something to do with the fact that the lashes in the hands of the winged woman (who is about to beat the neophyte) also fly through the air. Perhaps this is an Air ritual.[5]

The rites of the Bacchanalia were introduced to Rome in the third century, and were originally reserved for women only. Later, men were admitted. The external rites appear to have been orgiastic, the wild Maenads carrying serpents, and (it seems) in such delirium that they tore to bits with their own teeth the sacrificial animals presented to them. There are records of these wild women feeding such creatures as wolves with their own breast milk. It was while they were in this delirium that the god was supposed to appear to them.[6] In the midst of these orgiastic expressions, the initiates would hold their thyrsus, as wand of office.

That the thyrsus could be depicted in Mystery rites so far apart as flagellation and Bacchic frenzy indicates its importance as an emblem of initiate rank. Its importance as a symbol throws some light on what Plato meant – for, in his enigmatic line, he is saying that while many wish to

Alchemical Mercury, with the sigil above his head, and a caduceus in each hand. Detail from the second key to Basil Valentine's Duodecim Clavibus 1618.

hold the high office of initiation, few succeed in this quest for so high an honour. The thyrsus may be an outer emblem, but it marks also an inner transformation. It is one thing to carry openly this symbol of aspiration, but another thing to integrate the elements of this emblematic staff into the Self, and become an initiate.

There is every reason for supposing that the mercuric staff carried by Mercury (figure opposite) is a version of this thyrsus. In the mercuric staff, the vegetation – of ivy or vine – has transformed to a higher level of life, and has become a pair of intertwined snakes. The seed, or pine-cone, has sprouted wings. The sigil (above the head of Mercury, in the figure), which is used even today in astrology and astronomy to denote the planet Mercury, is a vestigial drawing of this Mercuric staff, and may therefore be traced back to the ancient Mysteries.[7] This hermetic staff is represented with wings, and is intended to symbolize a redemptive, or Spiritually transformed, version of the earlier stick. The redemptive element is quite fitting, as the god Mercury (the Hermes of the Greek tradition), besides being a healer, was a teacher of Mankind, and thus had access to initiate knowledge well beyond the possible evolution or capability of mere humans.

Some historians of the arcane[8] see this curious staff as a symbol of the human spine, with the serpent energies running freely up and down, and the wings as a symbol of emancipated Spiritual thought. It is more likely that the staff has a far deeper meaning, but, for the moment, the interpretation offered is sufficient to show that whatever its ultimate meaning, it is a redemption of the thyrsus carried by those who seek initiation.

The hermetic staff, like the thyrsus, is emblematic of stages on the sacred Way of Initiation. It is likely that the two staffs carried by the Fool in the Tarot card (see figure on page 22) are intended to symbolize the two extremes of the Way of the Fool. With one stick the Fool explores the visible world, while with the other, he guards the hidden, or noumenal world. One thing is sure – that the sticks of the Fool are throwbacks to the thyrsus carried by the hopeful neophyte in ancient times.

Is there any point in setting out on such a difficult Path with such slim chances of success? The question, of course, is, 'What do you mean by success?' In some respects, the fact of being on the Path is itself a redemptive element: one may not become a high initiate, but one will learn a great deal about the Self and about the cosmos, on a level which cannot be learned in the ordinary way. In view of this, those who fail on the Path only appear to fail, for in a subsequent incarnation they will be able to take up the Path or a related Way again, and continue the struggle.

We are tempted to amend Plato's dictum pertaining to the Mysteries, and say, 'Many are the Thyrsus-bearers, but few join the Mystes in a single lifetime.' In fact, we have to amend Plato, because our educational system and our modern superstitions tend to prevent us from reading his words in the spirit in which they were written. However, we may be sure that those initiates who read his words in ancient times knew exactly what he meant. Reincarnation was simply a fact of life for such initiates.

The Path of initiation is not an easy one; men and women are called to follow it for a multitude of reasons, but in almost every case there is an overwhelming desire for enlightenment which persuades the individual to undertake the Spiritual activity demanded of the Path. Those who enter the Path are driven by inner necessity, and one day will achieve initiation. But, we may ask, what happens to those thousands of individuals who do not even take up the thyrsus?

When the initiate of initiates, Hermes, was asked about the nature of ordinary man – that is, of man who had not entered the stream of development which leads to initiation – he said that such a man or woman was merely a 'procession of Fate'.[9]

In modern times, the idea of Fate is difficult for us to grasp. We are accustomed to believe that we control our own destinies – if not as individuals, then in political groups, or through national endeavour. We are so deeply rooted in a firm belief in the supremacy of the Ego that it is not easy for us to believe that the gods made a 'fiat', which determined the nature of a fate over a sequence of lifetimes.[10] It is not easy for us to imagine that we are under the sway of god-made destinies, which override much of our own personal volition and desires. This was not always the case in former times. In the past, the majority of humans could sense a connection between the will of the gods and their own lives on Earth. Indeed, the sacred oracle centres which were scattered throughout the ancient Greek world, in such places as Dodona, Ephyra and Delphi, were consulted by millions of people who had no doubt that, because the gods made and controlled fate, they could also reveal what this fate would be in the future.

The initiate was the individual who decided to wrestle with Fate – to, as it were, take the ordinances of the gods in hand, and by changing his or her own inner world, change the personal destiny. This meant becoming aware of what the fiat of the gods intended, and collaborating with the Higher Beings, either working this out or amending it in some way. The individual who wished to change this procession of Fate had to wake up to his or her condition: they could no longer afford to be a Sleeper during the journey through the cosmos.

In the Greek and Roman epics, it is a commonplace for the poets to visualize the gods spinning fate around a man, as though his body were nothing more than a spindle, the inner core being wrapped in the threads from which his destiny was being spun. This notion was extended into the fatalistic activities of the *Moirae*. The Greek word *moira*, which meant 'portion', was eventually applied to the fate apportioned to an individual, and the three Moirae were adopted as personifications of this notion of allotted destiny.[11]

The myths of Selene and the Moirae are not really too far removed from the ancient hermetic view which traced a link between the Moon and Fate. In early cosmologies, it was the Moon who was regarded as the controller of human destiny. The six-handed moon-goddess Hecate, who represented the new Moon, bereft of the light of the Sun, incorporates the three symbols of the *Moirae* – in her top pair of hands she carries a knife, which represents the shears of Atropos.[12] In her middle pair of hands she carries a scourge, which is said to represent her punitive side, but which is really little more than a thread on a stick – very close to the thread of Clotho.

We see from this image that something of the *fiat* of the gods, which was *fate* for mankind, was, to some extent, enacted on the human plane by the goddess Hecate, whose three heads looked towards the past, the present and the future. This goddess, whatever her origins, was regarded by the Romans as a goddess of magical arts, and among the sacrifices she was offered were black puppies and black female lambs. It was said that her triple form permitted her to keep at least one of her six eyes on the four tracks of the crossroads over which she had rule. While this is true, it is also likely that the triple heads are derived from the three phases of the Moon – crescent, gibbous and full. The Greek name Hecate means 'worker from afar', and captures perfectly the notion of an influence cast from a distant satellite. It would seem that Hecate is the tutelary lunar goddess of the Sleepers, of those who have not yet found their way to a Path.

Somehow, personifications such as Selene or Hecate seem remote to us nowadays. In modern times, most people tend to think of space as being empty of living beings: it is 'empty space' – save, of course, for the stars, planets and cosmic dust. This soul-less vision is however quite modern. In previous ages, there was never much doubt that the heavens were filled with Spiritual beings. The Christian tradition of angelology, which lies behind most arcane systems of the West, is no exception, for it describes the skies as a series of concentric heavens, each filled with spirits, with each spirit dedicated to a specialist service of God and Man.

The Graeco-Roman mythology seems remote mainly because it has been overlaid by Christian beliefs, and by a Christian system of angelology which has replaced the classical gods.[13] However, the early Christians did not believe that space was empty – they, too, believed that the heavens were filled with Spiritual beings.

The most extraordinary documents pertaining to ancient initiation knowledge are those which have survived in a collection of ancient manuscripts known as the *Hermetic Corpus*.[14] Although this Graeco-Egyptian literature is known only to a handful of scholars and hermeticists, some of its ideas have been made familiar to millions of people through what is probably the most remarkable poem of modern times. This is the *Four Quartets* of the Anglo-American poet, T. S. Eliot.[15] In this masterpiece, Eliot reflected upon the nature of time and certain deep Spiritual experiences in terms with which any initiate into the Schools of Osiris and Isis would feel comfortable.[16]

While reading these remarkable quartets, one forms the distinct impression that they are far more than ancient ideas dressed up in modern verbiage – far more than a clever poesic play with cosmological ideas. One feels, indeed, that Eliot must have been personally initiated, in a previous lifetime, into the Mysteries of Isis and Osiris, the secret teachings of which form the basis of this hermetic literature. Only such an explanation will account for the fact that he unerringly revealed the nature of the secret organ which lay dormant in ordinary man and woman, but which would begin to grow as they developed Spiritually.[17]

The Greek texts of the hermetic literature are themselves based on early Egyptian texts. It was only when scholars learned to interpret the ancient hieroglyphics, and a number of Egyptian names (during the 19th century), that the full esoteric depth of the original hermetic literature began to become apparent. It is for this reason that it is legitimate for us to insist that the secret core of hermetic literature has remained hidden for thousands of years, and has only recently begun to reveal its arcane contents. We might also add that the esoteric nature of these documents is such that it can be understood fully only by those who have received some form of initiation. This explains why so many modern academic scholars who have dealt with the material have done so only with considerable difficulty.[18]

Four thousand years ago, the principles of initiation were understood by almost any educated person, and to some extent it is true to say that such people strove towards initiation by serving the temple in one way or another. Nowadays, the external temples are gone, or are ruins, yet the human soul is still longing, with no less a fervour than in ancient times, for initiation. In modern times, we feel – howsoever dimly – that we are locked in a prison of watery plasms.[19] We feel instinctively that this body is not our true home, and whether we realize it or not, we look back to the ancient wisdom of Egypt for a release from this Spiritual prison.

When, in the early 15th century, a Florentine monk brought from Greece a manuscript which seemed to offer a clue to the meaning of the Egyptian hieroglyphics, the leaders of Western esotericism were in a high state of excitement.[20] They felt that through readings offered by the Egyptian hieroglyphics they would discover lost secrets. It had long been recognized that the secret writings of the Eygptian temples must contain a lost hermetic lore, but it was also recognized that the key to this language had been mislaid. Suddenly, the book which purported to give the meanings of some of these hieroglyphics seemed to have been discovered.

Significantly, in view of later developments, which saw Florence as the centre for the Renaissance which galvanized Western civilization, the book first turned up in this Italian city.[21]

Perhaps those angelic beings who oversee the development of mankind took satisfaction from the fact that the ancient wisdom relating to the secret arcane key should be brought to Florence. The word Florence is derived from the same word which gave us florescence, linked with the Latin *flores*, flowers.[22] The name of the key to Spiritual enlightenment in the hermetic documents was the *secret flower*.[23]

When we had studied under our Master in New York, he had explained to us how the hermetic literature was an expression of the Egyptian secret knowledge. When he began this account, we assumed that he intended his central theme to be that of initiation. It was only later that we realized his intention was to compare the esoteric idea of fission in the human being with fission among the cosmic bodies.

He began by discussing the Egyptian sacred lore.

'The Egyptian *Book of the Master of the Hidden Places*[24] is the supreme initiation document, and it is not surprising that it has been misunderstood by modern Egyptologists.

'Anyone who wishes to study the ancient initiation methods of the Egyptians could do no better than to follow the steps of certain masons, and relate the documents to the inner structure of the Great Pyramid, at Gizah. It is not our purpose to do this here – sufficient indication of how closely the rituals for initiation are linked with the secret corridors and chambers of the pyramid has already been published.[25]

'However, it will be instructive for us to examine briefly one of the corridors in the pyramid. Since the pyramid is a model of the cosmos, and since the cosmos has impressed its majesty upon the whole of Egypt, we can do no better than glance at the map of Egypt, even before we enter the pyramid.

'The country of Egypt was divided into 42 provinces, or nomes. Each of these provinces was accorded a sacred temple and a series of initiation rites, pertaining to a particular god.

'These 42 gods are described in many sacred papyri. They are the Judges in the Double Hall of Truth, which the candidate must pass on his way to initiation.

'These 42 are the "assessors" of the witness Osiris, and the deceased (or the initiates) must exonerate themselves of the 42 corresponding sins before passing through to the next phase of existence. This probably explains why, in the papyri of the dead, it is said that the impurities "are shed to the Earth", while what is pure "rises to the horizon".[26] This is the *fission* required in the Underworld to allow the newly dead, or the initiate, to continue on his or her way.

'Between the ancient world of the Egyptians, and our own world, lies the mediaeval realm. The Christians had tended to demote the Egyptian gods, which they so lamentably failed to understand: the Christians made of these strange creatures monsters. It is an amusing activity to look through the detailed descriptions of the 72 demons of Solomon in the mediaeval grimoires, and trace in these Egyptian gods.[27] This demoting of the *neters* has led to much misunderstanding, for the Egyptian gods were archetypes, and could therefore be found on all levels – in Heaven, and on Earth, as much as in the Purgatorial realms.

'It is easy to understand why the Christians were anxious to demote these gods to demons, for some of them appear in guises which are indeed terrible to behold. In the papyri and tomb frescos, they are painted in theriomorphic forms (figure 30). In these monstrous forms lies the *cheta* or "secret" of ancient Egyptian knowledge. Consider, for example, the montrous hippopotamus god, sometimes called *Apet*, at other times *Taurt*.

'The female *Taurt*, pot-bellied, and open-mouthed, with the crocodile god *Sebek* clambering over her back, was painted on a wall of the sarcophagus chamber of Seti I, in the Valley of the Kings (opposite). Why is such a pair of clowning monsters found in the tomb of a Pharoah? They are found because neither is merely a demon, but a star. *Taurt* is the same

*Egyptian constellation images on the wall of the lower sarcophagus chamber
of Seti I in the Valley of the Kings, near Luxor, Egypt.*

star-god as figures in the zodiac on the roof of the small temple in the roof
of the Temple of Hathor at Denderah, where she appears also in the form
of a hippopotamus. Her variant name, Apet, links the creature with the
sky (*pet* in Egyptian), and so perhaps we should not be surprised to find
the hippopotamus in the Heavens. Both Apet and Taurt were names for
the star we now designate as *gamma Draconis*.

'Up to about 7,000 years ago this star was of especial importance to the
Egyptians, as it was circumpolar: in the Egyptian sky-lore it marked the
head of the Hippopotamus. Archaeologists affirm that about 3500 BC, it
was visible through the central passages of the Hathor temples at
Denderah.[28]

'Why did the Egyptians go to so much trouble to establish links
between their architecture and this star? What is the function of this
neter?

'*Taurt* is the *neter* of multiplication – or, more precisely, of the
principle of numbers which permit multiplication. She has been
described as a womb, as the "sky" when considered in terms of material
volume, and she is a mammal with pouched belly and hanging breasts
because she represents the function of nourishment, by which forms are
maintained in a multiplied, or engendered, entity. One sees why it is
misleading to describe *Apet* in her form as *Taurt* as merely the goddess of
fertility, the presider over childbirth: in fact, she presides over all
extension into space and time. In this secret resides the importance

237

accorded to *Taurt* by the temple builders, who arranged passageways (that in the Rameses temple was 1,500 feet long!) to allow the star to pour its influence into the interior of the temples and pyramids. In this way, the influences of the star could multiply into the Earth: the builders were literally involved in a sort of stellar sexuality, aimed at a conception which would give birth to form, from the stellar heights.

'The passage in the Great Pyramid was so oriented to allow the light of the star *Taurt* to pour into the pyramid itself. It is not surprising that we should find the image of Taurt on the insides of the tombs, built into the solid rock of Egypt, to show that this imprint of Taurt has been received. The symbol is indeed an indication that Man is in touch with the heavens, and is himself a mediator between the heavens and Earth.

'Now, while it is true that the *neters* – such as *Taurt* – have an objective existence, and are used by the priests to bind heaven to Earth, so also are these creatures found in man. The esoteric tradition has always insisted that the outer may be found as part of the inner. Just so, the 42 nomes are found in the inner structure of the pyramid. Just so, the 42 gods are found in the inner being of the initiate.

'Even the masonry of the pyramid reflects this macrocosmic–microcosmic relationship, for from the point where the candidate for initiation appears before the judges in the Double Hall of Truth, to the point where he receives the Crown of Illumination, there are 42 courses in the brickwork.

'The candidate must walk by these 42 beings, symbolized in the stonework. No doubt, he or she will be protected by powerful charms, amulets and the knowledge they carry, but it is unlikely that they would be able to pass if any trace of the sin ruled by even one of those gods was within his being. At some point in his preparation for initiation, the candidate would have to have divested himself of this darkness. This fission would have been necessary, for otherwise he would have been burned up by the power of the guardians in that passage, the Double Hall of Truth. Do you see, now, the role of certain demons? They are, truly speaking, guardians of the Upper World. Not all demons are guardians of the Upper World, however. Some guard the Lower World.

'Now, the only glyph on the outside of the pyramid was that on the portal of the double arch, cut into the 17th course of the exterior of the pyramid: ⌣ . This hieroglyph is the horizon line.

'Of course, wherever you stand, the horizon is level with your own eyes. If you stand on the steps in front of this entrance, your own eyes will be almost level with the glyph, and the horizon line will properly cut the pyramid at this point. It therefore marks the point where the pyramid and the human candidate for initiation become one. The door marks the point between the outer world of Egypt and the inner world of initiation. This sacred point marks the double way of vertical space and horizontal space – the Way Up and the Way Down, the Way Out and the Way In. It marks a cross in space and time. This extension in space is reflected within the pyramid itself, for the the passageway into the pyramid leads downwards.

'Almost any popular handbook on the Pyramids will tell you that this steep angle of descent is by no means accidental. From the bottom of this passageway, it was once possible to see the ancient polar star, *Thuban*.[29] The candidate walks with the marked star symbolically shining down the passageway, on his back. As he walks downwards, he is driven, as it were, by the star – towards a chamber which has rightly been called the Chamber of Ordeal.[30] This chamber is below the foundation rock on which the pyramid stands.

'Spatially, this Ordeal Chamber is exactly below the Chamber of the Open Tomb, buried in the masonry of the pyramid. Now, from our point of view . . .' – our Master began to draw a simple diagram on the blackboard – '. . . the divisor between this underground cell and the sacred Tomb Chamber is *not* the foundation rock. The actual dividing point is found on the outside of the pyramid, in the glyph we have just examined, set above the double arch of the entrance. This means that the ancient hieroglyphic for the Place of the Horizon, which eventually turned into the modern sigil for Libra, is that which separates the infernal from the celestial.

'Of course, it is interesting to reflect that modern astrologers, who unwittingly trace the horizon line from east to west whenever they locate Libra in a horoscope, are indulging in symbols derived from the ancient Mysteries of initiation. The position of the glyph indicates that Mankind – even that small part of Mankind that seeks initiation – may go no higher than the second death of the Open Tomb. It also implies that all humans must, at some time or another, descend into the Well of Ordeal. The esoteric Christian Mysteries, which had Christ resurrected and then descending into Hell, constitute a parable on this ancient Mystery lore.

'You see, the pyramids are places of fission. They are designed to allow the higher to separate from the lower.'

In the following exposition, our Master told us a great deal about the secret initiation chambers and methods of the ancient Egyptians. He showed us why the actual place of initiation lay between the Chamber of Ordeal and that of the Open Tomb. He told us how the methods of initiation involved the priests engrafting pictures on to the detached

Spiritual bodies of the initiates. The wisdom in these pictures would become part of their own being, when the Spiritual bodies were once again united to their physical bodies. From this we learned that the pictures on the walls of the tombs, like the physical movements required by the passages and chambers of the pyramids, became pictures in the souls of those who sought initiation (plate 4).

This description was an elegant confirmation of what we had already begun to suspect from our reading of the extraordinary conclusions of the Egyptologist, Schwaller de Lubicz.[31] Our Master's words were sufficient to change the entire direction of our outer life. So deeply were we moved by this vision of the ancient Mysteries of initiation, that we resolved to travel the sacred sites of the world ourselves in search of the remnants of this lost knowledge.[32] We knew that to bring these things to life, we had to experience them for ourself.

In the meeting prior to his death, our Master fulfilled his promise to speak about the secrets of the Moon. Normally, he would wait for someone in our midst to ask a question. This time he began to speak without preamble.

'In the esoteric literature, you will find many records indicating that the Moon was at one time part of the Earth. It had to leave the Earth, in order to allow life on Earth to continue its Spiritual development unimpeded.

'It is important that anyone on the Path should attempt to form a clear picture of what this separation was like. Not only was it of considerable evolutionary importance in the cosmogenesis of the Earth, but it is played, in miniature, in many of our Spiritual activities. It is the archetypal form of fission. Now, unfortunately, in modern times even our imaginative faculties have been materialized, and it is difficult for us to form a picture of what this Moon-loss was really like. It is difficult for us to form clear images of the fission which lies at the root of all Spiritual activity. It is difficult for modern man and woman to visualize things in purely Spiritual terms. This is because the picture-making which lies at the basis of our imaginative faculty longs for mythology, since mythology is itself an agency of Spirituality.

'If you cannot imagine in this way at present, you must perforce cling to materialistic images . . .' – he touched the glass of water on the round table in front of him – '. . . then imagine a glass of water clouded with a pigment. If the glass is left to stand, the particles will settle to the bottom in a thick dross, leaving the water above clear. This is much nearer to the Spiritual reality of what happened when the Moon left the Earth, taking with it certain forms of dross materiality. Now, in your imagination, try to link this separation with the sigil for Libra, the sign of the Balance, and consider the place of this seventh sign in the rest of the zodiac. Consider also that Libra is not a violent sign. Of course, I realize that this imagery would not please those of the Velikovsky School, who imagine cata-strophic assaults on the Earth at fairly frequent intervals.[33] Even so, the fact is that in the remote past, neither the Earth nor the Moon were as material as they are now.

'The schema which depicts the planets in extended space pertains only to physical vision. You must understand this, or there will be no way in which you can approach some of the greater Mysteries of the cosmos. What appears to be on the outside is more accurately described as being on the inside: our Earthly vision is extremely limited, for, under normal circumstances, we see outwards from the central Ego to the cosmic periphery. However, this is not the cosmic vision. We are so used to this limited vision that we are not sufficiently tolerant to accept that there can be others – including a vision from the periphery into the centre.

'In the case of the Moon, the matter is made more complex by the fact that the physical matter of the Moon did once form part of what we now call the Earth. Within the context of the lunar sphere, the two centres did once coincide. A tremendous effort of meditative power is required to follow these connections, however, and the bald statement I have made can result in misconceptions.'

'Why,' asked Philip, 'did the Moon have to separate from the Earth?'

'It was a cosmic fission. The Moon represents the harder mineraliza-tion of the Earth. In the body of the Moon is the matter which, had it remained with the Earth, would have weighed down human develop-ment too deeply. Man would not have been able to bear the weight of those forces in his own body. Just as we know from our own observations of ourselves that we must slough off darkness to reach into the light, so the planetary bodies must also involve themselves in a similar fission. Even so, it is true that the weight of the Moon, albeit removed by half a million miles, still contorts the physical body of the Earth and its inhabitants through what are usually called 'gravitational' effects.[34]

'Now we must touch upon the connection between the Moon and clairvoyance. We must do this because one of our members has – wisely or unwisely – become involved with mediumistic groups.'

'It is important that we set out very clearly the dangers inherent in opening the soul to such activities. It is not for me to forbid such activity. I have no power to forbid, and would relish no such power. Much as I would wish to protect you, I cannot. The best I can do is make the dangers clear to you. After that, your beliefs and your conduct remain your own.'

He look around at our faces, as though to indicate that he had arrived at the most important point of the evening.

'And so now we must look at an esoteric truth which touches on the very edge of what is permissible. What I have to say will be greatly disturbing for many people of modern times. It will disturb, because it is generally taken for granted that clairvoyance, mediumship and Spiritualistic activity are somehow linked with Spiritual development, and consequently of benefit to mankind. Unfortunately, this is far from the truth. A vast amount of our modern so-called "Spiritualist" literature pertains to channelling and clairvoyancy which is far from beneficial for the development of mankind. Indeed, not to mince words, I should tell you that it is distinctly harmful.

'I must now make a statement which will introduce you to a concept which was, until comparatively recently, one of the deepest secrets of the esoteric Schools: In some ways, the Moon is the greatest problem of esoteric lore. The Moon is not at all what it appears to be.

'At the end of the last century an astounding revelation was made, as a result of dissent among members of secret Schools. Information, hitherto guarded jealously by the most enclosed of the inner Orders, was made public. The secrets disclosed pertained to a far deeper level of knowledge than has hitherto been made exoteric by the Schools – even in this enlightened age.'

His trace of cynicism seemed to go by unnoticed.

'Our purpose here is not to document how so deep an esoteric idea was made public – or even to assess whether it was wise for this idea to be brought out into the open. All this has been dealt with in the literature – and if any of you wish to follow this up, I will give you a few titles later.[35]

'In a nutshell, what was made public during this conflict in the Schools was the truth that our Moon is a sort of counterweight to another sphere, which remains invisible to ordinary vision. This counterweighted sphere is called in esoteric circles the Eighth Sphere.

'We must be careful with these words, for, in spite of what I have just said, this region is not itself a sphere, nor is it a moon. Even to locate it behind the physical Moon is not correct, for in the Spiritual realm spaces and distances are different. The truth is that this Eighth Sphere does not pertain to anything we are familiar with on the physical plane, yet we must use words from our own vocabularies whenever we wish to denote its existence. Were we to use a word which fits most appropriately this Sphere, then we should really call it a vacuum. Certainly, *vacuum* is a more appropriate term than sphere, for the Eighth Sphere sucks things into its own shadowy existence.

'This Sphere is lower in the scale of being than the Seventh Sphere (which is the Earth). It acts as a sort of demonic conduit to suck into its maws certain degenerate Spiritual forms on the Earth. It is a shadow Sphere, controlled by shadow beings. However, the fact that they are shadow beings should not lead us to demote or underestimate their capabilities and intelligence. In many respects they are more intelligent than Man, for they are not limited by the power of love, as is Mankind.

'The operation of this Eighth Sphere is complex. Its denizens – those shadowy beings for whom it is home – wish to people their Sphere with humanity, or (more accurately) with human souls. Towards this end, it has erected what we might call terminals on the Earth: these terminals are soul-conduits, which will suck into the lower Sphere a certain form of materialized Spiritual energy that is engendered on the Earth plane. The most usual circumstances where this materialization or engendering takes place is in seances, and in other localities wherein human beings attempt to meddle – against the cosmic law – with the lower Etheric planes.'[36]

Philip was having difficulties with this curious account of the lunar powers, and asked: 'Are you saying that Spiritualist activity is itself victimized by the Eighth Sphere?'

'Yes, Philip. Certain Spiritualist activity is coloured by the erroneous belief that the realm of the dead is accessible to the living. In truth, mediumistic activity *cannot* penetrate through into the true realm of the dead: it is therefore dealing only with shadows. In so doing, it is creating fodder for the nourishment of the Eighth Sphere. This sucking of certain forms of human soul-matter into the Eighth Sphere is not, by any means, intended for the benefit of humanity. The aim of the denizens of this world is to enhance and populate a world which may truly be described as the realm of the damned. The efforts of these denizens, or demons, is contrary to the evolutionary development which has been planned for the world. In truth, the human being was not designed to become a shadow being, captive in a demonic sphere: it was designed to become a god.

'It is less than one hundred years since this knowledge of the Eighth Sphere was made public.[37] At first there was an outcry at this breach in initiate knowledge, but now we can see that it has proved something of a blessing that the demonic threat has been brought out into the open. In some ways, it is easier to deal with a visible enemy. Those who dabble in the supposed communications with the dead, and with that spirit-land which they fondly imagine lies beyond the veil, have not gone unwarned.

'In fact, the School which revealed the secret of the Eighth Sphere made a very bad job of it. The person delegated (if that is the word) to reveal the secret was not a very advanced or accomplished occultist. His name was Sinnett[38] and he worked within the group of Theosophists who were, in the last decades of the 19th century, busy promulgating the wisdom of Eastern esotericism through the Theosophical Society, at the behest of H. P. Blavatsky.[39] The story of Sinnett's incompetence need not trouble us here: Blavatsky recognized his errors, but, for reasons best known to herself, refrained from correcting them in a systematic or informative way.[40]

'What is of real interest to us is the source of the opposition which was raised to Sinnett. This opposition was raised by a Christian religious group – a High Church group – who elected as their spokesman a very learned initiate, C. G. Harrison. Now this gentleman, while a deeply committed Christian, was far more learned in esotericism than Sinnett, or the majority of Theosophists. His analysis of the situation pertaining to the Eighth Sphere was quite masterly, and it was clear that he was attempting to rectify some of the errors made by Sinnett because he recognized how terrible their consequences might be. In fact, as a consequence of his decision to correct the mistakes made by Sinnett, Harrison became the first initiate to set out in public lectures the nature of the conflicts arising between the Secret Schools in 19th-century Europe and America.[41]

'Of course, it may astound some of you to learn that a highly informed stream of initiate knowledge has been preserved within the Church – even if this religious stream was associated with dissenters. One is often persuaded by the history of the Church that almost everything of esoteric worth either degenerated or was forgotten, as inner content gave way to outer form. Indeed, when in search of esoteric knowledge, it is often more productive to look through the literature of the Apocrypha, or the heretical Schools, than to search through official ecclesiastical literature. However, this is a mistake. Not only does the Bible – and the related apocryphal literature – remain the supreme arcane literature of the West, but certain of the hidden truths derived ultimately from the ancient Mystery Schools are still preserved within the Church itself.

'Such observations might remind you that there is much talk in certain circles about the esoteric and heretical lore hidden away in the Secret Library of the Vatican.[42] Some years ago, I was privileged to work in this archive, and I can tell you that while there must be hundreds of arcane documents in its 20 miles of corridors, this has little to do with the esoteric traditions of Christianity. The true knowledge cannot be preserved in documents. The parchments, palimpsests and papers of libraries are ideas in their death-throes, the dark rejects of fission.

'It is of profound importance that you realize this. True esoteric knowledge is revealed in deeds, not in words. When it is preserved in what we may call libraries, then it is preserved in symbols which can be read by very few. This is one of the deeper secrets of initiation, and it is a secret well preserved in esoteric circles. In spite of what you may think, the secret doctrine is not contained in books. Arcane knowledge – indeed, all forms of knowledge – can be preserved only in the souls and spirits of human beings.'

At the time, none of us realized that these would be the last sentences spoken by our Master in the group.

Perhaps the most remarkable of the texts among the Egypto-Greek hermetic time-capsules is that known to scholars as *The Virgin of the World*.[43] The text purports to be an account given by the Egyptian goddess Isis to her son Horus, nominally describing the creation of the world, and the relationship which this created realm holds to the Spiritual worlds. We write 'nominally', because the text is entirely esoteric, and the cosmological account of Creation is pertinent also to any initiation development in the life of one on the Path.

As with so many of the hermetic texts, *The Virgin of the World* is designed to be read on at least three levels, and this is a fact which has tripped up so many of the academics who have dealt with the material. We should observe that the text makes it quite clear that the Isis who permissibly reveals the secrets of the Isiac lore is not the goddess herself, but a priestess of the order. While Isis was the name of a goddess, the word was also used as one of the names for a grade of initiation.

The hermetic texts tell us that, shortly before those souls which were to be human were compelled to descend into the 'watery plasms' bodies, there arose from the Earth 'a Mighty Spirit which no mass of body could contain, whose strength consisted in his intellect'. This mighty Spirit was Momos.[44]

Momos demanded of his fellow gods what these new earthlings were to be called. After learning that they were to be called 'men', Momos said to Hermes: 'This is daring work, this making of man, with eyes inquisitive, and talkative of tongue . . . Have you, the generator of this Earthling, judged it well to leave him free from care? Would you leave him free of grief?'[45]

Hermes, who had been ordered to complete the work of making Man, responded with characteristic inventive wit. To bring grief to Mankind, he linked men and women with all their actions, thoughts and words. He appointed as the overseer of Man the sharp–eyed goddess Adrasteia, and devised an instrument 'possessed of power of sight that cannot err, and cannot be escaped . . . from birth to final dissolution – an instrument which binds together all that's done'.[46] This instrument is what modern esotericists call *karma*.

For all the care exercised in these preparations, things in the world of Man did not prosper well, for Man did not know about karma, or of its consequences. 'Having naught to fear, Mankind sinned in everthing.' At length, all the gods groaned at the wickedness of Mankind, and demanded that something be done. God responded to the prayers of the Spiritual beings, and sent another Efflux of His Nature down to Earth on a mission to change Mankind. At this point in the story told by the Virgin of the World, Horus asks her, 'How was it, and in what way did the Earth receive God's Efflux?'

But Isis refused to answer her son, saying that it was forbidden in the Mysteries for such knowledge to be divulged. She could not speak of so great a Mystery, since this *Ru*, this 'way-of-birth', of the immortal gods could never be known to Mankind.[47]

Yet, in spite of her refusal to break her vows of silence, Isis did consider it permissible to reveal other Mysteries to her neophyte son, and she set out astounding details of the secret consequences of the coming of this Efflux. Whoever and whatever this Efflux was, the effect of its coming was to bring initiation Schools to Earth, and to spread the teachings of the magical praxes which they held secret. From the great Osiris and Isis – who seemed to be emissaries of the Efflux – men learned the sacred art of divining sites for holy buildings and rites. They learned the hidden truths in the records of Hermes, the Master of Initiation, and they learned which of these truths could be imparted to mortal men. It was Osiris and Isis who taught the Mysteries of mummification, the awesome secrets of Death, and the reasons why the human deceased long with such ardour to return to physical form. It is they who taught that the whole of space was filled with daimons and spirits, and that the ancient lore of Hermes was engraved on hidden stones.[48]

If, as our Teacher had intimated, the staff over the shoulder of the Fool is a throwback to the feather of *Maat*, then we have a responsibility to examine our own karma, which remains ever hidden from our own sight in the bag dangling on the *clava* stick over our shoulder.[49] In a great deal of modern literature – even that which pretends to be written from a high Spiritual standpoint – karma is usually misunderstood. In such literature, it is suggested that one can 'deal' with karma by all sorts of techniques. Among these techniques are hypnotism and hypnotic regression. Such methods may appear to propose easy ways to rid one of unwanted karmic consequences, yet, when examined in the light of Spiritual truths, they turn out to be very dangerous.

Hypnotism is really a throwback to ancient techniques practised in the temples of Egypt by priests of high initiation.[50] These priests knew what they were doing when it came to dealing with karma and reincarnation, for they worked under the control of hierophants who had plumbed the deepest secrets of the human soul. Few modern hypnotists are likely to have the qualifications and initiate insight of these priests, with the result that what is practised through hypnotherapeutic techniques usually hovers on the edge of black magic.[51]

In spite of the obvious dangers and risks attendant on such methods, hypnotic techniques (and related regressional methods) are used in certain modern arcane schools which serve the Left-Hand Path. A perverted version of the Black Rite, mentioned in the Isiac hermetic *Virgin of the World*, and which seems to have been an initiation process much anterior to the Isiac initiations, is nowadays used in certain Schools of our acquaintance, concerning which we are not permitted to speak or write. This Black Rite, before it sank into the degenerate forms used in black magical schools, was one used in the initiation of highly developed individuals in the innermost temples of the Egyptian god, Ammon, whose name lingers still even in the finial to many Christian prayers as the dedicatory *Amen*.[52]

Man is not an angel, yet he has a knowledge, based on experience of the Earth, which is beyond the understanding of the angels. Man understands about the lower depths, about the Earth plane to which he was plunged so long ago, and which has remained permanently inaccessible to the angels, who do not have the material bodies to explore the depths. Just as Man cannot see the pleromic light (the great Spiritual light of the numinal world) which is perpetually before the gaze of the angels, the angels themselves cannot see the dense materiality which is constantly before the gaze of Man.

If this sacred lore is true, we must ask, What is it that Man and the angels have in common? In the answer to this question lies a profundity which takes us to the heart of the initiation Schools. *Developed almost to perfection in the angels is love. Love is scarcely developed at all in Man, and confused with many entities sprung from the realms of desire.*

Unlike the angels, Man has not been bequeathed the gift of pure love: to develop further, human beings must so perfect themselves as to learn to love unconditionally and to love without desire. One aspect of the Mysteries which Isis did not feel free to discuss with her son, and which was linked with the descent of the Efflux into the lower realms, was that Mankind has been offered the extraordinary destiny of becoming greater than the angels. The great sacrifice behind the descent of the Efflux is the way-of-birth which is Man's own initiatory way-of-birth into the future.

There have been two related experiences in this life of a Fool to which we look back with a particular sense of gratitude to the angels. We write these words with some reluctance, as we now have sufficient insight to recognize that angelic beings play a part in every moment of the lives of each human being. We know also that writing about an event can change that event – not merely in memory, but as an event in itself, for all human deeds are spread through space and time, as though on a weaving frame wherein the designs may be picked and re-picked to make new patterns.

We know now that it is simply not possible to cross a road in safety without the guidance and protection of angels. Yet, if we are to present a rounded picture of this Fool's growth, we must point to two life experiences during which the angelic activity was of profound importance.

In the middle of February, 1964, the heavens opened for us, and we saw the Higher World for what it is – the home of creative Spiritual beings. How easy it is to write such words, and with what sense of discomfort one recognizes just how difficult it is for mere words to capture the sense of what really happened at that remarkable moment in our lives, when the heavens revealed something of their splendour.

There had been no intimation that a vision would be given to us. We had just been to visit a newly discovered Necromanteion, in Western Greece, where, in ancient times, demons were raised for oracular purposes.[53] The land upon which we had recently been driving had once been a brooding marsh, called in ancient times *The Lake of the Dead*.[54]

In the small village of Ephyra, which was once the site of an ancient city, bordering on the River Acheron, are the extraordinary Graeco-Roman remains of the Oracle of the Dead. The upper part now consists of a maze of roofless walls, but the most remarkable survival of this ancient oracle is the underground cell, hidden, until recently, beneath the foundations of a church and cemetery. When we visited it, excavations were not yet complete, and descent into the cell was by means of a temporary ladder. The inside was lit by means of a single 100-watt bulb, which emphasized the shadows of the arch vaults, and grotesqued the shadows on the uneven earthen floor. Perhaps this eerie glow was the best light in which to gaze back over three or even four millennia.

The excavation of the site had begun in 1958, and had only just reached completion.[55] However, a considerable amount was already known about it from classical literature, and from passing references in late Roman sources.

It was at this oracle – sometimes in the subterranean cell (plate 21), and sometimes in the maze of religious buildings above – that the spirits of the dead were raised by specially trained priests, reciting the names of the infernal demons, and directing the truth-seekers to special sacrifices of rams or sheep.

The site had been a famous oracle in ancient times, and several records have survived giving accounts of those who visited Ephyra to ask questions of the deceased. Periander, the sixth-century BC tyrant of Corinth, sent messengers to ask the priests to consult the shade of his wife, Melissa (whom he had murdered), to determine where she had hidden some valuables.[56] Even earlier, the poet, Homer, describes how his hero, Odysseus, sacrificed a black goat and consulted the spirits at this same oracle. Odysseus was surprised at what came to meet him from the nether regions, for not only the shades of former companions appeared, but also the spirit of his mother, whom he had not realized was dead.[57]

It is difficult to determine how ancient the oracle of Ephyra is. The indications are that the surviving buildings are, on the whole, Roman, but the subterranean cell is certainly more ancient. The upper sanctuary appears to have been destroyed by fire, some time in the second century BC, after which the oracle appears to have fallen into disuse. However, the fact that the oracle is mentioned by Homer, who wrote in the ninth century BC, points to this as one of the most ancient surviving oracles of the dead in the Western world.

One might hardly imagine such a site to be conducive to contact with the *higher* world: in ancient times, the demons and spirits of Hades were firmly located in the darkness of Earth. Yet, it was while driving away from this place that the heavens opened themselves up to us. We suspect that this experience was not something we had earned, or deserved, and that it was nothing other than a gift bestowed by the heavens. Our daily Spiritual exercises had been conducted with the usual attention and lack of attention – with what our Master had once called 'quite normal, and quite unforgivable, human inertia'. Our life was going well, but not so well as to cause us to indulge in any sense of overweening pride. We were neither in love nor out of love, neither hungry nor surfeited. Everything was very ordinary – which is to say that we were pressed between the quite usual miracles which surround all humans, and which generally pass by unseen. No doubt, the angels who guide us must have seen that something was necessary. Perhaps we needed a shock, or an insight.

On that Thursday, we were driving in a sports car between Ephyra and Corinth. The weather was warm yet sultry and cloudy. We had a strangely claustrophobic sense that it was going to rain, and that we should stop the car to pull up the roof. Instead of stopping, however, we felt in our glove-compartment for a tape, and found Josquin des Pres' *Missa La sol fa re mi*, a musical mantra which, the moment it began to unfold on the cassette player, seemed to find a corresponding vibration in our soul.[58] We were intensely happy, though for no reason we could put our finger on.

We looked up over the windscreen towards the skies, to where clouds should be, and could no longer see clouds. A large bird was wheeling in the skies, without moving its wings. Suddenly, as though from within ourselves, a hitherto unrecognized joy cascaded on to the outside, and became part of the outer joy of the world. The clouds, as it were, dissolved, and in their place was light. But this was no ordinary light: it might be more accurate to describe it as life, though in truth one word would be insufficient to describe what we perceived, for besides looking upon a different sky, we could also see the car on the road below, driving in the central lane at considerable speed. In the car we could see our own body, about the size of a thumb.

There are probably many ways of putting it, yet all ways would be periphrastic. We might picture ourselves standing on the beach of a desert island, and wading thigh-deep into the turquoise waters. When we look down into the limpid surface, through the shafts of bright undulating greens which pattern the shifts of sunlight, we are enthralled to see the waters teeming with a myriad fishes of rainbow hues. Are these fishes scintillas of the sunlight, or are they splinters from the five-note phrases of Josquin's glorious Mass? They are musical fish, quite unlike the fish of this world.[59] Yet again, are these living creatures merely sweat-born from our own soul's joy – the reason why Isis herself was called the Lady of the Sea? Such questions do not make much sense for one who does not stand thigh-deep in those blue-green waters, or in the familiar world of senses, yet in the world where we were then immersed, the words approximate to sense: the outer and the inner were reflections of one another, and there was no me and thee, nor any that. Perhaps the ancient Greek word *zodia*, which has been so misunderstood in modern times, catches the feeling of the teeming life of spirit which we saw in the skies, as we drove in a sports car which was itself made from sky-metal, on a motorway which would lead anywhere, and forever, because to say it had an end would be to place it in time.

Tell me, they will say. What was it like, Master Fool, this *seeing*? This seeing into the higher world? And you will sigh, for there are no words to describe such a thing properly. However, you may say: 'Yes, I was there. I saw it. Yes, it is not quite what you might imagine. Indeed, it is beyond belief. Angels, you know, and living beings.'

And those to whom you speak will look at you blankly. You will learn from such looks, and you will even stop trying to explain, reserving that impenetrable silence which one was ever supposed to keep about the secret things. From their looks, you know that there is no point, any longer, in trying to tell the truth with ordinary words.

'It is the seeing of the little man,' you may say to them, speaking the truth, and thinking of the thumb-sized figure in the car below the vision.[60]

'Of the microcosm?' they ask, revealing that they do not understand.

'No, of the *little man*. Of the man no larger than the size of the letter *i* on the page you read. He looks upwards, and finds himself in the skies, looking downwards, at himself. He reflects himself, just as the *i* on the page before you must see itself reflected in your eye, because that is the nature of reality. The *i* is on the page and in your eye, and on the page in your eye . . . No, perhaps it is not wise to tell you of these things. Let me say merely that it was worth the furious gazing and all the pains to see Heaven's beauty – a beauty that seemed a thing removed, and in a different time set apart.'[61]

Yet now they know that because you are speaking as a poet, you no longer tell the truth. And yet you persist in erecting this barrier of words, because you sense that only poetry, spoken by a true poet, can tell how the sunlight splinters into myriads of fish that make rainbows seem colourless.

We must never have left the sports car, for we were still driving, and the sky above, filled with denizens of spirit, was fading. For one final moment of hubris, we had expected this vision to last forever, and we found ourselves wondering how we might lead an ordinary life while participating in this splendour which was so unutterably true, yet at that moment a shadow fell, as though a cloud had passed, and it was over.

'How did this vision change your world?' they will ask. You understand their question, but the words you issue in reply sound coarse and far from the truth.

'We saw that we are all sustained,' one might say, really trying to catch the essence of the thing. 'It is true that there are such things as spirit-catchers. Not only catchers in the rye, but above the skies which look down upon the rye, and in the Earth which nourishes the rye, and in the Celestial Nile where the rye has turned to reeds and is infested with the benu birds. We are caught and sustained, and all our tears and all our sadness is nothing more than an affront to those beings who sustain, for they know that the universe began with seven great peals of laughter, and the echo of this laughter rumbles on still.'

'Now do you understand?' you will ask, as you offer such words.

And they will reply, 'Yes, we understand!' But you know that they cannot understand, and will not, until they too stand thigh-deep in those waters which Paracelsus had called the Celestial Sea and the Virgin Waters, and which in the Isiac literature was called the Celestial Nile.[62]

From the vision we learned something of what might be for all men, and that a time will come when many men and women will wish to earn such a commerce with the Spiritual realm. Through the vision we had captured an insight into the future development of those among humanity who will be saved, and who, through such salvation, will progress into a Higher World.

The vision never returned – perhaps because it had achieved its purpose, and shown us a little of what would be possible for all striving humanity. For a while after the experience, the familiar world seemed flat, though charged with a Spiritual energy which could be felt pulsating behind the outer appearance of things. Yet even that passed away, and the world eventually became once again the familiar shadow-world, the reflection of the higher, the Isis-world reflecting the pleromic light of Osiris. The world returned to normal, but in our memory to this day we recall the beauty and promise of that vision, as though it had been a glimpse of the Grail. We know that if every person could be vouchsafed this vision only once in their lives, then the world would change in the instant, for it is to know the secret of secrets, when one really understands that the angels are here and there and everywhere.

As it happened, it was not the sound of angels' wings, or the sight of an Etheric feather floating Earthwards from the skies, which alerted us to an angelic presence in later times. It was something more like a small explosion of light, almost like a nova star, which would illumine itself in the air, yet illuminate nothing around it. Perhaps this was what the alchemists had called the *floral fire*,[63] for it resembled the expanding calyx of a flower, formed from a flame that did not burn. This flower-star pulsates, and seems to hover in the air, yet it is unlike any star one might see in the skies. It is a pinprick of exploding soft light, and so clearly of a Spiritual genesis that one has no need to ask anyone in the room, or in the street, if they too can see it. This star was not designed for ordinary eyes. It might even be the same type of star which guided the Magi of old, save – in the hermetic accounts – this warning star does not move.[64] The star appeared, a circle of light beckoning from another plane of being.

At that time – the third week of November, 1979 – we were exploring Monument Valley, staying in a motel on the road which passes between Death Valley and Mexican Hat. Both places are still so heavily charged with the powerful shamanistic magic of the dispossessed North American Indians that one might not be surprised to see star-bursts in the Etheric skies. Yet this star was fixed in our Etheric vision, and we knew that it was intended for us alone.

It would be a long drive to Los Angeles, and the Sunday night traffic would be bad, yet we knew that this was where we had to go. We climbed into the car. The star had already left us, but our knowledge urged us on.

In Los Angeles we had a considerable number of friends and acquaintances. One was an American psychologist, who had become deeply involved with a healing School based on a modern interpretation of traditions relating to the Egyptian god *Kneph*, the blue-black Old One of ancient rites.[65] The School centred its healing activities on erasing unwanted tendencies carried over from past lives, and seemed not to recognize the awesome Spiritual dangers in such manipulations.

Because we could not approve of his choice of Teacher, School or direction, our friendship had gone into abeyance. We had not seen him for over 12 years, ever since he had permitted us to witness – even participate in – one of the Knephian rites of healing. Even so, we knew from the stellar message that we had to call upon this man, whom, for the sake of convenience, we will name Arne Topolski.[66]

Early one Saturday afternoon, towards the middle of a bitterly cold day in November, 1966, while on a short trip to the States, we had called upon Arne Topolski in Los Angeles. His wife, Elke, had answered the door, and told us that Arne was with a patient in the surgery. She offered us a drink, and whiled away the time showing us snapshots of their recent holidays, and of their two children, who were now away at European universities. An hour or so later, Arne emerged from the room, followed by an attractive woman whom we instantly recognized as the well-known English novelist, Persephone Seabrooke.[67] Arne introduced us, but a few minutes later Persephone left, explaining that, much as she would love to stay and talk, she had a previous engagement. We had read a couple of her books, at least one of which had carried her portrait on the flyleaf, and from this we had formed an agreeable idea of her appearance. However, we were totally unprepared to discover that she had a mild form of glossoplegia, which made it difficult for her to speak with any clarity. Whenever she spoke, her whole face pulled into a grimace, and some of her words were almost unintelligible.

After the usual pleasantries, during which we were invited to stay for lunch, Arne brought the conversation around to Persephone by talking about her latest novel. This seems to have been a discreet way of touching upon her condition, which was giving him considerable trouble.

'Glossoplegia. A curious affliction. I might tell you that we have struggled with this now for almost three months.'

'She is seeking a cause through Knephian healing?' we asked, knowing that Arne specialized in the psychiatric system based on the exploration of the influence of past-life trauma on present-life ailments. The expressed aim was to bring the crises in past lives into consciousness, thus diminishing or even removing entirely their pernicious influences in the present life.

'Not just a cause, but also a cure. But in this case, we're foxed.'

'I thought that revealing the cause was in itself sufficient to set the patient on the path to recovery?' We tried not to sound cynical. While this was the theory, it did not always work in practice, and even those proficient in the art were not always aware of the long-term consequences. On the other hand, while we mistrusted the method and its ultimate outcome, we had heard of some fairly dramatic cures. Our concern was not so much for the present life, as for the effect that this kind of tinkering by amateurs could have on future development.

'In most cases, that is so. But with Persephone I seem to have come up against a blank wall. We have located the past-life engram[68] which has given rise to the glossoplegia, yet – for reasons which are not clear – we cannot get beyond this. I wonder if it might interest you to sit in on the next session. I would value your opinion.'

'If Persephone agrees.'

'How long will you be in Los Angeles?'

'Five days. I must fly on to Mexico City.'

'I'll ring her, and see if we can arrange another therapy before you go.'

Another session was arranged for lunchtime on the following Wednesday, the 16th. Persephone gave her permission for us to be present during the hypnosis, regression and later examination.

Arne decided to go through the case history with us, prior to the next session. He told us that, under hypnotic regression, Persephone had revealed that her present affliction was connected with an experience she had undergone in North America, during a previous lifetime. It seemed that during this life, she had been an Indian brave. He had been captured by white settlers, who had tortured him to death.

Almost as soon as Arne had hypnotized her, and asked her to go back to the middle of May, 1618, Persephone began to talk, her glossoplegia very much in evidence.

'The agony is almost unendurable, yet I know that I must show no pain . . .' We could see from the stiffening of her face, and from the physiological changes impressed upon it, that she was living through the torture experience once again. 'I am lying on the floor. On the hard rocks. My arms are tied behind my back. One man has already cut off my ears. Now he is pushing a skewer through my tongue. No, it is not a skewer. It is more like a huge wooden needle. Through the eye of the needle he has pushed the end of a cow-hide thong. I know what they are going to do, and I know that when they do it I will no longer be able to talk.' She was gulping and swallowing.

'Yes you will,' said Arne. 'Persephone, it is no longer you. Now you will have the power to tell us. Try to speak. Whatever happens to you, it will be possible for you to speak.'

'The thong has been threaded through my tongue. The man throws the end of the thong over a tree branch, and begins to pull it in jerks upon my tongue. Now the pain is more than I can bear, yet I cannot shout out. Terrible noises come from my mouth, but they are not the noises I wish to make.'

'What noises do you wish to make?'

'I wish to beg them to stop. Yet I know that I am a brave, and must show no pain to the face of an enemy.'

'Can you not leave your body behind?' suggested Arne. 'Can you not escape?'

'I have been shown such things. But the pain draws me down. I think that the shaman who instructed me did not know that such pain was possible.'

Her face was sweating. 'It is this same man. My tormentor. Now he has pulled me to my feet by dragging on the thong. Now I am hanging from the tree by my tongue. Below is a sharpened spike. He swings his gun around his head and hits me in the stomach. Now it is over. My tongue is split, and my body falls to the ground, and is skewered by the spike. I see my body fall, but now I am above the tree, looking down. The pain seems to be a long way away. I no longer think of the pain, but I wish to be with my young squaw, back in the mountains. I should not have left those mountains. What will become of my squaw, now?'

Persephone was brought out of her trance.

'It was the same as before?' she asked.

'You cannot remember?'

'No, I cannot remember. Was I a brave? Did that man pull out my tongue?'

'Yes.'

'If this is true – and I cannot see how it could be otherwise – and the pain is as you recall, then I cannot understand why you are not already healing,' said Arne.

He looked towards us. 'Do you have any views, Mark?'

We had a suggestion, yet did not feel free to make it in front of Persephone, who was, after all, a patient. Arne sensed this.

'Do you want to speak to me alone?'

She interrupted. 'Please feel free,' she said, awkwardly. 'I would be grateful for any suggestions that might help.'

Even though she had offered to listen, we still did not feel inclined to speak too openly. We were puzzled that she had referred to her tormentors as white men, and by other details of her account. Even so, we did not wish to interfere with her version, or complicate the issue.

'Have you thought of the mirror . . . the *mercuric speculum*?' we asked him.[69]

Arne was sufficiently versed in arcane matters to know what we meant, and he nodded slowly, before turning to Persephone.

'May I hypnotize you again?' he asked her.

Once more, Arne put her into a trance where regression became possible, and once again he led her to the trauma.

'I want you to go back to 1618. To 14 May of that year. There is an Indian brave. He is tied securely, lying upon the ground. Someone has cut off his ears. Around him are white men. They are his tormentors. They mean to kill him.

'How many men are there around that Indian, Persephone?'

'I can see three.'

'They are white men?'

'Yes. They are white men.'

'Why do you not call them pale-faces?'

'Why should I?'

'You are an Indian. You must call them pale-faces.'

'Yes, they are pale-faces.'

'How many do you see?'

'Three pale-faces.'

'Perhaps you are making a mistake, Persephone. Please, look again.'

'No. There are three. I see only three.'

'Look more closely, Persephone. This is very important. The year 1618 is gone. The Indian is gone, the white men have gone. Look again, most carefully. Where is the other white man? Look, and tell us about the one with the knife. That man – the one who has already slipped the Indian's ears into his pouch. He has sharpened a branch into the form of a wooden needle. Now he has threaded it with cow-hide thong. Where is this man, now? This white man? Where is he, Persephone?'

'I am looking. I cannot see him,' she said. Then suddenly she lifted her head and gave a most piteous howl. She started sobbing uncontrollably, pushing away a vision from her eyes.

'Oh, no. Oh, no. I would not do such a thing. It cannot be.' She was shaking her head from side to side, tears streaming down her face. 'There are *four* white men. I could see only three, because I am the fourth: *I was the tormentor, not the brave*. Oh, no. It is I. I am the one who does these terrible things to that Indian!'

A few months later, when we had returned to Europe, we asked a Teacher we knew about the Knephian School.

'Almost without exception, hypnosis in modern times is a dangerous undertaking. We are all like the demon-infested boxes of Epimetheus, and it is a courageous man – or perhaps a foolish man – who will lift that lid which separates the conscious from the unconscious.[70]

'This was not the case in former times. In former times – when the Egypto-Greek healing was at its height in such places as Alexandria, Oropus and the island of Cos – a form of hypnosis was used in what we now call sleep-healing, or serpent-healing.[71] However, this hypnosis and its associated snake-healing was practised by high initiates who knew what they were doing. Such priest-doctors knew precisely how the Etheric body would react to pictures and how that body is especially designed to absorb images during periods when the physical body itself is in suspended animation. There was a considerable body of knowledge concerning this incubation as the methods were derived from initiation methods developed by the Egyptian priests.

'However, the practice of temple-sleep – incubation as it was called – was controlled by initiates of immense learning. This is certainly more than can be claimed in modern times. In the hermetic texts, you will find many injunctions against the use of magic – "the Spiritual man who knows himself should not seek to accomplish anything by means of magic, but should allow nature to accomplish her own work according to her own decree". These are said to be the words of Hermes himself, and are as applicable to your Knephians as to ourselves.[72]

'But you did not come to see me to talk about incubation: you wanted to talk about the Knephians and their practices. I can tell you only one thing, and then I must leave you to come to your own conclusions as to how you should relate to this group, and to any individuals you know in this group.'

He cleared his throat. 'The young man who founded the Knephians was far from being an initiate of any standing.[73] He had however dabbled in various magical praxes before entering a monastic system of initiation established in a community related to Mount Athos. Although he did swear the usual secrecy oaths, he later broke them, and began to use some of the most extraordinary esoteric techniques for commercial purposes. He began to use pictorial manipulation of Etheric images on hypnotized patients. Of course, the results were extraordinary, when considered out of context. It is possible to heal – or seem to heal – with such techniques. Of course, with such healing techniques it is possible to make a great deal of money, for people are looking for such miracle-working. The young man was keen upon making considerable amounts of money. However, you yourself have witnessed already just how dangerous hermetic lore may be when it is leaked into the ordinary realm by people of an immoral tendency, or by people of an insufficiency of grade in initiation. In a word, the Knephian rites are both stolen and misapplied.

'I am not free to say anything more than I have said. Now you must exercise your own Will, and come to your own decisions about these matters.'

It was to Arne Topolski, a practitioner in this dangeous Knephian school, that the flower-star had directed us from the hot deserts around the outlandish Mexican Hat. It took many hours to reach Los Angeles, and we did not arrive until near lunchtime on 19 November. Wearily, we pulled up at the kerbside of one of the back streets behind the Masonic hall, outside the house in which Arne had lived in the days when he had been our friend. We were not supposed to park in this particular stretch of road, yet, somehow, we knew that it was essential that we should.

We walked down the stone steps of the tenement building to the lower flat, and rang the bell. Instantaneously – so that one had the impression that the ringing of the bell had caused the noise – there followed the shattering of glass, and a loud scream. It was a girl's scream. We rang the bell again, and the door was flung open by a white-faced girl whose wild stare identified her as the screamer. We did not know her.

'Come, quickly.' She motioned down the passageway.

Arne was in the small kitchen at the end of the hall. One of his hands was still pushed through the broken window pane, caught upon a sharp edge. Blood was spurting on to the floor and ceiling, and the jagged teeth of the broken window were red: we remember observing how this red contrasted strangely with the intense greens of the trees in the garden beyond. There was a sense that an everyday horror had been rendered eternal because it was frozen in time – rather like an expressionist water-colour by George Grosz.[74]

Removing as much of the splintered glass as we were able, we wrapped Arne's arms in towels, bundled him into the car, and, with the girl directing us, drove to the hospital.

'Why?' we asked, as we supported him into the hospital, not expecting him to reply through the pain.

'Elke died . . .' he began, but stopped short, adding almost inaudibly, 'Guilt.'

We nodded, but we knew that the real reason for suicide is always too intense a love of life.

It was only long afterwards that we thought back over the day's long journey, attempting to marshal it in reversed images. What would have happened, we asked ourselves, had the soft flower-star not appeared to us in the desert? Are there such angel-given stars for everyone at these times of the soul's perturbation? we wondered. And what would have happened had we not responded to that floral call?

And still we have no answer to this question, other than in the clue found in the fragmentary gospels now called *The Acts of John*.

The Disciple cries out, 'I would flee.'

The Master says, 'I would rather have you stay.'[75] The angels, no less than a Master, are not permitted to issue imperative commands. However, it seems that they may warn or persuade us with signs and wonders, even if these are no more substantial than floral stars illumined for a second or two in the air.

Chapter Six

Was not all the knowledge
Of the Egyptians writ in mystic symbols?
Speak not the Scriptures, oft, in parables?
Are not the choicest fables of the poets,
That were the fountains, and first springs of wisdom,
Wrapped in perplexed allegories?

(The pseudo–alchemist, Subtle, talking to Mammon, in Ben
Jonson's *The Alchemist*, II, iii)

The first-century AD priest, Plutarch, was one of the few early initiates to write openly about the Mysteries. It seems, therefore, that he may have been the first high initiate to break an oath of silence concerning the sacred Egyptian rites.

Plutarch, born in Chaeroneia in Greece, had been initiated into the ancient Egyptian mysteries of Osiris at Delphi, and held high office in several of the initiation rites at this beautiful sacred site. Since his book, *Isis and Osiris*,[1] was written at Delphi, we may reasonably question whether he was in breach of a sacred oath, for if he had been there would have been little difficulty in the priestcraft supressing the text, and punishing so serious a breach. However, since there may be no doubt that this remarkable work does contain a wealth of secret information about the Mysteries of Isis and Osiris, it does appear, at first glance, that he did in some way break his vows of silence.

The book itself is a loose collection of essays on the Mysteries. These essays deal with issues pertaining to certain levels of initiation and arcane mythology. They are specifically addressed to his friend Klea. Now, this Klea was herself a priestess at Delphi, and was also an initiate. It is this fact which enables us to remove any charge that Plutarch, in revealing the Mysteries of Isis, was in breach of his vows, for he was merely instructing a fellow initiate in the same Mysteries of Isis as his own. It is the fact that the collection of essays was later made available to the public which seems to offend the vow of silence enforced upon Plutarch. We do not know how this breach took place – it may not have been Plutarch's intention to publish these essays. Certainly, there is no indication that he was punished by the Delphic Mystery Centres for this seeming breach of his vow of silence.

In one part of the book, in which Plutarch appears to deal with the issue as to why the priests of Isis appeared shaven and wore only linen, he quotes a couple of lines from a Mystery wisdom which was ancient, even in his day.[2]

the fire-bloomed five branched

Some believed that the intriguing 'five branched' was the human hand. On the basis of this, it was argued by some modern scholars that the reference was to a prohibition against paring the nails at a Feast of the Gods. It almost goes without saying that, in so esoteric a context, the phrase has a much deeper meaning.

Almost any initiate of the ancient world would have recognized that 'five branched' was not a reference to the human hand, but to the Etheric body of man. This is a Spiritual body which is invisible to all but initiates and other clairvoyants.

In ancient Egyptian symbolism the 'five branched' Etheric was represented in the form of the *sba* star,[3] which was one of the more important hieroglyphics:

This *sba* star was so intimately linked with death that it appears on the inside of many tombs. At the sixth-dynasty tomb of Teti, the entire inner chamber is covered in the five-pointed radiants.

In early Christian symbolism, the star symbolism of this sarcophagus *sba* was humanized, so to speak. In the subterranean chambers of the catacombs in Rome, where ceremonies and ritual meals for the dead were held, the newly dead are depicted precisely as 'five branched', or in star-shape. They are portrayed with arms stretched upwards, the legs being the lower two points, the head the fifth (see over). Perhaps this explains why some sacred texts claim that the newly dead 'become stars'.[4] Esoteric writers insist that this five-fold gesture was used to indicate that the person so depicted was 'dead' – which is to say they were Etheric forms, bereft of the physical body.[5]

The post-mortem etheric gesture of a departed soul (a so-called 'orans', or praying figure) painted in the 3rd century catacomb of Callistus, Rome.

In later arcane texts, this Etheric *five-branched man* was expressed in the image of the pentagrammic man which so obsessed the mediaeval initiate Paracelsus, and which Agrippa, aware of its arcane origins, attempted to link with the planets.[6]

In modern times, the invisible five-fold body is called the Etheric body. In Greek times it bore a similar name, and because it was believed to be derived from the sun's Etherial radiance, was described as *the body of shadowless light*. Even Plutarch went so far as to speak of the Spiritual body of man as having the property of 'not casting a shadow'.[7] He recognized that such a body was composed of the light of the Etheric, the light of the Sun.

Now, the fragment quoted by Plutarch mentions more than the idea of merely the 'five branched'. It refers also to the *fire-blooming*. This fire-blooming was an esoteric reference to the 'burning' which had to be endured in the early stages of initiation. The initiate Schools recognized that, as a result of initiation, the higher pentagrammic Etheric emerged, hands held up in wonder at the Spiritual world newly revealed to it. In some respects, this stage of

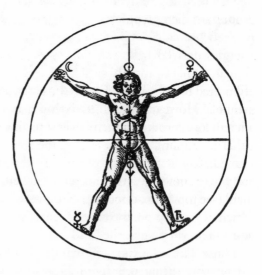

The pentagrammic man – the etheric gesture – from Cornelius Agrippa De Occulta Philosophia, *1534.*

initiation closely resembled death itself, for after the death of the physical, the Etheric automatically adopts the position of the five-pointed star, with hands held up in adoration. The gesture which modern art-historians usually refer to as the 'orans', or praying gesture, is the image of the Etheric as it was preserved in esoteric art.[8]

In these terms, therefore, we see that Plutarch's 'five-branched' is more than man: once the human has been through the painful burning of initiation, he becomes the *purified man*,[9] that man from whom all dross has been burned away. In alchemy – in which the burning away of dross to reveal the inner gold is a main theme – the pentagrammatic man is called 'the star of the microcosm', *stella microcosmi*.[10] This redeemed man – or woman – is a star which does not shine in the heavens (the *macrocosm*), but on the Earth itself, which is the realm of the little-cosmos, or *microcosm*.

Traditions of reincarnation maintain that Mankind consists of two systems, each of which penetrate, yet have separate existences. One system is that centred on the head, which pertains to thinking. The other centres on the human body, which pertains to Will. The mediaeval alchemists bound together these different systems by means of a numerology derived from Pythagoras and the *mathematici*, or astrologers, who linked the Etheric with the power of the sun. This knowledge was hidden from ordinary history for some centuries, but surfaced in the 19th century, in the writings of the Theosophists.[11]

To a very large extent – and in the face of some opposition from other groups – the Theosophists openly taught some of the great secrets of the hermetic schools.[12] They taught that the Etheric was a body of light, its energies derived from the Sun, with a predisposition to retain a form similar to that of the physical.[13] Few of the earlier Mystery Schools had attempted to portray the Etheric directly, and had remained content with symbols. However, the Theosophists, in their anxiety to publicise the ancient lore, produced many diagrams illustrating the distribution of the Etheric. Among the points made by the Theosophists was that, immediately at the death of the physical, the Etheric would disengage and hover above it, with arms outstretched, in the gesture of the 'praying man' (see top figure opposite). Strangely enough, it had been this gesture which was adopted by the ancient Egyptians for their own Etheric-equivalent, the spirit called *ka* ⊔Ⴗ [14]

Those Theosophists who popularized the idea of the Etheric did not fully expose the deeper significance of its symbolism. Madam Blavatsky, in her epoch-making break with esoteric silence, *The Secret Doctrine*, revealed that, in the Secret Schools of India and Egypt, this five-pointed star had been 'emblematically transformed into a crocodile', which was sometimes called the *Makara*.[15] It is a fact that one of the deepest secrets of arcane symbolism hinges on the fact that this same union of star and crocodile is linked with the secret principles of reincarnation.

It seems that the star of light is symbol of the pure and undefiled Etheric, while the crocodile is symbol of the Etheric which is still defiled by karma, and thus destined for rebirth.

Reincarnation is still one of the great secrets of the hermetic Schools. This may seem to be a nonsensical claim, for nowadays there are thousands of books, and no small number of esoteric-seeming groups, that teach various forms of reincarnational theory. Indeed, there is virtually an industry on the fringes of psychology that deals with regressions seemingly linked with reincarnation. In fact, a true knowledge of the laws pertaining to reincarnation is beyond the grasp of all those who have not undergone special training in Schools. An ability to deal with knowledge and insights derived from a study of reincarnation depends upon the development of psychic organs which is simply not available at present for the majority of people.

One of the problems with revealing or discussing the previous incarnations of famous men and women is that, once one has named a line of rebirths for a particular individual, ordinary people demand proof. If these people cannot see into the Spiritual realm where these truths are preserved, then it is quite impossible to offer proof which will be acceptable to them.

Of course, as an alternative to attempting to speak or write from one's own personal experience of reincarnation, it is quite possible to point to an extensive and reliable literature dealing with reincarnation. Certain writers in this field are prepared to list interesting connections between incarnated individuals who have been famous in different historical periods. For example, one author may connect St Augustine with a later incarnation of Leonardo da Vinci.[16] Another may trace an earlier incarnation of the American poet, Ralph Waldo Emerson, to the first-century AD Roman historian, Tacitus.[17] Another, perhaps touched a little by human egocentricity, might delight in tracing his or her own previous lives back to such an important personality as Mary Queen of Scots.[18]

Hundreds, if not thousands, of such examples of 'famous' incarnations are now on record, and form some of the most fascinating reading for those interested in occult matters. This should not surprise us, perhaps, as well over a century ago, one pioneer in the field pointed out that over 600,000,000 people believed firmly in reincarnation.[19] Of course, that figure must have doubled or even trebled in a century. It is mainly those in the West who have difficulty in feeling the inner truth of reincarnation. Many Westerners have to undergo special meditations and disciplines to arrive at an understanding of reincarnation which the majority of those in the East take for granted.

We speak of *famous* individuals because it is in this area that one can, through studying the extended biographies of influential men and women, reach most easily into the secrets of history. It is in this area that the interest of most occultists lies. One other reason why occultists continue to show an interest in the exploration of the facts of reincarnation – facts which they do not for one moment doubt – is that through a detailed study of the laws behind this phenomenon it is possible to learn a great deal about the cosmos. In tracing the influences which persist (in a transformed state) between lifetime and lifetime, the practised hermeticist can explain, if only for himself, many curious and otherwise inexplicable details of history.

For example, one may wonder why some people who find themselves in a crowd suffering infectious diseases do not catch these themselves. How, for example, could Florence Nightingale,[20] who worked for up to 20 hours per day among those dying of the terrible fever which raged during the Crimean War of 1853-6, have survived that scourge herself?[21] There may be no answer to this question in ordinary terms – many of her colleagues and patients died in that service, yet she did not. Was this really a question of accident? The trained esotericist recognizes that this is not accidental, but rather an effect of personal karma. Nightingale could survive because she did not have a karmic disposition towards infectious diseases.

There is meaning in this survival. Had she not survived, then she would not have been able to establish in England the principles and practices of modern nursing: her own personal destiny, and certain trends in Victorian England, would not have come to useful fruition. Florence Nightingale's Spiritual life had been touched by contact with the last of the esoteric medical orders, in the form of the Sisters of Charity, founded by St Vincent de Paul.[22] Such a contact reminds one that, in the beginning at least, such female Orders had intimate contact with the Orders of Hospitallers in Palestine, which had been formed to serve the Templars and the pilgrims they protected. There can be no doubt that these were esoteric groups – hermetic Orders – who had a profound effect on the development of late mediaeval European history. If one meditates on such things, one begins to perceive, in the life of the remarkable Florence Nightingale, her connection – established in a previous lifetime – with the crusading Templars.

What does the hermetic tradition teach concerning the Spiritual origins of infectious diseases? What events in one lifetime are likely to give a predisposition towards infectious diseases, such as the Crimean fever, in a following lifetime?

The arcane tradition teaches that the acquisitive urge in man – an urge which might properly be described as a psychic illness – colours the Etheric body in a particular way. Just as an ordinary person may look at the face of another and sense – even see – in that face physiognomic characteristics which suggest a strong acquisitive urge, so may a trained occultist look at the Etheric body of a person and see certain qualities which even more forcefully reveal a disposition towards such an acquisitive urge. The trained initiate will see, encased over the light-form of the morally weakened Etheric, the denser form of what it will become in bodily form. This encasing of darkness over the star is conveniently symbolized as a thick-skinned leathern crocodile.[23] Perhaps it was the knowledge of such hermetic truths that led to the mediaeval pharmacists and alchemists hanging stuffed crocodiles from the ceilings of their laboratories – to remind them of the dark star which is exhaled, as they perfect and solarize their own inner star of Etheric.[24]

What the trained occultist will recognize which the ordinary person will usually fail to recognize is that this 'Etheric illness' of acquisitiveness will work its way down into the physical body of a following incarnation. To put it crudely, the urge to acquire things on the material plane is transformed, in a subsequent incarnation, into a propensity to 'acquire' infectious diseases. Immorality, or a misapprehension about the true nature of the material world, will, as Blavatsky intimated, darken into a crocodile form, from which the soul must struggle free.

Among the vows taken by the Templars were those of poverty and chastity.[25] Being esotericists, they would have recognized that this would lead, in a future lifetime (among other things), to their being in a good position to resist certain infectious diseases. Viewed in the light of esoteric thought, we see that the way of such preparations was intended as a preparation for them to become healers.[26] It is almost certainly in this wisdom that we may trace the strange and dedicated life of Florence Nightingale, in her 19th-century incarnation. It is in such mysteries, as revealed in history, that we begin to sense the significance of the symbolism in the five-fold man – the *five-branched* of Plutarch. One of the great secrets of reincarnation rests on the relationship between the Etheric body and the physical. As we have already intimated, what is absorbed by the Etheric body in one lifetime is transformed, to colour the life of the body in a following incarnation.

It is perhaps reasonable for us to assume that what we breathe in one moment we breathe out, transformed, a few moments later. According to the hermetic wisdom, the lower world is like the higher, and it is therefore reasonable to assume that this same relationship of in-breathing and exhaling may be perceived in man and woman over a period of lifetimes. To adopt the imagery of the ancient world – if we do not involve ourselves on a programme of cleansing (such as is offered by initiation), then from lifetime to lifetime, we may breathe in the light of the Sun, yet we will breathe out the darkness of a crocodile.

'We are very proud of our heads, nowadays,' our Master had said, shortly before his death. 'Indeed, it is not too much of an exaggeration to say that we are far too proud of our thinking. We do not appreciate the extent to which human thinking casts a veil over reality. Part of the absurdity of of view of thinking is that we have the temerity to believe that thinking is something we do, something we own! As a matter of fact, it is very difficult to have a thought which is our own. A particular ability is required to create a new thought by means of thinking.

'So far as our personalities and persona are concerned, we identify far more with thinking than we do with feeling. One consequence of this is that we usually value more highly what a person says and thinks than what a person does. This suggests that we have become hypnotized by image, by surface-appearance, which is held to be so very important in modern times. By means of image, it is possible to create, with words and pictures, outer impressions which do not correspond to inner reality. I need hardly remind you that another word for this activity of such image-creation is lying.

'Let me create a truthful image for you, in the hope that this will help transform your own thinking.' He glanced around the room, indicating that what he was to say was of special importance. 'I must tell you that the human being is a somewhat uneasy union of past and future. I hope that what I mean by this will become clear to you later. For the moment, I merely wish you to consider that the head of each human being belongs to an entirely different time-system than the body and limbs.

'If we reflect upon plant life, we can see that the metaphor which links the head with the plant points to a mystery. The truth, recognized in alchemy, is that a flower is not a product of the present year's Earthly and Spiritual activity at all. It is always the manifestation of forces engendered in the previous year: a flower is the glorified reflection of last year's Sun. The flower really belongs to the past. Something of this knowledge – well known in initiation Schools – seemed to attract the remarkable polymath, the 17th-century Jesuit, Kircher,[27] who exercised himself with what he considered "alchemical" operations in order to bring back into visible form the ashes of burned flowers. Kircher called this *floral palingenisis*,[28] and he records that he was successful in creating in a bottle the simulacrum – what he called an Astral image – of destroyed flowers. Inevitably, Kircher's discoveries (which, I repeat, were well known to arcane Schools) degenerated in the hands of less scrupulous men in attempts to create mannikins or golems. However, that is another story, and is remembered nowadays mainly in connection with the story of *Frankenstein*.[29] It is most interesting, given the relationship between the Etheric and the *makara* crocodile, that Spiritual exercises involved with the Etheric should eventually degenerate into a monster that has fascinated the European world.

'I do not want you to accept my word that the flower of any plant is a memory of last year's Sun. You should know me better than this, by now. I would prefer that you look at a plant carefully, and discover this truth for yourself. When you begin to see that the plant is an image of last year's Sun, then you will be on the way to understanding how your own head is an image of your own previous incarnation.'

The head-forces of man are the transformed forces carried over from a previous growth, into a present lifetime. If we look at the human head with sufficient meditative attention, we can see very precisely this distinction in time and Spiritual intensity. The head is enclosed. It is a hard shell containing a cerebral nut of grey matter. The orifices which pierce this hard shell – the eyes, the nostrils, the ears and mouth – all reach into the centre, and are ultimately linked with the brain. If we attempt to *feel* the human head, by meditation, then we feel its existence as a closed unit, and understand the old mythologies which tend to present the image of the head as a castle, from which the soul, or princess, peers out from one of the windows. In the fairy lore, the castellated head is the guardian of our Spiritual activity. A comely knight rides out of the castle in quest of the Holy Grail. By means of such meditation, we might even form an inkling of a notion as to why the alchemists could insist that the philosophers' mystic mount should have within it a deep and mysterious cave.[30] It is within this cave that the true alchemy takes place – the transformation by means of images, smells and sounds of the external world.

In contrast to the head, the body which balances this fortress-mountain is not enclosed. It is open – it feels more vulnerable to the world. The hands and feet reach out into the periphery, as though they were designed to explore the extremes of this world in which it finds itself: as much as the head seems to be centripetal, the body seems to be centrifugal. If the head seems to us somehow old and skull-like, the body seems somehow untutored and innocent. The beauty of the body is quite distinct from the beauty of the head. We can literally fall in love with a body, without being in love with its head, or fall in love with a face, without being in love with its body – simply because the two represent different forces in the human being. The body is the guardian of our Will-forces: in the fairy lore it is often symbolized as a stupid and heavy giant.

This contrast between the head and body is of great importance in the study of reincarnation. The arcane tradition insists that the head of a given lifetime is a summation of the Spiritual forces in the previous lifetime. The head is a sort of seed, carried over from the past: it is like the flower, born of a previous solar warmth. Indeed, if one contemplates with sufficient intensity the head of an individual, one can sense its antiquity: one can sense that the head has soaked up the past in the way that the body has not. One can always sense the skull beneath the face. The head always exudes the feeling of being old. This is not surprising, for it belongs to a world which is, in many other respects, lost in the past.

One with a sufficiently developed Spiritual vision can read into the very soul of an individual from the form of the head. Whether a head is elongated or square; whether it is coarse or refined; whether it is ill-proportioned or beautiful – into all these factors the initiate can read the past directions which moulded the personality presently before his or her gaze. It is in this fact that the truth behind certain mysteries of art and literature may be perceived. In his notebooks, Leonardo da Vinci tell us about how, when he was in Milan, painting the huge fresco of *The Last Supper* in 1497, he faced great difficulties in finding a suitable person on whom to base his portrayal of Judas.[31] Leonardo told his patron, Ludovico, the Duke of Milan, that he would go into the seedy quarter of the city each morning in search of a Judas face, but had not been able to find anyone suitable. Most certainly, he did not encounter this difficulty because there was any lack of deformed or intense faces available in Milan in the 15th century. Leonardo, as an initiate, recognized that the destiny of Judas had been very, very complex.[32] In view of this difficulty, we can appreciate a little more fully why Leonardo never finished the face of Christ in this fresco.

Now, as the head is a sort of kernel summary of previous lifetimes, it is evident that, enclosed in every human being, is a chain of memories pertaining to every previous lifetime. It is in this fact that we begin to see something of the deep wisdom of Plato when he spoke of knowledge in terms of remembrance (see page 126). Everything we have ever experienced and known, from lifetime to lifetime, is contained within our being. The only problem is that our external knowledge – the knowledge of the Outworld – does not normally teach us how to recall this knowledge. This, of course, is where arcane training and knowledge comes in, for the true esoteric development eventually allows the one on the Path to contact this hidden knowledge, and learn the secrets of his or her own seeding.

In terms of cosmic economy, it is no accident that the Moon appears to resemble a skull. There is, indeed, a very strange yet powerful connection between the Moon and the human head. Esotericists recognize that this connection rests on the fact that the Moon symbolizes the past: it is seen by *reflected* light, second-hand light. In a similar way, the head of an individual is a summation of – a reflection of – the past of the person to whom it belongs.

The priest-bankers of Mesopotamia, seeking for an esoteric basis for their new coinage, related the value of silver and gold to the circle of 360 degrees: they recognized that silver was the metal of the Moon, and gold the metal of the Sun. They were fixing the value against the cosmos, or zodiac. They valued the gold at one unit, the silver at 13 and a half.[33] These priest-bankers, who were of course initiates, recognized that the metal gold was ruled by the Sun, the metal silver by the Moon, and that, in one day, the Sun moves one degree, while the Moon moves, on average, 13 and a half degrees. The values they chose were not determined merely by rarity, but by cosmic ratios. They recognized, also, that the periodicities in the heavens were reflected in the being of man. They knew that the Sun dominated and fed the Spiritual body we now call the Etheric, while the Moon was the force which regulated the physical body. The Etheric was a sign in the body not only of how the man or woman lived in the present life, but partly of the destiny they would fulfil in the coming life. The priest-bankers knew that the Sun was connected with the future. This meant, of course, that the silver of the Moon was connected with the past.

The important distinction between Moon and Sun, between the inert cold of death-like Moon, and the active warmth of the Sun, is found also in the polarity of head and body in Mankind. This polarity is reflected in another numerology. This is far more complex than that used by the priest-bankers of Mesopotamia, and while it was certainly recognized by the mediaeval alchemists, it was not brought into the light of day until the beginning of the 20th century.

Several occultists have pointed out a fact – well known in esoteric centres – that the heartbeat and human breathing is linked with the different cosmic rhythms of the Sun and the Moon.[34] As Mankind is child of the cosmos, it is perhaps not surprising that we should find in the human being – in what used to be called the *microcosm* – reflections of rhythms which can be measured in the macrocosm, or cosmos. However, what interests us here is that these two rhythms – the blood rhythm of the heart and lung rhythms of breathing – are involved in numerologies which are accorded profound importance in arcane literature.

In addition to this interest in the actual numerologies involved, we should also pay attention to the fact that the blood-rhythm and the lung-rhythm of the human body appear to operate as two separate systems, united only in ratios, or numerological laws. Let us examine this tradition in some depth, for a full understanding of its significance will throw much light on reincarnation.

On average, in one minute, we breathe 18 times. On average, in one minute, our pulse beats 72 times. This indicates that the number 18 is in some way linked with breathing, while the number 72 is somehow linked with the circulation of the blood.

This mystical number 72 is linked with the Sun. It is a numerological expression of the slow movement of the Sun, against the stars, called precession. This is a somewhat complex motion, and, for our present purposes, we do not have to understand it in detail.[35] It is sufficient to note that every 72 years the sun moves by precession exactly one degree of the zodiac. Arcanists have not been slow to link this period (during which time the Sun stays with, but then separates from, a degree occupied by a particular star) with the length of human life. One is born with a particular star, which is, by astronomical definition, located firmly in a single degree: one dies when the Sun severs from that star, through precession. This fact may explain yet another meaning in the hermetic dictum which holds that man is a 'star of the microcosm'.[36] Certainly, it is this magical precession which accounts for the reason why, in the arcane tradition, the number 72 is regarded as being so deeply esoteric.[37]

While the number 72 is linked with a solar periodicity, the number 18 is linked with a lunar periodicity. The period in which the axis of the Earth describes an imaginary cone around the axis of its orb is called the 'Nutational period'. It is an 18-year cycle.

Since the lunar 18 operates through our breathing, and the solar 72 operates through the circulation of the blood, these two numbers may be said to operate in Man. The esoteric tradition insists that Man is at once a lunar and a solar being. To put this more precisely, the esoteric tradition recognizes that there exists in the Spiritual composition of Man a lunar and a solar periodicity, expressed in the numerology of 18 and 72.

The ratio of 18:72 is 1:4. The solar activity in man seems to move four times more quickly than the lunar activity. The life force is four times more rapid than the death force.[38]

Like many of our contemporaries in the 1950s and 1960s, we went to India, partly in search of Spiritual clarification, and partly because we had learned that in India there were still men who had a practical knowledge of the effects that numbers and sounds could have on the material plane. Our Teacher, who before his death had anticipated and even encouraged such a visit, had warned us that under no circumstances should we involve ourselves in the regulation of breathing techniques, or in any of those Oriental systems which were based upon the control of breathing, such as the tantric.

His advice was sound. The Way of the Fool was designed to allow for initiation into the Mysteries by quite different ways than what our Master called 'the regulation of the furnace'. We presumed from this phrase that he had in mind the notion (which is seen in certain alchemical documents) that the human body is a combustion chamber, in which heat is fed by oxygen from the air.[39]

He insisted that the normal ratio of 1:4 should not be disturbed, for, under most circumstances, it was a ratio ideal for the Spiritual unfoldment of Western man. We saw that in many ashrams, the Schools of instruction in India, rapid developments were seen to take place as a result of breathing exercises, yet, because of what our Master had said, we ourselves never participated in these. For similar reasons we did not indulge in the drug-taking which was another mainstay of supposed Spiritual development in certain Oriental schools.

To some extent, we were disappointed by what we found in the Schools of India. There seemed to be little point in following the teachings of these sophisticated conjurors, and so we decided to explore some of the holy sites, to study the symbols of the arcane Schools which built them. In addition, to satisfy our growing interest in arcane astrology, we visited some of the surviving observatories in the north of the sub-continent.

The gigantic stellar observatory in Jaipur is one of the wonders of the world (plate 29), and we have visited it on several occasions while following our programme of research into ancient initiation lore.[40] The 18 weird-looking instruments which still survive on this site are the condensed dream of Jai Singh II, who founded the new city of Jaipur in 1728, and built this extraordinary observatory at about the same time.

The court astrologers of Jai Singh's father, Raja Bishan Singh, had foreseen the greatness of the child, Jai Singh. They had predicted that he would 'shine like Jupiter' among the galaxy of princes, and would be the brightest star of the royal house. The reference to Jupiter was in itself meaningful, for this planet was in Capricorn at the time of Jai Singh's birth – a placing which has always been regarded as an indication of excellence in architecture, or profit from building. The horoscope of Sawai Jai Singh II, cast for 1688, reveals him as a man of extraordinary vision, yet one who lived in a whirlwind of indulgent vanities. His own astrologers put great importance on the degree of his *Lagnam* (Ascendant) in Libra, since from it they saw an overwhelming lust for women, a deep love for music and a fondness for astronomical works. However, perhaps little insight was required for such a reading, since, by the time the astrologer made these pronouncements, Jai Singh had 31 wives, a vast number of concubines, several private orchestras, and had been, from his early youth, passionately interested in astrology.

Whatever the weaknesses in his personality, Jai Singh's energy was boundless. His construction of the city of Jaipur, and its observatory – involving thousands of labourers and the equivalent of millions of pounds – would have been a sufficient life-work for any man, yet this was merely one of five other observatories he constructed, all of which survive into the present time.

Jai Singh built 18 instruments in Jaipur to measure the relationship between the Sun, stars and Earth. There was a conscious magic even in his numerology, for it united the lunar 18 with the 72 of the Sun, which these structures measured. It is not surprising that the Indian words used to denote these massive structures, *Jantar Mantar*, are from the Sanskrit *Yantra* (instrument) and *Mantar* (calculation, or magic formula).[41]

The idea for these Jantar Mantars was no febrile fantasy of a dictator, anxious to impose his rule. The notion came to him through scholarship, when he discovered that the instruments of Ulug Beg[42] had produced tables of measurements which were insufficiently accurate for his own purposes. Eventually, as a result of the calculations afforded by his other observatory at Delhi, Jai Singh published his own remarkable tables. It was largely through these planetary, stellar and zodiacal tabulations that his fame as an astronomer spread through the civilized world. In recognition of his achievements, the Jesuits, who were at that time well established in Goa,[43] presented him with the mathematical and astronomical works of Copernicus, Galileo and Kepler. Jai Singh received these with quiet dignity, even though it is clear from the surviving documentation and manuscripts at Jaipur that, not only was he intimately familiar with the Western tradition of astro-measurement, but he also recognized that his own instruments were more accurate.

If outlandish in appearance, the names of the observatory instruments are so poetic in sound that one easily forgets that they are practical instruments of measurement.[44]

Undoubtedly, the most extraordinary of the instruments at Jaipur is the massive *Samrat Yantra*, which is still sufficiently accurate to determine local time within an error of 2 seconds. The central wall, which towers over 90 feet high, is essentially the gnomon pointer, the equivalent of the raised portion of an ordinary sundial. Inside this giant gnomon are flights of steps, designed to offer access to the top tower, for inspection purposes. The quadrants to this gnomon are on either side: a pin-hole of light in a dark camera-room near to the quadrants permits a ray of sunlight to fall on a graduated arc (28 feet in radius) when the Sun crosses the local meridian. Besides giving accurate time-reading, the instrument is also used in Hindu rituals conducted on the full Moon of June or July, mainly to determine coming weather, and the year's crops.

The *Jaiprakash Yantra* appears to have been the only instrument actually invented by Jai Singh II – all the others being perfections on extant instrument-designs. This marble structure was typical of Jai Singh's attitude, for it was designed to verify the readings and calculations derived from all the other instruments. It is really an inverted model of the section of the Earth's globe, a sunken hemisphere let into the flat platform of the observatory, and designed so as to permit the astrologer to stand inside for the purpose of taking measurements from shadows.

Thanks to the omnipresent Indian Sun, we were able to participate in the workings of these instruments, in much the same way as the ancient astrologers. We did this by climbing down into the sunken bowls, or up the steep steps of what are, in effect, gigantic sundials, to watch the perceptible motion of gnomon shadows as they touched significant calibrations, and actually participate in the mysteries of moving light. As we moved, we breathed, and this motion was paralleled by the movement of the Sun. We recognized that we were living within an inner framework of the lunar 18, through our breathing. At the same time, the outer objects we explored were measures of the solar Mysteries of 72. We felt that the structures were somehow more alive than we were.

274

The feeling of actually participating in the breathing and circulation of light was uncanny, and our meditations on the meanings of this magical numerology led to far-reaching insights. In the mornings, we would watch the shadow of the *Samrat Yantra* gnomon (the largest of the glorified sundials) fall on the top of the western quadrant, some 50 feet away. With the solar rising, the shadow descends along the arc of the quadrant until apparent local noon, at which point it disappears, only to reappear on the other side, and begins to climb the eastern quadrant until the lengthening shadow disappears at sunset.

In terms of the magical numerology of the place, the shadow-movement was symbol of birth and rebirth, of the mystery of reincarnation, which in India is linked especially with the zodiacal sign Capricorn, the *Makara*. In view of this, it is scarcely surprising that we should find on one of the walls below an image of this crocodile-like monster. The 12 instruments with graduated quadrants, set in an area of their own, are called the *Rashivalaya Yantra*. These are essential to practical astrologers, as they are used for reading the positions of the zodiacal signs. Underneath each of the arches near the bases of these instruments are the images of the corresponding zodiacal sign. That painted on the Rashivalaya of Capricorn is the *Makara* crocodile – a very different creature from the goat-fish which is used in the West as a symbol for Capricorn.

The *Makara* of Capricorn was of interest to Jai Singh personally, for he knew of its esoteric import through its connection with Saturn. It is in the sphere of Saturn that the soul begins its return journey through the planetary spheres, back to incarnation. When, after descending the spheres, it reaches the Moon, then the soul will take stock of the cosmos. It will await the right moment – the right horoscope, so to speak – to descend back into the incarnation of flesh and blood.

Our own Western image of Capricorn has been demoted to a goat. In mediaeval times, it was (usually, and more properly) a goat-fish. In the very earliest surviving Babylonian images, it was a fish-tailed goat:

This dual image was of profound arcane importance, for Capricorn has rule over the inner and outer man. This ancient rulership is enshrined in the earliest images of the zodiacal man, with the signs apportioned to different parts of his body. This tradition teaches that Capricorn rules the skeleton and the skin.

If we reflect on this rulership, we see it implies that Capricorn holds together the inner and outer frame of man. Without the inner skeleton, man would be a jelly. Without the skin, he would have no protection from the outer world. The goat-half, with its long horns, seems to be the hard part of mankind – representative of that which gives structure to things. The fish-half seems to be the soft part of Capricorn, which is held in place by this outer structured framework. Capricorn is ruled by Saturn, the time-god, and has thus been linked with the old image of that other scythe-carrier, Death.

The duality of rigidity and softness is meant to symbolize (among other things) the body of Man, in that it contrasts the castellated skull of the head with the softness of the body below the head. This duality of hardness and softness, which is found in the Capricorn sigil, is found also in the structure of the zodiac, for opposite to the goat-fish is the watery sign, Cancer. There can be fewer more telling contrasts with this structure-bound Earth sign Capricorn than the soft, fluidic Water sign Cancer. Just as Capricorn rules the physical death, so Cancer rules the opposite, which is birth into the physical. In the arcane astrology, Cancer represents the descent into life, or incarnation. This polarity of life and death is echoed in the great zodiacs placed in mediaeval churches in the 13th century, for these were orientated along the nave, with Capricorn near the portal, and Cancer directed towards the altar.[45] One entered the church at the point of death, and walked towards the freedom of the higher Spiritual life promised by Christ.

Our experiences in the temples and observatories of India had confirmed what we had discovered in the mediaeval cathedrals. In the buildings of both great cultures, the architectural manipulation of number and light seemed to be linked with the arcane mysteries of Capricorn, the oriental *Makara*.

'You are right to trace a connection between the sign Capricorn and the cathedral builders,' our Master had once said. 'Indeed, I personally have no doubt that Capricorn is one of the Mysteries behind the entire Masonic movement. The sigil for Capricorn . . .' – he reached forward, and with a deft movement, drew the sigil invisibly on the table in front of him:

'. . . which some see as a vestigial drawing of the goat-fish itself, has a profound meaning. Half the symbol consists of the rectilinear angle – the masonic square. This is what was called in the ancient hermetic circles the *kan*:[46]

In some symbolic forms it is associated with a curvilinear form, much like a knot. This knot is also derived from the Egyptian Mysteries.[47] In terms of esoteric symbolism, this simple curve and angle is really a unification of the cosmic duality of angle-square and fish. If you look at them with attention, you will see that there can be fewer more contrasting graphics than the rectilinear V form and the fluidic curve.

'Both symbols may be traced to ancient Egypt. The angle is the jewel placed upon the sacred mummy, informing us that at least half of Capricorn is linked with death. This is the *Pat-aik* symbol, the 'Golden Angle':

This symbol was carried only by the highest gods – for example, by the god Ptah, who fashioned Man from Earth.[48]

'As we know, much of the ancient Egyptian Mystery wisdom was directed towards preparing the insights and symbols which would nourish the future Mysteries of Christ. Among the multitude of symbols which were borrowed by the early Christians from the Egyptian priestcraft was the hieroglyphic *kan*. This hieroglyphic represents the corner-stone, and is clearly linked with the primal masonic symbol of the right-angle.[49]

'What we have here is the right-angle of the Masonic craft, in union with Pisces, which figures in the Mystery wisdom of the Templars. However, I should tell you that this Mystery was depicted in stone on the west front of Chartres Cathedral, and survives to this day. It is, indeed, one of the most arcane symbols of Christianity.'

He leaned back in his chair. 'Have you considered the relationship between the *liberia* cap of the Mithraic rites and the *makara*?'

The question seemed to be quite astonishing. What possible relationship could there be between that curious flop-over head-gear of Mithras (plate 23) and the fish-tailed goat?

Trying to hide our surprise, we said merely, 'I have not.'

'Imagine that the form of this cap is meant to represent a fish-tail – the curved part of the goat. Now, if this represents the fish – the Pisces – when it is placed upon the head, which is ruled by Aries, you have a symbolic completion of the zodiacal circle. The fish tail flops over the head, so to speak. The human head is ruled by Aries, while Pisces rules the feet. Can you see the implications of this symbolism?'

'The *liberia* curves over and pulls towards the feet?'

'Precisely. Aries, which begins the zodiac, touches Pisces, which completes the circle. In this guise, it is a symbol of completion. It is more than that, however: it is a symbolical reminder of the truth of re-incarnation – that the rigid skull of the head must be softened by the curvilinear *liberia*: that the inner hardness must transform to outer softness. Could it be that the initiates who were permitted to wear such caps were "completed men", who knew of the truths of reincarnation? These ancient initiation symbols are important, for they must always have meanings within meanings.'

Although we had been astonished by his original question, we realized immediately that our Master was talking sense: within a few minutes he had transformed our understanding of the symbolism of that curious head-gear. 'So,' we asked, 'when we find the hat depicted in images outside the Mithraic tradition – for example, in Christian images – it is still a badge of initiation?'

'Yes. In the sense that it is emblematic of completed work within the cosmos. *The completing of the circle.* Yes – it is true that when the *liberia* appears in early Christian art it is meant as reference to initiation. However, it is important to remember that, in the first few centuries, it is reference only to the Old Initiation. During the early centuries, the Christians adopted other symbols for the Fish and Aries, to represent the idea of completion.'

He paused, and raised his eyebrows. 'You know that the curious alchemist figure among the towers of Notre Dame in Paris wears a *liberia*?'

'Yes. Fulcanelli says that he is an alchemist.'[50]

'Fulcanelli is right. The Mithraic cap survives into alchemical symbolism, but by the 17th century it is no longer a reference to the ancient initiation, but to the modern, Rosicrucian initiation.'

We could recall many alchemical and Rosicrucian engravings which depicted the Mithraic hat (plate 30). Until that moment, however, we had not really perceived the implications of the symbolism.

'It is most interesting to study this Rosicrucian symbolism when it is handled by a Rosicrucian artist . . .'

'Whom do you have in mind?'

'William Blake. the most talented of all Rosicrucian artists.'

'When did Blake use the Mithraic cap?'

278

'You will find it in his engraving of *Joseph of Arimathea among the Rocks of Albion*. Blake has decked Joseph in the Phrygian cap to indicate his initiate status as a Christian.'

We recalled the print immediately (figure on page 79). Our Master had been right: Joseph did wear the *liberia*. We remembered that the picture was meant to be a copy, after Michelangelo. Did the original also wear a Phrygian cap?[51]

Blake was no stranger to the idea of Christian initiation. This had been the main theme of Blake's chief esoteric mentor, Jakob Boehme. According to an inscription written by Blake, one might be forgiven for believing that he seemed to think that Joseph of Arimathea was 'One of the Gothic Artists who Built the Cathedrals in what we call the Dark Ages'.[52] Such a belief would, of course, be nonsensical. In fact, Blake knew perfectly well that Joseph of Arimathea was the one who had been present at the crucifixion of Christ, and who had arranged for the burial of His body: such would be known by anyone familiar with holy writ. Blake was also familiar – if only through his reading of Milton – with the tradition that Joseph of Arimathea had subsequently visited England, bringing with him the Holy Chalice, which he buried under Glastonbury Tor.[53] When Blake describes Joseph as 'the one who Built the Cathedrals', he is writing periphrastically of the Christian impulse which swept through England, consequent to the visits of the first Christians. It was the Arimathean impulse which led to the establishing of Christianity in England, and the building of the cathedrals. In Blake's view, this Joseph was, like the Christians (and, we might add, in view of the Mithraic cap, like the initiates) of all ages, misunderstood.[54]

'It is certainly intriguing that Blake should turn this image into Joseph of Arimathea, the mythological founder of the English Church (or, to use Blake's poetic version, 'the one who Built the Cathedrals'). That Blake should return to it – a not very inspired copy – in later life and pick it out for special comment is even more intriguing.

'What is Blake really saying about this engraving? Surely he is not pointing to his genius as a student at Basire's, in whose print-shop he served his apprenticeship as an engraver: the engraving does not warrant such treatment.?[55] Perhaps the reason for his interest lies in the cap, which he recognized as a symbol of initiation. The background of the engraving aside, the only significant deviation Blake made from the Michelangelo figure is the addition of the Mithraic cap.'

Our Master had dipped his head, so that the grey pupils of his eyes were quizzically high, and gazed at us with some amusement.

'These Christian symbols fascinate you. Already you know that this is because of what you knew and did in a previous lifetime. All knowledge is remembrance, but your own remembrance pushes through with unusual force. One day, Mark, you will go back to France to study. With what you have learned in the past 20 years, you will be able to see the cathedrals in an altogether different level of esotericism as the remains of arcane knowledge. The Fool carries a stick over his shoulder, and uses the other as a guide to support him on his way.

'Why two sticks? You must try to answer this question, without my help. *Why two sticks?*'

He signed that the interview was over, but before he left the room, he turned to us. 'When you do find yourself once more in Chartres, you might like to confirm what I say. When you have discovered this outstanding arcane symbolism of fish and square, you may feel free to write about it. *Someone* should record its existence for posterity, for soon such things will be lost to the world, save for being stored in the secret records, the Akashic Chronicles. All these clever gentlemen who have written about the significance of the Templars' influence on the building of Chartres have missed it: you should try to avoid this error. For sure, it would be a pity for this thread of arcane wisdom to be lost to the world, because a Fool cannot use his eyes. I would make it a task for you to decipher this symbolism.' His eyes once again sought out mine, and he said something which I understood only later: 'It will give me great pleasure to watch you confirm my words in Chartres.'

What the modern expert on the dark path, Kenneth Grant,[56] has called 'the dual modes of the Moon' are of great importance in the magic of Aleister Crowley, whose influence on certain modern Schools of magic has been most profound.

Crowley knew that, in arcane astrology, Capricorn the goat is the representative of the male organ, the Phallus, while Cancer is the representative of the receptive female organ, the Kteis. These associations are clearly represented in the ancient sigils for the two signs.

CAPRICORN $\mathcal{V}$ CANCER $\mathcal{G}$

That for Capricorn is dual – it is both hard and soft (see page 277). That for Cancer is constructed wholly from curves and circles, which together describe the form of the ancient Egyptian *Ru*, $\bigcirc$, which was an emblem of the eye, the mouth and a uterus.

The Devil card, which Crowley designed for his book on the Tarot,[57] shows the goat, with powerful curvilinear horns (plate 31). The goat backs on to what at first may look like a tree, but which is in fact an erect penis, with two huge translucent balls, in which are humanoids. The two water-like balls recall the sigil for Cancer, and certainly draw a connection with the notion of 'birth' or conception. We need not concern ourselves with the symbolism of this card here, but we should observe that the card points to the duality of both Capricorn and Cancer, for the two balls represent the generative power of the Moon, prior to the enfoldment of the sexual energies by Capricorn.

Some of the more potent modern magical praxes pertaining to the Moon are derived from the influence of Crowley and his followers.[58] It is very likely that his *Babalon*, or Scarlet Woman, who was supposed to participate in his sex magic, takes her name-colour from the blood of the lunar menstruum.[59] This is intelligent symbolism, for the name combines the solar (blood) with the lunar (cycle), and hence suggests the magical numerology of 72 and 18 – the ratio of 4:1 (see page 271ff). There may be no doubt whatsoever that Crowley's Scarlet Woman was a lunar personification, and this fact throws some light on the link drawn by Crowley between Capricorn the goat, as a symbol of sexual prowess, and the Scarlet Woman, as an object of desire.

Capricorn the goat is associated, in its darker strains of symbolism, with the *Baphometic Goat*[60] of the witchcraft rites, and is in turn linked with the word *svd*, meaning the Secret, or the Secret Eye. In fact, modern witchcraft lore recognizes this *svd* as the anus of the goat, which symbolism perhaps explains some of the more lurid misunderstandings regarding goat-worship in the sabbats, and the 'profane kiss' on the buttocks. This *svd*, for all it is a Sanskrit term, is clearly related to the *Ru*, $\bigcirc$, of the ancient Egyptian hieroglyphics. On a cosmic level, the *svd* is the secret eye looking from the far side of the zodiac from Capricorn – towards the opposite sign, Cancer, which is governed by the Moon.

The cabbalistic systems, which influenced the thought and explorations of Crowley, were more circumspect about the sacred activity of sex than Crowley or his followers. Even so, within the prolix teachings of cabbalism, it is quite evident that the sexual element is linked with the Moon, and with all the lunar associations we may trace in alchemy and astrology. In fact, the cabbalistic teachings are far more explicit in pointing to profound esoteric connections between the Moon and the human imaginative faculty.

In the microcosmic image of the *Microprosopus*, or *Cosmic Face*, the Hebraic letter *qoph* is apportioned to the human brain, the source of imagination and directed imagination, which is fantasy. An interesting confirmation of this can be seen, almost hidden in the portrayal of the head of Adam Kadmon, the archetypal man, in Knorr von Rosenroth's famous engraving (below). In this picture, the skull of Adam Kadmon has been trepanned to reveal the brain. Superimposed over the maze-like convolutions of the brain is the Hebrew letter *qoph*. This letter is accorded an external and internal rule. It rules over the physical brain, and over one of its products – namely, imagination.

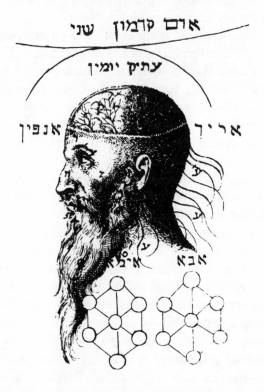

The cabbalistic Cosmic Face, with the letter qoph on the brain.
From C. Knorr von Rosenroth, Kabbalah Denudata, *1684.*

As the Knorr von Rosenroth engraving suggests, the human brain is a reflection of the greater brain, the cabbalistic *Macroprosopus*. This is the cosmic visage which keeps perpetually open its one visible eye, perpetually image-making Creation. It is said that if this eye were to close, even for an instant, the whole of existence would come to an end. The *qoph* of this cosmic visage is what perpetuates the entire Spiritual life of the cosmos.

In all other respects, this Great Countenance is found in the greater, or archetypal, image of a human face. Perhaps we need not labour the point that it is our own brain – our perceptual apparatus – which maintains the external universe. Just as the higher brain maintains with its single eye the entire cosmos, so our own brains maintain, with their pairs of eyes, the entire material fabric of the illusion which we call *the* World, but which is really *our* World. This suggests an interesting parallel between Creator and created. If the entire created cosmos is a thought of God, then our own world is a lesser created thought of our own. The Hebraic *qoph* is the intermediary, the communal element, in this greater and lesser brain, of God and Man.

The great Rosicrucian, Jakob Boehme,[61] played in a most creative and imaginative way with this idea of reflected countenances, and reflected eyes. He proposes the idea that God could be represented by the letter A, which stands for *Auge*, the German for 'eye'. This Spiritual eye would look with its creative power into the darkness below and see . . . and see *itself*. The A of the Auge would reflect its own A. As Boehme points out, this gives rise to a lozenge-shaped sigil:

For Boehme this sigil was the image of the interpenetration of Cosmos and Man, of Macrocosm and Microcosm.[62] This interesting view of the Eye, or Auge, was perpetuated in many Rosicrucian, Cabbalistic or occult images of the eye itself. The symbolism here was less graphically direct, but was rooted in the notion that an eye printed upon a page could be seen only by another eye – that is, the eye of the beholder. The two eyes interpenetrate in the act of vision, pulled together by the invisible strings of vision.

We find echoes of this reflective light-magic in the description of the head of the *Macroprosopus* in the Jewish *Zohar*.[63] Here we learn that its skull is made from light – a light so pervasive that it extends into 40,000 worlds superior to our own. This is a 'solar' light. The interior brain of the Macroprosopus is of a crystalline dew, but this dew is also lit internally with a light which extends into 13,000 myriads of worlds. This is a 'lunar' light. One of the magical qualities of this lit dew is that it it can flow down into the lower world (that is, our own Earth) and reawaken the sleeping dead, which is humanity.

From the membrane around the greater brain there extend 32 paths. This numerology links the Macroprosopus with the Sephirothic Tree (see over). The number of discernible paths in this tree is 32. The lowest path, linked with Tau, runs from Yesod to Malkuth – that is from the Moon to the World of Man. This lowest pathway is the Path of Imagination.[64]

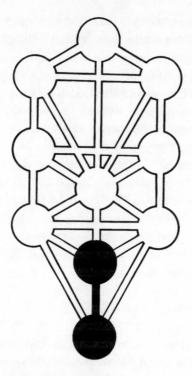

The cabbalistic Sephirothic Tree, with the centres for Yesod connected to Malkuth –
this is the connexion between Mercury and Earth (in some systems, Mercury and Moon), and
marks the 32nd path, the Path of Saturn.

In numerology the *qoph* is accorded the numerical value of 100.[65] This is a sexual number. As Kenneth Grant has pointed out, this century may be broken down numerologically to the 20 of K (*caph*),and the 80 of P (*pay*), which stand respectively for K(teis) and P(hallus).[66] With such sexual connotations it is proper that this letter be associated with the path from Venus, the planet of love and concupiscence.

The sigil for Capricorn is dual, but the two elements are in graphic conflict, one being rectilinear, the other curvilinear. This 'conflict' may be reduced to the ancient Egyptian symbols of the *kan* Γ and the *anke-te* ካ . The sigil for Cancer is also dual, but there is no conflict between them: indeed they appear to almost reflect each other. The sigil for Cancer is itself a mirror-image – because the Moon itself is a reflector of light.

The celestial dew of the alchemists (see page 297) is that emitted by the Phallus, and collected in the Kteis. It is in such connections that we begin to see the esoteric lines which tie together alchemy and astrology.

Once we begin to see the deeper implications of the symbols for

Capricorn and Cancer, along with their deep associations, both in the ancient Mysteries and in Christianity, we will be in a position to see more clearly the deeper significance of the idea of sexual restraint, and even chastity, in the development of the human psyche. The 'natural' connection between Cancer and Capricorn is in the curvilinear elements: Cancer is entirely curvilinear, while Capricorn is only half curvilinear. This symbolism contains a depth of esoteric meaning. The life forces, which lead to birth and incarnation in Cancer, are a natural progression. The rectilinear element in Capricorn fights against this natural progression: it holds back the natural flow of energies, of seed, by discipline and control. Through this control, the natural flow of energies into the material lunar realm is impeded. Those lunar forces which are not emitted (to use a sexual term) can be directed and transformed into Spirit powers. This is 'the working against Nature' which is the essence of initiation: from the point of view of ordinary life, such work is unnatural, or illusionist.

As we have seen, in the cabbalistic system, the century of *qoph* is the number of illusion. Just as the Secret Eye (*svd*) sees beyond illusion, so the undeveloped ordinary eye (or *Ru*) remains immersed in illusion. This means that the sexual activity itself is the outcome of, and generator of, illusion. This is an illusion in which cosmic powers work unseen.[67]

The non-illusionist Nature works from Capricorn to Cancer. The initiate – working invisibly in the world – strives not to follow the natural path, into that incarnation represented by the Moon of Cancer: he or she strives to work from Cancer to Capricorn, from the formless to form. This is probably why the arcane literature refers to Capricorn specifically as the sign of initiation – the sign of Spiritual development – for in Spiritual terms, when one has arrived at the balance of Capricorn, one has achieved initiation. This notion, which develops the image of the crocodile of Capricorn descending into the waters of Cancer, is expressed in the hermetic literature.

In his *Isis and Osiris*, Plutarch tells us that the crocodile is honoured as a god because, when it is in the waters, a transparent membrane covers its eyes. In this way, the crocodile can see without being seen, even though it straddles the cosmos, between Earthy Capricorn and watery Cancer.[68] It is the initiate who sees and is not seen – it is the initiate who is controller of this particular illusion offered by form.

We finished our work at Jai Singh's Jaipur observatory in May, and, after a trip northwards to visit Nepal, had returned to the Indian capital by late June, 1972, when the monsoons were at their worst. Early in the morning, during our first day – which happened to be the last Saturday in the month[69] – we were invited for supper in Delhi, at one of those splendid houses between Shakar Road and Talkatora, in the Raj centre.

At that time we were travelling with a delightful girl whom we had met in Kathmandu, under strange circumstances. As we had passed each other, on the steps of the *Swayambhunath*,[70] our eyes had met, and we had recognized each other, even though we had never met before. We had both stopped instantly, and smiled at the double recognition. After walking around the temple for an hour or so, we decided to travel together for a few days. Silvia had been finding it difficult as a lone girl in Nepal and she said that she would be happy to have a companion for her journey through India.

A few days after our meeting, as we both travelled south to India by train, Silvia leaned back against the wooden slats of the seat and laughed to herself.

'What are you thinking of?'

'I'm laughing because when we met, there were eyes everywhere. When we met, we were overlooked by 12 cosmic eyes.'

We could not understand what she meant.

'We met on the Swayambhunath steps: above us were the three eyes on the tower wall of the temple. There are three eyes on each wall.'

She was right. On each of the four towers were painted the distinctive pairs of eyes for which the Swayambhunath was famous. Between them, hanging down like a giant question mark, was the Nepalese *ek*, the symbol of unity (plate 32). This was an image of the third eye, the invisible eye of higher Buddhic wisdom.[71]

It was night-time in Delhi, and we knew that the grasslands abutting the roads were already covered in linen-wrapped bodies, laid out in rows like the shrouded dead, under primitive awnings which might keep off the monsoon rains. These sleepers were the poor, who had nowhere to go, and who survived by begging. Inside the house, there was no sign of poverty: indeed, everything was designed to reveal opulence. Such a social contrast, which makes a Westerner uneasy, is quite normal in India. Wealth is not a matter of shame, but of pride. It is, perhaps, the only defence against having to live shrouded on the grasslands, or on the intersections and roundabouts of the motorways. It is no wonder that the ancients apportioned India to zodiacal Capricorn, with its joyless cosmic tug-of-war between an ambitious goat, striving for differentiation, and a fish lost in shoals of anonymity.

While we ate the exquisite food, served with great deference by servants, we observed that the bookshelves alongside the European-style fireplace were stacked not with the books for which they were designed, but with magnetic tapes for our host's reel-to-reel recorder, each marked with codes which seemed to denote places and dates. There must have been several hundred of these. Our host observed our attention, yet did not elect to explain their presence. Later, when the meal was over, he took us into an even more splendid room, as though to demonstrate that he *did* indeed have shelves loaded with books. The library was enormous – multilingual in titles and demonstrative of a wide interest.

We took from a high shelf a monograph on Jai Singh, and began to flick through it. Inserted in the glossy pages was a sheet of paper bearing a horoscope, Indian style, with the dragon's head and tail, the Ketu and Rahu, figured as Oriental symbols. We held the horoscope between our figures, and glanced at it.

'You are interested in astrology?' our host asked. It was scarcely a question an Indian could ask of another Indian, for in that country everyone is almost fatalistic about astrology. But posed by an Indian of a Westerner, it was a matter of politeness.

We nodded. 'We have been to Jaipur, to study the observatory there.'

'And it is our own equally impressive *Yantra Mantra* which brings you to Delhi, I hope?'

Again we nodded. 'Silvia is anxious to see it.'

We did not mention that we had already visited the observatory several times before. For reasons which were not clear to us, we felt uneasy with our host. We had been introduced to him by a friend in England and had talked together over the phone for the first time this morning: this was our first meeting. He had studied at Balliol and had a magnificent command of English, supported by carefully cultivated English mannerisms.

From the instant of our meeting, as we climbed from the taxi outside the gates of his house, to his greetings, we had felt ill at ease. We sensed that there was something dark about him, yet we could not quite put our finger on what it was. We had glanced at Silvia, to see what impression she had formed, yet she seemed to be entirely charmed by the man's suave manner and his opulent home. Later, the darkness began to reveal itself more insistently, but for the moment, we were unsure. The Orientals have a most wonderful natural faculty for disguising their thoughts and feelings, and it is far from easy to perceive what is really going on in their soul. We in the West have developed the Ego and consciousness to a level of refinement which means that the group-soul, within which the sub-continent is still submerged, is foreign to us. Most Indians or Pakistanis still live their lives with an acute awareness of kith and kin, and willing submergence of Ego, which is both foreign and enigmatic to the Western mind. It is this, more than any barrier of language or religion, which makes for misunderstandings on a personal level.

Silvia was very beautiful. She had the long blond hair and soft English features which Indian men find attractive, and our host could hardly take his eyes off her. During the meal, he had put a great deal of attention into his conversation with her. And now, as we stood at the far side of the enormous library, looking through the books, we observed that he was talking to her with a proximity and body language which revealed a manipulative sexual interest. At one point, a part of their conversation drifted over to us. He seemed to be talking about magic. In order to hear the better, we edged nearer to them, though retained some distance.

'Yes, it is possible to do real magic.' Our host was speaking. 'Of course, the majority of fakirs are usually mere tricksters. Often the best fakirs are entertainers of the most sophisticated kind. For all their lean and hungry look, and for all they wear the simplest of *dhotis* around their loins, they usually have clever accomplices in the crowd, and a whole charabanc full of invisible wires and concealed cabinets. They are, in their own way, far more sophisticated than even the most advanced of your European stage-performers. Perhaps, if you will excuse me mentioning it, this explains why so many of your performers in the West don the costumes of the Indians. They will dress in exotic costumes such as no Oriental magician would wear, merely to lend credence to their art – the mystique and expertise of India. Perhaps this is a quite natural obeisance to our Oriental culture. Rarely do the two cultures meet, even after the admirable efforts of Madam Blavatsky and your inestimable Leadbeater.'[72]

We wondered if, with these names of Theosophists who had lived for a few years near Madras,[73] he was leading up to his own allegiance. Was he a Theosophist? It would seem unlikely, for the darkness in his aura was of a most disturbing kind.

'For example,' he continued, 'if you look around, you will see in various rooms images and statues of the incarnations of the great Vishnu.' He moved over to an ornately carved table, on which was a golden statue. 'Here is Vishnu as *Matsya*.[74] See, the god has the lower form of a fish. Has he not the most exquisitely wrought scales on the lower part of his body? But of course, you are well-educated people, and you will know of the *Mahabharata* stories, and the connection between the fish and initiation.'[75]

We moved closer to them, ostensibly to examine the object, but really because we were uneasy about the way the monologue was developing. The statue was beautifully wrought in gold, and the scales were, as he had said, exquisitely carved.

'This image reminds one of your fish-man, Capricorn.'

'Except that our Capricorn is a fish-tailed goat.'

'Are not all men goats?' He could not resist looking towards Silvia, to add a nuance to his words. 'Is there not some reference in your occult lore to the hornless goat? And is this hornless goat not a symbol for Man?'

He was right. In some black magical cults, the hornless goat was the periphrastic name for a human sacrifice.[76]

We held our silence, but nodded. The hint of a smile touched his lips: he recognized that he had scored a point over us.

'How different our Vishnu is from this *Ekadas*.'[77] He had swung round, and lifted from a pedestal an image of the *Samantamukha*.' This was the 11-headed god, with a five-tier cluster of heads, looking in triple directions. The figure had eight arms. 'You know the legend?' In his steady eyes we sensed a challenge.

'I think it is *Avalokiteswara*?'

'Avalokiteswara in his manifestation of Samantamukha.'

'Didn't he go down to Hell to liberate the wicked?'

'After converting them.' The man seemed anxious to correct us, to demonstrate that we were wrong. This would not be a difficult thing to do: for all our language was English, we were in a foreign culture. Clearly, he was intent on impressing Silvia at our expense.

'Avalokiteswara found that for every human he converted from sin, another instantly took its place. Horror filled his soul as he realized that he would never be able to save the whole of Mankind. In grief at this realization, his head split into ten pieces.

'If he split into ten pieces, why does he have 11 heads?' asked Silvia.

'The god Ambitaba changed each of the split parts into separate heads, and arranged them in tiers of three, all looking in different directions. He placed the tenth on top, and then added his own head as finial.'

'He had 22 eyes . . .' she observed.

'As befits one named the "One-looking Lord". He sees everywhere. Like the Swayanbunath. The Swayanbunath looks into the four directions of space. This Avalokiteswara looks into the three worlds of desire, whence sin arises.'[78]

He replaced the statue on its pedestal, allowing the idea of sin to hover in the room, like an Astral smoke.

'It is not surprising to find an image of the first incarnation of Vishnu in a household such as our own, and even a statue of Avalokiteswara . . . But . . .' – he permitted a dramatic delay – '. . . there would be some wonderment to find . . .'

He did not finish the sentence. Instead, with his right hand, he picked up a small bell from the glass top of a table, and rang it. At the same time as the bell tinkled, he made with his left hand the kind of flourish one might associate with a stage magician, as though he were picking some object from the air. When he opened the palm of his left hand, it contained a small pectoral cross.

'Perhaps a Christian cross is not a symbol which you might expect to find in a house such as our own?'

Silvia seemed to have been impressed by the trick: for sure, it had been done with incredible dexterity. Fortunately, our own attention had not been on the trick itself, but upon the face of our magician host, and upon the fact that he had used a bell. For reasons which were not clear to us, we had suddenly remembered that Paracelsus had written about a similar experience with a Spanish magician who had used a bell, engraved with magical characters, to practise 'angel magic' – which was then a politically correct term for black magic.[79]

We could see from his eyes that there was something afoot which was not intended for our benefit. We had the distinct impression that the man intended to hypnotize Silvia in some way – perhaps with a view to seduction.

'Do you believe that it is possible to bring something from the thin air?' His eyes were fixed upon Silvia. 'Our finest magicians can do this. It is well known that even the simple fakirs can make ashes appear from nowhere in the palms of their hands. I think that your wise lady – Blavatsky, who did us the honour of living for a while in Madras[80] – called this precipitation. She herself claimed the ability to bring things over great distances by magic – to incarnate them, so to speak. I belief your Theosophists used the term "precipitate"?[81] He glanced towards us, as though to obtain a response to his question. 'Indeed, I believe your Blavatsky would also transvect things – if that is the right word. She, like our own magicians, could cause objects in one room to dematerialize, and reappear unscathed in another room. This was the true magic. We are no strangers to such true magic in India.'

He held out the cross towards Silvia. At that moment, we knew instinctively that it was of utmost importance that Silvia should not touch the object. We could see around it a flickering aura of darkness – a darkness all the more surprising in view of its link with Christianity.

We were seized with a sense of panic: perhaps Silvia would take the cross from the man? Pretending an interest, we leaned between them, and lifted the cross from his fingers. We could not detect even a flicker in the eyes of our host, yet the Spiritual atmosphere in the room suddenly became charged.

'Can you tell me whence this cross came?'

He looked at me as though he were surprised, and there was a touch of resentment in his voice. 'Why, it was materialized in front of your eyes. In front of your *very* eyes, as they say in England.'

We did not respond. Instead, we reached over to the glass-topped table, picked up the bell and glanced at it. As we had expected, around the inner rim were scratched several occult-seeming characters, and three Sanskrit words. Our knowledge of Sanskrit was scanty, yet the name *Meru* was sufficiently well known for us to recognize it. The word was from a Tantric spell, and confirmed our suspicions about the dark sexual intent of our host.[82] We said nothing, but turned the mouth of the upturned bell towards him, to show what we had seen.

In silence, we sat down in one of the huge leather-bound chairs and took the cross in our fingers, running the papillary ridges of our fingertips over it, prior to dropping it in the middle of our palm. We then summoned all our energy into the palmar area, searching for the inner atmosphere of the cross by means of psychometry.[83] We knew instinctively that we had to counter his own black magic by means of another form of white or natural magic. It is forbidden to use such knowledge for one's own advancement, yet it is not forbidden to use it to help someone else in danger.

We looked up at him, forcing his eyes to meet our own.

'Do you really not know whence this cross came?'

'From the thin air, my friend.' His voice was perfectly controlled, with no taste of defensiveness in it. 'You saw that for yourself, did you not?'

We lowered our voice to a whisper, in order that Silvia would not hear. 'I will tell you where this cross came from. Then perhaps you will leave her alone?'

In former times, occultists had maintained that there were such things as eyebeams – extrusion rays of vision which were ejected from the eyes against the stream of light. We could almost feel our own eyebeams twisting around those of our host as he stared down at us. There was an icy coldness in his eyes, yet he said nothing.

The cross rested on our left palm, and our right palm was hovering over it.

After a little adjustment of thought, the usual rapid cinematographic images began to reveal the source of the cross.[84]

We spoke loudly as we traced the stages of our vision, so that Silvia and our host could hear.

'I feel the coldness of the tomb. I can see the loam at the side of a grave. The Earth is being scratched from the pit walls above me. The hands are wielding a cutting tool. We cannot see the face clearly, but it is an Indian in a *dhoti*. He is digging an old burial . . . I think that it is a Jesuit burial ground in Goa. The man is in search of valuable objects. Now he is rooting his hand among the bone-strewn loam at the bottom of the grave: his fingers close over me. I can feel the pressure of his dirty fingers. He is not yet done. His fingers reach again into the bones, and he removes some other objects. He tucks these into the folds of his *dhoti*, alongside me.'

The vision transmitted by the cross was instantaneous and utterly undeniable in its truth.

'You may not know this yourself . . .' – we said deliberately, to allow our host to save face – '. . . but there may be no doubt that the cross was taken from a Jesuit cemetery by a grave robber.'

Our host's eyes scarcely moved, yet there was a sufficient change in them for us to recognize that he knew where the cross had come from. An almost imperceptible smile hovered over his lips, and he signed to one of the servants to fill our glasses. He knew that we were speaking the truth.

No more was said about the event for the rest of the evening. He took the cross from the table, where I had placed it, and put it in a silver snuff box: he did this with some deliberation, to announce that the whole thing had been forgotten. The battle of wills had been abandoned.

In the conversations which followed, he revealed a considerable knowledge of the history of the shadowy division between magic and the supranatural. He talked about the work on Indian magic by Jacolliot,[85] and on Blavatsky's little-known contact with the remarkable English medium, Wiliam Eglinton, during their meeting in India.[86] At first, wc had the impression that his purpose in talking about events almost a century old was to divert interest away from recent events, and to hint at how even a renowned British medium was supposedly guilty of fraud. But within a few minutes, his real motive became clear to us, for he wandered over to one of the shelves and lifted down a first edition of Farmer's book on the mediumistic exploits of Eglinton,' *Twixt Two Worlds*.[87]

'Look . . .' He opened the book at the end-papers, where a newspaper report had been tipped in – '. . . I took the trouble to insert Kellar's famous challenge to Eglinton.' The faded yellow-brown cutting was from the *Indian Daily News*.[88] He flicked through the pages of the book. 'Yet I am sure that it is the lithographs which will interest you in Farmer's account of Eglinton's mediumship. Look, they are still in perfect order . . .' The chromolithos, among the earliest colour images of psychic phenomena, were almost in pristine condition.

His production of the book had broken the tension, and the discussion once again became animated. Our host proposed that while it was clear that Blavatsky had practised fraud on a massive scale, William Eglinton had been a true magician, and had been drawn into fraud merely by his involvement with the famous Madame. We each had our own theories about the extent to which psychic phenomena were involved with such sleight of hand or conjuring, and because the subject matter was historical, rather than contemporary, we each felt free to speak our minds.

'And the famous rope trick?' our host asked, signing imperiously for our glasses to be refilled. 'Have you ever seen the rope trick?' His question was unashamedly designed to lead to the fact that *he* had seen this rare wonder.

'You have seen the trick?' we asked dutifully.

'Yes, but only once. It was performed in front of an especially invited audience in one of those remote islands in the Lakshadweeps.[89] The evening was not at all dark – in fact, the stars were unusually bright. After the usual incantations, and the fire-lighting ceremony, which was performed on the beach, the fakir succeeded in throwing the rope into the air in such a way that it stayed upright. Naturally, he invited a member of the audience to test the rope by pulling on it. Then the usual drama with the small boy ensued. The boy refused to climb the rope, and the fakir threatened him with a knife . . .'

'Did his boy climb the rope in the end?' Silvia asked, fascinated by the account.

'The boy not only climbed it, but vanished at the top, as is generally expected in stage performances of the rope trick. Of course, I knew a little about conjuring, and I looked for wires strung between trees – perhaps between the high palms which fringed the beach – or from the mast of a boat, moored over the corals, yet I saw nothing. To this day, I would swear it was real magic. No other explanation – short of mass-hypnotism – could account for the display. The sky was not dark enough for black bags and blankets to be used to hide the boy. No doubt, when the fakir climbed up the rope, in pursuit of the boy, his knife gripped between his teeth, he did not find the boy. No doubt, the bloody remains he threw down to Earth were the severed limbs of a monkey – for that is usually the case. Yet, while we might anticipate that the murder of a small boy would be fraud, the fact of his disappearance could scarcely be fraudulent. Real magic and stage magic merged . . .'

'All for a few rupees?' we asked, perhaps rather cynically.

'Yes, my friend. A few rupees are important to such men. One must live. Even the fakirs must eat. Even the great Jacolliot paid his remarkable savant a few rupees.'

Dawn was breaking as our host called a taxi, and we left his house for our hotel.

'What happened?' asked Silvia, as she settled back into the leather cushions of the taxi, and closed her eyes with fatigue. Her voice sounded irritated. 'Why did you put on such a frightful mask, and refuse to explain the cross further?'

'Did you not know?'

'Know what?'

The man tried to control you. He was trying to hypnotize you.'

'I felt nothing,' she said. 'He was dark – I'll give you that – but probably harmless. Charming, silver-tongued and a bit of a show-off. His own worse enemy, I would say.'

'If you had touched that object – the cross – my guess is that you would have become his victim.'

'He had that power?' She was suddenly alert, surprised. 'The power of the *vama marg*?' This was Sanskrit for the powerful sexual black magic of India, practised by certain followers of the Left Hand Path. 'What could he want with me?'

'Something evil, whatever it was. At least, a good time for himself sexually – at worst . . . Well, I'm not sure . . . Perhaps to make you a *suvasini*.'

For a brief moment, the sexual embraces carved on the Vishvanath Temple at Khajuraho flashed through our mind.[90] What were the secrets of that sexual bliss? These women were not being coerced, for they were just as caught in the cosmic bliss of sexual fulfilment as the men with whom they coupled (plate 33).

'A holy whore?'

'Who knows?'

Holy whore sounds such a terrible contradiction in our own language, but in the Sanskrit it has no such connotation. Even so, I wonder if the *suvasinis* of the tantric cult are always willing in their sacrifice. To what extent may they be the victims of Astral manipulation? I sometimes ask myself if they smell as sweetly to themselves, as they do to their lovers.[91]

'Why did you tell him about the theft of the cross? You used psychometry, didn't you?'

'I told him about the grave robber to show him that I was on to his little game. I showed him the bell rim to indicate that I knew he was using tantric magic. He would not know if I had other powers. In a situation such as this, where deceit is being practised, the only thing to which one can resort is truth.'

She nodded. 'Yet I thought psychometry was forbidden.'

'It is. But then, so is sexual coercion by means of black magic.'

This was not the only time in our lives that we used – or were forced to use – powers which might be taken as exhibition of the magical. However, it was the only time that we had used a Capricornian magical technique, which involved countering the curvature of black magic with the rectitude of the angle, or *Kan*.[92]

There may have been some deep karmic significance why it had fallen to our lot to exercise a Capricornian technique in a Capricornian land, but this mystery would have to remain unsolved until after our death, when all the secrets of one's life are revealed.

Chapter Seven

I am the same Perseus who conquered the snaky-tressed
Gorgon, the man who dared to travel through the airy
breezes on beating wings.

(Ovid, *Metamorphoses*, IV. 697)

Among the most remarkable of modern initiates who were prepared to
reveal hermetic secrets to the profane was the mysterious Fulcanelli. In
keeping with the secret Green Language, which he studied and practised
with great acomplishment, he used a pen-name to disguise his real
identity. 'Fulcanelli' meant 'little Vulcan',[1] a reference to the mythological Vulcan, the smith of the gods, who was believed to be the first
alchemist, and who was certainly the ancient patron of the spagyric art.
As a pseudonym, this name seems to have worked very well, for no one
has been able to determine with any certainty just who Fulcanelli was: all
that is known about him is that he was extremely learned in the realm of
hermetic and alchemical thought.

As we have seen, this mysterious alchemist paid especial attention to
the alchemical images which are still found in the sculpted fabric of
French cathedrals. In particular, Fulcanelli dealt with the secrets within
the alchemical imagery of Notre Dame in Paris, and the cathedral at
Amiens.

Among the most arcane of the many arcane stone quatrefoils on the
western façade of Amiens cathedral which intrigued Fulcanelli is a
curious image of a heavenly rain.[2] The sheet of water streams like a
veritable Niagara from the clouds which, for the mediaeval mind,
symbolized Heaven (see plate 34). It streams down to the Earth, where,
in defiance of natural laws, it gathers into a ball of water which seems to
pulsate and tremble, as though it were a ball of flame, rather than a
magical liquid.

In the quatrefoil, an alchemist looks upon this cascade in awe, pointing with his right hand at the ball of water as though to show that it is a miracle, or something of profound importance. Could he be pointing to this water-ball to indicate that it is something dangerous? The phenomenon is portrayed in distinctly unnatural terms to show that this is no ordinary dew.

All the arcane images of the west front of Amiens are contained in quatrefoils. This in itself is a significant thing, for the quatrefoil is made up of four crescents – symbolic of the four phases of the Moon throughout the month. In the quatrefoil which contains the Niagara of water, the heavens open in the uppermost crescent, as if to indicate that this is a lunar Heaven (or sphere), and the magic water it dispenses is a lunar dew. In fact, it is the 'philosophical dew' of the alchemists – one of the great Mysteries of this mysterious art. It is not straining ancient mythology too far to see in this cascade the dual streams of the tears of the 'weeping sisters', the Egyptian goddesses, Isis and Nephthys, the combined influence of the light and dark Moons.

In Latin, this dew is *Ros*. As we have seen, some hermetic experts argue that the three letters form the beginning of the word Rosicrucian, a word which pertains to the most important secret brotherhood in late mediaeval Europe.[3] These initiates, who united the secret of the lunar dew with the cross (*crucis*, the genitive of the Latin *crux*), were practising Christians who sought to evolve spiritually by means of meditation through arcane alchemical processes.

The meditative practices were, in a very real sense, inner disciplines. They were concerned with inducing picture-formation into the imaginative realm governed by the Moon. Thus, the structure of the cross (itself a symbol, on one level at least, of the intersection of matter and spirit) was laid upon the chaotic lunar influences of imagination through Spiritual disciplines. The aim of imposing such a structure was to turn these lunar forces into what was called, in the mediaeval world, *fantasy*. In this sense, fantasy could be squeezed from the dew of the Moon. The *Ros* dew was subjected to the directional organization of the cross (*crucis*).

While it is quite clear that some alchemists did actually go out into the fields at certain times of the year, to collect the early dew on specially spread blankets (plate 35), the imagery of dew was really intended as a hermeneutic parable for early morning meditation, through which the lunar forces streaming into the microscosm (which is Man) were channelled into fantasy.[4]

In the alchemical tradition, one of the names for the lunar dew was *nostoc*.[5] As Fulcanelli reminds us, this word is from the Greek *nox*, which meant 'night' and, in some contexts, 'darkness'. This *nostoc* was a heavenly power which came to Earth during the night, and remained on the Earth only for a short time before being dispelled by the rays of the Sun.

Here we see an arcane parable, so beloved by the alchemists. The free-flowing and chaotic stream of imagination bestowed by the Moon on the Earth can be directed by mental activity and attention into fantasy. Imagination, like all thought-pictures, is visualized as coming from the dark skies, from the dark Moon, in the form of *nostoc*. The germination of the imaginative faculty, like the germination of plants, can take place only through the operations of lunar darkness. When the occultists say that darkness must mix with light to give form, we now begin to see what they mean, for without the human mind being continually fructified with the element of lunar fantasy, no creation can take place. The dark Moon militates against the light of the Sun.

Fulcanelli points out that the healthy development of the chick in an egg depends upon darkness, as does the survival of the silver-based photographic image in the light-excluding camera. However, what Fulcanelli does not reveal is the secret in the word *nostoc* itself: it is evident that he knew what the word really meant, yet he elected not to reveal it in his published works. No doubt, he felt that the time was not yet right for him to reveal the secret of *nostoc*, save in a way protected by occult blinds which could be interpreted only by those familiar with the arcane langauge.

In fact, the Greek word *nostos* means 'return', both in the sense of a journey and in financial terms – such as a return on an investment. The return homeward of the Greek heroes after the fall of Troy was called the *Nostoi*. How could this word possibly relate to the arcane term *nostoc*? To understand the connection, we must look at another level of Green Languge interpretation.

In the arcane tongue, the word breaks down into *nos stoch*. The Greek *stoch* is a word with several meanings, including to 'aim at': in certain compounds, it is linked with the art of divination. The final Greek letter, *chi*, is conveniently preserved in the Latin form *C*, which is an image of the crescent Moon – a conversion which is often used in occult and Christian symbolism.[6] It is the Moon of the Night (*nox*). We trust that it is not too fantastical to read this uncomplicated Green Language as implying that when we exercise our (*Nos*) imagination, and become fantastical, we are aiming at the Moon, and expecting a certain return, a payment back, or even the return of the thing aimed. Perhaps this concept explains the most curious graphic detail of the Tarot deck, which shows influence lines streaming like tears (or could those tears be dew?) towards the Moon, from the Earth. This upward, vertical stream of tears (or rain) may seem unnatural, as though the card depicted some unexplained phenomenon. However, in esoteric terms, it actually depicts the true influence of the Moon.

The Moon card of the Tarot pack (18 is a lunar number). The cosmic tears stream towards the Moon. The card is based on a design published in the late 18th century.

Esotericists see the Moon as having the power to suck out the vital solar forces of man: it will augment the growth of physical forms, at the expense of the Spiritual. The lunar power had sway over human 'imagination' and was seen by the esotericists as a dream-like or soporific influence on mankind, recalling again the Greek myth of Selene (see page 197). The images flowed naturally into the human brain, and maintained that brain in a natural sleep, as it was inundated with lunar-derived images. They saw this natural sleep as the antithesis of the Spiritual growth which was the purpose of initiation.

In order to permit certain individuals to escape this natural lunar influence, the alchemists and Rosicrucians devised methods of meditation – of mental picture-building – which worked against the Moon. Such picture-building sought to redirect the 'natural' flow of Spiritual energies away from the the influence of the Moon itself. In this sense, the meditative techniques taught in the Schools were 'against nature' – which is to say that they were against the lunar power under which the greater proportion of Mankind lives. The 'directed' picture-making was said to be to be solar.[7]

The poet-artist, William Blake, was intimately familiar with 'attention directed' imagination through his reading of such alchemists and Rosicrucians as Jakob Boehme. One of his powerful poetic creations is *Los*, an expression on the Earth plane of creative imagination.[8] Blake portrays this creative imagination as a reversal of the lunar imagination: to encapsulate this point in the name of his hero, Blake has made his name from the reversal of the Latin word for the Sun (*Sol*): this reminds us that the Greek *nostos* meant 'to go back, or return'. Blake admits that it is this Los, or solar force, who is the source of his own poetic imagination, and is the creator of all things in the human imagination. However, this is not ordinary imagination, but the 'fire-wrought' imagination of creative activity: Blake emphasizes this by making Los into a blacksmith, who casts the old molten iron into new forms.[9] We see, then, that the name *Los* gets very close to the meaning in the name Fulcanelli, and evokes the idea of the primal alchemist, Vulcan.

The type of meditative picture-making to which Los pertains is based on an inner alchemy through which images are *created* by the attentive mind, as forms are hammered into shape on a forge. While the lunar pictures are, in a sense, mechanical, and given by Nature (in that they require no attention in the making), the solarized image-making is born of directed attention – they are created by the one meditating – by the activity of the blacksmith, Los.

The arcane meanings in the word *nostoc* should now be clear. The *nostoc*, which the botanists recognize as a lucifuge algae, is a plant of darkness. This is one reason why it is called witch-butter, in traditional witchcraft literature. Besides fleeing the Sun, and seeming to melt away in daytime, it was believed, perhaps rightly, to have been a watery extrusion (dew) from the Moon. It was therefore a shadowy radiation of a lunar kind.

In the occultism of the cabbala, the shadow beings which have been born of ordinary human imagination are called *klippoth*. These are shadow beings, which have an existence of their own, even though they are nothing more than projections of human thinking, or image-making. They are truly *revenants* – shadow beings which come back, or return, from the human activity of imagination, or picture-making. The relevance of the word *nostos* now begins to make itself clear: these creatures are born of the operation of imagination and fantasy governed by the Moon, and they come back into the world of man (almost in a *nostoi*) as shadow beings, which not so much flee the light, but cannot be seen in the light. These creatures make their own dark odyssey back into the world, and when they are charged with a special energy by magical processes, they can exert distinct power in the world.

The solar image-making (imagination), born of the creative activity latent in human beings, was of a different category to this natural flow of image-making.

The collecting of *nostoc* was the subject of one or two plates in a famous alchemical book – a book which contained so few words that it was called 'The Silent Book' – in Latin, the *Mutus Liber*.[10] One of the arcane figures from this book is of great interest (plate 35), for it shows two alchemists – male and female – collecting dew, in blankets. At top right and left are the roundels of the Sun and Moon. They are within a few degrees of each other, on either side of the magnificent influx of celestial power to the Earth. The coming together of the male Sun and female Moon is usually a symbol of sexual imagery in alchemical literature, even when the exchange is symbolic of something beyond the sexual. On the Earth below, this celestial union is expressed in animal imagery, to show that the events are to be visualized as taking place on the Astral plane.[11]

The ram of Aries faces the bull of Taurus. Now, in the astrological tradition, Aries is ruled by Mars, and Taurus is ruled by Venus, so the image is a slightly disguised analogy of the meeting of the archetypal male with the archetypal female, in the guise of Mars and Venus. It is their sexual symbolism, rather than the fact that their relationship in the zodiac intimates a particular time of the year, which is of paramount importance. Between these animals are spread five blankets, mounted on upright stakes, to catch the lunar dew, the *Ros*.

This arrangement of blankets is of profound arcane importance, and has several levels of meaning. On one level is the fact that there are five points to the numerology of the higher body – to what Paracelsus called the *pentagrammic* or Five-fold Man. The number five is important, because not only does it refer to the Five Elements (which include the Quintessence), but also to the five-pointed star of the Etheric (see page 262).

On another level, we see that the innermost blanket of the bottom row is represented in the form of a lozenge, and is surrounded by the other four. The lozenge is an ancient symbol for the Quintessence, the fifth element, which completes the work of the Four Elements.[12] We see, then, that the Quintessence is subtly portrayed as the purpose behind this collection of dew. The ejaculation of semen (or of *nostoc*) is aimed not at the making of a child, but at the bringing of a higher energy, the Quintessence, down to the earthly plane.

The symbolism in this plate is complex, yet one single theme is that the natural flow of *nostoc* must be prepared by human beings in a special way: to become of alchemical value, it must be put through a process by which it is transformed into the Quintessence. This is a parable for solarization, as the Quintessence is a product of the Sun, just as the *nostoc* is a product of the Moon.

The 'creative' element in the picture-making derived from such directed attention of 'solarization' is represented in this plate in sexual terms. The fact that the two people are represented as male and female in itself supports our supposition that a sexual connotation may be read into the imagery. This should encourage us to examine the symbolism engendered by this couple.

We see that the pair are squeezing the the blanket. Instead of being laid out flat, the blanket is now in a phallic shape. It is being squeezed to release the dew (which is a sort of semen, or seed) into the dish. The phallic blanket and the kteis-like dish seem to speak almost too openly of the sexual implications of this act. If we look a little more closely at this detail, we shall see that it suggests an even deeper level of meaning, for the downward spray of dew forms a square. This spray drops into a circular dish. Taken together, the two represent the age-old conundrum, which so occupied the mediaeval magicians – the squaring of the circle.

This 'squaring of the circle' is, on one level, the ancient paradigm of the uniting of the male and female (the solar and the lunar) in a single union. To phrase a question in alchemical terms, we may ask, How can the lunar female unite with the solar male? This is not a question which can be answered lightly, save in terms of the Etheric, or Quintessential, power which the alchemists are evoking, in their attempt to transform the *nostoc* dew.

The engraver has shown that this sheet of dew casts a shadow, while the dish itself and the phallic blanket do not. This is no ordinary dish, no ordinary blanket.

Fulcanelli, through his familiarity with the *nostoc* images of the cathedrals and spagyric texts, was able to throw a great deal of light upon the secret symbolism of the cathedrals and churches of France. Those who had the hermetic knowledge to read his books in depth could see that he was dealing, in parables protected by occult blinds, with the nature of human image-making, or imagination – distinguishing the non-creative lunar imagination from the creative solar imagination. Like many esotericists, Fulcanelli was aware that the human imagination is in danger of atrophy, and that a revolution in human Spiritual thinking and image-making is desperately needed.[13]

Like many of those taking esoteric instruction in the 1950s and 1960s, we sometimes harboured the passing thought that one or others of our Teachers might be that mysterious alchemist, Fulcanelli.[14] This initiate, possessed of an extraordinary erudition, had a profound influence on the secret world of Schools, and an even deeper impression on us.

However, there could be no doubt, after our talks with many people we knew at that time, that Fulcanelli was dead. This was a reasonable conclusion. His most important work had been published in the 1920s, and he seems to have disappeared from the view of even his closest pupils by the end of that decade.[15] Even Canseliet, his pupil, had admitted, in the 1925 preface to *Le Mystère des Cathédrales*, that 'Fulcanelli is no more'.

We had assumed that Jacques Bergier, who claimed to have met Fulcanelli in 1937, had probably – to put it kindly – imagined this meeting.[16] Perhaps he had all too easily foisted the renowned name on the strange gentleman he met in the laboratory of the Parisian Gas Board. Indeed, there were one or two details in the published account of this meeting which indicated that the man Bergier met, for all his seeming wisdom, could not have been an initiate of any great order.[17] This much must be assumed because he spoke in material terms about issues which could be discussed only in Spiritual terms.[18]

However, a remark, made by a friend in Florence in the May of 1978, pulled us up short, and made us call into question what we knew about this mysterious alchemist.

Our friend was an old man, whom we had met on a trip to Florence in 1968. He was a well-known figure in the old city, for he tended to frequent the great square of the Signoria – an aged patrician figure in a voluminous cape, always dangling a few books on the end of a leather strap.

A casual observer – and there are many such in Florence – might have taken him for a tramp. The observant, however, might have noted that while his own appearance changed little, the books changed with remarkable frequency. We knew him well enough to be sure that he read each one, before returning it to his shelves. He had one of the largest private libraries in Florence, and was probably the most widely cultured arcanist in that city, where esoteric learning is highly esteemed, even in modern times. When we looked at our friend, we did not see the outer appearance of a tramp, but the inner light of one of the mediaeval wandering poets, or *vagantes*.[19]

As with so many deeply learned men, his knowledge seemed to have become a part of him. It was reflected in his finely chiselled face, browned with age – in the extraordinary upward sweep of his forehead which was edged over with pure white hair, and in the pensive kindness of his mouth. Yet, beyond the physical, there was something else. His learning seemed to exude an aura of light around him, and we used to marvel that other people could not see his inner beauty.

Whenever we met in the Signoria, we had only two courses of action open to us. Either we could sit outside, to drink coffee, and endure the tourist noise, or we could take a taxi to one of the hills. It has always been a source of surprise to us that within five minutes' drive of Florence one can find the quiet of the countryside, smell the magical aroma of basil and listen to the chattering hum of cicadas.

The short walks we used to take together, in the quiet streets beyond the Franciscan church of the Salvatore, along the leafy via Giramonte which skirted the ancient cemetery behind the monastic San Miniato, were instructions in themselves, for every stone and tree held a message for our friend. He was a true Rosicrucian, which meant that he had developed the ability to see through the phenomena of nature, and pierce its innermost secrets. Once, he pointed with his stick over the old villas which dotted the hilly landscape beyond via Giramonte, and mused out loud: 'The early Christians were buried in this stretch of Earth. Then, a couple of centuries later, came the martyrs. San Miniato, whose church is behind us, was one of these unfortunates, yet he was by no means the earliest. They were buried in this land, which is now used for vines and olives. Can you not feel the holiness of the place? Dante, Leonardo, Michelangelo – they would come here to meditate because they had knowledge of such things. They knew that places of the dead were helpful in the meditation which precedes the travail of creative thought. Even the sound of the birds is different here. It is peopled with antiquity – it is not a place of old ghosts but of old love. One does not need great powers to break through the veil in this place – to reach into a different time.'

On this occasion, however, we were standing on the generous pavement which frames the huge square of the Piazzale Michelangelo. We were leaning on the balustrade, overlooking Florence. As we talked, our eyes skimmed like swallows over the trees towards the lovely *ponte vecchio*.

We were talking about symbolism. Indeed, we were talking about a most exciting book on the secret symbolism of three Catalan cloisters, which, when decoded, revealed sacred musical notation. The book had been written by a German, Marius Schneider, but, to the delight of Italian Masons, had recently been published in an Italian translation, in Milan.[20]

This text, which we read avidly, raised many questions about the symbols Schneider had studied, and threw considerable light over certain of the mysteries on which Fulcanelli had touched. As we were already conversant with the methods of mediaeval arcane symbolism, we did not always come to the same conclusions as Schneider. Even so, as we read the enthralling book, we found ourselves in the familiar position of having in our mind far more questions than answers.

One of the capitals about which Schneider had written had left us with a particular question. In the mediaeval cloister of St Mary, at Ripoll in Catalonia, was a stone capital which displayed a register of six distinctive five-petalled flowers. These were divided by a roundel in which was a curious lozenge, with vertical lines, picked out in relief. The entire lozenge was enclosed in an eight-petalled flower (plate 36). Now, while we were able to establish that this device was heraldic, we could not understand why it appeared in such profusion in the cloisters.

We knew that the lozenge itself was an arcane symbol. The four bounding lines were symbolic of the four Elements of Fire, Earth, Air and Water, which, according to arcane knowledge, frame the outer structure of the phenomenal world. The space they bound is the Etheric, or life-force, hidden behind the Elemental Four. It is a 'space' invisible to ordinary vision, which is normally ensnared on the illusory Elemental realm. The lozenge is one of the basic symbols of esoteric lore, representing as it does a sort of doorway into the Etheric Spiritual World.

The arcane magic of the lozenge, as symbol of the Etheric plane, is nowhere more openly announced than in Notre-Dame, in Semur-en-Auxois, France. In a detail of statuary, a figure is displayed within a huge lozenge, the bounds of which are decorated with small lozenges. Altogether, there are 41 lozenges in this single architectural detail. What is the importance of the figure which occupies such a clearly defined Etheric space? The image within the space is that of a Master Mason, and initiate. We know that he is a Master Mason because he carries the tools – even the emblems – of this trade, in the form of the square and plumb. We know that he is an initiate because, besides being enthroned in the Spiritual Etheric, he wears the Phrygian cap, or liberia.[21] This portrayal is iconic – it is intended to record the fact that this remarkable building was raised by initiates. It is a page in a book of stone, which offers a glimpse through its lozenge form into the Spiritual world beyond.

So far as the lozenge-symbolism at Ripoll[22] is concerned, however, the arcane symbolism seems to have been taken to a much deeper level of meaning. We reasoned that while the verticals were, on an exoteric level, heraldic, yet they must also have an esoteric meaning. Not quite knowing where to look for such a meaning, we decided to leaf once again through Fulcanelli's masterpiece. Perhaps this old alchemist would be able to help us to understand the meaning of the verticals within the lozenge. However, even a careful re-reading of *Le Mystère* did not help us solve the problem. We could not understand why the lozenge was set with verticals.[23]

Finally, trained as we now were not to waste questions when in the presence of a wise man, we did decide to put the problem to our Florentine friend.

'You may not have found the answer in Fulcanelli,' he said, 'yet I assure you that the clue is there, nonetheless. You understand, sometimes even Fulcanelli wraps his mysteries in mysteries, for he knows that some things may not be spoken, even today.' He glanced at us, almost mischievously. 'Look again at what he writes of *Saturne* as an anagram of *natures.*'

As was usually the case, when considering the symbolism of alchemy, my friend's brief injunction proved to be correct. Fulcanelli *had* left a clue, after all.[24] The Quintessence (for that was the thing expressed in the lozenge) did contain the two natures, in the different levels of the bas-relief (plate 36). What more explicit arcane symbol might one have of the Quintessential power which stands behind the illusory duality of the world? It was as though the Ripoll sculptor had wished to make the Etheric visible.

'Fulcanelli is far wiser than most of his readers know. He sets down less in words than he could, and delivers parables in parables. In this there is real wisdom. The alchemists insisted that one should heat the retort many times before making the final distillation. This is an emblem of true thought: one must pass one's thinking through the furnace many times, to be sure. One should think with a hammer, rather than with a brain, as one shapes our thought from dross matter.'

As though imitating the hammer blows of Vulcan, he tapped his stick on top of the balustrade. 'Iron, you see. Cast iron. *Yet it looks like stone*. That is the true Philosopher's Stone, which never appears to be what it is. One almost has the impression that these balustrades, which make a prison for the great statue of David,[25] were built by men learned in alchemy. There are deeper secrets in stone than in iron.'

He paused, and sighed. 'You know, one day, some scholar will claim that they have finally discovered who Fulcanelli was. But that scholar will be wrong, for he or she will not know of how initiates really work. They will not know of how casually an initiate may change his clothing. They will not even be able to identify an initiate from his words, or from his eyes. Such knowledge, which was taken for granted 100 years ago, is already almost lost.' Once again he paused, and then he asked us a most extraordinary question. 'Did you ever meet Fulcanelli?'

It was the very question we should have put to him, yet, much to our astonishment, we found him asking it of us. We looked at him in some wonderment. 'I would have been an adolescent when Fulcanelli died.' It was a lame response, but at least honest.

Our friend laughed. 'Oh, I do not think that is the case at all. Fulcanelli is alive. Fulcanelli is even older than me, yet he is still alive. He lives here in Florence.'

We tried to hold back our emotions. Our whole body seemed to quiver, as though it were no longer our own to control. This was perhaps not so much at the surprise, as at the confirmation of something we had always known. We were in the presence of a man – a man with whom we were privileged to converse almost at will – and now we had learned that he knew personally the greatest alchemist of our century.

'You *know* Fulcanelli? Even today?'

'I have met him,' he confirmed. 'I meet him, from time to time.'

Did we dare ask the most daring question of all? To this day, we wonder if we should have asked. Yet, on reflection, we see that there could be little point in our seeking an introduction, other than to know – perhaps even casually boast – that we had met Fulcanelli. We knew that we had no currency to offer in return.

The old man sipped at his coffee, and as he did so, he raised his eyes towards us, and said, 'Perhaps you might like to join our little gathering in via de' Vagellai? We meet there to talk about such things. About Fulcanelli. About alchemy. About this and that.' He put his coffee down, and could not resist laughing out loud. 'How long have we – you and I – how long have we known each other?'

'A decade, perhaps.'

'Yes, ten years. Yet I knew *of* you long before then.'

'Of me? How so?' We were intrigued. It is true that before we had been introduced to him in the Signoria square, those ten years ago, we had occasionally seen him wandering around in various parts of Florence, like some Italian scholar gipsy,[26] but there was no reason to imagine that he had known who we were.

'I knew your Master long before he moved to Siena. A learned man, and a merry one in his youth. He told me a little about you, and your difficulties in Siena – in Montereggione ... Of your loss ...' He tightened his lips. 'I had asked him then if it was likely you would like to join our group, but he said that you were not ready. Would you like to join us now?'

So, our old Florentine friend was a Teacher!

Siena had been a long time ago. One can be almost healed of such a tragedy in 16 years. We nodded. 'Yes, it would be wonderful to study in such a School once more.'

He patted the back of our hand. 'A good decision, made at the right time, I think. If you glance at the ephemeris for today . . .' He fumbled at the buckle around his books '. . . you will find that Saturn is in 25 degrees of Leo – the famous Astrologer's Degree.[27] In former times, on the day the Sun entered this sign, the hermetic groups who were interested in the esoteric traditions of astrology and alchemy would meet together, for a meal and conversations about the sacred things.'[28]

'During one of the Egypt rites of Isis, the neophyte was shown the buttocks of a goat.'

It was the voice of our Florentine friend. The studio above the via de' Vagellai was in total silence, yet from the outside filtered a reminder of Florentine traffic. 'The Egyptian neophyte was forced to kiss the anus of this goat. He had, of course, sworn an oath to follow the biddings of the initiatory priest, and had no choice in the matter . . . However reluctant in spirit, the neophyte would force his head forward towards the repellent orifice, and press his lips to it. Yet, he found that, instead of his lips brushing against it, he was kissing the lips of a virgin priestess of Isis.[29]

'In this story lies the key to one of the great Mysteries of initiation. As Fulcanelli would have said, the story shows how closely connected is the mother, the *mere*, and the bestial *mare*.[30] It is a mystery which is, among other things, rooted in both the lore relating to the duality of the Moon, and the sexual mystery of the *svd*. The *svd*, as you will all know, is the Secret Eye which permits the possessor to see beyond the illusion of the ordinary and familiar. It is what we might nowadays call the developed Third Eye. The *svd* is also the seeing-eye *Ru*, $\bigcirc$, the Egyptian hieroglyphic of birth, of the portal between the two worlds.

'As you might imagine, the hermetic language of symbolism has suffered enormously due to secrets hidden in the "buttocks kiss".[31] Even so, this should not disguise from us that certain arcane imagery – even the arcane imagery of the churches – still hints at the real import behind this lewd-seeming imagery.

'The Fool in the 15th-century stall at Nejara [see figure on page 12] wears a robe which is so designed as to fall open at both front and back, so that his private parts are always visible.[32] This "naked" Fool has a long ancestry. We may read this anal-scrotal nakedness as a sign that the true Fool is prepared to show those things (including, one imagines, Spiritual things) which others prefer to hide. Of course, those who are prepared to reveal the way to higher vision – to that vision which arises from initiation – are often seen by the Sleepers as foolish.

'It might be tempting to link this imagery with what has been called *l'offrande anale* in French. This *offrande* is the offering of the buttocks to the kiss which has been made infamous by the witchcraft literature.[33] In fact, there is a considerable artistic and literary heritage to indicate that there were esoteric groups who, for entirely arcane reasons, favoured imagery depicting this *offrande*.[34] The buttock-kiss appears in rituals which are not always intended to be derisory.[35] It is perhaps true that such groups recognize a sanctity in "the repositories of human lineage" – implying that the buttock kiss is actully intended for the scrotum and penis, rather than the buttocks: it requires no stretch of imagination to see in this an obeisance to the rigid Capricorn, set between the two great buttock-balls of Cancer (plate 31). One thing is sure, however – the symbolism of the *offrande* is rooted in a ritual recognition of fission. As you know full well, fission takes place when a thing separates into light and darkness. On an arcane physiological level, fission takes place in the lungs when, through the operation of breathing, light (*phos*) is taken from the oxygen, and the dark carbon monoxide is rejected. This same fission takes place in digestion, when nourishment (a support for the "light" of the Spiritual man) abstracts energies and rejects unwanted material through the private parts. The dark reject is received by the cosmos, in one form or another, and eventually regenerated.

'A surviving 15th-century banner from the "Mad Mother" – perhaps linked with the confraternity of the *Mere Folle*, centred on Dijon, in France[36] – confirms this reading. Two clowns, each dressed in yellow and red, hug each other in such a way that their heads appear between the legs of the other, as though they are about to make the *offrande*. In fact, they are both savouring a fart, which is depicted as issuing from both sets of buttocks at the same time. This truth is recognized in the popular title of the image – *Le Petengueules* (the "fart-mugs"). This gaseous reject from the bowels is the dark element of the fission that makes life possible: it is the dark reject of the process of fission which maintains the "light" of perception.

'The curious shadows cast by these two figures reveal the esoteric meaning of the image, for the darkness of the shadow does not reflect the forms of the couple. In each case, the shadows take on shapes of their own, to form bellows. The bellows are being pumped towards two heads, and symbolize the winds. In the esoteric tradition, these winds are far more than representations of winds in the modern sense of the word – they are cosmic movers.[37] Thus, the wind which comes from the bodies of the two Fools is seen as being returned to their cosmic equivalent. The fart is seen as a part of the cosmic rhythm which maintains the light of human life. In this image, we find an extension of the notion that the Fool is prepared to reveal more than ordinary people, if only to lay bare the basic structure of the Spiritual world. This view of the esoteric background to an image which may be interpreted in terms of mere Earthy bawdy, enables one to see many mediaeval images on a different level. It is this esoteric strain which alone explains why so many *petengueules* are found in the fabric of mediaeval churches.[38] This imagery is linked with what the French esotericists call the *marotte*, or "small mother".[39] This, of course, brings us back to the connection between *mere* and *mare*.'

He paused, and looked carefully around, to ensure that we were all following his line of argument.

'In the arcane tradition there are two Moons. These pairs have very many names. Such names are usually derived from mythological personifications – yet all these pairs relate to the idea that one Moon is a reflector of sunlight, while the other, if not always in darkness, is invisible.

'The light Moon dispenses a beneficient influence, while the dark Moon is evil. One lies behind the other, so to speak much as the goat obscured the priestess of Isis. Now, the sexual undertones of this ritual of Isis are not particularly distinguished – there is a relationship between the anus and the lips. This relationship was recognized by the ancient Egyptians, who constructed their hieroglyphic $\bigcirc$ with the sound value *Ru*, to encapsulate their lore. Something of the magic in this hieroglyphic is dramatized in the obscene-seeming story of the neophyte's kiss.'

He left a short silence in his monologue, presumably to allow for questions, but such questions as we did carry in our souls remained unexpressed.

'From the very beginning of civilization, the Moon has been a mystery, because it has always stared down upon the Earth with one single face. As the Moon circles the Earth, it keeps one side of its globular face presented towards humanity. This means that (before the recent achievements of space travel, at least) no ordinary man had gazed upon the far side of the Moon. There was, quite literally, a hidden side, an unexplored side, a dark side, to the Moon. It would seem that Isis, the goddess of the Moon, did indeed veil part of herself from the gaze of men. This cosmological truth is expressed in more than one image of Isis and her dark sister, Nephthys.

'The hermetic streams which feed Western occultism have tended, until comparatively recent times, to emphasize only the light side of the Moon. Even so, hints of the dark Moon are encapsulated in even the most overt-seeming symbolism.

'In the Christian tradition, the archangel Gabriel is the ruler of the Moon – that is, of the light side of the Moon. His role as messenger at the Annunciation is well established, even if his arcane role (symbolized by the white lilies) is only imperfectly understood outside the secret Schools. The lilies of Gabriel are very profound symbols indeed. They are recognized, in the Mysteries, as symbols of the descent of a God.[40]

'Furthermore, in the same Christian tradition, images of the Assumption of the Virgin show the lunar crescent beneath the feet of the Virgin.

'In these two different symbols, we have a clue to how the Virgin of Light is linked with the angelic ruler of the Moon at the conception of the Child, and with the lunar crescent at her own translation from Earth to Heaven – at her death. It is as though this symbolism was designed to show . . .' He paused '. . . to show that the very same lunar forces which announced her destiny as the Mother of God were also lifting her to Heaven, at the end of her life.

'Now, Gabriel is the Christian equivalent of the personified light Moon. The name is, of course, Hebraic, and we must look to the same language in our search for the name of the Christian dark Moon. This name is Lilith, the mother of the *lilin*, or brood of demons. We see, then, that it is no great mystery that the angel Gabriel should carry lilies at the Annunciation. There is rarely such a thing as accident in the confluence of sounds in arcane symbolism.'[41]

Our old friend – now our Teacher – looked around, to ascertain that we had understood the connection he was attempting to draw between the lilin and the lilies, and then continued: 'The word "embarrassed" is perhaps not quite right, yet I have to say that the early Christian Church was *embarrassed* by the vast numbers of demonologies which prowled around the cosmologies of the pagan religions. These demons were especially numerous in the Gnostic tradition which the Church felt proper to dismiss. It seems to me that this rejection of the Gnostic tradition was part of a peculiar programme adopted by the early Church. The early followers of Christ were prepossessed with the Light – almost blinded by the light of the new Christian message. They seemed to have forgotten all too easily that every light casts a shadow. At all events, the huge pagan literature and tradition pertaining to the lilin and demons was not properly transmitted into Christian lore.

'When, in the fourth century, Theodosius – who was an initiate of the highest order – closed down the ancient oracle centres, such as Delphi, he recognized that their old power had already been lost. When he began to promote a programme of scholarship which turned the ancient

311

Egyptian gods into demons, then he should have known that he was doing something which was bound to lead to misunderstandings.

'It is a natural enough impulse to demonize the gods of a conquered religion. However, initiates should not always follow the natural impulse. In the confusion which followed, even the roles of Satan, the Devil and Mephistopheles were confused in the early Christian literature. I am sure that I am not telling you anything which you do not already know when I insist that Satan, the Devil and Mephistopheles were once recognized as distinct individualities.

'I should point out that it is scarcely surprising that the role of Lilith – so important, and so clearly delineated in Jewish arcane literature – should be relegated from the Christian literature, and left to survive only in misunderstood symbols. With this rejection of Lilith went a rejection of the importance of her Egyptian equivalent, the shadow-goddess *Nephthys*.[42]

'The great mother Isis is the womb of all things which come into the light of the Sun, from the preserving darkness of her womb. Yet the lunar Isis is not a single goddess, but dual. Her sister, Nephthys, was the dark Moon: in the ancient Egyptian *Book of the Dead*, Nephthys is portrayed standing opposite her sister, like a shadow-neter (opposite). In addition to being sister of Isis, this black virgin Nephthys was sister and wife of the dark *Set*. Like her sister, Nephthys was a great magician, with a command of the secret words. This may explain why she has been given such an important resurrectional role in certain modern black magic cults, after so many centuries of near oblivion.[43] The pair – Isis and Nephthys – were called *the weeping sisters*. Their tears stream to Earth, just as the tears of sleeping humanity stream towards the Moon in the Tarot card (see figure on page 299). This, it is said, was because they both wept at the death of Osiris, though, as we shall see, there may be a far deeper reason for this description.'

He paused once again, and his bright eyes rested on our own face. 'We have a new member with us here tonight. His name is Mark Hedsel. Like us, Mark is deeply interested in the works of Fulcanelli. Unlike most of us, he has already had an opportunity to study at first hand many of the symbols which the master wrote about.'

Not knowing what to do, we stood up and made a salaam.

'Mark – I recognize that you have taken an especial interest in the occult imagery of Christian churches and cathedrals. Can you think of any mediaeval image which expresses this idea of the tears of Isis and Nephthys?'

Reluctantly, we shook our head. The Tarot cards which first came to mind belong to a much later stream of imagery than the cathedrals, even

The goddess Isis (left), with her dark twin-sister, Nephthys, adoring the Tat of Osiris. From the Hunefer section of the Egyptian Book of the Dead *(after the Budge edition).*

though some of this initiation imagery was derived directly from the fabric of the cathedrals.[44]

'Then, Mark, I must tell you that such images exist. In your future travels, you might be advised to look for them among the cathedrals of northern France. To a very large extent, the imagery of the light side of the Moon, as expressed in the Isis symbolism, was integrated into Christianity in the form of Mary, the Mother of God. Just as Isis had been a star goddess, so was Mary, as the star called the *Stella Maris* (plate 37) on her shoulder, or on her maphorium, indicates.[45] I must say, indeed, that the very fact that Mary is depicted with a maphorium is itself a throwback to the initiation lore, which has Isis famously veiled against profane sight. Just as Isis was linked with the Moon, so was Mary, as is evident in thousands of images which portray her standing upon the Moon.[46] Just as Isis gave birth to a Child without sexual congress with Osiris, so was Mary famed for her virgin birth.

'We see, then, that strains of the hermetic Isiac lore survive – if somewhat mutilated – in even popular Christian imagery. However, her dark sister Nephthys does not.' He looked around, his eyes resting upon each of us in turn. He then nodded, to indicate that we had reach a point where it would be advisable to take a break.

Our new Master began again without preamble.

'I said that much of the ancient lore pertaining to the dark Moon was lost with the emergence of Christianity as the dominant method of initiation. With the loss of the dark Moon, several related symbols were either lost or obscured. Among these was the *kteis* symbol – the representation of the female sexual organ. This had been an important Egyptian hieroglyphic, in the form of the *Ru*. The sacred *Ru*, garnered from the secret parts of the dark goddess, was changed, and survived in a disguised form in certain Christian art forms.

'The *Sheelah-na-gig*, for example, is one of the strangest of all survivals of pagan lore still found on the fabric of certain European churches.[47] I am sure that you are all familiar with this symbolic lady? If you are not, then I think we could ask Ricardo to show you photographs of some of the finest. Do you have such photographs, Ricardo?'

'I have some bromides of the *Sheelah* at Kilpeck and Oxford in England and Dreieichen in Germany.'

'I am not familiar with the Oxford image. Is it in a church?'

'It is in St Michael's,' Ricardo said. 'Once it was part of the external fabric, but now it is kept inside the church.'

'If it is possible, Ricardo, some time in the future you might care to show your picture of the Kilpeck *Sheelah* to all those who are interested. For the moment, it is probably sufficient for me to tell you that the *Sheelah-na-gig* is the image of a woman so disporting her private parts as to make of them a gaping door, or opening (plate 38). It is clearly a reference to the vulva as a birth-passage, and may (even for the pagans) have had initiatory undertones. When one meditates on such an image, one has the impression that the Earthly *kteis* – the backside of the Earthly goat, so to speak – has turned into the mouth of a virgin priestess. The vertical mouth makes promises of a doorway to initiation beyond the physical body of the Sheelah.

'One might argue, perhaps, that the Sheelah is no longer pagan. She might be demonstrating the human birth of Christ. Or, again, one might argue that she symbolizes the Christ as the portal of life. Yet such arguments are self-defeating, for the Sheelah is much older than Christianity, and a change in interpretation does not change the meaning of a symbol. How these prurient mediaeval images have survived on so many Christian churches is a wonder in itself, perhaps even an entire history in itself.[48]

'Our own Master Fulcanelli learned a great deal from the remarkable Gerald Massey.[49] Some of you here may be familiar with his works, even though they have not yet been translated from the English. Massey wrote one of the most profound and disturbing etymological studies of the 19th century. His mind had been especially prepared for this undertaking by the fact that, as a child and boy, he had received virtually no education. He learned to read and write only late in life. Such an education has a very powerful effect on the Spiritual body of Man, and in this case, it entitled Massey to release vast energies into a narrow spectrum of intellectual research. Having learned to read and write, he became fascinated – that is not too strong a word – he became fascinated by language. He spent many years, working in the Reading Room of the British Museum, establishing the link which bound together the sacred language of Egypt first with the English language, then with other languages. He came to many far-reaching proposals which have never been adequately countered.[50]

'Now, Massey proposed that the name Sheelah is from the Egyptian *Sherah*. *Sherah* meant "source", or "waters of source". *Sherah* also meant "to reveal" or "exhibit". It is precisely this which the Sheelah does on the façades and towers of mediaeval churches: she exhibits her private parts, her *kteis*.

'Of course, what you will see straight away is that, if the image, like the name, is in origin Egyptian, then the Sheelah is exhibiting the *Ru*.' Without getting up from the chair, he leaned over and drew on the blackboard alongside the two curves which make up the Ru. His movement was dramatized to show that the Ru was made up from two lunar crescents.

$$\big)\big($$

'This ancient Egyptian hieroglyphic was at one and the same time a *kteis*, a mouth, and a doorway, made up of two crescent symbols. It was a doorway into the Spiritual world. It was a doorway into an initiation hall. It was the birth passage between the material realm and the Spiritual. The link with initiation is maintained in the fact that the Sheelah is sometimes called, in Ireland, Patrick's Mother. Here we have a reminder that it was Patrick who introduced to Ireland the Christian form of initiation. He replaced the older Hibernian methods of the Druids with the more advanced methods of Christ. The conversion was done gradually, with little disturbance of the older images and sacred sites. This in itself is interesting. The result is that there are many pagan images of the Sheelah in Ireland. Indeed, if there is one land in the world where the pagan initiation sites still live, it is Ireland.

'However, let me return to the *Ru*. The *Ru* may have survived in the semi-lewd image of Sheelah, but it also survived in a less prurient Christian symbol. It survives as the *vesica piscis*, or aureole, which surrounds such beings as the Virgin Mary, and sometimes the Christ, in mediaeval art.[51] Like the *Ru*, this vesica is made up of two crescents meeting. Of course, I am sure that you will appreciate just how surprising it is that the Sheelah should have survived at all in ecclesiastical art. The *kteis*, however well disguised, is scarcely a Christian symbol – yet the Sheelah is not inclined to disguise her wares at all.'

'If Massey is correct, and the *gig* of the name is from the Egyptian *kekh*, then even the full name points to its initiate origins, and explains why the image is uniquely found on church walls, for the ancient Egyptian *kekh* meant "sanctuary". Sheelah was the exhibitor of the sanctuary. Could it be that the image has an even deeper meaning? Could it be that the Sheelah is a survival – perhaps the only survival in Christian art – of the ancient sexual magic which was so widely practised in the pagan world, and which is still practised in the Orient among the tantrics? I think that the more you look into this question, the more you will be inclined to see the Sheelah as precisely such a survival. Perhaps, now, we might find ourselves inclined to think again about the black virgins. These statues, hidden in the crypts of certain ancient European churches, may not have been images of Isis, but of her sister, Nephthys.'

He turned his face towards us. 'Mark's own interest in the arcane insights of Fulcanelli has led him into some interesting byways. Among these byways he has explored some of the traditions of the mediaeval artists. Many a pleasant hour have I spent with Mark, here in Florence, talking about painting and sculpture. His own knowledge of the history of esoteric things could prove useful to us. I shall invite him to say a few words about the *Ru* as it appeared in Christian art.'

We took up the invitation with some diffidence, but found that almost as soon as we started to speak, the words came naturally, as though from a higher source within our being. 'Because the *Ru* is an Egyptian hieroglyphic, most people tend to think that it has disappeared – along with all the other detritus of ancient Egyptian knowledge. This is not the case. The initiates who guided the transfer of some of the ancient teachings of the Egyptians to Rome, that they might serve the new Mysteries of Christ, recognized the esoteric value of the *Ru*, and introduced it into the new Christian symbolism. This explains why it has survived in mediaeval art.

'There are many examples of this survival, but there are few works that

316

exhibit the *Ru* with such esoteric depth as the great altarpiece of the Apocalypse which was painted in the 14th century by initiate-artists in the school of Bertram.[52] This huge altarpiece is now in the Victoria and Albert Museum, London. It is a distinctly arcane work, and undoubtedly the product of an hermetic school. We recommend anyone in London to visit that museum, and examine the picture with care. The symbols within the 57 panels represent the highest level of esoteric imagery in a work designed for inclusion in a Christian church.[53]

'If you look closely at this altarpiece, you will find no fewer than six *Ru* symbols. Of course, in the Christian tradition they were no longer called *Ru*. Among the Christians that curious form has long been called the *vesica piscis*, yet even so, it still carries much the same hermetic meaning as the old Egyptian *Ru*. In Christian art, the purpose of this distinctive form is to show that the personages represented within them are in the Spiritual world – that they are on the other side of that portal which separates the material from the Spiritual.

'On the back of the left-wing is a panel showing the death of the Virgin. The Virgin lies flat on a bed, her hands crossed over to show that

The vesica piscis (or Ru), related to the posture of the dying Virgin. Drawing of detail of a panel from the Betram Altarpiece.

she is dead. Clearly, the world around her is the familiar material world. Above and behind her is the *vesica piscis* – a doorway into the Spiritual plane – through which we can see Christ. This is a very strange image, for He is carrying himself. In his left arm, He cradles the young Jesus, perhaps as a reminder of the Virgin birth.' We paused, to lend emphasis to the last word. This was a technique we had seen used to great effect by our first Master, in Paris.

'*Birth* – another link with the *Ru* symbolism of the ancients.[54] Now, what is of profound interest to us is that this *Ru* – for all its Christian context – still carries with it certain of the sexual implications which were expressed in the Egyptian form. The *vesica piscis* of this detail is so arranged on this painted panel that, if we complete the two arcs of the bottom part (presently hidden by the dead body of the Virgin), then we find that the point of intersection rests upon her crossed hands. Thus, it is a reference to the death of her Son, who was crucified by the hands. More pertinently, however, that same point also rests upon her sexual parts. This dead Virgin is making the equivalent of what is called the *Venus pudica* gesture, protecting her own private parts with her crossed hands. The full power of the *Ru* seems to have extended itself over a 5,000-year interlude in this picture of a woman who was, like Isis, a Virgin who gave birth to a Child from a Higher Realm.'

We had been really delighted by the invitation to join this group, *la Cantonata*, which met under the gentle direction of our alchemist friend. We were impressed to discover how many young people were among the 15 or so members.

It had long been our ambition to study in a group which concentrated on Fulcanelli and the Green Language, but we had never before been put in touch with such a group. How typical it should be that a path we needed to follow should have been at our feet for so many years, in the guise of this wise old man. Fulcanelli once admitted to his pupil Canseliet that he had spent 25 years searching for the Philosopher's Gold, only to find that it had been all around him, 'under his hand, before his eyes'.[55] If we did take part in this group, we might begin to find answers to some of the questions which Fulcanelli had raised in our soul.

Fulcanelli may well be a great initiate into the hermetic lore, yet he is an infuriating Teacher. He teaches, or enlightens, by means of hints and guesses, demanding all the while the full cooperation and attention of his reader. Fulcanelli seems to practise the *sol lente*,[56] the 'slow-heat' method of the alchemist, for he recognizes that a more fierce heat, which may be raised with the bellows, would kill the germinating life within the vessel.

A word or a phrase by Fulcanelli can do two things. Either it will spark off unconnected links in one's mind, yoking together unsuspected words or ideas, and thereby engendering enlightenment. Or, it can have one scurrying in ignorance to the old alchemical and occult books, or resorting to the active contemplation of symbols, which he so often recommends. Both these methods of learning are conducted through the slow inner heat, so beloved by alchemical teachers.

For the student, it is an infuriatingly slow method. All too often even the alchemical books prove too obscure for elucidation, and the questioning soul is left without answers to the questions raised by Fulcanelli. In some cases, years may pass before one arrives at the answers one seeks. We have to admit that, more than once, we have encountered great difficulties in following some of the indications left by Fulcanelli as he skipped along the Way of the Fool, juggling with words, occasionally allowing one to fall to the floor for the benefit of his followers.

As a practising Fool ourself, we had been puzzled by the fact that Fulcanelli seems merely to have glossed over what must have been the most interesting aspect of mediaeval festivities – the Feast of the Fools. We suspected that, hidden away in the esoteric account of the Feast of Fools, there would be some important lessons to learn about the inner life of the Fool. One of Fulcanelli's unwritten precepts was that most of the pagan-like festivities of the mediaeval period reflected esoteric doctrines. The Feast of the Fool, with its bawdy, its strange language, its open mockery of the religious life and of God's servants – its election of a boy as a mock-Bishop[57] – must offer a reservoir of arcane material for such a man as Fulcanelli. Yet, much to our surprise, he had given only passing reference to the Feast of Fools, 'and its Mad Mother'. This was infuriating: what was the esoteric background to the Feast of Fools? Who was that Mad Mother?

These deliberations led to my first question at the meeting of *la Cantonata*, which gathered with such sartorial elegance in an artist's studio overlooking the via de' Vagellai.

We cannot offer an account of our contact with this group without explaining their carefully-chosen hermetic name. The Italian means 'corner' or 'angle of a building', and evokes both 'Peter's corner', and 'the corner of the stone', a play on words which was entirely consistent with Fulcanelli's view of things. In the earliest of his published works, Fulcanelli had written of the mysterious stone image, known in French as *Maitre Pierre du Coignet* (Master Peter of the Corner). The word Pierre, besides meaning Peter, also means 'stone'.[58] This Peter-stone used to be near the corner of the choir rail in Notre Dame de Paris. It was mysterious because, in spite of its position in the heart of the church, it was an image of a Devil. When we first heard of this Pierre, we were reminded of that devilish Asmodeus water-stoup in the church at Rennes-le-Château.[59] This Notre Dame example had been removed years ago, but the image had been an embarrasment to archaeologists, and presumably to those churchmen ignorant of alchemical lore. The Italian group-name was intended as a similar play on the double meaning of Pietro, for the Italian *pietra* is also stone. The group identified with this stone because they realized that their ideas, stemming from their studies of Fulcanelli, would be an embarrassment 'to archaeologists', as to historians, and all those ignorant of the hermetic stream of knowledge with which the master dealt.

We ourselves recognized that this 'stone corner' was also the Masonic square, the *kan*, which we had traced in the hermetic lore of the ancient Egyptians. Our group was essentially a Rosicrucian group – which meant that it would be aware of the rich stream of Masonic symbolism that had been used in the cathedrals which Fulcanelli had studied.

The knowledge of the meaning in the name of the *Cantonata* had been divulged by our friend, a few minutes before we went into the studio. After revealing to us some of these interlinked levels of meanings in their chosen title, he rubbed his hands together with some glee: 'In any case – what an excellent disguise. It suggests we all gather here in the via de' Vagellai to sing! That indeed is the Language of the Birds.'[60]

Our old friend had introduced us during his preliminary talk, so we felt free to raise a question early in the proceedings. In theory, the questions were put to the group as a whole, yet, in deference to the wisdom of our friend, it was tacitly agreed that he should be the first to offer a response.

We cleared our throat, to indicate that we wished to ask a question. 'What was the psychological and cosmic purpose behind the the Feast of the Fools? For all the arcane promise in such festivities, Fulcanelli gives the Fool Feast short shrift. Have you any idea why?'

The sun-browned face of our friend lit up. 'What a delight to be presented with such a question! I too had observed that Fulcanelli did not deal with the Feast of Fools as he might have done. This puzzled me too, for the evidence of the Fool is scattered through many of the mediaeval documents with which he was familiar. Such fooling is also frozen in stone on the very cathedrals he discussed in such arcane detail.' He settled back in his chair. 'In the pre-Christian world it was recognized by the initiate groups that those who led ordinary lives required safety-valves. For this reason, certain calendrical days were set aside when all the norms of society were released, or even inverted. In the Roman Mysteries, the important period of such misrule had been the *Saturnalia*.[61] Important elements from this festival were carried over, almost intact, to the mediaeval Feast of Fools.

'During this Feast, the priests would dress as clowns or women, and generally "act the Fool". Clerics and priests would wear monstrous masks to perform their duties, and – according to their innate dispositions – would sing bawdy songs. Surprisingly, these practices did not degenerate into black magical practices, though all the tendencies were there.[62] Later, they would give displays of unlicensed bawdy in the streets, drinking, sporting, and spending their money wildly.[63] In a word, the clerics played the Fool. The nominal purpose of the riot was the bawdy worship of the ass which had carried Christ during His Entry into Jerusalem, and it is this which accounts for the fact that above the cacophonous music one could hear the constant imitation of the braying of an ass.

'It is reasonable to assume that the Fool Feast was a throwback to the Roman Saturnalia, during which slaves were allowed to change places with their masters. They might, for example, behave with the same lack of decorum, as the masters served them at table. The distinction between master and slave was very pronounced in ancient times – under normal circumstances the master was entirely protected by the law, while the slave had virtually no legal protection or redress. A master could use his male and female slaves more or less as he wished. The masters could be cruel, vindictive, licentious and arrogant, and slaves had no respite from this behaviour. Imagine the chaos of the Saturnalia when the laws were put into temporary abeyance. This was indeed the release of a safety-valve which held back the pent-up steam of a whole culture.

'The inversion was almost total. Something of this inversion of the "natural order" of society was continued into the Feast of Fools in the mediaeval period. Now, the festivities of Saturnalia of the ancient worlds poured over into the Christian world with such exuberance that the ecclesiastical authorities had no power to stop the celebrations completely. Indeed, it was as though the priests, who were most directly in contact with the populace, could see the importance of releasing such safety-valves from time to time, and, in the later mediaeval period, it was the priests themselves who were most vociferous and active in playing the Fool. The Christmas mummers of the English pre-Christmas festivities are the last remains of this extraordinary festival. There is good reason for believing that the long period of the original Feast of Fools was transferred to the single day's misrule of the All Fools' Day of 1 April. It seems to have come to England as a practice in the 16th century, from France.

'Of course, even those among the ecclesiastical hierarchies who understood the purpose of these rites pretended not to approve of them. Indeed, some authorities believed that they had got out of hand – that what had once been a safety-valve release had become an actual threat to the good order and morals of society. In consequence, there were numerous attempts to censure and redirect the energies of the great festival, yet it was too deep-rooted in the popular need for the Church to remove it.[64]

'I have to ask myself, though, whether there were elements in the Fool Feast which did not belong to the pagan world. More than once I have pondered whether there were Christian symbols and rituals hidden in this fooling and bawdy, beyond the nominal worship of the ass. Surprisingly, I came to the conclusion that the answer is yes. In the first few centuries of Christianity, there was still an official line of esotericism – a recognition that not all the Mysteries of Christ could be revealed to the congregation. This attitude was expressed mainly in what is now called the *arcani disciplina*,[65] and in the limitation of the study of hermetic documents to certain monks and other religious people. In those days, education was in the hands of the Church, and such arcane studies could be regulated. This separation of a religious élite meant that the general populace, denied access to hermetic thought, clung to the ancient festivals and beliefs which had once enshrined sacred knowledge.

'The more I looked into this matter of the Feast of the Fool, the more I came up against one recurring symbol . . .' He motioned towards us. 'Mark, you too have looked into these things. Have you any idea what this symbol might be?'

'The *fish*?' We gave the response as though it were a question, but we were fairly confident in his response. 'Yes, I too found a fish lurking – if fishes can be said to lurk – behind the non-pagan elements in the Fool Feast. This should not surprise us: the fish is the great Christian symbol. It is a symbol found in the earliest pictures and incisions in the old meeting places of the early Christians, the catacombs of Rome.[66] It is a symbol made famous by that great father of the Church, Augustine, who traced in the Greek word, *I-ch-th-u-s*, an acrostic for Christ as Son of God.[67] It is a symbol which even to this day overlooks the whole of our beautiful Florence, from the façade of San Miniato al Monte, the hill beyond the Arno.'[68]

'What first led you to the fish, Mark?'

'The extraordinary custom of the priests who officiated at the Feast of Fools. They would rip the soles from their shoes, and burn these in their censers, to fill the church with the unholy stink of smoke.'

'And this was the fish?' Our friend pretended confusion. Yet, he had known what we meant, and had asked the question merely for the benefit of those present.

Christ symbolized as a fish: the unidentified man is a Christian initiate, looking upon the Crucified Christ. Drawing of a detail from a 12th century manuscript.

We smiled. 'The feet are ruled by Pisces, the sign of the fish. The priests were making a fish sacrifice to the Fish – that is, Christ – who had sacrificed for them.'

'Thus, in the midst of the fooling, the Christian element was still reasserting itself.'

'That's what I had imagined. But some of the priests wore masks with fish-heads, and while some wore the tails of donkeys, others wore the scaled tails of fish . . .'

'There are calendrical considerations too, are there not?'

'Yes, although the origins of the Feast are obscure, it is evident that there *was* a link with what was later called April Fools' Day. The link has something to do with the calendrical changes when the calendrical date for New Year's Day was moved from 1 April to 1 January.[69] The first of April, our own April Fools' Day, had been intimately linked with the beginning of the zodiacal year, with the germinal month of Aries.'

'Could you develop on this idea, and perhaps relate it to Fulcanelli?'

We were not sure how we might link it with the Master, yet we felt that it would be worth raising some other important issues.

'You may have heard of *April fish*? There is some indication that, in France, the gifts formerly made between friends at this April time were called "fishes of April", intended to mark the beginning of a new year. In pagan times, this transition was of great importance, for it was far more than the passage of one month into another – it was the passage from one zodiac into another. The zodiac is circular, so it cannot properly be said to have a beginning or an end. However, the circle is said to begin in Aries and end in Pisces. This "severed" zodiac explains why the top of man, the head, is ruled by Aries, while his lower extremity, the feet, is ruled by Pisces. Men and women are the lengthened zodiac.

'This first day of April marked the transition from the Pisces of March to the Aries of April. Was it not reasonable that a day of chaos or fooling should ensue, to separate the old from the new? The fish-gifts seem to be a token exchanged between friends in recognition of this cosmic death of the old, and birth of the new. A fish, the *April Fish*, was an excellent symbol of the cutting of the circle at the end of Pisces.'[70]

'Thank you, Mark.' The old man brought our response to an abrupt and somewhat indecorous end. 'Now,' he went on, 'Mark asked me what was the purpose of these festivities in ancient times. As I have suggested, my impression is that they worked much like released safety-valves. Just as the cosmos has its own system of safety-valves for the Earth, in the eclipses, so society must have its own method of release. Without such a release, a society would quickly fall into total internal chaos. The festivities were a sign of just how well society was regulated in the days when initiate Schools – rather than politicians and bankers – were in charge of society. Do I sound cynical? Perhaps I am. Perhaps our modern societies could be regulated with a little more insight, and with just a little less reliance on Capricornian bureaucracy . . .'[71]

As we left via de' Vagellai, and walked into via dei Benci, to cross the Grazie bridge, the old man rested his arm on our shoulder. 'Perhaps you would like to take a meal with me?'

'I'd be delighted.'

'You are vegetarian? Yes? Then, let us try the *Sorelle* in San Niccolo. The food is good, and there will be silence enough for us to talk.'

From the way our friend was welcomed by the manager, we realized that he ate here frequently. He was ushered to what must have been his favourite table.

'Are the sisters the Fates?'[72] We were thinking of the name, *Sorelle*.

'The Parcae?' He smiled. 'Those sisters are everywhere. And you are right to ask, for everything in Florence has many meanings. But I think that the place was run by three sisters years ago. Before and during the War, I think. It is best not to ask. Who knows what skeletons will tumble from their closets. It is enough for me that the morning coffee is good. I love the ordinary streets of Florence: the streets of San Niccolo rather than the Repubblica, or even the Signoria. When I am in the Piazza

Emanuele, I see the destruction of Florence in the name of tourism.[73] When in the Signoria, I see the burning of Savonarola.[74] In these streets of San Niccolo, the tragedies are more private, and less talked about.'

Was our friend merely relaxing? He rarely spoke without there being a direction to his thoughts. Why was he lamenting the passing of the old world? Perhaps he sensed what was passing through our mind, for he asked, 'What is that saying – an English saying, "Young men think old men are fools . . ."'

'I think it is, "Young men think old men fools. Old men known young men are." '[75] Did he imagine that I was thinking him a fool?

'Yes, that's right. Only an Englishman could have said that. Was he a famous Englishman?'

'Not famous. Yet George Chapman was considered something of a rival to Shakespeare in his time. He was a big fish in a sea of big fishes.'

He nodded to show that he had understood our point, and returned to his own theme: 'In Italy, they still have respect for old men, even though they may well *think* they are fools.'

'I know you are old, but I do not think you are a fool.'

'Our friendship rests on that. Why else would you spend time with an old man, trudging the roads along the cemeteries?[76] You know that *friendship* has nothing to do with age, while *wisdom* does. You seek me out, and put up with my physical slowness, because you have glimpsed into my heart, which still races fast. You admire my wisdom. The wisdom of an old man is quite different from the wisdom of a young man.'

'I set out to learn how to be a Fool.'

'No, you set out to follow the Way of the Fool. There is a difference. And what is the result of such a journey? The result is *a wise Fool*. A fool is the one who gives up everything for an idea. The wise Fool is the one who knows that he never had anything to give up in the first place. Is that foolish?'

We opened our hands upwards, to show that we had understood.

'Yet your English saying is full of its own wisdom. It really asks, What is the difference between an old man and a young man, if they are both fools?' We had thought the question was rhetorical, but he repeated it. 'What is the difference, Mark?'

'Is it commitment? The old man has committed himself, while the young one has not?'

'Yes, exactly so. The old man has committed himself. He has made a stand. Life has made him do that. He has drawn a circle around himself, and said, "This is where I stand, this is what I must do." He has committed himself to an action. Because he has drawn a circle around himself, others can see where he stands. He can be attacked by others. His position is weak. Those who have not committed themselves can mock, if they are so inclined. This is the age-old battle between youth and age. The one who has committed himself appears to be in a weak position. Yet the Spiritual truth is quite otherwise. It is the one who accepts commitment who is strong. The true commitment is the artistic one. This is why artists are so often attacked. They are attacked for their morals, for their ideas – even for their work. Yet their essence – their commitment – is the secret which is unassailable. The true artist knows that creativity is its own reward. Ordinary people fear commitment, you see. Ordinary people fear creativity. They know that if they allow that seething cauldron of yellow liquid to boil over within themselves,[77] then their whole lives will be changed. People fear change. People do not wish to be creative and artistic in any real sense. They wish to decorate, perhaps, and to make things around themselves pleasant – but this has little to do with creativity.'

'Are you saying that the Way of the Fool should be a creative way?'

'All Spiritual Paths should be creative. Creativity is involved with sacrifice. That stew of yellow liquid which boils in everyone is a sacrificial broth . . .'

'The sulphur?'

'Yes, the sulphur. The first of the Three Principles. It is in a sacrificial cauldron. It is an *excess*. Creativity is Spiritual delight, an overpouring of sulphur.'

'Then all creative activity must be foolish? In which case, thinking must be foolish?'

He laughed at our sophistry. 'Perhaps thinking is foolish. Certain forms of thinking undoubtedly are foolish. After all, most people are vulnerable in their ideas: they fear to think for themselves. The Fool learns to think for himself: he or she makes it an exercise of the soul. Others refuse that Way. This is why our civilization is so under threat. We are living in a world where every effort is being made to ensure that the body is comfortable, yet little is done for the growing soul. Sometimes, I think we should dismantle our civilization, brick by brick, and rebuild.'

'You are an anarchist?'

He laughed once more. 'No, civilizations have a way of dismantling themselves. Listen to the traffic outside. That is already the sound of the retreating tide.'

'As I understand your words, you say that creativity is itself a form of selflessness?'

'Exactly so. Creativity is the giving away of Spiritual energy. Creativity is the soul in the expenditure of a bottomless purse. One gives sulphur away – initially perhaps through an excess of joy – for that is the foolishness of young men. Later, one gives away energy through commitment to an idea.'

'Creativity is the ultimate deed of unselfishness?'

'Yes. You speak from your heart now, rather than from your head. Now I see that you are almost ready.'

'Ready?'

'When a man really knows that creativity is its own reward . . . Well, then he is ready to work with people.'

'That is a strange thing to say.'

'It is mainly what I came here to say to you. I listened to you talking in the group this evening. You were not asking questions. You were giving answers. You were the Teacher, not thinking of payment, or reward. The attention of the group was electric. Of course, the Feast of Fools, to celebrate an ass, is a fascination in itself – *but it was also the way you spoke.*'

'I spoke with authority?' We were surprised.

'Thank goodness, no. You spoke in such a way as to allow the Spiritual world to work through you. The atmosphere you worked in – let us call it an aura – was an indication to me that the time has come for you to change your personal direction.'

We ate in silence for a while. Our own silence was a result of the inner doubts which assailed us. We had been a pupil for so long that we had not considered it would become incumbent upon us to teach. Finally, we broke the silence.

'Why do you say I am ready to work with people?'

'Because, my friend, you think of yourself as a loner. You do not see how much you are needed. You are needed to point the way.'

'But I know nothing.'

'This is what all Teachers think. You do not really believe that when you sit before a group you do so alone? You are there as a representative of the Spiritual world. You must know all these things.'

We nodded assent.

'You know these things, because you are a Fool.'

He had finished his spaghetti basilico. After wiping his mouth with his napkin and sipping water, he leaned back in his chair, looking directly at us. 'Let me tell that Fools like myself become Teachers, *because we find suddenly that there is no one else*. It is as simple as that. One day, you are wandering through Florence, after a day in the libraries, surrounded by books. You are carrying under your arm further books, to pursue further dreams. You see a young child playing with a ball near the Baptistery. His mother stands some way off. She is paying no attention to the child. She has a cigarette dangling from her mouth. You can tell a great deal about that woman, and about the future of her child. Suddenly, there is an illumination. You realize how great is the gulf between yourself and those others. There is a curtain between you. Now you understand that this curtain is good for neither of you. The house out there is burning. You can see the flames, but those others cannot see the flames. All you have learned from those books, and from those conversations with wise men, from all those meditations, is to see the flames. Now the question is, can you leave those people in the flames? Would it not be the act of a Fool to snatch one, or perhaps two, out of the conflagration?'

'If that is what they want.'

'They cannot see the flames, but they do not wish to be burned. You see, my friend, you are an alchemist. You know that there are two sorts of flame. There is the soft and slow flame of the inner heat, and that terrible burning flame which consumes, and which feels no human pain. Both are the flames of burning sulphur, but they produce very different results.'

'You are telling me that I should become a flame for others – a Teacher?'

'No one may instruct another in such things. One can only open doors. The matters of personal destiny are mysteries beyond words. When the time is right, you will know. All I suggest is that you stop thinking of yourself as the Fool, and see yourself as the wise Fool.'

'I shall need time to think.'

'"Thus we play the fools with time, and the spirits of the wise sit in the clouds and mock us."' He quoted the Shakespeare in English.[78]

'You cannot continue widening this gap between yourself and the world. By now you should know that the secret of the Way lies in fission. How can you slough off the darkness if you refuse to own it? Teaching is a way of learning to own one's darkness. In a sense, the Teacher needs the pupils more than the pupils need the Teacher.'

'The darkness remains, awaiting fission,' we said. Of this we were quite sure.

'But teaching is fission. What for others is light is for the Teacher an old light – another word for darkness.' He took the bill even as we reached for our wallet. 'No, this is my treat. Well, Mark, play the Fool with time. But do not take too long. We live a foolish paradox, for while we have forever, we do not have much time.'

'Meanwhile, the sulphur burns, and one seeks to be creative?'

We were leaving the *Sorelle*, and I knew that we would be parting for some time. My question had been badly phrased, but it was heart-felt.

'Listen, Mark.' He stood clutching the lapel of our jacket for a moment or two, as though to reinforce the urgency of his words. 'Some time ago you asked me about the word *sulphur*. We both agreed that Fulcanelli was right, and alchemical sulphur is the equivalent of the sexual energies in man and woman.[79] The sexual energies may come out in a selfish way or in a creative way. This is fission. Fulcanelli is working from the alchemical tradition, so he is right to see it in this way. Jakob Boehme was more of a Rosicrucian than ever Fulcanelli was.[80] Boehme saw the division in the word sulphur in a slightly different way. He divided the word itself, and said *Sul* was the soul of a thing, the oil.[81] This *sul* is born of the *phur*, the light.[82] This separation in sulphur – the oil and the light – is of tremendous importance to you. The oil clings to things, to physical form. Have you ever looked at spilt oil? Under certain conditions it can look like a thin filament of a rainbow. This is the light imprisoned in the oil.

'The light rises upwards. It liberates the rainbow. It is as simple as that. You must become more clear about the inner workings of your sulphur. It is this, rather than your thinking, which will enable you to commit.'

'Commit to what?'

'Ah, my friend, only you can answer that question. Only you.'

We should record that, in later years (in the early 1970s, to be precise), we *did* journey through France fairly extensively, as our old Teacher had intimated we would.

We made these journeys as part of a systematic study of the arcane legacy of the Templars. In the course of these studies, we spent several days at Chartres, contemplating the arcane astrology of the exterior portals and inner windows, yet we had to return to this great cathedral several times before we began to see what our Master had meant. In accordance with his instructions, we set down our observations about this extraordinary detail of sculpture, which ties the Masonic square (the ancient *kan*) with the Templars.

We had attempted to prepare ourselves for this task by reading as widely as possible, looking into the methods of the mediaeval builders, and into the arcane Schools which directed them. While involved in this reading, we discovered that one of the Mysteries of the zodiac of Hermes, which had been published by the Jesuit Kircher,[83] is that the image of Pisces is half-fish, half-man, and that he is carrying the *kan*, or Masonic

Detail of the Ichton of Pisces, from the Hermean zodiac recorded by the Jesuit polymath, Athanasius Kircher in Oedipus Aegyptiacus, *1652-55.*

square. Kircher did not name his sources, but it is evident that he had been looking into the astrology and mythology of the ancient Babylonians. The fish-man was one of the esoteric symbols for the initiate in that ancient culture. No doubt it was taught that the man or woman who has so developed themselves as to have free access to the Spiritual world could be regarded as being dual. Such people would be regarded as being equally content to walk on the Earthly plane, or swim in the watery. Such initiates can live on the material plane, with the body of flesh and blood, and they can also live in the Spiritual, in the aqueous world of the Astral, for which the fish-tail is an appropriate symbol, and where the physical body would be an encumbrance. The initiate's control over the two worlds is expressed in the mer-man form.

Now why does the mer-man Ichton in Kircher's zodiac carry the *kan* square? The *kan* is susceptible to many levels of interpretation within esoteric contexts, which explains why it is so important in the programme of Masonic symbolism. In an interiorizing sense, it pertains to the idea of a person being 'on the square', or properly oriented to a good moral life. In one sense, this wholesomeness is expressed creatively. It comes out in the wholesome human being as a wish to create – to introduce order, to construct and to build. One who seeks to create in a wholesome way always feels the urge to link his or her work of art with the cosmos: he or she feels the impulse to bring Spiritual ideas down to

Earth. This partly explains why, in ancient times, no building would be erected without an astrologer naming a propitious time, derived from a study of the skies.[84] In ancient times, the foundations of all important buildings were always determined according to stellar or planetary fiducials. This squaring of the cosmic circle was done with the aid of sacred ropes and metal squares.

In the sigil for Capricorn, $\vee^{\rho}$, we trace a vestigial drawing of the square and the rope (often symbolized as a knot), which to serve its purpose would have to be pulled tight, from the point of the square. It is this curious and unlikely union of fish and square, of curve and line, which we discovered in a remarkable programme of symbolism at Chartres.

On the façade of Chartres, it is quite possible to find images of half-fishes, half-men, and even distinctive squares, but there is only one place where each of the Capricornian parts falls into one specific group. This point – scarcely visible from the ground – is in the sculpted stonework which surrounds the south door of the west front. At this point – which, we repeat, is not easy to see in its entirety from the ground level – are a pair of Templars, who are intrinsically bound into the programme of zodiacal symbolism which is so important to the cathedral.[85]

The pair of Templars shelter behind a single shield (plate 39). The symbolism here partly the idea of armour, partly connotes the mythology of the metal-worker Vulcan (see page 300), and is also a play on the famous Seal, or Sigillum, of the Order of the Templars, which depicted two Templars sharing a single horse.[86] The bottom of the shield points downwards. It points to a single fish, which is the Christ-fish of Pisces (plate 40).

The fish is scarcely visible from the ground level. It can be seen most easily by a person who is prepared either to use binoculars, and examine it from a distance, or to climb the present wall and gate which protect the portal. There is a deep meaning in this requirement – intentionally imposed by the builders of Chartres. The full appreciation of this symbolism demands that one must move to a higher level than the normal to see the Resurrected Christ-fish above the sharp socle.

Now, what is of great importance to this arcane device is that the single fish of Pisces is hidden by a rectangular corner: this corner is itself the *kan* or square. Just as the true nature of dual Pisces is hidden in this single fish, so the *kan* – the equivalent of the Masonic square – is hidden by the most outrageous disguise imaginable: it is hidden by the form of an actual corner, which would have been sculpted with the aid of a square, and which is itself a square! As though to emphasize this rectangularity, the socle above (upon which the pair of Templars stand behind their single shield) is not squared, but of a curvilinear form.

One might imagine that this profound symbolism could be accidental, were it not attended by the down-cast eyes of the pair of Templars, who, arms crossed over their bodies, gaze upon the world in wonderment. Just in case we might be tempted to doubt even this almost overt symbolism, we should note that the cunning architects have placed the point of the shield between the two feet of the Templars, reminding us that the feet of the human being are ruled by Pisces.

Whatever conclusions we might draw about the Masonic influences (or even about the Templar influences) in this detail of arcane symbolism, we may have no doubt that the designer had the urge to bring together the fish and the square. This is the arcane symbolism of Capricorn laid out as an open secret. It is the stone equivalent of the fish-tail *anke-ti*, 𓃾 , and the rectilinear *kan*, 𐤓 , which are the two components of the sigil for Capricorn.[87]

Those who have troubled to measure in time and space such things as emotions insist that we can assess another person in a millisecond. Was this instant character-assessment the reason why we felt uneasy, in spite of all the other emotions which welled up from within? It was early in the second week of September, 1980, and we were sitting outside a café in the cathedral square at Chartres, talking to a girl we had just met.

In the cathedral, we had seen her walking down the south aisle towards the great floor-maze (see figure bottom of page 69). The bright hues from the stained-glass windows had flooded upon her, like coloured celestial music. She had walked directly across the spiralling arcs of the maze-like dancing ground. When she reached the centre, she stood quite still. She did not appear to notice us. We were in the shadows, leaning against a column, contemplating the maze. She looked down at her feet, as though to ensure that they were correctly placed, and raising her arms above her head, strained upwards on tiptoes. When she saw us, beyond the edge of the circle, she showed no embarrassment, but merely smiled. Perhaps she did not realize that when she had lifted her arms, we had seen the full sweep of her breast through the armhole of her loose blouse.

We had been contemplating the mediaeval dancing ground, and remained a short distance from the floor pattern while we studied its orientations to the details of interior architecture. Strangely, although the cathedral had been crowded only minutes before, we two were now the only ones near the floor maze.

'I am at the centre,' she said, with the soft accent of a Bostonian. She had lowered her arms and heels, but was still smiling towards us. Her voice was almost lost in the vastness of the cathedral space.

We laughed, but it was not in mockery. 'There is no centre to a maze.' We had said this only to continue the conversation.

'This is not a maze.' She sounded slightly upset as she corrected us. The tone of her voice insinuated that we had failed to understand. She was right, and we felt foolish. Of course it was not a maze: we had assumed that she had no knowledge of such things.

'It is a six-petalled centre,' we offered, to prove that we were not really foolish.

'Six petals. Yes, and a stalk because it is a flower.' Then, as though to show she forgave us, she once again stretched her arms above her head, and balanced on her toes. 'You see – I am Virgo standing on the Flower of the Virgin.'

We wondered if she could see the sexual implications in her words. We could not guess her personal horoscope, but she was right about the centre of the dancing ground being the *flos Virginis*.[88] We were already fascinated by this girl who was, whether she knew it or not, dancing the secret Way.

She crossed the maze towards us, offering her hand.

'Latona Hussay,' she said, introducing herself in the American way.[89]

'Mark Hedsel.'

'Pleased to meet you, Mark. You were paying great attention to the floor pattern.'

'And you went one stage further, Latona. You danced upon it.'

'That is what it was made for.'

'For *sacred* dance. For the dance of the inner Spirit.'

Latona smiled, and for a moment, we thought she was going to say something. However, instead of speaking, she began to walk towards the great west doors. We followed.

The sunlight flushed pink light over us as we stepped into the outer world, beneath the plethora of zodiacal images on the walls.

Now, as we sat in *Le Week-End* café to the north of the cathedral façade, her skin was no longer supercharged with celestial hues from the windows. Her black hair, swept upwards into a loose bun, framed her ebony skin to perfection. She had that finely chiselled negroid beauty, set with high cheekbones, striking green eyes, and a well-defined yet sensual mouth. She was wearing a perfume by Lentheric – perhaps *Femme*. It was clear from the two books she carried in her hand that she was not only bilingual, but also interested in esoteric thought.[90]

'Fulcanelli,' we said, nodding down to one of the books. It was the French version.

She smiled. Her teeth were a perfect white.

'I read the book while in Paris, and then again in Amiens. The astrological and alchemical quatrefoils at Amiens are filled with secret cyphers, but so few visitors seem to realize this. Fulcanelli is right in everything he says. It was he who introduced me to the secret tongue, yet now I hear joking songbirds everywhere.'[91]

'The jokes which few understand?'

'Few, yet *some*. It astonishes me that people who have no knowledge of the Bible will look at cathedrals, and not realize that they are shut off from reading the stone book by their own ignorance. It is foolish, when so many of the statues hold books, as though in warning.'

'But are those books Bibles? Could they not be the Book of Life, or esoteric books?'

'I had thought they were all biblical texts.'

'That's unlikely.' We nodded in the direction of the cathedral. 'In the archivolt of the central door is a small image of Grammar. She's teaching children. In one hand she holds a scourge, to show the need for discipline. In the other she holds an open book. This is merely a symbol of learning. Against the central pillar of the south transept is Christ, who is also holding a book. The decorative symbols on the cover show that it is the Book of Life.[92] This is no ordinary book, but a text derived from the ancient Mysteries.'

Latona smiled again. 'You could write a book about the books at Chartres.'

'Heaven forbid,' we laughed. 'The masons who built the cathedral left a message in this book, however.'

'A book which cannot be opened?' she suggested.

'No. A light mystery.'

'What do you mean?'

'The book is so located that in July the Sun edges up the central statue of Christ, until it cuts an arc exactly framing the book cover. At the same time, the serpent at Christ's feet is completely illumined. The masons are drawing a connection between the Book of Life and the Serpent.'

Latona twisted round to hang her bag on the back of her chair, and rose gracefully.

'I'm going to look at that serpent. Keep an eye on my things.'

We watched her sway sensually towards the southern part of the cathedral, and reached for the Fulcanelli. She was gone for about five minutes.

'Well?' we asked, when she returned, her face beaming.

'There are two monsters at the feet of Christ. Is it the serpent to the right which is lit up at the same time as the Book of Life?'

'Yes.'

'What are the two monsters?'

'They disappeared from Christian art after the 12th or 13th century – perhaps because their meaning had been forgotten. Perhaps because they hinted at heresy. They are the dualist monsters of the Zoroastrians. One is leonine in form, and represents the solar forces. The other is serpentine in form, and represents the lunar forces. In this image, Christ is dominant over both the solar and the lunar – the great Mazdao and Ahriman of the ancient cults.'[93]

'So why is the serpent lit at the same time as the Book of Life?'

'Perhaps to show that the Book of Life keeps records of all the dark lunar secrets of Man. All the dark deeds are recorded. *Nothing is hidden*. For those few moments of light magic, the Sun forces fall upon the lunar forces, lighting up in symbolism the darkest inner contents of Mankind.'

'Christ sees all?'

'Yes. And all is recorded in the book He carries.'

Latona did a silent whistle to show that she was beginning to see the implications of this light magic.

'One day, I shall return to Chartres in July. Is there any special time, or day?'

'The best time to study it is towards the end of July – during the last week.'

She nodded slowly.

'And Chartres, Latona? Why are you in Chartres?'

'I'm here to see the Black Virgin.'

'In the crypt?' Again foolishness. Where else would one see the Black Virgin of Chartres?

'"The smell of the grave . . ."' She was quoting from Fulcanelli.[94]

'Do you think the Virgin was an Isis? Or was she something else?'

'I don't know. It is enough for me that the cathedral protects a pagan goddess – and that she is black.' She leaned back on her chair, and pursed her lips, as though trying to sum us up.

'Do you know anything about the Black Virgins?'

We shrugged. 'I've read a little.'

'Fulcanelli says that they bear the inscription, To the Virgin about to give birth".'[95]

'Fulcanelli is right. Some do have those words inscribed on the socles.'[96]

'Well, that inscription fascinates me. I think it's the inscription alone which brought me in search of the Black Virgins. I feel always in that condition myself. I feel as though I am always about to give birth.'

'The great idea?' We could feel a trembling in our spine, for she was almost touching upon the idea which lay behind the word *idiot*.[97] We nodded, to show that we understood.

'Fulcanelli said that the Black Virgin was also called the Mother of God, the great idea.'

'*Matri deum, magnae ideae,*' we intoned. 'Difficult to translate, as *idea* is a play on the feminine for goddess, *dea*.[98]

'Great idea could be Great Goddess?'

'Or both. Fulcanelli often incorporated two or more meanings in a single phrase. On the other hand, it could be an error.' We were leaving our options open, as we did not know how much this girl knew of such things. We had no doubt that Fulcanelli was taking the goddess back to the Platonic ideas. The word *idea* had a closer correspondence to his archetypes than any other Latin equivalent.

'Is there such a thing as accident in art?' she asked, almost innocently. 'If you rule out accident in art, then you dismiss a great deal that presently passes for art . . . In any case, I will stick with *idea*. The notion of a Black Virgin as the mother of gods appeals to me.'

'Which other Black Virgins have you seen?'

'Not enough. The best so far was at Montserrat.'[99]

'*La Moreneta?*'

'Yes. There are vine plants and ears of corn on the Black Virgin at Puy.'

'The Eucharistic symbols of wine and bread?' we asked, even though we suspected that we already knew the answer.

'No – beyond that, to Mysteries more ancient than those of Christ.'

We talked until dusk fell, and the streets around the cathedral came to life in the glare of the café lights. We were reminded of the intense vision of Van Gogh in his paintings of café scenes at night in Arles, the empty glasses on the café tables reflecting the light of the stars, and symbolizing Vincent's loneliness. One could feel the peripheral life in the streets as transitory, against the quiet and massive bulk of the cathedral. The stone angel which held the great arc of the sundial at the foot of the *Clocher Vieux* was not measuring time for the eternal cathedral fabric, but moonlight for sleeping humans.

On impulse, we motioned Latona to follow us to the foot of the south tower.

We walked up to the walls of the high tower, stark against the artificial light. Leaning back, to watch the the massive stonework moving against the wisps of clouds, we remarked: 'It's called the Old Bell Tower.'

'Why?'

'Because its companion – the one to the north – was struck by lightning. In the first decade of the 16th century, Jean de Beauce repaired it with that Gothic spire which has no relationship to the rest of the cathedral. The locals, tongue in cheek, called it the New Tower, when they could have been a little more scurrilous. As a result, the original was renamed the Old.'

We had reached the marvellous *horloge* sundial.

'The angel is said to be Michael. Each of the four archangels of space ruled a cardinal direction. Michael was originally the guardian of the south. The sundial was added later, but I cannot help thinking that it had been intended from the very beginning.'

'Why?'

'Partly because Michael rules the south, and partly because it's well placed to measure the passage of the Sun through the skies. That, after all, is what the arc on the slab is designed to do. But there's another reason . . .'

We swung round slightly and pointed to the grotesque creature to the right of the horloge angel.

'This is my other reason.' We pointed upwards. 'One of my favourite images at Chartres.' The statue was of a fat donkey supporting its back vertically against the wall of the cathedral (plate 41). It was playing a mediaeval hurdy-gurdy,[100] and might have been the ass so boisterously worshipped during the Feast of Fools.

'And what is that?'

'He is called *L'ane qui vielle*.'

'"The ass which grows old"?' she questioned, obviously aware that the phrase was not easy to translate.

'Well, that's as good an approximation as any other. But you've read Fulcanelli – you know about the hidden language . . .'

'The Green Language . . . The *argotique* . . .'

We nodded. 'Well, as I see it, this phrase, *L'ane qui vielle*, means "The donkey who plays the hurdy-gurdy". The phrase seems to have something of a second meaning, for the verb *languir* is derived from *L'ane qui*, and means "to languish" or "become stagnant". Perhaps it is a symbol of people.'

'Of ordinary people?' she asked, glancing up at us sharply, but not allowing a space for us to reply. 'And *vielle*? That means "hurdy gurdy"?'

'In a manner of speaking. The word *vielle* seems to have been the old French name of the instrument itself.[101] As I see it, this musical donkey is the ordinary human soul who has not sought initiation: the drone keynote of the *vielle* makes him deaf to the higher music of the planets. It is the foolish soul who has not striven to hear the planetary Music of the Spheres, and contents itself with cacophony. It has refused to gaze on the cosmic intervals marked out in the arc of the sundial, in the hands of Michael. Such people languish into old age . . .'

'Become stagnant under the death forces of the planet Saturn?' she interjected. Latona had certainly understood Fulcanelli.

'Precisely. Saturn, the ruler of physical weight, stagnation and physical death. The planet opposite to the Moon which governs the imaginative life.'

'I'm impressed. What are you going to do with all this stuff you know?' Again, she did not wait for an answer. 'But, Mark – is there any chance you could be reading too much into a phrase and the juxtaposition of two statues?'

We shrugged, as though to indicate that all things are possible. Even so, we knew from other details of statuary that our interpretation was sound. 'It's always a danger – it's always possible to read too much into symbols, but we have to remember that the cathedral builders were initiates. They *knew* that real symbols had to work on seven levels. Perhaps we have penetrated to the second or third level with this angel and donkey . . .'

She nodded seriously.

We liked her question, and decided to suggest a possible answer. 'I suspect that when you were meditating in your dance on the labyrinth, you did not know that you were enacting a ritual connected with the Mysteries of the hurdy-gurdy donkey.'

She looked at us sharply. 'Whatever do you mean?'

'Follow me: there's another angel and ass you should see.'

We walked round the western façade, and turned right towards the great portal of the north transept. There, we gazed up at the three figures from the Old Testament.

'The figure to the left is King Solomon, the builder of the original esoteric Temple. When he appears in mediaeval architecture, you can always expect to find some hidden Masonic symbolism. The woman at his side is the Queen of Sheba . . .'

'And the man on the other side?'

'Balaam. The Bible tells how Balaam could not see the angel sent by the Lord to warn him.[102] The angel appeared three times, but Balaam could not see it. The angel was seen only by Balaam's ass. At length, exasperated by the failure of his master to see the angel in the Spiritual world, the creature finally refused to carry him further. Only in this way was Balaam persuaded to hear the words of the angel. The ass was no ass, but a wise Fool. Look! The ass is shown at the feet of Balaam.'

'Yes.'

'But what is special about this donkey?'

'I cannot see anything.'

'Remember that the cathedral builders dealt always in double meanings. Look at the crest.'

She studied it for a moment or two, and then, as recognition dawned, murmured almost reverentially, 'The crest is also a horn. The donkey has a single horn growing from its forehead. It is a *unicorn*!'

'Quite! Whoever has heard of a unicorn donkey? The wisemen sculptors have transformed Balaam's ass into the magical unicorn. The horn of the unicorn is symbol of the Third Eye. It was the Secret Eye which enabled the donkey to see angels – Spiritual beings which were hidden from its master.'

'Yes. Fulcanelli would have called it *an ass that is not an ass*.'

'Yes – or perhaps, a *wise Fool*.'

'Mark – you were going to explain why, when I stood at the centre of the maze, I was involved with the hurdy-gurdy ass. I can see what this unicorn has to do with the maze . . . Of course, because it's a donkey of sorts, it could be linked with the other, on the south side. Yet, I can't see a connection with the maze.'

'It is a hidden connection: at least, it is hidden to outer eyes. If you draw a line across the nave floor, connecting the image of *L'ane qui vielle* and Balaam's unicorn ass, you will find that the line *passes through the centre of the maze*.'

She looked at us in astonishment.

'The fact is, Latona, you were standing exactly on the midpoint between the two donkeys when you began your dance. You stood exactly between a foolish musician and a foolish visionary. Perhaps it was a deep instinct within yourself, but that centre is the most important point in the entire cathedral.'

Latona seemed to be too moved to say anything. Silently, barred by the gates from walking around the cathedral, we turned. From time to time, Latona would stop, and gaze up at a statue, and, while it was clear that she wished to ask a question, she held her tongue. Finally, after we had walked around the accessible sides of the cathedral a couple of times, she pointed to a detail of statuary and asked, 'Who's that falling from the horse?'

'It's the mediaeval image of Pride.'

'"Pride comes before a fall"?'

'I suppose so. A superb image. Even the horse is stumbling.'

Latona stopped, and swung round to face us. 'As I talk to you, I feel that I'm drinking at a great fountain of wisdom. Does that sound horribly pretentious? Well, even if it does – thank you.' She was embarrassed, yet she continued. 'Fulcanelli is a *book* – but you are a *living book*. Where do you get such wisdom? Where do you teach?'

The question passed through our soul like a burning rapier. It was the question we were asking ourselves: where do we teach? Should we teach? We hid our discomfort. We laughed and were evasive.

'You ask many questions. As for where I find such wisdom? You are asking me how do I know what I know? Come – what sort of question is that? How does *anyone* know what they know? Where *do* ideas come from?'

'And my question, *where* do you teach, could have been more circumspect. *Do you teach?*' She seemed to realize that she had touched a tender spot.

'I do not teach.' There was a finality in our voice.

Perhaps we had replied a little too forcefully, but some delicate thread in our relationship had broken. We had drifted towards *Le Week-End* once again, and Latona moved over to the menu displayed near the door, as though contemplating having a meal. In our absence, the café had filled up, and we had lost our places outside.

Suddenly, she turned back towards us. 'Which hotel are you staying in?'

'*Le Grand Monarque.*' It was a short walk from the cathedral. 'Where are *you* staying?'

'I haven't found a place yet. My things are in the car. Perhaps I could stay with you tonight?'

The question was asked as though it carried no sexual undertones, yet we were totally surprised. There had been nothing in her comportment, or in what had been spoken about, which had suggested such an intimacy. She was beautiful, and we felt a strong attraction to her, yet, at the same time, there was something which made us uneasy. Something we could not bring into consciousness. Perhaps we should have said no, but, instead, we nodded.

'It cannot be sexual,' she said, her eyes meeting mine. 'Will that make any difference?'

We shook our head. What were we letting ourself in for? The sense of embarrassment deepened.

Perhaps a little too abruptly, she said, 'I'll fetch my things.'

We watched her as she crossed the cobbles, to disappear behind the west front of the cathedral. There was something feline about her movement, and the sway of her hips was almost lascivious.

There was only one bed in the room. We offered to sleep in a chair, but Latona signed that this would not be necessary: 'We can share the bed.' Perhaps it would have been better if we had insisted, for the following hours proved to be among the most difficult in our life.

We showered first, and climbed into bed. We had expected Latona to change in the shower, as we had done, but she chose to strip in the bedroom. The electric lights were out, but as the French windows were still open, the moonlight cascaded into the room, lighting up Latona in silhouette. She was certainly aware that we could see her, and there seemed to be something intentionally provocative in the way she removed her clothes. We began to suspect that she was enjoying our discomfort. Why was it not pleasurable to see such a beautiful woman take off her clothes before coming to bed? It was not pleasurable because Latona had insisted that we should not touch her.

To our horror, she climbed into bed completely naked. While our bodies did not touch, we could feel each other's presence. Never before had I realized just how strong a source of spiritual power is the human body: it is a magnet of immense force. It is this power – a power which can descent into desire – that keeps the Moon swinging in pursuit of the Earth, and the Earth spiralling after the Sun.

There was a long silence. It seemed that when at last she spoke, her voice was deeper. She was a stranger. 'I am sorry that we cannot touch. I cannot explain.'

'I agreed.' That was true. We were foolish, and we had agreed. The intimacy we had slipped into earlier had completely dispersed. We were now held apart by almost tangible tensions. To offer some release, we observed, 'You were wearing a stone around your neck. What is it?'

'A sapphire. My birth-stone. I was born in September.'

Then, and only then, did we begin to sense the import of the inner warnings we had received at the moment of meeting. In her one-sidedness, this girl was too deeply under the influence of the Moon. All stones are symbols: the sapphire was worn in ancient times as an antidote for lunacy. Did she know? Did it matter if she knew?

We remained silent, and directed our attention to wrestling with the inner demons of desire. It is quite impossible to describe the way our body was racked with pain during that night in Chartres. We could feel ourselves trembling with desire. Fearful that our desire would induce us to reach out towards her, even in sleep, we reached up and grasped the brass bedrail above our head. All night we lay like a manacled prisoner, our arms stretched upwards in prayer, our fatigued mind in a fitful half-slumber, desire pumping through our limbs.

341

At some point, shortly before morning light spread over Chartres, we must have dozed. When we came to, the inner burning was no longer there. We could no longer feel that feminine magnetism on the other side of the bed, and when we turned to look we found that Latona was gone. The bed sheets beneath us were wet through, as though a dew had fallen through the ceiling. We were swamped in our own sweat.

As we showered away the misery of the night, we suddenly remembered the story told of Latona in classical times. On the island of Delos, she had knelt by a fountain to quench her thirst. Perhaps her clothes had been blown a little by the wind, or perhaps the two children in her arms were crying, but, for whatever reason, two Lycian clowns who watched her attempt to drink had foolishly mocked the goddess. Latona was so affronted that she had turned them into frogs.

On the dressing table, Latona had left a note. It was written in a precise and scholarly script. As we picked it up we caught a whiff of her perfume. The script and the scent reminded us of the two sides to her nature: the questioning soul and the woman. The note read:

> There is a hurdy-gurdy playing in my mind, and I cannot hear. If we meet again, I will explain. I think you are a Teacher, and this changes normal things. You deserve an explanation: I think that you are Perseus, riding a donkey, rather than a winged horse. But, for now, thank you for that other angel and that other donkey. I hope that your horse will resume its journey, and is not too bruised.

The note was not signed, but there was a sigil in place of signature.[103]

Not only the horse had been bruised. We ourself had been turned into a frog by this black princess. We were the sweat-born, and had spent the night bathed in a pool of our own pores' dew. Yet, in truth, we had never mocked her. Was it possible that she had been ill-used by others, and sought to punish all men? Was the feeling of unease we felt when we first saw her a measure not of her, but of our own guilt?

We found no answers to these questions, yet that night in Chartres had been burned into our soul. We recalled it ever afterwards as an emblem of the power of the human body. The body may well be merely an illusion constructed by our senses. It may well be a four-legged donkey, dangling on strings from the higher world of stars . . . Yet, when the creature is used by a soft-fingered goddess – who was herself the mother of the Moon – then the terrible secret of its power is revealed. Those women who displayed their secret places were less powerful than those who kept them hidden away. Yet it was not the sulphuric power of the tortured body which had been our real tutor. Our tutors were shadow images created in the mind of our imprisoned body – the creatures struck like sparks from the dark lunar imagination.

At last, we had learned what must have been obvious to our friend in Florence. We had learned that it was time for us to become a Teacher. We should teach others the Way of the Fool, and end this strange emptiness which had invaded our soul.

We never met Latona again, but we knew what she had meant when she referred to the Perseus of Ovid: perhaps it was time to change our donkey for a winged horse.[104]

Last Words

There is no death of anyone, save in appearance, just as there is no birth of any, save only in seeming.

(Apollonius of Tyana, from a letter to P. Valerius Asiaticus, *circa* AD 70. See A. E. Chaignet, *Pythagore et la Philosophie pythagoricienne*, 1874 ed.)

The last time I saw Mark Hedsel alive was in the Caribbean, in 1997. The moment I saw him at the airport, I was astonished by the change in his appearance. He no longer looked young: the years had suddenly thrown a web of wrinkles over his face and hands. His thick hair had turned white, and his face was haggard and lined. His vigour was spent, and he seemed almost like an insubstantial ghost of his former self. Yet his eyes still burned with their usual intense energy. Not for the first time, I found myself wondering just how old he really was. But if his body was in decay, his mind certainly was not, and the light of his intellect was reflected in the warm animation of his voice. At least nothing had changed in the mellifluous and intense content of his speech, even when the topics he discussed were not pertaining to initiation.

He told me that he had come to the island of Grenada mainly because of his weakening health, and because it was now his favourite Caribbean island. On one or two occasions, we had met in Galley Bay, in Antigua, which he had insisted was the most beautiful resort he knew, for one who sought rest. Yet, two or three years earlier, this old resort had been destroyed in a hurricane, and he had been compelled to look for another place of similar beauty and tranquillity, until he found a small hotel on the western coast of Grenada, near La Sagesse.

After we had been together for a few hours, he intimated that the main reason for his suggesting that we meet in Grenada on this occasion was because from here we would be reasonably sure of seeing the eclipse of the Moon, which should become visible in the last hours of 24 March.[1] We could sense from the sound of his voice that he already knew it would be the last eclipse he would witness in his present lifetime.

There was a symbolism of sorts behind his wish to see the eclipse with me, for the Way of the Fool has always been intimately linked with giving direction to lunar forces. For Mark, who had learned to apprehend the world in symbols, the putting out of the Moon by the dragon Atalia was a fitting symbolism for the end of a Fool's lifetime.[2]

I had flown out to meet Mark because we had various ideas to discuss in connection with his book – especially those issues relating to footnotes and bibliographic sources – but, for one reason or another, we did not get around to these questions at all. On the night of the eclipse, we sat on one of the hillsides which rise between Grand Anse and Pink Gin Beach, and watched the slow motion of the Moon as it edged towards the drama of its eclipse. Our view was complete, undisturbed even by a wisp of cloud.

Few humans have the attention span the cosmos deserves. An eclipse is a great wonder: it is a great cosmic wonder, as the shadow of the Earth slowly intrudes an arc of darkness on the mountainous surface of its satellite. The darkness nibbles away the skull-face of the Western tradition[3], just as inexorably as it devours the hare of the Oriental tradition.[4] One is aware not only of the fact that one is witnessing a cosmic drama, but also of how imperfectly developed is the sense of wonder in modern Man. One imagines that in former times, a person might have fallen down on their knees – perhaps the sense of wonder intermingled with fear – because their appreciation of the cosmos was more visceral than our own.

'Why,' I asked, 'is the eclipse such a *deep* experience? What is this sense of sadness one feels? It is a far deeper experience than one would expect of the temporary shutting off of the light. I have not seen many eclipses, yet I know that it is an experience . . . rather, as they say, "as though someone were walking over my grave". What is this experience?'

Mark had smiled at my outworn image, and, when I had finished the question, nodded: 'This feeling of death is there because the symbolism of the eclipse reaches into the very fundament of the human soul. There is a sort of presage of death, but not in the way one might immediately imagine. You'll remember, from your readings of the hermetic literature, that there's mention of *Ishon*, the small man?'[5]

I nodded.

'This small man is linked with the eye and vision of Isis, herelf a *kore* or maiden, herself "a pupil of the eye".[6] There is deep significance in this ancient link with the eye, and with vision. Isis is the Moon goddess, and her consort-brother Osiris is the Sun god. The number 28 is linked with Isis, for in the period of a month (which is between 28 and 30 days in length, depending upon how it is measured), the appearance of the Moon goes through 28 or 30 transformations, from new, through the full, back to new.

'Now, in man and woman, this number of 28 or 30 is represented in the structure of the backbone. If you count the outer protuberances on the spine, you will find between 28 and 30 (those on the sacrum are almost vestigial). It is as though the leaping of the Moon through the skies has somehow been ossified in the embryo, imprinting a lunar impulse on the human spine.

'I am sure that I do not have to tell you that the energies within the spinal frame are transmitted throughout the body, and reach even into the furthermost cells. Of course, the ancient hermetic tradition has always recognized that the optic nerve is a transformation of the spine.[7] There are between 28 and 30 nerve threads in the optic eye which links the dark brain with the light-seeing eye.

'In this arcane physiognomy, we reach almost into the depths of the Mysteries concerning which it is forbidden to speak. However, I am free to tell you that the *Ishon*, or little man, of the hermetic tradition is visualized as sitting at the place between the human eyes, where the lunar nerves and the olfactory nerves meet. This *Ishon* can only be perceived by the higher senses. It is the development of this Astral dwarf which was a central programme in certain of the initiation Schools of ancient times.[8]

'I seem to have gone a long way from your question – yet this is not the case. When we experience an eclipse, we feel, as it were, the "death" of this dwarf. We feel that he has been dropped into a narcotic state. The human spine, which grows upwards towards the Sun, loses for a few seconds its upward thrust towards verticality.[9] It wishes to "sleep" – to become horizontal to the surface of the Earth. In this respect, it feels the impulse to become like the backbones of the animal realm – parallel to the Earth, and completely under the dominion of the Moon. The human is suddenly pulled back into its atavistic animal-like state. It needs to be led out of this state of being, which, in comparison with the human state, is virtually a sleep.'

We were leaning back into an incline of hillside, in a position from which we could most easily watch the Moon, which was almost reaching the zenith. From below came the distant thud of waves as the Atlantic broke on the sands of Pink Gin Beach. In the distance were the lights of houses and restaurants on the further side of the great bay around which nestled the port of St George's. Here was peace, and I could see why Mark had adopted it as a retreat.

He reached into his pocket and handed me a folded envelope. 'This small gift will be more personal than the other things I have left you in my will. It is my horoscope, which I am sure will interest you. The envelope is sealed, and I would ask you not to open it until after my death.'

I murmured my thanks, but a wave of sadness washed over me. It was the first time he had mentioned his end in so many words. I knew that there is no such thing as death in the conventional sense of the word, yet I knew also that no one wished to part from friends, even when one knows that they return again, in a future lifetime.

Mark was looking out to sea, perhaps so our eyes would not meet, or perhaps because he was dreaming of Europe beyond, which he had so much loved, and where he had studied with such depth and commitment. 'From the chart, you will have the answer to one question you have never asked me.'

'That is?'

'My age.' He was smiling, eyes wide.

'I have always thought of you as being a few years older than myself.'

'Well, the horoscope will show you otherwise. It amused me to leave you with that impression, but the chart I have given you will enable you to make sense of some of the autobiographical details you may still need for our famous book. Listen to those waves, David. If you meditate in a certain way, you can hear the pulse of your own blood, which sounds just like this surf.'

In the eerie light of the Moon, I felt as though I was in a shadow realm. Mark seemed like a ghost. Only the growl and roar of the sea on the bay sands below, and the high wash of surf surging against the rocks, seemed real. Mark Hedsel's voice, soft and assured, seemed to come from the seas, rather than from the phantom-man before me.

With an abrupt movement, he sat up, leaned over on to his elbow, and said, 'We should talk.'

'The footnotes?'

'No, not the footnotes. May I offer you three questions?' He had craned his head towards me as he spoke. 'I think you are wise enough, now, to know what sort of questions you can ask an old Fool.'

'Three questions?' I echoed him rather stupidly. Mark had never spoken to me in this way – he had never before presented himself in the role of my Teacher.

'No more, no less.'

'Must I ask them now?'

He glanced up at me in the darkness, and it was as though his eyes had collected all the starlight in the skies. 'Never forget that the Fool progresses only by means of the questions he asks.'

Looking back over that curious interlude, I now realize that I panicked. In the months I had worked with Mark Hedsel, I had found myself nurturing many questions: there were questions about the inner sanctum in Man and the cosmos, about the meaning of life, about the structure of the universe and the secrets of the descent of the soul, about certain words which were preserved in the arcane hermetic literature, and which had not been understood by modern scholars, about the relationship between Christ and karma, about the rules of conduct required of neophytes – even questions about the deepest levels of initiation, which I suspected that no initiate would be permitted to answer. Yet now, when brought to the test, I failed, for I could only ask a question – indeed, to put it more accurately, blurt out a question – which had been most recently circulating in my mind. When the poor fisherman dredges up the green bottle, and sees within it the mannikin geni begging for release, he too is so unprepared for three wishes that he panics.

'Why *is* the Fool of the Tarot pack accorded the number zero?' I asked.

On more than one occasion, Mark had told me how the Masters would often respond to a question as though answering the questioner, rather than the question. Now I had a taste of this myself.

'I did become a Teacher, David. That much is evident to both of us. Yet I am not a guru. A Teacher can indicate the Way, but he cannot show the Way. There are the two Ways – the Way Up and the Way Down – and among the ways up is the Way of the Fool. The zero marks the intersection between the Way Up and the Way down, where there is neither Up nor Down. After all, a wheel in motion must have some point at its centre which does not move – this is the still point mentioned in the hermetic literature. Even a ladder pitched between Heaven and Hell must have a point where there is neither up nor down: this much Dante recognized, with his usual genius, when he wrote in his *Inferno* about his experience at the centre of the Earth when the movement up suddenly became the movement down.[10] This could perhaps be the zero place.

'Of course, there are other reasons why the Fool should be linked with the zero. Some you already know, for we have discussed them.[11] Perhaps, to keep my promise, I could glance at one more.'

He folded his arms around his knees, and looked seawards. 'To what purpose, we must ask, would anyone wish to follow the Way of the Fool?

It is no easy role to play. The Way of the Fool is so open to mis-understanding and mockery. To the casual glance – which is the glance of most people – it does not even appear to be a Way at all. At least, not a Way in the ancient meaning of a sacred Way, or an initiatory Way, like the Isiac *Ancient Road* of Hermes, or the Way of the Monk, with its hidden pomp of outer clothes, pectoral crosses and other symbols, fronting its dour seriousness.[12] Yet there is such Way, even if it is only one followed by men and women striving to establish a Spiritual identity for themselves, divested of outer trappings.

'On this way, the Fool is sensitive to symbols. Indeed, if the Fool is alert enough, sufficiently progressed along the Path, then everything becomes a symbol. Consider this zero of yours carefully. It is almost a circle, a symbol of Spirit. We are trained, by our mental inertia, to think of the zero as a circle containing nothing. But a circle is also a shape which *circumscribes* everything. When you draw nothing, in the form of a zero, then by default you draw everything outside it. There are secrets here which can scarcely be put into words. Why did the Indian gurus express the Etheric, their *akashya*, as a circle?[13] Why did the Hebrew esotericists insist that the open letter *aleph* was to be accorded the enclosed zero?

'And so, if everything is a symbol, so is this circle we sit in – this place and time. It can be no accident that we sit in a place when a eclipse is taking place.'

I had almost forgotten about the eclipse. I looked towards the Moon, to see that the shadow of the Earth had sliced an arc across its surface. Mark continued to speak.

'Here, in this eclipse, my own mind perceives a meaning which is different from the one you perceive, yet however we define it, an eclipse is a meeting of circles which are zeros. See how the shadow of the Earth's rim cuts the Moon down to a crescent. Soon, in a few minutes, the crescent will be gone. For a while, the Moon will appear to be a dark zero – a nothing. Then the cycle will begin again, breathing a new life of light into the Moon. Soon, it will become a great zero of light in the skies. This is a conjuring trick on a cosmic scale, which is repeated relatively few times in any lifetime.

'Could this be one reason why the Fool of the Tarot pack is given the strange number zero? It is a curious number, for any esotericist will tell you that there is no such thing as nothing. Yet even the Fool, and even the eclipsed Moon, is not nothing, as behind appearance there is always spirit. In the past, scientists used to say that Nature abhors a vacuum – this may be true in a scientific sense, but it is certainly true in a Spiritual sense. There is no such thing as a vacuum, for the entire cosmos is a conspiracy against nothingness. Everywhere is filled with God: perhaps this is the secret of the zero?'

I nodded my head to indicate my thanks. After such a speech, one had to allow a silence. I took advantage of this to consider my second question. Even so, it did not seem to be much wiser than my first. It was certainly an honest question, yet – given that I could ask anything – it seemed, like my first one, to be strangely flat and unambitious.

'Is there any practical advice you can give to someone contemplating studying and following the Way of the Fool?'

'Yes,' Mark said without hesitation. 'The keyword for all the Paths is *commitment*. Always remember that when you have committed yourself to an action, then the whole cosmos will conspire to help you.

'It was recognition of this truth which encouraged the ancients to institute rituals to mark out their undertakings – they did this to mark their intentions clearly for the eyes of the Spiritual beings. In those days, everyone knew that vows were literally sacred things, which would be prefaced by prayers to the gods. Perhaps prayers are still necessary to clarify such things, yet the fact is that the cosmos recognizes commitment, which is in itself a kind of prayer. If you commit yourself, then you will find that the angels are ranged on your side.

'And so, make a commitment. Remember it. Stick to it. And if you choose the Way of the Fool, do not fear appearing to be a Fool in the eyes of the world, for, if you do not stray too far from the ancient road, in the eyes of God you will always remain the beloved Fool. The Way of the Fool is a moral Path, which perhaps explains Hermes' own curious saying – that a man on the Path should become more lofty than all heights, and lower than all depths, for morality is beyond measure. Hermes' closing words in this same instruction to his pupil, Tat, are even more puzzling. He wrote that if you wished to make yourself like unto God, then you should be in the same time in every place, both not yet begotten and in the after-death state.[14]

'I have meditated on these words for a considerable time, and can only say that I do not fully understand them. Perhaps they mean that it is impossible to be like unto God. Yet, this is certainly no mystical injunction to forget the world, for the hermeticist is trained never to forget the world – as it is his or her forging ground. The hermeticist is ever prepared to burn in exchange for *gnosis*, or to peel away the onion skins which wrap up the world's Mysteries, and himself. No, I suspect that Hermes is pointing to a level of development which is even above that of many exalted ranks recognized in the initiation grades – higher than the *Alethophilote*, and perhaps even higher than *Equus*.[15] While it is undoubtedly true that God is out of space and time, only the highest levels of being are of a similar nature. By this I mean the Buddhas, and the Boddhisatvas of Oriental wisdom, and the Prophets of the Western wisdom.'

'It makes the Godhead seem so inaccessible.' I was voicing an objection which I had lodged against many Christian rituals.

'One must never think of God as inaccessible, for such a thought will forge a weight of iron to drag on your natural chains. There is a mediaeval sermon which pictures Man moving towards God: yet the movement is not one way. For every faltering step taken by Man, God in His Stillness bounds towards Man a hundred steps.'

He mused for a few moments. 'You know the old adage that when you are ready for a Teacher, a Teacher will come?'

I nodded.

'Well,' he continued, 'as is usually the case with such wisdom, it was set down by Hermes long ago. In writing of what he called the *Straight Way*, or the *Ancient Road* – to which main route the brambled path of the Fool meanders – Hermes said, "Once you set your foot upon it, then it will meet you everywhere. You will see it, both when you expect to and when you do not expect to. You will see it waking and sleeping, sailing or on the road, by day as by night, as clearly as when you speak and as when you reserve silence." It seems to me, David, that this is only possible, because God is everywhere, and as much the Lover as the Beloved.'[16]

He allowed a silence, for us both to savour the words. We both watched the Moon, which was now a half crescent.

'Yet, I suspect that all this seems to be far removed from your original question – is there, indeed, any practical advice one can give to someone on the Way of the Fool? I presume you wanted precepts?'

'Yes.' I had wanted a sermon of rules to ease the Path.

'Remember Feste the Clown . . .

> This fellow is wise enough to play the fool.
> And to do that well craves a kind of wit.[17]

'More than a kind of wit, in fact. The Fool needs a moral code, or at least a discipline to knock him into shape. Yet you are right. There is a need for discipline, otherwise the dwarf longs for things he cannot have.'

He smiled again. 'But you want rules. There are of course *diagrams . . . sigils . . .*'

Suddenly, everything began to fall into place. If the Way of the Fool was epoptic, *then there would have to be diagrams*. Could it be that I was on the threshold of learning about those 'secret writings and diagrams' to which the Rosicrucian literature referred, again and again, and which so many Rosicrucians used to obscure their texts from the uninitiated?[18]

'The diagrams I speak about are really meditative sigils, with short precepts attached. The magic lies in the diagrams, rather than in the words. They are meant to be epoptic, a sort of Mute Book. They are not my own, but I will pass them on to you. We need light, so I will draw them out when we return to the hotel. They are designed for meditation, and it would be wrong to make any attempt to explain them to others.'[19]

I nodded assent. I was no longer sure whether a last question remained to me. Perhaps he saw the flicker of doubt in my eyes, for he murmured, 'And your third question?'

In fact, a cacophony of questions jostled in my head. This could be the last question I formally addressed to Mark, yet I could not formulate one worthy of such an honour. I can no longer remember where I had read it, yet a phrase floated into my mind, as though from nowhere. 'The most illuminating answers are those which deal with questions asked about things other than oneself.' This was true, and I decided to make my last question one about Mark himself. His book was almost finished, and I asked him, as my final question, if he was satisfied with it.

Once again he laughed before speaking. 'David, what we are left with is nothing more than a few notes of a vision more or less lost – so many pencil sketches in the progress of a catharsis. If you are really asking whether I am satisfied with the catharsis offered by the past two years, then I must say that I am. It is always useful to be reminded about how little one knows. Yet, as for the book itself, well, I have to say that it was given to us at a strange time.'

'The *Kali Yuga*?' I asked, and almost immediately regretted the question. We were in the *Kali Yuga*, the Dark Age of the ancient Oriental system of world ages. This was the hardest time of all.

'I was not thinking of the Age – yet the *Kali Yuga* will serve just as well. It is a strange time. Do you know that wonderful passage from the Indian classic . . . I cannot recall which section, now . . . which deals with the question to Veda Vyasa about the nature of Spiritual development in the various ages?'

I nodded.

'Veda Vyasa called this *the vicious age of Kali*, yet he was kind about it – he understood it as a time of testing – claiming that it was by far the most satisfactory time for Spiritual development.'[20]

Mark was silent for a while, as though pondering whether he should say anything more. Then he continued. 'The *Kali Yuga* may not have been on our side, and Time was certainly not on our side, for, in my case, it was limited. I misjudged the time. Between us, we have not been able to set down all the things I want to say: in spite of what you imagine, the book is far from finished.

'The weakness in our book is that it is an *explanation* – furthermore, an explanation of an art which is the most complex of all arts. I suspect that, when dealing with such ethereal subjects as initiation, it is only when we break through into the fantasy realm of poetry that we will succeed in communicating anything of value. Initiation is an art, a Spiritual performance which can last a lifetime, and then pour into subsequent lifetimes, and I am no longer convinced that one can write about it intelligently. Perhaps it would have been better to simply quote passages from the hermetic literature – which is poesy itself – and allow people the freedom to read their own meaning into the seven levels contained within it. Anything else is a shadow-play with the puppets of maya.

'I had not overlooked these problems when we began the work, but I certainly have misjudged the times. Those who trouble to read the book may imagine that one can explain the Mysteries and that initiation in mere words, when this is not true.'

'At least you've tried.' My words were banal after his own impassioned speech. I could not think of anything to say which had any importance.

'Tried, yes. Yet, what have you and I tried to do? We have tried to explain the greatest Mysteries of all in words. Such might be done in poetry, perhaps – especially if such poetry were intermingled with dance and music, as in a Mystery drama – but we have elected to use only words.

'When I decided to ask you to help me write this book, I juggled with titles. I had in mind that we should call it *The Autobiography of a Fool*. But then, I reasoned, it would be unwise to expect anyone to read such a book, for in our hearts we all know that we are Fools. We keep this knowledge secret, of course, and we hide it with a variety of more or less sophisticated masks and uniforms. Few people dare approach closely this inner image of the Fool, for the danger is that they might actually be revealed as a Fool. If I had chosen a more honest title, and reverted to the word used so perspicaciously by my Teacher in Paris, then I would have called it *The Book of the Idiot*. While most people know, in their heart of hearts, that they are Fools, they do not suspect that they are also idiots. This is mainly because they do not really know what an idiot is, and how holy is that word.'

He seemed to have come to the end of the monologue, but then he added, 'There is only one complete illumination for one who dwells in the body. Then, at that marvellous moment of initiated insight, you will see that life itself is art: it is the art of the gods. The art of Man merely reflects the shadow of this creative exuberance. Initiation is the ultimate art of the gods, practised with more or less imperfection by men.'

There was only a thin silver line of Moon still visible.

'So, my friend, we are back to words. The things we so utterly believe in, and trip up over so easily. Yet, what we all overlook is that words are really understood only in silence: to understand, you must push back the sound of the voice, and listen to the silence behind the sound, tuning in to the soul who speaks. This is not mystical nonsense – this is realism; if you listen to the sound, there can be no understanding. *The meaning lies behind the sound*. Perhaps this is the secret of the zero.

'In any case, the eclipse is complete, and is answering your question about the zero. We are looking down the Earth's shadow into what appears to be nothing: yet it is really the dancing ground of angels.'

Appendix – The 12 Meditative Sigils

The 12 sigils passed on to me by Mark Hedsel appear to be vestigial drawings which can be linked (to some extent) with the curious *Book of Dyzan* that formed the basis for Blavatsky's *The Secret Doctrine*, and with certain of the alchemical sigils which circulated in the 16th and 17th centuries.

Altogether, they reminded me of those simple, yet deeply pregnant, alchemical sigils which appeared in the 18th-century *Aurea Catena Homeri* texts, in which ten sigils subtend from the *Chaos Confusum* to *Quintessentia Universalis*. It is sometimes said that this graphic chain was suggested by the opening words of book VIII in Homer's *Illiad*, but this, like all the other classical references I know, refers to what has been called 'The Great Chain of Being', which hangs between Heaven and Earth. The sigils of the alchemical *Aurea Catena Homeri* seem to have been constructed by a practising Rosicrucian alchemist, and, while they may partly reflect the nature of that Great Chain, they cannot be traced to any ancient prototype with which I am familiar.

However, these images given to me by Mark Hedsel were not ranged as a single connected descending chain, but in three groups. Mark Hedsel told me that any of the circles within these groups could be detached (mentally) and connected with any other, to work as a philosophical machine. I reproduce the 12 images here, copied as faithfully as possible from the manuscript which Mark gave to me. Although it is clear that each image is worthy of a lengthy commentary, in accordance with my agreement, I cannot (even were I able) comment further on their meanings.

Mark insisted that a full appreciation of the meaning within the sigils required that one should attempt to visualize each one separate from those contiguous to it, and in circular motion on an imaginary centre. Furthermore, the 12 images are to be visualized as forming a circle which offers no beginning or end to their sequence. Perhaps this suggestion was

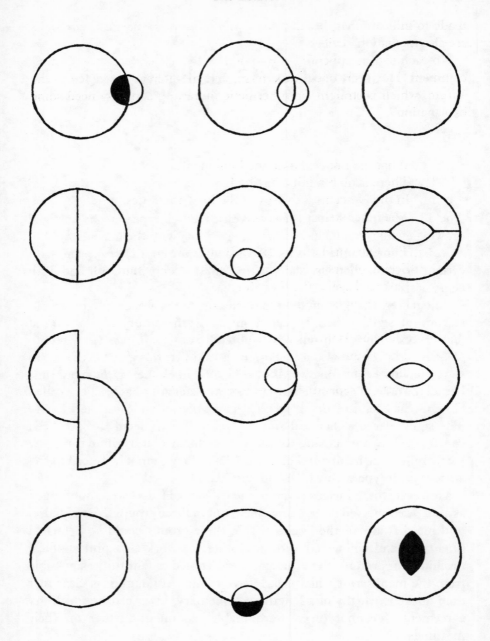

made to indicate that, besides being a philosophical machine, the sigils are also mediation devices.

To each sigil is appendid a gnomic line, which I reproduce without comment. However, one arcane term, and the literary reference to the Virgin, which is straight from hermetic literature, certainly need some explanation.

What the Fool exhales, the Fool inhales.
There is no feminine for Fool.
In the Descents,* the sex of the Fool alternates.
The inner strives to become the outer.

The Outworld others are self reflected.
Seeing others as Self, the soul seeks to make amends.
Balanced again, the Fool descends.
New thoughts become wrought deeds.

All below is image, and names perish.
The Virgin in the Fool's eye does not perish.**
The Virgin Waters generate their own light.
Without separation, there is no illumination.

* Passage of lifetimes, from the hermetic literature which describes such descents and ascents through the planetary spheres.
** The Virgin of the Eye is a reference to the Greek, *kore*, which besides meaning 'pupil of the eye' also means 'maiden' or 'virgin'. Just so, the English 'pupil' can also mean 'someone who is learning'.

Bibliographic Notes

PROLOGUE

1. The exhibition opened on 25 October 1955. The catalogue is reproduced in A. R. Naylor, *From the Inferno to Zos: The Writings and Images of Austin Osman Spare*, 1993, vol. 1. One presumes that Spare had chosen the opening date for its astrological significance: Jupiter and Pluto were conjunct in the Astrologer's Arc (in 27–28 degrees Leo). Later in the day, the Moon would oppose this pair, also from the Astrologer's Arc. It will be observed that on this day, the Moon was in Aquarius (n.11). His close friend, Frank Letchford, recalls that Spare played the 'horse-racing' predictive system, which he had himself designed, to find out how many pictures he would sell. The numbers 200 and 44 turned up, and he was excited at the idea of selling as many as 200 pictures at one exhibition. He sold 44. See F. W. Letchford, *From the Inferno to Zos. Vol. III. Michelangelo in a Teacup: Austin Osman Spare*, 1995, p.285.

2. The unconventional Australian, Dr Morris, was one of the early followers of Rudolf Steiner, and was deeply interested in esoteric thought. While I never met her, some of my close friends did. As an agent, she charged 25 per cent of sales, while the more usual charge was 35 per cent. I have learned (from friends) that in spite of the facts given in her obituary (see below) she died of malnutrition.

   Morris was born in 1880. Her name, up to her marriage with the Reverend William Morris, in 1905, was Ethel Ida Remfrey. She qualified as a doctor, and worked for some time as Resident Medical Officer at Lady Lamington Hospital, Brisbane. In 1924, she became interested in working with handicapped children, and adopted the art-therapy theories of Rudolf Steiner. She was an Anthroposophist: a pathetic note in the register at Steiner House Library records that she remained a member, even though she could not afford to pay the subscription.

   Like Spare (see n.5) Dr Morris also had a miraculous escape from Hitler's bombing. When her studio in St Mary Abbots Terrace was bombed, two of her friends, who were standing alongside her, were killed outright and she was buried in the rubble for a considerable time. The Archer Gallery also suffered from Hitler's bombing, for a V1 flying bomb shattered the display window. Dr Morris put in its place a huge tarpaulin and began to live inside the cold gallery to guard the pictures on show. As a result of the bombing, her lungs were permanently damaged. She died on 7 November 1957. Her obituary in *The Times*, on 8 November 1957, described her as a well-known figure.

3. In 1954, Spare told Frank Letchford that he had only two years left to live. Spare lived a further 16 months, dying at 01.50 p.m., 15 May 1956. See F. W. Letchford, *From the Inferno to Zos. Vol. III. Michelangelo in a Teacup: Austin Osman Spare*, 1995.

4. Spare's studio was destroyed on 10 May 1941. In the following year, he set up a new studio in Leyden Street, Aldgate, and took personal accommodation at 5 Wynne Road, Brixton.

5. In response to the invitation to paint a portrait of the Führer, Spare sent a drawing of himself, hybrid with Hitler, by way of the German Embassy. A copy of the letter was preserved by Hannen Swaffer, and is printed in Letchford (op. cit., n.1, p.253). See also William Wallace, *The Later Work of Austin Osman Spare – 1917-1956* (1989), note 10, p.16. May we see the destruction of Spare's studio, with all his current work, in the bombing of London on 10 May 1941, as Hitler's definitive magical response?

   However, even if this view is correct, Hitler would have been merely an agent, as the destruction was promised in a most forthright way in the horoscope of Austin Spare. On 10 May 1941, the five progressed planets – Sun, Moon, Mercury, Venus and Mars – were conjunct in Pisces, in his fifth house, the Sun squared by Pluto, the Cauda squared by Neptune, with Saturn and Uranus in square. For Spare, 1941 marked a lunar return to the radical, so that the Moon in that heavy satellitium was just past conjunction with its radical self, and moving towards conjunction with the progressed Venus. The significations could scarcely be more clear.

   The miracle, of course, is that Spare survived at all – he was on warden duty outside the house, but his arm was severely damaged by other bomb debris.

6. The word *Spar* or *spare*, from the Old English *sperran*, 'to strike out or fight with a weapon', is related to the Old Norse, *sperrask*, 'to kick out'. Although young at the time of my visit to the Archer Gallery, I was familiar with the near-archaic use of the word from my relatives. My grandfather (unaware that he was using antique terms) would often say ruefully that I would drive him *spare*. The idea was that my behaviour would so dement him as to drive him berserk. It was, indeed, something of this mobile quality of the wild berserker which I saw in the face of Spare. It is clear that Spare was himself intrigued by the secondary meanings in his name, for he incorporated one into a sort of valedictory promissory note: 'If I come again, I will not spare.' See Letchford, op. cit., p.360.

   The last-known photograph of Spare was taken at 5 Wynne Road, Brixton, where he lived, about three weeks before his death (Letchford, p.341). The haunting mobility of the face is quite extraordinary: whichever part of the face one looks at, it seems not to belong to the rest. It is precisely this quality which one experiences in his finest works. In many ways, this mobility is identical to the drawing by Spare reproduced in William Wallace, *The Later Work of Austin Osman Spare 1917-1956*, (1989), where there is a photograph of Spare's *Metamorphosis – Fish Becoming Men*. When one gazes at this picture, the eye cannot rest, for it is always carried elsewhere by the inner dynamic of the spirallic design.

   In so far as Spare is remembered at all outside specialist circles, it is perhaps as a witch, and as a close associate of Crowley. Both traditions are only partly true, and depend very much on personal definitions. Spare had claimed a sort of initiation into witchcraft through Mrs Paterson, who was supposed to be descended from a Salem witch. However, I personally question both facts, for I doubt there was any genuine witchcraft at Salem. The idea of initiation in another direction – perhaps linked with Crowley – was confirmed in the perceptive *Appreciation* which Kenneth Grant wrote for the catalogue for the Archer exhibition, and it was this which first alerted me to the fact that Spare was an initiate. Of course, had I been more advanced on the Path, I would have recognized this from his work. In those days I was too young to ask the obvious question – an initiate into which Mystery? Grant was absolutely right – the exhibition itself offered a glance, as it were, into the inscrutable Mysteries. Certainly, Spare was initiated into the *Ordo Templi Orientis* by Crowley.

7. Dennis Bardens, *Mysterious Worlds*, 1970. See Chapter 11. See also Clive Harper, *Revised Notes Towards a Bibliography of Austin Osman Spare*, 1996, p.28.

8. It was hard to believe from his later appearance that, in his early days, Spare had been something of a dandy.

9. For an account of this remarkably sophisticated and urbane occultist, see Isabel Cooper-Oakley, *The Comte de St Germain. The Secret of Kings*, 1912.
10. The older lady was a well-known traveller and novelist. The younger is a painter, whom I met at the extraordinary exhibition at Batley Art Gallery, in 1952, organized by the farsighted curator, Gelsthorpe. It was this artist who eventually made over the Spare pastel into my care.
11. The title *Blood on the Moon* puzzled me for a very long time. Then, one day, I chanced upon a quotation from Seutonius' account of the life of Domitian, and the significance of the title dawned on me. On the day prior to his assassination, the Emperor Domitian had remarked, somewhat prophetically, 'There will be blood on the Moon as she enters Aquarius, and a deed will be done for everyone to talk about throughout the world.' On the following day, when he died, the Moon was in Aquarius . . .

    Of course, I doubt that Spare was deeply interested in the fate of Domitian, yet, through that pure chance by which the cosmos disguises itself, the Moon *was* in Aquarius on the day the picture was first exhibited at the Archer Gallery. It is more likely that the artist, who always sought the hidden depths in things, was attracted to the quotation because ot the light it threw upon the misunderstood 'Age of Aquarius'. The popular journalistic notion – already widespread in exoteric circles in the middle of the 20th century – held that the Age of Aquarius would be an age of freedom, of new communications, of developing spirit. However, esotericists cognizant of the rulership of Uranus over this sign were aware that (initially at least) the age would be full of violence, upheavals and disturbances. Spare saw that, rather than the inauguration of the New Age bringing peace and goodwill, it would bring Uranian blood on the Moon.

    If this interpretation is correct, then the deed which 'will be done for everyone to talk about throughout the world' will no longer be the murder of a mundane Emperor, but the resurrection of a murdered Son of God. The dual nature of Christ, and the dual rulership of Aquarius (with ancient Jupiter and modern Uranus), are superbly expressed in the uneasy duality of the picture, which portrays a human two-headed hermaphrodite dancing in sacred alignment.
12. The bookseller, John Watkins, was one of the four founder-members of the Ananda Lodge, in the Esoteric Section of the Theosophical Society.
13. His real name was Michael Houghton. He did however use the pseudonym *Michael Juste* for his occult autobiography, *The White Brother* (n.d.), and for his poems (for example), *Many Brightnesses*, and the anti-war, *Shoot – And be Damned*, 1935. He was a well-respected figure in the arcane world of London, and ran the Atlantis Bookshop, at 49a Museum Street, for over 30 years. He died in June, 1961.
14. I reproduce the drawing I did from Wren's house (see page 5) in order to demonstrate something of interest – just how closely my own pull to certain parts of London seemed to draw me near to Spare, even though I never spoke to him. In his fascinating account of Spare's life, Frank Letchford gives an account of a jaunt the two took together to Cardinal Cap Alley, adjacent to the Wren house. It seemed that Spare was considering the idea of having a house built on the site. Spare seems to have had a good knowledge of the history of that area, and I too (although very young at the time) explored the badly bombed areas around Bankside, 'The Anchor', the roads around the old Clink and Deadman's Place, soaking up the history of the place which still seemed alive in those days. Of course, subsequent rebuilding programmes seem to have erased everything but the names. The aura from the old brothels, the plague dead – even the unimpeded view of St Paul's – and the hordes of cats which Spare would feed in those streets, is now no more, and with this loss in substantiality has disappeared a part of living London. See F. W. Letchford, *From the Inferno to Zos. Vol. III. Michelangelo in a Teacup: Austin Osman Spare*, 1995, p.243.
15. This was true. For example, in 1949 Spare held an exhibition at The Temple Bar,

in Walworth Road, SE17. As Spare wrote, in his *Apologia* to the catalogue to this exhibition, 'it costs nothing to enter a Public House'. However, one suspects that he chose such places not for democratic reasons but because he could no longer find a dealer or gallery prepared to exhibit his works. In 1952 he mounted an exhibition at the Mansion House Tavern, in Kennington Park Road, SE11. One wonders what the casual and regular drinkers would make of Spare's catalogue notes. In these, Spare wrote of 'the uninhibited rendering of certain inherent levels and values, these usually being expressed through a deliberate matrix of ethical conventions: probably all deliberate expression is an arbitrary corruption or rectification of our "Ids" . . .' Accounts of the exhibitions are given in *From the Inferno to Zos: The Writings and Images of Austin Osman Spare*, edited and compiled by A. R. Naylor, 1993.

16. Cornelius Agrippa (1486-1535), John Dee (1527-1608), Johann Gichtel (1638-1710) and Franz Mercurius van Helmont (1618-1699). All these authors had been influential Rosicrucians. Dee and van Helmont had important roles to play in the unfolding of British history – Dee in the court of Elizabeth I (see, for example, F. A. Yates, *The Rosicrucian Enlightenment*, 1972, p.30ff), and van Helmont in the Rosicrucian school at Ragley, in Warwickshire (see, for example, P. M. Allen, *A Christian Rosenkreutz Anthology*, 1968, p.61ff.)

17. The Artzybasheff picture is reproduced in Alfred Kreymborg, *Funnybone Alley*, 1927, p.95. The naked woman in the blue night sky has a huge crescent over her forehead. In her right hand she hold the five-pointed star, which is the sacred *sba* of the Egyptian hieroglyphics (see page 464), and perhaps the most recurrent of all arcane symbols. Is there meaning in the chance flow of blood over a page, one wonders? The red rivulet had run between the crescent and the star, and through the woman's belly, as though it had been directed by some talented Cosmic Joker. No Dadaist artist – even Marcel Duchamp in his construction of that 'mystico-mechanical epic', *The Bride Struck Naked by the Bachelors, Even* (the discoveries within which Spare had explored earlier) – could have 'accidentally arranged' things better. In later life, to mark in retrospect the meeting with Mark, I purchased a copy of *Funnybone Alley*, signed in person by Artzybasheff. Ironically, beneath his signature, the artist had drawn a picture of a cat – that archetypal lunar creature.

18. Mercury was exactly conjunct with Saturn on that day, both square to Pluto in Leo. This would have been sufficient to persuade them to seek cosmic significance in the accident. However, it was clear from later conversations that the significance they did see was entirely alchemical. The fact is, that in the arcane correspondencies which govern occult thought, the blood is ruled by the Sun.

19. At that stage, I knew of Gurdjieff's occult movement through P. D. Ouspensky's *In Search of the Miraculous*, 1949. So far as I can recall, the first of the trilogy, *Beelzebub's Tales to his Grand-son*, 1949, was available only to members of the Gurdjieff groups.

20. Alice Bailey's remarkable *Unfinished Autobiography* had been published only four years previously, in 1951. It gives details of her telepathic channelling with the Tibetan Master whose influence lay behind most of her important books.

21. The Evans-Wentz edition of *The Tibetan Book of the Great Liberation* had been published in England in the previous year.

22. There does not appear to be any evidence that Theodor Reuss initiated Rudolf Steiner into the *Ordo Templi Orientis*, as is claimed by Francis King, *Ritual Magic in England*, 1970 – see Appendix E (p.163, 1972 ed.). King was undoubtely confusing the OTO with the *Memphis and Misraim Rite* (of which Reuss was Grand Master in Germany and Austria). It is clear that Steiner (then Secretary General of the German branch of the Theosophical Society) was granted a warrant, in 1906, to form a Chapter and Ground Council, the *Mystica Aeterna*, of which he was Deputy Grand Master. This information, preserved in Reuss' *Die Oriflamme*,

1906, V. i, pp.4–5, is quoted by Ellic Howe, *The Magicians of the Golden Dawn. A Documentary History of a Magical Order 1887-1923*, 1972, p.263.

23. Blavatsky, the originator of the Theosophical Society, appears to have been influenced by the Hermetic Brotherhood of Luxor, and by the teachings of the African-American, Paschal Beverly Randolph. See J. Godwin, C. Chanel and J. P. Devney, *The Hermetic Brotherhood of Luxor. Initiatic and Historical Documents of an Order of Practical Occultism*, 1995.

24. Curiously, the *mer* for 'chisel' is one of the hieroglyphics in the name Narmer, which takes us back to the protodynastic period in Egypt (*c*. 3000 BC). Narmer is the king identified with Menes, who unified Upper and Lower Egypt: his name is represented by the two hieroglyphics for the fish (*nar*) and the chisel (*mer*). See the Narmer palette, discovered by Quibell at Hierakonpolis, in 1894: M.Saleh, et al., *Official Catalogue. The Egyptian Museum, Cairo*, 1987, ex.8. For *mer* meaning 'to die', see G. Massey, *A Book of the Beginnings*, 1881, p.65. The esoteric undertones in this compound of fish and death are very profound indeed.

25. The Egyptian *neters* were both archetypes and gods. R. A. Schwaller de Lubicz has developed this truth in his studies of esoteric Egyptian thought – see, for example, his *Sacred Science*, Eng. trans., 1982, p.162ff.

26. It is this loss which explains why I have been compelled to construct most of the footnotes. I was fortunate to discuss almost all the points he raised in the book, during our last meeting in Grenada (see p.344ff), yet there were still a few lacunae which I have had to fill as best I could. Wherever possible, I completed the literary sources from his notebooks, and supplemented these with observations based on my own conversations with him, and from a knowledge of the arcane books he owned, or had read.

27. There are numerous references to Saint-Germain as an active initiate and Mason between the years 1710 up to the French Revolution of 1789. Baron von Gleichen, in his *Souvenirs*, 1868, records that several people, including the French Ambassador at Venice, testify to having met Saint-Germain in 1710, when he gave the appearance of being about 50 years old. This would suggest a birth round about 1660. See Isabel Cooper-Oakley, *Comte de St Germain*, 1912, 1985 rep., p.7. One hundred years later, in 1760, Cornet, in a letter to the Count de Haslang, dated 29 April, mentions that the Comte de Saint-Germain, 'who is said to be extremely rich and very well received at different Courts in Europe', had just disappeared when least expected. Op. cit., p.240. A Masonic register, pertaining to the *Grand Orient*, for which the earliest possible date could be 1775, contains the signature of Saint-Germain (op. cit., p.217).

28. See, for example, Jacques Sadoul, *Alchemists and Gold*, in the 1972 Eng. trans. by O. Sieveking, p.269. In this appendix, Sadoul lists nine well-known alchemists whose lives average 82 years. Saint-Germain lived in the late mediaeval period when less than half that age was the general average.

29. The Latin, *caput mortuum*, means 'death's head', and is sometimes translated as meaning 'skull'. However, in alchemy, the words are used in a different sense, to relate in a meaningful way to the alchemical hermetic practice. For example, the 16th-century alchemist, Paracelsus, often uses the term as the 'sulphureous subsidence' in matter. When this term is translated, in terms of the Three Principles which dominate alchemy, it is seen as referring to the unredeemed Will, or the unredeemed sexual forces in man and woman. See p.140, where the symbolism of the redeemed and unredeemed sexual element of sulphur is discussed.

30. For the connection between Mark Hedsel and the Sagrada di San Michele, see p.72ff.

31. An example of an invented initiatory system is that used in the Hermetic Order of the Golden Dawn. For a survey, see Ellic Howe, *The Magicians of the Golden Dawn. A Documentary History of a Magical Order 1887-1923*, 1972.

32. See Howe (n.31), p.259ff.
33. The esoteric roots of *King Lear* run very deep. 'Where's my fool, ho. I think the world's asleep', Lear shouts (i.4. l.50). For the sleeping world, see p.71. King Lear is the Fool who acts foolishly, for he cannot recognize the importance of love. He is accompanied by the wise Fool, who knows what love is. In his own book, Mark Hedsel points out that the Way of the Fool is a Way of Love.
34. He was quoting from a line by the troubadour Monk – see n.37.
35. Probably this was the Monk of Montaudon, who was of gentle birth, yet became a monk in the abbey of Orlac (the modern Aurillac, in southern France). For a while, he had the priorate of Montaudon, which may have been the modern Montauban. Only 16 of his poems have survived: the music for two of these has been preserved. See Anthony Bonner, *Songs of the Troubadours*, 1973 ed., pp.180 and 295.
36. The Green Language is the secret language of esotericists and alchemists.
37. The Monk's poem is No. 3 in the Bonner collection (n.39) 1, p.186. viii. The hare and ox lines are described by Bonner as probably the most famous three lines in all of Provençal literature. They appear in *En cest sonet coind'e leri* (No. 3 in the Bonner sequence), which I translate freely:
    > I am Arnaut, the gatherer of the wind
    > The one who hunts with ox the hare as hind
    > Who swims 'gainst the tides' turning bind
    In a later reference to these lines, Daniel himself develops on these claimed powers, insisting that it is knowledge (his *conning*) which is his strength. It is because he *knows* so much that he can stop the incoming tide, and his ox is faster than a hare. This fooling poet seems to have learned a secret or two from a magician. One cannot help feeling that the seeds of Rabelais were being set in the French soil by these humour-filled troubadours, who had looked into a world which was hidden from other men.
38. He was paraphrasing a poem, *Una ciutatz fo* (A city of fools) by the early 13th-century poet, Peire Cardenal. See René Lavaud, *Poésies complètes du troubadour Peire Cardenal*, 1957.
39. The French poet, François Rabelais (1494–1553), was born near Chinon. He was a Franciscan friar at Fontenay-le-Comte, in Poitou, but eventually became a monk with the Benedictines at Maillezais. He lectured in medicine at Lyons.
40. For Rabelais and the initiation theme, see page 50. For the mad poet theme, see the Navarre Society edition, *The Works of Mr Francis Rabelais . . . The Lives, Heroick Deeds and Sayings of Gargantua and his Sonne Pantagruel*, 1931, v. xlvi and xlvii. Some scholars argue that the Fifth Book is not entirely from the hand of Rabelais, yet the initiation theme is evident, and the humour just as trenchant as the earlier books.
41. Mark Hedsel used the French word *bavard*, for which there is no real English equivalent – in the sense he used it, the word means 'one who drinks and talks a great deal while in his cups'.
42. Hieronymus Bosch (*c.*1450–1516). Examples abound of the 'Fool' in his paintings. The most notable are *The Prodigal Son* in the Boymans-van Beuningen Museum (Rotterdam), and on the outer wings of the *Hay Wain*, in the Prado (Madrid). The titles of these two pictures are misleading, for the subject is the Fool: the art-historian, L. von Baldass, in *Hieronymus Bosch*, 1959, suggests that they depict the Vagrant. There is no ambiguity about Bosch's *Ship of Fools* in the Louvre.
43. The story of the Prodigal Son is told in *Luke*, 15. 11–32. It is difficult to trace a correspondence between this account and the paintings by Bosch.
44. C. A. W. Aymes, *The Pictorial Language of Hieronymus Bosch*, Eng. trans. 1975, examines some of the hidden symbolism relating to the Fool in the works of Bosch.
45. For some account of the *Feast of Fools*, see p.368, n.17. The Church lamented the excesses of the Feast of Fools from as early as the seventh century. A number of Councils in France (Rouen, 1435; Soissons, 1455; Sens, 1485 and Paris in 1528)

condemned the lewd and anarchic festivities, seemingly to little effect, as the Worship of the Ass was still drawing critical notice as late as 1644. The Feast, so outwardly inimical to the strictures of the Church, was deeply rooted in pagan consciousness. Henry VIII of England abolished the Feast in 1542, yet, under the pressure of popular demand, it was reinstituted by Mary, 12 years later. See T. Barns, 'Abbot of Unreason', in J. Hastings, *Encyclopaedia of Religion and Ethics*, 1971 ed., I, p.10a. For a survey of the *Festum Fatuorum*, see M. du Tilliot, *Memoires pour servir à l'histoire de la Fête des Foux*, 1741.

THE WAY OF THE FOOL

1. The language of the ancient Mysteries drew a distinction between ordinary ways of learning, and how, and what, one learned through initiation. The Greek verb, *mathein*, was applied to those things one learned through the intellect. It is from this root that we have our modern word 'mathematics'. This 'ordinary learning' was contrasted in the Mysteries with what one could learn through the inner experiences of the soul. The Greek verb *pathein*, which was used for this kind of learning, is usually translated as meaning 'suffering', but it represented more than suffering – it was 'a learning by way of direct contact with the material realm'. The Ego of the Fool travelled by way (the Path) of *pathein*. This partly explains why those not on this Path should look at the antics of the Fool with some suspicion – who, such people might well ask, would seek to learn by experience, when ordinary knowledge satisfies the majority? The uninitiated rarely see just how much ordinary learning represents an exitless maze, and does not satisfy the growing soul.

2. Since the word *Ego* is of such importance to the Way of the Fool, we should perhaps examine its meaning in the light of initiation. *Ego* is, of course, the first person nominative, the Latin for 'I'. It denotes that element within man and woman which is sacrosanct to that Self. The only person who can correctly address itself as 'I' is that Ego. Only the Ego can take responsibility for its decisions and actions. Just as, in the course of many thousands of years, the other Spiritual bodies of Man have been developed, through experience and through initiation, so the human Ego has been undergoing special development since the late 15th century. For a treatment of the Ego, or Higher Mind, from a Theosophical standpoint, see A. E. Powell, *The Mental Body*, 1927. In modern esotericism, the Ego is usually treated alongside the Consciousness Soul.

    In Jungian terms, the Ego is conceived as a sort of dynamic unity which binds together (or even fails to bind together) the individuality. On a different level, it is seen as that part of the individual which is perceived by others as being in touch with external reality. In both these views there is a passing resemblance to the truths taught in the esoteric Schools, save that (for the esotericist) the Ego is a distinct Spiritual body, a sort of 'over-soul' (to use Emerson's term: see Essay IX, 'The Over-Soul', in *Emerson's Essays*, in the Everyman Library, intro. by S. Paul, 1971 ed., p.149ff). In esoteric thought, the Ego is the user of the *persona*, or mask of personality. Furthermore, as the esotericist sees it, the Ego is still in conception in the majority of people, and still capable of extraordinary growth.

3. The word *Astral*, now widely used in occult literature, is derived from the Latin for 'star'. The Astral is a plane of being which is contiguous in space with the material realm, where thoughts and emotions have a reality of their own: on this plane, thoughts and emotions are entities. This plane is the realm of emotions, reminding us that the Astral body of man (which remains invisible to all but clairvoyants) is the body of emotions, and was in former times called the 'Desire Body'. As such a body, which seeks to descend into matter, and become entangled with the material realm, it is an instrument of the Ego. Stones and plants do not have an Astral body, while animals do. This explains why, in the esoteric tradition, animals are often used as symbols for the Astral plane. On one level, the animal

(dog or cat) which pursues the Fool in the Tarot card is meant to symbolize that part of the Fool's Astrality which has not yet been tamed. See, for example, A. E. Powell, *The Astral Body and Other Astral Phenomena*, 1928.

The word *Etheric* denotes that Spiritual plane in the cosmos which works upon inert matter to give it life. It is the ancient 'Fifth Element' (Quintessence) which was believed to hold together the chaos of the Four Elements in a distinctive organization of form. When the Etheric is operative, the molecular activity of matter is transformed into cellular activity. Stones and minerals do not have an Etheric activity, while plants do. This explains why, in the esoteric tradition, plants are often used as symbols for the Etheric plane. See for example, Guenther Wachsmuth, *The Etheric Formative Forces in Cosmos, Earth and Man*, 1932.

4. The Astral is called, in the mediaeval alchemical system, the *Ens Astrale*, and in some English systems the *Passional Body*. It is sometimes called the *Sidereal Body*, because its home is the realm of stars. In the Sanskrit, it is the *kama-rupa*.

5. The Etheric is called, in the mediaeval alchemical system, the *Ens Veneni*, and sometimes the *Ens Vegetabilis*: in some English systems it is the *Life Body*. The nearest equivalent, in the Sanskrit is *Linga-sharira*.

6. The Physical is usually called in the mediaeval alchemical tradition the *Elemental Body*. It is also the *Ass*, or the *Donkey*.

7. The resurrected body of Christ is sometimes called *Augoeideian* in the mystery literature: it is from the Greek meaning 'ray-like light'. We should observe that the same word was used of the robe of Osiris, the Egyptian god who resurrected from death and dismemberment.

8. We once had the pleasure of talking to one on the Path who had specialized in medicine, but who, in advanced age, had retired. We had asked him one or two questions about the Spirit, and how certain moral issues manifested on the material plane. He answered our questions clearly and concisely, and much to our satisfaction. Later, in the same talk, we asked him a question about the physical body, at which point he became slightly agitated, before saying, 'In truth, I know nothing about the physical body: it is the Great Mystery.'

9. The traditional divinatory Tarot pack consists of 78 cards, 22 of which are picture-cards, called the Major Arcana, or 'atouts'. The images of the original packs were clearly designed by initiate Schools, for their symbolism, iconographic and graphic permutations allow them to be used for meditation. All trace of the School or Schools is now lost. Of the 22 atouts, only the Fool is un-numbered, and usually ascribed the *zero*. For a wide selection of images of the Fool, see S. R. Kaplan, *The Encyclopedia of Tarot*, 1986. Kaplan intimates that it is possible that the card designs might have had a more 'mystical intention' than game-playing (see vol. II, p.391). That the Tarot cards are receptacles of arcane lore has been recognized for some considerable time, and the 17th-century Italian Minchiate set seems to be entirely arcane. However, the first writer to openly draw a connection between the 22 major Tarot cards and the 22 paths of the Hebraic Sephirothic tree seems to have been E. Poirel, in *Les 22 Arcanes du Tarot Kabbalistique*, 1889. For an interesting note on various changes made to this system by Aleister Crowley, see Kaplan, p.391. Not all the post-1889 Tarot cards accorded the Fool the *aleph*. For example, in a hand-drawn set reproduced by Kaplan (p.397), *Le Fou* is accorded the Hebrew letter *shin*, and the Juggler is accorded the *aleph*: it remains, however, the zero card. It is one of those fanciful images in which the crocodile lies in wait for the heedless wanderer. P. D. Ouspensky, in *A New Model of the Universe*, 1931, ch. V, examined the Fool card in the light of its being an esoteric symbol, 'a combination of Cabala, Alchemy, Magic and Astrology', but his claim that the designs go back to the 14th century is questionable. His description of the card seems to be based on a late 19th-century version, for he mentions the crocodile. *Meditations on the Tarot*, published anonymously by Element Classics Edition, 1993 (Eng. trans. Robert Powell), changes the order of the Fool, and ascribes it the

21 position in the sequence: there are other deviations proposed in the book which suggest an inadequate grasp of hermetic lore: this work relies too much on such inept esotericists as Eliphas Levi.

10. With this link (often made in the popular literature) we have a good example of how an occult blind works. The truth behind the blind is that, while the Fool is definitely linked with the Moon, his (or her) destiny is concerned with the Spiritual triad of Atman, Buddhi and Manas.

11. The opened Third Eye permits the possessor to see into the Spiritual world. It is not developed in the majority of people.

12. Karma is the 'law of consequences'. Karma is the accumulated consequences of action in present and previous incarnations. It is a sort of ragbag of unresolved past misdeeds, and there is good reason for believing that the bag hanging on the stick over the shoulder of the Fool was intended as a symbol of accumulated karma. Those early cards which depict the stick of the Fool coloured in yellow were really reaching into the esoteric tradition, for the feather of *Maat* was yellow (see n.14).

In its more sophisticated definitions, karma is seen as the determinative of birth, experience and destiny in a lifetime. During a given lifetime the incarnate entity is (usually unconsciously) working out karmic consequences carried over from previous incarnations. Since karma is a powerful driving force in the life of the individual, it appears often to militate against free will. The free will element is operative prior to birth, when the individual elects to return to the material plane – a return which alone permits the amending of previous action, and the cancelling of particular karmic debts. In this sense, karma is the binding force which keeps humanity tied to the wheel of rebirth.

Non-initiated humans carry within their Spiritual organism all the memories of past actions – of things which they have *done*. We emphasize the verb because karma, in its Sanskrit origin, emphasizes the act of doing, as it is from the root *kri*, 'to do'. What we do (in thought, word and deed) on the material plane has consequences for the future of the world, and for our own future lives. The karmic impulse is such that it drives us towards the redemption of all evil deeds, often in some future lifetime, where opportunity for such redemption is prepared. Karmic drives are not concerned merely with evil, however: our past good deeds flower in the future as some unexpected benefit.

13. In Latin, the *aetherius* was the realm of Heaven, or 'the upper world'. However, this *aether* could be found in living material bodies.

14. The name of the Egyptian goddess, *Maat*, means 'straight', and is associated with the idea of the 'straight way' of law and order. *Maat* is goddess of the Underworld, where she sits with Osiris as a judge of the dead. The feather she uses to weigh against the soul of the newly deceased is also called *Maat*. Thus, the word *Maat*, so intimately linked with the French *mat* and the Italian *matto*, both meaning Fool, is as straight as the stick in the hand of the Fool, and denotes also the balance. Just so, the Fool balances the stick over his shoulder, carrying the bag, his sin of *karma*. Let us hope that the bag is at least as light as a feather, or he will not pass Maat in the underworld.

15. The physical body is sometimes called 'the Great Mystery' in esoteric literature. In the arcane tradition, it is maintained that in the distant future the physical body will be redeemed and spiritualized: this will be the 'body of light rays', the *augoedeian body* in the hermetic terminology (see n.7). In the Theosophical terminology, this will be when the physical has been transformed to *Atman*. The redeemed physical – a level of glowing perfection – is evident in the Christian resurrectional traditions and images. Needless to say, the advanced imitation of Christ is limited to very few extremely developed initiates.

16. The tear in the clothing allows us to see the body within. On a symbolical level, it suggests that, in order to complete his journey, the Fool must be prepared to strip away his covering – to drop the *persona*, or mask, which hides his Spirit. The

personality must be burned in the *aestum* or fire. The Fool of the Tarot cards wears shoes, while the beggar of the French *Apocalypse* image is bare-footed. The bare feet are intended to show that the beggar, and the seated man he importunes, are not on the material plane. They are both Astral figures. In contrast, the Fool is walking the hard Earth.

17. The *Feast of Fools*, held in mediaeval times, was sometimes called the 'Feast of the Asses'. The custom seems to be a continuation of the Roman mockery of Mystery customs (*asini portant mysteria* – asses carry the mysteries), in which the symbols were carried in special ritual boxes on the backs of asses, during the time when the Mystery processions were being held. The truth recognized by the Fool is that the ass (the physical body) does indeed carry Mysteries.

   The word *Ass* has probably been adopted by those who follow the Way of the Fool because of certain secondary meanings within the Green Language. The esoteric strain of symbolism is linked with the origins of money: the *aes rude* was a weight of specific value, the equivalent of a 'pound'. When these 'weights' were later stamped with an image – as it happened, the images of animals – they were called after the imprint, the *pecus* or herd of cattle. This became *pecunia*, as a word for wealth or money in general. Our own English word *pecuniary* has this interesting origin.

   The *as* is virgin metal (or earth) stamped with the image of an animal (Etheric and Astral) to give it a value (Ego). Perhaps more important is the fact that the Latin *as* is linked with the 'perfect number'. The physical body is ascribed the earth-number 4 (because of the elements) and may be perfected. The perfect body is the resurrected body. It is ascribed the number 6, the *numerus perfectus*, on the grounds that $1 + 2 + 3 = 6$. This simple numerology seems to have been at the basis of the Roman system of dicing, and behind the importance accorded the six. The six-petalled flower, and for that matter, the six-petalled centre to the mediaeval mazes, is linked with the Mysteries of this number.

   In Latin *aes* was any crude metal dug from the ground (the Gothic *aiz* was copper or gold; the German *eisen*, for 'iron', seems to be derived from the same origins). We can sense in these meanings something of the alchemical ideal – to transmute crude metals – the *Ass* – to reveal the gold hidden within. St Francis' famous phrase, 'Brother Ass', in reference to his own body, takes on a different meaning in the light of these reflections.

18. In the second century AD, Apuleius wrote about the Isis mysteries in his *Golden Ass*, xi, yet would not reveal all the secret aspects of his initiation – no doubt because of his vow to withhold such knowledge from the profane. In spite of this, from the details he leaves, it is evident that he was initiated to a very high degree (see p.378, n.30). A year or so after his initiation into the Isis rites, Apuleius was initiated into the Osiris Mysteries.

   It is of interest to those on the Way of the Fool that Apuleius tells the story of his adventures among the initiation centres through the persona of Lucius, who, in consequence of being prepared to use black magic (of which he is ignorant), is turned into an ass. Lucius is finally changed back to human form by Isis.

19. Apuleius was writing in the second century of our era, and probably had in mind the explanation of the symbolism of the magical sistrum from Plutarch's *De Iside et Osiride*.

20. Those who read the wild Latin of Lucius Apuleius would have known that the Latin for rose, *Ros*, was also the name used for the dew-fall from Heaven, the secret liquor of the Moon, which was one of the mysteries of the *Ros*icrucians (see p.449).

21. The Italian esotericist, Marsilio Ficino (1433-1499), worked closely with the Medici, and in particular with Cosimo de' Medici. He has been accused of lack of originality, and of being a store of ill-digested erudition, yet he was a powerful instrument in the injection of the Neoplatonic stream of arcane thought, and of esoteric astrology, into Western esotericism.

22. The link between the Graces and the higher ternaries was widely explored in esoteric literature. See, for example, Edgar Wind's *Pagan Mysteries in the Renaissance*, 1967 rep., esp. ch. II, 'Seneca's Graces', and Appendix 6, 'Gafurius on the Harmony of the Spheres'. See Pico dell Mirandola, *Conclusiones*, xxxi. 8. Jean Seznec, *The Survival of the Pagan Gods. The Mythological Tradition and its Place in Renaissance Humanism and Art*, 1953 Eng. trans. (p.115), recognizes that Botticelli was inspired to adopt it as one of his themes for the esoteric work now wrongly entitled '*Primavera*', and for 'The Birth of Venus'.

23. *Maya* is a Sanskrit word conveniently translated as 'illusion'. However, it refers to all manifestations of matter in the material world – that is, to the notion that the whole of creation is an illusion, or a sort of shadow-projection of a higher realm. Indeed, some linguists trace the word back to a meaning linked with the shadow-puppet plays of the Orient.

24. I write of Shakespeare as though he were a single person, when Mark Hedsel insisted that, on serious investigation, Shakespeare turns out to be little more than a convenient myth. It would be rash to identify the person or persons who wrote the Shakespearean works, but there is a fair certainty that Francis Bacon was the main author. However, it is not a point I wish to labour here.

    The life-size bronze statue by James Butler on a pedestal in the road which fronts the western face of Shakespeare's house in Stratford-upon-Avon was unveiled in 1994. In its enthusiastic joy, this statue catches the very essence of the Fool. Perhaps more important, from our point of view, is that in its gesture it reaches into the secret symbolism of the Fool: the triple foolscap on the stick he holds aloft is reflected in the triple cap on his own head. Taken together, the two indicate that the Ego of the Fool (so beautifully represented in the hole, or *zero*, of the head covering) stands between the three upper 'bodies' and three lower 'bodies', as set out in Table 1, p.21.

25. In esotericism, the word *veil* is often used to denote the screen which hides the Spiritual world from the eyes of those without higher vision. In a sense, this *veil* is Nature herself. 'Lift not the painted veil, which those who live call Life', wrote Shelley, in a sonnet. Of course, the veil worn by Isis is even more famous than Shelley's painted veil: it is the covering of the goddess which must not be lifted by the uninitiated. In some accounts the outer veil is black, and the ones below studded with stars.

26. Goethe said that Hamlet was 'A soul quite unable to cope with any situation, nor be satisfied with it; a soul on which was laid a task it could not fulfil.' See R. Steiner, *The Gospel of St Mark*, 1950 trans. of stenographic notes taken during the 1912 Basel lectures, ch. I, p.13ff.

27. We suggest that some may see this as a mistake because the second card in the series, the Juggler, echoes in the positions of his arms the form of the *aleph*. The Juggler, through his outer actions, brings the *aleph* of 'one' into manifestation. The Fool is not involved in such display, but concentrates on the Way, upon the road before him. Many of the changes imposed upon the order, numeration and design of the Tarot cards in *soi-disant* hermetic groups at the end of the 19th century seem to have obscured much of the graphic wisdom in the older series.

28. *Hamlet*, III, i. It is significant that the soliloquy is hedged in by the word 'Lord' (spoken by Polonius to the King) and 'Good my Lord', spoken by Ophelia. In esotericism, the Ego is the Lord of the lower bodies – the Astral, Etheric and Physical.

29. Paracelsus' Latin motto read, *Alterius non sit, qui suus esse potest*. The motto heads the portrait of Paracelsus which appears in his *Opera Omnia*, but it is more available for modern readers in A. E. Waite, *The Hermetic and Alchemical Writings of . . . Paracelsus the Great*, 1894, 1967 University Books rep. The portrait shows an interesting parallel with the Fool card, for his right hand rests on the hilt (line, or upright I) of the sword, while his left hand rests on the round pommel (circle, or zero).

30. The French and Italian names, with their Sanskrit-like roots, were used on the earliest-known named images of the Fool which were printed on Tarot cards in the 16th and 17th centuries. It is possible that the esoteric groups which designed these cards were aware that there was another line of etymology, derived from ancient Egyptian, which added significance to the sound *ma*. See following n.31

31. It is most interesting, in view of the etymology mentioned in our text, that the Jacques Vievil deck (mid-17th century) gives simply *MA* as the printed version of *Le Mat*, or Fool, of the Tarot pack. The Italian name *Il Matto* was certainly used by 1534. The 16th-century French tradition generally eschews a name, yet one Parisian version, now in the Bibliothèque Nationale, gives *Le Fous*; however, by 1707, the word *Le Mat* began to dominate, with *Le Fol* a close second. The significance of the Sanskrit *Ma* is discussed by Mark Hedsel on p.149.

32. Van Eyck's extended signature was: *Joannes de eyck fuit hic. 1434*, in a legal script, and showed his own reflection in the mirror – possibly to record that he was witness to the marriage. The painting (No. 186 in the National Gallery Catalogue) shows the marriage of Giovanni Arnolfini and Giovanna Cenami. Perhaps it is no accident that this stamp of the Ego shows the artist reflected in a mirror which is in the shape of the zero. The signing of a work is witness to a change in outlook – the artist is now dedicating his or her work to the Self, to the Ego, rather than wholly to God.

33. For Herri met de Bles as an Adamite, see F. Gettings, *The Hidden Art*, 1978, p.71ff. For Hieronymus Bosch, see W. Fraenger, *The Millennium of Hieronymus Bosch*, 1952.

34. See Heinrich Khunrath, *Amphitheatrum Sapientiae Aeternae*, 1602. S. K. de Rola, *The Golden Game*, 1988, reproduces the Dutch version of the owl vignette, from the 1653 edition of Khunrath's work: just as *eule* (owl) in German had a hidden meaning (for *eulenspiegelei* meant 'fooling around', or 'practical joking'), so the Dutch *briln* (eyeglasses) is linked with light.

35. Translations of the commentaries on the *Book of Dzyan* appear in H. P. Blavatsky's *The Secret Doctrine*, 1888, which is, to all intents and purposes, an extensive commentary on these commentaries. G. S. Arundale (n.36) offers translations of the seven stanzas of Dzyan, in what he calls the Secret Doctrine Version and the 'original' (see p.23ff).

36. G. S. Arundale, *The Lotus Fire. A Study in Symbolic Yoga*, 1939.

37. As will be evident from the biographical details offered by Mark Hedsel, the Way of the Fool attempts to combine both the *epoptic* and *mystes* methods. However, it is clear that Mark Hedsel himself, in tune with his own temperamental disposition towards scholarship and research, worked mainly with the latter – with spoken words, dialogues and personal study. See however the epoptic symbols in the Appendix.

38. Rosicrucianism is the esoteric movement which, inspired by the legendary initiate Christian Rosenkreuz, introduced a working system of esotericism, informed with alchemical and astrological terminologies, which examined Christianity in the light of occult knowledge. It emerged from an underground stream of hermeticism just about the same time as the Catholic Church experienced the vast schismatic upheavals of Protestantism, which was itself a reflection of the imperatives within the newly developed Ego. In some respects, Rosicrucianism is the equivalent of Christian hermeticism, but many of its beliefs – particularly those relating to reincarnation and the Spiritual model of Man – prove unacceptable to the modern Church. For a profound modern study of the implications of this conflict, see S. O. Prokofieff, *The Case of Valentin Tomberg. Anthroposophy or Jesuitism*, 1997.

39. Esoteric Christianity is that stream of Christianity which may be traced back to the hermetic Schools of the first and second centuries of our own era. As a body of thought which lays great emphasis on personal responsibility, and upon the teaching of reincarnation, it has often been in conflict with the official doctrines of

the Church. The modern instrument of esoteric Christianity is the Rosicrucian stream.

40. See Paul M. Allen, *A Christian Rosenkreutz Anthology*, 1968, and Fr. Wittemans, *A New and Authentic History of the Rosicrucians*, Eng. trans. by Durvad, 1938. The latter, quite rightly, admits that the 'investigation of the origins of the Rosicrucians takes us to a distant past'. However, Michael Maier (whom Wittemans quotes) was writing of the hermetic tradition, rather than specifically of the 'German Brotherhood of the Rosy Cross': thus, when explaining the silence of the Brotherhood in regard to its applicants for membership (in his *Silentium post Clamores* of 1617), he seems to trace the latter back to the Hindu Brahmans, the Egyptians, Eleusis, Samothrace, and so on. Maier was merely confirming the authenticity of the Rosicrucian movement. By the early 17th century it was a commonplace to trace the roots of hermetic movements to Egyptian origins.

41. The progression from alchemy to chemistry, which followed on the fission of the esoteric line of the former, is well documented. The great Jean Baptiste van Helmont is rightly viewed as the father of modern chemistry (we owe to him even the simple word *gas*), as he was among the first to apply chemical remedies, yet even van Helmont was a disciple of Paracelsus. His son, who shares the father's portrait in the posthumous 1652 edition of *Ortus medicinae, id est, initia physicae inaudita*, was one of the most influential Rosicrucians of the 17th century (see p.405, n.44).

42. These are the 'Three Principles' of the alchemists: Salt appertains to the thinking life, Sulphur to the willing, or sexual, life, and Mercury is the mediator, in the zone of feeling. In accordance with the principles of 'veils' used in alchemy and Rosicrucianism, none of these three 'principles' is the substance itself.

For an esoteric view of the principles, see Jakob Boehme, *The Three Principles of the Divine Essence*, 1634, 1909 Masonic Temple, Chicago, rep. While Boehme sometimes uses other terms than the three alchemical words, the fact is that, for all his complex language, Boehme is really the first to take the lid off the secrets enshrined in the esoteric notion of the three principles. See, for example, what Boehme had to say about the principles in his *Clavis*: having remarked that the ancients do not use the terms in reference to the material but to the Spiritual aspect of things, he says: 'by *Salt* they understood the sharp metallic desire in nature; *Mercurius* symbolized to them the motion and differentiation of the former . . . *Sulphur* signifies the anguish of nature'. Boehme, like the ancients, recognized that the three have significance only in relation to the seven: see therefore F. Hartmann, *Jacob Boehme: Life and Doctrines*, 1891, p.71ff.

In the more recondite esoteric images, Mercury is represented in a dog-headed icon – consistent with the mercuric *Thoth* – while Sulphur is represented with a goat-headed icon. The sublimation of the goat was part of the great work of the Templars, which is why the goat-fish of Capricorn is so often associated with the Order.

43. The idea of there being a pre-Christian Christianity may appear absurd. However, there is a considerable body of evidence to show that the initiation Schools of pre-Christian cultures were preparing for the descent of the Logos, which appeared in the being of Christ – indeed, certain Schools saw their own validation in preparing for such a descent. The redemptive purpose of Christianity was recognized by advanced initiates long before Christ came to Earth, even if the cosmic implications were not perceived. The fact that there was a relationship between the old Mysteries and the inauguration of the New Mystery of Christ is reflected again and again in the uses made in the New Testament of phrases from the Egyptian Mysteries. Naturally, most of these references have been misunderstood by scholars not familiar with initiation lore. See, for example, G. Massey, *Lectures. The Logia of the Lord; or the Pre-Christian Sayings Ascribed to Jesus the Christ*, 1900.

44. Parthey has his information regarding Plato from Clement of Alexandria,

Stromateis; on Pythagoras and Eudoxus from Plutarch. His list includes Appuleius, Archimedes, Diodorus Siculus, Euripiedes, Herodotus, Melampus, Solon, Strabo and Thales.

45. The Egyptian goddess *Ast*, whose name means 'Throne', was called Isis by the Greeks. She was wife and sister of Osiris, and both a magician and teacher. This explains why (at least in the Greek phase of her Mysteries) the priestesses who taught within her Schools were often called Isis. Isis was the sister of Nephthys, and most modern esoteric Schools, which have adopted Egyptian mystery lore, tend to see Isis as representative of the Light Moon, Nephthys as representative of the Dark Moon. The teachings of the School of Isis and Osiris (but mainly in connection with the former) are partly revealed in Plutarch, *Concerning the Mysteries of Isis and Osiris*, of which the best translation and commentary is G. R. S. Mead, *Thrice-Greatest Hermes. Studies in Hellenistic Theosophy and Gnosis*, 1964 ed., p.178ff.

Osiris was probably the most important of all the Egyptian gods in the ancient Mysteries. There are very many myths about this god, some of which express esoteric ideas: he is the ruler of the Kingdom of the Dead. Since the pupil is often identified with the teacher in ancient times, those who die in an initiatory sense are sometimes referred to as Osiris.

46. Gnosticism is the word applied to the vast, mainly syncretic, literature which has its roots in a combination of Zoroastrian, Platonic and Christian teachings. It is the survival of the Gnostic literature, intermingled with the hermetic literature, which has contributed to the development of non-Judaic occultism in the Western world. See, for example, Jean Doresse, *The Secret Books of the Egyptian Gnostics*, 1958, in the Philip Mairet ed. Doresse's dedicatory quotation, from the Naassene Gnostics, in the *Philosophumena* (V.10.2), reads: 'I will unveil every mystery; I will denounce the appearances of the gods and, under the name of Gnosis, I will transmit the secrets of the holy way.'

47. The ancient Mysteries seem to have taught the secrets of reincarnation through the 'blind' of *metempsychosis*. The blind has worked so well that many modern scholars really believe that the ancients taught that human Spirits could be reborn in animal form. However, this misconception is corrected by both Plotinus and the early hermetic literature, the latter of which insists that 'the will of the Gods for ever preserves the human soul from such disgrace'. See Mead (op. cit., I, p.302ff).

The astrology of the hermetic texts rarely sinks to the level of modern astrology, which on the whole is designed to serve the lower demands of the Ego. It is entirely Spiritual, never failing to regard the planets and zodiacal signs as living beings. The planetary and Spiritual spheres – through which the departed soul ascends after death, and descends prior to rebirth – are far more clearly described in the hermetic texts than in modern arcane literature.

While the hermetic documents do not use the Sanskrit *karma*, they do refer to gods and goddesses who perform the functions of the karmic deities under the control of *Adrasteia*, or *Nemesis*, who have 'the instrument of power of sight that cannot err'. See 'The Virgin of the World', ch. XXV, p.71 of Mead (op. cit., III).

48. Shakespeare, *Hamlet*, III, 1. Mark Hedsel alluded to this play frequently because it is an initiate play specially written to set down the conditions relating to the growth of the human *Ego*, which would take place in the West, after the late 15th century. It is typical of the genius of the writer of *Hamlet* that throughout this famous lengthy 'To be, or not to be' soliloquy (which deals with the tribulations of the Ego) Hamlet does not once use the word 'I'. The soliloquy is sealed when Ophelia speaks to him, at which point Hamlet immediately resorts to the personal pronoun. The word is Hamlet's mask. In some esoteric Schools, preliminary exercises involve neophytes talking for relatively long periods without using the first personal pronoun. There is an amusing reference to this in the beautifully crafted *The Magical Dilemma of Victor Neuburg*, 1965, p.23, by Jean Overton Fuller.

We suspect that *Hamlet* can be understood in its full depth only when it is perceived as an initiation play, on the same level as Goethe's *Faust*. Just as Marguerite is a shadow embodiment of Faust's soul, so is Ophelia a shadow embodiment of Hamlet. Her name in Greek approximates to 'that which is bound by debt'.

49. The Language of the Birds is one of several names gives to the hermetic language of esotericism. As a language, it flourished in the late mediaeval period, especially in Rosicrucian and alchemical circles. For examples of use, see Fulcanelli, *Les Demeures Philosophales*, 1979 Pauvert ed., and (especially the glossary of techniques on p.394), D. Ovason, *The Secrets of Nostradamus*, 1997.

50. *Senzar* is described by Blavatsky as 'the early hieroglyphic cypher' of the mystery Schools. She says that this form of writing was invented by the Atlanteans (see *Secret Doctrine*, II, p.439 – but see also I, xliii, where she writes that it 'was known to the Initiates of every nation, when the forefathers of the Toltec understood it as easily as the inhabitants of the lost Atlantis . . .'). However, part of the mysterious *Stanzas of Dzyan* which form the background to *The Doctrine*, said to have been 'written' in Senzar, are similar to the *The Hymn of Creation* in the *Rigvedas*.

Blavatsky, while admitting that the *Book of Dyzan* is in the ancient language of Senzar, points out that the text appeals 'to the inner faculties rather than to the ordinary comprehension of the physical brain'. See *Secret Doctrine*, I, p.21. In fact, this is true of virtually any language of symbols (as opposed to secret alphabets).

51. G. Wachmuth, *The Evolution of Mankind*, 1961, Eng. trans. by N. Macbeth.

52. The Atlantis literature is now vast, but in the 19th century, the two most influential books were Ignatius Donnelly, *Atlantis. The Antediluvian World*, 1882, and W. Scott-Elliot, *The Story of Atlantis and The Lost Lemuria*, 1896. Scott-Elliot published some magnificent colour-maps, in surprising detail, showing the areas of Lemuria and Atlantis overprinted on the modern map of the world. In his *Lost Continents. The Atlantis Theme in History, Science and Literature* (1954, 1970 ed.), L. Sprague de Camp rightly calls these 'Theosophical Maps'.

53. The Atlantis myth persisted in many other sources, in addition to Plato: even Plutarch mentions an attempt made by Solon to write an epic poem about the 'island'. As late as the sixth century, Kosmas (better known as Indikopleustes, because he journeyed to India) was still mentioning Atlantis – ironically (for such a widely travelled man) to prove that the world was flat. For a balanced survey of Atlantis, and the migrations of people consequent to the cataclysms, see G.Wachmuth, op. cit., n.51, p.61ff.

54. The archives which Solon had claimed were in the ancient libraries of Egypt (see n.55) are either lost or indecipherable: we presume they were in the ancient Senzar, which is said in the initiate language to have been the prototype of the Egyptian hieroglyphics (see n.50). Those arcanists who investigate Atlantis do so by means of the *Akashic Records* – see page 459, n.92.

55. The 'History of Atlantis' which Plato had from the Egyptian teachers, by way of the Athenian law-giver, Solon, is told in his *Timaeus* and *Critias*, and forms the basis for many modern books and speculations about the lost continent. Plato tells us that Solon (who had lived in Egypt for ten years, during the sixth century BC) had learned this history from Egyptian priests, who had records in their ancient libraries. The last part of Atlantis seems to have sunk about 9500 BC, but prior to this, the continent had been through many catastrophic upheavals.

56. G. Wachmuth, op. cit., ch.5.

57. There is no satisfactory history of esotericism available in published form.

58. For brief definitions, see Powis Hoult, *A Dictionary of Some Theosophical Terms*, 1910.

59. Owen Barfield, *History in English Words*, 1953, 1969 rep., p.85.

60. Gerald Massey, *A Book of the Beginnings*, 1881.

61. Massey, op. cit., vol. I, pp.225-6.

62. Rudolf Steiner (1861-1925) was the foremost esotericist of his period. At the turn of the century, he was deeply involved in promulgating certain of the views of Theosophy, but he eventually broke away to establish his own 'Spiritual Science' under the name of Anthroposophy. He gave a prodigious number of lectures on a wide variety of arcane subjects.

63. Steiner gave many lectures on different aspects of Rosicrucian thought: a good introduction is probably the series of lectures he gave in Munich, in 1907: available in English as *Theosophy of the Rosicrucian*, 1966. See also the lectures he gave in Berlin, 1905: available in English as *Foundations of Esotericism*, 1983. Within Rosicrucianism lay strains of the hermetic traditions of Christianity which had been forgotten or lost by the Church. Its members undertook a rigorous programme of self-discipline and meditation with a view to establishing and understanding Christ on Earth. After the first flush of the Italian Renaissance (itself driven by esoteric groups) had died out in Europe, the Rosicrucians were the only Spiritual body with a sufficiency of arcane knowledge, and a sufficiently powerful organization, to influence the direction of European Spiritual life.

64. One may trace the roots of Rosicrucianism in ancient Egypt with equanimity only if one is prepared to admit that the ancient Egyptian Mysteries were themselves (among other things) in active preparation for the Mystery of Christ. This involves reading the teachings concerning the child Horus and the resurrection of Osiris as types of initiation which found fulfilment in the Christian Gospels. The fact that the Rosicrucian alchemists of the 17th century published documents and illustrations replete with Egyptian lore – or what they believed to be Egyptian lore – is some indication of this connection. The Rosicrucians themselves traced their heritage to the Egyptians – see for example Michael Maier's *Arcana Arcanissima* of 1614, which deals with 'the most secret secrets, which is to say, the Egyptian and Greek hieroglyphics, never hitherto known to the public . . .' Such literature is the result of the pressure of past-life memories flooding into consciousness. Maier is not unique in reacting in this way to what he knows within himself: we are all doing it, most of the time. Beyond such bibliographic arguments, we should point out that virtually all the main tenets of Rosicrucianism, such as reincarnation, the hierarchies of the Spirits, astrological theory, esoteric alchemy, etc., etc., were practised in ancient Egypt.

65. The idea that the *virga* stick of the Fool can give birth to a mannikin is expressed in a large number of popular images, and even in paintings by Hieronymus Bosch. For example, a detail from his *Ship of Fools*, in the Louvre, shows a Fool in a tree, drinking from a vessel, and carrying over his shoulder a stick carved at the end with a bulbous human head. Several of the Fools in woodcuts to Sebastian Brand's original book, *The Ship of Fools*, show similiar mannikin-heads, sometimes in the forms of tiny Fools, complete with cockscomb hats.

66. We use the word 'invite' to avoid polemics. In the magical tradition, one is supposed to *evoke* elementals and other lower beings, and to *invoke* higher Spirits. However, in modern times, there is so much confusion in magical circles as to what is lower and higher – as to what is demonic and what angelic – that the word *invoke* is rather in disrepute. Fortunately, the Way of the Fool has very little to do with either invoking or evoking. One *prays* by way of angels – one does not invoke them. The guardian angel, being alert to one's needs, does not need to be invoked, but sometimes things have to be clarifed by prayer.

   The word *magician* is usually explained in terms of the *Magians* of the ancient Persian cults, who were renowned for their power of magic working. However, the roots do go back to the Sanskrit *ma*, suggesting that the magician is the one who knows how to manipulate the Earth-forces (*matter*). This is more than mere etymological play – the fact is that the Magians of Persia seem to have been involved with shamanistic Earth magic which was very different from the Spiritual magic of the Egyptians. Shaman-magic takes its power from the ability to manipulate the Spirits of the lower Astral planes. The Egyptian magic, which informs the hermetic tradition of the West, is involved with the higher gods, and with what we would now call angels. The distinction is of profound importance, even in modern times. We should distinguish the magical operations which involve *mage*-working, or contact with Earth Spirits, and *im-mage*-working, which involves the use of images, derived from archetypes.

67. The cabbalist is the one who studies and practises the *Cabbala*, or esoteric tradition of the Jews. See W. Gray, *The Ladder of Lights*, 1971 ed., p.29. It is quite true that the intention to make a cup of tea may not appear to be magical, yet, because it involves the unconscious evoking of elemental Spirits, it is in fact a magical act. One cannot warm water without the aid of the salamanders; the water itself is the proper domain of the undines; the cup, utensils and the leaves being boiled are in the realm of the gnomes, while the steam is the domain of the sylphs. Once the veil is rent, the true Spiritual significance of even our most simple-seeming actions is revealed.

68. The term *Gnosis* is from the Greek word meaning 'Knowledge', and was adopted specifically to denote a Christian sect, arising early in the second century AD, which claimed to have a special form of knowledge – a magical system which combined Christian beliefs with earlier Platonic and Neoplatonic teachings. These *Gnostics* taught that knowledge, rather than merely faith, was the key to Spiritual growth.

The Albigensians were a large community of Christians, located in and around Albi, in the south of France, from the 11th to the 13th century. They were regarded by the Catholic Church as 'heretical' – probably because of their demonstrable connection with the Gnostic teachings, and perhaps with earlier streams of arcane Christian traditions. The Albigensians rejected sacraments, and were led by initiate-priests, the *Perfecti*, or 'perfected ones'. They were largely exterminated during the 'Albigensian Crusade' mounted by the Catholic Church. For the Templars, see p.331.

69. For Blake's spectre, see p.137ff.

70. *Fission* is an arcane term which relates very closely to its modern scientific use. Fission describes the separation of a given organism into two parts. One part is a released Spirituality which had been *in potentia* in the organism: this is liberated, and through the liberation finds its own development on the Spiritual plane. The other part represents a darkening, a solidification of the remaining part of the original organism. This darkens, and drops nearer to the Earth. The classical alchemical imagery for fission is the burning of a candle. The candle itself is separated into the light of the flame, and the darkness of the ash of the charred wick, and the smoke. Without fission, no development can take place. In terms of initiation, when a darkness in the soul begins to retard Spiritual development or evolution, it must be rejected. This rejection, with the corresponding liberation of Spirituality, is the actual fission. The new life which emerges from fission involves a kind of death. In effect, the constituent elements are being drawn to their natural habitations by this separation – the Spirit to the Heavenly planes, the darker elements to the Earth, or even to the demonic realms.

71. As we have noted, Plutarch in *Isis and Osiris*, and Apuleius in *The Golden Ass*, wrote about the Mysteries.

72. Rabelais in *Gargantua*, and (perhaps) the Comte de Saint-Germain in *La Trinosophie*, wrote about the Mysteries. For Rabelais, see *The Works of Mr Francis Rabelais . . . containing . . . the Lives, Heroick Deeds and Sayings of Gargantua and his Sonne Pantagruel*, 1653, 1931 Navarre ed. For Saint-Germain, see *The Most Holy Trinosophia of the Comte de St-Germain*, 1963 Philosophical Research ed.

73. Hedsel recognized that the three books of Dante's *Commedia* are an account of initiation experiences. See p.132.

74. Hedsel seems to have had in mind the Masonic opera, *The Magic Flute*, first produced in Vienna in 1791. In the final lines, the Priests of Isis sing:

Die Strahlen der Sonne vertreiben die Nacht,
Zernichten der Heuchler erschlichene Macht!
(The beams of the sun drive away the night
They destroy the stolen power of the Dissembler.)

The words are entirely Masonic, and while the opera-goer may get the general drift, it is unlikely that he or she will understand the meaning in its esoteric sense. Who is this *Heuchler*, or Dissembler, who became the 'hustler' of modern cant? And why is his power stolen, or gained by trickery (*erschlichene*)? With such questions we touch on the Secret of Secrets guarded by the priests of Isis.

75. Mark Hedsel seems to be quoting the dying prayer of the Roman Emperor, Claudius.

76. See Rabelais, op cit., n.71, bk, IV, p.144.

CHAPTER ONE

1. Hubert Butler, *Ten Thousand Saints. A Study in Irish and European Origins*, 1972, p.319.

2. Nigel Lewis, *The Book of Babel. Words and the Way We See Things*, 1994, p.201.

3. The word now widely used in occult literature for illusion, *maya*, is said to have been derived from the puppet-play images, in which shadows are cast on a screen from live-seeming puppets, which are in fact manipulated by means of strings.

4. Hermes Trismegistus, *Poemandres*, i. 3, 6-9. The quotation we use is from the fourth century, Firmianus Lactantius, *Divine Institutes*, iv.9., 1747 ed.

5. The word *Schrack* seems to be from the German verb, *schrecken*, which means 'to frighten' or 'terrify' – this is the effect of the planet Mars, when it is working through its negative aspect. Boehme's peculiar use of the word is unique. See for example C. A. Muses, *The Works of Dionysius Freher*, 1951.

6. In traditional astrology, Mars was accorded a rulership over Aries which was labelled 'positive', and a rule over Scorpio which was labelled 'negative': this classification goes back to pre-Ptolemaic structures. With the discovery of Pluto (first named Pluto–Lowell), in 1930, this new planet was accorded rule over Scorpio, and negative Mars was dispensed with. As a matter of fact, the Theosophist, Isabelle M. Pagan, pre-empted this change of rulership in *From Pioneer to Poet* (published in 1911), when she specified Pluto as the alternative to the traditional 'Negative side of Mars'. Pagan proposed a new sigil, a mirror image of Mars, which was not adopted by the astrological fraternity, and which was quickly replaced by the modern sigil that combines the initials for Pluto and Lowell.

7. This is a reference to the veil, or veils, worn by the statues of the goddesses in the ancient Mysteries. In the classical descriptions of the rites of Eleusis, when the final rite of the Degree of Perfection was attained, 'the sacred coverings dropped from the image of the Goddess, and she stood revealed in all her splendor'. See Albert Pike, *Morals and Dogma of the Ancient and Accepted Scottish Rite of Freemasonry*, 1871, p.433. Strictly speaking, the famous Isiac phrase probably means: 'No ordinary man may lift the clothing of Isis.'

8. When a new image of Buddha is made, a special rite of 'painting in the eye of Buddha' is held as a dedicatory ceremony.

9. For an account of *The Feast of Fools*, see p.368 n.17. The reference to Fulcanelli is *Fulcanelli: Master Alchemist. Le Mystère des Cathédrales*, 1971 Eng. ed., p.38.

10. The idea of the masked Fools walking into the nave of a church reminds us that the word *nave* meant 'ship', and is cognate with our *naval* or *navy*. This points to something of the meaning in the title *Ship of Fools*, the *Narranschiff*.

11. The *hamor* was the he-ass, the *athon* the she-ass. The resemblance between the four Hebrew characters for the latter and the alchemical *athanor*, or furnace, has excited many esotericists. The arcane relationship between the ass (which is symbol of the physical body) and the alchemical oven (which is also symbol of that

body) is reflected in other things than merely the similarities of sounds.

In biblical countries, due to a prohibition of the horse, there was no indignity in being seen riding an ass: indeed, asses were highly valued as saddle-creatures. Solomon was among the first notables to break the prohibition against riding the horse. The view of the ass as a creature of God goes back not merely to the symbolism of Christ riding the creature, when recognized as the Anointed King of Israel, but to the mystery of Balaam's ass, which could see into the spiritual world when its human rider could not (see p.338).

The alchemical oven, or *athanor*, is from the Arabic term *al tannur*, which means 'furnace'. The emphasis in the Arabic is on the function of the heating, while in the alchemical derivation emphasis is on the function of transformation. The *athanor* was a furnace-oven designed to maintain a steady temperature, maintained by a self-feeding system: it was therefore an ideal symbol for the human physical body, which is spiritually effective only within a narrow band of temperatures.

12. Jerusalem may be compounded of *yera* and *shalem*, 'foundation of peace'. A variant reading is *yerush* and *shalem*, 'possession of peace'.

13. Fulcanelli, op. cit., p.38, equates *Saba* with *Caba*.

14. The English version of 'land of Saba' is incorrect in Fulcanelli, op.cit., p.38. It should be 'land of Sabians', or even 'land of Sheba'.

15. The 13th-century monk Jacques de Voragine, in his *Legenda Aurea*, or *The Golden Legend*, tells the story of the Queen of Sheba's magical vision. The story is recounted in the magnificent fresco cycle of Piero della Francesca, in the church of San Francesco, Arezzo, finished about 1458.

16. The French pronunciation of *sabbat* is much closer to *saba* than the English. Fulcanelli might well be right in drawing a connection between these two words, as there is much dispute as to the origins of the word *sabbat*, as used in witchcraft. Nicholas Jacquier used the word about 1458, though descriptions of witch-parties, with the Devil as host, had been circulating ('fabricated', as Robbins says) among investigators and judges during the 14th and 15th centuries. Since the word *synagoga* was used in the early imaginative descriptions, and as Jews were often targets of religious oppression, it is quite possible that the *sabbath* could have been transferred to the other abused groups – the witches. See R. H. Robbins, *The Encyclopedia of Witchcraft and Demonology*, 1959 ed., p.415.

17. The esoteric nature of certain paper-marks probably explains the popularity of the Fool image in these designs. For a study of the influence of the early heretical groups on such designs, see Harold Bayley, *The Lost Language of Symbolism*. Bayley's thesis is that the early water-marks, which first appeared in the 13th century, when paper-making had been introduced from China to Europe, by way of the Arab traders, constituted a coherent system of emblems that enshrined esoteric knowledge.

18. K. von Eckartshausen, *The Cloud upon the Sanctuary*, quoted by H. Bayley, op. cit., 1988 ed. pp.30-31.

19. G. J. Witkowski, *L'Art profane à l'Eglise*, 1908. (For Fulcanelli's interest, see Fulcanelli, op. cit., p.38, where he discusses the Feast of Fools as *The Feast of the Donkey*; p.56, where he discusses the star in the stained-glass imagery of the *Conception of St Romain*; p.58, where he writes about Nôtre-Dame-du-Pilier at Chartres; p.60, where he mentions the *Isis* in *St Etienne, Metz*; and p.75, where he discusses the 'alchemical' image, in Brixen (Tyrol) of Christ mingling His blood with the milk of His mother, Mary.) Witkowski demonstrates little knowledge of arcane things, but is interested in pagan survivals and prurient symbolism, which he scarcely explains. It is likely that one reason why our Master delighted so much in his book is precisely because it is so deficient in explanation.

20. It would have been wonderful if our Master had been able to examine the magnificent modern work, *Art Profane et Religion Populaire au Moyen Age* by C. Gaignebet and J. D. Lajoux, published in 1985. To some extent this develops on

the work of Witkowski, though the text is far more charged with a knowledge of the arcane significance of the esoteric and popular art of the Middle Ages. It is a delight to see some of the images – of necessity engraved in Witkowski's book – reproduced in photographs. It is also instructive to see how certain erotic images, represented as undamaged by Witkowski, have, in less than a century, been damaged (see, for example. p.31).

21. See, for example, J. Cage, *Goethe on Art*, 1980, p.xv.
22. Witkowski, pp.180–1 (see plates 7 and 8). The two images depict sculpture in the west porch of St Pierre, Moissac. The porch has been badly eroded, and in some ways the Witkowski engravings are a greater aid to study than the originals.
23. Something of the symbolism of the toads is missed when the image is discussed in English. The French for toad, *crapaud*, is closely related in sound to *crapule*, a debauched or dissolute person.
24. Paracelsus called it the *ens veneni* – the principle of poison. It was more often called *ens vegetabilis* – see n.25.
25. For an example of *vegetabilis* for the Etheric, along with *animalis* for the Astral and *mineralis* for the physical, see the frontispiece engraving for J. J. Becher, *Mille Hypotheses Chymicae de Subterraneis*, 1668.
26. The Latin verb *seder* means 'to sit'. The prefix *pos* is from the Latin *potens*, powerful. The combination 'potent sitting' sums up the idea of demonic possession very well. In fact, the Latin verb *possidere*, meaning to take possession of, was used to denote demonic occupation from very early times.
27. According to Witkowski, this is from a translation (into French) of the biblical *Apocalypse of St John*, in the Bibliothèque Nationale, mss. no. 7013. In Witkowski, it is fig. 213 bis, p.181.
28. As is evident from the engraved version of the illumination, in mediaeval baptismal rituals the new convert was totally immersed in the water. Indeed, he or she was immersed three times, in the names of the Trinity. The mechanisms for such immersion still survive in some parts of Europe. See, for example, the great immersion well in the baptistry of Pisa, with the smaller dry protective wells intended to keep the officiating priests clear of the water, and the superb monolithic octagonal well in San Giovanni di Fonti, Verona. The initiatory role of the baptismal well is indicated in the *Splendor Solis* alchemical series, in which a bearded man is seated up to his shoulders in a huge vatlike cistern. The alchemist heats the water by blowing air on to the fire in the oven below the vat.
29. The Latin *idus* seems to have been linked with the idea of dividing, and hence marking half the month. The Ides fell on the 15th day of March, May, July and October, and upon the 13th of the other months. Since interest payments were legally due on this day, it was linked with making amends, with rectifying, and retained something of the lunar quality of the Sanskrit word from which it was derived.
30. Lucius Apuleius, *The Golden Ass*, bk XI, 25. Lucius records that as a consequence of his long initiation (prefaced by his trials as an ass) he was elected to the rank of the Pastophores (the college of shrine-bearers in the Isiac mysteries). Of course, the *Pastos* was a coffin, as well as a shrine. The word has survived into modern initiation Schools, and still symbolizes the outer form which contains the initiating Spirit. One recognizes that the ass was merely a *Pastos* form, which permitted Lucius to transform.
31. This was the *Isidis Navigium* of the Roman cult of Isis, which was celebrated on 5 March. A richly equipped and decorated ship was sent to sea as an offering to Isis. The *Pelusia* festivities of Isis, held on 20 March, were connected with the flooding of the Nile. The *Heuresis* festivities were in commemoration of the grief of Isis during her search for the body of her husband Osiris, on the last day of November.
32. See Apuleius, *The Golden Ass, Being the Metamorphoses of Lucius Apuleius*, bk XI, 23. His account is framed in the form of an occult blind (*per omnia vectus elementa*

remeavi – 'I was returned, borne through all the elements'). This indicates that he had been previously in an out-of-body experience, and now returned to the heavy physical body, composed of the elements.

33. Apuleius wrote, '*nocte media vidi solem candido coruscantem lumine*' ('at midnight, I saw the sun gleaming with a dazzling light'): see Apuleius, *The Golden Ass, Being the Metamorphoses of Lucius Apuleius*, bk XI, 23. We should mention the remarkable song 'Midnight Sun', which was popular in the early 1960s, and which we would listen to with great pleasure as a survival from such Mysteries. It was sung by June Christy, who had recorded it about 1959, in the 'Something Cool' album. In Christy's repertoire were several songs with distinct arcane associations, which she performed in such a way as to suggest that she knew about their inner contents. June Christy died in 1990.

34. For a note of the misunderstanding regarding the meaning of *peplon*, see Heinrich Zimmer, 'The Indian World Mother', in *The Mystic Vision. Papers from the Eranos Yearbooks*, 1969 (sixth vol.), p.78. What Zimmer does not tell his readers (perhaps because it is beyond his remit) is that the phrase is also mistranslated in regard to who, if anyone, is qualified to raise the clothing of the goddess. Just as *peplon* means woven clothing, so *thentos* means mortal. Such a word is often used to denote ordinary men, as opposed to the initiates, who are not liable to an ordinary death.

35. M. Briquet registered 1133 examples of the paper unicorn. See Bayley, op.cit., p.23.

36. In the mediaeval period, a sharp distinction was made between the religious and the laity. The religious had re-tied (*re-ligio*) their allegiance to Christ which not only permitted them to take the Blood and Body of Christ during the Mass, but to have access to parts of the church denied to the laity. The walled 'choir' at San Miniato al Monte, in Florence, was an area forbidden to the laity, and the pulpit was designed to serve this walled area as much as the remaining part of the church. The idea of exclusion in churches disappeared after the reforms of the 13th century, but traces of areas designed for initiates still survive. For example, Vezelay in Burgundy has a narthex, Chartres has the maze, San Miniato has the zodiac-circle, Sagrada di San Michele has the Staircase of the Dead, and so on. These are the points where the neophyte must stand before the Mysteries. Of course, the idea of the church fabric as a repository of arcane wisdom linked with initation law did not survive the mediaeval period. Even had it done so, it would have been strangled by the Council of Trent, which was the apotheosis of bureaucracy over art.

37. The word *Zelator* is derived from the Greek (by way of Latin) *zelotes*, denoting one who burns with jealousy. However, this is not ordinary jealousy, for the word contains within it the notion of an intense love, through the Latin *zelo*, 'to love ardently'. Within the hermetic literature, this burning jealousy is for higher things – a student is, for example, a jealous lover of the higher vision available to the Master, and one strives to attain this vision for oneself. The modern term *zealous* still retains some of the intensity of the original word.

38. The notion of all *matter* awaiting redemption is expressed in alchemy, and, in the hermetic literature, in the figure of the *prima materia* (pri*ma ma*teria) or 'first matter', being the basis of the work. In terms of the secret language (the Green Language) of esotericism, the *matter* is fissioned into *ma* and *ter*. The matter is the original Great Mother, the *mater*, the *Madonna*, the Spirit within things. The *ter* is the Earth, the dross, the *Terre* (Latin for 'Earth'). This separation into Spirit and Earth is described in many different ways in various esoteric groups, but the secret of the fission is rarely completely hidden. In the writings of Boehme, the *prima materia* is separated into *Fire* and *Earth*, though Boehme is careful to tell us that there are different forms of Fire. In this, Boehme is following a primal hermetic instruction, which points to the secret of the entire work. On the microcosmic, or human, level (as the initiate Albert Pike indicates), the Great Work is the creation

of Man by himself. (See A. Pike, *Morals and Dogma*, 1906 ed., p.773ff.) This is the creation of the Spiritual Man, the Fire-Man, the *Ignaeous Man*, from the Earth Man.

The *stone* of the alchemists (and for that matter, of the true Masons) is that which has to be *worked* and well squared. The *foundation stone* is the *prima materia*, which is why it is said to be inscribed with the Name. Whilst this Name is not sounded for anyone in the low degrees of initiation, it is the Name of the Godhead, that drop of the Godhead which must be released from the stone, to return to its origins. It is the *Sword in the Stone* of the Arthurian cycles.

39. Michael Maier was a German Rosicrucian and alchemist. He came to England in 1612, and learned the language with sufficient fluency to translate the alchemical work by Norton, *Ordinall of Alchemy*, into Latin. During his four years in England, he wrote several alchemical and Rosicrucian works, including the 'hieroglyphic' *Arcana Arcanissima* ('the most secret secrets'), 1614, which, as the modern scholar S. K. de Rola has shown (*The Golden Game*, 1988, p.60), was published in London.

40. The goddess of the Moon, Selene, put to sleep the shepherd Endymion, that she might possess him.

41. See Heinrich Khunrath's *Amphitheatrum sapientiae aeternae*, 1602, pl.5. The motto, *Dormiens vigila*, is at the foot of the architrave in the centre of the picture. Mark Hedsel chose his words with care: although printed on the eve of the 17th century, the privilege granted by Rudolph II indicates that the work was completed in 1598.

42. William Law, *The Works of Jacob Behmen, the Teutonic Theosopher*, 1772.

43. Hermes Trismegistus, the 'thrice-blessed Hermes', was the Greek name for the High Initiate, Thoth, the supposed fount of the hermetic literature. The quotation is one of the most widely quoted of dicta from the hermetic canon, and is usually taken from the *Poimandres*. After the blessing, the words open the hermetic *Emerald Tablet*, which had such a profound influence on alchemical and Rosicrucian literature. It is given in Latin by Henry Khunrath, *Amphitheatrum Sapientiae* . . . 1602. For a useful translation, see de Rola, op. cit., p.42.

44. The rich astrological tradition of the Arabs was funnelled, by way of translations, into Europe from as early as the 10th century, but did not reach its full momentum until the 11th and 12th centuries. It was at this time that astrological symbols were assimilated into Christian architecture. See, for example, F. Gettings, *The Secret Zodiac. The Hidden Art in Mediaeval Astrology*, 1987.

45. The constellation names on the bas-reliefs are Aquila, Delfinus, Pegasus, Deltoton, Orion, Lepus, Canis, Anticanis, Pistrix, Eridanus, Centaurus, Cetus, Nothius, Ara and Hidra. For a brief summary, see Giovanni Gaddo, *La Sacra di San Michele in Val di Susa*, 1977.

46. Hedsel appears to have got the day wrong. According to the surviving letter of invitation, the lecture was given at 12.30 on the afternoon of 25 August 1961 – a Friday, not Wednesday.

47. We had come across the sculptor Nicholas (or Nicholaus) who had carved the magnificent pulpit in the cathedral at Bitonto, but had to reject him on stylistic grounds. See, for example, G. Mongiello, *Bitonto nella Storia e Nell'Arte*, 1970, p.81. This Nicholas left his name on several 11th-century monuments in the south of Italy. It is possible that the Nicholaus of the Sagrada was altogether different, however.

48. Regrettably, even when we succeeded in interpreting the mediaeval code (see n.49), the identity of the sculptor was not revealed.

49. The uneasy dog-Latin, with its alchemical, astrological and even cabbalistic undertones, reads:

> *Dilexi secreta loca qui in arbore erant hostic factus est luminosus lapis cibus ante animalis et recedens de suprema rami arbor radicibus evulsa in terra quod ita domus ipsa fumabat*

50. In those days, it was possible to examine the bronze doors without impediment. Now, heavy wooden doors have been hung in front of them, partly obscuring the sunlight which used to pull out the figures with such distinction, as the afternoon passed.

51. In esotericism, the forces in the head (Aries) relate to the past life, while the forces in the feet (Pisces) relate to the future life. The panel is an imaginative illustration to Matthew xiv. 3-11. A series of monochrome plates depicting many of these panels is in Drutmar Cremer, *Ich Komme zu Euch. Bildmeditationen zur bronzetur der basilika San Zeno in Verona*, 1975.

52. Much mediaeval art depends for its symbolism on the Arabic traditions of astrology which had been newly adopted by Christian architects. This explains why historians who have not studied astrology fail to understand the deeper significance of mediaeval art.

53. The panel is wrought in what is called 'continuous representation', a device in which time is telescoped so that several actions, separated in the narrative, are represented in a single spatial plane. The technique actually goes back to Egyptian art, and is rooted in the notion that an image is eternal – which is to say that it is 'out of time'.

54. See J. J. Becher (op. cit., caption on page 25). The *vegetabilis* (that is, the Etheric) is represented as a tree.

55. They might also have called it the *Ens Veneni*, as it is likely that the term used by Paracelsus in the 16th century was even then in circulation among initiates. The men who sculpted these doors were certainly united with Paracelsus in initiate vision.

56. The 'discord in the pact of things' is from Boethius (*De Consolatione Philosophiae* V.iii), but Hedsel is probably thinking of that perfect poetical gloss by Helen Waddell, in the final pages of her Introduction to *The Wandering Scholars*, 1932 ed. Boethius is seeking out the hidden principles, behind form, admitting that our dull soul (the sleeping soul, which is encased in flesh – *caecis obruta membris*) does not know the secret laws which bind things in pact. In a word, he is lamenting that we cannot discern the Quintessence. The 'pact of things' is the pact between the Four Elements, which is maintained by the fifth, or Quintessence.

57. The relevant Latin inscription on the pillar read, *Flores cum beluis comixtos cernitis* ('You will see flowers and beasts mixed together'). In the secret language of the mediaeval world, the flowers relate to the Quintessential or Etheric plane, the animals to the Astral. The Latin is intentionally ambiguous, for besides pointing to the zodiacal roundels, it points also to the emblems above the earth beast and water siren on the capitals to the left side of the doorway. Above these two figures is a floral banderole with arcane roundel images of the planets. They are in a form which could be recognized only by initiates.

58. The flame-like *vesica piscis* is remarkably like the Egyptian hieroglyphic *Ru*. In fact, there are several interesting survivals from the hermetic tradition on this thoroughly Christian bronze door. The five-pointed star above the heads of the astonished shepherds is straight from the inside of the pyramids, a late development of the Egyptian *sba*.

59. For the eclipse, see p.345ff.

60. For an account of Joseph of Arimathea in England, see L. S. Lewis, *St Joseph of Arimathea at Glastonbury*, 1955. What Blake believed about Joseph is set down very clearly by S. Foster Damon, *A Blake Dictionary*, 1965. See in particular, pp.224-5, and the account of how Blake transformed his early copy of a Michelangelo engraving into an image of 'Joseph of Arimathea among the Rocks of Albion'. *Albion*, in Blake's vision, is England.

61. This has 44 fires on the periphery of the ring, but is designed to be viewed from both front and back, giving 88 flames.

62. For this star, see page 262ff.

63. The panel illustrates *Exodus* iv. 18 onwards, save that Moses is shown travelling without his family. The miracle-working rod (the Rod of God) in his hand is of profound importance in esoteric lore, for it is the first time that we read (in the Scriptures, at least) of a human being endowed with such power. The literary question is, who is 'the servant of the rod' – the magician who rides the ass, or the ass itself? ('Sad is it, thou servant of the rod, that the pack-saddle of ill luck hath stuck to thee', laments a mediaeval Irish poet, quoted by Helen Waddell. See W. Stokes, *Thesaurus Palaeohibernicus*, ii, p.290.)

64. In mediaeval mythology, the cat saved the ark of Noah (the symbol of arcane Schools) from a mouse, who was nibbling through the wood. While the cat devoured the offending mouse, a frog forced itself into the hole, thus saving the ark. The godly cat and demonic mouse is a popular theme in mediaeval literature and art. See, for example, the story of St Francis, in P. Dale-Green, *Cult of the Cat*, 1963, p.34. In the curious etymologies beloved by the mediaeval mind, the cat was one who 'lies in wait' (*captat*), and so sharp are her eyes that they penetrate the darkness with their own gleams of light. This light, as most classical sources, affirm, is a lunar light. See, for example, T. H. White, *The Book of Beasts*, 1956 ed., pp.90-1, which deals with both *Catus* and *Mus*.

    We must hazard a guess at the meaning intended by Mark Hedsel, as he left no notes as to what sort of response he expected from the girls. Perhaps he was drawing a link between the image and the Feast of Fools, which was a curious mockery of the Entry into Jerusalem. The Entry is an initiation image, representing even in ordinary symbolism Christ's triumph over death, as He enters the 'eternal city' of Solomon's Jerusalem. This 'triumph over death' motif is expressed in the Germanic term *Palmesel* (palm–donkey) used to denote the life-sized images of Christ on the ass which were used in processionals in mediaeval times. The palm – once an esoteric symbol – is now merely a symbol of triumph over death. In relation to the esoteric tradition of the cat, we should record that Fulcanelli notes that, in one sacred language, the word *ka* is used to denote the cat: the moustache of the cat is seen as sacred rays of light. This view is reflected in the esotericism behind the term *Chat-Noir*; the black cat is the dark cat – the dark *ka*, and is hence almost the opposite of what is normally believed. Surely, this is the human Etheric which is being carried by Christ to be reborn in Jerusalem. See Fulcanelli, *Les Demeures Philosophales*, vol. I, 1979 Pauvert ed., p.345.

65. The door was knocked through the façade in the late 19th century, and is entirely unsuitable, either aesthetically or structurally. Since the late 1980s, however, this original main doorway has been used.

66. P. d'Ancona, *The Schifanoia Months of Ferrara*, 1955. Seznec is correct in seeing the surviving images in the topmost registers of the frescos as representations of the 12 Olympian gods: however, the figures around them are not (as he claims) their 'children', but depictions of details from the mythology linked with the central Olympian. See J. Seznec, *The Survival of the Pagan Gods*, 1953 Eng. ed.

67. Francesco del Cossa (1435?-1477) worked extensively in Florence, and was influenced partly by Cosme Tura. It is very likely that del Cossa and his pupils did not paint the entire Schifanoia cycle. That relating to Libra was probably the work of the youthful Ercole Roberti.

68. The decans are Egyptian in origin. Perhaps the oldest lists are those on the coffin lids from Asyut, dated to *c.* 2300 BC. The 36 decans of the early Egyptian astrology seem to have been very different from those which came to Europe by way of the Arabian astrology. For some mention of the Egyptian 'ten-day star system', see C. Fagan, *Astrological Origins*, 1971, ch. 7: 'Decans or Pentades'. With some justification, Fagan regards the original decans as pentades, pertaining only to the visible vault of Heaven. It seems originally to have been applied to a six-fold division of the zodiacal arcs, into 72 divisions of 5 degrees each. There is no doubt, however, that by the time the mediaeval world had received the decan system, it

was believed to relate not to pentades, but to decans. For a standard academic view, see W. Gundel, *Dekane und Dekansternbilder*, 1936.

69. The Latin term *facies* or 'faces' is often used confusingly in the early literature – perhaps a reflection of the fact that the original 36 divisions appear to have been pentades, rather than decans: see n.68. In some mediaeval texts, the word also appears to have been applied to the 'images' – to the 36 so-called 'genii' which were supposed to inhabit the decans. However, by the Renaissance, the words 'face' and 'decan' (literally, 'a division into ten degrees') were regarded as being interchangeable. The three images in figure 17 are actually called 'facies' in the text.

70. The rulerships varied, from system to system. The one which was adopted by del Cossa seem to have been based on the idea that the first decan should be ruled by the ruler of the sign (thus, in the figure on page 82, the first decan of Pisces – itself ruled by the planet Saturn – is ruled by Saturn). The second decan should be ruled by the next planet in descending sequence in the heavens (which is Jupiter), while the third decan should be ruled by the planet next in descent after this one (which in the case of the Pisces image is Mars).

71. For the Egyptian god Thoth as a monkey-god, see figure on page 191.

72. The name Ferrara is etymologically connected with the *ferraio*, or blacksmith. The archetypal blacksmith was Vulcan, who is the patron saint of alchemy. In the mid-eighth century, Ferrara was originally the *ducatus ferrariae*. It may well be this etymological link which explains the importance accorded Vulcan in the section for Libra.

73. The Vestal Virgins served at the altar of Vesta: their external duty was to preserve the flame at this altar, but it is evident that they served an esoteric School, for which the flame was symbol. The link with the fire-god Vulcan is evident. There were originally two Vestal Virgins, and later four. By the time Rome emerges into the stream of history, there were six, each serving for 30 years. They were required, on threat of death, to remain chaste. Ilia knew that in sleeping with Mars, she would meet her death. Those interested in the arcane associations which link alchemy with the Way of the Fool will be intrigued to learn that Vesta's creature is the ass.

74. In the best alchemical symbolic manner, the seventh is hidden from view, guarding the far side of the chariot.

75. Not a very elegant joke, but an attempt to play with the name Ferrara in the same way that tradition had played with the name word Schifanoia (see n.76).

76. The name Schifanoia is from the Italian *schivar la noia*, meaning 'do away with boredom'. The original 14th-century building was a sort of folly, designed by the d'Este family for entertainment.

77. For a survey of the influence of this 12th-century prophet-monk, see M. Reeves, *The Influence of Prophecy in the Later Middle Ages. A Study in Joachimism*, 1969.

78. The Leo sigil is ♌ and the letter M ♏.

79. Richard was right about the authoress, but wrong about the book in which the verse appeared. This poem is quoted in its original Latin in Helen Waddell's immortal *The Wandering Scholars*, 1927 (1934 ed., p.75, fn.1).

80. The full solution to the code is beyond the remit of this present work. However, its codification, which was resolved initially as a result of Richard Dayton's insight into the three words of the poem, is indicated in n.85.

81. For Vettius Valens, see Riess, *Philogus. Supplem. Frag. I.* For some of the preserved horoscopes by Valens, see O. Neugebauer and H. B. Hosen, *Greek Horoscopes*, 1959.

82. The quotation is after the translation of the Greek by G. R. S. Mead, *Thrice-Greatest Hermes*, 1906.

83. Julian the Apostate, *Oratio* IV. There is a translation of the relevant passages, by W. C. Wright, in Hans Leisegang, 'The Mystery of the Serpent', in *The Mysteries*.

Papers from the Eranos Yearbooks, 1971 printing, p.202ff.
84. For the Ether sigils, see F. Gettings, *Dictionary of Occult, Hermetic and Alchemical Sigils*, 1981. See the entries under 'Akyasha,' 'Etheric' and 'Quintessence'.
85. We had suspected that the long phrasing of the code had to be broken down, but Richard Dayton's recognition of the importance of the first three words indicated the probable truncations. We reduced the whole to some semblance of order by breaking the continuous text into seven sections, according to a verbal sense. Seven is a number favoured in mediaeval coding systems. The following observations pull together notes derived over a considerable period of time. However, it is fair to say that the code was broken on that day in Ferrara. The proposed septenary is:

> Dilexi secret loca
> Qui in arbore erant
> Hostic factus est luminosus
> Lapis cibus ante animalis
> Et recedens de suprema rami
> Arbor radicibus evulsa in terra
> Quod ita domus ipsa fumabat

Although, before decoding, these seven lines do not make for perfect translation, the following may be proposed:

> I have loved the secret places
> That were in the tree
> The sacrifice was made luminous
> The stone before the food of air
> And falling from the highest branches
> The tree was pulled from the earth by its roots
> In such a way the house itself reeked

The reference is to the notion of an esoteric content for the remaining Latin, for later in the same poem is a mention of the nightingale's song – *Philomena iam cantat in alto* ('for the nightingale is singing on high'), which is a clear enough indication of the secret Language of the Birds – one of the names given to the secret language of occultism.

The ambiguous letter M in *luminosus* gave us a clue to the notion that the luminosity (third line) related to the Sun (Leo being ruled by the Sun). This was confirmed when we located one of the three (or perhaps four) sources of the poem.

Four of the first six sentences appear to have been abstracted in part from an esoteric Christian text dealing with a vision relating to John of Parma. (See *Archiv für Literature und Kirchengeschichte des Mittelalters*, 1885, II, pp.126–7 and 280–1, which proved invaluable in the decoding of four lines). When completed from this vision, the third line reads . . . *luminosus sicut Sol* ('as bright as the Sun'), and confirmed our view that the Leo–M code related to Leo or its ruler, the Sun.

The curious phrase in the fourth line, *cibus ante animalis* ('before the air-food'), has little meaning in modern times, but, in Roman and mediaeval times, related to the idea of food which could be derived from the air – that is to say, Quintessential food. This is clearly the sanctified invisible eucharistic body of Christ.

The encoding of the word *piscibus* (of the fish) in the fourth line suggests that the living food of the air (*cibus . . . animalis*) is the hidden nutriment which is Christ. This is a reasonable assumption, as Christ is often portrayed in mediaeval imagery in the symbolic guise of Fish. Since He swims in the element of Water, the secret Aerial nutriment has been brought down to Earth (by the Mystery of baptism, perhaps?).

At all events, according to the John of Parma source, those who do not drink of this *Aqua Vitae* will be lost when the tree is uprooted. The uprooting of the tree is susceptible to many different levels of interpretation, but we see it as relating to the 'tree' in man, which is the spine: the uprooting of the tree is death.

Once the codification principles had been established, and once the source had been discovered, it was a relatively easy matter to interpret some of the hidden meanings in the Latin.

For example, so far as we know, there is no *hostic* (third line) in Latin. However, *Hostia* pertains to a group of stars located by mediaeval astrologers in the constellation Centaurus (one of the Constellations listed at the Sagrada – see n.45). *Hostia* also means 'sacrifice' or 'victim', and it is the combination of the idea of stars and sacrifice which explains why the suffix *c* has been applied. During our experience in Ferrara, when it became evident that *Hostia* was intended, with all its Christological overtones, we recognized that the suffix *c* must represent the first letter of *Christ*, who came from the stars, and who was sacrificed. The 'host' of the modern Christian sacrament is derived from the Latin *hostia*. There are further meanings, which hinge upon the fact that the cancelled *a* of *hostia* is the equivalent of the Greek *alpha* and that the omega is seen, in the esoteric tradition, as being a repetition of C (ᘓ). This mutation of forms is standard symbolism in the Joachimite codifications of the 12th century.

We must assume in the *recedens* of the fourth line a missing letter, perhaps once marked by an abbreviation symbol. This missing lower-case n, was one of the late mediaeval sigils for Saturn.

The last line, which has the Earth reeking with the smell of destruction, seems to be from Cicero's *Oratio pro Sestio*. The significance of this last line lies not merely in the fact that the end of the world is seen as the after-effects of an excessive banquet, but that an otherwise Christian message ends in a quotation from a pagan. The final message is that only the pagans will be lost, perhaps reeking in Hell. In other words, Hell and Earth become one and the same.

It is clear that certain of the images on the constellation pillar are reflected in this quaint dog-Latin: the fish of Nothius, so close to the Ara, or altar, as a sacrifice, for example; and the direct reference to Centaurus. Clearly, it is beyond our present remit to examine the meaning of this Latin in full. It is sufficient that something of its relationship to the Sagrada has been established.

86. The *kalahansa* is 'the bird out of space and time', who can descend into space and time. The term Hansa (or Hamsa), which is Sanskrit for 'swan', has been explained in more materialistic terms which define it as a particular earth-bird, but this is quite unnecessary. Brahma is called the Hansa-Vahana because his vehicle, or body (vahana), is the swan, or goose. It seems to be the equivalent of the European pelican, and, as Blavatsky points out, the Ein-Soph (the Endless and Infinite) of the cabbalistic tree is called the 'Fiery Soul of the Pelican'. See for example H. P. Blavatsky, *The Theosophical Glossary*, 1892, p.134. The swan of the alchemical images is the equivalent of the hansa bird in Western esotericism. The priest of the Mysteries, depicted on a fifth-century Greek vase (see C. Kerenyi, 'The Mysteries of the Kabeiroi', in *The Mysteries. Papers from the Eranos Yearbooks*, 1971 ed.), has a swan by his side, reminding us that the Greeks regarded its song as the most beautiful among birds – albeit it sang only at the very end of its life. The death-song of the bird has its own level of meaning in view of the fact that the Mysteries lay, in their lower degrees at least, at the portals of Death.

87. In his *Four Quartets*, the poet T. S. Eliot wrote of history as a series of timeless moments ('Little Gidding', V), but it is evident that he was using the term 'timeless' in the sense of 'eternal'.

88. *Vale*, which is the Latin equivalent of 'farewell', is said to be repeated three times out of respect for the three (higher) bodies of the human constitution. In some esoteric literature, the word has been hidden behind such Green Language as 'three veils', or 'three valleys', and so on.

89. The Latin *Ros* means both 'dew' and 'rose', and has sometimes been linked in the Green Language with 'tears of the rose'. In Rosicrucianism, the Rose is the perfect blood of the One who died on the Cross.

90. For an account of the Azoth, see p.399, n.8.

CHAPTER TWO

1. See Fraser's *The Dying God*, 1911, p.75ff. Fraser, who was immensely learned in matters of mythology, but extremely lacking in esoteric knowledge, saw such a dance as an attempt to aid the progress of the Sun across the sky. In such a way are esoteric truths completely misunderstood, even by learned gentlemen.

2. Plutarch, *Theseus*, 21.

3. The *Granitos* is also a precious stone.

4. In this sense, the word was widely used in regard to the mechanical contrivance used to lift scenery, etc., on the stage.

5. We know from our own experience that, in certain states of meditation, it is possible to feel the Earth move in space. One feels the planet Earth not so much moving in a path through space, as slowly rocking or swinging. One feels it involved in a slow dance. However, as with all such experiences beyond the ordinary threshold of knowledge, it is difficult to describe this precisely.

6. *The Most Holy Trinosophia of the Comte de St Germain*. The book we have before us was printed in 1962, and is a poor-quality facsimile. With it is a passable English translation, with a commentary and biographical introduction by Manly P. Hall. Almost all the biographical material and quotations have been lifted from Isabel Cooper-Oakley's monograph, *The Comte de St Germain*, 1912, and the assumption that this is indeed 'the rarest of occult manuscripts', copied from a work of Saint-Germain, is entirely suppositious. It seems to be early 19th-century Masonic, perhaps linked with an Egyptian ritual, such as the Memphis Rites. The 'explanation' of the coded languages furnished by E. C. Getsinger is not very helpful: the arcane text itself is more translucent than the commentary.

7. *Trinosophia*, op. cit., Section 5.

8. *Trinosophia*, op. cit., Section 5, p.37. The secret codes on the four blocks have not yet been translated, and are referred to in the manuscript merely as 'emblems'.

9. *Trinosophia*, op. cit., Section 5, p.37. The bird, which hovers above the altar, has black feet, a silvery body, a red head, black wings and a golden neck. This means that it is an alchemical bird, as black is Saturn, silver the Moon, red Mars and gold the Sun. However, its form is that of a crane.

10. Siva was the male generative power in the Vedic religion, who assumed terrible aspects through his associations with Kali, and other gods. Siva is often portrayed in his role as *Nataraja*, the Lord of the Dance, through the performance of which he is said to have converted thousands to the faith. Even in this dance, he is shown as the ruler over sexual energies, the subterranean fires. Sometimes he is depicted dancing, four-armed and multiheaded, in a ring of flame. It is quite fascinating that some examples of the statuary portraying this fire-dance have 44 nodes of fires on the outer periphery (see, for example, the dancing Siva on p.94 of Paul Carus, *The History of the Devil and the Idea of Evil*, 1969 ed.), since the number 88 was often linked with solar imagery in the West (see n.61 on page 381 for example): in the Siva statuary, the flames could be viewed from front and back, giving a total of 88. Usually, each of Siva's heads has a Third Eye. Besides being destructive, he is also merciful: when he and his wife, Parvati, embrace in the sexual dance, the whole world trembles, reminding us that Siva will rule over the End of the World.

11. T. S. Eliot, *The Four Quartets*, 1943.

12. The *vasanas* are streams of karma breaking into time from the past, yet this is not a satisfactory definition since in the higher worlds the past runs parallel to the present and future. The *vasanas* may therefore be thought of as the nodes of interpenetration from one time sequence into another.

13. For notes on karma, see n.15.

14. The Greek *phos* can mean both 'man' and 'light' depending upon accentuation. This word, rather than Adam, is used to denote the developed man, or the initiate, in such texts. The Race of Adam, or the Men of Flame, are ordinary mankind. The Race of Phos, or Men of Light, are evolved mankind, or those who have been initiated.

This application of the idea of a body of light was extended into the very highest levels of esoteric thought. The Greek-derived term for the transformed body of Christ is *Augoeidean*, meaning 'ray-like', or 'shining like the Sun'. It was this body which appeared to John in the Gospel mentioned on page 91. An equivalent Greek, *to photoeides*, meaning 'ray-like', is used by Plutarch, when describing the sacred robe of Osiris, who also rose from the dead. See *The Mysteries of Isis and Osiris*, Lxxvii.

15. The speculations seem to rest upon the similarity of the sounds *dam*, blood, and *edom*, red. *Adam* is often used with this interplay of meanings in the alchemical texts. See, for example, Jean Doresse, *The Secret Books of the Egyptian Gnostics*, 1960 Eng. ed., p.175. The hidden meaning (on which Doresse does not appear to touch) is the fact that fire also is red. Adam is the unredeemed 'Man of Fire'. The higher man, the one who through initiation can redeem the inner fire, loses the heat and becomes light only.

16. Karma can be redeemed only through *doing*, through being incarnate in a physical body. Hence the need for rebirth. The observations in n.14 relating to the difference between the Fire Man and the Light Man make sense in terms of this observation, since the Fire Man dwells in the flames of karma, which keep him in the body of Adam, while the Light Man is freed of karma.

17. Yet Salt is also 'potentiall fire, and waterish, that is to say terrestriall water, impregnated with fire . . .' *A Discourse of Fire and Salt, Discovering Many Secret Mysteries*, the anonymous work, was printed by Richard Cotes, and sold by Andrew Crooke at the Green-dragon in St Paul's Churchyard, 1649. In alchemy, there is a visible fire and a secret fire. The flame which rises has two lights, one of which is white. In the root of this white flame is the colour blue. The flame which 'is fastened to the weik that it burneth' (that is, to the wick) is of the colour red. The burning residue – which is smoke – is black (above with a white flame, below with the blackness of matter). The adept sees in the play of the candle flame the perpetual endeavour of the red flame to destroy that which nourishes it. *A Discourse*, p.6.

18. *Numbers* xviii. 19.

19. *Matthew* v. 13 seems to be an important source for the saying 'salt of the Earth'. However, Christ does not refer to peasants, but to high initiates. Somewhere along the line, the idea has been misunderstood. The original idea, as expressed in *Matthew*, survived in alchemy, for Salt was supposed to be a compound (if such a word can be used in an alchemical sense) of Sulphur (with all the resultant sexual connotations, and its important link with Fire, set out in n.17) and mercurial waters. *Salt of the Earth* is actually an alchemical term, an alternative for 'Mercury of the Sages' – the finished product of the alchemical operation. This contrasts with the Adamic Salt, the *Red Salt* which was the sulphur of the Sages, and thus Man still in birth (which is to say, in the process of initiation): it is sometimes called *Pansal* or Universal Salt. There were, however, such a wide range of different salts, and salines – usually symbolic of different stages in the Great Work – that any discussion of the alchemical nature of Salt is beyond the confines of the present work.

20. The *salinium* is the mediaeval Latin for salt-cellar. The Latin for salt is *salus*, but it was from the word used to denote sprinking before a sacrifice, and therefore had a deep religious connotation. It was, indeed, as religious in its original connotation as the *Salii*, and almost certainly carries the same Sanskrit-root origins. The *salillum* of the Romans was 'a little salt-cellar', and (significantly) the word was used to denote a symbol for 'a short span of life'.

In mediaeval times the *salinium* had considerable social significance, for it was placed on a dining table in such a way as to distinguish those of importance (who sat 'above the salt', and therefore nearer the hosts). Leonardo da Vinci, in his fresco of The Last Supper, has Judas knock over the *salinium* by accident, to reflect upon his status at the supper. We suspect that the importance attached to the *salinium* is of much the same order as the importance attached to the alchemical furnace: it was an image of Man, for the salt had within it both the Adamic red and the Light. Salt was therefore an excellent symbol of the immutable division between men, who are either Adamic or Phosphoric, in alchemical terms (or, of course, in conception, in the making, between the two). In alchemical lore, Salt contains both the red and the white, and is therefore capable of fission. It is, of course, difficult to speak about such alchemical interpretations in modern language, which has lost its feeling for secondary meanings.

21. See, for example, the notes culled from his *Chirugia Magna* by Waite, in *The Hermetic and Alchemical Writings of Paracelsus*, 1894, vol. II, pp.28-9, notes.
22. See Mabel Collins, *Light on the Path*, 1888, p.29.
23. E. C. Brewer, *Brewer's Dictionary of Phrase and Fable*, 1963 ed., p.794: see 'Spilling salt' under *Salt*.
24. See, for example, the Rosicrucian *Geheime Figuren*. An ornate version is in plate 'Mysterium Magnum', on the third register, between the wings of the double-headed eagles, but this is disguised, to make it a Christian form of salt. In this guise, it is the initiation salt, in which the sigil for salt has been combined with the sigil for the World, the orb held in the hands of God or Christ in mediaeval imagery. Thus, it is the 'salt of the Earth', mentioned in *Matthew* v. 13 – see n.19. Other versions of the sigil abound in the Rosicrucian and alchemical books: see, for example, Manly Hall, *Codex Rosae Crucis*, 1938, p.49.
25. See quotation in n.17.
26. The Latin *salse* means 'witty' or 'facetious', and described a style of writing – the word had the undertone of 'pickled' as salt was widely used as a preservative in Roman times.
    Esotericism distinguishes two forms of thinking – that which is mimetic, or mechanical, and driven by dreams; and creative thinking, a perceptive and active form of thinking. Goethe's words *anschauende Urteilskraft* ('perceptive power of thinking'), which is not ordinary thinking, are discussed by the translator O. D. Wannamaker in the 'Note to the Reader' in the 1950 ed. of Rudolf Steiner's *Goethe the Scientist*.
27. In Rome, there were two companies of *Salii*, each 12 in number. They were garbed in the old Italian war-dress, and the conical *apex*. On their left arms they carried shields decorated with a lemniscate (figure of eight), said to be copies of the *ancile*, or shield, given by Jupiter to Numa. Their Martian origins were evident from the rituals enacted at the opening and closing of the campaigning seasons, on 19 March and 19 October. Their elaborate leaps and dances were sometimes accompanied by songs, the *axamenta*, religious hymns which were originally written on wooden strips. The word *Salii* is from the Latin verb *salire*, 'to dance'. It is interesting to observe that this word, and the Greek from which it was derived, came from the Sanskrit *sal*, 'to go', and that the Greek equivalent, *allomai* (there is an important accented breathing on the first letter), throws some light on the significance of the dancing of Salome (see n.76ff).
28. The Palladium was the mysterious sacred shield, gifted by Zeus to Dardanus, who founded Troy. It was believed that the well-being and safety (the *salus*) of the city depended upon its preservation. It was stolen by Diomede and Odysseus, who thus prepared the way for the destruction of Troy. Eventually, the Palladium found its way to Rome, where it was hidden in the penus Vestae (sanctuary of the Vestal Virgins), and became a symbol of the safety and well-being of the city. It was rescued from a fire in the temple in 241 BC. Legends, which may have some historical truth in them, have the Palladium being transferred to Constantinople, where, as a talisman of the city, it was buried beneath a pillar in the hippodrome. Legends as to its later destiny flourish, but its location is no longer known. There seem to have been different Palladia claimed by many cities, most of them – like the *ancila* – gifted by the protector, Zeus.

29. The Language of the Birds, or Green Language, is the secret language of esotericism.
30. The wine was called *guinguet* because it made you jump (*guinguer*). However, it has been sanitized, and in modern French the *guinguette* is a suburban tavern, usually with a small garden for drinkers.
31. Fulcanelli, *Le Mystère des Cathédrales*, 1926. Fulcanelli was the first esotericist to deal openly with the complexities of the arcane secret language.
32. See K. Rayner Johnson, *The Fulcanelli Phenomena*, 1980. Because no one really knew who Fulcanelli was, speculation contributed imaginative solutions. He was a surviving member of the Valois, he was a Parisian bookseller, specializing in occult books, he was Jolivet Castelot, the President of the Alchemists Society of France and a cabbalistic Rosicrucian, he was merely a front for Canseliet . . .
33. Fulcanelli, *Les Demeures Philosophales*, 1929.
34. We saw this being performed, round about August, 1952, near Changu Narayan. The boy appeared to be from a Tibetan monastery, and it was a tribute to the incredible eclecticism of the religious life of the Nepalese that a dance so steeped in esoteric Buddhism of the Tibetan school should be practised near images of the lion-headed Vishnu.
35. We were uneasy about this name, even when it was given and explained. It was only some years later, that, while reading through the Evans-Wentz version of *The Tibetan Book of the Great Liberation* (1965 ed., fn.3, p.223), we realized that the interpreter had not been very accurate. The Sanskrit would have been *mthah-drug*, and meant 'six directions'. The six directions included the four cardinals with the zenith and nadir. It expresses perfectly the nature of the dance, in which one was required to maintain contact with the zenith Heavens and the nadir Earth, even while moving the legs, arms, hands, spine and head to specific different rhythms. And this, we might add, pertained only to the outer movements.
36. See M. R. James, *The Acts of John*, p.228 of the 1975 ed. of *The Apocryphal New Testament*, 1924. The second council of Nicaea attacked and condemned these 'Acts'. At the time of this council, the dance round, with words sung by Christ, was widely believed to be a ritual of initiation, with Christ as the mystagogue. This seems to have been the earliest recognition, in published form, that Christ delivered a secret and incomprehensible initiation to his disciples. For the Latin dance round, *Salvare volo et salvari volo*, and a fuller account of its reception up to the fourth century, see Max Pulver, *Jesus' Round Dance and Crucifixion According to the Acts of St John*, in *The Mysteries. Papers from the Eranos Yearbooks*, 1955, 1971 ed., pp.172-3.
37. *The Acts of John*, 97, James version, p.254. After dancing with the Lord, the disciples were 'as men gone astray or dazed with sleep'.
38. Docetism was the heresy that the body of Christ had not been real, but a phantasm. By the fourth century the heresy of docetism seems to have lost much of its attraction, for it was recognized that if Christ had not suffered on the Cross, then there was no Resurrection, no real Christian Mystery. It had rightly been termed a heresy. The fact that the follower of a Master cannot always understand that Master is linked with the relationship which his or her higher body, or Ego, holds with the Master. In some Ways – but not in the Way we ourselves followed – the pupil is required to subordinate his or her Will to that of the Master. In such a case, it is no longer a question of understanding or not understanding. In the Rosicrucian methods which we followed, the primal approach was by way of understanding (Salt): from understanding, an impulse was directed to the emotional sphere (Mercury), which mediated a responding and significant action from the sphere of the Will (Sulphur). It was forbidden, in such Rosicrucian circles, to bypass this operation, and to allow ingress into one's being of another person's Will. This is the fundamental secret of the Rosicrucian method. We suspect that the inner meaning is in this section 97 of the *Acts* (see n.37) for after

the Crucifixion, the Lord sees John and admits that he had influenced his thinking and willing.

39. In the esoteric tradition, the depth of incarnation into the physical is an important indicator of personality traits, and of how the higher bodies (such as the Etheric) can work into that physical. Generally speaking, the male incarnates more deeply than the female. Many of the psychological differences between the two sexes are accounted for in terms of this depth of incarnation.

40. In fact, Hedsel uses the same esoteric expression in another context (see p.342). In the *Book of Dzyan* the Second (evolutionary) Race of Man was said to be sweat-born. The term seems to relate to a period of human evolution which was hermaphrodite, and perhaps Hedsel uses the term with another idea in mind. In certain Yogic practices (the Laya-Karma), the yogin is advised that during the three phases of breathing he or she should visualize that a new celestial body is being formed. This is in accordance with the creation of a higher life by moving from Fire to Water. This visualization makes a body of 'nectar', falling from the Moon. While there are overtones of the *Ros*, or dew, of the alchemical *nostoc* in this reference, we may also see in it Hedsel's image of the visualizations which accompany esoteric dancing as being born of the 'nectar', or a more earthly liquid, such as 'sweat'. For a translated note on the yoga visualization, see John Woodroffe, *The Serpent Power*, 1928, 1973 ed., p.243.

41. *The Epic of Gilgamesh* tells of the dissatisfaction of Gilgamesh, the King of Erech, with all his accomplishments. He meets with the desert-man, Enkidu, and they fight for possession of a temple prostitute who has ensnared the wild man. They become friends, and journey together in search of the Plant of Life. On the journey, Enkidu is slain, and Gilgamesh is allowed to visit his friend in the dark halls of the Underworld. Gilgamesh eventually gains the Plant, from the bottom of an ocean, but cannot stay away long enough to keep it. The Plant is stolen by a snake. Gilgamesh was a historic figure, the fifth king of the Sumerian Dynasty: he is said to have ruled for 126 years. For a summary of the myth, as it is preserved on the tablets found in the Library of Nabu, Nineveh, see E. A. Wallis Budge, *Babylonian Life and History*, 1884, 1925 ed., p.86 ff.

42. The name appears to be that of a Babylonian star – the equivalent of our Antares, the *alpha* of Scorpius. We discovered that it was linked with the 24th ecliptic constellation of the Babylonians, and meant something like 'Lord of the Seed'. However, its esoteric implications became clear to us only much later, when we began to see the connection between the the the shape of the human embryo (seed) and the ear. The portal of *Bilu* was designed to awaken the potential within hearing. Perhaps it is no surprise that, to this day, the Hindu cosmology still refers to the star as an 'Ear Jewel' in the ear of Indra. The notion of the star being a guardian-star is probably expressed in the early Greek (whence we have derived our modern name), recorded in Ptolemy, for *Antares* means something like 'rival of Ares, or Mars'. The general historian usually take this derivation as relating to the splendid red of the star, which rivals the red of Mars, but the esotericist will see it as rivalling the traditional role of Mars as the soldier-guardian.

43. 'The earliest Christian references to Satan are partly to blame for much of the later confusion and commentary.' See F. Gettings, *Dictionary of Demons. A Guide to Demons and Demonologists in Occult Lore*, 1988, pp.212-13.

44. The name of *Ladon* who guarded the apples is something of a mystery: so far as we can see, its meaning is not known. The Hesperides are 'Daughters of the Evening'. In the stellar lore, they are the Pleiades, a name which is from the Greek epic form *pleios*, 'many'. Perhaps we could look to the stars for a meaning of the word *Ladon*? The Draco, or dragon, of the stellar maps is very ancient – at least Persian, as *Azhdeha*, the 'Man-eating Serpent'. According to R. H. Allen, *Star-Names and Their Meanings*, 1899, Virgil called it *Maximus Anguis*, the Greatest Snake, and said that it glides in the manner of a river, between the two stellar bears. Allen suggests

that this river-simile may be the source of the dragon-name Ladon, for the same name is used of a river in Arcadia, which flows into the Alpheus, and which was visualized as being the border of the Garden of the Hesperides. Allen even records another name, *Custos Hesperidum*, 'Watcher over the Hesperides', but gives no source for the title. In the myth, Ladon was killed by Hercules before he took the golden apples. The esoteric background to the labours of Hercules is dealt with in Alice Bailey, *The Labours of Hercules*, 1977 ed. For the Golden Apples, which figure in the Third Labour, see p.26ff.

45. The world *chakra* is of Sanskrit origin, and means approximately 'wheel'. The chakras are wheels of light which may be perceived clairvoyantly on the surface of the human body; they are Spiritually connected with the activity of the spine. There are seven chakras, of which the topmost, and most splendid, is the head, or Crown, chakra.

46. The mediaeval writers made much of the fact that the Latin for apple, *malus*, also means 'evil', 'deformed' and 'anything bad'. The two words appear to have different origins, however. The malus of evil was from the Greek *melas*, meaning 'black', while the malus fruit was from the Greek *melea*, and meant apple tree. However, they may have a communal origin in the Sanskrit *mala*, meaning 'dirt'.

In *A Discourse of Fire and Salt, Discovering Many Secret Mysteries*, 1649, the Adept tells us, 'So that a man is but as a Spirituall tree planted in the Paradise of delights, which is the earth of the living . . .' This man-tree, as he admits, is planted in the earth 'by the roots of his haires'. Here the author reaches into the very essence of alchemy – that the head is the seed, which must be planted in the darkness of death, to flower again. For a modern reappraisal, see Ursula Grahl, *The Wisdom in Fairy Tales*, 1955, 1969 ed., p.16ff.

47. The three Hesperides were Aegle, Arethusa and Hesperis (sometimes Hesperethusa, which Maier reduced to Hespertusa). They were the Light guardians of the tree, while Ladon was the Dark guardian.

48. Michael Maier was born in Rendsburg in 1566, and studied at Rostock, Nuremburg, Padua and Basle universities. He was a well-connected alchemist, and worked with and for the Landgrave Maurice of Hesse and Prince Christian I of Anhalt, both of whom, besides being alchemists, were Rosicrucians. See Frances Yates, *The Rosicrucian Enlightenment*, 1972, esp. p.70ff. Maier's undoubted connection with the Rosicrucians is dealt with in A. E. Waite, *The Real History of the Rosicrucians*, 1887, 1977 rep., p.268ff.

49. Michael Maier, *Atalanta Fugiens, hoc est, Emblemata nova de Secretis Naturae Chymicae . . .* , 1618. The superb plates were engraved by Johann Theodor de Bry. This 1618 edition, although the second, is the first to contain the portrait of Maier to which we refer.

50. The Three Principles of Salt, Mercury and Sulphur are reflected in a considerable number of other ternaries, which reflect in turn the supercelestial world (the Holy Trinity), the created worlds (Spiritual, Earthly and Infernal), the planetary world (the three superiors and the three inferiors), and the Microcosm (thinking, feeling and willing). 'So that there is a Mystery in this number of 3 that must not bee forgotten', exclaims the anonymous alchemist-author of *A Discourse of Fire and Salt, Discovering Many Secret Mysteries*, 1649.

51. The esoteric message in this mythology is all too clear. The gods have a treasure, well guarded by three women and a dragon. An initiate hero is sent to kill the dragon, and take the fruit. Although dressed in the skin of a lion, he has open access to the gods, which means that he is an initiate. He is a man who has not yet sloughed off his animal nature, but is prepared to undertake a dangerous journey, and face many hardships, to redeem himself. Towards the end of his journeys, he recognizes the value of the golden fruit, and offers it as a worthy gift to the naked Venus. Now the apples make their way as a gift to the Earth, for Venus hands them over to Hippomenes. This is the 'chain of initiation', the ancient Golden Chain of

Homer. Hippomenes uses this golden fruit to obtain the object of his love, Atalanta, the swift-footed beauty. She may be his soul, the eternal anima, but this is of no great import, for his leaping desire proves to be stronger than love, and he takes the maiden by force. He, who had received a gift from the gods, pollutes the holy temple in return. His punishment is the worst possible: he is degraded from the stream of human evolution, and exiled from the temple. His victim-soul, though stainless of sin, is punished alongside him, and both must await redemption.

This could be the story of the human condition, for within it we read of one success (Hercules) and one failure (Hippomenes), and learn how it is not easy to use wisely the gifts bestowed upon us by Heaven, nor to distinguish between love and desire. It is all too easy to slip from humanity into the bestial (the name, Hippomenes, is related to the Greek meaning 'horse-keeper').

52. The talented 17th-century engraver, Theodor de Bry, shows Hercules, the slayer of Ladon, plucking the apples. The hero must have handed these (perhaps for favours granted) to Venus, as the semi-naked beauty is shown handing them, in turn, to Hippomenes. The race beyond the garden of the gods is also depicted, with Atalanta pausing in mid-flight to retrieve a thrown apple. Hippomenes is already in the lead, balancing the remaining two apples like a juggler, ready to throw them to gain an advantage in the race. The rape in the temple seems almost decorous, for the fact that Atalanta is an unwilling participant is shown only by her averting her face: perhaps, indeed, were the truth known, it was no rape at all. Perhaps the gods had connived that the pair should pollute a sacred place. Whatever the truth in the story, the couple are shown next transformed into a lion and lioness, walking away, side by side, with the male still showing interest in the female, as though no lesson had been learned.

The pair have been expelled from the paradise of the temple, just as the first pair were expelled from the garden. The pair who played with the golden apples of the gods have been turned into golden cats: their darker animal nature has swamped their humanity.

53. Reincarnation was not openly taught by Western esoteric circles until the late 17th century. The earliest published work dealing with reincarnation we know is the 'revolutions' diagram published by van Helmont, and perhaps shown to the Ragley Hall group organized by Lady Conway.

54. The alchemist, Jean d'Espagnet, quoted by S. K. de Rola, *The Golden Game. Alchemical Engravings of the Seventeenth Century*, 1988, p.68.

55. Quoted from the title-page of Maier's *Atalanta Fugiens, hoc est Emblemata Nova de Secretis Naturae Chymica . . .* , 1618. The Latin reads: *accommodata partim oculis & intellectui . . . partim auribus.*

56. The music is headed *fuga*, and each page faces on to the arcane engravings, under which are Latin emblems. Thus, each double-page spread offers the triad of hearing, seeing and thinking.

57. The symbolism of Saturn in this print is even more insistent than we have suggested. In the vase shown in the print (where we might reasonably expect a rose emblem of the Rosicrucians, to which arcane body Maier belonged) are a Morning Glory (*Ipomoea*) and Banewort (*Atropa belladonna*). As we might anticipate, both flowers are ruled by Saturn. The third flower is too crudely cut for us to identify it, but there is enough evidence in this vase alone to establish a link between the engraved portrait and the Saturnine intellect. What we must interpret painfully, line by line, Maier's 17th-century readers would have read immediately: it is only in our own century that we have needed a bevy of German art historians to remind us that Saturn is the planet of scholarship and intellect. See R. Klibansky, E. Panofsky and F. Saxl, *Saturn and Melancholy*, 1964.

58. The esoteric tradition insists that the planetary motions resound to a music which may be heard in certain high states of meditation, or when in the Spiritual realms.

Relevant to the Maier plate is the notion that the embryo in the womb is an ear listening to the strains of this celestial music, which it will no longer hear once it is born. For a brief summary of the history of the idea (usually traced to Pythagoras), see F. Gettings, *The Arkana Dictionary of Astrology*, 1985, 1990 ed., p.330ff.

59. The *Anima Mundi* is the Soul of the World. This soul is usually visualized in arcane literature as a naked woman. In a famous engraving which appeared in Fludd's *Utriusque Cosmi Historia*, the symbolism is extremely complex, for she stands on the Earth, holding by a chain a monkey (Earth intellect), and chained by her right hand to God. Her feet rest on the Earth, and her head is wreathed in an aureole of stars. Her hair rests upon the seven planetary spheres. As in the Maier plate, this Fludd woman is discharging a stellar milk from her breast, over which is a seven-pointed star. This 'milk', which looks more like a stellar dust, merges with the influence rays of all the planets to fructify the Earth. No doubt this portrayal of milk is intended to show that the *Anima Mundi* is discharging Magnesia.

60. In some versions of the story it was the goat of the nymph Amalthea, in others Amalthea herself, who suckled Zeus.

61. *Magnesia* is one of the words for the higher realm of the Etheric: it is of 'such a celestial and transcendent brightness that nothing on earth can be compared to it'. The word is clearly intended to evoke the magnet (*magnes*) with its invisible yet dramatic influence. The quotation is from 'A Short Lexicon of Alchemy', in A. E. Waite, *The Hermetic and Alchemical Writings of . . . Paracelsus the Great*, 1894, vol. II, p.372ff.

Magnesia, says Paracelsus (op. cit.), is incorruptible, and all things are nourished by her. She is everywhere and always, yet not all men may see her. She may be seen only by those who are ready for this birth into a new world of sight and hearing. As Maier himself admits, the seeing of Magnesia, the vision of this virgin, demands special eyes, like the innocent eyes of the unicorn. If we read between the pictorial lines, we see that Maier is dealing with Archetypes, the Ideas which lie behind manifest form.

Fulcanelli writes, in his terse and scholarly style, that in the Green Language of alchemy, Ariadne is a form of *araignée*, the spider. Is not the spider the soul, weaving our own body? he asks. But the Greek verb *airo* means to seize, or draw down, which is why the name arean is used for the lodestone, the magnet, the Latin *magnes*. This invisible magnetic virtue, shut up hermetically in the web of the body, is what the Philosophers call Magnesia.

62. In some versions of the myth, Amalthea nursed Zeus with the milk of a goat. Zeus broke off one of its horns, and filled it with a magical power which would allow it to fill to overflowing with anything the possessor wished for. This was said to be the origin of the cornucopia.

This ungainly mother (*mater*, in Latin) is the world mother, and her milk (the *Lac virginis* of the alchemists) is at first a snow-white water but later turns to her own heart blood, just as the alchemists have Salt returning to the red of Fire.

63. Hedsel is virtually quoting from Yeats' poem 'The Second Coming', first published in *Michael Robartes and the Dancer*, 1921.

64. In mythology, Romulus was the founder of Rome. When newly born, he and his twin brother, Remus, were saved from drowning, and both were eventually reared by a wolf.

Amalthea (see n.60) was a virgin, and we may see in this story an esoteric account of how the virgin milk of pagan times was turned into the eternal spring of the cornucopia, the sexual connotations of the horn scarcely hidden. In contrast, the wolf's milk which nourished Romulus and Remus led to the founding of the eternal city. Maier's emblem points to the two secret activities of the Secret Fraternities: they keep sacred and undefiled the waters of the Virgin, and maintain on Earth the life forces which make civilization possible.

65. For the *Emerald Tablet* of Hermes Trismegistus, see de Rola, n.54 and Mead n.97 below.

66. *Lac Virginis*, or Virgin's Milk, is the milk of *Magnesia*, (see n.61). It is white and transparent like the shining heavens, somewhat like quicksilver, yet neither animal, vegetable nor mineral. As Hedsel observed earlier, is is the Etheric. See, for example, A. E. Waite, *The Hermetic and Alchemical Writings of . . . Paracelsus the Great*, 1894, vol. II, p.373.

67. See Fulcanelli, *Le Mystère des Cathédrales*, 1971 Eng. ed., p.74.

68. Hedsel seems to have originated this term, for I can find it in none of the alchemical books with which I am familiar. *Alba Mater*, or White Mother (and perhaps 'White Matter', which is another alchemical term), may have been used to contrast with the Black Mother (see p.335ff). It is a useful name to supplement those many others applied to the Magnesia. The White (which is the Spiritual salt) may also be a reference to the salt tears of the *Mater Dolorosa* of Christianity, weeping for her Son (who came from the other alchemical extreme, the Fire of the Sun). In alchemy, the *Alba Lapis* (White Stone) is the Philosopher's Stone which has the power of turning dross metal into silver. The silver of the Moon is thus reduced to a white light, something like the white of Magnesia.

69. For an account of this pageant, see Frances A. Yates, *The Rosicrucian Enlightenment*, 1972, p.9ff.

70. In terms of ordinary history, it might be argued that Frederick V, at this time, was unlikely to be a Rosicrucian, as this secret society had not emerged into history. It is true that the Rosicrucian *Fama* was not published until 1614. However, it has been recognized by historians that long before this date Rosicrucianism was widespread, yet still secret. Simon Studion's *Naometria* of 1604 seems to have been the first to make use of Rosicrucian symbols which later were adopted by the movement. The inner history of the Rosicrucians is very different from that which can be reconstructed from surviving books and manuscripts. For a survey of the early literature, see *The Fame and Confession*, published by the Societas Rosicruciana in Anglia, 1923.

71. The Order of the Golden Fleece was certainly the most distinctive knightly order of the European esoteric tradition. It was founded in 1430 by Philip the Good of Burgundy, and was limited to 24 members, with the addition of the Grand Master, and the sovereign. Most of the mediaeval and late mediaeval orders were esoteric in origin, but without exception this esoteric element was lost within a few generations. The moral integrity of the Order still seemed to be intact in the years when Frederick was a member.

   The *Argo* was the name of the ship sailed by the 50 Argonauts, who sailed with their leader Jason in search of the dragon-guarded Golden Fleece. According to Fulcanelli, the *argotiers* – those who speak and write the argot of French – are the hermetic descendants of those earlier alchemists, who voyaged in search of a gold guarded by a dragon. In these terms, cant, or *argot*, is more than a secret language – it is hermetic in origin and purpose. Fulcanelli adds that the term *Art Gothique* (Gothic Art) was a reflection of the fact that *art got* was the art of Light. the Greek *cho* meaning precisely 'light'. See Fulcanelli, op. cit., 1971 ed., pp.42-3.

72. For the supernatural qualities of the fleece, see the interesting article by L. Deubner, in *Hastings*, VI. 51ff.

73. The designer was Salomon de Caus, a Rosicrucian. A plate from his *Hortus Palatinus* of 1620, showing the castle at Heidelberg with the gardens in the foreground, is probably the most famous view of this Rosicrucian centre. The raised walls to the extreme left of the print are still *in situ*, but almost everything else has vanished.

74. This is recorded by Frances Yates (op. cit., p.12), from an article by Lili Fehrle-Burger.

75. The mechanical horse is called after Hero of Alexandria, whose work on automata,

inventions and mechanical marvels had recently surfaced in Heidelberg.

76. The symbol for Aries is the ram: that for Pisces is the fish or the fishes. The Golden Ram is an esoteric symbol for Aries, which is ruled by the Sun, and therefore coloured in gold. It is the fleece of this stellar ram that was sacrificed, to make a new age of healing, as the Sun slipped back (by that little-understood phenomena we call precession) into the sign Pisces. The ship *Argo* is a symbol that the next sign will be watery. The following age, which is that of Pisces, is dominated by the fish, by the Fisher King, who is Christ.

77. See, for example, Steffan Michelspacher, *Cabala*, 1616. Plate 4 shows such a hermetic garden, with a complex fountain, and what may be automata of the planets. It is evident from the aureole of clouds that this is a heavenly garden, or the secret hermetic garden.

78. The author Michelspacher (see n.77) designed the illustrations, which probably explains the depth of their hermetic content: they are among the most original alchemical illustrations of the century. Plate 3 (marked *Mittel: coniunction*) depicts the Philosopher's Mountain, with the alchemical grades marked as steps to the laboratory inside the hollow mountain. On the flattened mountain top is a six-sided fountain, on which Hermes, who taught the secret art to mankind, is balanced on one leg. The curious figures on the foundations of this levelled hill are V W I W V. The numerical value is of course 31 (= V V V I V V V). The arrangment, however, is probably intended to denote the Astral Plane (which is to say that the Mercury is on the high level of the stellar world, as is confirmed by the six-pointed star in his left hand). The sigil V is derived from the early Christian symbol, which made of a repetition of the first letter of the Greek word *Nike*, that resembles the Roman V. When repeated, it mean double victory, or victory on the two planes (of Etheric and Astral). When tripled, as in this example, it means victory on all three planes (Etheric, Astral and physical) – and is therefore a reference to complete initiation. The doubling of the V V is a mirror-image, following the strict symmetry of the plate – a reference to the fact that the Spiritual World is a mirror image of the material. In a different context, the triple, VVV, is one of the arcane greetings in initiate circles – perhaps here is it an indication that the highest level of initiation permits one to say farewell to the world.

79. When, some years later, we travelled again to Prague, we discovered that the superb figurative sculpture on the façade of house *15/11, Kaprova ulice* was by the artist Richard Luksch. Naturally, we wondered if Adrian was any relative. By a strange coincidence, the beautiful statuary on *Kaprova ulice* portrays the relief of a young woman against a background of ten golden fish.

80. In the mediaeval chorographies, which assign planets and zodical rulerships to towns, cities and countries, Heidelberg is ruled by Virgo. Germany (more or less with its present borders) was assigned to Aries.

81. There is a magnificent photograph, by Charlie Waite, of this early morning gold in James Bentley, *The Rhine*, 1988. The image is much the same as we saw it, in 1958: the blue skies through the window reveal that it is a façade.

82. The laboratory was eventually opened up to the public as a museum of pharmacy, with scarcely any mention of its origins as an alchemical laboratory. The large picture in Wolf-Deiter Müller-Jahncke's 'Objecta pharmaceutica', in *Pharmazie und der gemeine Mann*, 1982, 1988 ed., p.134, shows the laboratory more or less in the state we saw it on a later visit in 1989.

83. The castle and grounds have almost been destroyed more times than they have been restored. Something of the destruction of four major wars still hangs in the atmosphere above the place. It is difficult to put a date to the castle, for it is a labyrinth of different styles. It was begun in the 13th century, and added to by subsequent rulers, the Renaissance wing known as the Freidrichsbau being added by Frederick IV. Frederick V, as a sign of what has generally been regarded as a true story-book love and marriage, added an equivalent western wing named the

Englishebau in 1618, at one time named after his wife, the English princess. The destruction begun in 1622 was thorough. It was further dismantled by the French at the end of the same century, and was severely damaged by lightning in 1764.

84. One cannot study the early official history of the Rosicrucians without coming across the *Naometria* of Simon Studion, which has very strong Joachimite influences – not merely in its approach to deriving prophecy from numerological considerations. It is a most interesting stepping stone from the realm of mediaeval Christian esotericism (which was, so far as the official standpoint of the Church was concerned, heretical) to the more esoteric Christianity of the Rosicrucians.

85. See p.374, n.63.

86. See, for example, *The Goetheanum. School of Spiritual Science*, 1961, with an introduction by Albert Steffen.

87. The symbolism here is of tremendous importance to esotericism, for the furnace in man is found in the lungs, where air is combusted to maintain the temperature of the body at a constant, no matter what the ambient temperature (this, of course, explains the insistence on the *athanor* symbolism). All human beings are walking and talking furnaces, and the symbolism of Steiner's suggestion is clear. Man, as an individual, must to some extent remain outside the formal buildings of Schools (in this particular case, the Goetheanum), if he is to retain the necessary independence and equilibrium of soul.

88. Charles IV was, in the words of Maximilian I, the step-father of the German Empire, and father of Bohemia. His famous Golden Bull, determining the rules pertaining to the election of kings and issued at Metz in 1356, was one of his major political achievements. Among his many lasting cultural achievements was the foundation of the university in Prague. This *Karlova Univerzita* was instrumental in spreading many of the ideas of John Wycliffe, brought to the city by Jerome of Prague. The importance of such reformations on the development of this part of Europe, in regard to the spread of Rosicrucian thought, was incalculable. Prague University was also a hotbed of alchemical, astrological and occult thought. For notes on the Karlstejn Castle, see Paul M. Allen, *A Christian Rosenkreutz Anthology*, 1968, 1974 ed., p.477ff. There are some minor differences betwen Allen's description of the castle and the one given by Mark Hedsel. However, Hedsel's description is without doubt based on personal observation. Some differences may be accounted for by the fact that the castle has been restored fairly recently. A report, dated 1693, shows that the Holy Rood Chapel was, at that time, in a very bad state of repair. Even before that, the state of the castle was so dire that the treasures and archives were moved to Prague Castle.

89. It is so called from a fresco on the side of the altar table, which Hedsel discusses in his text.

90. The stones were mined from the mountains near Cibousov. This incrustation technique was greatly favoured by Charles IV, and similar examples are found in the St Wenceslas Chapel in Prague Cathedral, and in the imperial castle at Tangermude.

91. The idea of a 'divine ruler', symbolized in the painting, makes sense only within a context of initiation. If a nation is being directed by those of superior knowledge, it is quite reasonable that they would follow the imperatives of the wisest among them – the person most intimately linked with the Spiritual Realm – the world of the gods. The Pharoah was literally appointed to divine rule, and was in communion with the gods. The idea of divine rule certainly seems to have lingered on in Europe into the 17th century, but, in practice, it had been defunct for some centuries.

92. The Bifrost Bridge was the 'rainbow bridge'. The Aesir were leaders, theoretically a group of 12, dedicated to the service of Odin. The great tower in the city of Asgard was the castle of Glaldsheim, in which was the vast hall of Valhalla.

93. Mark Hedsel is playing with the name Karlstejn, which means 'Charles' stone' –

stein is the German for 'stone'.

94. See, for example, W. T. Fernie, *The Occult and Curative Powers of Precious Stones*, 1907, 1973 ed., pp.171-2. The other ten stones, which have been inlaid in the gilded stucco, were sapphire, chalcedony, emerald, sardonyx, sardius, chrysolite, beryl, topax, chrysoprasus and jacinth. There are often certain differences between these mediaeval names and the modern classifications, particularly where the quartzes are concerned.

95. The hidden place seems to have been approached by way of a step below the altar. There was also an entrance from below, by means of steps built into the thick wall. The official guide to Karlstejn refers to the account in B. Balbin, *Miscellanea historica regni Bohemiae*, III, 1681.

96. The skull is said to be preserved still at Karlstejn, and is mentioned in the official modern guidebook. We were not able to see it ourselves, however.

97. See 'The Mystery of the Birth of Horus', in G. R. S. Mead, *Thrice-Greatest Hermes*, 1906, 1964 ed., vol. I, pp.53-4. The descent of Horus is, as Mead seems to recognize, the prototypal descent of all human incarnations, for every birth is divine. For a theosophical view of the *makara* crocodile, see p. 264ff.

98. The four elementals are the invisible creatures linked with the four elements of Earth, Air, Water and Fire. The gnomes express the element of Earth. In mediaeval times, the gnomes were usually called *pigmei*.

99. Prague is perhaps a strange place for a Danish astronomer to be buried. When his Danish supporter, Frederick II, died, Tycho left his wonderful observatory of Uraniborg, to work for the Emperor Rudolf II. He was given the castle of Bentatky to live in, and in the year before his death, Johann Kepler went there to live with him. Brahe died at this castle, and was buried with all honours in the Tyn, Prague.

100. For an explanatory diagram of this complicated horlogium, see Philippe Legin, *The Astronomical Clock in Pictures. Strasbourg*, 1986. The earlier Strasbourg clock, of which Legin offers an engraving, seems to have been even more complex. The great astrolabe-like face of this early clock showed the diurnal motion of the stars at the latitude of Strasbourg. There is a legend that the Council of Strasbourg was so jealous of this masterpiece that its members had the eyes of its inventor put out, to prevent him from building another. The present casing is 16th-century, of course, the earlier 14th.

101. The painter was Josef Mánes. The outer series roundels depict the 12 activities of the month. This is the human year, in contrast to the 'divine year' on the outer rim, which lists the 365 saint-day festivals. Between the outer roundels and the image of the celestial city is a series of 12 roundels depicting the zodiacal signs.

102. I doubt that Hedsel was claiming that *all* the triple-towered castles were not symbolic of Prague. His argument seems to be that an image central to the zodiac must be an ideal city, since it is located in Heaven.

103. When the clock was first constructed, the festival would almost certainly have been that of the seventh-century bishop, St Pamphilus, whose cult was widely spread in Germany, and into Bohemia.

   In fact, Michael points to the topmost part of the outer periphery, where the saint-day, or festival day, is marked out as a zenith of the whole circle. The choice of Michael as pointer is certainly determined by esoteric principles, as this archangel was regarded as the leader of the seven planetary angels (the Secundadeis) who ruled the passage of time in historical periodicities. When the 15th-century occultist, Trithemius, wrote his book on these periods, *De Secundadeis*, 1522, the tradition was already ancient.

104. This was in 1787. Just over 200 years later we attended in this same theatre the most stunning performance of Mozart's *The Magic Flute* we had ever seen.

105. In the mediaeval chorographic lists, both Bohemia and Prague are ruled by the regal Leo.

106. For the crocodile Makara, see p.264ff. We are not suggesting that Charles or his

architects would have been familiar with the hermetic texts relating to the crocodile, but the symbol, divested of its sacred setting, was well established in sacred literature as an image of human passions. It was a version of the lower nature, which has to be conquered by the higher man.

107. Plutarch, *The Mysteries of Isis and Osiris*, 'Why the Priests are shaven and wear linen.' See, for example, Mead, op. cit., p.186.

108. As he intimates, Hedsel seems to be paraphrasing Plato. The words resemble very closely those found in Plato's *Phaedo* (72e), where Cebes mentions the theory of *anamnesis*. It was developed more fully in the *Meno* (80d). We should observe that the teaching of this learning by remembrance touches only on a certain faculty of the soul, and that the more ordinary educative type of learning – the development of skills – is not part of this theory. *Anamnesis* is a knowledge derived from a capacity within the soul – even a memory-bank within the soul – rather than that knowledge gained experientially, or by inductive reasoning. In fact *anamnesis* is a tool of knowledge which is developed by meditation.

109. The Leonardo da Vinci, *Lady with an Ermine*, now in the Czartoryski in Cracow, is almost certainly a portrait of Cecilia Gallerani – the ermine was emblem of the Sforza family.

110. The *diwanir*, which is an important institution in most Arabic communities, is an informal daily gathering of men (though women are not excluded) to discuss events affecting the community. Since one of the functions of the *diwanir* is to resolve communal problems, and to answer questions put by strangers, we have been fortunate enough to be present at *diwanirs*, as a querent concerning aspects of Arab culture: we marvel at the fact that the talk does not appear to descend into gossip, and is entirely democratic. So far as we know, Goethe never heard of the *diwanir*, but had he done so, he would have had no need to propose the art of Goethean conversation as a novel thing. The institution of the *diwanir*, once the life-blood of nomadic culture, must be of extraordinary antiquity.

111. *Vale* is from the Latin verb *valeo*, meaning 'to be healthy', and cognate with our word 'valuable'. As we leave someone, we do not merely wish them 'well', we also acknowledge their worth. The Arabic greeting is more interiorized, but of the same kind, for the *salaam* is a bestowal of peace. The cunning old man was wishing us the very thing we had sought in the cycling of the dance, and in following the path of an alchemist through Europe. He was saying farewell with the age-old greeting.

CHAPTER THREE

1. Ignaz von Dollinger's farsighted view is quoted by Henry Corbin, *Temple and Contemplation*, 1986, p.263.

2. The Templars were arrested throughout France, in September, 1307, on the orders of Philip IV, who was supported by Pope Clement V. They were both driven by cupidity, for the wealth of the Templars was quite extraordinary. The reason why Hedsel insists that they should have known better is because it is impossible – given their standing at that time – that they were not both quite familiar with the esoteric nature of the Templars. Clement summoned the Council of Vienne to establish that the Templars were guilty of heresy, but the Council was unable to support such charges. Consequently (and under pressure from Philip, who had cleverly brought the Papacy under his control through his battles with Boniface VIII) he had the Order abolished. It is a sign of the financial interests involved that while the vast lands owned by the Templars were nominally given to the Knights Hospitallers, Philip actually kept them for himself.

This is no place to examine the esoteric credentials of Philip IV: it is sufficient to record that, largely through his own shrewd insight, character and judgement, the French monarchical system was put on a secure footing and important reforms were instituted in the State. It is not unreasonable to describe him as the late mediaeval founder of France.

3. To his credit, the young King of England, Edward II, did not believe the charges of heresy and refused to arrest any Knights, until the Pope later 'authorized' such arrests. There were none of the mass arrests and savage torture such as had occurred in France, although by 1309 Inquisitors had been sent to England from Rome. However, in England the Inquisition was not a tool of the State, and the subsequent history of the Templars in England was by no means as bleak as that in France. In a letter dated 1310, the Inquisitors complained that they could find no one prepared to carry out the torture of the Knights, as they deemed necessary. The story is well told in M. Barber, *The Trial of the Templars*, 1980 ed., p.193ff.

4. See H. F. Cary, *The Vision of Hell, Purgatory, and Paradise of Dante Alighieri*, 1814, p.322. See also n.9.

5. So far as we can see, the term *Dweller on the Threshold* came into English usage through the so-called 'Rosicrucian novel', *Zanoni*, of 1842, through which Sir Bulwer Lytton seems to have caught the Victorian penchant for an eclectism which was by no means unique to the 19th century. In a preface to this work, he intimates that he was himself an initiate. It is not difficult to see through Lytton's suggested claim to membership of what he called 'the Everlasting Brotherhood'. No initiate would write (as he did), 'our true nature is in our thoughts, not our deeds . . .' The true initiate knows that thoughts *are* deeds.

   Three years after its publication, he wrote of *Zanoni*, 'I love it not the less because it has been little understood, and superficially judged by the common herd. It was not meant for them.' This causes one to wonder exactly for whom it *was* intended. For further notes on the *Dweller*, see n.18.

6. Hell and Purgatory are clearly demarcated in Dante's poem: in the esoteric tradition, however, the emphasis is on Purgatory, as a place of purgation between lifetimes.

7. Dante's vision is divided into three parts, because he is following the Christian cosmology, which incorporates Heaven, Hell and Purgatory.

8. A few of these names will emerge as the theme develops. However, we should observe that Paracelsus uses the mysterious name *Azoc*, or *Azoth*, for the 'ripe Mercury' by which impure bodies are purified with the help of fire. This helps explain the true nature of the three-headed monster which is sometimes identified with *Azoth*, and which has been called the Mercurial Dragon. This monster is reproduced in a startling arcane image by Martin Rutland, in his *Lexicon Alchemiae*, 1612 (plate 17). The triple-headed monster which is associated with Azoth has heads composed of the three elements of the sigil for Mercury, to signify that they head a living creature: this is about as near as the alchemists ever got to identifying the real nature of the *Azoth*, as a hermetic guardian. In its monstrous form – and, we might emphasize, *only* in its monstrous form, – the Mercurial Dragon is the mediaeval equivalent of the Egyptian *Amemit*, who was also triple of form, and also a guardian of the Underworld. The transformative alchemical powder which is also called *Azoth* is, of course, the earthly equivalent ('that which is below') of the monster-guardian which is above: the three components of the Mercuric sigil (Moon, Sun and Cross) are the three principles of Salt, Mercury and Sulphur, combined into the one Mercuric principle which is Man. Thus the stellar (or more accurately, planetary) and Earthly combine in the single image. This is an arcane way of demonstrating that this monstrous triple-headed guardian is the unredeemed Man – that, indeed, the *monster is in Man*. The Mercuric wings on the feet of the monster are the most obvious clue to the hermetic intention of the design.

   These reflections indicate that the post-Paracelsians are right to interpret the *Azoth* as the formative power of the nascent *Ego*. The developed Ego will be the controller of the three bodies below, and will be active in their redemption.

9. In modern Italian, *lonza* certainly means 'panther', alongside the word *panthero*: however, the first word seems to have taken its meaning from readings of Dante,

which suggests that scholars find themselves in something of a *huis clos*. The Italian *lonza* means also loin of meat, and we suspect that it is this underlying meaning of death, of something newly killed, at which Dante is partly hinting in his choice of word. Dante tells us that the lonza moves quickly – that is perfectly in accord with the alchemical *Azoth*, which in its Spiritual monstrous aspect is the guardian of the Spiritual plane in mediaeval esotericism: Azoth is a corrosive form of Mercury, so renowned for its quickness and life that it was called quicksilver, or 'living silver'. We should also bear in mind that, in the following line, Dante tells us that the creature is distinguished by a 'stained skin' (*pel maculato*), which tends to confirm that the animal is symbol of the inner stains of sin, for, on the Astral levels on which Dante is presently straying, the inner has become the outer. Given the nature of the Dweller, which is a monstrous embodiment of sin, it is unlikely that Dante would have chosen a more precise meaning to symbolize the creature, and this may account for the confusion which the word *lonza* has brought into scholarship. We should record that, in spite of the fact that almost every translation into English offers the word 'panther' or its equivalent, there is by no means universal agreement among scholars that the *lonza* was indeed such a creature. In certain Florentine records contemporaneous with Dante (that is, dated 1285) there is a note of a *leuncia* in captivity: this could have been a lion, for the Latin *leunculus* meant 'small lion'. Perhaps, as the Italian scholar, Daniele Mattalia, has suggested, it was a lynx, the Italian having been derived from the French 'once'. See Daniele Mattalia, *La Divina Commedia. I: Inferno*, 1975 Rizzoli ed., note 32, p.15.

10. Austin Osman Spare. *Earth Inferno*, 1905, p.23. At the foot of the drawing, Spare quotes Dante's famous opening line to the *Inferno*: '*Nel mezzo del cammin di nostra vita*'. Like Dante, Spare intends two levels of meaning in his translation ('In midway of the journey of our life'). First, it relates to the age at which the vision of the Spiritual world took place. In 1300, Dante was in his 35th year. Esoteric wisdom recognizes this as an important year in the life of every human being, for it marks the fullest point of descent into matter. After this age, the individual begins gradually to excarnate, to reach back to the stellar realms. Astrologers and arcanists recognize the age as the Spiritual midpoint of life, and an important climacteric.

The man in Spare's picture, perhaps oblivious of the Spiritual beings around him, seems to be approximately at this age, though Spare himself was only 18 in 1904, when he drew the picture. It was an important time (in astrological terms, a Saturn return) in his life. It was due to the publication of this *Earth Inferno* that the two leading artists of the day, G. F. Watts and John Singer Sargent, hailed Spare as a genius. See W. Wallace, *The Early Work of Austin Osman Spare 1900–1919*, 1987.

However, there is another level of meaning in Dante's line. Both Dante and Spare's seated man are still in life, in the physical body, yet, for one reason or another, poised to look into the realm beyond the Dwellers: this is midway (*nel mezzo*) between the normal Inferno and the Spiritual Inferno, which is a reflection of the normal. The two dark feline creatures which prowl around the feet of the seated man are a typical Sparesque reference to the strange *lonza* which appears at the opening of Dante's *Inferno* (see n.9).

11. The term sky-walker is sometimes used in modern occult circles to denote someone who is travelling on the Astral plane. In fact, the word is very old indeed, and appears frequently in the hermetic literature.

12. Spare, op. cit., p.16.

13. Austin Osman Spare, *The Book of Pleasure (Self-Love). The Psychology of Ecstasy*, 1913, p.12.

14. If proof were ever needed that the *Odyssey* is based on initiate lore, then this mysterious root *moly* would probably be sufficient evidence.

Black was the root, but milky white the flower,

Moly the name, to mortals hard to find.

So Pope tells us in his version of the *Odyssey* (X. 365). The word survives in the magical expression *holy moly!*. In fact, it is much older than the ancient Greek language, into which it was transmitted from the Sanskrit, *mulam*. Exoterically, this meant 'root' (the *moly* used by Odysseus was the root of the herb), but esoterically it was linked with stages of transformation through karma. Thus, the black root is the unredeemed karma, the milky-white flower the redeemed, which has taken on the colour of purity. For an example of the use of this term, in connection with *Mulaprakriti*, see Blavatsky, *The Secret Doctrine*, 1988, vol. I, p.176. There are many other examples in this esoteric work, however.

15. In the later constellation lists, it became the Wolf, or *Lupus*, and is better known by this title in modern astrology. See R. H. Allen, *Star Names. Their Lore and Meaning*, 1963 rep. Dover ed. of the 1899 Stechert ed., p.278, under *Lupus, the Wolf.* Allen names Vitruvius as the source for the name *Bestia*, but we have found it in earlier sources.

   Inevitably, the various names of the constellation reflect the ferocious nature of the star-group. At one time, the creature was called *Hostia* (from which we take our word hostage), meaning victim. This accounts for the alternative name, *Victima Centauri*, suggesting that it is Centaurus who is carrying the unfortunate creature to sacrifice on the altar. The Greeks and Romans believed the pattern of stars marked out *Therion*, or the Wild Animal. The Arabs, as usual, borrowed the name for the classical charts, and called it *Al Sabu*, the Wild Beast.

16. In the astrological tradition, Saturn rules over lead. The Saturn of the body is the skeletal system. The Saturn in the soul is (essentially) motivating fear.

17. For some discussion of the wallet and staff of Hermas, see Mead, op. cit., vol. I, p.258ff.

18. See n.5. Bulwer Lytton's phrase, *Dweller on the Threshold*, was unwisely adopted by certain Theosophists, even though the term *dweller* was already in use in Spiritualist circles, pertaining to improperly demolished residues of the deceased. The occultist Blavatsky used the word Dweller as an equivalent of Diakka, however: the Diakka of the American seer, Andrew Jackson Davis, was an evil entity that had never lived in a human body, and could therefore not be described as being 'dead', for only Earth-dwellers may be said to die. In more modern times, the phrase *Dweller on the Threshold* has been used to denote the karmic guardian – which is to say that dark entity which embodies (if that is the correct term for a Spiritual being) the unredeemed karmic consequences of past actions. The would-be initiate must, at some point, confront this guardian to pass into higher initiation. The communal theme in these various uses suggests that the Dweller is a ghost, or former entity, which still haunts the living, and must be laid to rest. The Hebrew term *klippoth* (plural, *klippa*) is sometimes used of such soulless entities, who dwell on the plane of klippoth.

19. For the 'red-man Adam', see p. 94; for *phos*, see p. 425, n.83. These are the two extremes – the red and the white of alchemical colouring – in Man. The red is the natural man, the white the initiated. There are many grades of colour in between.

20. The Minotaur was conceived by Pasiphae, who had sexual union with a bull. The episode arose because Minos had prayed to Poseidon to send him a bull from the sea, that he might sacrifice it to determine the line of kingship in Crete. The bull was so beautiful that Minos could not sacrifice it: in punishment for defying the gods, Poseidon caused Pasiphae, the wife of Minos, to fall in love with the bull. Pasiphae had invited the monstrous union by concealing herself in a model cow (made by the archetypal alchemist, Daedalus), and presenting her sexual parts to the rear end of the model, that she might be taken by the white bull.

   The Minotaur was fed on the human flesh of youthful Athenians: a variation of the old adage that the sins of adults are manifest on the children who follow. The sin of Pasiphae was the greater because she was a daughter of the Sun god, and married to a king. She had no need to descend so deeply into matter, as to enclose herself in the body of beast.

Bestial sexuality is forbidden because, in the esoteric tradition, the animal (beast) is a reject of the evolving human being (the salt of fission). Esotericists insist that the animal kingdom was once part of humanity, and was rejected (by fission) in the remote past. Union with such rejects would be tantamount to returning to the former pro-fission state – a thoroughly involutory process. It would damage both the human and the animal by re-establishing atavistic connections best left severed.

21. While the *Dark Night of the Soul* is the title of a remarkable book by St John of the Cross, it is a phrase often used in esoteric circles to denote a crisis of the soul, or a period of testing.

22. See, for example, G. Wachsmuth, *The Evolution of Mankind*, English ed., 1961.

23. The sea-monster Tiamat, mentioned in the Assyrian Creation Tablets, is one of the ancient *Mater* figures, within this Creation mythology the source of all living things. She preserved her watery nature even into the 18th century, in the engravings which Blake made for his *Book of Job*, as the serpentine Leviathan, in which she is combined with the male land-monster Behemoth, as one of the two dual symbols of the inner monster. This arcane design, and the notes which accompany it, tells us a great deal about the nature of the inner Bestia. However, Blake's finest literary description of Leviathan emerging from the sea (see n.31) – which is perhaps the finest description of a monster in the English language – is in his visionary encounter with the angel in 'A Memorable Fancy'. This is quoted in full by Swinburne, op.cit., p.243.

24. William Blake gets very close to representing the demonic Behemoth and Leviathan as untamed powers within the unconscious mind. In another context, which we shall quote, he distinguishes between the emanation from within and the Spectre on the outside. In a famous engraving from his *Illustrations to the Book of Job*, Blake represents the two demonic forms in a great circle below the celestial and human realms. Behemoth, which is encased in a metallic armour, seems to represent the unredeemed interior, set in Time, while Leviathan, the coiled sea-serpent, represents the monster when it is compelled to approach from the outside – from Space. In this latter aspect, it is clearly the Spectre. The compelling description of Leviathan (see n.31) in Blake's 'A Memorable Fancy' begins with an account of how the Leviathan appears as a fiery crest above the waves. Blake tells us that it appears 'to the east, distant about three degrees . . .' Quite clearly, he is defining that aspect of the monster which appears from *space*. The contraries of colours on its forehead denote that it is born of inadequate thinking which has turned to the violence of the tiger.

25. The constellation *Bestia* is located in the zodiacal arc of 15 Scorpio to 7 Sagittarius, though its nearest point to the equator is 34S. This means that the influence of the constellation is profoundly conditioned by a number of stars located in other constellations, and great care must be taken in attempting to isolate such influences in a reading. It is evident that, in our search for the significance of Bestia, we should glance at the reputation of these stars. When we do this, we find that they divide themselves into two groups – one of which works through a sort of catalytic action, intensifying any planet or node with which it makes contact, and the other of which works through an influence which may only be described as evil.

The stars Zubeneschamali, Agena and Bungula appear to intensify the influence of any planet they conjunct. The star Unukalhai (from the Arabic meaning 'neck of the snake') is distinctly evil, and linked with poisoning. Dschubba is also evil, and is linked with immorality, as its placing in the claw of the Scorpion might suggest. Graffias, set in the head of the Scorpion, besides being evil, also has a reputation for malevolence, crime and disease.

26. The standard modern horoscope figure, which is usually drawn as a cross within a

circle is actually a disguised encircled point. In glyph-form, this was an arcane sigil which used to serve as an Egyptian hieroglyphic, a determinative for (among other things) Time. The birth, or nativity, takes place at the earth-centre, as the soul, newly invested with a body, emerges into Time at this central point. The soul and Spirit of the incarnating child are visualized as streaming to this point from the outer periphery of the zodiac. In this descent, the soul carries influences from the stars, and imbibes the necessary impulses from the planetary spheres through which it passes on its journey to Earth. This incarnation process is called, in the ancient arcane literature, the Egyptian Descent of the Soul. An esoteric account is given in the *Poemandres* literature. See, for example, Mead, op.cit., vol. 2, p.22ff. Blake recognized the circle and cross in his *Los* and *Enitharmion*, who were symbols of Time and Space.

27. It is perhaps a sign of hubris to mention Blake and Boehme in the same sentence in a work such as our own, which claims to pertain to arcane knowledge. In his perceptive criticism of the writings of the Swedish philosopher and clairvoyant, Emmanuel Swedenborg, William Blake wrote:

> Any man of mechanical talents may, from the writings of Paracelsus or Jacob Behmen, produce 10,000 volumes of equal value with Swedenborg's; and from those of Dante or Shakespeare, an infinite number.

It is with some trepidation that we note just how freely we have quoted three of these four geniuses in our own text. It is, of course, very disturbing to see the number of books published in modern times, purporting to deal with esotericism or the Mysteries, written by authors who reveal their ignorance of the subject in almost every word.

For the source of the above quotation, and for enlightenment on much of Blake's inner vision, see that masterpiece of biography, Algernon Charles Swinburne, *William Blake. A Critical Essay*, 1906. The quotation from the Swedenborg notes is on p.245.

28. The horoscope of William Blake which appears in modern collections of genitures was cast by his friend, the artist John Varley, who was among the most proficient astrologers of the period. See A. T. Story, *James Holmes and John Varley*, 1894. The Blake horoscope seems to have appeared first in *Urania: or, the Astrologer's Chronicle, and Mystical Magazine*, 1825. In view of the present theme, of the constellation Bestia, we feel free to add a few technical notes for astrologers, mindful that these may perplex the general reader. Observe the radical placings of Mercury and Jupiter:

> ME 27 Scorpio
> JU 2 Sagittarius

Due to precession, Mercury is near Bungula and Jupiter is on Graffias. The whole arc of Bestia overlays Blake's fifth house – a house of great importance to any artist. The specific reading for Mercury on Bungula is that the native is difficult to please, has good intellect yet disappointed ambitions (all relevant to Blake). The horoscope diagram is reproduced in Gettings, *The Hidden Art*, 1978, p.151. The chapter 'The Divine Principles' in this work touches on Blake's use of astrology.

29. Blake uses the symbol of the Spectre in many different contexts, and with several different meanings: see S. Foster Damon, *A Blake Dictionary*, 1973 ed., p.380ff. However, our quotation, which opens 'Poems and Fragments from the Note-Book' (see G. Keynes, *Blake. Complete Writings*, 1971 ed., p.415), is the same as the Spectre in the powerful creature in the *Four Zoas* (vii.304): 'Thou knowest that the Spectre is in Every Man insane, brutish, deform'd . . .'

30. Not surprisingly, in view of this dark mythology, the group of stars has attained a rather unfortunate reputation, even in astrology. Ptolemy claimed that the combined stars of *Bestia* have an effect similar to Saturn and Mars combined – that is, the influence of the two malefics. They is said to give strong and poorly controlled passions, along with all the usual Saturnine and Martian attributes. For

a brief modern mention, see V. Robson, *Fixed Stars and Constellations*, 1969 ed., p.50, under the name *Lupus*.

31. William Blake (see n.23) wrote:
    . . . slowly it reared, like a ridge of golden rocks, till we discovered two
    globes of crimson fire, from which the sea fled away in clouds of smoke: and
    now we saw it was the head of Leviathan; his forehead was divided into
    streaks of green and purple, like those on a tiger's forehead: soon we saw his
    mouth and red gills hang just above the raging foam, tinging the black deep
    with beams of blood, advancing toward us with all the fury of a Spiritual
    existence.'

In terms of this rulership over Time and Space which Blake seems to have
accorded his two monsters, it is worth quoting the hermetic literature. An Ophite
diagram mentioned by Origen portrays the ten Unseen Spaces, which were
divided into the three main divisions. The innermost of these contained a further
ten circles, surrounded by a single circle which was called *Leviathan*. The lower
space had in it a grouping of seven circles, associated with the ruling daemons: this
whole group was named *Behemoth*. Even the numerology might suggest that Blake
was familiar with this imagery, considering that he placed his two monsters in a
great circle, with the head of Leviathan marked out by ten serrated spines, and the
armoured Behemoth pressing a septenary of forms to the Earth (two tusks, four
feet and a pointed tail which drags on the Earth). See G. R. S. Mead, *Thrice-
Greatest Hermes*, 1964 ed., 'Concerning Leviathan and Behemoth', p.295.

32. See R. Steiner, *Karmic Relationships. Esoteric Studies*, 1972 ed. of the Eng. trans. of
    lectures given at Dornach in February and March, 1924, vol. I, lecture X, p.159ff.
33. For Comenius and the 'Invisible School', see P. M. Allen op. cit. n.44.
34. The phrase was used by Birch, in his 'Preface' to Boyle's *Works*, 1772.
35. While Robert Boyle (1627-1691) is not treated as an arcanist in most scientific
    studies, he at least finds his way into E. R. Dalmor, *Quien fue Y Quien Es en
    Ocultismo*, 1970, pp.86-7 – mainly because of his connection with alchemy. For a
    review of his occult interests, within a scientific context, see Lynn Thorndike,
    History of Magic and Experimental Science, 1958, VIII, p.170ff. This work also
    treats Francis Bacon from a similar standpoint – see VII, p.63ff.
36. We find an interesting survival of this in the later work of the homoeopathist, Dr
    Hahnemann, who lent a specific meaning to the word *miasma*, which is still used in
    modern homoeopathy. This latter is a system of curative medicine which has its
    roots in a highly respectable arcane lore of Paracelsus, transformed by scientific
    investigation and experimentation.
37. See Thorndike (op. cit., n.35 above), where this and other experiments are
    recorded. The tale of the conflicts faced by Boyle, as he moved away from what is
    now called magic to physical science, is told admirably in A. D. White, *A History
    of the Warfare of Science with Theology in Christendom*, 1955, p.405ff specifically.
38. For an excellent account of this Great Chain, see A. O. Lovejoy, *The Great Chain
    of Being. A Study of the History of an Idea*, 1960 Harper ed.
39. Hedsel delighted in constructing names with hidden meanings. The Italian
    Muscoso actually means 'mossy'. Fortunately, Hedsel left a footnote to indicate that
    Mosi is from the phrase *mosi oa tunya* (meaning 'the smoke which thunders'),
    applied by the Africans to what Livingstone called the Victoria Falls. No doubt, in
    terms of inner content, Hedsel had in mind the famous entry in Livingstone's
    diaries, made in 1855, shortly after he had looked upon this water: 'On sights as
    beautiful as this Angels in their flight must have gazed.' Perhaps a somewhat
    elaborate coding, yet appropriate for a man who could read the angelic script of the
    Silver Waters, or *Celestial River*. How (or even if) the Green Language coding
    relates to the actual name of this individual is not clear: Hedsel never told me the
    real name of this remarkable man, nor left any record of it.
40. Naturally, I asked Mark Hedsel about this intriguing weakness. He refused to

discuss it. 'A man's chief weakness is evident in everything he thinks, says and does: in consequence, it is more than evident in this present work. If you are interested in such things, then you should be able to unearth it without too much difficulty.'

41. So far as we can recall, he said, *Cotale colori sono soltanto coloratura*. Muscos' use of language was extremely elegant. It is impossible to translate this passable Italian *jocata* (a semi-humorous play on words), even though the Italian *coloratura* has entered into English musical terminology. The *coloraturi pentimenti* are (so far as English is concerned) overpainted brush-strokes or covered-over trill-like sounds, but the Italian words contain the idea of sin, or of moral error reflected upon later – in English, a sort of repentance. Even the word which is translated here as style (*moda*) has a moral implication (a *moda* was a struck attitude as much as a passing fashion, and once not a thing to be over-proud of), though this now seems to have disappeared from contemporary Italian. Hedsel left a note to the effect that this play with the Italian language reminded him more of Dante than of any other poet he knew: even so, Muscos was so evidently a man out of his time that there did not appear to be anything strange about it.

42. As it turned out, Muscos was right about our timing. Alkindi died round about 872 AD. Alkindi is the Romanized version of Abu Yusuf Yaqub ben Ishaq al-Kindi (*c*.800–872 AD).

43. The *Lac Virginis* or *Maris Virginis* (too close to Virgin Mary for the comfort of some) were some of the phrases used by Paracelsus when discussing the *Magnesia* as a memory bank of nature.

44. Franciscus (or Franz) van Helmont was certainly the Master Teacher at Ragley. There is no satisfactory assessement of his esoteric teachings: his remarkable book, the *Alphabet of Nature*, has been misunderstood as a work designed to help the deaf and dumb, while few, if any, of the arcane figures he designed, and which were published by Georg Welling, have been understood. They are probably still too arcane for wide publication. Sir Peter Lely painted van Helmont's portrait, and this was given by the sitter to Lady Conway. By way of Horace Walpole and the Marquis of Hertford, this magnificent picture found its way to the Tate Gallery. There is yet one other way in which van Helmont survives in the modern Spiritual life: van Helmont was the original wanderer of Matthew Arnold's poem, 'The Scholar Gipsy'. Arnold is supposed to have taken the story from Glanvill's *Vanity of Dogmatising*, 1661.

    When we visited Ragley Hall, we were disappointed to find that it had been rebuilt in an 18th-century English Palladian style. We made inquiries about the library, which had been famous among esotericists during the lifetime of Lady Conway, but found that it had been dispersed. Some of the books, and a number of manuscripts, are now in the British Library. Lady Conway's coffin – specially designed by van Helmont – is in nearby Arrow Church. There are some useful notes on Ragley, written from an esoteric point of view, in P. M. Allen, *A Christian Rosenkreutz Anthology*, 1968, 1974 ed., pp.647-9.

45. So far as I know, there is no treatment of the esoteric design of the fountain in *Piazza Vecchia* of *alta citta*, Bergamo. It is called *La Fontana del Contarini*, and like many other architectural elements and esoteric symbols in and around the square, reminds one of the time when Bergamo was under the control of Venice.

46. The 'horologium' is a mediaeval zodical time-keeper, constructed of marble, and bedded in the stonework of the *pavimento* beneath the undercroft of the Podesta. It measures the passing of the days, rather than hours, for it is so arranged that a radiant of sunlight glows upon the line each day, marking the position of the sun in the zodiac. The calibrations and zodiacal sigils are modern restorations, but the structure is very old.

47. The Cappella Colleoni is Renaissance, completed *c*. 1476. Its complex white and rose marble façade is too cluttered to be satisfying: however, this restlessness seems

to have been the aim of the architect, as the available planar surface is destroyed by the optical illusion of 'cubes' so beloved of Roman mosaic workers. The general effect is of the break-up of surface which is entirely contrary to the idea behind Renaissance architecture.

48. The two brazen columns of Solomon's Temple were *Jachin* on the right, and *Boaz* on the left. At the time, we saw these as representative of the polarity of 'Romanticism and Materialism' (respectively) – but this was probably because this polarity obsessed us then. In modern times, the two columns are often reversed, perhaps to symbolize the new dispensation of Christ, which changed the direction of worship to the East. According to Stieglitz, some *Boaz* columns were tripartite, the double columns twisting into each other twice to divide the whole into three parts. This represents Man, who is of triune nature. In contrast, the *Jachin* was dual, expressing the Godlike (three in one, if the nodus is counted). Two sample images derived from Steiglitz, *On Ancient German Architecture*, are reproduced in R. Macoy, an initiate of the 33rd degree Masonic, *A Dictionary of Freemasonry*, 1989 rep., p.176. When Macoy compiled his work, *c*. 1885, the two columns were in the cathedral of Wurzburg, and probably dated to 1042: the shaft-heads above the capitals are marked with the Romanized names, *Jachim* and *Boaz*. These forms (though not named in this remarkable way) are not uncommon in mediaeval architecture, but they are rarely explained by historians of the art outside the Masonic tradition.

49. Most of the useful material dealing with the esoteric meaning of the columns is found in Masonic sources. The American Mason, Albert Pike, tells us that the columns of *Jachin* and *Boaz*, erected in the Temple of Solomon, are (among other things) in 'the obscure language of the Kabalah', intended to symbolize the male and female in separation. They represent the letters of the Ineffable Name, divided. See A. Pike, *Morals and Dogma of the Ancient and Accept Scottish Rite of Freemasonry*, 1871, p.849. Just as in the later creation story of Genesis woman is taken from the body of Adam, so Minerva, goddess of wisdom, was born of the brain of the god Jove. The mythology is ancient, and reflected in many male-female relationships of gods. Its importance on the columns in the Capella Colleoni is reflected in the fact that one of the themes on the façade is the Consecration of the Temple at Jerusalem.

50. This is the view of several scholars. See for example the useful summary of views in A. Horne, *King Solomon's Temple in the Masonic Tradition*, 1972, 1977 ed., p.221ff.

51. According to esoteric thought, men and women have different thought-processes – on the whole, a healthy woman (one who is sexually differentiated from man) is more Spiritual in her thinking than a man, more in tune with Spiritual exigencies. This usually means that, all things being equal, the female is more mature in thought than the male. Men and women have even more pronounced differences in their emotional lives. Man is more inclined to be exploratory, while the female is inclined to be receptive and nourishing.

In contrast to Thinking and Feeling, the human faculty of Will is still undifferentiated. It may at times appear to be differentiated, however, simply because it is expressed through thinking and/or feeling. In alchemy there is a feminine and masculine Salt; there is also a masculine and feminine Mercury (which explains why this god is androgynous): however, there is only one Sulphur, neither masculine nor feminine. The differentiated forms of Sulphur one finds in the hermetic texts – such as White Sulphur, Black Sulphur, Gold Sulphur (which is Sulphur of Sol), Red Sulphur, Ligneous Sulphur, and so on – relate to the degree of refinement in the Will, not to sexual differentiations.

52. The basic philosophy of the *I Ching* seems to have been formulated over 5,000 years ago, but Chinese sages and scholars have added many amplification since that time. Few of the European translations capture the depth of this arcane text. See,

however, Wu Jing-Nuan, *Yi Jing*, 1991: this author is deeply interested in Chinese etymology, and has taken the trouble to relate some of the difficult characters to the oracle bone pictographs from which they originated. The hexagram of *Inner Truth* is No. 61, *Zhong Fu*, translated by Wu Jing-Nuan as 'Inner Sincerity'. It is the changing of the third line, from a yin to a yang, which gives rise to the text relating to the altercation of beating of a drum, and weeping or singing. The significance of the hexagram, in regard to human love, is that the inner space, which is open within, is being subjected to change, and must alternate between being open and closed. Being an esoteric diagram, the six lines relate, in pairs, to the three levels in man and woman (see n.51).

53. An excellent example is that given (albeit innocently) in 1965 by Lynn Thorndike in her treatment of the 13th-century magician, Michael Scot. In explaining the names of the seven hours of the night (which were *crepusulum*, *vespera* or *vespertinum*, *conticinium*, *intempestum*, *gallicinium*, *matucinum* and *diluculum* – historically speaking, watches, rather than hours), Michael Scot observes that these are not really hours, and may be called hours only 'through foolishness' or 'through ignorance'. In Latin, Scot wrote this latter phrase as *ab ydiotis* – an explanation which was clearly satisfactory for Thorndike, as being dismissive. However, the esotericist will recognize that Scot is using an occult blind, and referring to the deeper meanings (the Idiot's meanings) in the seven words. They denote progressive stages in initiation, the significance of which may be interpreted, in terms of secondary meanings, by analogy to the setting and rising of the Sun. For example, *conticinium*, marks the first part of the night: however, the word really means 'that time when all becomes still'. Similarly, the *gallicinium*, or *galli secundi* ('the second crowing of the cock') are terms from the Mysteries of Cybele, relating to the noises made by priests. Thorndike does not appear to have been aware of this initiation gradus. See, however, L. Thorndike, *Michael Scot*, 1965, p.57, where the scholar quotes from the Munich Staatsbibliothek, cod. lat. 10268 52r.

54. Edwin Zeydel, in his *Sebastian Brandt* (1967), has offered an excellent introduction to the history of Brandt's *Ship of Fools*. Although not writing in an esoteric tradition, Zeydel recognizes the importance of the *Narrenschiff* to what we have called the 'Ego-development' of the 15th century. Zeydel points out that the *Narrenschiff* presents, for the first time in German literature, a sense of the writer's personal philosophy of life. The world view in this philosophy reveals man as the central figure on Earth, faced with the necessity of deciding whether or not to take the Path of Wisdom. This Path of Wisdom involves becoming a microcosmic image of the macrocosm. The alternative path is that which leads to folly, and to subversion of that macrocosmic image. (See Zeydel, p.79.) No esotericist could have set out the purpose of Brandt's book more succinctly.

55. This was *Das nuv schiff vo Narragonia*, 1494. There is a facsimile edition of the Colmar edition (Inc. XI. 9821), published in Dortmund in 1981, in the W. Besch. S. Grosse and H. Menge, *Deutsche Wiegendrucke*, series.

56. The topmost trinity of the Sephirothic Tree, condensed by the cabbalists to the symbol *shin*, is composed of Kether, Hokhmah and Binah. These three generate the realm of living beings. They are the hidden trinity of the Realm of Lights. It is probably this Sephirothic placing which led to *Shin* being accorded the cabbalistic number 300. This symbolism, as Charles Poncé admits, is the reason why the cabbalistic literature accords so much importance to the upper trinity. See Charles Poncé, *Kabbalah*, 1974, p.111.

57. The 'defrocked priest' was Eliphas Levi, a *soi-disant* Hebraist whose unscholarly writings on the cabbala revealed that he could not read Hebrew with the ease he pretended. He was a romanticist, one of the earliest of a whole generation of journalistic writers on the occult – but one who (unaccountably) developed a considerable following. He knew but little occultism, yet invented much about it.

Without exception, all his writings are unreliable. See, for example, the survey in *Blavatsky: Collected Writings*, p.491ff, especially p.495. For an even more trenchant assessment, see A. E. Waite, *The Holy Kabbalah*, 1971 ed., p.487ff.

58. In Homer's *Odyssey* (12 39 184) Odysseus, following the advice of Circe, listens to the songs of the Sirens by stopping up the ears of his sailors, but having himself lashed to the mast. The mythology varies from poet to poet, but it seems that these sea sirens sing the song of Hades.

59. For the *Makara* in esoteric literature, see p.264ff.

60. We had imagined that our Master was merely applying the Green Language rule of homophony. However, we later discovered that what he said was absolutely correct. The *gest* of 'noble deeds' was from the Latin past participle, *gesta*, 'exploits'. The 16th-century English word *jest*, relating to the idea of humorous speech, and which is the root of *jester*, is from the same *gesta*. In a very real sense, the jester, or Fool, is one who does something of importance.

61. The Odysseus of Homer's great epic was an initiate, and he would have known in his heart that his men of the *Nostoi* would be turned into swine by the enchantress he chose as lover. Yet the purpose of the myth was to show how the higher magic of Hermes could counter that of Circe, and it was, after all, through this involvement with the enchantress that he obtained directions that would take him home. For an examination of *Nostoi*, see p.298.

62. The Teacher, Gurdjieff, had called this the 'Chief Feature'. See, for example, P. D. Ouspensky, *In Search of the Miraculous*, 1949.

63. There was always some initiatory lore in the beginnings of Gothic and other 'occult' literature of the 19th century. The doyen of them all, Mary Shelley's *Frankenstein* (1818), was certainly sparked off by stories of the genuine 17th-century alchemist, Konrad Dippel, which its author heard during her visit to the Castle Frankenstein. See Radu Florescu, *In Search of Frankenstein*, 1975, p.78ff.

In contrast, the 'Dweller on the Threshold' – a Spiritualized Frankenstein, in the sense that it was attached by invisible bonds to the creator – invented by the English novelist, Bulwer Lytton, in his *Zanoni* (1845), already showed a retreat from actual arcane history into fantasy: the 'Everlasting Brotherhood' to which Bulwer Lytton refers in this novel is a literary projection of Rosicrucian literature.

64. Circe, the sorceress of Aeaea, mentioned in Homer's *Odyssey*, transformed the companions of Odysseus into swine. The initiate leader was, however, protected from such transformation by Hermes' gift of the herb *moly*. Having resisted her magic, Odysseus took the sorceress as a lover. For a brief survey of the esoteric background to the word, see n.4.

65. We cast a horoscope for the day of the move, to see if this would throw any significance on the timing, in the middle of so cold a winter. We observed that Saturn had just moved into Aquarius, and that there was a preponderance of planets in Capricorn. The mediaeval tracts assign Siena to Libra (see, for example, the 17th-century Lucca mss. reproduced in F. Gettings, *The Hidden Art*, 1978, p.65, pl.65). However, we have always been of the opinion that this hill town is ruled by Capricorn: perhaps our Master agreed with this? Perhaps the date had nothing to do with astrology – the day marked the old festival of the Birth of Christ, before it was moved to 25 December.

66. Rafaelo had not read Dante with sufficient care. It is widely believed that Dante placed Montereggione in Hell. This is not true. In Canto XXXI 40, the poet offers Montereggione's castellated hill (*Montereggion di torri si corona . . .*) as a simile of the Well he encountered in Hell.

The modern Montereggioni is still girdled by the 13th-century walls with which Dante was familiar. As we recall, the wall is strengthened by 14 towers, but some symbolists prefer to count 12 – perhaps to draw a parallel between Dante's Well of Hell and the 12-arc'd zodiac of the Heavens. The general proposition behind this over-exerted symbolism is correct: Hell does house inversions of Heavenly things.

However, we wonder if Dante had in mind the *Puteus* (Well) which his near-contemporary, Michael Scot, wrote about so learnedly? One gets the impression that the location of *Puteus* in the skies was not clearly defined, even by mediaeval standards. The famous Alfonsine tables suggest that it is another name for *Ara* (Altar), and distinguishes it from *Sacrarius*, which Michael Scot never did. For Scot, the Pit and the Sacred Place were one and the same.

67. I found the quotation copied in manuscript in one of Hedsel's notebooks, yet unfortunately he omitted the source. Otherwise, the quotation was well annotated. He points out that 'the black soot of that ancient one' is a reference to the evil Egyptian god *Set*. We are told by etymologists that the name Set literally means 'black', and (perhaps with less reason – see Kenneth Grant, *The Magical Revival*, 1972, p.226) that our own word *soot* is derived from the name of this same shadow-god. If this etymology is correct, then just imagine what can we make of *sot*, which meant 'fool', and 'habitual drunkard', or *sot-weed*, which was, of course, tobacco. The entire quotation seems to be alchemical, yet it is an alchemy of a highly sophisticated kind. For example, the fingertips refer to the periphery, the eyes to the centre, of Man. This separation of Saturn and Sun, to the peripheric and innermost central dot, respectively, suggests that the alchemical work is almost finished, that the inner eye is almost developed. Even so, the pain is such that the would-be Adept cries out for release. Finally, and most appositely, Hedsel notes that only those who have been in this alchemical crucible are qualified to judge whether the text is over-dramatic.

68. These are the Moirae, or Fates, conceived as spinners at the loom of Life. Lachesis determines the length of the thread, Clotho spins it into a form, and Atropos cuts it with her shears.

69. This appears to be a reference to T. S. Eliot's poem, *The Waste Land*, 1922, pt III, 'The Fire Sermon'. It opens with near-quotes from Spenser's *Prothalamion*, which was written to celebrate a marriage (in fact, the double marriage of the daughters of the Earl of Worcester, in 1596), and continues into a reference derived from Shakespeare's *Tempest*, relating to a sea-wreck and death – a suitable progression of images, given the theme of Hedsel's narrative. One wonders to what extent Hedsel's references to the 'Well' in Dante's *Purgatorio* (see n.66) are also an attempt to evoke the notes to line 411 of Eliot's *The Waste Land* ('What the Thunder Said'), for this was truely a Waste Land experience in his life. Eliot, in his notes on the line '*Dayadhvam*: I have heard the key', quotes from *Inferno* XXXIII, from which the English is a translation, and adds a highly relevant gloss from F. H. Bradley, *Appearance and Reality*, p.306. The Sanskrit word, *Dayadhvam*, is from 'What the Thunder Said': it is a Sanskrit term, meaning 'sympathize'.

70. Once again (see n.69) Mark Hedsel is inviting parallel texts, to deepen the intellectual content of his imagery. In this case, the reference is to Eliot's poem *The Four Quartets*, 'The Dry Salvages', II, l.2, and evokes the idea of the 'soundless wailing' of grief.

71. The Egyptian goddess *Maat* is mistress of the Underworld, and participates in judgement over the dead.

72. The term *Shadow land* seems to have been used fairly widely in the 19th century, but was accorded some passing fame by the medium, 'Elizabeth d'Esperance' (1855-1919), in the title of her curious autobiography, *Shadow Land*, n.d. It is the autobiography of a person who lived between this world and the next, in which the impalpable impressions of others were confusingly real for her.

73. Andrew Jackson Davis, *The Diakka, and Their Earthly Victims*, 1873: his theme is that seances and clairvoyants attract very low-grade entities of a selfish disposition, which are not in the least interested in probity, yet will furnish information in order to maintain a kind of vampirish relationship with humans. Undoubtedly, Davis was the most remarkable of the American clairvoyants.

74. It may appear that we are now breaking this agreement. However, we have disguised her name, the site of the house, and the actual circumstances under which the circles were conducted. The important story we tell here is quite true, but we have changed the details sufficiently to avoid any possibility of those involved being identified.

75. Increase Mather (1639-1723) was President of Harvard for 16 years, and pastor in North Church, Boston, until his death. His son, Cotton Mather (1662-1728), took charge of North Church, after the death of his father, and is still famous, or infamous, for his support for the prosecution of the so-called Salem witches.

76. Apparently, William Mumler's first 'unexplained' images had appeared on his photographic glass plates unbidden, in 1862. These early Spirit photographs are now much sought after by collectors, but in the 1960s it was still possible to buy the occasional print, made from surviving plates, for only a few dollars. In particular, the sepia print which Mumler had made of the ghost of Abraham Lincoln was popular; we purchased two prints from separate sources.

    The fraud trial, held at Tombs Police Court, in New York, initiated by a journalist with an eye to obtaining material for the newspaper *World*, lasted several days, and was a sensation in its day. Mumler was exonerated of the charge. It is an indication of how widely spread Spiritualism was in the United States at that time, when we learn that Judge Edmonds of the US Court of Appeals, and a Senator for New York State, who was called as a witness at the trial, was a Spiritualist, and the author of a two-volume 1853 work, *Spiritualism*, 1853.

    One photograph by Mumler showed the supposed spirit of President Lincoln resting his arm on the shoulder of Mrs Lincoln, was copied by the photographer Hudson, and published in *Human Nature* in December 1874. All the Lincoln-ghost prints we have seen appear to have been copied from this Hudson version, which was probably touched up. When the historian of psychic photographers Coates, reproduced it on p. 23 of his *Photographing the Invisible*, 1912, he said that both the Spirit images on the print 'were almost too faint for reproduction'. The second 'extra' was said to be the image of Lincoln's son.

77. Mark Hedsel is either quoting directly from Longfellow, or is identifying Lady C with the medium, d'Esperance (see n.72) – perhaps suggesting that Lady C had been a pupil of d'Esperance. At all events, d'Esperance had opened the first chapter of her autobiography with the words of Longfellow:
    > All houses wherein men have lived and died
    > Are haunted houses, through the open doors
    > The harmless phantoms on their errands glide,
    > With feet that make no sound upon the floors.
    > We meet them at the doorway, on the stairs,
    > Among the passages they come and go,
    > Impalpable impressions on the air,
    > A sense of something moving to and fro.

78. Although Lady C was famous as a medium, she was by no means the only one in the United States. Indeed, the type of Spiritualism she advocated had become inordinately popular even in the 19th century. In America, the Spiritualist methods and literature became popular through the Reverend Hammond's *Pilgrimage of Thomas Payne*, which had appeared in New York, in 1852. However, the far more informative and intelligent works of Andrew Jackson Davis – especially his influential *Principles of Nature*, begun in 1845, and his *Penetralia*,1866 (which has still not been accorded the fame it merits) – were outstanding examples of the clairvoyant literary genre. Within this context of Bostonian Spiritualism, it is worth observing that there were several 'automatic writings' in Judge Edmond's book *Spiritualism*, which had appeared as early as 1853. It was this same Edmond who appeared on behalf of the Boston photographer, Mumler, at his trial for fraud (see n.76).

79. Automatic writing is a technique of contacting spirits for literary purposes, by which the medium gives himself or herself over to the controlling spirit, to act as an amanuensis (or to dictate to an amanuensis) at the dictate of the spirit. It is a cause of much self-delusion.

   This technique of spirit-writing was widespread in the 19th century, though most of the 'literature' produced is so turgid as to suggest the majority of spirits have poor literary ability. There are exceptions: some of the Theosophical literature of Madam Blavatsky and many of the works of Alice Bailey were produced in this way, but there may be no doubt that the spirits contacted were of high order, and supplemented by the considerable learning of the amanuenses.

   The main problem is that those who practised automatic writings often made high-sounding claims regarding their Spirit sources. For example, on the European continent, the 15-year-old Hermance Dufeaux had written a widely read life of Joan of Arc, allegedly dictated by the Maid herself. This pseudo-religious theme was developed by the medium Geraldine Cummins, who wrote to the dictate of *soi-disant* contempories of Christ, including Cleophas and Philip. The widespread practice of this Spiritualist literature appears to have resulted in little of genuine literary importance (*The Vision* of W. B. Yeats is a notable exception), but the 16th-century monks who oversaw the work of the archaeologist Frederick Bligh Bond certainly offered material which was new to the circle who operated under their control: see, for example, *The Gate of Remembrance*, 1918. The term 'automatic writing' – not to mention 'automatic speaking' and 'direct voice' – was changed, in relatively recent times, to 'channelling'. This change in name should not obscure the fact that the literature of the channellers seems to be of much the same low order of literary quality and intellectual calibre as of the earlier automaticists.

80. The individual *Egos* that had dwelled in such bodies as those of Cleophas or the Apostle Philip would have long ago taken other existences, in other bodies, and would not be available to dispense instruction in this way. The periods spent by disincarnate spirits in the Spiritual world, in between incarnations, is only a matter of a few hundred years duration at most.

81. Monitory, or monitorial spirits, were those which, in one way or another, furnished warning information about a future event.

82. *Ectoplasm* is the name given to a substance which is extruded from the bodies of mediums (usually from orifices, such as the mouth, eyes, or even the sexual parts). Those who have investigated the phenomenon have established that it is a semi-matter, invisible in its primal state, but visible and tangible at a later state: it does react badly to light, however, which makes investigation difficult. Madam d'Esperance (see n.72) said that the first stirrings of the substance ('a vaporous mass, quasi luminous') felt like being covered with spider webs. The name now in use was apparently coined by Dr Charles Richet (Professor of Physiology at the Faculty of Medicine, in Paris), from the Greek *ektos* and *plasma* – 'extending substance'. One wonders if Richet realized that *plasma* was straight from the hermetic literature, descriptive of the human bodies which spirits were compelled to descend into at rebirth? The phenomenon of ectoplasm was wide open to fraud in the seance rooms – there are thousands of photographs of 'ectoplasm' which look suspiciously like cotton wool.

83. See for example, Ronald Pearsall, *The Table Rappers*, 1972

84. This 'Phrygian cap' – a red cap of distinctive shape – seems to have been used to mark initiation into the cult of Mithras, and its ceremonial donning was an important element of the Mithraic rituals. This head-gear of Mithras, most clearly seen in the various Tauroctonous images, of the god as a bull-slayer (figure 00), survives in many later initiation images – for example, it is worn by the so-called Alchemist on the tower of Notre-Dame of Paris. In the Mithraic mysteries, the cap was called the *liberia*, which has led some scholars to suggest that the the rites of

Mithras was involved with freed slaves. Could this Sun-god liberate those sleepers in thrall to the Moon? It was adopted – possibly at the instigation of certain Masonic bodies – by the French revolutionaries as the red 'Cap of Liberty', who used it as a 'protective talisman in the midst of the revolutionary slaughter' – see Fulcanelli (op. cit., p.72). Surely, the *liberia* survives still in the phrase 'Liberty, Equality and Fraternity'? For an account of the Mithraic mysteries, see Franz Cumont, *The Mysteries of Mithra*, 1956 ed. There were seven degrees of initiation, ranging from the *Corax* (Raven), to *Heliodromus* (Sun-Runner), to the highest, Pater (Father): it is evident from the records that these titles were occult blinds, and that secret titles were bestowed. The masks, or *persona*, worn during certain rituals, were designed to reflect the attained grades (see Cumont, pp.152–4).

The sword accorded to the grade of *Miles* or soldier was handed at initiation to the *mystes* on a crown, which he would ever afterwards aver ~belonged to my god' – that is Mithras. This rite throws some light on the sword in the grasp of Paracelsus marked with the secret *Azoth*. It also explains why the rites of Mithras were so popular in the Roman armies. The Christian, Tertullian, recorded a ritual in the Mithraic cults involving the branding the forehead of the initiate (almost certainly the *Miles* grade) with a red-hot iron.

For some hint of the esoteric background to the Arabic headgear, see n.24.

85. In the late 1980s we heard a similar word, *flipper*, being applied in Kuwait to electronic 'space invader' machines, in which (of course) the side 'finger flippers' were non-existent. Many of the wealthy Kuwaitis were educated in France, England or the United States, so we need not look far for the source of the word. It is not often that one encounters etymologies in the making.

Unfortunately, we know very little about the rich etymology of the Arabic language, but it is worth observing that the word *Al Jabhah*, used for the distinctive head-scarf (which, for all its tribal significance, is essential to the desert climate) is almost certainly linked with the *Al Jabhah*, 'forehead', that appears no less than twice in the lunar manzils of the Arabian astrology. It is the Arabian name for the equivalent of the mediaeval *frons*, and appears again as the mediaeval *corona*, or crown'. In this latter form, it appears in the phrase *Iklil al Jabhah*, which means 'Crown of the Forehead', and is used to denote the 15th manzil. To the arcanist, this would suggest a connection either with the third eye of the forehead, or of the more resplendent Crown chakra of the head.

86. Perhaps the most famous is that from the North-western Palace at Nimrod, which is now in the British Museum.

87. The 'Baghdad Batteries' were found by the Iraq State Railways Department in June, 1936. They have been dated to the second century BC. In 1960, a replica was made in the University of North Carolina, using an electrolyte of 5 per cent vinegar solution, a charge of one half volt was obtained from the battery for a period of 18 days. It has been deduced from these experiments that the batteries could have been used for a primitive form of electroplating silver on to copper. See W. Winton, 'The Baghdad Batteries B.C.', *Sumer* 18 (1962), pp.87–9.

Ahmed was certainly exaggerating with the term *famed battery*. In fact, round about 1955, we had seen one battery on display in the museum, but did not have enough information to perceive its implications. The batteries were brought to the attention of the general public through the Pauwels and Bergier *The Morning of the Magicians*, 1963, which was one of the main source books for the ideas borrowed by Erich von Daniken for *The Chariot of the Gods?* There was never any adequate reason for von Daniken to promote the batteries as being of extraterrestrial origin. It is the survival, rather than the fact of their previous existence, which is the real wonder of the Baghdad batteries. For a well researched account, see Ronald Story, The Space Gods Revealed. *A Close Look at the Theories of Erich von Daniken*, 1976 ed, p.5.

88. Jalal al-din Rumi, known in Persian as *Maulana*, 'our Master' (1207-1273), was the

most influential esoteric teacher of the period, and one of Persia's greatest poets. Rumi was forced into the life of a wanderer due to the anger of his sovereign. He was the founder of the Mevlevi order of dervishes. He designed some of the order's dances, and wrote some of its sacred hymns. His great mystical work, the *Mathnavi* is in six books, and over 27,000 verses.

The two lines quoted are from the *Mathnawi*, bk I, 1504–5. For a delightful glance at the esoteric element in the work of Rumi, see Coleman Barks, *Rumi. One-Handed Basket Weaving*, 1991.

99. Dhu'l-Nun belonged to a ninth-century Egyptian sect of Sufi: his books on alchemy and magic have not yet been translated into English. Coleman Bark (op. cit., n.88) tells the treasure story in a slightly different version, pp.126–7. A story of Dhu'l-Nun 'Foolish Wisdom', or 'Instructive Madness', is told by Rumi in the *Mathnawi*, bk 2. The friends of the alchemist were surprised that a man of such profound wisdom could have become mad, and went to visit him. Dhu'l-Nun rushed from his house, and threw stones at them. They all ran away. 'See,' shouted Dhu'l-Nun, after them. 'How can you be friends, when friends do not run away from pain inflicted by a friend?'

90. Dhu'l-Nun's poetic conceit seemed to be that the 'treasure' which could be grasped was the sacred written Arabic name of God itself, for the final *h* of Allah is an enclosure, like a handle at which the faithful may grasp, in the certainty of being lifted by three upward-sweeping letters of the *a* and *l*s.

91. Sufism is the name now given to one of the most ihfluential of the mystic or esoteric streams of Islam. It is likely that the word is from the Arabic for wool (*suf*), as it was usual for the early Sufis to clothe themselves in the coarse woollen clothing, and renounce the ordinary world – a practice probably borrowed from early Christian recluse-monks. Among the most important of its Spiritual disciplines was *tawakkul*, or trust in God, which encouraged an individualistic approach to mysticism, in which the adherent sought to every deed in harmony with the will of God. Many of the early Sufis wandered from place to place, in some cases living on alms, in other cases from a craft or from labour, in a manner which (initially at least) did not encourage monastic or social structure. Although undoubtedly Islamic in inspiration, there are in the written works of the leading Sufis strains of early Christian mysticism, and Neoplatonic thought, carried over from the classical world. It is inevitable, in view of these influences, that the later Sufi movements became at loggerheads with the official doctrines of Islam. It was from the Sufi orders of the 11th century that the Dervish orders arose – groups of people who sought deeper relationship with God through ecstatic music, dancing and (in some cases) self-induced trance.

92. *Enkidu* was the name of the wild-man in the *Epic of Gilgamesh*. After a fierce fight with Gilgamesh, Enkidu became a close friend, and and set out with him in search of the Plant of Life. On the journey, Enkidu was killed, and taken to Hell. See n.93.

93. The Sumerian *Epic of Gilgamesh* seems to be of great antiquity, and has been traced back to the fourth millennium BC. In so far as Gilgamesh was a historical king, he seems to have been the fifth divine ruler after the Flood. The general drift of the Epic – of Gilgamesh's search for the Plant of Life, aided by his friend Enkidu – is told in the following dialogue between Mark Hedsel and his companion.

94. The four 'Great Markers', or 'Royal Stars' of the Persians, ib the third millennium BC, were Aldebaran (our *alpha Tauri*, which marked the vernal equinox), Antares (our *alpha Scorpii*, which marked the autumnal equinox), Regulus (our *alpha Leonis*, which marked the summer solstice), and Fomalhaut (our *alpha Piscis Australis*, which marked the winter solstice).

95. Typically, Ahmed gave the poetic name for the asterism. In the majority of star lists it is named *Al Jabbar*. The two words mean the same, however. Oddly enough, the name seems to have come not from a stellar giant, but from a sheep. *Al Jauzah* was a black sheep with a white spot on its body.

413

96. There seems to be a play on words here. *Algebar*, used as an alternative name for Orion among the Arabs, was also used by them to denote the *beta* of Orion. This star was also known by the Arabic name *Rigel*, which was from a descriptive phrase meaning 'the left leg of the asterism'. The left literally stood on the Earth, which explains Mark Hedsel's words. Another possible meaning in this play on words is that derived from the fact that the mediaeval Alzoph (who was almost certainly the tenth-century Persian astrolger, Al Sufi) called the star 'the Herdsman': once again, a very Earthly image in comparison with the stellar imagery of *Uruanna*.

97. According to R. H. Allen, the 16th-century scholar Joseph Justus Scaliger believed this. See Allen, *Star-Names and Their Meanings*, 1963 rep., p.307. Allen does not give a source for the reference.

98. He was Sahu in the fourth-millennium Ramesseum at Thebes, and in the *Egyptian Book of the Dead*.

99. The Arabic names Mintaka, Alnilam and Alintak were sometimes groupe dtogether under the title *Al Nijad* – 'the belt', as in European astronomy.

100. See, for example R. Bauval and A. Gilbert, *The Orion Mystery*, 1994.

101. See, for example, R. W. Buchanan's *Ballad of Judas Iscariot*, where '. . . round and round the frozen Pole Glideth the lean white bear . . .'

102. The story from the *Mathnawi*, 'The Man with a Bear', is told on p.24 of Barks, op cit. n.88. It is from R. Nicholson's translation, *The Mathnawi of Jalaluddin Rumi*, 1925–40.

103. It was the same Cotton Mather who had been buried near the home of Lady C (see n.75), who, in 1712, recorded that the North American Indians used the word *Okuari*, meaning 'bear', long before the Europeans came to their country.

104. The word *uzur* is the plural for the veil which covers the whole body. When Ahmed used the word, we thought at first that this was a reference to the fact that, in Arabic, there are a considerable number of different names for various forms of the veil. Later – given the context of 'illusion' – we came to the conclusion that Ahmed was thinking of the 70,000 veils of light and darkness which cover the splendour of God. If God were to raise these, anyone who gazed upon Him would be set alight.

105. The Arabic *Manzils* are the 'mansions of the moon', or the arcs of approximately 12 degrees, measured against fixed stars denoting the distance travelled by the Moon each day during the 28 days of the month. They correspond as arcs with the Hindu *nakshatras*.

106. Fomalhaut is the fixed star which is now classified as the alpha Piscis Australis. See n.112.

107. Mark Hedsel left no notes as to the source of the Arabic, but we observe that the lines resemble the Jastrow translation, noted in *Aspects of Religious Belief and Practice in Babylonia and Assyria* . . . p.374ff.

108. In Arabic, *Bayt nuri* is literally 'a house of light'. In fact, it is a term from the ancient initiation rites, which apportioned specific names to specific inner functions: these names were given to inner temples, shrines and courtyards within the main body of the temple proper.

109. It is almost impossible to translate the Arabic *wasta*, for even the nearest equivalents in European languages are remote from its true meaning. It would be almost correct to translate it as 'reflected influence' or 'social refulgency'. In an Arabic community, a person has *wasta* through his or her known associations with another individual of undeniable power or importance. It is a reflected power, a sub-status determined by an actual status possessed by another who is a protector or friend.

110. *Ishtar* was the Babylonian goddess of fertility, and her cult was of considerable (early) importance at Erech, the city of Gilgamesh. She is the *Ashtart* of the later Greek cults.

111. The phrase 'bilocated sky-walker' refers to the ability recorded of initiates of being

able to appear in two forms, contemporaneously, in very different places. The phenomenon is said to depend upon the fact that the initiate can subtend an 'astral' form as materially convincing as his or her physical.

112. In astrology, the *anaretic* is the planet, star or nodal point which brings about the death of the person for whom the horoscope has been cast. In the stellar tradition of astrology, when the star Fomalhaut was with the Sun (it was in 3 degrees of Pisces in Ahmed's chart) this was regarded as a sign of danger of death from snake bites. We were reminded of how careful Ahmed was to ensure fhat there were no snakes in the trench we sat in during that night in the desert: whether this was a primal fear, or a knowledge of his horoscope, we cannot tell. The Moon of his chart was in 9 degrees of Sagittarius, on the fixed star *Han* set in the knee of the giant *Ophiuchus* – a position always associated with ruin and diseases of the thigh There were other factors in the chart which predicted death by snake poison.

CHAPTER FOUR

1. *Adeptus* is from the Latin meaning 'an obtaining', or 'an arrival at'. In esoteric literature it simply means someone who has attained a particular grade – usually a high grade. In this sense, it denotes a 'Master of a particular craft' – the artist Elias was a Master Alchemist. In some initiation schools, an Adeptus is a specific title in a series of grades.

2. The identity of this Adept, who taught Helvetius what the latter called the *Artis Pyrotechnicae*, has never been established. Helvetius tells us only that he was *ex Batavia Septentrionali*, which is, from North Holland. One wonders if it was a colleague or pupil of the great Rosicrucian, Franciscus (Franz) Mercurius van Helmont. That the visitant was a fellow Rosicrucian is beyond doubt from a phrase used by Helvetius, in his description of the meeting.

   A fairly common appellation for the alchemist was 'artist' – a term indicating one who had become proficient in the spagyric art. However, there *was* a Dutch artist, Nicolaes Elias, a contemporary of Rembrandt, who worked as a portrait painter in Amsterdam. The problem is that, while the precise date of Elias' death has not been recorded, it is likely that he died in the decade prior to the encounter recorded by Helvetius. Such alchemical references (especially those pretending to identify Adepts) are usually well hidden behind occult veils, however. For the Biblical name, Elias, see n.5.

3. During their first meeting, on the VI Calends January, 1666, the artist Elias showed Helvetius three pieces of the substance, contained in a cunningly worked ivory box. These, he said, were sufficient to produce 20 tons of gold. See *Vitulus Aureus quem Mundus adorat . . .* , in the 1678 ed. of *Museum Hermeticum Reformata et Amplificatum*, p.815.

4. The astrology involved in the Helvetius account is quite fascinating. Helvetius would not have known the planet Neptune, of course, yet this still left four planets – the Sun, Saturn, Mercury and the Moon – in Capricorn on that day. It is highly significant that Saturn was placed in what is known, in the astrological tradition, as the 'scholarly degree' (21 degrees Capricorn, marking the first degree of the last decanate of the sign). For an easily available list of such degrees, see Nicholas Devore, *The Encyclopaedia of Astrology*, 1947, p.90ff. In the alchemical literature, most dates refer to meaningful horoscopes, and the Helvetius *Vitulus Aurea* is no exception. Indeed, it is the astrological data which accounts for the gap of three weeks (from 27 December 1666) which Helvetius tells us was allowed to pass between the first and second of his meetings with the mysterious alchemist. On 17 January 1667, the aspects were far more favourable to an alchemical operation, if only because the Sun was exactly conjunct the important Mercury, the hermetic planet. In addition, the Moon had moved to a point where it was exactly trine its first position (27 December 1666) and was also both sextile the January chart position and trine the Venus of that latter chart. Those modern scholars who

comment on *Vitulus Aurea* without reference to such important arcane lore (taken for granted by the alchemists themselves) are missing the whole point of such literature.

5. The name Elias appears several times in the New Testament, and is almost certainly a version of Elijah. Relevant to the mysterious, unknown alchemist is the quotation from *Matthew* 17.12: 'Elias is come already, and they know him not.'

6. See, for example, A. E. Waite, *The Real History of the Rosicrucians*, 1887, p.417. The first grade is *Zelator*.

7. A. Pike, *Morals and Dogma of the Ancient and Accepted Scottish Rite of Freemasonry*, 1871, 1906 ed.

8. As Owen Barfield records, the Greek word for 'potential' seems to take its modern meaning from Aristotle: it is one of those words which was transmitted to the West through Latin translations. The Greek word *posotes* (which Barfield delightfully translates as 'how-muchness') seems to have been an analogy for Plato's *poiotes*, ('whatness') which gave us the word 'quality' since Cicero took the Latin equivalent, *qualis*. The word was probably from the verb to quantify. It is, as Barfield remarks later in the same book, one of those many words which has grown and developed in the 'long, agonizing struggle' to express the relationship between Spirit and matter. See Owen Barfield, *History in English Words*, 1953, 1969 rep., p.106.

9. The well-worn phrase 'The magic of the minimum dose' is from the title of a book on homoeopathy.

10. The homoeopathist Tyler tells us that it was the triturated poison Aconitum which finished off medical 'bloodletting' because of the relief it gave to inflammatory conditions in which, until that time, it was regarded as tantamount to murder not to bleed. See M. L. Tyler, *Homoeopathic Drug Pictures*, 1942, 1952 ed., p.6. This is something of an exaggeration, for homoeopathy itself put an end to such practices.

11. It is often claimed that this principle was recognized by such earlier physicians as Paracelsus. However, almost certainly this is not true. Paracelsus certainly used medications which were derived from herbs and powdered stones, and even believed that, by means of what is called the Doctrine of Signatures, it was possible to cure an illness by means of a particular plant or stone: however, Paracelsus does not appear to have promulgated the theory of homoeopathy precisely in the form proposed by Hahnemann. The arcane *Doctrine of Signatures* is based on the idea that every created thing has some planetary or zodical rulership. Those things which have a rulership in common are related in some way, and may interact beneficially. This doctrine has been applied in medicine to the notion that (for example) a like plant will cure a like illness – that a plant of the Sun will cure a solar illness. Human blood is ruled by the Sun, which is why the crusaders of the Knights of St John of Jerusalem used the Sun-ruled plant *Hypericum perforatum* to heal the bleeding wounds of their knights and soldiers. In addition to the planetary doctrine, there was an echo of the idea of 'like cures like' in the fact that the leaf of *hypericum*, when held up to the light, seems to be covered with tiny punctures or wounds which it would 'therefore' cure. However, it is the planetary rulership which is of the greatest importance in the Doctrine of Signatures: in popular mediaeval lore, *hypericum* was called *Sol terrestis*, 'Sun of the Earth'.

12. Avicenna (979–1037) was the greatest of the Eastern Arabian philosophers, and under his guidance Arabic medicine reached its highest peak. His philosophy was deeply influenced by Neoplatonic theory, and his approach to medical theory was based on alert observation. His *Canon of Medicine*, albeit badly translated in the 12th century, remained a medical classic until the mid-17th century in European universities.

13. This Order was shortly to be remodelled, after the death of the last of the Knights, Hohenthal. See Trevor M. Cook, *Samuel Hahnemann. His Life and Times*, 1993 ed., p.108. For details of the Leipzig Lodge, see R. F. Gould, *The History of*

Freemasonry, n.d., vol. VI, p.271ff.

14. Such connections lead one to question the extent to which Hahnemann had been commanded by leaders of such arcane groups to bring the principles of homoeopathy into the mundane realm, from the exclusive protection of esoteric circles.

15. H. L. Tyler, *Homoeopathic Drug Pictures*, 1942, pp.568-9 of the 1952 ed.

16. J. T. Kent, *Lectures on Homoeopathic Philosophy*, 1900, 1987 rep., p.118.

17. Hahnemann's *potency* is a statement of a sort of inverse relationship between quantity and Spiritual content. See n.8. The word belongs to spiritual science, rather than to mechanical science: it is interesting to see how readily the doctors who took to the Spiritual Science of Rudolf Steiner adopted homoeopathy as their favoured curative practice.

18. If the phrase was not actually written by Paracelsus, it does appear in a marginal gloss of the four-volume 1658 Geneva edition of his works. In an essay of 1796, Hahnemann had used the phrase *similia similibus*. The expanded phrase of 1810 is from his *Organon der Rationellen Heilkunde*. The historian, Henry M. Pachter, recognizes that Paracelsus was not a homoeopathist in the sense that Hahnemann was: see his *Paracelsus. Magic into Science*, 1951, for example p.86. For an excellent survey of this aspect of the Paracelsian medicine, see E. Wolfram, *The Occult Causes of Disease*, n.d. but *c.* 1925, trans. from the German by Agnes Blake.

19. For the story of Selene and Endymion, see p.71.

20. This was being built not far from a site which would eventually turn into the Shea Stadium. Both were being constructed for the New York World's Fair, to be held in 1964.

21. The rebuilding reminded us of just how prodigal New York had been with its older architecture. There is a delightful story told of Prince Bernhard of the Netherlands, when visiting the Museum of the City of New York. He was studying a small model of New Amsterdam, as New York had been called in the 17th century. 'Are any of these buildings still standing?' he asked. The President of the Museum replied, 'None.' With a shrug, the Prince murmured, 'You do things very thoroughly in New York.' See J. E. Patterson, *The City of New York. A History Illustrated from the Collections of the Museum of the City of New York*, 1978.

22. He worked under a pseudonym. Hedsel has made it clear that this pseudonym should not be revealed, as it might lead to the true identity of his Teacher. In his day, he was well known as an authority in his field, even if his esoteric teaching was undertaken secretly.

23. Frederick Childe Hassam (1859-1935).

24. Hedsel probably had in mind the Museum of the City of New York, but there are fine examples of Hassam's work in Boston, Washington DC, and so on.

25. What we considered to be his most impressive painting did not come into the Museum until much later. This was the delicately handled *Winter Afternoon in New York*, of 1900, which was bequested to the collection in 1971 by Mr Giles Whiting.

26. We were never able to trace literary support for the tradition.

27. This was at a ritual conducted in 1946. In magical circles it is known as the Babalon Working: it was a magical operation performed by John Parsons, the head of Crowley's magical Order in California. For the background to this Working – which involved Cameron Parsons, W. T. Smith and L. Ron Hubbard – see, for example, Kenneth Grant, *The Magical Revival*, 1972, p.136.

28. For a reliable survey of the arcane hermetic literature, see G. R. S. Mead, *Thrice-Greatest Hermes. Studies in Hellenistic Theosophy and Gnosis*, 1906. We have used the 1964 reprint.

29. Crowley has supporters and detractors. For a view of Crowley as overbalanced (if not to say mad), see J. O. Fuller, *The Magical Dilemma of Victor Neuburg*, 1965. For a more supportive view, see Kenneth Grant, *Aleister Crowley and the Hidden God*, 1973.

30. Crowley's drawing of the extraterrestrial *Lam*, which must have been made some time after the Astral contact of 1919, was exhibited in that year in Greenwich Village, New York. The picture is reproduced by Kenneth Grant in *The Magical Revival*, 1972, pp.84–5. Perhaps our Master did not know the Tibetan meaning of *Lam*. Kenneth Grant, in *Cult of the Shadow*, 1975, records that *Lam* is a Tibetan word meaning 'god', or 'extraterrestrial intelligence'. An entity called *Lam* seems to have been contacted by several magicians in recent years: see, for example, Kenneth Grant, *Cults of the Shadow*, 1975, pp.192–3, notes 40, 42.

31. The Koranic *Bism Allah al-Rahman al-Rahim* ('In the name of God the Compassionate, the All-Merciful') is reduced to the 19 letters BSM ALLH AL-RHMN AL-RHIM. For a thorough survey of the relationship which the number 19 holds with the three sacred books, see 'The Science of the Balance', in Henry Corbin's *Temple and Contemplation*, 1986 ed., p.89ff. Corbin did not mention Crowley's use of the Amuli correspondences. However, it is worth pointing out that *Lam* is the fifth letter of the Basmallah, which is pronounced to defend the faithful from the demons. In the schema of correspondences which relate the *Koran* to the *Book of Horizons* and the *Book of Souls*, this Basmallic *Lam* corresponds (in the exterior world of *Mulk*) to the sphere of Saturn. The 15th letter, also a *Lam*, corresponds to the Earth. Thus, the name could be used, outside an Arabic context, to denote the descent of a being from the highest planetary sphere of Saturn, which marks out the realm of Time, to the Earth plane.

32. The 19 'henchmen of Hell' are mentioned in the holy *Koran*; see H. Corbin, *Temple and Contemplation*, 1986 ed., p.89ff.

33. The scholar to whom our Master referred is probably R. A. Schwaller de Lubicz, whose writings caused such a stir in the 1960s: see his *The Egyptian Miracle* of 1985, which is a translation of the French *Le Miracle Egyptien*, 1963. His wife, Isha Schwaller de Lubicz, wrote a magnificent trilogy on Egyptian initiation: at that time, we had read only the first of these, *Her Bak*, 1956. For recent works by R. A. Schwaller de Lubicz, see *Sacred Science. The King of Pharaonic Theocracy* (a translation of *Le Roie de la théocratie Pharaonique*, 1961). The German Egyptologist, Karl Richard Lepsius, seems to have been the first to call this collections of papyri *The Book of the Dead*, a title made famous by the monumental lithographic version by Budge. However, it is a title which has worried many specialists ever since. Two subsequent specialists, well versed in initiation lore, have given it very different titles. Marsham Adams, in *The House of the Hidden Places*, 1894, recognizes that the true title is found in the rubric of chapter CLXII, which reads, with true arcanist overtones: 'This Book is the Greatest of Mysteries. Do not let the eye of anyone look upon it – that were abomination. *The Book of the Master of the Hidden Places* is its name.'

34. Under the Hyksos of the 15th dynasty, *Set* had become one of the most important of the gods: however, when the Hyksos left Egypt, he rapidly became the chief power of evil. In this guise, he was often portrayed as the serpent, *Apep*. Undoubtedly, we may trace in this Apep the tempting serpent of the Garden of Eden (plate 22).

Of course, the cult of the snake was widespread in pre-Christian cults, wherein serious attempts were made to unite the Light with Darkness. The fact that the snake was linked in almost every culture with the dead, or with the realm of death, partly explains the biblical imagery. Asklepius (whose very name is linked with the Greek for 'serpent') was the god of healing who had dedicated to him shrines in which were kept snakes fed by virgin priestesses. In many cults, such captive snakes were fed with honey-cakes, in precisely the same way such cakes were offered to the shades of the dead. The connection between the Realm of Darkness and the serpent, which had been established in Egyptian times, was continued in many forms.

There may appear to be confusion between this snake of the dead and the snake which was the symbol of the initiate. In fact, there really is no confusion, as the initiate is the one who has unimpeded access to the Spiritual Realm of the Dead – he or she may glide silently between the two realms. Only the uninitiated dead must remain beyond the veil.

35. In the Egyptian pantheon, and rites for the dead, *Amset* was the canopic protector of the liver. *Duamutef* was the protector of the stomach. *Hapi,* the Nile god, was protector of the lungs. *Quebhsneuf* was the canopic protector of the intestines.

36. The *Chariot of the Gods* in Egyptian star lore is probably the square marked out by the stars (Dubhe, Merak, Phekda and Megrez) of our Ursa Major. Certainly, by the end of the Egyptian civilization, the *Chariot* was referred to more specifically as the Car of Osiris, and sometimes depicted as a boat.

37. The poet, Victor Neuburg (see n.29), said of his magical adventures with Crowley, 'We went to sea in a sieve.'

38. See 'The Oracle of the Dead on the Acheron' by S. Dakaris, in *Temples and Sanctuaries of Ancient Greece*, ed. Evi Melas, 1973, p.139ff.

39. In early accounts, Cerberus had as many as 100 heads, like his father, Typhon. The later attribution of three heads was clearly intended to make of the dog an image both of man, and of the man–dog, Thoth. Just as Thoth guarded the secrets of Egyptian initiation, so Cerberus guarded the secrets of the Netherworld. The canine's serpentine mane or tail reveals his mother, Echidna, who also bore, among other arcane monsters, the Sphinx. The Labours of Hercules are revealed as being thinly disguised initiation myths when we learn how the eponymous hero descends to Hades to drag the guardian dog to the upper world, in order to show the devilish creature to Eurystheus.

40. For a fascinating account of the monkey in mediaeval art – which is partly the story of the fall of Thoth – see H. W. Janson, *Apes and Ape Lore in the Middle Ages and the Renaissance*, 1952; see esp. ch. 1, '*Figura Diaboli*: the Ape in Early Christianity', and note 46, p.351.

41. Hedsel gave no satisfactory source in his notebooks. However, in my opinion, his Master must have been reading Robert Burton, rather than Rusca's *De Inferno*. In *The Anatomy of Melancholy* (Pt I, Sec. 2., Mem. 1, Subs. 2), Burton translates Rusca fairly closely in approximately the words given by the Master.

42. We have discovered similar sentiments relating to the esoteric nature of creativity in the writings of Goethe. For an interesting commentary, see R. Steiner, *Goethe the Scientist*, 1950, p.97.

43. It is interesting that Hedsel (writing of a period in the early 1960s) should mention the finale of the *Suite*, for in 1976 musicologists discovered that the lyric attached to the linear melodic of the finale was a German translation of Baudelaire's poem 'De profundis clamavi'. This idea – of a voice calling out from the depths – certainly has some relevance to the idea of words, arising from unknown depths, deeply influencing Hedsel's life. Even if Hedsel did not have this in mind, the entire *Suite* is esoteric in content. The Viennese composer Alban Berg (1885-1935), like his mentor Schonberg, was deeply interested in esotericism, and his *Lyric Suite* is a complex exercise in numerological and musicological arcane associations. The esoteric basis of sound was being explored by musicians at the same time as the esoteric basis of colour was being explored by abstract artists, such as Kandinsky. For an excellent survey, see Sixten Ringbom, *The Sounding Cosmos. A Study in the Spiritualism of Kandinsky and the Genesis of Abstract Painting*, 1970.

44. It is forbidden for us to record the actual word, but at least *Sassuwunnu* is a reasonable approximation. *Sassuwunnu* is the name of a Babylonian marine demon of hideous aspect, with serpentine head and the body of a starry fish. A full description is given by R. C. Thompson, *Devils and Evil Spirits of Babylonia*, vol. II, p.149 ff. We realize, of course, that our enforced silence regarding the name uttered by our Teacher will persuade the reader to disbelieve the story, which will be unfortunate, as the account is true.

45. The Sanskrit *Preta* means 'hungry ghost', but Theosophists have translated the word as meaning 'shells', or Astral images left by avarious or selfish men and women after death.

46. In alchemy, the word *Putrefaction* was used as a convenient 'blind' to denote fission – the disguise in the blind resting upon the emphasis being placed on the dark reject, rather than the ensuing light. In putrefaction, the dark matter becomes thick and dark: it settles down, and thus 'putrefies'. Above the darkness the shining colours of a rainbow develop. In the Ripley Scroll of the 15th century, the radiant Hermes Bird rises above the Lunar Dragon as symbol of putrefaction (see n.50).

47. Prayer is a form of self-induced meditation which permits fission to take place. Prayer is one form of petitioning for release from unwanted darkness. In some cases, it is the only ritual which will offer lasting protection from demonic entities.

48. Eleusis, on mainland Greece, to the west of Athens, was one of the most important of the ancient initiation centres, charged with the cult of Demeter and her daughter. *Halade Mystai* is a Greek injunction, meaning 'Go to the sea, initiates [literally: Mystes]'. Clearly, there are meanings within meanings in the two words, for while the initiates do proceed to the sea, the inner sea is also intended.

    The month of Boedromion at Eleusis saw the processionals of the initiates, culminating (on 20th and 21st) in the *Night of the Mysteries*. What took place within the confines of the sacred Mystery Centre, the Telesterion at Eleusis, is still a secret, for the profane ones were never allowed to witness the ceremonies or initiations. One unidentified Greek poet, who admitted that he had been initiated at Eleusis, refrained from speaking about his experiences because, as he put it, 'Reverence weakens my voice . . .' (See K. G. Kanta, *Eleusis*, 1979, p.9.) The Christian, Clement of Alexandria, records that during these rites, 'The temple shook, and there were terrifying visions and fearful spectres, portraying the fate which awaits the evil man after death.'

    The secret rites were called 'orgia' in all the sacred centres. The demotion of the word has led to many misunderstandings of what went on in the Mystery Centres.

49. The Moon passes through each 30-degree segment of a zodiacal sign in approximately two and a half days. In astrology, the Moon in the progressional chart marks out periodicities of seven years. This gives us the basic triad of lunar numerology – 3, 7 and 28, the number of days in a month. The three and the seven are the base numerologies of occultism: it has been remarked that a man who can see the cosmos working in terms of both the law of three and the law of seven must be of very high initiation indeed.

50. George Ripley was a 15th-century alchemist, an Augustine canon of the monastic settlement at Bridlington, England. His alchemical research was supported by the hermetic brotherhood of the Knights of St John of Jerusalem. Several of the long alchemical scrolls, known delightfully as *Ripley Scrowles*, have survived. At least one genuine copy is in the British Museum.

51. The *Hermes Bird* is one of the names given to the radiant light which rises upwards during the initiatory process of *fission*. It is the bird of Hermes because it is alchemical, and therefore linked with the supposed founder of alchemy, Hermes Trismegistus. The alchemist, George Ripley, painted the crowned bird of Hermes standing triumphant over the world with seven feathers projecting from the globe. These are the seven feathers of the 'planets', over which the bird has dominance. Ripley rightly portrays the bird above the Lunar Dragon, to illustrate that the process of *Putrefaction* or *fission* is complete. For accessible notes on the 12 stages (linked with the 12 zodiacal signs) which Ripley traced in the alchemical process, see F. Sherwood Taylor, *The Alchemists*, 1952, p.113ff. In this discussion is a note on the stage of *Putrefaction* which we considered in n.46 above. The idea of something which both dies and quickens is an arcane expression of the alchemical process of *putrefaction* or fission – see n.46. A section of the British Museum version of the Ripley Scroll is reproduced in Alexander Roob's magnificently

illustrated *Alchemie und Mystik*, 1996, p.417. The scroll is discussed briefly in C. Burland, *The Arts of the Alchemist*, 1967, p.76.

52. The *Lunar Dragon* is partly the dragon of the astrological tradition – the Atalia dragon which was supposed to wind around the Earth. Where the path of the Moon (marked out by this dragon) intersected with the orbit of the Sun, the dragon's head lay. At the opposite side lay the dragon's tail. These two points (the caput and cauda of the astrological tradition) are 'dragon holes'. Ripley calls the Lunar Dragon in his famous scroll, 'The serpent of Arabia' – no doubt because in his own day it was clear that astrology was pouring into the West from Arabic sources. The Lunar Dragon in the Ripley scroll is the reject darkness, the putrefied residue of the process of *fission*.

53. The ancient Egyptian teachings pertaining to the empty tomb are preserved in the imagery of the Holy Sepulchre at Jerusalem. It is no accident that the empty tomb, or sarcophagus, became the altar of the Christian liturgy and symbolism. The symbolism proclaims that while the tomb may appear to be empty, it is yet filled with the presence of the living Christ, over whose body the sacraments are held. Each of the four Evangelists gives a different account of the finding of the empty tomb, but the one issue which is communal is that the disciples saw only the bandages – the physical remains, which remind us of the mummified deceased. It was that most enigmatic of all New Testament women, Mary Magdalene (*John* 20), who saw, yet did not recognize, the resurrected Christ. She did not recognize Him because the Resurrectional body is different from the physical body.

Curiously, our Master did not point to the most obvious connection between the ancient Egyptian and Christian Mysteries of the open tomb. The fact is that the mediaeval images which portray Christ with his arms upstretched (the so-called *orans* gesture) when He is standing behind the tomb, or sitting on it, are throwbacks to the Egyptian hieroglyphic for the *ka* or liberated soul.

54. Various Scalae, or ladders of perfection, were given by the occultist, Cornelius Agrippa, derived from pre-16th-century sources: see, for example, the Scala Duodenari, in his *De Occulta Philosophia*, 1534, bk II, cxxxii.

55. We suspect that our Master had in mind the idea that in the great fission of what the Theosophists call *The Separation of the Races*, humanity will be divided into one third and two thirds. Only one third will be able to progress. No doubt this idea (which is expressed in the apocalyptic literature of the Old Testament, such as *Revelation*) explains the insistence on the third day.

56. The *gimmel*, like the C, is both a determinant of the horizon (level) and the vertical (square to the horizon), thus a definer of the upright man. The Hebraic *Caph* has the numerical value of 20, but in their wisdom the ancients ascribed the Roman C the value of 3, which, in the Hebrew, had been given to *Gimel*. The value 3 was also given to the Greek *kappa*. Long before the Greeks adopted this sound value, the Egyptians used the hieroglyphic for the *Throne* as the equivalent of the sound.

57. The esoteric traditions pertaining to the swastika are exceedingly complex. It is said to be laid on the breasts of initiates after death: it was widely used as a Buddhist symbol from very early times, and is classified by Blavatsky as 'the symbol of esoteric Buddhism' and of the Lotus School of China. See H. P. Blavatsky, *Theosophical Glossary*, 1892, p.315. It is found marked on the breast of many images and large statues of Buddhas in Oriental temples: the giant Buddha at Lantau, off Hong Kong, is a good modern example.

58. The Baal's Bridge Masonic Square, discovered in the foundations of a small bridge in Limerick, Ireland, in 1830, is inscribed with the words:

> I will strive to live with love & care
> Upon the level. By the Square.

The verso and obverse is reproduced in Alex Horne, *Sources of Masonic Symbolism*, 1981, p.19.

59. The Master was using an occult blind. He uses the word 'days' to apply to a

proportion of years. He has in mind that the period spent in Purgatory is approximately one third the length of a lifetime. Thus, the one third, to three thirds, makes four thirds – the very basis of the swastika.

60. The word *lucifuge* is Latin for 'fleer of the light'. While no demon appears to enjoy the light, there *was* one class of demons called Lucifuges in certain mediaeval scripts.

61. It has been recognized for some considerable time that the various shafts within the Great Pyramid were oriented to Sirius, the Belt of Orion, the Pole Star and Thuban. The Sirius connection was so important in the arcane structure of the Pyramid that the hieroglyphic for the star was precisely a pyramid, divested of its foundation line. The name Orion has always been something of a mystery: it is usually explained as being derived from the Theban Greek *Orion*, but this does not explain the origin of the Theban. The fact is that the Thebans had derived it from the ancient Egyptians, for their *Ur Oon* meant 'Great Being'. In fact, many of the meanings of ancient mythological names of the Greeks become clear the minute the Egyptian prototypes are applied to them. For example, as Marsham Adams points out, *Kas Pehu* (meaning 'Lake of Inundation') is the Egyptian proto-name for the Greek *Cassiopeia*, the oldest known name for the constellation. The mythologists will remember that Cassiopeia was bound into her uncomfortable chair in the heavens by the sea–nymphs.

62. Our Master never told us what this name was, but we suspect that it might have been *Lilith*. In the Talmud, it was Lilith who spawned the *lilin*, or demons.

63. L. Kolisko has shown that during a solar eclipse the normal working of gold-salts is radically changed, and that the normal working of silver-salts is sensitive to the Moon, lead-salts to Saturn, iron-salts to Mars, tin-salts to Jupiter, copper-salts to Venus and mercuric salts to the planet Mercury. The evidence of the litmus paper images is convincing, and startling in its artistry. Many useful Kolisko reports have been widely published, but see in particular the report, *The Total Eclipse of the Sun, 15th February, 1961, studied in Bordighera (Northern Italy) with 1% solutions of Gold chloride and Silver nitrate. Capillary Dynamolysis Tests by L. Kolisko*. Kolisko was working in the anthroposophical line of research suggested by Steiner. The Steiner material is lifted from a series of lectures given on 25 June to 2 July 1922, translated with the title of *Human Questions and Cosmic Answers*, 1960. An available paper in English touching on the litmus paper images is the Agnes Fyfe paper, 'The Signature of the Planet Mercury in Plants. Capillary Dynamic Studies,' reprinted from *The British Homoeopathic Journal*, LXII 4, 1973, LXIII 1, 1974 and LXIII 2, 1974.

64. For an excellent survey, see J. Godwin, C. Chanel and J. P. Deveney, *The Hermetic Brotherhood of Luxor*, 1995. The Golden Dawn – or to give it its full title, The Hermetic Order of the Golden Dawn – was a semi-arcane order, claiming affiliation with a shadowy Rosicrucian order, but seemingly founded by a Theosophist and Freemason, W. W. Wescott, an amiable enough scholar, but no hermetic leader or Adept. Its external history is peculiar, and far too saturated in personal interests and amateur theatricals to be representative of a genuine hermetic order: its so-called 'inner order' – that of the Rose of Ruby and the Cross of Gold – seems to have been dreamt up and manipulated by S. L. MacGregor Mathers. Perhaps the most satisfactory survey of the Golden Dawn is Ellic Howe, *The Magicians of the Golden Dawn. A Documentary History of a Magical Order. 1887-1923*, 1972.

65. For a brief but useful survey of Annie Horniman (1860-1937), daughter of the founder of the Horniman Museum in London, and a proficient magician in the order of the Golden Dawn, see I. Colquhoun, *Sword of Wisdom. MacGregor Mathers and the Golden Dawn*, 1975, p.159ff. (See also n.64.)

66. There are many useful, and unfortunately brief, studies of W. B. Yeats as a magician, touching upon his somewhat uneasy relationship with the Order of the

Golden Dawn, but for a glimpse into his true magic-working we would recommend Yeats' own *A Vision*, 1937. Colquhoun (n.65) lists his initiations, p.172ff. There is a useful booklet by Kathleen Raine, *Yeats, the Tarot and the Golden Dawn*, 1972.

67. The Aleister Crowley business is now a lucrative one, and there are very many works dealing with different aspects of this magician. See n.29, where contrasting versions are noted by the pro-Crowley Grant, and the anti-Crowley Neuburg. (See also n.64, as Howe deals admirably with Crowley's destructive approach to the Golden Dawn). It is not possible for anyone advanced on the Path to take Crowley seriously as an initiate, for all his cleverness, and for all his important-sounding self-appointed tituli.

68. In the Celtic mythology, Merlin (originally named Myrddin) was a magician–bard, whose mythology became entangled with that of the Arthurian legends relating to King Arthur. It was Merlin who gave Arthur the sword Excalibur. Vivien (sometimes called Nimue) was his mistress. Andrew Lang, *The Book of Romance*, 1902, 'The Passing of Merlin' (p.33ff) tells how Vivien used Merlin in order to obtain his secret knowledge. Tiring of him, she tricked him into entering a cave in the Earth, where, he had told her, many wonders lay. Once he had entered, she rolled over the entrance a huge rock, so that Merlin could not get out. '. . . the damsel departed with joy, and thought no more of him: now that she knew all the magic he could teach her'.

69. The Rosicrucian pectoral, or secret-symbol medallion, designed to be worn over the chest, had a tag marked *fortiter et recte*, the order-motto of Annie Horniman. The jenny-haniver, a 'dragon' made from manipulating the dried body of a fish, was either a skate or a ray. We have seen similar 'dragons' for sale in Chinese markets. The shamanistic thigh-bone trumpet was beautifully made, with grotesque skulls as both blow-hole and mouth-piece. The head of the thigh-bone was incised with a neat motto, *res non verba*, which suggests that it might have been used in rituals.

70. The book seems to have been divided into three sections, only one of which was of the 'Book of Shadows' form: see C. G. Leland, *Aradia. Gospel of the Witches*, 1890. The large leather-bound manuscript grimoire which Mark Hedsel showed to me was entitled *The Shadow of the Golden Fire*. I estimated that it was itself little more than a copy, made perhaps in the 1950s. I noted from a dedication that it, or an earlier copy, had belonged at one time to D. H. Murgatroyd, author of *The Knight of the Raven. Being a Biography of John Hunyadi*, n.d. On checking details of Murgatroyd, I discovered this latter work was not dated, but, since it contained a reference to R. T. McNally's *Dracula Was a Woman*, 1984, I was forced to assume Murgatroyd's book was post this date: however, it was published posthumously. I further discovered that Murgatroyd had published a version of the grimoire manuscript, under the original title. In a useful note on the manuscript, in this printed book, Murgatroyd claims to have found it during a house clearance. Through an address left in the book, Murgatroyd was drawn to the now-demolished offices of the Fathers of the Rosy Cross, who are supposed to have published the magazine *The Lamp of Thoth*, in Keighley, in what was then the West Riding of Yorkshire.

71. A friend who examined the grimoire, and who knew far more about this type of literature than I did, said that the Crowley signature did not look genuine. However, Murgatroyd had claimed friendship with Crowley. Aleister Crowley's wide use of the sigil for *caput draconis*, for the capital letter of his personal name, has been interpreted by many as a penis symbol. It may well be such a symbol, but in addition, Crowley intended to link himself with Atalia, the Lunar Dragon The penis-like symbol is also a representation of the astrological lunar node, the *dragon's head*.

72. The manuscript was a carefully annotated version of Avalon's majestic work on the

423

chakras, with additional material from his *Sakti and Sakta*. The manuscript was dated 1920, but there was no note of the identify of the copyist. Avalon was the pseudonym of Sir John Woodroffe.

73. Sir John Woodroffe, *The Serpent Power. Being the Sat-Cakra-Nirupana and Paduka-Pancaka.* The 1928 corrected edition is by far the most useful textually, though the colour plates are not of as good a quality as the earlier ones. We are delighted to note that on p.7ff of this edition Woodroffe is rightly disparaging of the view of the chakras promulgated by C. W. Leadbeater, in his works, *The Chakras*, and *The Inner Life*. This is not the first time that Leadbeater has been revealed as writing 'from clairvoyant vision' about things concerning which he was ignorant.

74. The temple of Surya, at Konarak, is near Puri. The temple, built in the ninth century, is in the form of huge chariot, or *jagamohana*, driven by the Sun-god to whom it is dedicated.

75. Surya is the Vedic Sun-god, whose chariot was driven by seven horses, representative of the planets. Originally, seven horses were depicted pulling the great Orissan temple at Konarak. The statue is in a niche on top of the chariot. Surya is the driver of the temple. The symbolism is obvious – the temple is Man, with the seven inner planets, the wheels of the zodiac and constellations (12 pairs), and the solar Ego in control.

76. The Oriental nations have developed control of certain aspects of the Astral body to a much higher degree than the Occidentals. What Western Man has lost in the Astral, however, he has gained in development of the Ego.

The folds and the dignity of Indian clothing reflect the Astrality of the Indian bodies behind the clothing. When such clothing is stuck upon a European, it reveals the poverty of the Astrality – or, to be more precise, the difference in the Astrality. When the inner forms and the outer clothing do not correspond, then there is a sort of lie which is immediately visible to the sensitive eye.

What we are saying is in no way intended to demote Western humanity. The Western human being has developed other faculties at the expense of Astrality: the Western stream has moved into realms quite foreign to the Oriental stream. In a word, the Western civilization has developed the Ego-consciousness at the expense of the group-consciousness favoured by the Astral development. This is why there is something innately comical in a Westerner wearing Indian clothing, for when so clothed, the outer and inner do not match. When clothing is worn as an empty mask, then it is at best funny, at worst frightening – perhaps like the demon masks of Indian sacred dancers. The masks look ferocious, even when those behind them are dancing in a state of serene trance, attempting to regulate the movement of their bodies to the music.

77. For an excellent survey of the story by Goethe, see R. Steiner, *Goethe's Standard of the Soul as illustrated in Faust and in the Fairy Story of 'The Green Snake and the Beautiful Lily'*, 1925.

78. Coffee is said to drive the Spiritual bodies more deeply into the physical. Our Master seems to be making a joke of this enforced removal from the Spiritual centre. The playwright Ibsen wrote his nordic drama *Peer Gynt* in the warmth of southern Italy. Ibsen had written, 'So far away from one's future readers, one becomes rather reckless.'

In esoteric lore, coffee is harmful because it draws the spirit deeply into matter: in this sense, it can be an aid to clear thinking. Tobacco smoking is harmful for many reasons, but mainly because it attracts low-grade spirits and obscures the Spiritual world, both for the smoker and for those in the environment. Alcohol attacks the organism which serves the development of the Ego, and enables spirits to take over the personality, by means of the blood. The whole issue of drug-abuse and hallucinogenics is of profound interest to esotericists.

79. In esotericism, love is virtually an aspiration – something which is not yet

developed adequately in ordinary people. Ordinary love is 'love of the veil' – a love directed at the outer appearances of things, for want of a knowledge of what is behind that veil. The initiate – like the mystic – aspires to develop the love of the Spiritual, for the sake of the Spiritual, without being trammelled in the deceptions and glamour of the veil. In mysticism, this is called Love of God.

80. The vision was of the *ajna*, which is like the Moon, beautifully white, and which is ruled by Hakini. A traditional description of the *ajna* is in *The Serpent Power*, p.395, but it is evident that Hedsel saw other things beyond the symbolic forms set out in the Sanskrit literature. It is significant that his Master *commanded* Hedsel to experience the vision, as the Sanskrit word *ajna* means 'command', and pertains to the place where commands from above may be experienced or 'heard'. 'It is here that Ajna of the Guru is communicated', writes Woodroffe, quoting the *Gautamiya-Tantra* (p.395).

81. The Sanskrit texts place in the hands of the divine Hakini a rosary and the skull. It is perhaps this latter symbol which explains why she is said to dwell in the marrow. Hakini makes the sign (*mudra*) called in the texts *Vidya-mudra*, which confers knowledge. She has six faces, coloured red (though they look like the Moon), with three eyes in each face. The 18 eyes confirm her lunar nature, for the Saros cycle, which measures the regression of the lunar nodes, has a cycle of just over 18 years. This lunar cycle repeats four times during the 72 years in which the Sun regresses a single degree. This numerology is involved in the breathing and circulation of man. For details of the interaction of the two cycles, see G. Wachsmuth, *Reincarnation as a Phenomenon of Metamorphosis*, 1937, p.65ff.

82. The idea of the inner sky-walker was difficult for us at first. Later, when we understood that the outer eye had been made by the sunlight, and that the inner eye could only be made by the human being, the notion of the inner sky-walker became more clear. With the dawning of this clarity, we began to understand the significance of the statue at Konarak (n.74): Surya was set in a niche on top of the structure, yet he drove or controlled the entire temple edifice. This latter was the body, with its planetary powers, and the seven Spiritual bodies. The Sun-god Surya was himself an inner sky-walker, in the skies above the temple: he was the developed Ajna, the one in command.

83. In ancient times, Venus was called *Phosphoros*, which is usually explained as applying to the planet only when she appeared in the morning. Venus has long been adopted as a symbol for the Etheric body, and with the five-fold star of the pentagrammic man. Within the word is the Greek *phos*, or 'light', which is used in the initiation circles to denote the developed or initiated man – the 'Man of Light'.

84. See, for example, R. Collin, *The Theory of Celestial Influence*, 1954, 1971 ed., p.138ff, where the spiral terminates in the pineal gland. See also p.153, where Collin points out that the function of the pineal gland remains unknown because it comes into operation only in higher states of consciousness. G. W. Perry, *The Zodiac and the Salts of Salvation*, 1971, appears more well-informed on occult matters than Collin: Perry also sees the pineal as undeveloped in ordinary man, and as the connection with the 'temple of the Spiritual Ego (which is the optic thalamus) and the third eye'. Perry follows tradition in ascribing this centre to the zodiacal sign Aries, with which is associated the cell-salt, *Kali Phosphorus*. This is perhaps a surprising insight in view of the original name for Venus.

85. See the song of the Egyptian god Atum, from the fourth-century BC creation myth in the *Bremner Rhind Papyrus* quoted at the head of the present chapter.

86. L. E. Arochi, *La Piramide de Kukulcan*, 1976. For an English appraisal, see P. Tompkins, *Mysteries of the Mexican Pyramids*, 1976, p.308.

87. Dr Marian Popenoe Hatch's observations are recorded by Tompkins, op. cit., p.297, while dealing with the *Tro-Cortesianus Codex*.

88. In the Latinized Arabic of the mediaeval tradition, the star to which Marian Hatch referred had been named *Al Dhibain*. Some historians of stellar lore thought that

the star marked the darting tongue of the serpent, but others considered it to be under the dragon's mouth. In the first century of our era, the Alexandrian astrologer, Ptolemy, had called it, in Greek, *Geneus*, which meant 'jaw'. The main astronomical discoveries of the graphic intentions behind the serpentine form were made by Samuel S. Block.

89. *Superior* and *inferior* in this context are technical astronomical terms, derived from the Ptolemaic model of the planetary system. A superior conjunction is one which takes place beyond the Sun (in Ptolemaic terms, higher than – that is, superior to – the Sun). An inferior conjunction is one which takes place in front of the Sun, which is to say in the sphere lower than the solar sphere, in geocentric terms.

90. A late Roman star map (with personifications of Sun and Moon, and the main Ptolemaic asterisms) is given in Georg Thiele's *Antike Himmelsbilder*, 1898.

91. For details of the ceiling zodiac in the Mithraeum on the island of Ponza, see R. Beck, 'Interpreting the Ponza Zodiac', in *Journal of Mithraic Studies*, 1976, I. i. One should note that this is not a zodiac but a constellation chart.

92. The cult of Mithras, based on a solar cult of ancient Persia, spread to Rome shortly before the birth of Christ, and was at one time the unofficial religion of the Roman army. The Mysteries of Mithras have never been fully explained, but it is clear that there was a well-established system of initiation. Mithras, usually represented as wearing a tunic and the distinctive Phrygian cap, is often depicted killing a bull. See F. Cumont, *The Mysteries of Mithra*, in Eng. trans. of 1956.

93. Dr Hatch (n.87 above) made this observation, based on the double meaning of *Tzab* for rattle and stars, recorded by Tompkins, p.297.

94. See R. C. Allen, *Star-Names. Their Lore and Meaning*, 1963 ed., p.392.

95. In the days when we did research into the connection between the Americas and the Middle East, the works of Zecharia Sitchin had not yet been published, so we were reluctant to step ahead of scholars, and link the planet-image of the Mayans directly with the solar-image of the Chaldeans.

96. In fact, Venus is one of the great problems of early astrology, even though this has not been adequately dealt with by historians of astrology.

    The Greeks called the planet *Phosphoros*, when it appeared as a morning star. Strangely enough, how the Latin name Venus became attached to Phosphorus is unclear. In pre-classical times, Venus seems to have been a relatively unimportant Italian goddess, though, from time to time, her name was used in Latin as an equivalent for beauty. In the early history of the goddess, there does not appear to be any indication that she was linked with fertility, or even with lasciviousness – two of the qualities of the later Venus. At some point, prior to the expansion of Rome in classical times, she became associated with Aphrodite, and took on something of the latter's sexual character. By the second century BC, for reasons which have never become clear, the Romans were dedicating temples to Venus. This brief history partly explains why there are two traditions attached to the planetary Venus, one of which finds expression through the Earthy rulership of Taurus, and the other of which finds a more refined expression through her rule over Libra.

97. See quotation heading chapter 4, p.177.

98. The 'Solar disc' classification which is so frequently applied in Egyptian archaeological summaries reminds us of the other catch-all classification, 'ritual object', which really means that those classifying the object have absolutely no idea as to what it was used for, or what it really symbolized.

99. In very ancient times, there was an Egyptian uraeus-goddess named *Uazet*, but she seems to have been absorbed into the personages (and imagery) of many other later gods and goddesses.

100. As the art historian Carl Linfert points out, for all the vast scholarly research which has gone into his life and work, Bosch still remains an enigma. See C. Linfert, *Hieronymus Bosch*, 1971, p.7. The artist's fantastic depictions of Heaven and Hell,

replete with sexual and hermetic innuendo, his delight in such themes as 'The Ship of Fools', and the bizarre panels of his 'Garden of Earthly Delights', have resulted in pictures which are still mysteries, so far as most art historians are concerned. From surviving documents, we know that he belonged to the Brotherhood of Our Lady in 's Hertogenbosch, and that the name by which he is now so famous was a pseudonym, his family name being Van Aken. We have no idea as to why he painted his remarkable images, which seem to represent a hiatus in the development of late mediaeval symbolism. He had no artistic precursors, and, while he left behind a bevy of imitators, he left no School which could develop his painterly ideas: if his life is something of an enigma, his paintings are even more so.

Several attempts have been made to explain what Linfert called his 'cryptic language', and among the most convincing of these attempts is that by Wilhelm Fraenger. This German historian connects Bosch with the heretics, the Adamites, groups of which survived in his day in various guises in France and the Netherlands. See W. Fraenger, *The Millennium of Hieronymus Bosch*, Eng. trans., 1976. For the heretical group, the *Homines Intelligentiae*, the Brothers and Sisters of the Free Spirit, see p.16ff. We should observe that Linfert does not appear to agree with Fraenger's thesis that Bosch was a member of the Free Spirits.

101. For Philip II's role in developing esoteric thought, see R. Taylor, 'Architecture and Magic: Considerations on the *Idea* of the Escorial', in *Essays in the History of Architecture Presented to Rudolf Wittkower*, ed. D. Fraser, H. Hibbard and M. J. Lewine, 1967, p.81ff.

102. The Latin reads: *Cave, Cave, Deus Videt*.

103. The Hebrew *Ishon* means literally, 'little man', but was wrongly translated in the Authorized Version of the *Bible* as 'apple of the eye'. In dealing with this 'little man' in the hermetic literature, Mead quotes the *Kathopanishad*: 'The Man, the size of a thumb, like flame free from smoke, of past and of future the Lord, the same today, tomorrow the same will be. This Man is the *purusha.*' Mead's section on 'Ishon', in his *Thrice-Greatest Hermes*, III, p.102ff, is worth reading for its esoteric content.

104. Bosch has included in each of the seven images a detail of symbolism which points to a possible way to the higher life. For example, Sloth (*Accidia*) is represented as a man, sleeping in front of a fire: above the fireplace is a circular plate against which burns a candle. The light, like the pupil of the eye, is at the centre of the circle. This light is symbol of the Light of the World which can save the man: he cannot see it, only because he is asleep.

Bosch has painted a nun hurrying towards the sleeping man, holding out a rosary towards him. Bosch is suggesting that the sleeper may slough off his *accidia* with the help of Christ. It is not an easy Way that is being offered, but Christ will accompany the man. As the hermits who retired to the desert caves to tackle their own inner demons found to their cost, the sevenfold way through sin is no easy way, for it is a fight with the inner nature, a fight with what the mediaeval writers would have called 'the natural man', who is at all times beset by inner demons and temptations.

105. The painting was done for an unpublished work on Egyptian mythology, and is one of a series of 12 large monochromes (private communication from the artist).

106. Five Venus years ($5 \times 584 = 2920$) were equal to eight solar years ($8 \times 365 = 2920$). The sacred, solar and Venusian calendars conjuncted every 104 years. At one time, Venus was identified by the mythologists with the plumed serpent of the Toltecs and Aztecs, Quetzalcoatl – a most curious association as the feathered serpent was male, and Venus was female. However, this has since been shown to have been an error.

107. The *Liber Divinorum* illumination we have in mind is that showing the Spiritual structure of the sphere of the Earth. A reproduction is given by C. Singer, *From Magic to Science. Essays on the Scientific Twilight*, 1928, p.202: on p.222 is a

description. We were amazed to find this remarkable initiation-visionary manuscript of *Liber Divinorum* virtually on the open shelves of the municipal library, when we visited Lucca to examine the manuscript, in 1960. Hildegarde had herself overseen and instructed the artists, to ensure that her vision was correctly represented.

108. In an explanation of our experience described on p.211ff.

109. For *chasca*, see the article by S. Hagar, in Hastings, *Encylopaedia of Religion and Ethics*, XII, p.69.

110. The visit by Elizabeth to John Dee was on 16 March 1575. The passage is quoted in full in G. F. Kunz, *The Curious Lore of Precious Stones*, 1913, p.189ff. The visit is not mentioned in J. O. Halliwell's edited version of *The Diary of Dr John Dee*, 1842, as this is really an astrological day-book, listing only such things as births, curious events and deaths.

111. In the Aztec Creation Legend, the creator-god Tezcatlipoca was the god who ordered *Nata* (an Aztec equivalent of Noah) to build an ark, to save his family from the Deluge shortly to be released by the god, *Atonatiuh*. This last god was associated with the later rain-god, *Tlaloc*, to whom large numbers of children were sacrificed annually to avert further floods. According to Prescott, his polished shield was magical, for in it he could see all the deeds of the world. For the horror of the sacrifices in his honour, see Prescott (op. cit., n.120), I. 382.

112. For the significance of *Phos*, see n.83.

113. A number of these orientation markers have been published by Tompkins, op. cit., p.318ff. Among these are the Bennyhoff and the Harleston series. These diagrams reveal that, as in Callanish, the local mountains are used at as fiducials. The arc of sunrises between May 19 and July 25, which extends over an arc of 40 degrees, is indicated on the marker on the hill of Chiconautia. The Harleston marker, which was discovered accidentally due to rainfall, also indicated surrounding mountain tops and declivities.

114. Monte Alban seems to have been founded about 600 BC. The present ceremonial centre is vast, covering an area of about two and a half square miles, with over 20 well-defined pyramidal buildings, including an extraordinary observatory. The dancers (as they are called) are in bas-relief on a series of vertical stones: these rather static human dancers are overlaid with complex hieroglyphics. They are now located between the two major pyramidal temples of what is called System M, to the south of the ceremonial area.

115. Even when we last visited Monte Alban, in the late 1980s, the site had not yet been completely restored, and the pyramid angles (intended as viewing niches, or fiducials) were still undefined. Even so, the astronomers' viewing ports, and the ample niches in which they stood, were still perfectly preserved. The three-dimensional level on which the Mexican astronomers had worked was still evident. Those who attempt to reduce such analyses to two-dimensional geometric diagrams are unwise: the geometry is three-dimensional, and extended also into temporal co-ordinates. The viewing chambers built into the faces of the pyramids, intended for astrologers watching the sunsets and sunrises, are still intact.

116. The astronomers and historians who confirmed such things in 1974 were A. F. Aveni, S. L. Gibbs and H. Hartung. Their conclusions as to the stellar observations, and as to the connection between the Pleiades and the transit of Venus past such apertures and portholes, are outlined in Tompkins (op. cit., n.86), pp.309–10.

117. Hugh Fox, *Gods of the Cataclysm*, 1976.

118. It has not surprised us that so many modern historians have suggested that the Babylonians and Phoenicians of antiquity had contact with the Americas. The similarities in art-forms, mathematics and astronomical knowledge are far too close to be ignored, as they are by conventional historians. See Z. Sitchin, *The Twelfth Planet*, 1976.

119. The Bennyhoff marker on the southern flank of Malinalli had been discovered in 1963, but was not published until a decade later – in the introduction to the Teotihuacan Map, 1973. See Tompkins, op. cit., p.319.
120. The fact that the cross did figure in Aztec and Mayan symbolism had impressed the first priests to oversee with such piety the slaughter of the ancient Mexicans. Indeed, the similarity between some of the Aztec rituals at Palenque (where a great floriated cross was discovered) and their own Christian rituals was recorded forcefully by W. H. Prescott, *The Conquest of Mexico*, 1843, 1965 Everyman ed., II, p.381. Images of gods carrying crosses are found even in the few books which survived the Spanish book-burnings, and very many must have been seen before this holocaust. However, these crosses had a different symbolic import to the Christian cross. So far as we have been able to determine, the unobtrusive encircled orientation crosses were brought to the attention of Europeans only in the 1960s (see, for example, n.119). In fact, we now recognized that the cross links more directly with Venus than with any other planet. In the legends of North and South American tribes alike, the morning Venus comes in advance to announce the coming of her solar master. In this form, Venus is symbolized in the form of an equal-armed red cross. A similar cross is found encircled in the so-called winged globe of the Babylonian symbolism, which is supposed to be a version of the solar Ahura Mazda. Perhaps we should not be surprised that the hanging vertical of the Greek sigil should eventually become a cross: ♀

   In his remarkable book, *The Twelfth Planet*, Sitchen points out that the cuneiform sign for the god *Anu*, which also meant 'divine', was: ⋙

   This evolved into the Semitic form *tau* ⋙ ,which was one of the forms for the cross. Sitchen records that it was called, in this later development, 'the sign' (op. cit., 1976, p.218).

CHAPTER FIVE

1. Plato was the pupil of Sechnuphis of On (better known now as Heliopolis), which was the oldest capital of Egypt, and, as a sacred centre, even more ancient than Memphis.
2. We use the English phrase given by Mead in *Thrice Greatest Hermes*, 1906, 1968 ed., vol. iii, p.215.
3. The Roman city of Pompeii was partly destroyed by an earthquake (in 63 AD), and then covered in volcanic ash during the eruption of Vesuvius in 79 AD. The buried city was not rediscovered until 1748. For information on the Villa of the Mysteries, see M. P. Nilsson, *The Dionysiac Mysteries of the Hellenistic and Roman Age*, 1957.
4. The picture in Room No. 5 of the Villa of the Mysteries is beautifully preserved because it remained untouched until it was excavated in 1909. Although catalogued as a fresco, the painting appears to be in tempera.
5. In the Mysteries, the rituals are often linked with the Five Elements of Earth, Air, Fire, Water and Quintessence. A lash, whipping through the air, represents the Air element.
6. Maenads were women incited to ecstatic states by the influence of Dionysius. They displayed disordered hair, wore panther skins, and carried snakes or torches. While thus inspired, they had no fear of wild animals. The play by Euripides, *Bacchae*, offers considerable insight into the activities of the Maenads, who were sometimes called *Bacchae* or *Thyiades*. The sexual licence and orgiastic practices of the *Maenads* eventually led to a senatorial decree (second century BC), which banned them on Italian soil, save under extraordinary circumstances. In spite of the ban, these Mysteries flourished.
7. The Mercuric staff survives on many Roman sarcophagus reliefs, of which a fine

example is on public view in the painting gallery corridor of the Uffizi, in Florence. The sigil, in slightly different variants – yet quite clearly related to the mercuric staff – is found in the earliest surviving Graeco–Byzantine horoscopes. See O. Neugebauer and H. B. van Hosen, *Greek Horoscopes*, 1959. The great esotericist, John Dee, used the Mercuric version as the basis for his *Monas*, the 'hieroglyphic' which was adopted as a trademark by the Rosicrucians: see his *Monas Hieroglyphica*, 1564.

8. The hermetic staff was seen as a representation of the human spine, with the *ida* and *pingala* currents running up through the body in early Theosophical literature. See for example the diagrams in the unreliable work by C. W. Leadbeater, *The Chakras*, 1927.

9. In the passage 'Concerning the Inner Door', usually quoted in the Trismegistian literature through the writings of the fourth–century AD alchemist, Zosimus, in his notes on the 'great work distinguished by the letter Omega'. The title 'Inner Door' (*enaulia*) has given Greek specialists much trouble. See Mead, vol. iii, p.179, n.5.

10. The word fate is derived from the Latin *fatum*, from the verb *facere*, 'to do' – thus, it is something done, or something decreed. Fate was the doing of the gods. When, in later mythology, the Fates were named after the Parcae, the idea of the triple beings was linked with the Moon, and then with Hecate.

11. The Moriae were: *Lachesis*, the goddess who assigns the apportioned term of life to humans, *Clotho*, who spins the thread of this fate, and *Atropos* who ends the fate by snipping it with her shears.

12. It was this dagger which became the *athame*, or ritual knife of the modern wiccan groups. The scourge of this Moon goddess is perhaps less evident, but certain wiccan rituals which we have been honoured to witness do include the use of whips. In other images, Hecate carries also a lit torch, perhaps to remind us that she accompanied Demeter in the Underworld, while the latter goddess was seeking her lost daughter. This torch may even be a throwback to the ancient belief that the planets – including the Earth's satellite – besides reflecting the light of the Sun, also had their own intrinsic light. The weak 'light' of the darkened portions of the Moon was the reflection of sunlight thrown back from the Earth: this also had a symbolic importance in the Hecate rituals, further tying the Moon to the Earth.

13. The classical planetary gods were replaced by angels by the School associated with the pseudo–Dionysius, who wrote in the fifth century AD. The following list gives one variant classical name, the late mediaeval planetary name, and the angelic name:

Selene	Luna	Angel
Hermes	Mercury	Archangel
Aphrodite	Venus	Archai
Apollo	Sol	Exsusiai
Ares	Mars	Dynamis
Zeus	Jupiter	Kyriotetes
Chronus	Saturn	Thrones

For a more hermetic analysis, see A. E. Thierens, *Elements of Esoteric Astrology*, 1931, App. III, p.285. It is important to distinguish in this list Helios the Sun-god (which is equated with Ra, or Aten) from Apollo (which is equated with Knepth – see p.435, n.65).

Dante's hierarchies of the spheres in his *Commedia* correspond to those set out above. He is always prepared to interchange names and systems within the appropriate rank or sphere, in the agreeable manner of the poet. His Mount Purgatory in *Purgatorio* is a mirror image (or inversion) of the Spiritual hierarchies, as reflected in the mediaeval concept of perverted love. On the bottom Cornice are the Proud (pride being the sin of Saturn); on the seventh Cornice the Lustful, consumed with the lunar sin. For a list of anglicized titles of the angels, see Dorothy L. Sayers trans., *The Comedy of Dante Alighieri*, 1955, 1974 ed., *Purgatory*, p.352.

14. The hermetic corpus is perhaps best studied in English through G. R. S. Mead's three-volume work. See n.2. We do however refer from time to time to other authorities.
15. Thomas Stearns Eliot (1888-1965) was probably the most important modern English poet to give expression to his arcane interests in his published poetry. His *Four Quartets* is a superb example of esoteric poetizing.
16. For the time-references of the *Four Quartets*, see (for example) *Of Time*, p.19, and *Of the Decans and the Stars*, in Mead (n.2), vol. iii, p.28ff. Mead was not intimately familiar with the astrological nature of the decans, however, and some of his notes must be ignored.
17. In *Burnt Norton*, of *The Four Quartets*, Eliot visualizes the lotus rising quietly, its surface glittering out of the heart of light. There is a play on the double meaning (as noun and verb) in the word *rose*. The seven flower-chakras are each composed of light, but in this context the 'heart of light' is a direct reference to the heart chakra, or *anahata*. We are aware that many modern commentators on the poem have tended to miss or skate over the hermetic sources: for example, G. Williamson, *A Reader's Guide to T.S. Eliot*, 1967 ed., sees the ideas in terms of The Gospel of St John and Christian mysticism.
18. The scholar G. R. S. Mead (see n.2) was proficient in many languages touching upon the hermetic literature, and he was also deeply involved in the early Theosophical Schools. However, even Mead confessed to not understanding fully the hermetic texts.
19. This was one of the hermetic terms for the human body, which the initiate Schools recognized was composed essentially of warm water.
20. The literature is supposed to have been introduced to Italy in 1419 by the Florentine priest, de' Buondelmonti, who claimed to have found it during a journey to Greece. See, for example, R. Wittkower, *Allegory and the Migration of Symbols*, 1977: 'Hieroglyphics of the Early Renaissance', p.114ff.
21. The esoteric movement in Florence, which eventually gave rise to the Renaissance, and the spread of a new vision through Europe, seems to have been directed by the Medici.
22. The modern Italian *Firenze* is from the Latin name *Florentia*, which is from the verb *florio*, to bloom or blossom.
23. The 'flower' which is the key to modern Spiritual development is the ajna, the chakra located between the eyes. This flower is dual-lobed, which is why some literature describes it as having only two petals. It is said to be presided over by Hakini.
24. The German Egyptologist, Karl Richard Lepsius, seems to have been the first to call this collections of texts *The Book of the Dead* – a title which has worried many specialists ever since.
25. See Marsham Adams, *The Book of the Master of the Hidden Places*, 1933. This is a combination of his two works, *The House of the Hidden Places*, 1895, and the *Book of the Master*.
26. See for example the *Papyrus Carlsberg I* of the second century AD. This is quoted in E. C. Krupp, *Echoes of the Ancient Skies. The Astronomy of Lost Civilizations*, 1983, p.108. The 'pure' arising from this fission is said to appear in the horizon like Sirius.
27. The *grimoires* are the mediaeval books of demonic lore. Among the most widely used in mediaeval times was the *Solomonic* literature, the *Idea Salomonis et Eutocta*, most versions of which listed the names of 72 demons, their corresponding sigils, and their specializations. For an account, see F. Gettings, *Dictionary of Demons*, 1988, p.123ff and p.228ff. To judge from the descriptions, many of these demons were demoted Egyptian gods.
28. J. N. Lockyer, *The Dawn of Astronomy* 1894, (ch. XXX, esp. p.310ff), saw the star as such a visible fiducial in several Egyptian temples.

29. According to A. Badawy (and V. Trimble), the star now called Thuban was visible down the shaft from the main corridor of the Great Pyramid, *circa* 2600 BC. See 'The Stellar Destiny of Pharaoh and the So-called Air-Shafts in Cheop's Pyramid', *Mitteilungen des Deutschen Archeologischen Instituts*, 1964, vol. 10, p.189ff.

30. It is called the Chamber of Ordeal by Adams (see n.25), who was a Mason, following a line of reasoning in pursuit of Masonic nomenclatures.

31. Isha Schwaller de Lubicz was the wife and student of R. A. Schwaller de Lubicz. She and her husband dedicated their lives to the study and revelation of Egyptian sacred science. See n.32. See R. A. Schwaller de Lubicz, *The Egyptian Miracle*, 1985 Eng. trans. For a brief survey of the life of R. A., see the 'Foreword', by R. and D. Lawlor to his work *The Temple is Man. The Secrets of Ancient Egypt*, 1977.

32. Isha Schwaller de Lubicz, *Her-Bak. Egyptian Initiate*, 1967 ed., p.339. She is absolutely right to insist that while Egyptian priestcraft did not popularize knowledge, it did not conceal it. The Egyptians recognized that the secrets would remain secret for all those who had not been initiated into the higher lore.

33. Immanuel Velikovsky popularized the notion that a series of physical and cosmic catastrophes, in prehistoric and historic times, have shaped the history of the world. See his *Worlds in Collision*, 1950. See also the supplement based on his Princeton University address of 1953, in his *Earth in Upheaval*, 1956, p.233.

34. The effect of the Moon on all physical bodies has been demonstrated very ably in recent years by Kolisko. See, for example, p.422, n.63.

35. This must have slipped our Master's mind, for he never did give us the bibliography he promised. However, see n.37, where we make some attempt to remedy this oversight.

36. Etheric planes may seem to be beside the point, but they are absolutely relevant. Our Master rarely misused words. The truth, as we now understand it, is that the reason why mediumship, clairvoyance and channelling do not pertain to the Spiritual realms they aspire to is because they do not penetrate into the Astral world at all. They remain bound upon the Etheric plane, which, in contrast with the Light realm of the Astral, is little more than a shadow plane. They therefore can offer no possibility of communication with the Higher Beings. They remain in the shadow realms, which partly explains their great danger. The early Spiritualist, Andrew Jackson Davis, saw something of this danger, and expressed it in his remarkable book, *The Diakka and Their Earthly Victims*, 1873.

37. See E. G. Harrison, *The Transcendental Universe*, and Steiner's commentary upon this, and upon the corresponding Theosophical literature of Sinnet and Blavatsky, in his group of lectures, *Occult Movements in the Nineteenth Century* . . . The choice of the name 'Eighth Sphere' to denote that Spiritual realm which the Earth's Moon counterweighted was very unfortunate. The truth is that in the Spiritual chain of being, which was derived from the Ptolemaic astrology (itself merely the outer fragmentation of ancient Mystery wisdom), there existed already an eighth sphere. In this system, the spheres were numbered outwards, from the geocentric centre of the cosmos. The seventh sphere was that of Saturn, while the eighth was, in some systems, the zodiac itself, in yet other systems, the Stellatum.

38. Alfred Percy Sinnett (1840–1921), perhaps best known for his *Incidents in the Life of Madame Blavatsky*, 1886. The text which confused the issue of the Eighth Sphere was his *Esoteric Buddhism*, 1883. Sinnett, for all his connection with the Theosophical Society, had no deep knowledge of esoteric lore.

39. For Blavatsky, see p.33.

40. It is true that the learned Madame Blavatsky criticized the book most strongly in *The Secret Doctrine*, vol. I, pointing out that it has produced 'a very fatal impression upon the minds of many Theosophists'.

41. The analysis by C. G. Harrison, *The Transcendental Universe*, written around a series of lectures given in 1893 before the Berean Society, while admitting that he recognized 'many occulists who say the subject ought not to be brought before the

public at all', gave a much more thoroughly esoteric account of the Eighth Sphere. He recognized that Sinnett had been the first to profane this mystery, but that in doing so he had been working unconsciously, and in any case succeeded in getting many of his facts wrong. There is a less partisan analysis in Steiner's lectures, given in Dornach, in October 1915, now available in *Occult Movements in the Nineteenth Century*, 1973.

42. M. L. Ambrosini, *The Secret Archives of the Vatican*, 1970 Eng. ed. Our Master spoke of there being 20 miles of secret archives in the library, while Ambrosini writes of 25 miles.

43. In so far as there was a Greek title, it was probably *Kore Kosmon*, but the text has been given many titles, not all of which represent this Anima Mundi idea. The title 'Virgin of the World' is that favoured by Mead, who recognized the text as a sacred sermon of initiation into the Hermes-lore, the first initiation of which is always issued by the hierophant by word of mouth. Mead's commentary on the text, although perhaps marred a little by his adherence to Theosophical terms, is by far the best analysis available. Patrizzi offers the titles *Minerva Mundi* and *Pupilla Mundi*, the latter of which has been translated as 'Apple of the Eye of the World'. It is highly likely that this manuscript is the 'Sacred Book', mentioned in other hermetic texts. For a brief survey, with sources, see Mead, III, p.59, note 2. In fact, none of these titles adequately represents the contents of this hermetic text, which deals with the Mysteries well beyond the limits suggested by the Anima Mundi theme.

44. The synopsis is from *Kore Kosmon* (see n.43), p.25ff. For Momos, see n.18. Momos is generally regarded as being the personification of fault-finding in Greek poesy and mythology.

45. In the *Kore Kosmon* (see n.43) p.25.

46. *Adrasteia*, the keen-eyed goddess, seems to be one of the names of Nemesis, which G. R. S. Mead correctly identifies as a 'karmic deity', karma being that 'instrument, mysterious, possessed of power of sight that cannot err, and cannot be escaped . . .' See Mead, op.cit., III, p.71.

47. The Egyptian hieroglyphic *Ru*, $\bigcirc$, represents the place of birth.

It is a vestigial drawing of the kteis, and of the mouth, from which words are born. By extension, it became the place where secret knowledge was delivered, from the secret Schools, and the process nowadays known as 'rite of passage'. Something of this hermetic lore was expressed in the Christian symbolism which adopted the *Ru* as the vesica piscis, which is sometimes used to sheath Christ, Mary and certain saints. In this use, it represents the Spiritual world beyond the 'door' of the *Ru*.

48. No synopsis can do justice to this hermetic text. By far the best commentary and translation we know is G. R. S. Mead, op. cit., III, pp.59-117. Mead has the advantage over most other commentators in having a profound knowledge of initiation literature and terminology.

49. The true symbolism of the staff in the hand of the Fool of the Tarot card, and even of the stick he carries over his shoulder, is revealed by such terms as 'the feather of Maat', bearing in mind that the French for Fool is *Mat*. The *clava* staff is clearly linked with the *clavis*, or key.

50. Modern historians usually trace the origins of hypnotism back to India, but this is largely because modern history is so rigorously based on documentary evidence. The initiates of ancient Egypt were versed in hypnotism, and passed this knowledge on to the ancient Greeks. Modern hypnotism in the West has its roots in this initiation lore.

51. Black magic is a term often used to denote forms of magic which were once white, but which lost their Spiritual direction. While it is undoubedly true that there are 'black Schools' which devote their energies to regressive techniques which do not advance humanity, these must be distinguished from certain practices termed

'black', which are derived from ancient Mystery Schools, and which still have a hermetic validity. The Egyptian god of the Underworld, Osiris, was called the 'dark god'. He was the 'Lord in the perfecting black', which may be taken as meaning that he was endowed with the power of perfecting the darker side of man (what we have elsewhere called the double, but which in the hermetic literature was sometimes called the shadow). In this work he seems to cooperate with the goddess Isis, and perhaps with her darker counterpart, Nephthys.

These observations should show that, in a former time, what we might call 'black magic' had a Spiritual validity. It may have been practised in initiation Schools, but in some cases we have no doubt that its techniques may have fallen into incompetent or ill-trained hands. A consequence of this fall is that hypnotism, which was once used to develop the soul of the neophyte towards freedom and love, was later used to demote these two principles: hypnotism eventually became the tool of those interested in demoting freedom and love.

Techniques which worked on neophytes when the psycho-physical composition of man and woman was different from what it is now will no longer work beneficially, even were they to be conducted by initiates. Hypnotism is precisely one of these 'laggard' techniques. It is against the cosmic lore because it can be used with such ease to subvert the will of another, even in those cases where the hypnotized has give his or her permission for the hypnosis. The human will is sacred in the esoteric White Schools. The Dark Schools will work upon and subvert the will.

52. The Black Rite is mentioned in the hermetic texts in connection with Ammon. In turn, this Egyptian god was associated with Kneph, who seems to have been a form of Ammon. See Mead, op. cit., III, p.91ff. The texts mention by name *Kamephis*, who is probably the great hierophant of an initiation School which eventually gave rise to the Isis Schools.

53. Evi Melas (ed.), *Temples and Sanctuaries of Ancient Greece*, 1973, trans. from the German of 1970. See S. Dakaris, 'The Oracle of the Dead on the Acheron'. The Acheron runs into the Bay of Ammoudia.

54. This was Lake Acherusia, in Epirus.

55. Dakaris (see n.53), working with the Greek Archaeological Society, completed the first part of the archaeological survey and excavations in 1964. The site was not in a fit state for tourism when we visited the underground necromanteion.

56. The Periander story is told by Herodotus, *History*, V.92.

57. Homer, *Odyssey*, bk x, l. 487ff (p.129 in the Loomis 1944 ed. of the Butler trans.), recorded the location of the site, as well as the directions given by the magician Circe to Odysseus for consulting the oracle, which required the sacrifice of a ram and a sheep at the site, and promise of the further sacrifice of a black ram and cow, when he had finally reached his home. Odysseus' experience at the site is related in bk xi. Dakaris (op. cit., n.53 above) quotes from later sources, such as Lucian's *Menippus*, which give similar directions for the consultation of the shades of the dead in other oracular sites.

58. Josquin des Pres, *Miss La sol fa re mi*. The entire Mass is based on the single five-note phrase, and is no doubt linked with the magical numeration of the pentagram (see p.262, bottom figure).

59. So far as I can see from his notebooks, Hedsel is paraphrasing a quotation from the writings of the clairvoyant, Andrew Jackson Davis (1826-1910) – probably from his *Penetralia*, in which the American describes a bird he saw through clairvoyant vision. Hedsel had copied the quotation in full, yet left no indication of pagination.

60. This little man, the size of a thumb, is the *Ishon* of the hermetic and Old Testament texts. In discussing the idea, Mead (op. cit., n.2) compares the *Kathopanishad* (II.ii.iv. 112, 12) in the Chattopadhyaya translation of 1896. 'The Man, of the size of a thumb, resides in the midst, within the self, of the past and the future the lord; from him a man hath no desire to hide.'

61. Hedsel was quoting directly from the Hermetic texts. "'Twas worth the furious gazing and the pains to see Heaven's beauty, beauty that seemed like God – God who was yet unknown, and the rich majesty of Night, who weaves her web with rapid light, though it be less than Sun's, and of the other mysteries in turn that move in Heaven, with ordered motions and with periods of times, with certain hidden influences bestowing order on the things below and co-increasing them.'

62. For the *Celestial Nile*, see 'The Mystery of the Birth of Horus', in Mead (op.cit., n.2), III, p.101.

63. This is not a literary invention, for *flos ignis* is straight from the alchemical literature. The background of the word *flos*, or flower, in the alchemical literature indicates that it is a reference to the Etheric level of being. This is perhaps not surprising, as the alchemical terminology (at least in Western use) was developed during the late mediaeval period, when artists also began to adopt floral motives, incised (sometimes pricked or embossed) into the gold-painted gesso of their religious icons, to indicate that events depicted in the paintings were taking place, not on the Earthly plane, but on the Spiritual level.

    The Paracelsian alchemical term *flos ignis*, which Mark Hedsel translated as 'floral fire', is sometimes used to denote the red colour, similar to the *flos Solis* (flower of the Sun), which is of a reddish citrine. However, the *colours* in alchemy are merely a convenient shield for indicating the stages of the process, or levels of perfection. That mere colour is not intended may be seen from the fact that *flos aeris* (flower of Air) does not denote a colour, but the important alchemical dew (*ros*) which penetrates from the upper realms into the lower. This is clearly an interpenetration from one elemental level into the next. Just so is the *flos ignis* a penetration from the 'fire element', which is supposed to ring the Earth, into the Earth plane.

    The method of the alchemical symbolism is perfect, for flowers are colours which break through from the dark loam into the realm of ordinary day. This imagery reminds us that Osiris, the Egyptian god of the Underworld, was called 'Lord of perfecting black' (see n.51). Even though the imagery is perfect, it is only when one has experienced the sight of this floral flower that it is really possible to understand what Hedsel is writing about.

    In spite of this long note on the alchemical origins of the floral fire, I should point out that in his own notes, Hedsel refers to 'the flower of fire' in the Chaldean Oracles mentioned by Mead, op. cit., vol. iii, p.83.

64. As St Chrysostom recognized, the Star of the Magi was no ordinary star (see Fulcanelli, op. cit., p.13), which goes a long way to explaining why astronomers and astrologers have made little headway in identifying the celestial phenomena. A star which could be followed, and which would stand over a given spot on Earth (like the Magian star), is no celestial body. See in this context, however, R. Powell, *Christian Hermetic Astrology. The Star of the Magi and the Life of Christ*, 1991. Powell rightly views the hearing of the *music of the spheres* as marking a high stage of initiation. The Magi, as the last representatives of a Spiritual tradition linked with the esoteric cult of Zoroastrianism, read not merely the stars, but, as Powell puts it, 'the occult script of the stars'.

65. *Kneph* is mentioned in the early hermetic literature as a black-god (some say that he was blue-black): see n.51. Plutarch, in his *Isis and Osiris*, regards him as an immortal. Recent research suggests that the darkness is cyclical, for Kneph is an aspect of Ammon, and 'When he closes his eyes, all things becomes dark'. According to Porphyry (quoted by Mead, op. cit., iii, pp.92-3), his skin was blue-black, he held a sceptre and wore a winged crown. The modern revival of the name in the Knephian School seems to be directed by the union of something which is 'black', but which is 'intellectually energized' (for thus Porphyry reads the symbolism of the winged crown). This degeneration of an Egyptian *neter*, or god-archetype, reminds us that even the mighty Amon was reduced by the occult-

journalist, Collin de Plancy, to an owl-headed serpent-tailed monster, with the body of a wolf, raised by magicians to teach knowledge of past and future, and the secrets of love. See de Plancy, *Dictionnaire Infernal*, 1863.

66. Hedsel did not reveal to me the identity of Arne Topolski. Nor did he offer more details of this man's connection with the Knephian School (see n.65). However, the coding of the name he used certainly points to the Egyptian, *Har-nebeschenis*, or *Arnebeschenis*, which is a name of Horus when represented as Lord of the city of *Letopolis*, formerly in the Nile delta. Of course, the first part of the name is Egyptian, the latter Greek, and concerned with the birthing of Apollo on the island of Delos. The temple-sleep healing centres (the incubation temples – see n.71) were almost always associated with Apollo, and seem to have been involved with a legitimate form of what we would now call hypnosis.

67. Hedsel did identify the novelist he called Persephone Seabrooke, but for legal reasons we are obliged to remain silent about her real name.

The encoding of the pseudonym is of interest, however, for it shows how Hedsel usually attempts to provide meanings within meanings, even when masking individuals. The classical reference to *Persephone*, as one condemned to live for periods of time in the Underworld, may appear to be fairly obvious, as the lady in question was periodically put in touch with her own unconscious through hypnosis. Just so, the name *Seabrooke* redoubles the watery nature of this Isiac voyage. However, the reference may be even more specific, because, in the *Odyssey* where Circe advises the sea-voyaging hero to consult the dark oracle at Ephyra, the magician says that the place of the dead is near the 'grove of Persephone'.

The important encoding is found in the first three letters of her two names, which combine to give the word *Persea*. In ancient Egyptian symbolism, the persea was one of the attributes of Isis, when she was called by her Mystery-name, 'The Lady of the Heart and Tongue'. The point was that the fruit of the persea looked like a heart, while its leaf was shaped like a tongue.

68. Whether the application of the word *engram* is made by Mark Hedsel or by Arne Topolski is far from clear, yet it is very illuminating. In the 19th century the word was used to denote a tendency imparted to the nucleus of a cell, whilst this is undergoing variation. This tendency becomes heritable by transference to the nuclei of the germ cell.

69. The *mercuric speculum* is the Astrum Mercury of the alchemists, a term for the quintessence of mercury, or the Astral Plane, in which events may be seen clairvoyantly in reverse. No doubt Hedsel was using the term to disguise his meaning from Persephone Seabrooke. In the arcane tradition, it is recognized that the events of the material realm are visualized as though in a mirror – that is, reversed. On certain levels, this reversal is not only spatial, but temporal, so that the end of the Astral experience brings one to the beginning of the Earthly experience. When Hedsel suggested that Persephone Seabrooke was blocking her vision, he did so by pointing out to Arne Topolski the fact that she was not prepared to look into the Astral 'mirror' for fear of what she would see.

70. Although perhaps rather academic, Mark's description is correct – the gift usually referred to as Pandora's box was actually gifted to Epimetheus by Zeus: Pandora merely opened it. In the hermetic literature, the gift is that of Fate, or what we would now call 'karma'. The fourth-century alchemist, Zosimus (quoted in Mead, op. cit., iii, 180), interprets it in this light. In terms of strict hermeticism, the gods alone are allowed to deal with, or manipulate, a person's karma. This is probably the reason why Hedsel introduced the idea of Pandora's box in this context: however successful he may have been in his own terms, Arne Topolski was interfering in the work of the gods.

71. Sleep-healing, or incubation, was a method of healing used in ancient Greek hospitals. It was based on the fact that the Etheric body was itself a sort of memory-body, where images of past perceptions, events and deeds were stored. Certain of

the images arising from evil deeds or events would work their way into the physical body, and create disease. The method of incubation involved the priests adjusting the images, before the damage had been done on the material plane, so that they could no longer work through into the physical body, as disease or illness. The 'sleep' was not hypnotic, in the modern sense of the word, but it did involve the complete removal of the Etheric, to leave the physical in a state of suspended animation. One important difference between this and certain modern techniques is that the healers worked not on the physical, but on the Etheric. Surviving incubation centres are at Cos and Oropus; both served Apollonian temples.

72. For the hermetic injunction against magic, see Zosimus, *Against Magic*, quoted from *About the Inner Door*, from vol. iii, p.180 of G. R. S. Mead (op. cit.). For an indication of the modern *Knephians*, or followers of the Egyptian *Kneph*, see n.65. Hedsel insisted that he had never personally worked in this School, but had, in the early 1960s, known some of those involved in the higher levels of the groups. He made it clear that he considered their work unwholesome.

73. Hedsel did not identify the individual. There is no indication in his notebooks as to the identity. Mark told me that he had been dead for some years, yet he did not wish to give the name.

74. Georg Grosz (1893-1959), German satirical painter. See *A Little Yes and a Big No. The Autobiography of George Grosz*, trans. L. S. Dorin, 1946. One does not know which drawings are the most perceptive – those which strip bare society by representing the thoughts of those depicted (for example, the drawing on p.116 which shows Man rendered bestial in face because of his desires, stripping bare in his mind the women who sit with him at table) or those showing the consequences of murder and mutilation (p.253).

75. M. R. James, *Apocrypha Anecdota*, ii, 1897, in *Texts and Studies*: pp.432-3.

CHAPTER SIX

1. Plutarch, *De Iside et Osiride*. By far the best scholarly treatment of this hermetic Egyptian-derived Greek text on initiation is that prepared by G. R. S. Mead, 'Concerning the Mysteries of Isis and Osiris', in *Thrice-Greatest Hermes. Studies in Hellenistic Theosophy and Gnosis*, 1906, 1964 ed., I, p.178ff. G. R. S. Mead calls the hermetic fragments 'a scrap of ancient gnomic wisdom', and claims that they were preserved by Hesiod, in the seventh century BC, from the arcane Orphic fragments, or perhaps from a lost treatise of the third-century BC Egyptian priest, Manetho, who wrote in Greek. Plutarch lived well into the first century AD, but makes no direct reference to Christianity, which was at that time changing the ancient initiation practices.

2. Plutarch is quoting Hesiod: 'Nor from five-branched at fire-blooming of Gods . . .' See Mead (op. cit., n.1 above), 'Why the Priests are Shaven and Wear Linen', I, p.185.

3. The arcane significance of the *sba* star has not received the scholarly attention it deserves. See, however, F. Gettings, *Dictionary of Occult, Hermetic and Alchemical Sigils*, 1981, p.23, where the star is linked with the Christian image of the *orans*. The similarity between the orans and the gestures of certain gods in Egyptian art is very striking. For excellent pictures of the *sba*-star in initiation chambers and so-called tombs, see W. Forman and S. Quirke, *Hieroglyphics and the Afterlife in Ancient Egypt*, 1996, for example, p.54 and pp.56-7.

4. The arcane tradition insists that Man is already a star in his invisible Spirit: at death, the elemental body drops away, leaving the star free. Plato, in *Timaeus*, 41, records that the demiurge assigned each newly created soul to a star. It is fascinating, in view of the themes of Hedsel's present chapter, that Plutarch (see Mead, op. cit., I, p.248) mentions the star and the crocodile in contiguous texts. Plutarch says that the asp, 'because it does not age, and moves without limbs', is likened to a star: we may trace here the notion of the 'limbless' (that is, without

physical limbs) Spiritual body of the Etheric. The crocodile is paid honour because it is without a tongue: this too is inoperative on the physical plane (that is, it cannot speak of the Mysteries above). While no doubt biologically incorrect, the Egyptian symbolism is indeed profound.

5. See H. P. Blavatsky, *Secret Doctrine*, 1888, I, 219, where she refers to the Egyptian star as symbolizing 'the defunct man', and where she sees this as emblematically transformed into a crocodile. Blavatsky seems to have derived the idea from Gerald Massey, but she might just as well have had it from the hermetic documents.

6. C. Agrippa, *De Occulta Philosophia*, 1534, p.clxiii. The arcane element is not in the text, but in the distribution of seven planets in the pentagrammic man: one observes that the Sun and the Moon are not integrated.

7. See Plutarch, 'The Mysteries of Isis and Osiris', XLVII.7 – 'But in the end, Hades fails, and men shall be happy, neither requiring food nor casting shadow.' This is reference to the post-mortem state, for most men, or to that body-free state enjoyed by initiates. The shadow-casters are ordinary humans.

8. For the *orans*, or praying gesture, as image of the Etheric departed, see E. Bock and R. Goebel, *Die Katakomben*, 1931, in the A. Heidenreich Eng. ed., *The Catacombs. Pictures from The Life of Early Christianity*, 1962 ed., pp.24–5.

9. The 'purified man' can only refer to the initiate, as only the initiate dies with a cleansed Etheric body.

10. Paracelsus, 'The Composition of Metals', in the Waite translation (op.cit.), pp.116–17: 'the interior or invisible man is a kind of constellation or firmament'. One of the themes of this remarkable text is that all created things (from stones to metals, from metals to plants) are alive, and reflect the stars.

11. The Theosophical Society (intended initially to promote occult research), in New York, in 1878. Significantly, the idea for such a Society was mooted by Colonel Olcott, after a lecture, delivered by the architect George Felt, in the rooms of Blavatsky, at Irving Place, New York, on the lost canon of proportion used by the ancient Egyptians, and in particular on what he called 'the Star of Perfection'. This historical detail has been amended by Annie Besant to an account of how the Invisible Masters really founded the Society – see *Lucifer*, April, 1895, p.105. By that time, Madame Blavatsky was already a Mason of the 32 degree. See H. P. Blavatsky, *Collected Writings. Volume One. 1874–1878*, p.281. The Esoteric Section of the Theosophical Society was formed in 1888.

12. C. G. Harrison, *The Transcendental Universe*, 1894, was the first openly to publish material relating to the warfare and dissent among the esoteric bodies as to the utility of opening up esoteric lore. See also the ten lectures of 1915, by R. Steiner, published as *Occult Movements in the Nineteenth Century*, 1973, which draws heavily on the Harrison material.

13. The Theosophical view of Etheric was coloured by the orientalizing tendency which was established in this movement by Blavatsky, and by the somewhat dubious clairvoyancy of C. W. Leadbeater. An excellent summary of the Theosophical teaching relating to the Etheric is A. E. Powell, *The Etheric Double and Allied Phenomena*, 1925. We consulted the 1969 ed.

14. The tomb is called the 'house of the Ka', and certain priests 'priests of the Ka' – see R. A. Schwaller de Lubicz, *Sacred Science. The King of Pharaonic Theocracy*, 1982 Eng. trans., p.217. We do not have to turn to esoteric books to offer examples of the *ka* hieroglyphic in Egyptian art. In R. T. Rundle Clark, *Myth and Symbol in Ancient Egypt*, 1978 ed., p.233, an image is reproduced showing a child being nursed by its own ka.

15. Blavatsky's treatment of the zodiacal *Makara* is extremely complex. She is at her best when quoting from the astrological writings of Subba Row, *Five Years of Philosophy*, in her *The Secret Doctrine*, II, p.576ff. She reminds us that goats are still sacrificed in India to Durga Kali, who is 'only the black side of Lakshmi (Venus), the white side of Sakti'. This line of thought leads her to 'a Mystery which the

writer dares not dwell upon at length, not being sure of being understood'.

16. R. Steiner, *Karmic Relationships. Esoteric Studies*, 1974 ed. (revised version of the 1956 trans. of *Esoterische Betrachtungen karmischer Zusammenhange*, based on the lectures given at Dornach in 1924), is by far the most useful and comprehensive study we know of personal reincarnation histories of famous individualities.

17. See 'Studies in Successive Earth-Lives', in *The Golden Blade*, 29th issue, 1977, p.71ff.

18. Lady Caithness, to whom Blavatsky granted the charter to establish a lodge of the Theosophical Society in France, was dominated by the belief that, in a previous life, she had been Mary, Queen of Scots. See J. Symonds, *Madam Blavatsky. Medium and Magician*, 1959, p.168ff. Caithness was not the only lady to have such high retro-expectations – Annie Besant revealed her previous incarnation as the unfortunate Giordano Bruno. The 'Great Beast', Aleister Crowley, firmly believed that he was a reincarnation of the 19th-century magician, Eliphas Levi, and indeed they did have certain things in common – though that is no proof of Spiritual unity.

19. W. R. Alger, *A Critical History of the Doctrine of a Future Life*, 1860. The figures are quoted from C. J. Ducasse, in the forward to I. Stevenson, *Twenty Cases Suggestive of Reincarnation*, 1966.

20. Florence Nightingale (1820–1910) first studied medicine with the Sisters of Charity of St Vincent de Paul, in Egypt, and later underwent formal training as a nurse, both in London and Edinburgh, and became superintendent of a hospital in Harley Street, London. Hearing of the terrible suffering of the sick and wounded in the hopital at Scutari, during the Crimean War, she volunteered to serve there. Part of her heroic tale is the story of the struggle of one who knows what is right against the inertia and prejudice of bureaucracy. She was the founder of the nursing system in England.

21. In fact, Florence Nighingale *did* catch that fever. She lay on the point of death herself for over a week. Yet she survived, when so many soldiers and nurses did not.

22. The Sisters of Charity was a religious order founded by St Vincent de Paul in 1634, now spread extensively throughout Europe and the United States. The sisters' external work is through nursing in hospitals, orphanages and so on.

23. In the Egyptian hermetic text dealing with the Mystery of the birth of Horus (see Mead, op.cit., I, 54) we learn that the newly dead soul finally takes the semblance of a crocodile, to symbolize the passions of humanity. We presume that this crocodile-form is an expression of the passions experienced in the preceding life, and which now await sublimation.

   Blavatsky (see n.5) was quite right to link the crocodile imagery with the defunct, in ch. lxxxviii of the Egyptian *The Book of the Dead*: under the glyph of a mummiform god with a crocodile's head, the text reads:

   > I am the god (crocodile) presiding at the fear . . . at the arrival of his Soul among men. I am the god-crocodile brought for destruction, when man acquires the knowledge of good and evil . . . I am the fish of the great Horus.

24. We observe that there is a stuffed crocodile on the ceiling of the newly restored 'mediaeval' laboratory in the Pharmacological Museum in Basle.

25. The founders of the Templars, Hugues de Payns and Godefroi de Saint-Omer, in 1119, insisted that their followers should take and keep an oath of chastity, obedience and poverty. The original secret Rule of the Temple has been lost, though it was referred to in later literature. Their vow specified that they could not own property in perpetuity. Property was in fact given to their Order, if only to render them operative as knights. They were permitted to have land, houses (which they might furnish), servants and serfs (see H. de Curzon, *La Regle du Temple*, 1886, p.58ff.). They were closely following the Rule of Benedict, and the Knights themselves seem to have adhered very closely to this throughout their

existence. The surviving mediaeval constitution was drawn up by Bernard of Clairvaux: significantly, it contains 72 articles. Beyond their extraordinary achievements, it is this hermetic number, and the fact that it provides for a Grand Master as head, that confirms externally that the Order was esoteric. The Templars took their name from the houses given them by Baldwin II, King of Jerusalem, as their dwellings: these were alongside the remains of what was assumed to have been the Temple of Solomon. See M. Barber, *The Trial of the Templars*, 1980 ed.

26. All things being equal, humans incarnate from lifetime to lifetime, in alternate sexes. This implies that, generally speaking, the knights who had fought in the 12th and 13th centuries with such courage would reincarnate later in female bodies in the 18th and 19th centuries.

27. Athanasius Kircher (1601-1680) was probably the most learned German of his day. A Jesuit and polymath of extraordinary erudition, he taught mathematics in the Collegio Romano, but at the age of 42 dedicated himself to the study of archaeology. His *Lingua Aegyptiaca Restituta*, which he completed in the year of his resignation, was one of the first serious studies of the arcane literature of Egypt – marred only by the fact that no one at that time knew how to read the hieroglyphics.

28. In fact, perhaps for rather obvious reasons, this palingenesy has been treated in several books dealing with magic, which have failed to point to a large number of experiments of a palingenesic type. These were recorded by Kircher's main disciple, J. Kestler, *Physiologia Kicheriana Experimentalis*, 1680. This text records that Kircher tried to reproduce from supposedly dead matter a wide variety of living forms, including earthworms, bees and scorpions. These were not Astral images, as in the case of the rose, but actual creatures of flesh. In each case, some remains of the dead creatures were required to ensure the success of the experiments.

   It is certainly in these experiments that we can trace the alchemical roots of the *Frankenstein* story. As one might expect, the Kircher experiments (which, to judge from contemporaneous records, do not appear to have been unique to his laboratory) led to more sophisticated attempts to bring back to life dead people. All that was needed was their surviving remains or ashes. According to C. F. Garmann, *De Miraculis mortuorum*, 1709, the alchemical bibliographer, Pierre Borel, called this 'licit necromancy', and claimed that one could represent in a glass phial one's father, or any other ancestors (Thorndike, op. cit., VIII, p.634).

29. For an account of the genesis of the novel *Frankenstein* from the true story of the experiments of the alchemist Conrad Dippel (1673-1734), see R. Florescu, *In Search of Frankenstein*, 1975, p.78ff. There is no doubt that Mary Shelley heard of the Dippel story when she visited Castle Frankenstein.

30. Virtually all the images of the *Mons Philosophorum*, or alchemical mountains, in the classical alchemical texts have caves excavated into them. Often, these caves are inbuilt with oratories. The most artistic representation is plate 3 in S. Michelspacher, *Cabala*, 1616.

31. Leonardo da Vinci's fresco of the Last Supper is in what used to be the refectory of Santa Maria delle Grazie, in Milan. Typically, he never quite completed the picture, and the experiments he made with the technique of fresco ensured its rapid ruination. The fresco now *in situ* has been overpainted many times: it is unlikely that a single stroke of the original painting survives.

   According to his own notes, Leonardo began this work in 1495. The same notes indicate his search for the figure of Christ. He visualized one model for the face, and another for the hands. I. A. Richter, *Selections from the Notebooks of Leonardo da Vinci*, 1966 ed., p.322, gives an account (almost contemporaneous) of how Leonardo would establish the nature, social standing and expressions of the persons he wished to paint, and would then visit the places where such people would gather, to study their mannerisms, faces, gestures, and so on. In a letter to his patron, the Duke of Milan, he regrets that he has not been able to find any face which caught his imagination for Judas.

What is of importance, from a point of esoteric history, is that Leonardo was in search of models at all. This search reflected the independence of the artist under the influence of the new Ego-consciousness which gave rise to the Renaissance. Until the late 16th century, artists had tended to use model-books, or to depict their human subjects in terms of the ancient temperaments. Judas, for example, was always portrayed in late mediaeval art as a melancholic, under the influence of the Earth element (see R. Klibansky, E. Panofsky and F. Saxl, *Saturn and Melancholy. Studies in the History of Natural Philosophy, Religion and Art*, 1964, pp.195 and 286).

32. The esoteric view of Judas hinges on the question as to why a person should betray by means of so tender a symbolic gesture as a kiss (*Matthew* 26.49). In addition, the esotericist finds it necessary to ask why Judas – or anyone – had to identify, or 'betray', the Christ, who, consequent to His miracles, was certainly the most famous person in Jerusalem at that time. There are several other unresolved issues in the story of Judas – for example, it is quite possible to read the identifying incident at the Last Supper as an indication that Judas himself did not know that he was to be the traitor, until that moment. There is no doubt from the Gospels themselves that Judas was a traitor, but the story is told in such a way as to suggest that it points to one of those great Mysteries of Christianity which still await revelation in the future.

33. Those alchemical images which portray men with solarized heads and women with lunarized heads are misleading to those who have not learned to interpret esoteric imagery. These are not portrayals of ordinary humans, but of initiates. In this context, an initiate is one who has redeemed the head forces, and imbued the degenerative lunar imaginative powers (seen most clearly in 'associations') with phantasy, or creative image-making. This development of the lunar past is illustrated in those alchemical pictures which show a flower inside a vessel, for the flower is symbol of the previous year's Sun, which, after alchemical treatment, becomes symbol of the Spiritual future. A fine example is the three-rooted flower from Sloane Mss. 256 (British Library). The hermetic vessel is in the form of a human face, with the spout a nose. The seven-leafed flower is the developed planetary forces, which manifest through the seven chakras. The triple roots are the Three Principles, which are the foundations of the alchemical Great Work. In this way, the lunar forces are transformed into solar forces for the future. The Sloane Mss. illustration is reproduced by Burckhardt (op.cit., n.38, between pp.168 and 169).

34. At first glance, the connection between the two different systems of Sun and Moon appears to be merely numerological: the movement of the blood is ascribed 72 because there are 72 pulse beats in one minute. In one minute we breath 18 times. Thus, the solar (warm) blood and the lunar (cold) air meet in the 60 seconds of the minute. However, this numerology finds a cosmological correspondence in the 72 of solar precession and the 18 of the lunar nutational period. For details, see R. Schubert, 'Kosmische und menschliche Rhythmen', quoted in English by G. Wachsmuth, *Reincarnation*, 1937, p.65.

There is another way of looking at this curious relationship between the lunar 18 and the solar 72. Arising from the nutational period is another lunar cycle, also linked with the number 18, which, in a most remarkable way, ties together lunar and solar activities through the phenomenon of eclipses. The Saros cycle, much used in astrological cycles theory, is 18 years, 11 days and 8 hours. The Saros cycle consists of 223 lunar months; during this cycle, there are 70 eclipses, 41 of which are solar, 29 of which are lunar. This cycle of eclipses is framed by the ending and beginning of the cycle, making 72 eclipses in all.

35. The precession of the equinoxes is a phenomenon which is connected with the gradual slipping back of the Vernal Equinox, one degree in 72 years. In exactly 25,920 years, the sun precesses the entire 360 degrees of the zodiac. This vast cycle is the so-called Platonic Year. In the Platonic Year, each degree is precessed in 72 years. This solar precessional numerology is represented in the lunar. Since we breathe on average 18 breaths per minute, we breath 25,920 times in a day. Thus, the two figures – solar and lunar – are expressed very precisely in a cosmic event.

36. For man as 'star of the Microcosm', see n.4.

37. The mystery of the precessional and blood-number 72 (see n.34) is expressed in a very large number of arcane stories from the hermetic lore. King Solomon is supposed to have imprisoned 72 demons in his brass bottle. Certainly, there are 72 demons in the grimoires of the Solomonic literature. The cake, or tablet, made for Mithridate (King of Pontus and Bithynia, first century BC), which was supposed to render the eater immune from all poisons, had 72 named ingredients. The Arabic scholar, Haydar Amuli (1320-85), wrote works on esoteric lore culminating in the 'Balance of Seventy-two', a treatise which, he claimed, embraced the entire history of religion.

38. The fascinating thing is that this does not appear to be the ratio of the initiates who designed the Jaipur observatory. The breathing-number confirmed by the Indian system of time-measurement at Jaipur is itself based on their recognized times of human breathing rates. Our question is whether this is normal or initiate breathing. The Indian astronomer-priests divided one sidereal day into 60 dandas. One danda was divided into 60 vicalas. One vicala was equal to 6 respirations. The 6 respirations were called the pala, and this was the equivalent of 24 seconds of our time system. This implies that in 72 seconds there were 18 respirations, which is one sixth slower than that recorded for the West. This seems to be a measure of initiate breathing. While the ratio is different, there is still an adherence to the solar (72) and lunar (18) numerology.

39. The majority of the breathing systems, designed to accelerate Spiritual development, were taught originally in Eastern Schools – for example in Tantric yoga and among the Sufis. Undoubtedly, these were of value in inducing certain advanced states of being within those of Oriental psycho-physical makeup, and already proficient in certain arcane techniques of development. However, when transferred to the West, and practised by individuals of an Occidental psycho-physical makeup *not* proficient in arcane techniques, such breathing systems may be distinctly harmful. No one should practise breathing techniques without the supervision of a Master.

   As regards my Master's reference to 'the furnace', alchemists recognized that the heat of the blood (and hence of the entire body) is maintained by combustion in the lungs. This is the 'natural' fire of the three fires mentioned by the alchemists – the others being the artificial and the anti-natural. This 'natural' is also the latent heat, which implies that the *athanor* (the 'oven', from the Arabic *at-tannur*) is the whole human body – the dross of the work. See, for example, T. Burckhardt, *Alchemy. Science of the Cosmos, Science of the Soul*, 1986 ed. of the Eng. trans., p.161ff.

40. B. L. Dhama, *A Guide to the Jaipur Astronomic Observatory*, n.d. The standard work is A. Garrett, *The Jaipur Observatory and its Builder*, 1902.

41. Technically, the *Yantra* is the visible and knowable, while a *Mantra* is a form of words, or sound, designed to make specific vibrations of a magical kind. The *mantrabija* is the mantra 'seed', the keynote of a mantra, usually the first syllable.

42. Ulug Beg (1394-1449) was grandson of Tamberlain, and the creative power behind Tartar astronomy and astrology which deeply influenced Chinese and Oriental cosmoconceptions. In 1420 he built the great observatory at Samarkand, which he then used to correct the positions of the classical stellar positions recorded by Ptolemy.

43. Jesuits, the members of the Society of Jesus, were influential in India from the middle of the 16th century, consequent to the achievements of St Francis Xavier. They were greatly respected in India for their scholarship and knowledge of the stars.

44. The smaller sun dial is called the *Laghu Samrat Yantra*. The *Dhruva Darshak Yantra*, inclined at an angle of 27 degrees (the latitude of Jaipur), is designed to reveal the position of the pole star. The instrument made of two brass circles, and designed to measure celestial latitude and longitude, is called the *Kranti Writa*. The *Yantra Raj* is a circular disc of seven alloys, made in such a way as to remain the same size whatever the temperature: this is used to calculate the positions of the main planets. The *Unnatasah Yantra* is a huge graduated brass circle, some 18 feet in diameter, and hung vertically: this is designed to give readings of altitudes. The *Dakshinobhitti Yantra* looks something like a wall with two equal quadrants, some 20 feet in radius: this gives readings of the altitudes of heavenly bodies, and thus is on the north-south line of the meridian. The *Shasthansa Yantra*, which is really a huge sextant, is used to determine zenith distance and declination.

45. For example, the pavement zodiac in the basilican church of San Miniato al Monte, in Florence (dated 1207), is oriented with Cancer towards the altar, and Capricorn towards the central door. Cancer is thus promissory of Life. In walking the orientation, one walks from Capricornian Death to the Life promised by Christ.

    Such arrangements point to the esoteric teaching which reveals Capricorn as cosmic symbol of initiation – the Path from the rigidity and control of Capricorn, to the life of Cancer, is the Path of initiation. Some esoteric astrologers, and even some poets, have recognized the higher constructive power of Capricorn, as the transformer of elemental earth into imaginative forms. The great poet and playwright, J. C. F. Schiller, in his trilogy, *Wallenstein*, 1799, writes of the ruler Saturn as 'Lord of the secret birth of things . . . within the lap of earth, and in the depths of the imagination'. Isabelle Pagan was discussing the more advanced Capricornian when she called the sign 'the Priest or Ambassador', in her remarkable *From Pioneer to Poet*, 1911. The unconventional astrologer, John Varley (who taught William Blake astrology), intuited the deep relationship between Capricorn and the opposite sign Cancer, though he drew his conclusions from the ancient position of the 'fish-star' Fomalhaut in Capricorn in classical times. See J. Varley, *A Treatise on Zodiacal Physiognomy*, 1828. This star, our own *alpha* of Piscis Australis (now in Pisces), marked the winter solstice in ancient times. The link with the ancient Ichton, the fish-man who holds the *kan*, could not be more precisely stated.

46. The hieroglyphic *kan* is the corner-symbol, or square. See G. Massey, *The Book of the Beginnings*, 1881, vol. II, p.49. Massey rightly sees the hieroglyphic sound equivalent of *kan* as surviving in the Hebrew *kanph*, 'the corner or extremities of the Earth'.

47. The curvilinear knot-half of the Capricornian sigil is the sacred Egyptian symbol, called by Blavatsky the *Ankhe-te* (op. cit., II, p.546ff) – it is 'a mere loop which contains both a circle and a cross in one image'. In the Egyptian Mysteries, the Ankhe-te was used for the measurment of buildings, which implies a connection between the square and the curvilinear form of the Capricornian sigil. Blavatsky rightly links this Ankhe-te with the *Pasa*, or cord, in the hand of the Hindu god. Mead (op. cit., I, p.43, 'Thoth the Master of Wisdom') rightly sees this as the 'Noose of Ptah', which became the Noose of Hercules, which probably represented the binding together of the male and female, in the line and circle. This idea of sexual congress links very well with the idea of birth and nourishment in the sign Cancer. How Spiritually deep are these ancient sigils, such as the one for Capricorn.

48. The *Pat-aik* is the emblem of Ptah and Osiris, its name in Egyptian meaning

'dedication of the angle'. Marshall Adams traced even the name of Sicily to this angle, for the tribe of the Sikeli took their name from the Egyptian meaning 'Sons of the Angle'. See M. Adams, *The Book of the Master of the Hidden Places*, 1933 ed., p.167ff. It might be argued that as the Masonic square may be traced back to the *kan*, it would be more accurate to trace the *pat-aik* to the Masonic compass. This is a reasonable argument, as the jewel of the Past Deputy Grand Master of the Grand Lodge of England combines the compass and the square, to create the sigil for the Quintessence. See, for example, R. F. Gould, *The History of Freemasonry*, pl. II, no. 3.

49. The importance of the square is reflected in both speculative and operative Masonry. A curious word used in Masonic catechisms is *giblim*, which is one of the names for 'Mason'. The word appears in the Masonic *Wilkinson MS* (dated about 1727) as *Giblin*. This term may come from the town-name Gebal, for it is believed that the Giblemites did the stone-work for the building of the Temple of Solomon. The Hebrew word *haggiblim* is translated in the Bible as 'stone-squarers'. There is a useful survey of the word in A. Horne, *King Solomon's Temple in the Masonic Tradition*, 1977 ed., p.172ff.

    In his fascinating examination of the operative Masons' techniques, John James points to the measurement known as the *pied-du-roi* (the King's foot), which was supposed to have been a gift from the great initiate, Haroun-al-Raschid, to Charlemagne, *circa* 789 AD. This measurement was certainly used in the building of Chartres, and in the construction of the 'true measure' which, James shows, was derived from the square with sides measuring 230mm, for the diagonals to that square give the 325mm of the King's Foot. See J. James, *Chartres. The Masons who Built a Legend*, 1982, p.36ff.

    The two streams of Masonry seem to merge in the inscribed square, dated 1507, which was left as a foundation deposit in the building of the old Baal's Bridge in Limerick. See A. Horne, *Sources of Masonic Symbolism*, 1981, pp.18–19. Horne quotes from Rudyard Kipling's delightful Masonic poem, 'The Mother Lodge', which seems to be the Lodge in Lahore, where he was initiated: 'We met upon the Level, an'/We parted on the Square.' Our own interest in the above notes rests on the fact that the Hebrew root *gib* pertains to height, or to a high place (for example, *Gibeon* is identified with the village of *El-Jib*, which stands on top of an isolated hill). The true Mason, the true man who stands on the square, and who, further, stands on the foot of the king, is one who stands also on the Spiritual heights. The place of Capricorn is symbolically at the highest point (the *medium coeli*) of the horoscope figure.

50. There is a picture of the 'Alchemist' wearing his liberia, on the tower of Notre Dame, Paris, in Fulcanelli, op. cit., plate III, opposite p.18.

51. Blake says that the engraving was after a drawing by Salviati, after Michelangelo – detail from the Crucifixion of St Peter.

52. Blake inscribed his new engraving, which he completed about 1810, 'Joseph of Arimathea among The Rocks of Albion. This is One of the Gothic Artists who Built the Cathedrals in what we call the Dark Ages'.

53. For the Arimathea legend, see L. S. Lewis, *St Joseph of Arimathea at Glastonbury*, 1964 ed. In fact, the Arimathea legend was widespread, and Blake could have been familiar with it through his reading of the 16th-century Italian writer on English History, Polydore Vergil, the Bishop of Bath, whose views on Arimathea are quoted by Lewis, p.15.

54. Blake actually wrote: '. . . One of the Gothic Artists who Built the Cathedrals in what we call the Dark Ages, Wandering about in sheep skins & goat skins, of whom the world was not worthy; such were the Christians in all Ages.' See n.52. For notes on the biblical associations behind the quotation, see S. F. Damon, *A Blake Dictionary*, 1973 ed., p.225.

55. Blake had autographed a surviving print of this drawing, 'Engraved when I was a

beginner at Basires/from a drawing by Salviati after Michael Angelo'. In fact, this autographed note is misleading, for Blake copied the picture from a print attributed to Beatrizet, after a drawing (perhaps by Salviati – see n.51) which is supposed to have been copied from Michelangelo's fresco, *Crucifixion of St Peter*, in the Pauline Chapel. For details, see D. Bindman, *Blake as an Artist*, 1977, p.14. The iconography of Blake's engraving is given a thorough treatment by Bindman, though the significance of the Mithraic cap is passed by without comment. For details of John Varley, see A. T. Story, *James Holmes and John Varley*, 1894.

56. Kenneth Grant, *The Magical Revival*, 1972, p.63.

57. The cards, designed by Crowley for his *The Book of Thoth*, were painted by Lady Frieda Harris (1877-1962). Lady Harris, although a disciple of the notorious Crowley, was well connected, the wife of a Member of Parliament who was Chief Whip of the Liberal Party. In 1912 Crowley had published his first survey of the Tarot in *The Equinox*, and it is likely that some of the information in this account was published in breach of his initiation vows made in the Hermetic Order of the Golden Dawn. The Harris cards were published in 1944, with Crowley's *The Book of Thoth* (written under his pseudonym, Master Therion), in a limited edition of 200 in England, and 200 in New York. In his series of associations and numbers, Crowley made the Fool card (as we have seen, the zero of the traditional series) the number 20, which seems to have been in accordance with Golden Dawn practice. For a brief survey of the Crowley cards, see M. Dummett, *The Game of Tarot*, 1980, p.158ff.

58. Aleister Crowley, for all he has been misunderstood in modern times, and for all he was morally deficient, was a very learned occultist. It is unlikely that his much-publicized adoption of the number 666 was abstracted merely from the number of the Beast, mentioned in *Revelation*, as is so widely believed. He would have been aware of the occult tradition, set out in one of the earliest printed books on occult lore, the *De Occulta Philosophia* of Agrippa, that 666 is the number of the Demon of the Sun, Sorath. Now, this meant that, in cosmological terms, Crowley, in taking as his own the number of the demon of the Sun, was identifying himself with Sorath. In turn, this meant that he could seek to have sexual congress ideally with a demon of the Moon, whom he called, among other things, the Scarlet Woman. In the occult tradition recorded by Agrippa, the name of the Demon of the Moon was Hasmodai, whose number was 369. This numerology is of no great importance within the present context, yet it is worth observing that the 69 (itself a sexual joke in French, as the famous *soixante neuf*) is itself a numerical image of the sigil for Cancer. This alone would have confirmed Crowley's view that the Scarlet Woman would pertain to the dark side of the Moon. Further, we must bear in mind that Hecate, the infernal demon of the classical world, was a lunar goddess with 3 heads, thus reifying the 69 with the initial 3. Of course, other numerologies have been recorded: see for example Kenneth Grant, *The Magical Revival*, 1972, pp.43-4.

59. See Kenneth Grant, *Aleister Crowley and the Hidden God*, 1973, p.19ff. For some very intelligent comments on Crowley's actual view of the Scarlet Woman, as opposed to his literary view, see Phil Hine, 'Love Under Will – Magick, Sexuality and Liberation', *Chaos International*, Issue 4, 1988, p.13ff.

60. The Devil-goat was a popular image in the witchcraft literature, but we must recall that much of this imagery was put into the mouths of suspects by priests, while the former were undergoing intolerable and sadistic torture. The Frenchman, Eliphas Levi – a poor scholar, and worse magician – popularized the image of what he called the 'Sabbatic Goat, or the Baphomet of Mendes', in his *Transcendant Magic* (1896 Eng. ed., p.174), but what he had to say about it (p.xxii) is largely nonsensical, and merely describes his own magically irresponsible syncretism. It is possible that the word *Baphomet* was a corruption of *Mohammed*, which name was misunderstood by the mediaeval Crusaders. In this connection, see M. Barber, op. cit., n.25, p.62.

61. Jakob Boehme (1575–1624) was a German Rosicrucianist, who worked for most of his life as a shoemaker. He wrote his first work, (the *Aurora*) as a result of an illumination, in 1612. See F. Hartmann, *Jacob Boehme: Life and Doctrines*, 1891.

62. The *Auge* or 'Eye of Eternity' in Boehme's graphic symbolism is discussed by F. Gettings (op. cit.), p.113. The use of the eye – often linked with interpenetrating triangular forms, which link Spirit to man – predominates in the Boehmian symbolism, as may be seen from the *Theosophische Wercken* of 1682.

63. The Hebraic cabbalistic literature dealing with the Microprosopus is complex. The image seems to revolve around the idea that Man was created in the image of God, and that there are two faces, the Micro (lesser) and the Macro (greater), reflecting each other – though the literature admits that this is not a perfect reflection. The greater is hidden (and therefore cannot reflect), which is why his face is described as being in profile while the Microprosopus is depicted full face. In the cabbalistic literature, every detail of the two faces is accorded a symbolism, but we are interested here only in the *qoph* of the brain. The illustration on page 282 is from Knorr von Rosenroth, *Kabbala Denudata*, 1684, and belongs to Christian cabbalism: it is portrayed in profile, as Adam Kadmon. This image is the result of the emanation-ray from the En Soph which later made the Sephirothic Tree.

64. In the Sephirothic Tree, two other paths join up with the Malkuth Earth. One path runs from Hod (Mercury), which is linked with the Hebraic letter *shin*, while one runs from Netzach (Venus), which is linked with the Hebraic letter *qoph*.

65. Each letter of the Hebrew letter was accorded a numerical value. There are minor differences, but the list given by C. Poncé (*Kabbalah*, 1974, p.173) is valid. The system of ascribing numerical values to letters and letter-sounds is very ancient.

66. Kenneth Grant, *Cults of the Shadow*, 1975, p.27.

67. The active discounting of the illusions engendered by sexual impulses – what in esotericism is sometimes called the Thrall of the Moon – and the creation of shadow beings, is possible only for those who have gone through very arduous training.

68. Capricorn is diametrically opposite Cancer in the zodiac.

69. We remember this, after all these years, because this was the day of Saturn and the Sun was in Cancer. The fight between Saturn and the ruler Moon seemed to set the theme for the entire evening.

70. The *Swayambunath* temple, built on a hill to the west of Kathmandu, is the most famous Buddhist temple in Nepal. The four pairs of eyes, on the central tower, have a circular third eye between them – and the Nepalese figure one, the *ek*, which looks rather like a nose. The 13 gilded rings above the tower represent the three degrees of knowledge, leading to nirvana: they might also be taken as a reference to the lunar periodicity.

71. Many years later, in 1992, we returned to the Swayambunath alone, and saw those eyes in a different light. We discovered, on a wall within the precinct of the temple, yet within full view of the two eyes and the secret *ek*, some inscriptions in Nepalese. These were beautifully written, yet quite evidently they were graffiti. As it seemed unlikely that any Nepalese writer would deface a temple in this way, we decided to ask one of the English-speaking monks to translate it for us.

The monk examined us carefully before agreeing. Running his finger beneath the dance of curvilinear characters, he said, 'These are memorials. They record the reincarnations of those Tibetan monks who were put to death by the Chinese in their own monasteries in Tibet.' He turned round and looked reverentially up at the three eyes. 'They have been inscribed on the temple wall to remind everyone that the Spiritual sees all – even those things which are believed to have been done in secret. Even in those places where screams cannot be heard, there also the screaming is heard.'

He saw that we were looking up to the pair of eyes and the nasal *ek*. His own eyes followed our gaze.

'Yes, the eyes see all. Even when we can no longer see those eyes, they follow us everywhere. Buddha sees all.'

72. Leadbeater is given a deservedly rough biographical treatment in various sections of P. Washington, *Madame Blavatsky's Baboon*, 1995 ed.

73. The Indian headquarters of the Theosophical Society were established on the banks of the Adyar river, outside Madras, in a house with extensive grounds, in what had been called the Huddlestone Gardens, on 19 December 1882. It was purchased on behalf of the Society by Ilalu Naidu, for 600 pounds: Naidu was eventually repaid. It seemed to early Theosophists a 'fairy place'. See J. Ransom, *A Short History of the Theosophical Society*, 1938, p.174ff. The Theosophists were received by a deputation of 50 Fellows of the Society at Madras station, and conducted in triumph to Adyar. There could hardly have been a more unsatisfactory timing, from an astrological point of view (Uranus was square the opposed Jupiter and Mars, which was conjunct Sun and Mercury in Sagittarius). This horoscope might well explain the subsequent unfortunate history of events at Adyar. When we last visited Adyar, in 1985, it was still active, though the Temple of Peace was beginning to fall into ruin.

74. *Matsya* is the name given to the first avatar of Vishnu. The fish-form reflects the mythology which tells how he descended to save Vaivasvata (the Spiritual world ruler, or Manu) from the great Flood. The myth has been linked by more than one mythologist with that told of the Babylonian fish-god Oannes. This suggests that our Indian host might have been right in seeing in the Western goat-fish of Capricorn a connection, however tenuous, with Matsya.

75. The epic of the *Mahabharata* forms the backbone of the Vedic mythology, telling (among other things) of the conquest of India. The mythology of the epic mingles with recorded history. Yalambar, the first Kirati ruler (*circa* eighth century BC) was a high initiate, who had contact with the gods: his meeting with Indra is mentioned in the *Mahabharata*. Yalambar was slain in one of the great battles described in the epic.

76. Hassoldt Davis, *Sorcerers' Village*, 1956, records that the term 'hornless goat' was used in the old Ivory Coast for a human sacrifice. The term was certainly adopted into Voodoo, in which human sacrifices were recorded in Haiti well into the 19th century. See, for example, the *affaire Bizoton* of 1863, mentioned in A. Metraux, *Voodoo in Haiti*, 1959 Eng. trans.

77. *Ekadas Lokeswar* is one of the names for Valokiteswara, whose story develops in the text.

78. This is Samantamukha, a god of 22 eyes. The name means, approximately, 'All-sided One': in this form, the god is a manifestation of Avalokiteswara. The details of the legend attached to his deeds emerge in the conversation.

Our host was not entirely correct. He looked into the world of desire, but he also looked into the worlds of *rupa* and *arupa* – the realms of 'form' and 'no-form'. These were respectively the created world and the Spiritual world. To avoid confusion regarding these Sanskrit terms, we should observe that the Higher World always appears to be 'formless' from the point of view of the ordinary vision of the lower world contiguous to it. In Oriental esotericism, the Mystery of the *Makara* is connected with the fact that the Spiritual beings sometimes called the *Makara* invest the formless with form. This is one of the esoteric principles of the Western Capricorn, to reveal the formless through form.

79. Paracelsus wrote, 'But I cannot refrain from telling a miracle which I saw in Spain when I was at the house of a certain necromancer. He had a bell weighing, perhaps, two pounds, and by a stroke of this bell he used to summon (and to bring, too) visions of many different spectres and Spirits. In the interior of the bell he had engraved certain words and characters, and as soon as the sound and tinkle were heard, Spirits appeared in any form he desired. Moreover, the stroke of this bell

was so powerful that he produced in the midst many visions of Spirits, of men, and even of cattle, whatever he wished, and then drove them away again. I saw many instances of this, but what I particularly noticed was that when he was going to do anything new, he renewed and changed the characters and the names.' (See Paracelsus in the Waite translation, Vol I, p.116.)

80. Among the more readable accounts of Blavatsky's journey to, and progress through, India, is J. Symonds, *Madame Blavatsky. Medium and Magician*, 1959.

81. In the sense it was used in the early days of Theosophy, *precipitation* was applied to phenomena by which solid objects were passed through other solid objects – for example, letters, through walls, and often from great distances – by unknown means. The word reflects the idea that for this transfer to take place the object had to be 'precipitated' into its radical atoms, which, after passage through the solid, were then reassembled into the old form. The sending of 'mental letters', which were answered by precipitated responses, was indulged in by some of the early Theosophists. For example, A. P. Sinnett established an entire correspondence, over a period of years, with a Master. The information he derived in this way seems to have been the basis for his *Esoteric Buddhism*, 1883, a rather turgid book which seems to deal neither with Buddhism nor with esotericism. A collection of such letters, published as *The Mahatma Letters to A. P. Sinnett*, 1923, is in the British Library. A brief survey (following the official Theosophical line) of precipitation in reference to the Mahatma letters in general is in G. de Perucker, *Studies in Occult Philosophy*, 1945, 1949 ed., p.703ff.

82. The word *Meru*, which was the only word we recognized, refers to the fabled Mount Meru. However, it is also used of one of the three chief postures, or *prastara*, adopted by the *suvasini*, or temple prostitutes, in the tantric sexual practices of the *Kala Marg*. In this posture, the woman sits upon the man, who is also in a seated position: she is the sacred mountain. The other two postures are *Bhu*, in which the woman lies on the earth, with the man over her, and the *Kailasa*, in which the woman is on top of the man, thus forming another Spiritual mountain over him. The last word is taken from the name of a mountain in the Himalayas.

83. Psychometry is the faculty by which one reads the psychic impressions left on material objects. The implication is that all objects have a memory of the conditions through which they have retained form: however, it is more likely that the person practising pyschometry is merely using the form as an aid to contacting the Akashic Records. The word psychometry seems to have been coined by the American J. R. Buchanan, but it is difficult to differentiate his view of actual psychometry from Spiritualist intervention. See his *Manual of Psychometry*, 1889, which is less zany than his later works.

84. It was the French psychometrist D'Aute-Hooper who so wisely chose the word 'cinematographic'. The images move so quickly that there is no opportunity for words, scripted or auditory, to cover all details of what is seen. Said D'Aute-Hooper, 'It is far too rapid. They are like cinematographic pictures. I seem to be in flight, . . . without thinking power but seeing things and happenings around me.' *Spirit Psychometry*, quoted p.318 Fodor.

85. L. Jacolliot, *Occult Science in India and Among the Ancients*, n.d. in Eng. trans. but *c*. 1890.

86. William Eglinton was an English medium of quite remarkable abilities. He was in India (first in Calcutta, then in Howran) from 1881 to 1882. During his stay in Howran, he converted Lord William Beresford to Spiritualism. Two years later he converted in a similar way W. E. Gladstone. In the following year, he so impressed the French artist Tissot that the latter painted a picture, later made into a mezzotint, entitled *Apparition Médianimique*. Among the psychic researchers who investigated him, and were satisfied that he was a genuine medium, were Richet, Alfred Russel Wallace and the Baron du Prel. Eglinton's involvement with Blavatsky seems to have led him into the practice of fraud. See *Proceedings of the*

Society for Psychical Research, III, p.254. See also IV, p.460.

87. J. S. Farmer, *'Twixt two worlds: a Narrative of the Life and Work of William Eglinton*, 1886. The full-page chromolithographs in this work are said to be the earliest colour pictures of materializations. His visit to India is described p.89ff, the Kellar incident p.92ff.

88. Harry Kellar was a well-known stage magician, and was extremely impressed by Eglinton's work, in which he could see no trace of ordinary trickery. The letters in the *Indian Daily News*, which follow the challenge to Eglinton, first published on 13 January 1882, confirm this view. However, as Farmer points out, Kellar later 'ratted' to the American press (see Farmer, op. cit., n.87, p.94.). The issue is clouded by the fact that both Eglinton and Kellar were Masons.

89. The *Lakshadweeps* are a group of 28 tropical open-reef islands in the Arabian Ocean, about 300 miles to the west of the Kerala coast. They are better known among English travellers as the Laccadives.

90. The Vishnavanath at Khajuraho, in Madhya Pradesh, is the most important of the Shiva temples of the 22 surviving masterpieces at this extraordinary site. It seems to have been built *circa* 1000 AD.

91. *Suvasini* is the Sanskrit for the temple prostitutes of the Kali Tantra, and means 'sweet smelling woman'. The notion seems to be that the *yoni* is a perfumed flower.

92. Hedsel did not leave a note on this comment, but his meaning is clear enough. I see in this endeavour just how great a struggle there is in Capricorn to maintain rigidity and moral probity against the insistent tendency to deflect the line, implicit in the structure of the curved knot. Contemplation of this struggle between angle and curve, between *kan* and *anke-te*, leads us to see something of the compensatory nature of karma, which ever strives to make straight the crooked, by means of the adjustment permitted by reincarnation.

CHAPTER SEVEN

1. For examples of 'secret names' given by Fulcanelli, see *Les Demeures Philosophales*, 1979 ed., I, pp.158-9.

2. This image is, significantly, in the Porch of the Virgin Mother – the great Creatrix – rather than in the alchemist's porch.

3. For the double meaning of Ros, see p.368, n.20. See plate 4 of the *Mutus Liber*, which shows the alchemist and his lunar sister squeezing dew from such a blanket (see n.10). The solar Ram and the lunar Taurus indicate that this is the beginning of spring, when the Fire of the Sun meets with the Earthly (that is, dark) Moon. In fact, the symbolism of the picture is of a far higher order than a mere definition of time and alchemical process. A modern version of the *Mutus Liber* is available in Adam McLean's *A Commentary on the Mutus Liber*, 1982, published as Number 11 of the Magnum Opus Hermetic Sourceworks Series.

4. Fantasy – more properly, in the Greek form, *phantasia* - was used among the mediaeval thinkers (who moulded the Western occult forms of thought) in a very special way. In Chaucer the word is used in the sense of a mental image or reflection, or as an image of something which has no real existence. See 'Imagination', in O. Barfield, *History in English Words*, 1969 ed., p.208ff. This idea of an i-mage which is a reflection links it with the esoteric view that the lunar realm is itself a reflective realm. The ability to give a name, or a picture, to an imagination-derived image is the genius of poetry.

5. In botany, *Nostoc* is a genus of freshwater algae which forms greenish globular masses in damp places, in water and so on. It is a lucifuge, and sometimes called 'witches' butter' and 'star-jelly'. Clearly, this algae is used in alchemy as a symbol for something of a very different nature: it resembles semen, more than dew.

6. In Christian symbolism, the letter C is used mainly as a symbol of the lunar forces, on the basis that it is a crescent shape. This may appear to be simplistic, until one recalls that the C was derived, by way of the early Greek and Egyptian hieratic,

from the hieroglyphic for the throne. One of the versions of the throne, the *ast*, was the symbol, and name-hieroglyphic of the goddess Isis.

7. In Blake's mythologies, Los is the vehicle for Urthona, and his planet is the Spiritual Sun. For an excellent (albeit non-esoteric) account of Los, see S. Foster Damon, *A Blake Dictionary*, 1965 ed., p.246ff.

8. See Blake's poem, *Milton* 22:4.

9. See Blake's poem, *Jerusalem* 88:49.

10. The *Mutus Liber*, or 'Wordless Book, in which the hermetic philosophy is depicted in hieroglyphic figures', was compiled by 'Altus', and published in 1677. Altus (which means 'raised' or 'high') is probably one of the several anagrammatic references to Jacob Sulat, or Saulat, in the book – which suggests that was the name of the author.

11. In esoteric imagery, plant forms (including flowers) are usually intended to point to the Etheric plane, while animal forms are intended to indicate the Astral plane. Our Master had already explained to us that the Astral plane was, in certain mediaeval texts, called the *ens animale*, 'the principle of animality'. We have since discovered a useful table of such ancient nomenclatures in the anonymous *Aurea Catena Homeri*, 1723.

12. The lozenge is a symbol of the Quintessence because it is bounded by four lines. The importance of the symbol lies in the fact that it contains 'empty space' – this is the 'fifth element' (the Quintessence), which is normally invisible, but which keeps in place the activity of the Four Elements of Fire, Earth, Air and Water.

13. Elémire Zolla, *The Uses of Imagination and the Decline of the West*, in the 1978 Golgonooza rep.

14. Surprisingly little is known about the hermetist and alchemist Fulcanelli, save what may be seen of his thought in his two books. For an assessment, see Kenneth Rayner Johnson, *The Fulcanelli Phenomenon*, 1980.

15. It has been suggested that Eugène Canseliet was the outer mask of Fulcanelli. Canseliet claims merely to have been his pupil. Intriguingly, in his Preface of 1925 to *Le Mystère des Cathédrales*, p.7, Canseliet remarks that Fulcanelli had told him, round about 1915, that the much sought-after key to the major arcanum of alchemy was given 'quite openly' in one of the figures in that book.

16. Louis Pauwels and Jacques Bergier, *Le Matin des Magiciens*, 1960, in the 1988 Dorset Press ed., *The Morning of the Magicians*, p.77ff. The meeting with what Bergier supposed (with little evidence) to be Fulcanelli took place in June 1937. The Pauwels/Bergier book is rather sensationalist, and not always reliable.

17. The 'initiate' quotes from Frederick Soddy's *The Interpretation of Radium*, in which the author claims that civilizations in the past were familiar with atomic energy, and that by misusing it were totally destroyed. In fact, Soddy's view is based entirely upon what Blavatsky had claimed. Surely, an initiate such as Fulcanelli (who was not given to quoting so explicit material) would not have referred to the writings of a non-initiate which were, at best, second-hand? In fact, the mysterious stranger was wrong in his opinion that these ancient techniques have partially survived. The invention and release of atomic energy may have been unwise, but had nothing to do with the knowledge of the ancient Atlanteans, to which Soddy is referring.

18. Bergier's 'initiate' account of alchemy as being involved with the creation of 'force-fields' is ludicrous. It is an entirely materialistic description of a Spiritual activity, as Fulcanelli himself recognized. On these grounds alone, we must claim that the 'initiate' whom Jacques Bergier ambiguously described as the one 'for whom there was good reason to believe' was Fulcanelli was wrongly identified.

19. The Latin *Vagantes* was used in the mediaeval period to denote the wandering scholars. See Helen Waddell, *The Wandering Scholars*, 1927: but see also Hedsel's observations on p.16ff, where he mentions the early French wandering scholars and poets. Naturally, a word used to denote a group of poets who were interested

in arcane lore must have hidden meanings. The word is from *vagus*, for 'strolling about' or 'wandering', but in mediaeval times the word *vagans* was used as a loose equivalent of the Greek 'erratic, or wandering', to denote the planets, as opposed to the 'fixed' stars. In this sense, the *vagantes* were the planet-men, wandering as much in the Spiritual spheres as in the material.

20. Marius Schneider, *Pietro che cantano. Studi sul ritmodi tre chiostri catalani di stile romanico*, 1976.

21. 'A veritable rebus' is how Gaignebet and Lajoux (op. cit., p.271) describe the Masonic figure with the Phrygian cap: it is, they say (coining an interesting word), paramasonic. Their analysis of the arcane significance of the orientation symbolism is both accurate and profound, but we cannot agree that the image is in any way a prelude to the secret Masonic work: it is Masonic, and initiatory.

22. The mystery of the church at Ripoll seems to lie in the extraordinary zodiac images on the portal. These are not in the traditional order, and the purpose behind the sequence is hard to grasp.

23. We record this footnote to the story of our development because it illustrates so well how a mere word from a Master can take one enormous distances towards understanding. As so often happens with the search for meaning in an alchemical symbol, once we had understood the significance of the verticals, the meaning of the entire capital became clear. The Quintessence contains 'manifest nature' in the dualities which are the basis of the perceptive act. This small lozenge therefore represents a particular doorway into the material world: it is more powerful than the huge *Ru* over the portal at Chartres. Around are the flowers, birds and animals which represent the Etheric world and the material world. The bird is esconced in the Etheric acanthus leaves and spirals, with the patera of eight leaves: all these symbols point to the Etheric. The two beasts (lionesses perhaps) fight, indicating both the animal nature, and the conflicts, within the Astral plane. Fulcanelli discusses Saturne as an anagram for Natures, in connection with the shallow grooving on a plinth, (op.cit., p.115). The hermetic secret is that nature can manifest only through dualities – hence the grooving, and hence the relevance of this Fulcanelli passage to our own search.

24. *Fulcanelli Master Alchemist. Le Mystère des Cathédrales*, Eng. ed., 1971, p.115.

25. The old man is developing a rather complex conceit. He imagines that the copy of Michelangelo's giant statue of David (which is in the square wherein we stood) was imprisoned behind the bars of the 'stone' balustrades around the square. This was a play on the idea expressed by Michelangelo himself, that the form of his statues were imprisoned within his marble blocks. For his belief in the dependence of the outer on the inner, see Sonnet 44 in Michelangelo Buonarroti, *Rime* (intro. G. Testori), 1975, p.87.

26. See Matthew Arnold's poem, 'The Scholar Gypsy', 1853.

27. The old man was right about the position of Saturn. Astrologer's degree is the four-degree arc of 25 to 29 Leo. What fascinated us more, however, was that Jupiter was in Cancer, exactly opposite the conjunction of Venus and Mars which had occurred on the day our Teacher had moved to Siena.

28. The Society of Astrologers, formed in London, used to hold annual dinners from 1649 onwards. As Keith Thomas observes, it constituted a would-be scientific organization a full decade before the formation of the Royal Society. See K. Thomas, *Religion and the Decline of Magic*, 1971, p.304. There is a printed version of one of the sermons 'Preached before the learned Society of Astrologers' by Robert Gell. The sermon was delivered in August, 1649.

29. Hedsel left no reference which enables us to locate the source of this interesting story. The obscene kiss, *osculum obscoenum*, was regarded as the highlight of the witch Sabbats. However, it would appear that the Sabbat itself seems to have been dreamed up or fabricated in the 15th century by judges and ecclesiastical investigators in the service of the Church. The concept of the Sabbat made it very

easy for them to establish guilt, with the aid of horrendous torture, for the imagined trip to the sabbat was just as lethal as the supposedly genuine trip.

30. He used the words *la mere* and *le merde*, yet the idea of the kiss of the lips of the woman being contrasted so powerfully with the kiss of the buttocks of a goat seems to be expressed just as well in the English, as Canseliet had been anxious to draw the Green Language insistence that *mere* (mother) and *mer* (sea) are the same.

31. Buttock kiss, or *osculum infame*, seems to have been developed as part of the imaginative mythology of the witchcraft hunters (see n.29). Certainly, it was given great prominence in trials – perhaps because it figured in the text and illustrations of Guazzo's important *Compendium Maleficarum*, 1608. Perhaps there was also a misunderstanding of the Egyptian *ru* symbolism among the churchmen who supported the inhuman witchhunts?

32. Our Master had talked to the group about the Fool carving at Najera. In fact, the penis of this fool has been cut away by a vandal. See C. Gaignebet and J. D. Lajoux, *Art Profane et Religion Populaire au Moyen Âge*, 1985, p.165.

33. For all the diabolical associations enforced upon the buttocks kiss by the priestcraft, it remained a surprisingly popular image in ecclesiastical sculpture. No doubt, this is partly due to the fact that the hermetic tradition still lived among the Masons, who knew precisely what the Egyptian *ru* had been. Some evidence of this is preserved at Fribourg, for a 15th-century *offrande*, in the form of a gargoyle, has the anus in the distinctive form of the *ru*.

34. The French, *offrande*, carries the same double-meaning as the English, 'offering' – the religious and everyday meaning.

35. Gaignebet and Lajoux, op.cit., p.200.

36. Gaignebet and Lajoux, op.cit., p.213.

37. The mediaeval respect for the winds and their significant place in the mediaeval cosmology may be understood only within the mediaeval view of the effect of the Fall of Man. As a consequence of the Fall, all nature was thrown into disarray, as the Quintessence lost its harmonic grip on the Four Elements. However, something of the old harmony was still preserved in the celestial spheres, and in the higher (though non-planetary) spheres where the four airs (or winds) had their origin. These winds were the celestial equivalents of the four lower elements. This theory, in relation to the rich symbolism of Hildegard of Bingen, is discussed by Charles Singer, *From Magic to Science*, 1928, p.211ff.

38. Gaignebet and Lajoux reproduced examples from Diest (p.212), Aosta (p.213), Montemart, Massay and Chezal-Benoit (all three on p.215), Saint-Claude, Troyes. These are in Continental churches: it would be easy to provide as many examples from English churches.

39. *La marotte* is one of the names given in French for 'the small mother'. There is every reason for seeing this as a cosmological image of the inner dwarf, or *Ishon*, no bigger than a thumb – the Tom-thumb of the fairy-tales – which is also prepared to reveal the things which are normally hidden. Certainly, the *offrande* finial on the staff in the hand of Metsys' Fool is a *marotte*, and certainly it is meant to symbolize an esoteric aspect of Spiritual development. The larger Fool – who wears a cock, with the full force of the double meaning implied in this term, upon his cap – carries this *marotte* as an arcane symbol. As the image makes quite clear, he is required to keep silent concerning what he learns from this small inner man, even though it is not the natural disposition of the cock to hold its silence.

It is worth bearing in mind that, in materialistic terms, the inner man must be smaller than the outer man. This inner man is linked with the spine: this is because, quite literally, the space occupied by the Ishon is at the end of the extension of the spinal cord, which serves, among other things, the eyes. This, in a strictly physiological sense, explains why the *marotte* is represented on a staff. In esoteric lore – as in fairytales – the staff is the symbol of the spine, and thus of the nervous system. This symbolism applies to the staves in the hands of the Tarot Fool: one staff is the spine of the outer Fool, the other that of the inner Fool.

40. The story of how the lilies of the classical mythology, linked with the seduction of Alcamene by Zeus which led to the creation of the Milky Way in the Heavens, and the white lilies on Earth, is told in the Byzantine *Geoponica*.

41. Such 'confluence of sounds' is the very basis of the Green Language which Fulcanelli explored with such rigour, and which Nostradamus used with such remarkable insight. See D. Ovason, *The Secrets of Nostradamus*, 1997, pp.134ff and 394ff.

42. Nephthys, the sister of Isis and Osiris, is the dark–goddess. The two sisters cry in lamentation at the death of Osiris. Their tears are a result of the temporary loss of the solar power. Some of the attributes of Nephthys are examined in the following text.

43. Isis and Nephthys play increasingly important role in modern wicca cults. No doubt this is due to a weakening in the power of official Christianity, for much of the Isiac wisdom had been transferred to the new Virgin, with the coming of the new dispensation of Christianity. In consequence the Isis cult, which is inseparable from the Nephthys cult (as the hermetic texts reveal), went underground and continued only in forbidden, heretical or occult groups. Some of these traditions have survived, if only in a dislocated form, into modern times. It is quite possible that the Black Virgins of the Christian churches in Europe are survivals from pagan Isis or Nephthys cults. However, the notion of the 'shadow' of the idea, the *eidolon* which was connected in ancient times with the irrational soul, seen as a shadow of the rational soul, has survived in literature with less distortion. See G. R. S. Mead, *The Doctrine of the Subtle Body in Western Tradition*, 1919, 1967 setting, p.44. There does not appear to be any ancient rite of worship directed to Nephthys herself, but this is probably a reflection of the fact that she is the shadow, or dark side, of Isis, who was the object of widespread worship throughout the ancient world. Her Egyptian hieroglyphic probably means 'Lady of the House'. As a guardian of the canopic jars in which were placed the organs of the dead, this 'house' might be the 'house of the ka' – or the tomb.

The 'Great Beast', Aleister Crowley, did a great deal to introduce a romanticized form of Egyptian imagery into modern magic. He was attached to the mythology which he fondly believed was expressed in the ancient Egyptian rites. However – and this was more important to so egocentric a person – his interest in Egyptian things was increased when he traced some of his previous incarnations to an important phase of this culture. These two factors tend to explain why he represented the dual Moon in terms of Set, as representative of the dark Moon, and Horus as the Child who was born and waxed to strength with the new (horned) Moon. Whether this view of Egyptian lore is mythologically correct is not really relevant – what is important is that the father of modern black magic praxes recognized the essential duality of the Moon, and the validity of its traditional division into dark and light.

44. Some occult writers ascribe a quite fabulous origin to the Tarot cards. However, it is unlikely that the cards were used for divination until the late 16th century. That the designs were promulgated by an arcane School may hardly be denied. However, as with so many such products, their origins, purpose, designers, and even their original names, are lost. For the record, the earliest card we know which depicts the Fool more or less in the traditional form is from the Pierre Madenie set of 1709. For a useful assessment as to when the cards (as game cards) were invented, and for a survey of the cards in a strictly occult setting, see M. Dummett, *The Game of Tarot*, 1980, p.102ff. For a survey of the cards in a less esoteric setting, see S. R. Kaplan, *The Encyclopedia of Tarot*, 1986.

45. The *Stellar Maris* is said sometimes to be the 'Star of Mary', at other times, the 'Star of the Sea' – an ambiguity which would have delighted Fulcanelli. However, in mediaeval art, the star is usually placed either over the heart of the Virgin Mary

(in the place where the Child would be) or on her head-veil, her mapharion. The print plate 37 on page 495 shows the eight-fold star as an indispensable symbol of the Virgin. The star has very many meanings, but its prime significance is that it links the Virgin with *Spica*, the main star of the constellation Virgo. The star marks the head of an ear of corn (from which the eucharistic bread may be made) in the sheaf held against the body of the Virgin.

46. The image of the Virgin Mary standing on the Moon, to indicate that the lower demonic energies are under control, is essentially an apocalyptic icon. It is now used to denote the Virgin of the Assumption. The most impressive image we know is that giant statue which dominates the skyline of Santiago, in Chile. This iconography must be compared with the earlier images (of which one survives on the west front of Notre Dame in Paris) which show Mary trampling upon the serpent which had brought about the Fall of Man. This imagery shows the Mother of God as the new Eve: see Gertrud Schiller, *Iconography of Christian Art*, 1971 Eng. trans., I, p.108.

47. As our Master intimated, the best image of the Sheelah-na-gig is in the form of a soffit on the south-eastern wall of the 12th-century church at Kilpeck, in Herefordshire (plate 38). Significantly, she is so placed that on certain days she greets the sunrise with her opened *kteis*.

48. We can give no adequate account of why the Sheelah-na-gig, with such obvious pagan origins, has survived on the fabric of Christian churches. Usually, she is not very much in evidence, and (as at Kilpeck) is among other grotesques. The huge Sheelah carved on the great stone on the south wall of the church at Whittlesford, south-east of Cambridge, is very much in evidence, yet it would take considerable effort to reach it in order to efface the design. One wonders just how many of these images have not survived, however. We learn from Massey that the Sheelah was also called 'Cicely of the Branch' – II, p.681. Undoubtedly, this sound is linked with Sicily.

49. The question is, did Fulcanelli ever meet Massey? Given their remarkable occult insights and influence, they both remain very shadowy figures, but there are indications that the Englishman did influence the Frenchman, in method and ideology as much as in anything else.

    Gerald Massey is sometimes confused with the Theosophist and Freemason, Charles Carleton Massey, a man of considerable literary ability and social standing, a founder of the Society for Psychical Research (1882) and a chief organizer and President of the British Theosophical Society (from 1878).

50. See Gerald Massey, *The Book of the Beginnings*, I, p.466.

51. According to most accounts, it is called the *vesica piscis* because it is supposed to resemble the shape of the bladder of a fish. However, a mediaeval sigil for Pisces, ℞, consisted of two interlocking crescents, just as does the *Ru*. The connection between the Piscean Christ, who descended from the Spiritual world – through the door of space and time – and the Egyptian *Ru* must be evident. The *vesica piscis* is sometimes called the *mandorla* because it is supposed to resemble the shape of an almond. One presumes that the mediaeval ecclesiastical seals were intended to show that the waxen impressions left on documents were invested with power from another, higher world.

52. The Master Bertram may have been born *circa* 1340, and it is suspected that he came from Minden, in Westphalia. See C. M. Kauffmann, *The Altarpiece of the Apocalypse from Master Bertram's Workshop in Hamburg*, 1968.

53. It is likely that the altarpiece was painted round about 1400 for the friary of Mary Magdalen in Hamburg. The iconography is certainly based on the commentary of the Franciscan friar, Alexander, on the *Apocalypse*, for some of the images are derived from known manuscript illuminations to this text. See Kauffmann, op. cit., n.52, pp.7 and 32.

54. Once again, a birth-theme associated with the *Ru*. It may be argued that the figure

holding the Jesus child is not Christ, but God. In fact, the Christ in a burning aureole of *vesica piscis* form is a conventional image of the Resurrected Christ, so we have here a combination of the Spiritual Christ with the physical Jesus. The emphasis in both cases is on birth, for the Jesus Child descended by way of ordinary birth into the Earthly plane, while Christ was born again (that is, resurrected) from the Spiritual plane. The *Ru* is the portal for both births.

55. The story is told by E. Canseliet in the Preface to Fulcanelli, *Demeures Philosophales*, 1964 ed.

56. The *sol lente* is the 'slow Sun', or *fuoco lente*, 'slow fire'. The alchemists often draw parallels between the heat they apply to their various receptacles, and the heat of the Sun. Indeed, the *Fire of the Philosophers*, which may be *fuoco* or *sol*, is an aerial fire, a fire on the Etheric plane, which is circular, and bright like the Sun, 'but which is not the Sun'. The alchemist Philalethes, in his tenth rule of the art, takes the matter even further, insisting that the entire secret of the art depends upon the two types of heat used by the Masters. The secret internal fire is the instrument of God, and its qualities are imperceptible to men. (See *Règles du Philalethe pour se Conduire dans l'Oeuvre Hermétique*, 1979, Genoa ed.. In fact, *sol lente* is Green Language, for its sound incorporates the word *sollennis*, pertaining to a religious feast, or sacrifice. Our own phrase 'solemn festival' originally denoted a sacrificial festival. In just such a way is the *sol lente*, which uses the secret fire of God, a sacrificial fire.

57. In part, Santa Claus is a direct throwback to the Boy Bishop, the *Episcopus Puerorum*, elected on St Nicholas' Day (6 December), with authority to rule until Childermas (28 December). King Edward I regarded the Boy with such seriousness that he permitted him to say vespers in his own presence on 7 December 1299. In Santa Claus there are also traces of Nicholas of Bari: the Boy Bishop was sometimes called St Nicholas' Bishop.

58. Fulcanelli, op. cit., p.46, likens the stone Peter to the corner stone of the philosophers' Great Work. This is why the image of the devil, so frequently found on the outside of gothic cathedrals in the gargoyles, should be found at the important point of intersection of the cruciform of the ground-plan of the cathedral. It is the *Peter* (pierre = 'stone') upon which the Church is founded – a symbol which takes one well beyond the vexing confines of the Apostolic succession.

59. In the church of the Madeleine, at Rennes-le-Château, the enigmatic priest, Saunière, placed a demonic water-stoup, which has been called the Asmodeus figure. Although somewhat garish and strangely placed so near the doorway, there is nothing strange in the image of a demon in mediaeval churches. However, Saunière did not introduce the demon until the late 19th century: this late dating is perhaps what makes the figure curious. The Devil is acting in the church as bearer of the holy water, a bénitier. This should remind followers of Fulcanelli that the French benêt means 'Fool'. There are mysteries at Rennes-le-Château which, for all the spilt ink, have not yet been fully explored.

60. Our friend explained that the word *cantonata*, which is an architectural name for an interior corner, is close to *can'tonato*, an abbreviation of *cantare intonato*, 'to sing in tune'. This cant almost takes us back to the musical capitals of Catalonia.

61. The Roman *Saturnalia* was (in its later phases) a festival which lasted for seven days, from 19 December. During that time, all normal business activity was curtailed, schools closed, and there was a general merrymaking which involved a special licence to slaves. Small presents were exchanged at this time, and it is therefore tempting to trace our own Christmas festivities to the Saturnalia. In fact, the key date in the West – 25 December, as the supposed birthdate of Jesus – was derived from Mithraic rites involving worship of the Sun-god.

62. He probably made this observation because he recognized that only a priest can offer a Black Mass. No one out of holy orders – let alone a devil – could offer a Mass

which, by definition (being Black, rather than White), is intended to invert the holy rituals in every way. Thus, he is recognizing that only one empowered to offer the genuine Christian ritual could officiate in a Black Mass. With this fundamental truth collapses the majority of stories of Black Masses with which the history of the mediaeval period is punctuated.

63. Satirical coins – the Fool's jetons – were issued in some cities during the times of the Feast of Fools. Records of such issue have survived for Amiens, Chartres, Reims, Laon, and as far south as Besançon. Presumably used for the purchase of goods at the fairs, their purpose and origin is unknown. One coin with which we are familiar shows on the obverse a Fool (in Mithraic-like cap) addressing a Pope: the inscription runs: *.MONETA.NOVA.ADRINI. STULTORU.PAPE* ('New money of Adrian, the Pope of the Fools'). On the reverse is what is sometimes called in English 'My Mad Mother', or 'Mother Folly', with an Ishon-like stick in her hand. The inscription runs: *+STULTORU.INFINITUS. EST.NUMERUS* ('The number of Fools is infinite').

64. Even as late as 1644, it was recognized by a correspondent of the great astronomer, Gassendi, that the Feast of Fools at Antiles was beyond the control of the Church. See the article by T. Barns, 'Abbot of Unreason', in Hastings, *Encyclopaedia of Religion and Ethics*, 1971 imp., vol. I, p.10. By 1555, the Festival of the Fool had been suppressed in Scotland. No astrologer would be surprised by this, as Scotland is ruled by Cancer, the sign opposite to Capricorn, the zodiacal governor of the Saturnalia.

65. The *arcani disciplina* is the name given in the early Church to a practice of preserving the Mystery of the rites of Baptism and the Holy Supper and their doctrines secret. The Arcani, or Mysteria, were preserved from all those who did not enter them without considerable preparation. In this practice, the Church was merely continuing the hermetic practices of the ancient Mystery Schools. Those interested in esoteric Christianity might argue that the full import of the Mysteries of Baptism and the Eucharists are still not public knowledge. We must not forget that many of the early Christians refer to the 'unwritten teaching' of Christianity – to a living tradition which is not found in the Gospels, or in other sacred writ. In this context, the fourth-century bishop, Basil the Great, *De Spiritu*, 27, is often quoted.

66. In some cases the catacomb paintings and incisions use the actual image of a fish to represent Christ, following the acrostic recorded by Augustine (see n.67). In other cases, the Greek word for the fish (*I-ch-th-y-s*) is used. A beautiful example of the former is in the Catacomb of Domitilla, where the emphasis is on the dual fish of Pisces. The fresco in the 'Chapel of the Sacrament' in the catacomb of Callixtus not only shows the two fishes of the holy meal, but depicts the table in the form of a fish. The celebrants are eating the body of Christ from the body of Christ.

67. The famous acrostic for *I-ch-th-y-s*, or fish, seems to have been old even when Augustine recorded it. Augustine claims that he had taken it from a prophecy written by the Erythraean Sibyl, which was one way of linking the new Christ Mysteries with the ancient pagan Mysteries. The 'prophecy' is a Latin verse, translated from the Greek. The opening letter of each line spells out the words *JESOUS CHREISTOS THEOU UIOS SOTER* ('Jesus Christ, the Son of God, the Saviour'). See Augustine, *City of God*, XVIII, 23.

68. We owe our delight in seeing these hidden fishes on the façade of the church of San Miniato to our Florentine friend. In fact, they are so well hidden that a pair of binoculars is needed to see them. They are held to the mouths of initiate figures (men-fish) in marble work below the cross in the apex of the façade, below the ornate socle on which stands the bronze eagle (the symbol of the Calimala Guild which probably funded the rebuilding of the church, in 1207). The fishes are both zodiacal and eucharistic.

69. 1 March marked the beginning of the ecclesiastical year in many parts of Europe,

even though the secular calendar of Julius Caesar had commenced the year on 1 January. This distinction explains the phrase 'In the year of our Lord' in mediaeval texts, for the ecclesiastical year was different from the secular, and the phrase pins the dating down to the former.

70. They marked this transition with reference to the passing of the fishes of Pisces: the Fish of Christ was being renewed. Thomas Barns argues against this, on the grounds that there are records of such presents being made between Christmas Day and 4 February in the early 15th century. More reasonable is Barns' suggestion that the April Fool custom may be traced to the Welsh Spring festival of Llew, the Sun-hero of the *Mabinogion*. See article by T. Barns, 'All Fools' Day', in Hastings, vol. I, p.332ff. Although the origin of the festivities is the subject of dispute among scholars, the fact of its being a zodiacal celebration is preserved in one of the mediaeval words for the festival – *Kalendae*.

71. Capricorn rules over bureaucracy. The Capricornian has a great ability to organize, and to put things in order, and to lay careful plans. Without such abilities, without the inner rectitude of the Capricornians, the great cathedrals could not have been built. The point being made in this meeting is that Capricorn must temper itself by organizing outbreaks of Cancerian riot, when people may fall back to their Earth-bound roots. Behind every Capricornian move towards regulation falls the shadow of inner Cancerian rebellion.

72. The three *Moirae* are the Greek equivalent of the Roman Fates, or *Parcae*.

73. Our friend was being old fashioned, and monarchist. The modern Piazza della Repubblica had been formerly Piazza Vittorio Emanuele, and was renamed to accord with republican sympathies. The misconceived project of modernization, to produce this soulless square, involved the wholesale destruction of much of old Florence, including the Mercato Vecchio, and the tangle of ancient streets which were famous in the annals of Florentine history. Our friend was lamenting the destruction of the old fabric of Florence.

74. The powerful monk, Savonarola, once the Spiritual leader of Florence, was arrested in 1498, on a trumped-up charge of heresy. He was tortured savagely for 40 days in order to obtain a confession. He was hanged, with two of his disciples, in the Signoria, in front of the Palazzo Vecchio, and his body was publicly burned in the square. His ashes were thrown into the Arno. To this day, annually, on the anniversary of his death (23 May) flowers are strewn on the place where this courageous man died. Our friend was lamenting the destruction of the old Spirit of Florence.

75. Chapman, *All Fools*, V. ii, 1599.

76. He was referring to the cemetery of San Miniato al Monte. We used to walk for hours in the shade of the cypress trees which grew alongside the walls of this place.

77. He is talking of the inner sulphur – see n.81. In the microcosm, *sulphur* is the Will, which is the source of sexual energies.

78. Shakespeare, *Henry IV*, II.2.

79. Fulcanelli, like all good alchemists, recognizes that there are different forms of sulphur. Concerning the sulphur of the Will (see n.81) he quotes the Cosmopolite, *Nouvelle Lumière chymique. Traité du Soufre*, 1647: 'The Wise man will find our stone even in the dung heap.' This is true, for it is the dung heap yet in the bowels, near the sexual parts.

80. For details of the Rosicrucian, Jakob Boehme (1575-1624), see p.53, p.283 and p.371, n.42.

81. The relevant discussion of sulphur is in Boehme, *Von der Dreien Principien*, 1624, ii.7. The three principles are those of Sulphur, Salt and Mercury (Willing, Thinking and Feeling), seen in a spiritual light. Boehme wrote in German, and the play on words does not come out well in the Italian. The German for sulphur is *Schwefel* but in this case Boehme uses the Latin *sulphur*. Boehme clearly regards the *Sul* as sufficiently similar in sound to the German *Seele* to warrant a play on

words. Curiously, the play is more obvious in English, when the *sul* resonates in *soul*. See also n.82.

82. The sound, *phur*, of the Latin *sulphur* (see n.81) is equated by Boehme with the German *feuer*, for fire. Boehme was one of the Masters of the Green Language, yet often made his meanings clear in the way that few Masters did.

83. For Kircher, see p.268 and 440, n.28.

84. No mediaeval architect would have dreamed of laying a foundation stone without having a horoscope cast for the moment of laying. Such horoscopes were usually called foundation charts. The theory was that the planetary positions at the foundation of a building would colour the nature, duration and Spiritual history of the building. In even earlier times – in ancient Rome, Greece or Egypt – buildings were oriented to specific stars or star-groups. The principles in each case were much the same, reflecting the notion that a building, to be beneficial to men and gods, should reflect the cosmos in a harmonious and meaningful way. A standard – and eminently readable – account of such stellar orientation in Egyptian times is J. N. Lockyer, *The Dawn of Astronomy. A Study of The Temple-Worship and Mythology of the Ancient Egyptians*, 1894.

85. The Templars are represented as twins, each with their arms crossed over their chests, as though they are in effigy – that is, suggesting that they are 'dead to the world', or in the Spiritual realm. Their eyes appear to be closed. For a treatment of this symbolism, see F. Gettings, *The Hidden Art*, 1978, p.45ff.

86. The Seal, or *sigillum*, of the Templars shows two knights, with two shields, sharing a single horse. There is an example on display in the Templar Museum at La Rochelle, France. This is inscribed with the Latin which translates: Seal of the Soldiers of Christ.

87. See p.280.

88. The girl seems to have assumed that the *Flos Virginis* was the *Flos Caeli*, or Heavenly Flower, mentioned by Paracelsus and Fulcanelli. However, she was wrong. Paracelsus is more explicit than Fulcanelli, and tells us that the heavenly flower is a species of manna: the Flower of the Virgin is really the Virgin's Milk (*Lac Virginis*), the Spiritual white extract which marks an important stage in the alchemical process. It may be the same as the Flower of the Earth, when it has become dew. However, the Flower of the Virgin is sometimes five-petalled, and appears in this form widely in mediaeval Christian art. The mediaeval architects who designed their dancing floor with a six-petalled flower could not have been more explicit: the pathway to this flower is itself the stalk of the plant. The girl was doing this dance on 9 September, when there were five planets in Virgo.

89. Hedsel does throw some light on the personal name of Latona Hussay, for he links it firmly with the Latin name of Leto, which is Latona. This mythological identification is evident in the stream of light which bathes the girl when he first sees her, and in her disappointed reaction to his words. The surname, Hussay, is not so clearly defined, even in Hedsel's notes. He merely pencilled alongside the name – *degeneration*. We must presume from this that he visualizes *Ussay* (which would be a French pronunciation of hussy) as a degenerate form of *housewife*, which, in etymological terms, is precisely what hussy is. What is now used in contempt was once a word applied to a woman as a term of honour. Hussy, or even Ussay, is an excellent term for a degraded woman. Could we see the girl as a degradation of the Roman goddess Latona? Or could it be that Hedsel wished to show the two sides of the woman: the goddess and the degenerate? Even though he changed the name of his companion, Hedsel's story is undoubtedly true, and he does seem to resort to this theme in more than one detail of narrative. In the penultimate paragraph of his account, the phrase *when the creature is used by a soft-fingered goddess* reminds us that the French verb *user*, which sounds like 'Ussay', has a distinct sexual connotation.

90. Both the books were by Fulcanelli: *Les Demeures Philosophales* and an English

edition of his *Le Mystère des Cathédrales*.

91. She meant, of course, the *Language of the Birds*. She reveals a considerable knowledge of the tradition of this language in her reference to 'the joking bird-song'. The alchemist, Michael Maier, printed an engraving of a conference of the birds, as symbol of the Green Language, in his *Jocus Severus* (1617): this was the 'serious joke', expressed in the idea of a group of birds assembled to determine which of them deserved the palm. Although the Egyptian Phoenix presided over this meeting, the owl was eventually designated the wisest among them. This perhaps explains why the owl was adopted by some Rosicrucians as a symbol of their initiation into the Mysteries.

92. The *Book of Life* is mentioned in many different scriptures throughout the world. Esotericists recognize this 'Book' as the equivalent of the *Akashic Chronicles*, which record all human thoughts, words and deeds, to apportion karmic adjustment. In *Revelation* (4–5), the first thing that St John is shown when he enters, in Spirit, the door into Heaven is the One who sits upon the throne, who has, as it were, a rainbow around him. To the right side of this being is a book, sealed with seven seals. This is the *Book of Life* which no man is deemed worthy to open and read. No doubt Latona had this book in mind when she used the term. At the time when the Chartres statuary was being carved, there developed, as a dark counterpart, the idea of a *Book of Death*, or the *Black Book*. This was the book given by the Devil to those witches who agreed to have their names scratched from the Book of Life, in exchange for this dubious gift.

93. In ancient Persia, Mazdao and Ahriman were the two Zoroastrian beings of Light and Darkness respectively – the leaders of the contending dualistic principles behind the Zoroastrian system. Modern esotericists – who are aware that the cosmos may be understood only in terms of such dualism – have tended to identify the principle of Light with Lucifer, as the modern equivalent of Mazdao. The dark Ahriman (the word Ahrimanus was used even in the Egyptian hermetic texts) still retains the ancient name, and still wears the black hat as leader of the baddies: he is the Prince of Lies, the Prince of Materialism.

94. Morien, quoted by Fulcanelli in a brief mention of *La Clef du Cabinet hermétique*, says of the black matter used in the alchemical process of refinement that it must show some acidity and have 'a certain smell of the grave'. See Fulcanelli, op. cit., 1971 Eng. ed., p.80.

95. The inscription is *Virgini pariturae*, but this does not make the statues Isiac. See C. Bigarne, *Considérations sur le Culte d'Isis chez les Eduens*, 1862. However, one should note what Fulcanelli has to say about this, op.cit., pp.57–8.

96. It seems curious to me that Latona was not aware that the *Nôtre-Dame-sous-Terre* at Chartres was inscribed with *Virgini pariturae* on its pedestal.

97. For the relationship between *idiot* and *idea*, see p.65ff.

98. Was Fulcanelli offering an occult blind with a seeming-error in the passage where he quotes *Matri deum, magnae ideae*? This is not the actual quotation at Die. In the same paragraph, quite uncharacteristically, he misspells the name of the authority Bigarne (which name he gives as Bigarre, even though he has it perfectly in the footnote on the previous page). Of course, *bigarre* is a French word meaning 'motley' – a strange word to apply in a context referring to the Black Virgin. Clearly Fulcanelli (or his editors) is hiding something.

99. The Black Virgin at Montserrat is called *La Moreneta* and is supposed to have been brought to the region by St Peter. The one we have seen is no older than the 12th century, however, but this is very impressive. We wonder if the pine-cone in the hand of the Child on her knee has anything to do with the pine-cone of the hermetic thrysus.

100. This mediaeval 'hurdy-gurdy' carried by the donkey was a guitar-like stringed instrument, played by the friction of a rosined wheel, turned by hand. One of its popular French names was *vielle* (see n.101). Almost certainly, the symbolism at

Chartres is linked with the fact that the instrument has a permanent keynote, or drone, which drowns the sound of the planetary music. In the light of this, the symbolism of the music at the Feast of Fools becomes more clear.

101. This mediaeval instrument was still called a *vielle*, or *vielle à roue* (wheeled vielle) up to the 18th century. Precisely when it was linked with the hurdy-gurdy, or street piano, is not certain. All the instruments have in common is that they were both played by turning a handle. While the *vielle* was essentially a street-instrument, Haydn had sufficient respect for it to write concertos and nocturnes for the instrument.

102. The biblical account of Balaam and his ass is in *Numbers* 22. The idea of the ass or donkey being able to see into the Spiritual world, when the self-important Balaam could not, clearly appealed to Hedsel, as much as to the mediaeval sculptors at Chartres. To gather from his notes, Hedsel seems to have found the meaning of Balaam ('One who swallows down') important.

103. We recognized the circled N as a letter L, for Latona, from the secret writing called 'Supercelestial Script' (see, for example, J. Marques-Riviere, *Amulettes, Talismans et Pentacles dans les Traditions Orientales et Occidentales*, 1938). We presumed that the upper circle (which played no part in the secret alphabet form) represented a star, and the lower one the circle of the maze, or (less likely) the Earth. Latona had stretched between Heaven and Earth while standing on the maze, when first we met. Of course, she may have added two circles simply to make of her initial a six, thus linking with the six petals of the dancing floor, and with the *Flos Virginis*.

104. Ovid, *Metamorphoses*, IV. 697 – see quote at head of the present chapter.

LAST WORDS

1. The eclipse began shortly before 11.30p.m. Caribbean local time. The comet Hale-Bopp was, in theory at least, visible to the north-west, below Perseus and Cassiopeia. Unfortunately, neither I nor Mark Hedsel saw the comet on that occasion.

2. *Atalia* is one of the names given to the Lunar Dragon which was, in former times, symbolically held to swallow the eclipsing luminary.

3. In the Western arcane literature the skull-face of the moon is recognised as the detritus of fission. It is a cosmic symbol of the ossifying darkness that had to be removed from the planet earth, to allow human beings to develop spiritually. Its darkness is illuminated externally, bereft of an inner source of light.

4. The Chinese, and several Oriental cultures, claim to trace the form of a hare in the Moon. Some Buddhist stories tell how the hare was translated to the Moon because it allowed a starving man to eat it. The connection between the hare and the Moon is extremely widespread – it is found in Mexican and African mythology. Among the North American Indians, the Great Hare in the skies is Manibozho, hero of the Creation Legends: some stories link him with the Moon, others with the Sun.

5. The Hebrew *Ishon* means 'dwarf', but in the Authorized Version of the Bible it is translated as 'apple of the eye'. The association is almost certainly linked with the hermetic *kore*. In *The Lamentations of Jeremiah* (ii, 18), the translation offered is 'let not the apple of thine eye cease', suggesting that the apple of the eye is weeping. However, it could, with a much deeper meaning, be translated, 'let not the small man within cease'.

6. For the double meaning of *kore*, see p.357, footnote.

7. It is clear from the notes left by Mark Hedsel that he had in mind a lecture given on 12 January 1924 by Rudolf Steiner, at Dornach. In the library which Hedsel bequeathed me, there was a typescript, which had been formerly in the Myrdhin Library (London), marked on the paper jacket, in script, *Teachings and Initiations of the Old Rosecrucians* (sic). The typescript seems to be one of the copies made from stenographic notes made during Steiner's lecture. The second lecture in this typescript deals with the lunar spinal cord, and while it mentions the 'Astral man',

it does not use the hermetic word *Ishon.*

8. See n.5. The Ishon sits inside the pupil of the eyes. Hedsel's conceit is that Ishon is blind to things of the world, but can see things Spiritual – the dwarf is blocking his own view of the world.

9. This relationship of the human spine to the Earth is symbolized in the upright vertical of the I. The *Ego* can develop only because it is poised upright between Earth and the cosmos, working as a sort of vertical antenna, transmitting the cosmic forces into the Earthly.

10. In the *Inferno*, Lucifer stands at the centre of Hell, and hence at the centre of the geocentric universe. At one point, Dante is climbing down his figure, and suddenly finds himself climbing up. He has been at the still point, where up and down meet. See Canto xxxiv. l.76ff.

11. For previous references to the Fool and Zero, see pp. 00 and 00.

12. The Way of the Monk has been radically misunderstood in modern times. Before the Church began to lose its connection with Spirituality, as a consequence of the Council of Trent, the Way of the Monk was a Spiritual search which continued the Gnostic streams of initiation. See the useful essay by Ernesto Buonaiuti, 'Symbols and Rites in the Religious Life of Certain Monastic Orders' (1934–5), in *The Mystic Vision. Papers from the Eranos Yearbooks*, 1969, p.168ff.

13. For the Akashya as a circle in the Oriental and Occidental traditions, see F. Gettings, *The Dictionary of Occult, Hermetic and Alchemical Sigils*, 1981.

14. The closing words of Hermes' address to Tat (op. cit. Mead), in this same instruction to his pupil, are even more puzzling. He wrote that if you wished to make yourself like unto God, then you should be in the same time in every place, both not yet begotten and in the after-death state.

15. Hedsel's grades seem to pertain to the *African Brothers* of Masonry. I suspect that these curious references must have been a continuation of Hedsel's thought-patterns: he had been speaking about the Egyptian dialogues between Hermes and his disciple, Tat, and continued this Egyptian theme. Now his reference to the hierarchy of grades in an Egyptian system of Masonry. The Italian hermeticist, Balsamo (1743–94), who worked and wrote under the name of 'Cagliostro', had introduced into the Masonic stream a series of Egyptian rites, seemingly designed to renew the respect for the goddess Isis, and hence for the hermetic texts. This was merely one of several serious attempts to reintroduce Egyptian mysticism into Masonry – perhaps to redirect these rites to their original source. The *African Brothers* were instituted in 1767, and named the first of their 11 degrees 'Apprentice of Egyptian Secrets', the fifth 'Initiate in the Egyptian secrets', and the eighth 'Master of the Egyptian Secrets'. This latter was also known by the Greek title *Alethophilote*, meaning 'Lover of Truth'. The three higher degrees were 'Armiger', 'Miles' and 'Eques', supporting the idea put forward by Albert Pike, in his examination of the Masonic grade of 'Knight Kadosh' (*Morals and Dogma*, 1871, p.823), that Cagliostro had been working in the Templar stream of initiation. The *Eques* or 'rider' is a reference to the Order of Knights, which probably refers to the initiation image of the Templars on their Grand Seal. For a list of the African Brothers grades, see Isabel Cooper-Oakley, *Masonry and Medieval Mysticism*, 1900, 1977 ed., pp.56–7.

Long after Mark Hedsel's death, when reflecting upon this conversation, it struck me that his reference to this relatively obscure Masonic stream was intended to point a truth. The most striking literature to emerge from the Egyptian moralizing (strengthened politically by Napoleon's involvement in the Egyptian form of Masonry) was the *Trinosophia* attributed to Saint-Germain. I had always felt that there was a connection between Mark Hedsel and this great initiate. Was Mark providing hints that my guess was well founded?

16. For a more poetic translation, see Mead, op. cit., iii, p.218.

17. Shakespeare, *Twelfth Night*, iii. I. The quotation is from the mouth of the

disguised Viola, who knows full well that the Fool is no Fool, for, as she says of playing the Fool, 'This is a practice/As full of labour as a wise man's art.' In fact the first 75 lines of Act iii, scene I of *Twelfth Night* are virtually a succinct case for the hermetic nature of the Fool. Note, for example, 'how quickly the wrong side may be turned outward'.

18. At least 50 per cent of the Rosicrucian literature is presented in the form of arcane diagrams and secret languages, and concentrates on the Green Language of the alchemists. Among the earliest Rosicrucian work to be brought into the light of day by the Order was *The Chymical Wedding of Christian Rosenkreutz*, admirably translated by the Rosicrucian, Ezechiel Foxcroft, in 1690 as *The Hermetick Romance: or the Chymical Wedding*. Foxcroft was undoubtedly involved in the Rosicrucian enterprise run by Lady Conway at Ragley Hall, and, indeed, his wife, Elizabeth, lived with Lady Conway during his seven-year absence in the West Indies. It has been posited that it was the Teacher of the Ragley group, Franz van Helmont, who suggested to Foxcroft that he should translate this hermetic work.

    On the Fifth Day of this hermetic romance, the hero, being led to the cellar of a castle through an iron door, finds affixed on this a number of great copper letters, in a secret script. This is by no means the first such cryptographic encounter he has been presented with. Significantly, the hero copies it down in his book, but does not explain it.

    The Chymical Wedding is one of those initiatory texts which can only be read with the aid of an explanatory gloss, or with profound knowledge of alchemy and Rosicrucian lore. The text identifies its Rosicrucian origins in many symbols, not least of which is the famous *Monad Hieroglyphica* of Dr John Dee (1526–1607). This was a single sigil, concerning which Dee had propounded a whole book of theorems in explanation.

    Among the alphabetical riddles in the *Chymical Wedding* is: 'My name contains five and fifty, and yet hath only eight letters.' The riddle was solved by the scientist, Leibnitz, in the late 17th century, when he offered the solution as the eight-letter word ALCHIMIA. In the cabbalistic method of Gematria, letters of the alphabet are ascribed numerical values. The most simple of these *keys* is that in which the letter A is ascribed the value 1, B the number 2, and so on. In this schema the numerical value of ALCHIMIA is 'five and fifty' – provided one misses out the second I.

19. After some thought, I decided that that the 12 sigils which Mark Hedsel drew, and the 12 lines of text, warranted a separate treatment – see Appendix.

20. The ancient Sages asked Veda Vyasa which Age (Yuga) was the most suitable for Spiritual improvement. Veda Vyasa said that the fruits of asceticism practised for ten years in the Krita (Golden) were equal to one year in the Treta (Silver) and one month in the Dwapara (Bronze). However, the same fruits may be obtained in the Kali Age (the Dark Age, in which mankind presently dwells) when a similar asceticism is practised for only 24 hours. This is the secret, 'the one great virtue of the otherwise vicious Kali age'. From the *Vishnupuranam*, vi. sec.2. The short quoted section is from George S. Arundale, *The Lotus Fire: a Study in Symbolic Yoga*, 1939, p.607. The usual 'translations' for the Ages, in terms of the metals, are questionable. See Arundale, op. cit., p.69. In these terms, Kali Yuga is the 'enforced yoke'.

*1. A.O. Spare, **Blood on the Moon**, pastel, 1954. Private collection.*

2. *'I'd be very onely sitting up here all alone' – illustration by Boris Artzybasheff for Alfred Kreymborg's* **Funnybone Alley**, *1927.*

*3. The Fool, or the Prodigal Son – artwork based on Hieronymus Bosch, **Prodigal Son**.*
The original is in the Boymans–van Beuningen Museum.

4. *Initition of the spirit of the deceased, identified with Osiris. Detail from the Hunefer papyrus of the Budge lithographic version of* **The Egyptian Book of the Dead.**

*5. Garden of Eden, with Fountain of Life, unicorn, and other alchemical
or hermetic symbols. Detail from Verard's, **L'Abre de la Science**, 1505.*

6. 'From Byss to Abyss' – illustration of the cosmic chain from the Godhead to Man, from
William Law's edition of **The Works of Jacob Behmen, the Teutonic Philosopher**, 1772.

*7. Bas-relief of the zodiacal sign Scorpio, with the balance
of Libra in its claws (or chelae). Detail of the zodiacal column at the top of the
Staircase of the Dead, Sagrada di San Michele, Val di Susa.*

8. Dance of Salome, in front of Herod. Detail of bronze panel from the left-hand wing of the bronze doors on the west front of San Zeno, Verona.

9. Detail of the Crucifixion panel, with personified Sun and Moon, from the left-hand wing of the bronze doors on the west front of San Zeno, Verona.

*10. Moses riding the Ass. Detail from the right-hand wing of the bronze doors
on the west front of San Zeno, Verona.*

11. Aries the Ram with the three Arietan decan symbols.
Detail of the 'Months' fresco in the Palazzo Schifanoia, Ferrara.

12. Mars and Ilia in bed. Detail of the 'Months' fresco in the Palazzo Schifanoi, Ferrara.

*13. Title-page of Michael Maier's **Atalanta Fugiens** 1618.*
The story of the three golden apples is told in the marginal illustrations.

14. Portait of the alchemist-Rosicrucian, Michael Maier, at the age of 49.
*From **Atalanta Fugiens**, 1618.*

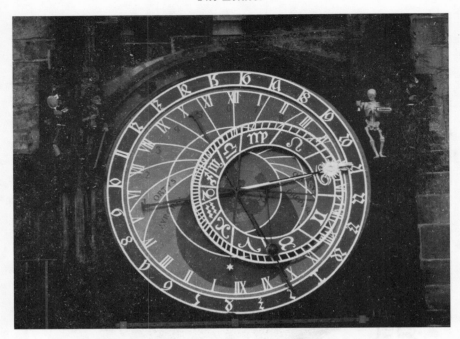

15. Upper dial of the great zodiacal clock in the mediaeval centre of Prague.

16. Lower dial of the great zodiacal clock in the mediaeval centre of Prague.
The outer concentric is calendrical, the inner roundels pertain to the monthly activities.

17. Hand coloured woodcut of circa 1530 based on a drawing of the Azoth used to illustrate the works of Paracelsus. The three extended heads are allegories of Mercury.

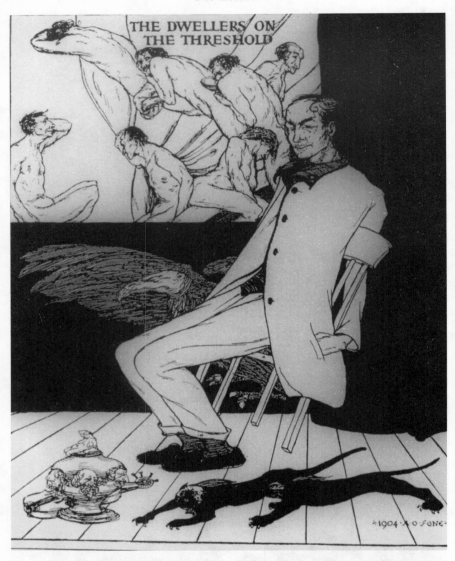

18. *'The Dwellers on the Threshold' – illustration to lines from Dante's **Commedia**, by A.O. Spare for his **Earth Inferno**, 1905.*

19. Centaurus with Bestia in his grasp. Detail of the constellation column at the top of the Staircase of the Dead, Sagrada di San Michele, Val di Susa.

20. The 'Fool' of the tarot pack, as visualized by Oswald Wirth, designed in 1889
under the influence of the occultist, de Guaita.

21. The underground cell of the Necromanteion at Ephyra, on the Acheron, where the ancients used to raise and consult the spirits of the dead, and infernal spirits.

22. The Egyptian serpent-god, Apep: detail from the Budge version of
The Egyptian Book of the Dead.

23. Mithras slaying the bull in the Cave. The blood pouring from the wound is the nama sebesion,
or 'sacred spring'. Engraving after the Borghesi Monument in the Louvre.

482

*24. Head of the giant statue of Ramses II in the Temple of Luxor, ancient Thebes.
The uraeus serpent between the eyes is a sign of initiate vision.*

25. Hieronymus Bosch – detail of central part of the 'Seven Deadly Sins', designed in the form of a giant eye, with Christ as the pupil. Prado Museum, Madrid.

26. Fay Pomerance, **Union of Isis with Osiris,** *monochrome tone illustration, 1959.*

27. One of the temple-pyramids of System M at the ceremonial site of Monte Alban (Oxaca) in Mexico. The upright stones are incised with dancing figures, some of which are marked with hieroglyphics that have been linked with the chakras.

28. Initiation ceremony – fresco in the Villa of the Mysteries at Pompeii.
The Mystery School to which the fresco refers is not known.

29. The Samrat Yantra, or giant sundial (a masonry gnomon) in the observatory at Jaipur. It is still an accurate time-keeper for the city, which is regulated according to solar time.

*30. Alchemist working in his laboratory: note the liberia worn
by the alchemist.*

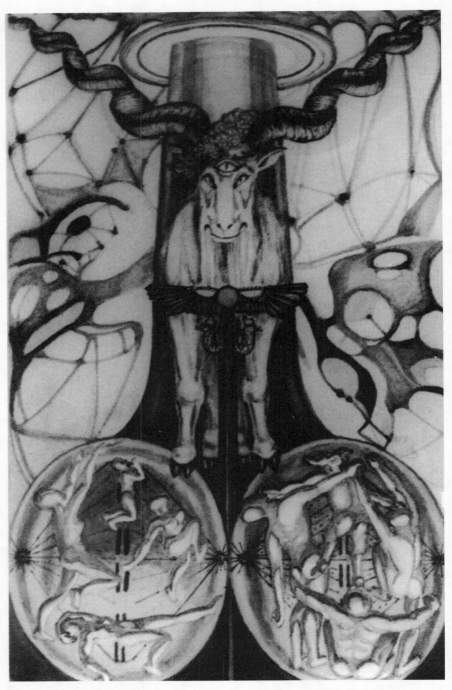

31. *The Devil card of the Tarot pack –* **The Book of Thoth** *– designed by Lady Frieda Harris, on the instructions of Alester Crowley. The sexual overtones are not found in the traditional tarot card design.*

32. The central tower of the Swayambhunath temple in Kathmandu, Nepal. A pair of eyes, with the third-eye ek (Nepalse number one), is painted on each of the four faces of the tower.

33. Erotic embrace in stone: relief on the 10th century Lakshmana temple dedicated to Vishnu at Kajuraho, India.

34. *The fall of the nostoc, or the Philosopher's Dew, from heaven, watched by an alchemist.*
From the alchemist portal of Amiens Cathedral, France.

35. Male and female alchemists gathering Philosopher's Dew collected in blankets.
Plate 4 from the alchemical 'wordless book', or **Mutus Liber***, probably by Jacob Saulat, 1677.*

36. Detail of heraldic lozenge and five-petal etheric flowers on the medieval capitals in the cloisters of the Catalan church of Santa Maria, Ripoll.

37. Christian symbols, including the mysterious Stella Maris (below the banderolle, top right), on a woodcut of Circa 1505.

38. The pagan Sheela-na-gig to the south east of the Norman church at Kilpeck, near Hereford. He Sheela's vulva is in the form of a ru.

*39. The Knights Templar on the west front of Chartres Cathedral. This pair correspond
to the sign Gemini displaced from the zodiacal arch of the portal to the north.
Their single shield points to the fish of Pisces below.*

*40. The Fish of Chartres, hidden from casual view by the projecting ledge below.
It is, however, indicated by the shield of the Knights above. It is the hidden Christ,
and symbol of Pisces, the ruler of the secrets of initiation.*

41. L'ane qui vielle – the ass with the hurdy gurdy – on the south wall of Chartres Cathedral. The figure in the background is the Archangel Michael carrying the sun-dial.